MW01055897

HOW TO KEEP YOUR TOYOTA PICKUP ALIVE

STEP-BY-STEP PROCEDURES FOR THE COMPLEAT IDIOT

FOR 1975-1987/2 & 4WD

BY LARRY OWENS
ILLUSTRATED BY JOE LEAHY

JOHN MUIR PUBLICATIONS

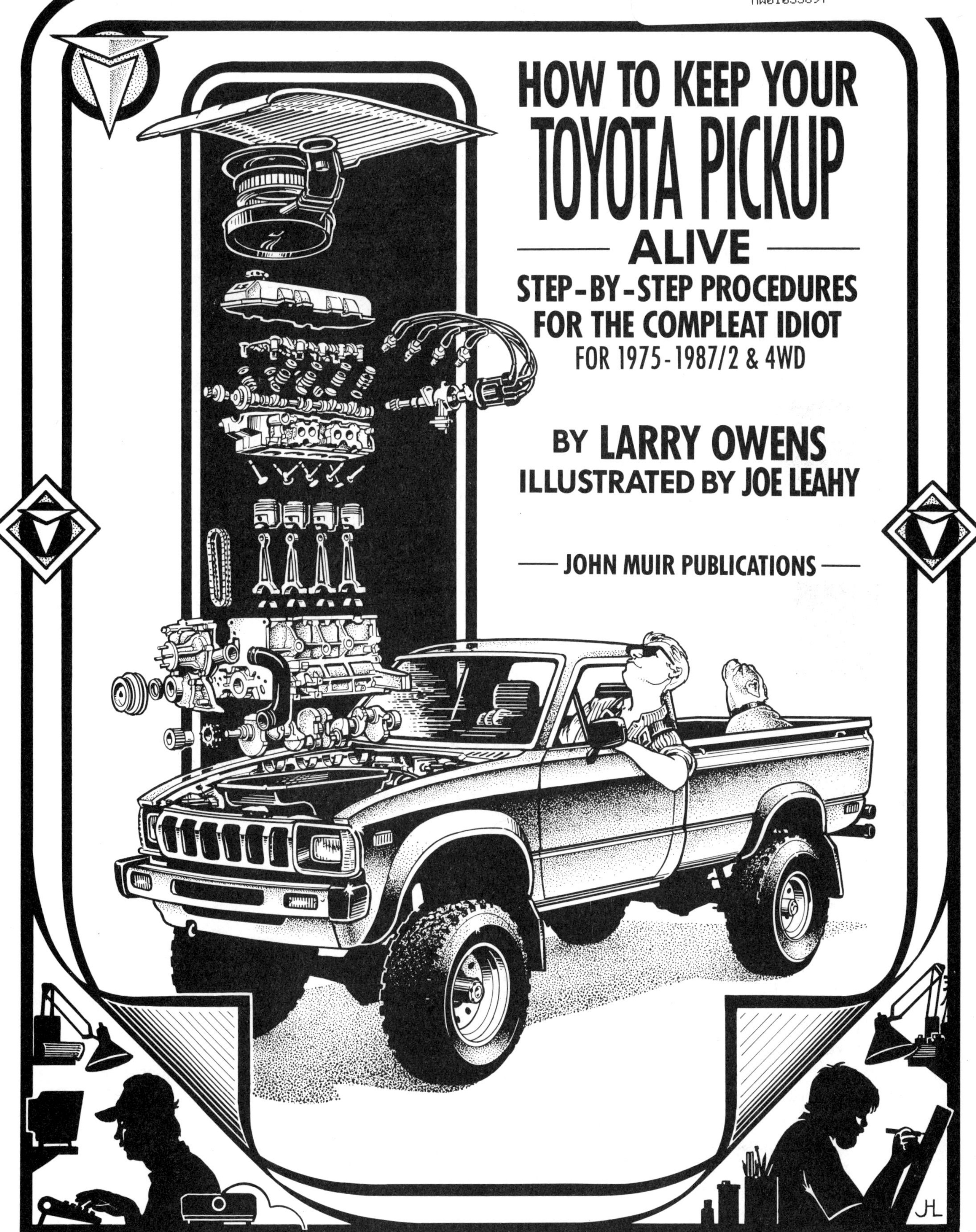

Production Credits:
Cover: Peter Aschwanden
Illustrations: Joe Leahy
Design and Production: Jim Wood
Editor: Richard Harris
Typography: Copygraphics, Santa Fe NM
Typeface: Times Roman
Printed on Recycled Paper

Copyright © 1988 by John Muir Publications
All Rights Reserved

Published by:
John Muir Publications
P.O. Box 613
Santa Fe, NM 87504

Printed in the U.S.A.

Library of Congress Catalogue No. 87-043130
ISBN 0-912528-89-3

First Edition, December 1994

PLEASE NOTE:

The repair and maintenance procedures in this book are based on the training, personal experiences and research of the author, and on recommendations of responsible automotive professionals. If you follow all the directions specifically, you should be able to complete the procedures in this book successfully and safely.

Please understand that the recommendations and warnings herein cannot cover all conceivable ways in which service procedures may be done, or every possible hazard and risk involved. The author, illustrator and publisher are not responsible for any adverse consequences that may occur in connection with the procedures explained in this book. Please do not use the book unless you are willing to assume the risk of adverse consequences. We urge you to consult with a qualified mechanic before using any procedure where there is any question as to its completeness or appropriateness.

We especially advise you to heed all WARNINGS and CAUTIONS, to use all recommended safety precautions called for throughout the book—and to use common sense. Thanks.

ACKNOWLEDGMENTS

Although my name is on the cover, there are several other people who deserve an equal share of the credit for this manual. Without them the project would have floundered many times over. So with great pleasure I now get to thank them publicly for their efforts.

Thanks to all the people at John Muir Publications for their support throughout the project. Especially Ken Luboff and Steven Cary for backing the project, Richard Harris for the difficult task of translating my writing into English, and Jim Wood for book design, layout and paste up.

I can't thank Joe Leahy enough for the great illustrations. Joe's pictures really are worth thousands of words. And thanks to Peter Aschwanden for the cover design.

Thanks to Mike Michels, Jim Pond and Scott Goldenberg at Toyota Motor Sales, U.S.A., Inc., who offered friendly, enthusiastic support for the project.

Special thanks to three top notch Toyota mechanics at Joe Redford's Toyota in Goleta, California, Niko Norton, Dave Harris and Alan Pratini for the valuable technical assistance and suggestions about how to do things easier and/or better.

Others who helped with the project are: Sol Morrison, Paul Miller, Peter and Jonathan Porinsh, Alec and Cindy Chambers, David Norrie, John Alper, Kevin Robinson and Billy J. Trucker.

This book is dedicated to my wife Camille (Mimi) and my son Oscar (Oz). Thanks for keeping me going when the going got tough, and when it seemed like it would never end.

TABLE OF CONTENTS

INTRODUCTION

Contrary to popular belief, modern cars and trucks are not too complicated for the average owner to maintain, often at a savings of $100-1000 per year!

The basic things that professional and amateur mechanics have dealt with since cars were invented haven't really changed that much—except that a lot of things have gotten easier. For example, some of the most common sources of trouble, like breaker points in the distributor and carburetor adjustments, have been eliminated on later models. Changing the oil and filter is just as messy now as it was when Henry Ford did it on his first car, but even this bothersome chore doesn't have to be done as often as it did in the old days, thanks to higher quality oils and engine materials. And it's much easier to replace the pads on disc brakes than it is to replace brake shoes. Your truck has disc brakes up front where most brake wear occurs, so maintaining the brakes is easier now than in the old days.

What I'm getting at is that in most cases it's easier now to do the maintenance on your truck than it ever was.

Yes, it's true. Cars and trucks built in the last few years have computers and other complicated gadgets that are beyond the home mechanic's means to deal with. But there's no need to mess with these systems unless they start causing problems, which is very rarely. All those wires, hoses and mysterious looking gizmos under the hood just make things *look* a lot more complicated than they really are.

So what's left to do? Basically, simple things like replacing the spark plugs (a task very similar to replacing a light bulb), replacing other parts periodically (like the air, oil and fuel filters which are a piece of cake to replace), and doing a few other simple things like keeping the tires inflated properly and rotating them regularly.

How To Keep Your Toyota Pickup Alive was written for people with little or no mechanical experience. Normal people like you who, with a little friendly direction, can do most of the work on their truck. I've tried to write it so you'll feel as if my friendly hand is on your shoulder as you go through the procedures. Using this manual you can do the things that you would otherwise pay someone else a wad of money to do. I'll warn you up front if a procedure requires special tools or expertise.

The heart of this book is a detailed lubrication, maintenance and tune-up chapter. In this chapter engine tune-ups, the maintenance of all other vital systems such as brakes, cooling, suspension and steering systems, as well as checking the condition of almost all other vital parts on the truck like tires, wiper blades, lights, and so on are arranged in a logical maintenance schedule based on recommendations by the Toyota factory as well as my own experience.

This book includes maintenance, diagnosis and repair instructions for all 1975-87 gasoline powered Toyota pickups, 4 Runners and Cab and Chassis models. Due to special tools, safety factors, and/or complexity, instructions for the following models and systems are not covered: Landcruisers, diesel engines, air conditioning and power steering. Also, there are peculiarities on some Cab and Chassis models that have campers, flat beds or utility beds that are not covered.

Toyota trucks are renowned for their toughness, dependability and ease of maintenance. But, like almost everything else, they need to be fondled occasionally to stay in tip-top shape. With a minimum amount of attention they will stay looking good and running great almost indefinitely.

Professional mechanics, machinists and parts store personnel are almost always willing to help inexperienced mechanics who get stuck with catastrophes like a broken bolt or crossed wire. In fact, they generally seem to be impressed by people who want to maintain their own vehicles. Be sure to reward those who help you with a cold six-pack, a dozen donuts or something—you never know when you'll need their help again.

If you are unsure of your mechanical abilities, read Chapter 1: *How To Use This Book*, then do the Vital (yet simple) chapters and procedures listed at the end of that chapter, to slowly wade into the book. As you build up confidence, gradually go deeper and deeper into Chapter 5. Soon you'll be changing the oil and filter, massaging away your truck's aches and pains, and eventually you'll be doing thorough, competent tune-ups and repairs. Also, you'll be replacing worn parts before they fail completely, which might have left you on the side of the road with a roast in the oven, the kids stranded at school, a hungry date waiting to be picked up, ad infinitum.

Write to me at John Muir Publications, P.O. Box 613, Santa Fe, New Mexico 87504, to let me know how it goes. I'm always open to suggestions for easier or better ways to do things, interesting stories, pictures of my readers with their machines, compliments and complaints.

Thanks,

Larry Owens

Larry Owens

CHAPTER 1
HOW TO USE THIS BOOK

To get your money's worth from this book, you gotta read it. Skipping paragraphs, sentences, and sometimes even skipping a word can defeat hours of otherwise meticulous attention to instructions. When helping Volkswagen and Subaru owners who got stuck using the *How To Keep Your Volkswagen Alive* and *How To Keep Your Subaru Alive* books, and when testing this book on inexperienced mechanics, the most common problem was that people were skipping part of the instructions. The information was there, they just weren't using it.

To make this book really work for you, please read Chapter 2: *Orientation, Safety, and Driving Tips* before getting your nose and hands greasy. Orientation will define some very important terms so you can correctly follow the instructions. "Right side" and "left side" sound simple and concrete, but they are actually relative to where you're standing when reading the instructions. The Safety part of Chapter 2 will tell you how to do things safely. A trip to the emergency room could quickly wipe out the money you were trying to save by doing the work yourself. I want you to come through the procedures with nary a scratch, let alone major damage (to your body or your ego). Driving Tips will give you some pointers on how to drive to minimize wear and tear on your Toy.

Nobody knows it all! There are times when you'll need to ask questions of the pros. The people at the Toyota dealer will help you when they have time. I also urge you to seek out advice at a friendly, well-equipped independent garage that specializes in Toyotas. I'll warn you about procedures which require special tools, skills and/or experience that are beyond the home mechanic's means. That's when it's time to seek professional help. Procedures labeled "Phase 2" mean a greater degree of difficulty is involved. So if you aren't a somewhat experienced mechanic or unless you have a good friend who is, take the truck to the professionals for Phase 2 procedures.

Almost every car has idiosyncracies that give it character and personality. For example, your truck may make horrible scraping sounds when you step on the brake pedal, or a glove box door may open every time you hit a bump. Maybe you can live with an open glove box door but the brake thing should be checked out right away. The idea is to keep a sense of priorities. Get what's important fixed right away, then mess with the true idiosyncracies as you choose.

There are three types of procedures in this book: *Maintenance*, *Diagnostic* and *Repair*.

Maintenance Procedures: By regularly performing the maintenance procedures, which include checking the condition of almost everything, the likelihood of having to use the diagnostic and repair procedures will be reduced considerably. You'll know when some of the parts, like brakes, belts and hoses, are nearing the end of the trail and should be replaced. Waiting for something to break before replacing it won't save you money by squeezing a few extra miles out of the part. When it breaks, other parts could be damaged that were otherwise in good condition. It's a lot easier on the nerves as well as the bank account to replace certain parts during your maintenance procedures rather than at the side of the road—or after having a tow truck haul you back home. The AAA estimates that 80% of road emergencies are caused by neglected maintenance.

When you buy a used pickup or 4 Runner, assume the maintenance *hasn't* been done even if the seller swears on his mother's grave that it was faithfully performed daily (she might be alive and playing tennis every day). Go through the 12,000 mile and 30,000 mile maintenance procedures (Chapter 5, Procedures 5-15) to replace all the vital fluids and to check the condition of the various systems such as brakes, cooling, steering and suspension. This will acquaint you intimately with your "pre-owned" Toy.

Diagnostic Procedures: When there's a clue that something's amiss, from fresh spots of oil on the driveway to an engine that won't start or dies suddenly, don't take it personally. Just use the diagnostic procedures in Chapter 4: *Troubleshooting and Emergency Repair* to identify the problem. Troubleshooting describes the symptoms of various maladies, then either tells you how to fix the problem or directs you to the appropriate chapter. Oftentimes, diagnosing a problem is much more difficult than fixing it. But Chapter 4 and the Conditions paragraphs will help you.

Repair Procedures: Eventually some parts, like the radiator hoses and drive belts, will give up the ghost due to normal wear, no matter how well the truck is maintained. When the telltale symptoms appear, use the diagnostic procedures in Chapter 4 to identify the problem, then turn to the appropriate repair procedure. Fix it as soon as possible so you don't end up stranded in rush hour traffic or in the middle of the desert.

PROCEDURE LAYOUT

The chapters are broken down into **Procedures** which are broken down into **Steps**. Occasionally I'll have a few words to say about the system at the start of a procedure.

At the beginning of each procedure in this book, a **Conditions** paragraph describes the *existing conditions of the truck* under which the procedure should be performed.

Next comes the **Tools and Materials** paragraph, which will tell you what tools, parts and supplies (such as brake fluid, gaskets, gasket sealer, or whatever) are needed to do the procedure. The word "Friend" is capitalized because there are times when two people are required to perform the procedures. Don't macho out and try to do everything yourself—you might get hurt or become so frustrated you give up. Having a Friend around to help and give you support and encouragement will make the procedures go faster and they'll probably be more fun.

The **Remarks** section gives you special instructions for the procedure and reminds you about things that should be done before starting the procedure.

Especially important are the **Cautions!** and **WARNINGS!** that alert you to possible dangers you might encounter in the procedure. Do not pass Go until you read and heed them.

Read the entire procedure through before you begin, and read each step and be sure you understand it before you do it.

To eliminate duplicating procedures throughout the book, you will occasionally be instructed to turn to a different place in the book to perform a task. For example, "Do Chapter 5, Procedure 1, Step 1"', means turn to Chapter 5, Procedure 1, Step 1, and follow the instructions. Only perform the indicated procedure and/or step. To make it easy to find your way, the chapter, procedure and step numbers are indexed at the top left of each page and the procedure, step number and chapter title are indexed at the top right of each page. (How organized can you get?) If the instructions don't include a chapter number, it means the procedure and step you're looking for are in the same chapter you're reading. Likewise, if only a step number is given it means the step is within the procedure you're reading. To save time, mark your place with a piece of paper before turning to the new instructions.

YEAR AND MODEL VARIATIONS

Toyotas covered in this book are 1975 through 1987 two and four wheel drive pickups, 4 Runners, and Cab and Chassis models. Engine types covered are the 20R, 22R, 22R-E and 22R-TE. Diagnosis, maintenance and repair of diesel engines is not included in this manual. However, other than the engine, the various systems (brakes, suspension, steering, etc.) on diesel powered models are essentially the same as those on models with gasoline engines.

Within several procedures, different tools, parts or techniques are required for working on the various models. When there are differences, I'll indicate in boldface type which years and models the instructions are for. If the years are followed by **models**, it means the instructions are for all models within those years. For example, **'79-'87 models:** means *all* models (two and four wheel drive pickups, Cab and Chassis and 4 Runners) made from 1979 through 1987. Specific instructions for 4 Runners are always indicated by **4 Runners** and specific instructions for Cab and Chassis models by **C & C** after the applicable years.

Occasionally there are variations between ½ ton, ¾ ton and 1 ton trucks. If there are differences, I'll indicate which vehicles the instructions are for.

Instructions that apply only to long bed pickups will be indicated by **long bed** and, you guessed it, instructions for short bed (also called standard bed) will be indicated by **short bed**.

Instructions that only apply to two wheel drive vehicles will be indicated by **2WD**. Likewise, instructions that only apply to four wheel drive vehicles will be indicated by **4WD**.

Instructions that are specific for the various engines will be indicated by the engine model number: **20R**, **22R**, **22R-E** or **22R-TE**. The engine model number is on a sticker on the top front of the engine and on a sticker on the underside of the hood.

Toyotas designed to California specifications are called **California models** and all others are called **Non-California** or **Federal models**.

Don't worry about trying to remember all these code names and abbreviations right now. You'll "pickup" on them as you get into the procedures.

When you come to a section that applies to your particular model, follow the instructions to the end of the step, or until you come to a section in the step that doesn't apply to your particular vehicle. Skip down through the section that doesn't apply until you either come to another section that applies to your year and model or one that begins with the word **EVERYONE**. Obviously, everyone should do the **EVERYONE** section.

Using a yellow marking pen to highlight the sections appropriate to your year and model as you do the preliminary read-through will save you time and possible confusion later while you're actually doing the procedure.

STEP-BY-STEP

Read each procedure all the way through before starting to work. Often something that doesn't make sense in the first part of the procedure will become obvious a little further along. I've seen people become very perplexed and waste a lot of time trying to figure something out, whereas if they had only read the entire procedure before starting they wouldn't have gotten hung up.

If possible, have someone read the steps to you as you perform the work so you don't have to stop and find your place in the book so often. Also, there's nothing worse than trying to turn pages with greasy hands or trying to read while lying under the truck with dirt falling in your eyes. Have a pencil and paper handy so you or your reader can jot down notes as you go along—about parts needed, disassembly sequence, or if there's a discrepancy between what you have and what the book says you should have.

Take your time! Do the job once and do it right. DON'T IMPROVISE! Just do it the way the book says. When you strip a thread, twist off a stud, break a bolt and disasters like that, don't slit your wrists—turn to Chapter 15. It was written for just these contingencies. Smile and get on with it!

Keep everything clean as you go along. Clean parts so they shine, or bribe your Friend to do it. The job will go easier with fewer frustrations. When you're through working on your Toy, clean your tools and put them away before you take your funky clothes off. Then clean yourself and change your clothes before you drive the truck, or at least cover the seat so you don't get the inside greasy. Old sheets, large towels or blankets work well.

NOW WHAT?

Now that you know how to use this book, and before you jump into some of the full-scale repair procedures, I suggest you read and perform the simple, yet vital, chapters and/or procedures listed below to familiarize yourself with your Toyota and the actual doing of procedures. The only tools required are the lugwrench, jack and jack handle that came with the truck, a rag, and safety glasses. If you're missing any of these tools, get them as soon as possible. Just knowing how to change a flat tire and check the vital fluid levels in the engine compartment will give you confidence that you can perform the more complicated procedures when necessary.

SIMPLE, YET VITAL CHAPTERS AND PROCEDURES

Chapter 2: Orientation, Safety and Driving Tips. Learn the names and locations of some of the important parts in the engine compartment. While you're at it, copy the vital numbers for your Toyota in the "My Specs" chart in Chapter 5.

Please read the *Safety* rap, then pretend you have a flat tire and follow the instructions in Procedure 1 to practice changing a tire. Having leisurely changed a tire in your garage or driveway, you'll be assured the necessary tools are on board, you'll know how to use them, and you'll have the confidence that you're prepared to do the job if and when the dreaded event actually happens. Even if you belong to an auto club that will change the tire for you for free, think of the time you'll save and the sense of pride you'll experience by confidently handling the situation yourself!

Driving Tips will give you some tips on driving that will make your Toy last longer.

Chapter 5: Maintenance, Lubrication, and Tune-up. Read the introduction to the chapter, then do Procedures 1 and 2 to check the vital fluid levels and condition of the drive belts in the engine compartment. Doing these two procedures regularly (and Procedures 1 and 2 in Chapter 6) will probably eliminate the causes of 80 percent of roadside breakdowns!

Chapter 6: Cooling. Procedure 2 tells you how to check and replace the rubber cooling system hoses. If any hoses look suspect (I tell you what to look for), replace them as soon as possible. It's a great way to get hands-on experience taking things apart and putting them back together, and it's almost as easy as eating homemade apple pie.

CHAPTER 2
ORIENTATION, SAFETY AND DRIVING TIPS

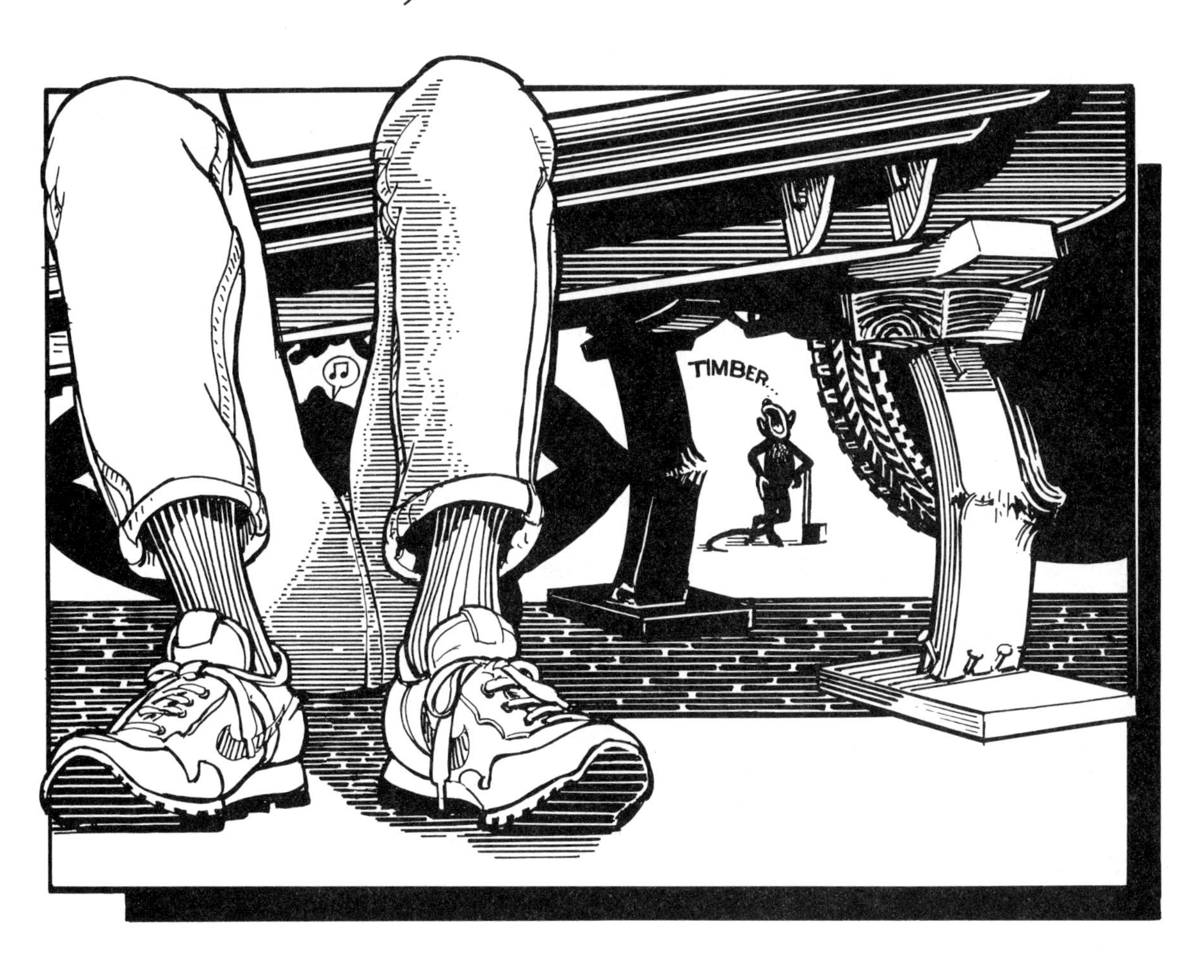

ORIENTATION: WHICH WAY IS UP?

As a great philosopher once said, "Before we speak, let us first define terms." That's exactly what we need to do before jumping into the maintenance and repair procedures. It's important to eliminate directions that may be ambiguous because they're relative to things that change. For instance, you know which is your right hand and which is your left hand, but that won't necessarily help you when the directions say something like, "The widget is on the right side of the gizmo." Sounds simple, but right is relative to which side of the gizmo you're standing on.

To keep things straight, throughout the book **right** will mean the **passenger's side** of the car; **left** will be the **driver's side**. Therefore, if you're standing in front of the car looking at the engine, the right side will be to your left because right is *always* the passenger's side. Got it?

The front of the car is the end with the headlights, and the rear end of the car has the taillights. So **front** always means toward the front of the car, **rear** means toward the back of the car. Assuming your Toy is standing on its wheels, the **top** is the shiny side and the **bottom** is the mysterious underneath side you seldom see. And that goes for every part on the vehicle. In other words, all directions (front, back, top, bottom) relate to the car itself.

Here are two more: **inboard** means toward the center of the car; **outboard** means away from the center of the car.

When the instructions say, "Turn the key to ON," it means turn the key until the dash lights blaze but don't start the engine. "Turn the engine ON," or "Start the engine," mean just that, so turn the key all the way and start it.

Although it's technically inaccurate, for convenience I'll refer to nut and bolt sizes throughout the book by whatever size wrench it takes to fit the nut or head of the bolt. (Technically, the size is determined by the size of the threaded portion, not the wrench size.) If you have to replace a bolt or nut, take the old one (or one just like it) to the parts store with you to be sure you're getting exactly the same bolt or nut.

All bolts and nuts on your Toyota (at least all which you'll be removing or installing) have *right-hand threads*. Right-hand threads mean you screw the nut or bolt *clockwise* to tighten it and *counterclockwise* to remove it. That means *clockwise* or *counterclockwise* as viewed from the end of the bolt or nut you're turning. It gets a little confusing when you're on your back under the car and removing a nut screwed on from the top. You need to imagine an out-of-body experience so you can view the nut from above—the end which you are turning. *Clockwise* and *counterclockwise* are sometimes italicized just to get your attention.

THINGS IN THE ENGINE COMPARTMENT

Knowing the names of some "under hood" parts common to all Toyotas will help you locate lesser-known parts. For example, telling you the distributor is on the left front corner of the cylinder head won't help much if you don't know where the cylinder head is located. Please learn the names of the major parts in this section (indicated in boldface) and where they are located in the engine compartment.

While reading this section, it's best to be looking at your engine so you'll know exactly how the parts look on your model. The illustrations are great, but there's no substitute for the real thing since there are slight differences in the location and appearance of some of the various parts, depending on which engine you have. This section is only to familiarize you with the **name** and **location** of common parts. What the parts do and how they do it is explained in the rap at the beginning of the chapter that covers maintenance and repair of the part or system.

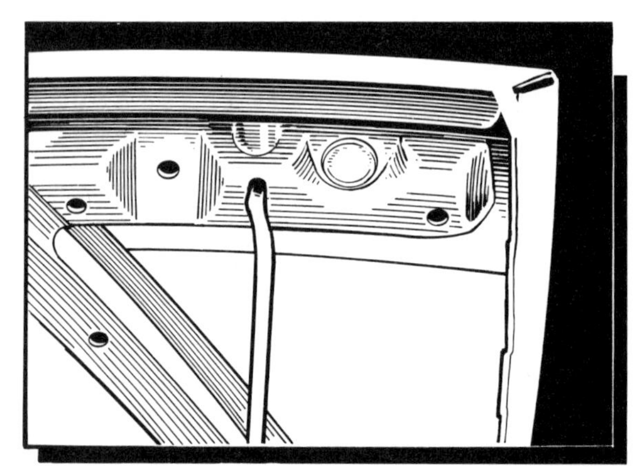

Starting with the basics: To open the hood, find the small black knob underneath the dashboard on the left, near your left knee when sitting in the driver's seat. (There's probably a small picture of a car with an open hood on the knob.) Pull on the knob until you see the front of the hood jump slightly. Go to the front of the car and grope around between the hood and the top of the grille (slightly toward the driver's side from the center) for a little flat lever that releases the safety latch. Lift up on the lever and the hood will rise before you. Hold the hood up with your left hand while you look for a long thin prop rod across the top of the grille, held in place by a rubber or plastic clip on the right (passenger's) side. With your right hand, lift up on the right end of the rod (the crooked end with a rubber coating) and it will pivot in a rubber grommet on the left (driver's side) end. The free end of the rod hooks into a hole punched into the bracing near the front edge of the hood. There should be an illustration of the hole somewhere nearby. (If you absolutely can't get the hood open, sell this book and go fishing!)

WHICH ENGINE DO YOU HAVE?

There's usually a sticker on the front center of the engine with a series of numbers and letters indicating the engine type. There's also a white sticker on the underside of the hood that tells the engine type, if the emission control system complies to California specifications, and whether there's an exhaust catalyst or not. Here's a

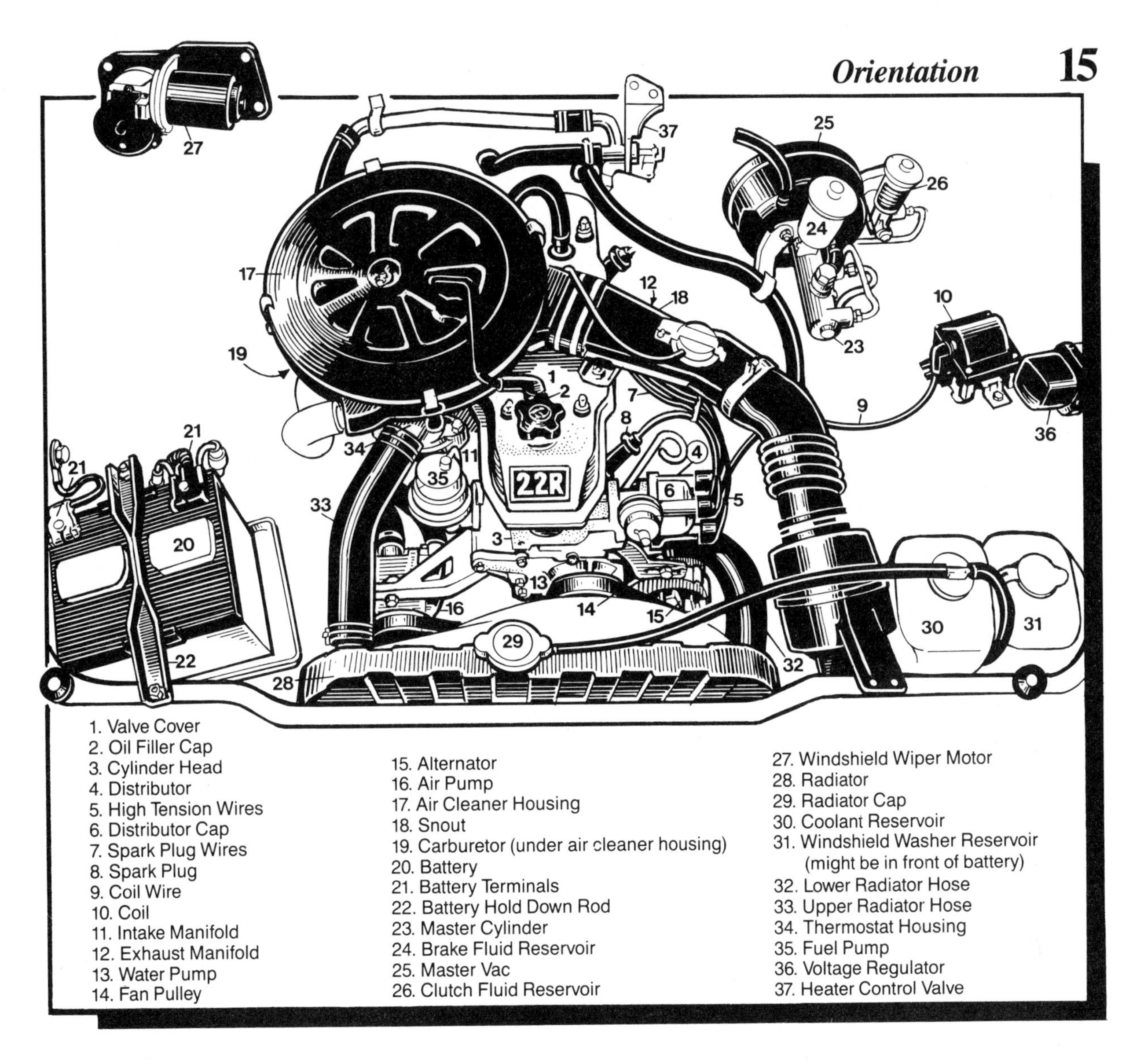

basic rundown of the various engine types covered in this manual, when they were offered, their size, and what kind of fuel system they have. EFI stands for Electronic Fuel Injection.

ENGINE	YEARS	SIZE	FUEL SYSTEM
20R	1975-1980	2189cc	Carburetor
22R	1981-1987	2563cc	Carburetor
22R-E	1984-1987	2366cc	EFI
22R-TE	1985-1987	2366cc	EFI and Turbocharger

Now, to continue with the tour, look at the top of the engine.

The first thing you'll probably notice is the long aluminum **valve cover** running front to rear covering the top of the engine. TOYOTA is proudly stamped into the cover. Lurking inside the valve cover are such mysterious things as the **camshaft**, **rocker arms**, **valves** and **valve springs**. The round flat black cap on the top front of the valve cover is the **oil filler cap**. To remove the cap, unscrew it *counterclockwise* (as viewed from the top). This is where you put fresh oil into the engine.

Just below the valve cover is a 3" thick slab of aluminum known as the **cylinder head**. The **distributor** is a fist-sized thing sticking out of the left front corner of the cylinder head. The distributor has five large **high tension wires** plugged into the plastic **distributor cap**. The four wires around the edge of the distributor cap are **spark plug wires**. They carry electricity to the four **spark plugs** located on the left side of the cylinder head (just follow the wires to find the spark plugs). The **coil wire** is plugged into the center of the distributor cap and connects the distributor to the **ignition coil**, which is bolted to the inside of the left fender.

A hollow aluminum **intake manifold** is bolted to the right side of the cylinder head and a hollow cast iron **exhaust manifold** is bolted to the left side of the cylinder head.

The large hunk of steel below the cylinder head is the engine **crankcase** (also called the "block"). Within the crankcase are the **cylinders**, **pistons**, **crankshaft** and **connecting rods**.

Bolted to the rear end of the engine crankcase is the round **flywheel housing** (also called a bell housing), and to the back of that the **transmission**. The engine and transmission are held in place by steel and rubber **engine mounts** bolted to the engine and the chassis (frame).

On the front of the engine you will see at least three round pulleys. The pulley on the bottom front center of the engine is attached to the end of the crankshaft and is approriately called the **crankshaft pulley**. It turns whenever the engine is running. Licorice-looking **drive belts** (also called V-belts or fan belts) around the crankshaft pulley turn pulleys on other things—for instance, the **water pump**, bolted to the left front of the engine; the engine **fan**, bolted to the front of the water pump pulley; and the **alternator**, mounted by brackets to the bottom front left corner of the engine. The alternator is about the size of a short fat coffee can sitting on edge. It has wires connected to its back and a metal fan-bladed thing with a pulley on the front which is turned by the drive belt from the crankshaft pulley.

On some models an **air pump** (which looks a lot like an alternator) is bolted to the bottom right side of the engine. Two thumb-size hoses connect the air pump to other things on the engine. A second drive belt from the crank pulley turns the air pump.

If you have air conditioning, the large, clunky looking **air conditioner compressor** will be bolted to the top right front side of the engine. Two hoses are attached to the compressor—*DON'T mess with these two hoses!* If your model has an air pump, the drive belt which turns the air pump also turns the air conditioner compressor. On models without an air pump a separate drive belt turns the compressor.

If you have power steering, you'll have a **hydraulic power steering pump**, located near the top front of the engine on the driver's side. It is driven by another drive belt from the crank pulley.

Things are quite different on the right side of the various engine types so let's take them one at a time.

20R and 22R engines: A large, round, black **air cleaner housing** is on the top right (passenger's side) of the engine. Inside the air cleaner housing is the engine **air filter element** which filters out the dust, bugs and gravel before the air enters the engine. There's a long oval air intake **"snout"**" on the left (driver's) side of the housing which points toward the left front headlight.

The **carburetor** is directly below the air cleaner housing, in amongst some pipes and wires. The carburetor is bolted to the top of the engine's **intake manifold**; a hollow chunk of aluminum which connects the carburetor to the cylinder head.

22R-E engines: A long, hollow, aluminum **air intake chamber** is bolted to the passenger's side of the cylinder head. The **throttle body**, which controls engine speed, is bolted to the front of the air intake chamber. A large, round rubber **air intake connector** connects the throttle body to the engine air cleaner located in the left front corner of the engine compartment.

22R-TE engines: These engines look very similar to 22R-E engines (see above) except that the **air intake connector** tube connects the **throttle body** to the **turbocharger**, which is bolted to the left side of the engine. Another large round rubber hose, the **air cleaner hose**, connects the turbocharger to the **air cleaner** which is mounted in the left front corner of the engine compartment.

EVERYONE: Here is where some other exciting parts of your engine are located:

The round **oil filter** sticks out of the right side of the engine crankcase, just below the intake manifold.

Here's where the **engine oil** and **automatic transmission fluid dipsticks** are located:

'75-'77 models: The wire-loop handle of the **engine oil dipstick** is located on the right front side of the engine.

'78-'87 models: The engine oil dipstick sticks up on the left side of the engine, just behind the distributor.

Automatic transmission models: You have a second wire-loop handled **fluid level dipstick** for checking the level of fluid in the transmission. On '75-'78 models the fluid level dipstick is on the right rear of the engine. On '79-'87 models the fluid level dipstick is on the left side of the engine below the **brake master cylinder**.

EVERYONE: Let's move away from the engine now and explore other delights under your hood:

The **battery** is the big, rectangular plastic box in the right front corner of the engine compartment. Two **battery cables** attach by clamps to **terminal posts** on opposite ends of the battery. A **hold-down rod** across the top center of the battery holds it in place. Some Turbo models also have a second battery located in the left front corner of the engine compartment.

The brake **master cylinder** with one or two **brake fluid reservoirs** mounted on top sticks straight out of the **firewall** (the wall between the engine and passenger compartments). It's near the left rear corner of the engine compartment. See the plastic filler cap(s) on top of it? A large, round black **Master Vac** (vacuum assist unit) is between the master cylinder and the firewall.

Tucked in the far left corner of the engine compartment is the **clutch master cylinder**. A white plastic **clutch fluid reservoir** sits on top.

The soup can sized thing in the top, right, rear corner of the engine compartment is the **windshield wiper motor**.

The **radiator** is that large, flat black thing with a corrugated surface attached vertically to the body between the engine and grille. The **radiator cap** is on the top center of the radiator. A white plastic **coolant reservoir** is just to the left of the radiator.

Somewhere near the front of the engine compartment you'll find a white plastic **windshield washer fluid reservoir**. On '75-'83 models it's just to the left of the coolant reservoir. Don't confuse it with the coolant reservoir. On '84-'87 models the windshield washer fluid reservoir is located in the right front corner, between the battery and the grille.

Two large black rubber hoses attach to the back of the radiator. The **lower radiator hose** goes from the lower left corner of the radiator to the water pump; the **upper radiator hose** goes from the upper right corner of the radiator to the bulbous looking **thermostat housing** on the intake manifold.

We have now covered the main parts visible underneath the hood of your Toyota. Yes, there are sundry other pipes, hoses and wires. Many of them deal with emissions, and I'll get to them in Chapter 10: *Exhaust and Emission Control Systems*.

NUMBERS

This little section tells you how to locate the engine and body serial numbers, the production date (when the car was made), and the engine type. I urge you to find the numbers now, then copy them down in the "My Specs" chart in Chapter 5. Always take these numbers with you when buying parts. Changes in parts are sometimes made during a model year run, so you may need more than just the year model of your truck.

Production Date and Vehicle Identification Number (VIN): Open the driver's door and look for a metal plate on the rear pillar the door closes against. You'll see a month and a year stamped on the plate indicating the month and year the car was manufactured. That's the **production date**. Also on the plate there will be a long **Vehicle Identification Number (VIN)**. A similar plate is also riveted to the body someplace inside the engine compartment. The VIN is also on the top of the dash and you can read it by looking through the lower left corner of the windshield.

Engine Serial Number: The engine serial number is stamped on a flat place on the crankcase. The number is followed by the engine type. On '75-'78 models the engine serial number is stamped on the right (passenger's) side of the engine crankcase. On '79-'87 models the engine serial number is stamped on the left side of the crankcase, near the alternator.

Engine Type: A sticker on the front of the valve cover tells the engine type you have. The number is also on the underhood sticker mentioned below.

UNDERHOOD STICKERS

Most models have a white **Emission Control Information** sticker on the underside of the hood which contains valuable information about your particular Toyota. If your sticker is missing, try to get a new one from the Toyota dealer. Be sure and take your vehicle identification number, engine type and serial number with you to insure getting the correct sticker.

Here's the pertinent information the sticker can tell you: If your model has an exhaust **catalyst**, or if it's a **non-catalyst** model (if the sticker doesn't mention a catalyst, you don't have one); some of the **tune-up specifications** for your engine (timing, valve clearance, idle speed, etc.); and the **model year**. If the truck was built to **California specifications**, the sticker will say something like, "This model complies with State of California regulations applicable to 19?? model year trucks sold in the state of California." If California *isn't* mentioned on the sticker you have a **non-California (federal)** truck.

You might also have a handy **vacuum hose connections** sticker. You can use the sticker to identify some of the emission control gizmos and to see that all the vacuum hoses are connected to them correctly.

OK, that's it for orientation. To lower the hood, lift it up with one hand while you lower the prop rod and stick it in the clip on the right side above the grille. Lower the hood until it's open about a foot, clear your fingers, and let it drop. Pull up on it to check that the safety catch has grabbed hold and will keep it snugly down.

SAFETY!

Please read this section all the way through, but don't let it scare you. It shouldn't intimidate you out of working on your truck, but it will make you aware of a few simple safety precautions that will prevent common accidents. We're here to have fun, not go for a joy ride to the emergency room. Read on.

Besides being a fine piece of automotive engineering, your Toyota, dealt with thoughtlessly, can also be dangerous and deadly. When working on your truck, *concentrate* on what you're doing. If something is distracting you, STOP, deal with the interference, then go back to work with all your attention focused on the task at hand. It's hard to keep track of what you've done and what you're to do next when being constantly interrupted. No matter how tired, cold, miserable or pissed off you get, don't make borderline decisions *against* safety and *for* convenience.

Work at your own pace. Don't rush a job. And do EVERYTHING it says to do in the procedures. It's wise to allow at least twice the time you think you'll need. Remember, cleanup is part of the procedure, and that takes time too. It's especially important to be patient near the end of a job. That's when you may be a little tired and tempted to take shortcuts or rush things. Don't. It's often toward the end of the job that mistakes and accidents happen.

I can't possibly come up with every bizarre situation you might run into, but I'll list the most common causes of accidents, and how to avoid them:

EXHAUST GAS: Carbon monoxide first makes you drowsy and careless, then kills you. So *never* run the engine in a garage with the large garage door closed. It's best to roll the truck out of the garage far enough so the exhaust pipe is outside. I stick a ten-foot piece of rain gutter downpipe on the end of the exhaust pipe to get the fumes as far away from me as possible.

FIRE DANGERS: The combination of a spark and a puddle of gasoline can turn your truck into a nasty black carcass in about ten minutes. Have you ever seen a car destroyed by fire? It's sickening. To prevent this from happening to you, wipe up all drips, spills and puddles of gasoline right when they happen.

Don't smoke *anything* while working on your truck. If you smoke, take a break away from the car (you can read the procedure or step you're about to perform while you light up).

Keep a modern fire extinguisher handy. Be sure it's capable of putting out gasoline fires. Check it regularly. Inform helpers of its whereabouts.

SAFETY GLASSES: Always wear clean safety glasses when you're banging on something with a hammer, messing with any kind of spring, checking the battery, using a spray can of cleaner (carb cleaner, brake cleaner, etc.), or working under the truck or dashboard where crud could fall in your eyes. Your sight is much too precious to even think about risking by not wearing safety glasses in these situations. I know there aren't any designer safety goggles around and most people look pretty foolish in them, but swallow your vanity and wear 'em.

CLOTHING: Take off all jewelry, including rings. Also remove scarves, neckties or any loose clothing, and tuck long hair into a stocking cap when working on a car. Wear comfortable clothing. If you have long sleeves, either roll them up or button them properly (loose cuffs are notorious for finding their way into moving parts).

RUNNING ENGINE: When the engine is running, some of the pulleys, fans and drive belts spin so fast you can't even tell they're moving. When doing a tune-up, *Be Aware* and keep fingers, tools, rags, hair, clothing, and the wires from the timing light and/or the tach/dwell meter well away from the front of the engine. Remember also that some engine parts get *very hot* soon after the engine is started.

BATTERY ACID: Battery acid loves to eat clothing and it should be kept away from your eyes at all costs. The vapor around the battery caps is explosive, so never check the battery fluid level with a match or lighter.

DUST MASK OR RESPIRATOR: Wear at least a dust mask (a painter's respirator is better) when working on the brakes or clutch. They contain asbestos, which can cause cancer if inhaled too often.

AIR CONDITIONING: If you have air conditioning (A/C), be very careful around the hoses attached to the A/C compressor. They contain gases under high pressure. If any A/C stuff has to be taken apart, have your Toyota dealer or a garage do it.

LIGHTING: You'll frequently need some kind of light to see what you're doing. Groping around in dim light is dangerous as well as frustrating. Use either a **flashlight** or a **"drop light"** (the kind with the bulb surrounded by a steel safety cage). Use "rough service" light bulbs. Never use a household type standing lamp. If it's knocked over, the bulb can shatter, exposing the metal filament. If any combustible fuels contact the filament, hope that your insurance is up to date. My recommendations for good work lights are in Chapter 3: *Tools, Parts and Books*.

OILY RAGS: Don't stash a pile of oily rags in the corner of your garage. They have this weird ability to build up heat and ignite themselves. Put them in a metal trash can outside. There are companies that supply rags in bundles you can buy or rent.

WASTE MATERIALS: Drain oil, coolant and other fluids into a catch pan, then transfer them into a sealed metal or plastic container marked POISON. Dispose of waste materials properly—not down the drain. Recycling centers can tell you who accepts used oil if they don't.

BATTLE SCARS: Anyone who has worked on a car has experienced the skinned knuckle syndrome. To protect your pinkies, think about where your hand will end up if the wrench slips or the stubborn bolt suddenly breaks loose. If possible, position the wrench so you're pulling it toward you rather than pushing on it.

CLEANLINESS: Keep your work area clean and well organized as you go along. It's easier to find dropped screws, bolts and washers on a clean floor rather than having to dig through dirt clods, grease blobs and squished cigarette butts to find them. Stash the parts you remove from the truck someplace where you won't be tripping over them, causing damage to the parts or yourself.

GETTING UNDER THE TRUCK

Knowing the right way to jack up your truck safely is very important. It can be very dangerous if you don't do it right. Improper jacking is the most common cause of injury when working on a car.

When you need to support the truck to work under it, support it well on level ground. Always put the gearshift in FIRST or REVERSE (manual transmission) or PARK (automatic transmission), set the handbrake, and chock the wheels on the opposite end from the end you're raising with blocks of wood so the truck can't roll. Stuff the chocks under there snugly on both front and back of the tire. Use good quality **jackstands** to support the weight of the truck once it's jacked up. Jacks are notorious for slipping or falling over, so don't get under the truck when it's only supported by a jack.

Keep kids and spectators away from the truck while it's jacked up. Have them take a walk or fix snacks.

I recommend buying, borrowing or renting an inexpensive hydraulic **floor jack** (they cost less than $50 now) and two good jackstands (about $10 each) to safely raise and support the truck if you're going to be working on the brakes, suspension, steering, axles, etc. The jack that came with the truck is meant for raising one corner so a tire can be changed. They work fine for that but they aren't designed to raise the truck high enough to make repair work convenient or safe. If you have 4WD and/or over-size tires, you'll need taller than normal jackstands and a larger floor jack.

Here are a few *NEVERS* to keep in mind before getting under the truck.

NEVER use a bumper jack to raise your truck. The bumpers might get bent and ruined.

NEVER use cinder (cement) blocks to support the weight of your truck. They look strong and feel heavy, but they are very brittle. Without warning they can crumble into a pile of dust. I would never get under a car supported by cinder blocks and you shouldn't either.

NEVER use a stack of lumber to support the truck if you're going to be working under it. Unless you're using heavy beams at least 12 inches wide and several inches thick, the stack would be so wobbly by the time the truck is high enough to crawl under that it would be unsafe.

OK, with all the warnings from never never land taken care of, here's how to properly *Chock, Jack and Block* your Toy. Procedure 1 tells you how to safely use the Toyota jack or a floor jack and jackstands to change a flat tire or rotate the tires so they'll wear evenly, and how to use jackstands to get both front or both rear wheels off the ground so you can work underneath the truck safely. You'll be referred to this procedure throughout the book, so be sure you have the equipment and know-how to do it correctly. Procedure 2 tells you how to tow a distressed truck safely. Remember, read each procedure all the way through before you start the work.

PROCEDURE 1: CHOCK, JACK AND BLOCK

Condition: The truck needs to be raised so the wheels can be removed; OR you need to get under the truck to work on it.

Tools and Materials: Toyota jack and jack handle or a hydraulic floor jack, two jackstands unless you're only changing a flat or rotating the tires, at least two chocks to keep the truck from rolling. The chocks can be blocks of wood (4x4 blocks six to 12 inches long work well), wedge-shaped blocks of wood, or store-bought metal wheel chocks. If you've got oversize tires on your Toy, you'll need larger chocks.

If you're removing one or more of the wheels, you'll need a **lug wrench** or socket and ratchet that fits your lug nuts. Some lug nuts for custom wheels are larger than the original lug nuts, so the Toyota lug wrench won't fit them. Be sure you have the correct size on board at all times.

It's a good idea to stash a strong, flat piece of wood (about 12" x12") with the jack, just in case the ground is soft where you're trying to jack up the truck.

Remark: If you need to remove a wheel, brake drum or disc, loosen the lug nuts a little (about a half turn) *before* raising the truck.

SAFETY FIRST! If a tire goes flat while you're driving, don't slam on the brakes. Just carefully pull over to the side of the road and switch on the **emergency flashers**. *Don't* change a tire in the middle of the road, no matter how deserted it may seem. As soon as you get the truck jacked up, sure enough someone will come blasting by in a semi-truck.

Ask your passengers to get out and keep well away from the road. Safety! The shoulder on a busy highway is one of the most dangerous places on earth. Have someone hold on to small children and keep pets in the truck so they can't run around and cause havoc.

Step 1. Park the Truck.

Try to park on a level, hard, smooth surface, completely off the road. Turn the engine off, pull the handbrake on, then put the transmission in FIRST or REVERSE (manual), or PARK (automatics). Even though a flat tire isn't a true emergency, if you're parked at the side of the road, turn on the **emergency flashers** to warn others that you're temporarily immobilized.

Remember, jacking a vehicle up on even a slight incline greatly increases the chance of an accident. If the ground is soft or muddy, you'll need to round up a large, thick, flat piece of wood to set the jack on or you'll end up lowering the jack into the ground instead of raising the truck.

Step 2. Chock the Wheels.

Place wood or steel blocks (called *chocks*) in front of and behind at least one of the wheels on the opposite end of the truck from the end you're raising. It's especially important to chock the front wheels before raising the rear end of the truck because the emergency brake and transmission gears only lock the rear wheels. The fronts are free to roll once the rears are off the ground. If you're stuck at the side of the road, find some big rocks, bricks or chunks of wood to use for chocks. Force the chocks into the gap where the tire meets the road.

Wheel Chocks

Step 3. Locate and Assemble the Toyota Jack and Jackhandle.

Even if you're using a hydraulic floor jack, you'll need this step to locate the Toyota jack handle and lug wrench in order to remove the spare tire and lug nuts. If you don't need to use the spare tire or lug wrench, skip down to Step 5.

The Toyota jack is a screw-type jack that looks like a short fat bottle. There are three parts to the jack handle: a long extension with a hook on one end, a short extension with a round collar and lockbolt on one end, and a crank that fits onto the end of the short extension. The short extension, crank and lug wrench are all stored in a small tool bag. Here's where to look for the jack, long extension and tool bag.

Pickups and Cab and Chassis models: You'll find the Toyota jack stashed behind the seat. You'll have to flop the back of the seat forward to get to the jack and/or the tool bag. On Xtracab models the jack is beneath the shelf behind the seats.

The jack is held in place either on the floorboard with a small wingnut and clamp near the base of the jack, or in a horizontal bracket. To remove the jack, loosen the wingnut *counterclockwise* enough so you can wiggle the jack out from under the hold down brackets if yours is that type, or turn the tab on the jack *counterclockwise* to loosen the jack in the bracket.

The long jack handle extension is a two-foot steel bar about the same diameter as your pinky and held in place by metal clips. On '75-'78 models it's stashed vertically in the right rear corner behind the passenger's seat. On '79-'87 models it's stashed horizontally against the center of the rear wall of the cab. On Xtra-cab models it's near the bottom of the rear cab wall.

The tool bag should be somewhere behind or under the seat(s), or maybe even in the glove box. Or did someone take it out thinking it would never be needed? Anyway, it contains the other two parts of the jack handle assembly and the lug wrench. You'll have to dig around until you find it. Once you have the jack, jack handle extension and tool bag located, skip down to the EVERYONE section.

4 Runners: The jack and long jack handle extension are stashed in the little compartment in the left rear corner of the cab, near the left taillight. Remove them. The tool bag containing the other two parts of the jack handle is stashed in the compartment in the right rear corner. Pull it out.

EVERYONE: Slip the round collar that's on one end of the short extension onto the square end of the long extension. Position them so the screw on the collar will screw into the small dimple near the end of the long ex-

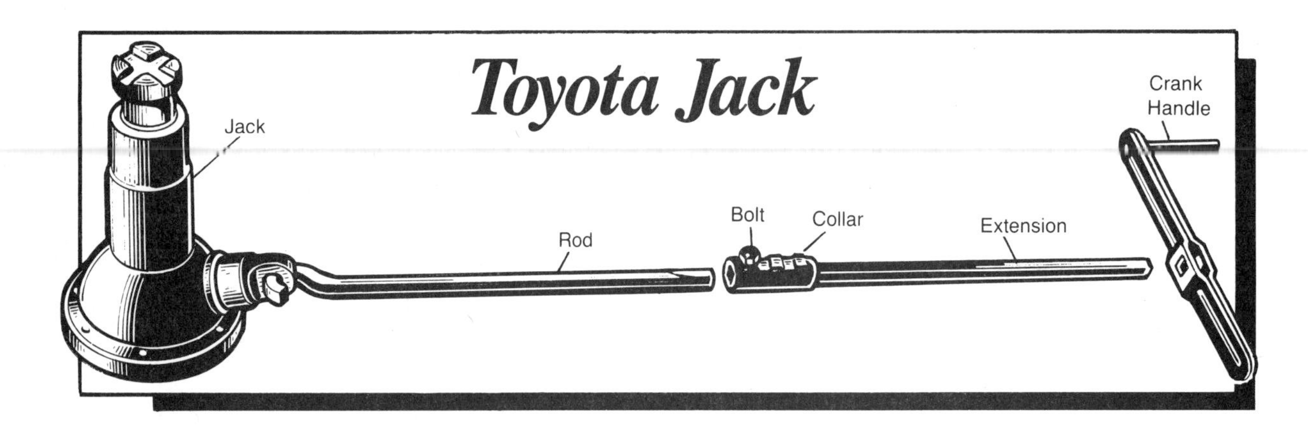

tension. Use either the square hole in the handle crank, a 10mm wrench, or a crescent wrench to snug down the lock bolt on the collar (*clockwise*). OK, the jack handle is assembled. If you're changing a flat tire, be sure to do the next step. If you're removing and installing the same tire, or rotating the tires and don't need the spare, skip the next step.

Step 4: Remove Spare Tire.

The spare tire is mounted beneath the rear of the truck, just in front of the rear bumper. To remove the spare, slide the hooked end of the long jack handle extension through the key hole located just above the rear license plate (or through the bumper on 4 Runners). Push the handle in until the hook engages in a slot that's in a round hole in the frame (look at the illustration). Now fit the square hole in the crank over the end of the jack handle. Hold the jack handle with one hand while you turn the crank handle *counterclockwise* (as viewed from the rear of the truck) with your other hand. Keep turning the crank until the spare tire is on the ground and there's enough slack in the chain so you can unhook the flat bracket on the end of the chain from the spare. To unhook the bracket, push it down through the center hole in the wheel, then turn it to a vertical position and pull it up through the hole.

Step 5. Loosen Lug Nuts.

If you aren't removing any wheels, skip to Step 6.

If you are going to remove a wheel from the truck, use the lug wrench or a socket and ratchet to loosen the lug nuts about one-half turn before raising the wheel off the ground. Otherwise, a turn on the lug nut will simply make the wheel turn around.

If a plastic or metal hub cap or ornament is in the way so you can't get to the lug nuts with the lug wrench, use the tapered end of the lug wrench or a screwdriver to gently pry all around the edge of the cap or ornament until it pops off.

Next, fit the lug wrench squarely onto a lug nut so the handle is sticking out to your left. Push down on the end of the handle so the lug nut is loosened *counterclockwise* (as viewed from the end of the nut). Think about where your hands will end up if the wrench slips. Loosen the nut about one-half turn, then loosen the other lug nuts on the wheel the same way. Lug nut won't loosen? Then it was probably installed by some sadistic gorilla with an air impact wrench. If the lug nuts were torqued on with a torque wrench you should be able to remove them with minimal effort. Anyway, if they're stuck, you'll have to really throw your weight into it. Try this: be sure the handle of the lug wrench is sticking out to the left and as horizontal as possible. Be sure the wrench is fully and firmly engaged on the lug nut because if it slips you could end up with an ugly black and blue bruise on you shin. Put one foot on the handle, and press down with all your weight. Put your hands on the car for balance. Now bounce (carefully) on the handle, lightly at first. Get all the lug nuts loose—just a half turn or so—we'll take them off later.

Step 6. Jack It Up Using Toyota Jack.

If you are using a hydraulic floor jack, skip down to Step 7. If you are using the Toyota jack, here's where to place the jack to raise the truck.

'75-'87 2WD front: Look under the side of the truck, just to the rear of the front wheel. About six inches inboard from the body you'll see the square steel frame running front to rear. Just about where the frame swoops upward toward the front of the truck, a short steel arm is attached on the outboard side of the frame. Position the jack directly under the frame near where the arm is attached.

'79-'85 4WD front: Find the front axle that runs across the bottom front of the truck between the front wheels. Place the jack beneath the front axle, about six inches inboard from the wheel you're raising.

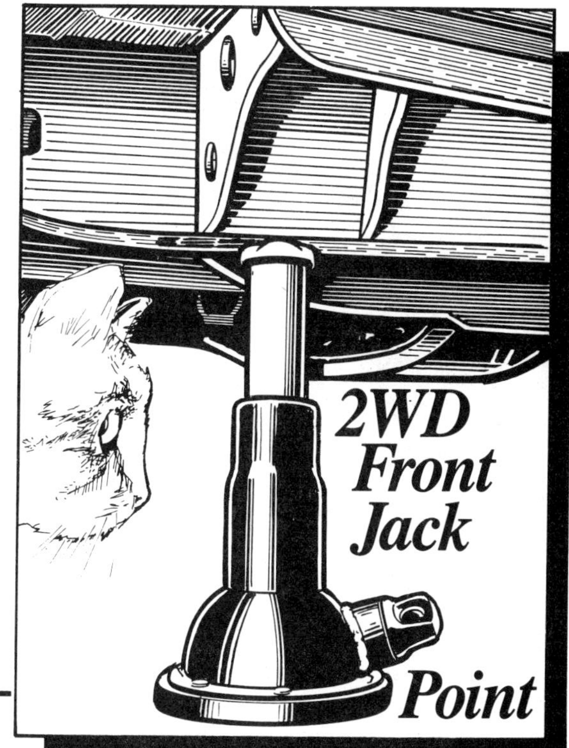

'86-'87 4WD front: Place the jack below the front crossmember (that piece of steel that runs across the bottom of the engine between the front wheels). Position the jack so it's near the end of the cross member that's closest to the wheel your replacing.

'75-'87 rear: Place the jack beneath the rear axle, about 12 inches inboard from the wheel you're raising.

EVERYONE: Set the jack so the flat tab near the bottom is pointed in a direction so you can easily hook the end of the jack handle in the hole in the flat tab. If you're using one of the axles to jack up the truck, rotate the round top of the jack so one of the grooves is aligned with the axle.

Be sure the jack is sitting squarely on the ground, then use your fingers to turn the flat tab *clockwise* until the top of the jack reaches the jack point. Thread the hooked end of the jack handle through the hole in the flat tab. Fit the crank onto the jack handle if it isn't already, then hold the jack handle with one hand while you rotate the crank handle *clockwise* with your other hand. If the ground is soft or muddy, you'll have to round up a flat piece of wood to put under the jack to keep it from sinking. It's also probably getting dark and starting to rain. Anyway, keep turning the handle to jack the truck up until the bottom of the flat tire clears the ground by at least an inch. To jack the truck up higher than the jack will raise it, put a flat block of wood under the jack before raising the truck. Be sure the block solidly supports the jack.

Step 7. Jack It Up Using a Hydraulic Jack.

Front 2WD: To raise both front wheels at once, place the business end of the jack beneath the crossmember that runs side to side beneath the engine. When it's jacked up high enough, place jackstands under the frame behind the front wheels, right where you would place the Toyota jack to raise the truck (Step 6).

If you only need to raise one of the front wheels, you can use the Toyota jack point on the side. It's safer than raising both wheels unnecessarily.

'79-'85 4WD Front: Place the end of the hydraulic jack directly beneath the front differential. It's the large round part of the front axle.

'86-'87 4WD Front: Place the jack beneath the center of the crossmember that goes across the front of the truck below the engine.

'75-'87 Rear: Place the jack directly beneath the round differential housing located in the center of the rear axle.

Step 8. Block it Up With Jackstands.

Do this every time the truck is going to be up for more than just a quick wheel change. Never stick any part of your body under there without the jackstands in place.

If you're changing a flat tire and don't have a jackstand, slip the spare tire under the truck where you would normally put the jackstand. That way if the truck falls off the jack while the tire is removed, the spare tire will hold the frame off the ground. Otherwise you'd have a hard time getting the jack back in position.

Front: Place jackstands under the reinforced area of the frame that runs along the bottom sides of the truck. If you're using the Toyota jack, place the jackstand as close as possible to the jack.

Rear: Place the jackstands under the rear axle, as close to the wheels as possible. If you are using the Toyota jack, place the jackstand under the axle as close as possible to the jack.

EVERYONE: If your jackstands are adjustable, adjust them so the top is as close as possible to the frame or axle. Be sure the *adjusting pin* or *lever* on the jackstand is locked securely in place. Slowly lower the jack so the jackstand supports the weight of the truck. If you are using a floor jack and it won't be in your way, leave it in position with just a slight amount of pressure on the jacking point for added safety. (If the jackhandle is removable, remove it. If it isn't removable, be aware the handle's there, and try not to trip over it.) Check the bottoms of the jackstands to be sure they are squarely on the floor or ground and not tilted.

Now you can remove or work on the wheels, brakes, suspension parts, or whatever, without worrying about getting squashed.

Step 9. Exchange Wheels.

Remove all the lug nuts from the wheel you're removing. Put them in the hub cap, your pocket, or someplace where they won't get lost. Gently remove the wheel, using both hands and balancing your weight. If you're changing tires, roll the spare tire over to where you're working. If you used it for a safety block, drag it out from under the truck and put the tire you removed in its place. Rotate the wheel until the holes in the wheel line up with the threaded **lug studs**. Lift the spare into position on the **wheel hub** and screw on one lug nut by hand. Then screw on the others. Spin them down with the lugwrench until they are just firm. If you try to tighten them completely before the truck has been lowered to the ground, the wheel itself will spin, or you might force the truck off the jack and onto your foot.

Remark: When rotating radial tires, all you do is put the front tires on the rear and the rear tires on the front. (Don't criss-cross the tires on the truck). Follow the directions in this procedure and substitute the spare for each tire you remove while you mount it on the other end of the truck, then replace the spare with the tire you just dismounted from the other end. I keep the spare strictly as a spare so I only have to buy four tires instead of five when the old ones wear out.

Step 10. Lower Truck, Tighten Lug Nuts.

Toyota Jack: Remove the block, tire, or jackstand from under the truck, then lower the jack by turning its handle *counterclockwise* until you can pull the jack out.

Hydraulic Jack: Be sure the wheel chocks are still in place, then use the floor jack to raise the truck high enough so the jackstands or blocks can be removed. Lower the jack until the truck is back on all fours. Pull the jack out from under.

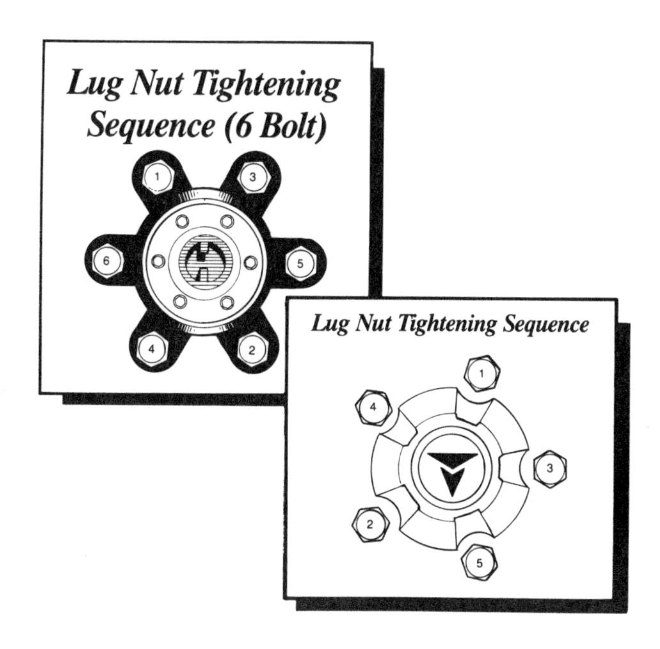

EVERYONE: Using the lug wrench, socket and ratchet, or your torque wrench if it's with you, tighten one lug nut, then the one directly across from it, then the one opposite it until they're all tight (look at the illustration). Starting with the first nut you tightened, go around in a circle to be sure you got them all. If you aren't very strong or have a bad back, try using a foot and the weight of your body on the lug wrench handle. Careful, don't slip. One bounce on each lug nut should do it.

If your torque wrench wasn't handy, torque the nuts when you get home or have a garage torque them for you. The correct torque is 65-87 ft.lbs. (I torque mine to 75). The reason for using a torque wrench is to be sure each lug nut is tight enough so it can't loosen and fall off, but not so tight it strips the threads on the bolt or will be a hassle to remove next time. Unevenly tightened lug nuts can warp the front brake discs or rear brake drums, reducing the braking efficiency and causing premature wear on the brake parts.

If you have regular hubcaps, align the valve stem that sticks out from the wheel with the hole in the hubcap, then hold the hubcap in position and bump it around the edge with the heel of your hand until it's seated firmly.

On 4WD models you might have to use the U-shaped installation tool in the tool bag to install the ornament. Here's how. Slip the ornament over the end of the axle, then fit the tool on so the inner shoulders of the tool are resting on the outer edge of the ornament. Squeeze the tool tightly with one hand so it can't spread apart while you hit the end of the tool with the heel of your other hand.

Step 11. Finish the Job.

Put your tools away. If you had a flat, toss the flat tire in the bed or stash it in its proper place underneath. Head for the nearest service station or tire store. Paranoia will lurk in your mind in the shape of a flat tire until you take care of it, so get it fixed right away.

PROCEDURE 2: TOWING

Condition: Your Toy is broken down at the side of the road; OR you're being a good samaritan and helping a fellow motorist.

Tools and Materials: Friend, tow car, and good quality tow rope, chain or cable (See Chapter 3: *Tools, Parts and Books*).

Remarks: You're broken down on the side of the highway without the necessary tools or parts to get you mobile again. It's 110 degrees in the shade, you're tired and hungry, the first mate is complaining, the kids are all crying, and all you can think about is getting the car towed to a safe harbor.

Step 1. On Your Mark.

When help arrives, attach the towing chain or rope to one of the **towing hooks** below the bumper (some models have only one towing hook on the front), and attach the other end securely to the vehicle doing the towing. It's very important that you don't tie the rope or chain around the front or rear bumper of either vehicle. A jerky tow driver could yank them off. Don't wrap it around any of the steering or suspension parts under the front of the truck—could be costly and dangerous. On the rear you can tie the tow rope or chain to the place where the rear end of the spring attaches to the body.

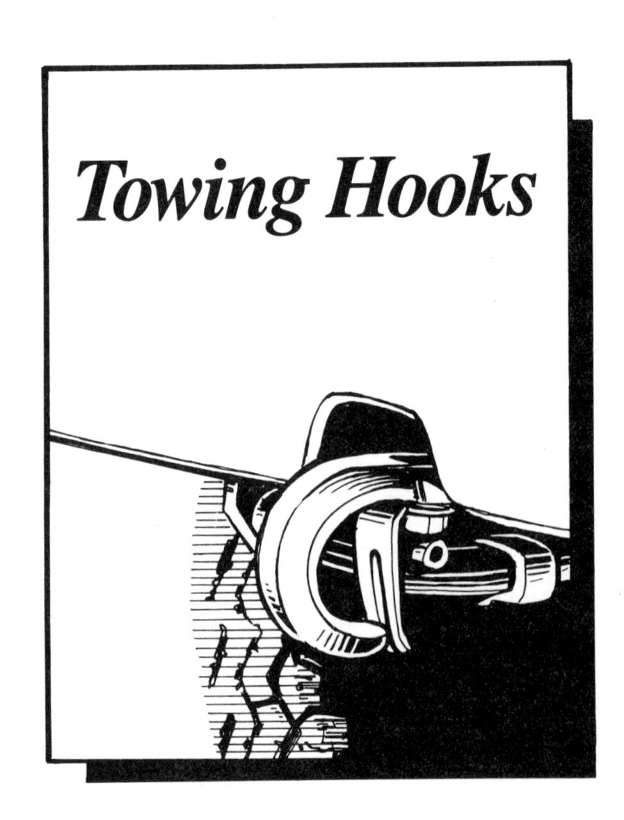

Whatever rope or cable you use, the length between the two vehicles should be no longer than 15 feet, nor shorter than eight feet. If it's longer, other drivers may not realize you're being towed and try to cut in between the tower and towee, with quite spectacular and alarming results! If you have a rag handy, tie it in the middle of the tow rope as a marker. If the rope's too short, you won't have much margin for error if Friend stops or slows abruptly, and you may have trouble going around turns.

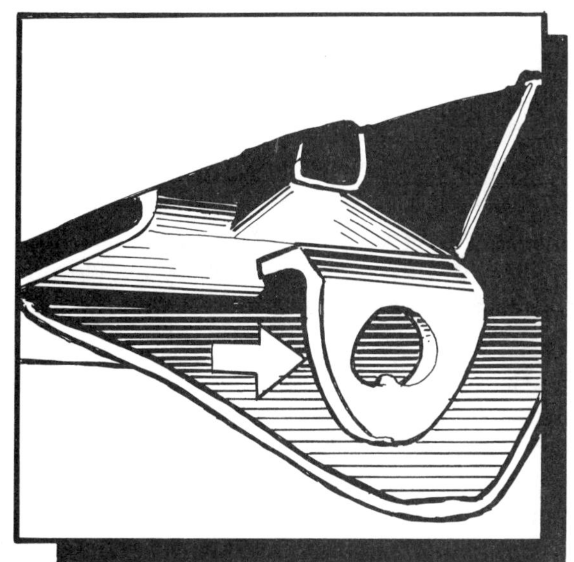

If you have some paper or cardboard and a magic marker handy, make a sign reading "Car in Tow" and stick it in the rear window. Turn the **emergency flashers** for both vehicles ON.

Step 2. Get Set.

Before towing, be sure the parking brake is released and the transmission is in NEUTRAL. Turn the ignition key out of the lock position so the steering wheel can turn.

Automatic Transmission models: Keep the towing speed under 30 miles per hour and don't tow it more than 50 miles. Here's why. The automatic transmission has an oil pump, which pumps only when the engine is working. If the engine isn't turning over while the truck is moving, the transmission isn't being lubricated. The 50 mile, 30 mph towing limit is *absolutely crucial*. The dollars you try to save by towing the truck a few extra miles will soon be in the hands of the transmission shop owner. If it's more than 50 miles to the nearest garage, or you absolutely must tow faster than 30 mph, and Scotty isn't around to beam you up, disconnect the driveshaft from the rear differential (Chapter 11, Procedure 6). Otherwise a tow truck will be needed to lift the rear wheels off the ground.

Manual Transmission models: The towing speed should be held to a 30 mph limit for safety reasons, but you can tow it almost any distance. You should stop at least every 50 miles, however, to give everything a chance to cool down.

Step 3. Tow!

Once again, be sure the handbrake is OFF, the ignition key is ON, and the transmission is in NEUTRAL.

Your Toyota has vacuum assisted brakes, so you'll have to press on the brake pedal harder than usual to slow the car.

Have the tow car driver wave his arm when approaching a stop sign, or whenever he needs to slow down, then the driver of the car being towed should do the braking for both vehicles. The trick is to keep the tow line tight at all times. If the tow line goes slack and the tow car takes off suddenly, extra stress is placed on both vehicles, the tow line (it might even break), and you. If the tow line does break while moving, don't slam on the brakes—someone might be close behind. Just coast until you find a safe place to stop.

Above all, if you're in the car being towed, keep your eyes on the towing car and the traffic ahead. If you doze off and the tow car has to slow or stop, your grille will end up eating his bumper. Remember, you're a team, and it's your job to get on the brakes when your Friend signals you to slow or stop. If you're on a downhill grade, keep your foot lightly on the brake to keep the tow rape, chain or cable taught. Slack (in the chain or in your brain) is your enemy.

Tow the truck to a Toyota dealer if you're still under warranty. If you attempt to repair a covered part or system while it's still under warranty, you may end up paying to have them complete the job.

DRIVING FOR ECONOMY AND LONGEVITY

This little section is about how to help keep your Toyota alive and efficient without even picking up a wrench or getting greasy. Driving for economy means more than just getting good gas mileage; it also includes saving on repairs that can be avoided if the car is driven correctly, promptly making repairs that would end up costing more if not done right away, and planning ahead to purchase parts when they're on sale rather than be stuck with the full price on the day of the tune-up or repair. Getting into the habit of driving for economy and longevity will not only save you a bunch of money; you'll also become a safer driver because you'll be more aware of driving conditions. Driving will be more interesting because every time you drive your Toy you'll be challenging yourself to get the most possible value from your motoring dollar. Consider it a game played by the rules of physics, where you can come out a winner.

GAS MILEAGE

Gas mileage alone isn't everything. As far as I know, Toyotas have never won a major gas mileage test, so don't expect your Toy to get the same mileage as the cars at the top of the government's annual gas miser list. Toyotas are, however, usually at or near the top of the list in overall economy when repair bills over a period of time are also tallied. Even a car that gets 50 miles per gallon (mpg) isn't economical to drive if it takes $50 a month to keep it on the road.

What kind of gas mileage do Toyota trucks usually get? From talking with dozens of Toyota owners and owning several myself, I've deduced that with a manual transmission you should get 20 to 30 mpg on the highway and 18 to 25 mpg driving around town. Two wheel drive models with 5-speed transmissions will probably get mileage close to the high end of the scale, while models with options like 4WD, air conditioning and power steering will probably be closer to the lower figures. Toys with automatic transmissions usually get about five mpg less than models with stick shift.

Here are a few good reasons to keep track of your gas mileage: (1) you'll know if something in the engine has changed causing gas consumption to change (usually for the worse), (2) you'll know approximately how many miles you can drive on a tank of gas so you won't be as likely to run out, (3) you can use mileage calculations to see which brand of gas gives you the best mileage, and (4) you'll find out if changing your driving habits as outlined below will really save you some money. (If it doesn't, drive as you've driven all along and don't worry about it.)

HOW TO CALCULATE GAS MILEAGE

To calculate gas mileage all you need is a pencil, a notebook, and a working **odometer** or **trip meter**. The odometer is that row of numbers in the speedometer that tells how many miles the car has gone. A trip meter is a short odometer, on which you can reset the numbers to zero by pushing a button. Most of the fancier models (SR 5, Sport) come with a trip meter.

You can calculate gas mileage two ways: by the tankful or by a cumulative average taken over a long period of time, which is probably more accurate.

With a pencil and notebook at your side, drive to a gas station and fill the tank. Let the automatic shutoff on the pump do its thing twice to be sure the tank is really full, then quit adding gas. *Don't* fill the tank so full you can see the gas in the filler neck. And *don't* forget to put the gas cap back on. Now write down the miles on the odometer and set the trip meter (if you have one) to zero.

The next time you fill the tank, try to fill it exactly the same way you did the first time. Check the gas pump to see how many gallons of gas it took to fill the tank (include the tenths figure). Write that number in your notebook. If you have a trip meter, just divide the number on the meter by the number of gallons it took to fill the tank, and that's your gas mileage (mpg). No trip meter? To see how many miles you've gone on the first tankful, write the *present* mileage on the odometer in your notebook, then *subtract* the number you wrote down the first time you filled the tank. Divide the number of miles you went by the number of gallons it took to fill the tank this time, and that's your gas mileage.

It's more accurate if you keep track of the mileage over several fill-ups. Write down the mileage number on the odometer at the start of the test. Keep track of the number of gallons you add at every fill-up. You don't have to check the odometer, however, until the end of the test. When you decide to check your overall mileage, fill the tank, then subtract the original odometer figure from the present reading. That's the number of miles you've driven since the test began. Add up the number of gallons of gas you've put in the truck since writing down the original odometer reading. (*Don't* include the gallons it took to fill the tank at the start of the test!) To determine your mpg, divide the number of miles you've driven by the total number of gallons.

For example, the odometer reads 45,650 miles when you fill the tank at the start of the gas mileage check. At the next fill-up the odometer reads 45,855 and it takes 9.7 gallons to fill the tank. Subtract 45,650 miles from 45,855 miles. Aha! You've gone 205 miles. Divide 205 by the number of gallons it took to fill the tank (9.7) and you have your gas mileage. In this case you got 21.13402 mpg.

To do the longer overall gas mileage test, write down the original mileage (45,650) and subtract it from the mileage at the end of the test. Let's say the mileage is 47,975 at the end of the test and you've added 95.3 gallons of gas during the test. OK, 45,650 subtracted from 47,975 equals 2,325 miles. Divide 2,325 by 95.3 and you get 24.396642 mpg. Hmmm, not bad.

If you have a home computer capable of running BASIC (or you need a good reason to buy one), here's a little program you can run to calculate gas mileage. First, enter the program (be sure to include all the quote marks (") and semicolons (;), then run it. It will ask you for the necessary numbers. Here goes:

```
10 REM COMPUTE GAS MILEAGE
20 PRINT "ODOMETER READING LAST FILLUP";
30 INPUT L
40 PRINT "ODOMETER READING THIS FILLUP";
50 INPUT T
60 PRINT "NUMBER OF GALLONS THIS FILLUP";
70 INPUT G
80 LET M=(T-L)/G
90 PRINT "YOUR GAS MILEAGE IS";M;"MILES PER GALLON"
100 PRINT
110 IF M<20 THEN PRINT "YOU NEED A TUNEUP!"
120 IF M>35 THEN PRINT "CONGRATULATIONS!"

140 END
```

FACTORS AFFECTING ECONOMY

Tune-ups: No matter how you drive, your Toy won't perform as economically as possible if the engine isn't operating at peak efficiency. Therefore, the single most important factor in getting good gas mileage is to keep the engine well tuned. Chapter 5 tells you the appropriate intervals for performing the various tune-up procedures.

Tire inflation: Keep the tires properly inflated to decrease the resistance (sluggishness) of the tires as they roll along the road. The higher the tire pressure, the better gas mileage you'll get. However, don't inflate the tires above the maximum pressure rating stamped on the tire just to squeeze out a few extra miles. It isn't safe.

Extra Weight: Hauling around excess weight in the bed can lower your gas mileage.

Models with Carburetors: In order for your engine to perform satisfactorily under a wide range of conditions (such as cold weather, quick acceleration or climbing hills) the carburetor has three devices built into it which operate only under certain conditions. The devices are the **choke**, the **accelerator pump** and the **power system**. You have at least partial control over these devices and the less you use them the better gas mileage you'll get. Here's how they work and how you can control them to your advantage:

Choke: A richer (more gas to air) mixture is required to start a cold engine and keep it running until it warms up. A flap on the top of the carburetor called the *choke plate* makes this adjustment. The choke is activated automatically on all models. Since the engine uses more gas when the choke is "on" (flap closed), it makes sense to warm up the engine as quickly as possible. However, racing the engine or holding it at a very fast idle to warm it up causes excess wear on the engine parts. Driving warms up the engine quicker than idling. As a compromise between thoroughly warming up the engine at idle and wasting a lot of gas or jumping into traffic before the engine is warmed up enough to run properly, let the engine idle just a short while—just long enough to get the oil flowing. Warm up the engine enough to drive conservatively in traffic without lugging or racing the engine, which should take from one to five minutes depending on how cold it is outside.

Accelerator Pump: When you push the gas pedal down suddenly (to pass a car or make a quick getaway after a bank robbery) the sudden rush of air into the engine would cause a temporary loss of power if it weren't for the accelerator pump. To keep the gas/air mixture in a proper ratio, the accelerator pump squirts an extra shot of gas into the engine when the gas pedal is pushed down quickly. Pushing the gas pedal down slowly doesn't activate the accelerator pump, so the slower and smoother you operate the gas pedal, the less extra gas you squirt into the engine.

Power System: The further you press the gas pedal towards the floorboard during rapid acceleration, while climbing steep hills, pulling heavy trailers, etc., the more the power system in the carburetor is turned on. The power system allows more fuel to be drawn into the engine under these conditions. If you keep your right foot away from the floor and drive so you use the power system as little as possible, you'll save a lot of gas.

Brakes: It takes a certain investment in energy (i.e., gas) to get your car up to driving speed. Once you're cruising, less energy is required because you've gained some momentum from the initial investment. When you take your foot off the gas pedal, the car will coast for some distance without using much gas, thus repaying some of your initial investment in momentum. To get the car back up to the desired driving speed another investment is required to regain the momentum. Using the brakes to slow the car not only wears out the brake parts, but also quickly reduces the momentum you've achieved, without getting the repayment by coasting. Staying aware of the traffic conditions ahead so you can slow down just by letting up on the gas pedal, rather than having to apply the brakes, allows you to get the most from the momentum you've already paid for. For example, when approaching stop signs, ease up on the gas pedal as soon as traffic will allow and let the momentum carry you close to the stop sign. This way you'll need to use the brakes a lot less. If you drive with a minimal use of the brakes, you'll save a lot of gas as well as wear and tear on the brake system.

Transmissions: When you're driving your Toy, the engine has an optimum revolutions per minute (rpm) range that gives you the best economy, power and longevity. Driving with the engine below this range is called "lugging" the engine, and driving with the engine above the optimum range is called "over-revving." The proper rpm range is between 2300 rpm and 3700 rpm. For economy driving, it's generally best to keep the rpms to the lower end of the range rather than the higher end. There are exceptions, though. For example, it's better to shift to a lower gear when going up a steep hill so the engine is turning easily at a higher rpm rather than lugging and struggling along at a lower rpm. The **tachometer** (if your model has one) is there so you can keep the engine in the proper rpm range. If you don't have a tachometer, you can learn to regulate the rpms by the sound of the engine.

Manual Transmissions: You can easily use the transmission gears to keep the engine within its optimum range under varying circumstances. While driving, don't rev the engine to the top of the rpm range between every shift; just rev it high enough so that when you shift up through gears the engine will still be turning fast enough so it won't bog down or lug when you release the clutch. Shift up to higher gears as soon as you can without slowing the engine down below the optimum rpm range.

Automatic Transmissions: These are notorious for reducing gas mileage. Regardless of what the EPA says, if you have an automatic, count on getting about 5 to 10 miles per gallon less than your neighbor with a manual transmission.

The shifting in automatics is controlled by the engine speed, demands on the engine (going uphill or downhill, or carrying a heavy load) and the position of the gas pedal. The only economy driving tip I can give you about automatics is to let up on the gas pedal slightly when you feel the rpms are high enough to change to the next higher gear. This will cause it to go ahead and shift. Holding the pedal in one position tends to make the engine rev higher than I think is necessary. One good thing about automatics is that they shift into a lower gear by themselves whenever the engine is about to lug (which a lot of people don't do).

FACTORS AFFECTING LONGEVITY (AND THUS ECONOMY)

Stay on top of your Toy's overall condition and make necessary repairs or adjustments *right away*. If you put off things like tuning the engine when it starts running poorly or having the front end aligned when the tires start wearing on the edges, it will probably end up costing you more than if you attended to them right away.

When parking the truck (especially on hills), set the handbrake *before* releasing the clutch pedal or putting the transmission in PARK. This way the truck is held by the brakes (which are relatively inexpensive and easy to replace) and no strain is placed on the more expensive drive train parts that are involved when the engine and transmission are used to hold the car.

Plan ahead when it comes to anticipated maintenance replacements (see Chapter 5). Buying tune-up and replacement parts (such as oil, filters and brake shoes) when they're on sale at the local parts store can save you quite a lot of money over the course of a couple of years.

Always having the spare parts and tools listed in Chapter 3 on board will let you repair the most common causes of roadside breakdowns and thus eliminate expensive towing bills.

Buying a cheap **magnetic key holder** so you can hide a spare key under the bumper or fender can save you the time and expense of having a locksmith unlock your truck on that fateful occasion when you absentmindedly lock the keys inside or lose them while camping at Lake Wobegon.

Toyota Passing Lane

CHAPTER 3
TOOLS, PARTS AND BOOKS

Some professional mechanics have been known to spend more for tools each week than for food. Others can do quality work with a handful of tools they've collected from pawn shops, surplus stores and swap meets. My tools have somehow found their way from the far ends of the earth into my tool box. Each one has a specific purpose, so I'm not lugging around extra weight.

Tool selection is easiest if you're going to be working on the same car or the same make of car all the time. Toyotas use metric sizes, fortunately, so you'll want to have metric tools. Keep a basic set in the car at all times so that if you're stuck on the road and a Mack truck driver stops to help, you'll have the right tools (and this book, of course) to get you rolling down the road again. Most of his truck tools won't fit.

There are two ways you can approach buying tools. If you have the money, just go out and buy what's on the list. If you can't afford to buy them all at once, read through the procedure you are getting ready to do and buy only the tools you need for that procedure. Gradually you will build up a full-fledged tool set. Dropping hints around Christmas time and birthdays sometimes works if the right people are around to catch them.

Ultimately, how much you need to invest in tools comes down to how independent of garages and dealerships you want to become. At the current hourly shop rates for garages, your tools will pay for themselves just by doing a couple of tune-ups or simple repairs yourself. Bashing around off-road in your four wheel drive will be more fun knowing you have the tools, this book, and a few spare parts to get you back to civilization.

If you have a stash of tools for American cars, don't throw them away, because some of them can be used on your Toyota. Here's a list of direct conversions:

13mm = 1/2"	17mm = 11/16"	21mm = 13/16"
14mm = 9/16"	19mm = 3/4"	22mm = 7/8"

Tool prices vary radically from brand to brand. The most expensive and generally considered the best are **Snap-on** and **Mac Tools**. They look good, feel like silver jewelry in your hand, come with a lifetime guarantee, and cost about a third more than good medium-priced tools. If your last name is Rockefeller or Springsteen, go ahead and buy all Snap-on or Mac tools. They're sold mainly to shops and garages out of the large company vans you've probably seen around town. Even if you don't buy any tools, it's fun to look through the van. **Stahlwille** tools are my favorites, but they're not always easy to find. Sears' **Craftsman** tools are also good, guaranteed for life, and rather expensive. They sell a cheaper line too, just labeled "Sears." The most common tool sizes used on Toyotas are 10, 12, 14, 17 and 19mm wrenches and sockets. If you want to splurge, get the expensive wrenches in those sizes.

You can buy good medium-priced tools at auto parts stores, swap meets, surplus stores and reputable department stores such as Sears. Medium-priced tools work as well as the more expensive ones, they just don't feel as good and usually aren't guaranteed. I've gotten a lot of good, hard use out of **Stahlwille**, **S-K Wayne** and **New Britain** tools.

The really cheap brands (99 cents for a half dozen wrenches or screwdrivers) work once or twice, then break or bend—sometimes taking large hunks of flesh with them. Those bargain sets of 40 sockets and a ratchet wrench for $5-10 you find at the discount stores also fall in this category. Watch out!

The large "tool sets" often on sale at department stores aren't a good deal because you end up paying for (and hauling around) tools that you'll never use. On the other hand, good pliers and screwdriver sets can save you some money. It never hurts to have extra screwdrivers and pliers around.

When shopping for tools, here are some things to consider in addition to price:

Wrenches: *Combination wrenches* have a "box end" on one end and an "open end" on the other. They're generally the most useful. Buy wrenches with 12-point box ends because they allow you to get the wrench on bolts and nuts in twice as many positions as six-point box ends. Very handy in tight spots.

Most bolts and nuts on Toyotas are 10, 12, 14, 17 or 19mm. Having a selection of different lengths, shapes, and box end "offsets" of these sizes will make things easier. I like the way the box end of Stahlwille wrenches is attached: it's slightly offset and slightly angled so you won't scrape your knuckles as often. I get Stahlwille wrenches from the Mac Tool salesman.

Sockets: Buy six-point sockets—they're stronger than ones with 12 points. (You don't need the 12 points in sockets because the ratchet gives you an almost infinite option of angles for getting the socket onto the bolt or nut.)

Ratchets: For 3/8" drive sockets, ratchets with about six-inch handles are the most versatile. As you become a tool aficionado you'll want one with a three-inch handle for working in tight places and one with a nine-inch handle for added leverage. For ½" drive sockets, get a ratchet with a 12-inch handle.

Torque Wrench: Torque wrenches are a necessity for evenly tightening some nuts and bolts so they won't be so loose they unscrew themselves or so tight they break, strip the threads, or can't be removed the next time. The cheapest kind of torque wrench is a *beam type*. They're very accurate, but when using them in certain positions it's hard to read the indicator needle. I prefer the *"clicker"* type that you set at the desired torque, then the wrench clicks when that torque is reached. To keep clicker types accurate, they must always be unwound to the lowest setting after use to relieve the tension on the spring inside. They should be checked and recalibrated occasionally (every six months to two years depending on how much they're used).

A torque wrench capable of torquing nuts and bolts to 100 ft.lbs. will be adequate for all repairs on your truck.

PHASE 1 TOOL SET

The following list of tools and materials will get you through most of the procedures in this book. Again, you can buy 'em all at once, or just as you need them. Parts required are listed in the Tools and Materials list at the beginning of each procedure.

Safety Glasses: An absolute necessity if you value your eyesight. And who doesn't? Modern plastic ones are adequate and inexpensive.

Flashlight: One with a magnet attached to the side so you don't have to hold it, or one small enough to hold in your mouth. (Sometimes you need three or four hands anyway, so why waste one holding a flashlight?) The mini mag-lites are very versatile because you can focus the light beam, or unscrew and remove the lens and it becomes a lantern. Check the batteries regularly.

Jack: The one that comes with the car is OK for changing flat tires but don't crawl under the car while it's being held up by that little thing. See Chapter 2, Safety.

Lug Wrench: One should have come with the car. If it's missing, find either an original type or an X type ("'star wrench") at a salvage yard or parts counter.

Oil Filter Wrench: Since the oil filter is rather difficult to reach on some models, get a heavy duty band-type (preferably with a swivel handle) or the kind that fits over the end of the filter and has a place to fit a ratchet to unscrew the filter. I've gone through several cheap filter wrenches.

Combination Wrenches: 6, 8, 10, 12, 14, 17, and 19mm. This is your basic wrench set. "Open end" at one end and "box end" at the other. It's nice to have a complete set of regular length wrenches plus longer 12, 14, 17 and 19mm wrenches for added leverage on stubborn bolts and nuts. You can't have too many different lengths and shapes of 10, 12 and 14mm wrenches.

3/8" Drive Sockets: Same sizes as the combination wrenches. I urge you to get the six-point type sockets.

3/8" Drive Ratchet: Get a good one. I got my favorite ratchet in the '60s when it cost only $12; the same ratchet now costs about $35 (which is probably too much). I'll tell you what it is, though—an S-K Wayne #3870. It's long and has the kind of swivel head I like!

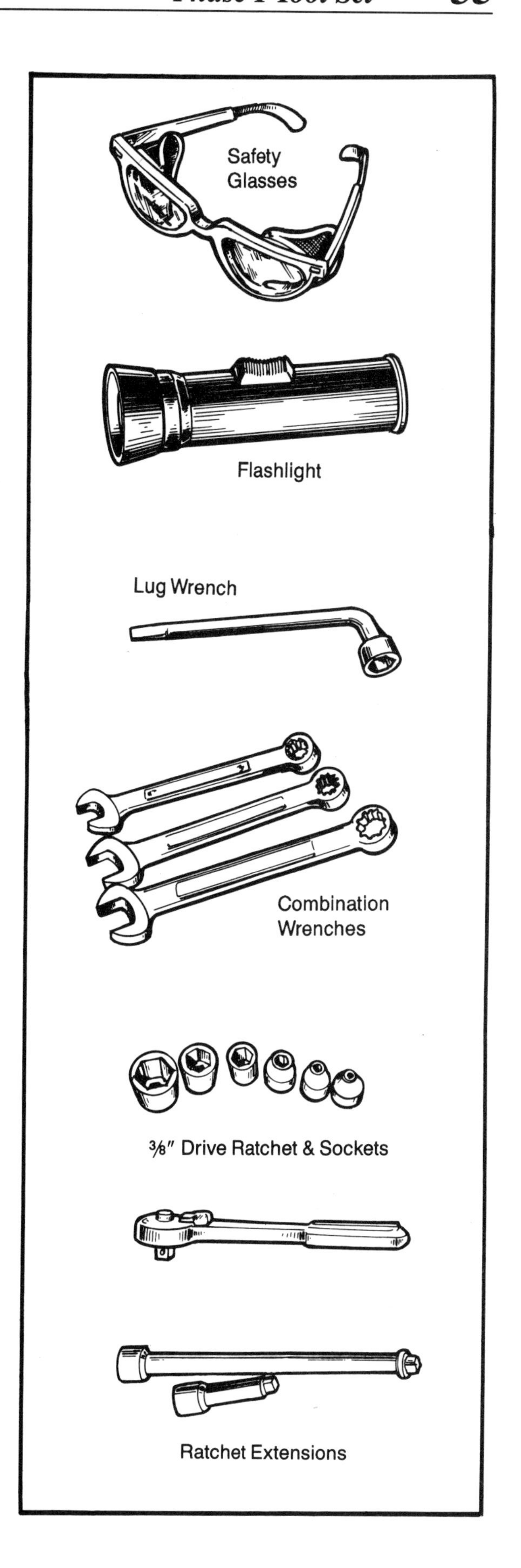

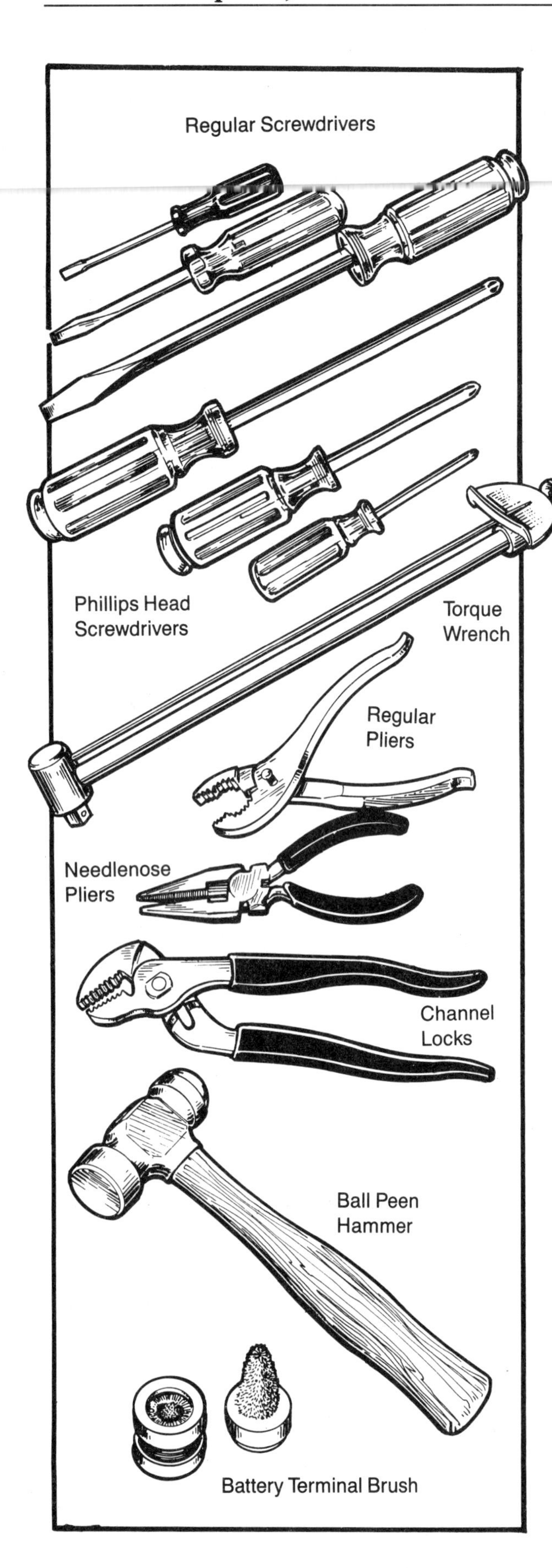

3/8" Drive Ratchet Extensions: Several, ranging from one inch to 12 inches. These make things easier to reach. They snap on between the ratchet and socket.

Screwdrivers: A variety, including short, medium and long ones with narrow and regular width blades. Get one giant one (16 inches to 24 inches long and strong).

Phillips Head Screwdrivers: Get good quality small, medium and large ones. The cheap ones wear out quickly and ruin the screws. These screwdrivers are for dealing with all those screws with cross-shaped slots in their heads.

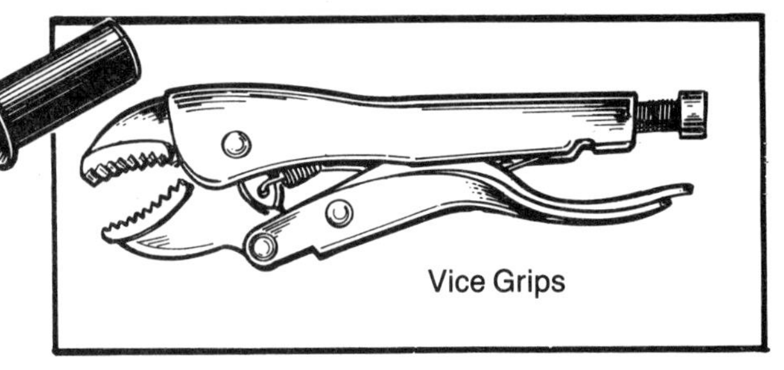

Torque Wrench: See the Torque Wrench rap earlier in this chapter. It tells about the kinds available. How to use a torque wrench is explained in Chapter 15.

Pliers: Regular and needlenose, and one set of large **Channel Locks**. Channel Locks are long-handled pliers with adjustable jaws.

Vise Grips: One medium size (eight-inch) with flat jaws. Vise Grip is a brand name of locking pliers. You'll learn to love this tool—it's like having an extra hand.

Ball Peen Hammer: A 12-16 oz. model. Carpenter's hammers are not safe for use on cars.

Battery Terminal Cleaner: The kind with internal and external wire brushes. These are handy, cheap and readily available, but you can get by with a knife or the small wire brush mentioned below.

12 Volt Test Light: For finding shorts (electrical) and checking for "juice" in your wiring and electrical components.

Crescent Wrench: Handy when you can't find the wrench size you need. Get a four-inch and eight-inch. Don't use them when the right-size combination wrench is available—they're not as safe and tend to round off the edges of nuts and bolts.

Pocket Knife: Swiss Army type with as many gizmo blades as you can afford. That corkscrew or bottle opener could save the day at a picnic.

Small Wire Brush: Get one about the size of a toothbrush. I've found good cheap ones in art supply stores.

GOOD Tire Gauge: Absolutely necessary for radial tires. The cheap pencil types don't stay accurate for very long.

Rags and Paper Towels: To clean your hands and tools, and to mop up spills. Worn out clothing works well for rags.

½" Drive Sockets: 17, 19, 21, 22 and 24mm. Again, go for quality six-point sockets.

½" Drive Ratchet or "Breaker Bar" and a six-inch Extension: For the ½" drive sockets. Get a big one with about a 12-inch long handle. A breaker bar is a socket handle without a ratchet mechanism—it's wonderful on really stubborn bolts.

1/2" to 3/8" Adapter: So you can use the 3/8" sockets on the 1/2" ratchet, breaker bar and torque wrench.

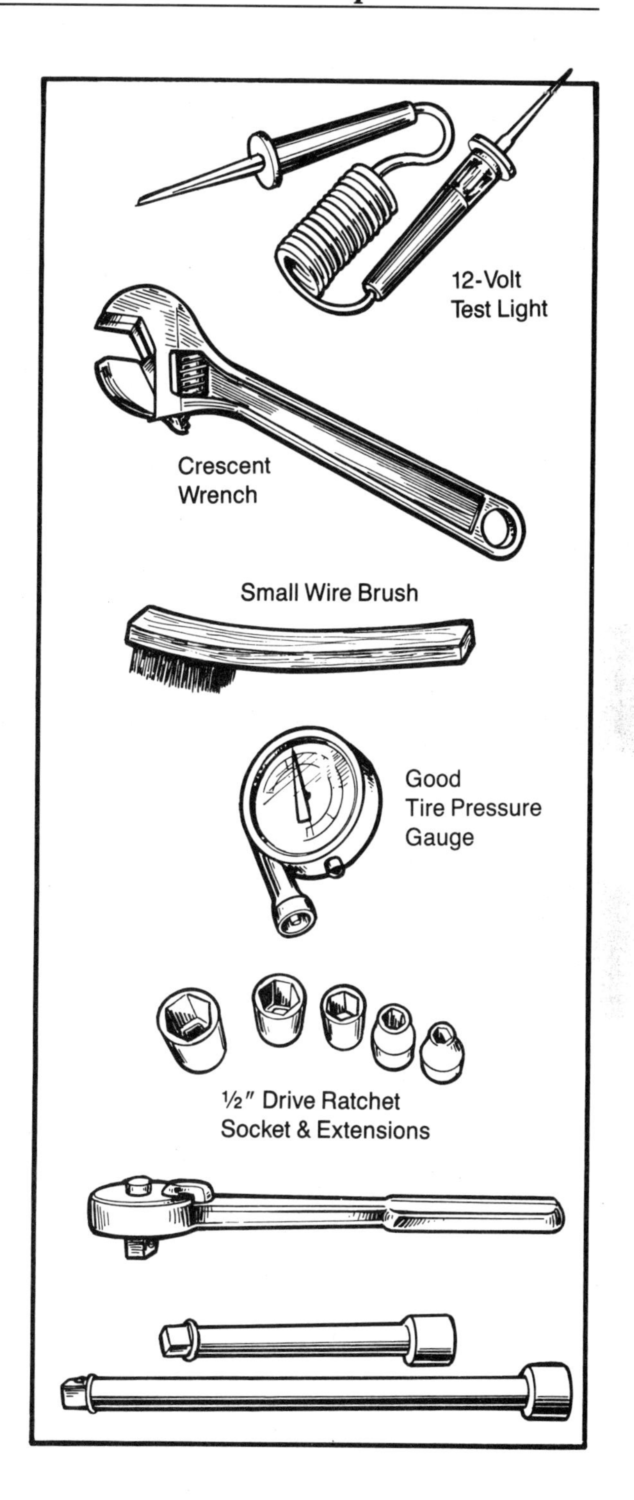

TUNE-UP TOOLS

These tools are used only when tuning the engine. Several more are illustrated in Chapter 5.

Spark Plug Socket: Right. It's for checking or changing the spark plugs. There should be a rubber boot inside to grab the spark plug.

Feeler Gauges: The "Go/No-Go" kind are the easiest to use. What they are and how to use them is explained in Chapter 5, Procedure 8, Step 4. '78-'87 models also require .008-.016in brass feeler gauges.

Spark Plug Gapper: Bosch makes a really nice one. A cheap one will do, though.

Strobe Timing Light: For setting the ignition timing. The inductive kind are easiest to use. Get the kind that connects to the car's battery for power. Avoid the cheapies, which are practically useless unless you live in a cave or mine shaft.

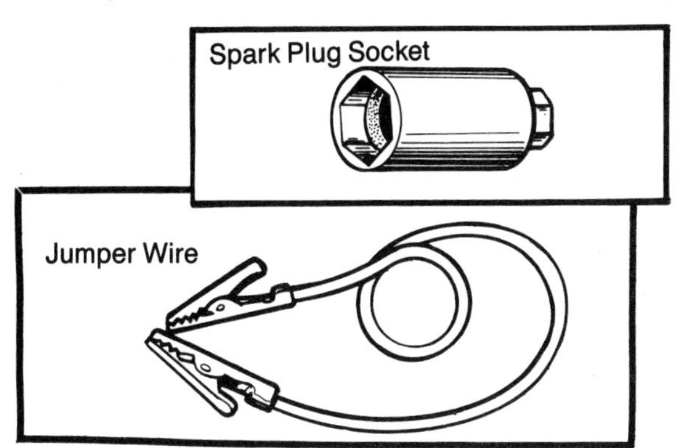

Jumper Wire: A jumper is a wire with an alligator clip on each end. EFI models also need a short piece of wire with ¼" of insulation stripped from each end.

Tach/Dwell Gauge: For setting engine idle speed and the points dwell on distributors with breaker points.

Compression Gauge: The kind that screws into the spark plug hole will eliminate the need for a helper. The cheaper kind that you just push into the hole is OK—if you have a Friend.

1/8" (4mm) Vacuum Hose: Get about 12 to 18 inches of this rubber hosing. It's for checking vacuum operated gizmos on the engine. Don't use the brake bleeding hose for this.

Ruler or Small Tape Measure: For measuring things like clutch and brake pedal "free play." Either inches or centimeters is OK.

Grease Gun: A small mini grease gun will be adequate. Keep a couple of spare tubes of grease around because you can't tell when the gun is almost empty.

Grease Gun Attachment ('79-'83 4WD only): An attachment for the grease gun is required to get to the driveshaft grease zerks. One should be in the tool kit that came with the truck. If it's missing you'll probably have to get it from the Toyota dealer.

File: A small, flat, hard steel one to file burrs off of parts.

Magnet: The kind about the size of a pencil is adequate. Fancy ones have radio antennae type extension handles.

PHASE II: OPTIONAL AND SPECIAL TOOLS

Consider getting these tools as need arises.

3/16" (5mm) Clear Plastic Tubing and Glass Jar: For bleeding the brake system (see Chapter 7). Old suction tubing from hospitals works well.

Chisel: One with a sharp ½" to ¾" wide tip. Make sure it's one designed for use on steel. Do not use woodworking chisels: you'll ruin them, and probably your eyes too.

Cheater Pipe: A piece of pipe a couple of feet long that will fit over the handle of the ½" drive ratchet or breaker bar. It's for persuading extremely tight bolts or nuts.

Hacksaw and Blades (fine and coarse): For when the going really gets tough.

Snap Ring Pliers (for circlips): Wait to buy these until you definitely need them. If possible, get the kind that can convert to work on either internal or external snap rings. The kind with changeable tips of different sizes and shapes are the most versatile. Sears sells a nice set.

Lock Ring Pliers: They are like snap ring pliers except that they have flat tips.

Volt/Ohm Meter: A Volt/Ohm meter (VOM) is very handy to have around. Radio Shack sells good cheap ones. Minimum requirements are listed in Chapter 15. How to use a VOM is also explained in that chapter.

Jumper Cables: For when the battery runs down because you left the headlights or radio on, etc.

Tow Rope, Chain or Cable: To tow a disabled vehicle. Or (gulp) to be towed with. Canvas-like towing straps are good, lightweight and easy to store beneath the seats.

Funnel with a Long Skinny Neck: To add oil to the automatic transmission.

Syringe, Eye Dropper or Turkey Baster: To suck brake fluid out of the brake and clutch master cylinder reservoirs when you change the brake fluid.

Oil Suction Gun, Large Syringe or Turkey Baster: You need one to get oil into the manual transmission, differential(s), or the transfer case on 4WD models.

Pickle Forks or Small Two Jaw Puller: For removing ball joints and/or tie rods on the steering and suspension systems. It takes a larger pickle fork for the ball joints than for the tie rods.

Battery Terminal Puller: It's a small two jaw puller for separating stuck battery cable clamps from the battery posts.

Rubber Gloves: To keep your pinkies pink.

Tire Pump: You can buy inexpensive pumps that plug into a spark plug hole on the engine. Or, if you enjoy aerobic exercise, get a good manual bicycle pump.

PHASE III: DON'T LEAVE TOWN WITHOUT 'EM

Following is a list of tools and parts that should be considered part of the truck. This survival kit will cover 90% of road emergencies (and several repair procedures). I roll the tools up in old towels and stash them under the seats.

Jack, jack handle and **lug wrench**, small and medium **regular** and **phillips screwdrivers**, **pliers** (regular and needlenose), **Vise Grips**, **feeler gauges**, **plug gapper**, **crescent wrench**, **10, 12, 14, 17 and 19mm wrenches and sockets**, **ratchet**, **ratchet extension**, **spark plug socket**, **12-volt test light**, **pocket knife**, **tire gauge**, **rags**.

Here's a list of spare parts that could save you hours of despair and a large towing fee. Most of them can be stashed under the front seat. **Ignition points** ('75-'77 models only), **distributor cap and rotor**, a set of **spark plugs**, spare **fuses**, **fusible links**, **drive belt(s)**, and a couple of quarts of **oil**.

If you bash around off-road a lot, **jumper cables**, a **tow strap** and a **tire pump** (manual or engine operated) should be on board at all times. You should also consider a **first aid kit** and some **survival gear** (spare water, clothing, matches, etc.). I've listed the source for several survival books for hard core off-roaders in Chapter 14.

GARAGE MATERIALS

The following materials are frequently needed for the maintenance and repair procedures. They're handy to have around to avoid trips to the parts store early Saturday or Sunday morning:

Hand Cleaner: Get the kind with lanolin to keep your hands soft and lily white. Ivory Liquid dish detergent is a good substitute if you're caught dirty handed. Goop it on full strength, then wash it off. Incidentally, Goop is also a brand name of hand cleaner.

Rags and Paper Towels: Seems like you can never have too many rags around. Don't use fuzzy ones that might shed on things. Old bath towels are my favorites.

Catch Pan: To drain oil and antifreeze into. You can also use it for cleaning parts. Plastic ones are cheap these days. Get one that will hold at least five quarts.

Parts Cleaning Brush: Get a brush with long, stiff, fiber bristles. An old toothbrush is also very good for cleaning small parts.

Spray Cans of Cleaner: *Berryman B-12 Carburetor Cleaner* and *Solder Seal Brake Cleaner* are handy to have around. When sprayed on parts, they dissolve the crud so it runs off, then they evaporate without leaving a residue. Try not to breathe too much of the stuff and be sure and wear safety glasses to protect your eyes.

Penetrating Oil: *Liquid Wrench*, *WD-40* and *Marvel Mystery Oil* all work well, but my favorite is *Sili Kroil* made by Kano Labs in Nashville, Tenn. It penetrates, then lubricates with silicone. (And it's pink!)

Wheel Bearing Grease: A small can of high-temperature wheel bearing grease is always handy to have around. You may even need it to grease the wheel bearings.

Cleaning Solvent: You can buy this by the gallon at some filling stations, parts stores and machine shops. It's safer than using gasoline. *Never* use gasoline in a closed area or near heat or flame. In fact, it's best to use the same precaution with all cleaning solvents.

Drop Light: Get the kind that has a metal cage around the bulb (the plastic ones melt, then stink). Also good (but more expensive) are the fluorescent drop lights called "Sunlights."

Extension Cord: Get one with at least 14-gauge wire (12-gauge is even better). The length you need depends on how handily your wall outlets are located.

Silicone Gasket Sealer: A tube of the blue stuff works on nearly all gaskets except those exposed to gasoline. Also available is high temperature silicone sealer (it's red).

Hydraulic Floor Jack and Jackstands: You can pick these up pretty cheaply these days. They make working on your truck a lot faster, easier and safer. Jackstands are a must if you plan to crawl under the truck.

Fire Extinguisher: The kind that puts out gasoline fires. Keep it handy and check it regularly. A small one (or two) will do.

Conveniences and Odds n' Ends: A role of soft tie wire (baling wire, machinist's wire), pair of coveralls, stocking cap for long hair, low stool to sit on while you work, a large piece of cardboard or plastic to lie on, a few sheets of fine emery paper, plastic sandwich baggies, masking tape, rubber bands, indelible pen.

PARTS

Prices for Toyota parts vary radically from store to store. Store A might have good prices on some parts but not on others. The price markup in Store B might be exactly the opposite from Store A. And the same applies to the Toyota dealer parts department: some of their prices are the best you can find, while others are two or three times more than for the same part in the parts stores. A few phone calls or a little legwork can save you quite a bundle.

When trekking to the parts store, be armed with your Toy's *production date*, *vehicle identification number (VIN)*, and *engine serial number*. These will maximize your chances of getting the right part the first time. How to find these numbers is in Chapter 2.

OTHER SOURCES OF INFORMATION

You should find a copy of the *Owner's Manual* stashed in the glove box. It has lots of little tidbits about your particular year and model. If yours has disappeared, I urge you to get one from the parts department at the Toyota dealer. As of 1987 the Owner's Manuals cost $3.95 each.

A Toyota factory repair manual for your model is handy to have around. They have lots of pictures, and cover things not included in this manual, like transmission and differential repair, replacing body parts, etc. As of 1987 the books cost $29.95 and are available through the parts department at the Toyota dealer.

The Toyota *Owner's Manual* and factory workshop manuals can be ordered by phone and charged on your credit card. The phone numbers are 1-800-443-7656 for California residents or 1-800-622-2033 for non-Californians.

The *Toyota Pickup Truck Service Manual* by Robert Bentley is good. It has lots of photos but the instructions are rather abbreviated. Unless you're quite experienced (mechanically speaking), you may find the manual difficult to understand. You can buy the Bentley manual at automotive parts stores.

I've included a list of magazines and catalogs applicable to Toyota trucks in Chapter 14.

SAFETY WITH TOOLS

Use your head! Not as a substitute for a 10 pound hammer, but to select the correct tool for each job. Take the time to pick out the right wrench, extension, etc., for the task. Wear your safety glasses when underneath the vehicle and wherever else called for to protect your eyes while working. Wear a painter's mask or respirator when dealing with dust, especially during brake and clutch jobs. Regardless of what else you might snort, keep the black brake and clutch powder out of your nose. That asbestos stuff is very nasty.

If you haven't worked with hand tools before, gradually get the feel of them. Make sure sockets and wrenches are fully on the nut or bolt head before you pull, and anticipate where your elbow or knuckles might land if a tool slips. Clean your tools after each use so you can look forward to fondling them the next time. Unless you've skipped ahead to this chapter, you have already read my safety rap in Chapter 2. It's friendly—and essential. I want you to make it through each procedure without so much as a scratch. Thank you.

CHAPTER 4
TROUBLESHOOTING

Club Fred

Whatever's wrong, it is rarely as bad as you first expect. (Only very occasionally is it far worse than you could ever imagine.)

You are here because your Toy is misbehaving in one way or another, right? If you're stuck on the side of a busy road, you also have sweaty palms and a sick feeling in the pit of your stomach. Regardless of your present situation, there's NO need to panic! Take one step at a time in a logical order, and you can probably diagnose the problem—then either fix it on the spot (if you have the necessary tools and parts onboard), nurse it home, resign yourself to taking the car to a garage or, in rare cases, call for a tow truck. At the very least, you'll know how serious the problem is or isn't.

This chapter lists some of the most likely problems you may encounter and tells you which chapter and procedure tells how to fix the problem. To use this troubleshooting guide, find the section that applies to your problem (Engine, Brakes, Noises, etc.), then locate the symptom that sent you here in the first place (engine won't start, brakes squeal, steering wheel vibrates, etc.). I'll tell you how to fix the problem, direct you to the appropriate chapter and procedure in the book, or advise you to seek professional help. Oftentimes diagnosing the problem is the hardest part. If you can't identify the problem, take the truck to the Toyota dealer or a garage for a professional diagnosis, which should cost little, provided you insist that it's just a diagnosis you want. Once the problem is diagnosed, read through the appropriate chapter and procedure, then decide whether it's something you feel confident tackling or whether you'd rather have someone else fix it for you.

If you don't know what the various components mentioned in this chapter look like and where they are located, read the Orientation part of Chapter 2.

ENGINE PROBLEMS

1. Engine Stops and/or Won't Start.

A. Starter Doesn't Turn the Engine or Turns It Very Slowly:

Turn the ignition key to ON and check the dashboard lights, headlights, horn, and other electrical gizmos.

1. Lights and electrical things DON'T work or JUST BARELY work (dim lights, etc.): See Chapter 8, Procedure 2, Step 3, to check the fusible links. If the links are OK, see Chapter 8, Procedure 1, Step 1, to check and add battery fluid, and Step 3 in that procedure to clean the battery terminal connections. If you don't have the proper tools, try *gently* tapping with the lug wrench, a rock, or whatever's handy on each cable clamp where it attaches to the battery, then try to start the engine. The tapping might temporarily make the connection good enough to start the engine. You might also try wiggling the ends of the battery cables where they attach to the engine and starter (Chapter 8, Procedure 1, Step 4). If the engine starts, clean both ends of the battery cables as soon as possible.

If the electrical equipment still doesn't work after cleaning the terminals, the battery is discharged. You'll need a jump start (Chapter 8, Procedure 1, Step 8), or else you'll have to remove the battery (Chapter 8, Procedure 1, Step 7) and take it to a garage or service station to be trickle charged. Why did the battery lose its charge? Check the alternator drive belt and if necessary, tighten or replace it (Chapter 8, Procedure 3, Step 2). If the drive belt is in good condition and properly adjusted, see Chapter 8, Procedure 1, Step 5, to check the battery condition, and Chapter 8, Procedure 6, to check the charging system.

2. Lights and electrical things all work normally but the starter won't turn the engine: The problem is in the cranking system. Chapter 8, Procedure 9, tells you how to check the cranking system.

B. Starter Cranks Engine Normally but Engine Won't Start:

To make the engine run, three elements are necessary: air, fuel and a spark to ignite the fuel and air. Unless you live in a vacuum, there's plenty of air available so let's check the other two.

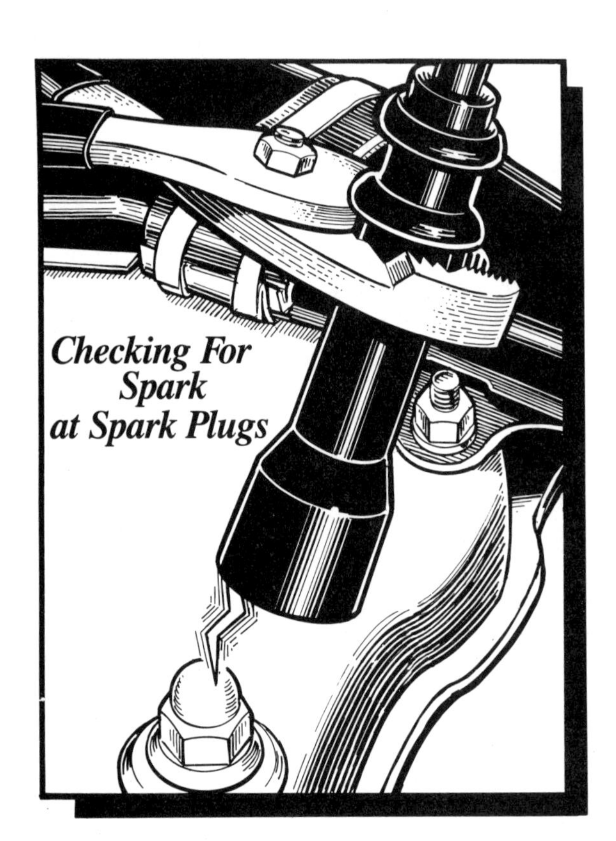
Checking For Spark at Spark Plugs

1. Spark plug wire test: Remove one of the spark plugs from the engine (Chapter 5, Procedure 7, Step 2), or use a spare plug if you have one handy. Connect the spark plug wire to the spark plug, then use a plastic or wood handled screwdriver or insulated pliers to hold the metal part of the spark plug against a metal part of the engine. Have Friend crank the engine while you watch for a spark across the electrodes on the end of the spark plug. If a spark intermittently jumps the gap, the ignition system is OK; skip down to *4. Fuel Test*. No spark across the spark plug electrodes? Do the coil test below.

2. Coil tests: Disconnect the coil wire from the distributor cap and test it for spark (Chapter 8, Procedure 11, Step 1). If a Friend isn't available to help you, just prop or tie the end of the wire close to bare metal (away from the carburetor or fuel pump) where you can see it from the driver's seat. Then crank the engine with the key to START while you watch the end of the wire. If juice is getting to the end of the coil wire, you'll be able to see (and probably hear) a strong blue spark as you crank the engine.

If there's no spark, check all of the wire connections on the end of the coil for tightness. Tighten them if necessary. Wire connections all tight? Check the fusible links and the fuse labeled IGN in the fuse box (Chapter 8, Procedure 2, Step 1). If you have a 12-volt test light, turn the ignition switch to ON, then do the quick coil checks in Chapter 8, Procedure 1, Step 1. If the coil isn't getting juice, the problem is probably in the electrical part of the ignition switch. Chapter 8, Procedure 14, tells how to replace the switch. Or have the Toyota dealer or a garage check the switch for you. If the coil is getting juice but the spark plugs aren't, the problem is in the distributor (see below).

3. Distributor checks: If there's a small wire terminal on the outside of the distributor, check the connection for tightness and tighten the little nut or screw if necessary. Remove and inspect the distributor cap and rotor (Chapter 5, Procedure 9, Steps 1-4). Look for broken or loose wires inside the distributor.

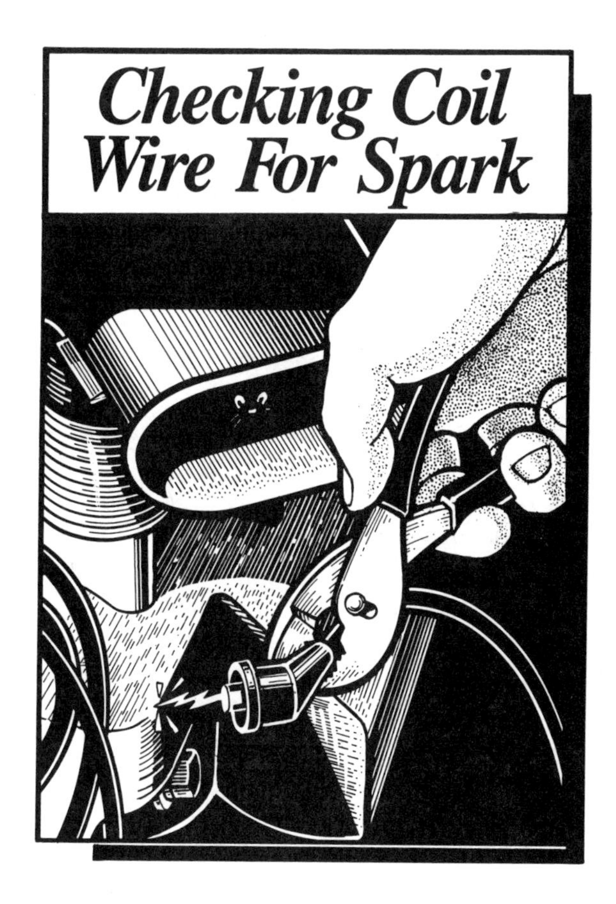

If the small wires from the distributor are connected to a plastic connector a few inches away from the distributor, disconnect the two halves of the connector and check that the contact points inside the connector are clean and free of corrosion. If you find corrosion, use a wire brush to clean the contacts, then reconnect the two connector halves. Be sure they are locked together.

'75-'77 models: Do Chapter 5, Procedure 11 to inspect and adjust the points. If the points are adjusted correctly and open and close as you rotate the engine, rotate the engine so the points are closed (no gap). Turn the ignition switch to ON, then use a plastic or wooden handled screwdriver to push the moveable arm of the points set away from the stationary arm. You should see a spark when the moveable arm breaks contact with the stationary arm. No spark? Check the wire between the wire terminal on the side of the distributor and the points set, and the little ground wire that connects the body of the distributor to one of the points set attaching screws. If either wire is broken or disconnected, reattach or replace it as necessary.

If there's still no spark when you move the points arm, the plastic insulator for the wire terminal bolt on the side of the distributor might be broken or missing, allowing the bolt to touch the distributor body. Replace the insulator if necessary.

Still no spark? It's time for professional advice.

'78-'87 models: If the truck starts OK when the engine is cold but not after it's warmed up, the signal generator (electronic pick-up unit) in the distributor might be shot. Chapter 8, Procedure 11, Step 3, tells how to check it.

4. Fuel tests: You're sure there's gas in the gas tank, and you've checked the ignition system and you're sure electricity is getting to the spark plugs, right? OK. '80-'87 20R and 22R models, do Chapter 9, Procedure 4, to see if fuel is getting to the carburetor. '75-'79 and 22R-E and 22R-TE models should do Chapter 9, Procedure 6, Step 3, to see if the fuel pump is working. You'll be directed where to turn according to the results of the checks.

2. Engine Starts OK, but Doesn't Run Right

You can get the engine to start, but it isn't running the way you know it should. Symptoms are rough running, hesitation, lack of power, poor gas mileage, backfiring or "pinging." Lack of power and/or poor gas mileage can be caused by any or all of the following problems.

A. Engine Pinging:

Engine pinging (also called pre-ignition) sounds like someone's in the engine compartment shaking a coffee can full of small pebbles. It usually occurs during rapid acceleration or when going up hills. What's happening is that the fuel/air mixture is being prematurely ignited in the cylinders.

The problem could be that you're "lugging" the engine by using too high a gear for the driving conditions. Even a well-tuned engine in good condition will ping when it's lugged down. Try driving the truck at a higher engine rpm. If lugging isn't your problem, here are some other causes and cures for pinging.

1. Wrong fuel: The fuel octane is too low; use gas with a higher octane rating.

2. Ignition timing: The ignition timing is too far advanced. Adjust it. Chapter 5, Procedure 12 tells you how.

3. Faulty vacuum advance unit (20R and 22R engines): Check and if necessary replace the unit (Chapter 5, Procedure 9, Step 7).

4. Buildup of carbon in the combustion chambers: 20R and 22R models should check the automatic choke (Chapter 9, Procedure 9). Everyone should check the spark plugs and do a compression check to see if excess oil is getting into the combustion chambers (Chapter 5, Procedure 7).

B. Rough Running:

Your engine feels and sounds like it's not running on all its cylinders all the time. Often there's a drop in power and gas mileage.

1. Vacuum leaks: If the engine has suddenly started running like a three legged dog, look for a vacuum hose that has come off its fitting. The open line will probably make a hissing noise when the engine is running. If you find the culprit, reconnect the hose or replace it if it's cracked or stretched on the end.

2. Check spark plug wire connections, spark plugs, and engine compression: Are the spark plug wires securely connected to the distributor cap and spark plugs? Check 'em: push down on both ends of each wire. Remove the spark plugs and check their condition. Do a compression test while the spark plugs are out and evaluate the results. How to do all this is in Chapter 5, Procedure 7.

3. Coil and coil wire connections: Check the coil and the wires attached to it (Chapter 8, Procedure 11). Replace the coil or tighten the wires if necessary.

4. Carburetor checks on 20R and 22R engines: For these checks you'll need to remove the air cleaner (Chapter 5, Procedure 6, Step 1).

Choke: To see if the choke is working, see Chapter 9, Procedure 9.

Anti-diesel valve: The symptom of a faulty anti-diesel valve is that the engine runs OK at high rpm but won't idle. Have the Toyota dealer or a garage check the anti-diesel valve on the carburetor for you.

Electrical connections on the carburetor: Follow all of the wires attached to the carburetor to where they connect to the wiring harness. Be sure the connections are clean and tight.

5. Check for water in the gas tank: See Chapter 9, Procedure 7, to see if enough water has condensed in the tank to make the engine run poorly.

6. Clogged EGR system: See Chapter 10, Procedure 2. If the EGR valve is stuck in the open position, the engine won't idle properly.

C. Engine Backfires:

If your Toy occasionally makes loud explosions that cause nearby motorists to duck for cover, check the following systems as soon as possible or you run the risk of blowing the exhaust system apart.

1. Idle speed: If the backfire only happens when you turn the ignition key OFF, the engine might be idling too fast. Check and adjust the idle speed (Chapter 5, Procedure 13).

2. Improper ignition timing: See Chapter 5, Procedure 12, to check the timing.

3. Distributor problems: See Chapter 5, Procedure 9, to do several easy distributor checks.

4. Crossed spark plug wires: Be sure the rotor is pointing to the #1 spark plug wire when the timing marks on the pulley are aligned with the pointer (Chapter 5, Procedure 5, Step 3); then trace the wires, going counterclockwise from the #1 wire on the distributor cap—the wires should go to cylinders #1, #2, #4 and #3, in order.

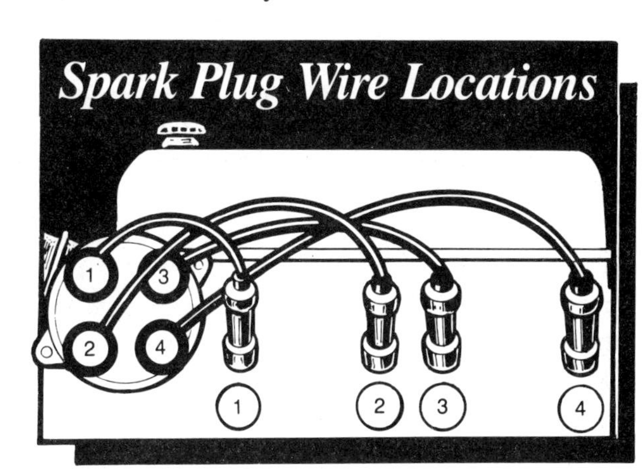

5. Clogged EGR system: See Chapter 10, Procedure 2.

6. Leaking or sticking exhaust valves: A compression test will tell you if the valves are leaking (Chapter 5, Procedure 7). An oil and filter change might prevent the valves from sticking.

7. Leaking or worn out exhaust system: The engine normally creates some backfires but you don't hear them because the muffler(s) muffle the sound. If the inside of the muffler is worn out or there are leaks in the exhaust system, you'll hear these normal backfires. Tighten the clamps if they're loose, or replace the exhaust pipe, catalyst or muffler/tailpipe assembly. It's all in Chapter 10, Procedure 6.

D. Engine Hesitates When Accelerator Pedal Is Pressed Down Suddenly:

This symptom is called a "flat spot" and is usually caused by not enough fuel being pumped into the engine when the pedal is pressed down.

1. Check accelerator pump on 20R and 22R models: Remove the air cleaner lid (Chapter 5, Procedure 4, Step 3). Use a finger or screwdriver to hold the choke plate in the top right side of the carburetor in a vertical position.

With the engine OFF and the choke plate in a vertical position, have Friend pump the gas pedal a few times while you peer into the barrel on the right side of the carb. If a Friend isn't available, you'll have to rotate the throttle arm on the side of the carb where the accelerator mechanism attaches. You should see a healthy stream of gas squirt into the barrel from a small brass nozzle each time the pedal is pushed down or the throttle arm is rotated. A weak, puny stream, or no gas at all, means the accelerator pump nozzle is clogged or the accelerator pump diaphragm is broken. Have the Toyota dealer or a garage fix it for you, or buy a carburetor rebuild kit and replace the accelerator pump diaphragm yourself.

2. Check mechanical and vacuum advance unit on the distributor: If the accelerator pump in the carb is working correctly but there's still a flat spot, see Chapter 5, Procedure 9, to check the advance mechanisms in the distributor.

E. High Tech Self-Diagnosing Capability On '84-'87 EFI Models:

'84-'87 Toyotas with EFI have an onboard computer to diagnose problems in the electrical sensors and components related to the electronically controlled fuel injection system.

I'll explain how the self-diagnosis works because it's so fascinating (to me anyway) and probably indicates how high-technology gizmos will be involved in automotive diagnosis in the future. Before long our cars will probably moan and cry when something is wrong. To do these checks you'll need a short piece of insulated wire with about ¼" of insulation stripped from each end. To understand what the codes mean you'll need the Toyota workshop manual for your year so you can look up the code numbers for the various components. Here's how the miracle works:

If there's a problem in one of the electrical sensors or components of the EFI, the CHECK ENGINE light on the dash goes on while the engine is running and the computer stores a code for the problem in its memory. To make the computer tell you what's wrong, the throttle valve must be fully closed (take your foot off the gas pedal), the battery must have at least 11 volts of juice, the transmission must be in NEUTRAL, all accessories must be off and the engine must be at normal operating temperature. Turn the ignition key to ON but don't start the engine. Now see Chapter 5, Procedure 12, to turn off the electronic advance mechanism in the distributor. (You use a short piece of wire to bridge two terminals.) When the terminals are bridged, the CHECK ENGINE light on the dash will flash a numerical code to identify problems in one or more of the components. One flash every 4.5 seconds means the computer doesn't detect any problems in the system. When you're through playing with the computer, remove the jumper wire and fit the test connector back into its rubber boot ('84-'86 models), or put the lid back on the little box ('87 models).

This high-tech stuff is nifty, eh? It's great for identifying which system has a problem but it doesn't tell you which part of the system is broken—whether it's the electrical component, the wiring for the component, or maybe even the ECU unit itself has a problem. The Toyota workshop manuals devote pages and pages of flow charts to using a volt/ohm meter and dwell meter to diagnose the various engine electrical systems. If you're electronically inclined, let the ECU diagnose which system is malfunctioning, then buy the workshop manual for your year and follow the flow charts. Otherwise, have Toyota diagnose the problem and replace the faulty part for you.

3. Engine Overheating.

Most overheating is caused by owners not taking the time to do periodic tune-up, lubrication and maintenance of their cars. If your engine starts running a little hotter than normal, run through the following checks *before* you get stuck in rush hour traffic with your hood up and your radiator and temper bellowing clouds of steam.

A. Emergency Overheating:

If you are ever cruising along and suddenly notice the needle on the temperature gauge is indicating HOT, what should you do? What would Captain Kirk do?

If the alternator charge light is on, the alternator drive belt is probably broken and not turning the water pump. Check, then adjust or replace the alternator drive belt if necessary (Chapter 8, Procedure 3).

If you're driving up a steep grade on a hot day with a heavy load, there's probably nothing wrong with the truck. It's just being overworked. When the temperature gauge drops to normal, start the engine and drive on—with one eye on the temperature gauge. If you have a tachometer, use a gear that allows the engine to turn between 2,500 and 3,000 RPM. If the engine quickly overheats again, pull over and go through Steps 1 through 8, below. If everything seems OK, you'll need to do Step 9.

1. Don't Panic—Just Act! Turn the air conditioner OFF if it's on. Set the heater control to HOT and the fan switch to ON. As soon as it's safe, pull off the road and turn the engine off. These moves will release excess engine heat into the air.

Open and prop the hood. **Do not remove the radiator cap.** Check the coolant level in the reservoir and add some if necessary (Chapter 5, Procedure 2, Step 7).

Check the following things while the engine cools. If you are in an emergency situation, be careful—everything under the hood will be HOT.

2. Check drive belts: See Chapter 8, Procedure 3 to check the drive belt(s). Too loose or broken? Wait until the engine has cooled a little before trying to adjust or replace the drive belts. You do have spare drive belts and the tools necessary to change them stashed somewhere, don't you?

3. Look for coolant leaks on the engine and radiator: See the Pressure Leaks section below to see everywhere the cooling system could be leaking. Pay particular attention to the hoses and clamps.

4. Check the engine oil level: See Chapter 5, Procedure 2, Step 1.

5. Tap on thermostat housing: Use the handle of a hammer, screwdriver, or the lug wrench to tap (not bang) on the thermostat housing. It's on the engine end of the large black radiator hose that's attached to the top rear side of the radiator. If the thermostat is stuck closed, the tapping might jar it loose.

6. Check front of radiator: See if a newspaper or something is blocking the flow of air through the front of the radiator. If necessary, remove the grille (Chapter 5, Procedure 4, Step 10), then remove the offending obstacle. Install the grille.

7. Check water pump: Symptoms of a worn out water pump are: (1) squeals up front when you first start the car in the morning; (2) the pulley on the water pump can be wiggled up and down or side to side by hand; and (3) coolant leaking from the water pump. To be sure it's the pump leaking, use a small mirror to peek behind the bottom of the water pump pulley. There's a little hole in the water pump housing where coolant will leak if the seals in the water pump are worn out. You'll see drips or other signs of water residue at the hole. If you determine the water pump needs to be replaced, see Chapter 6, Procedure 4.

8. Check coolant level: If the reservoir was completely empty, wait at least 15 minutes, then put a rag over the radiator cap and *slowly* turn it *counterclockwise*. If you hear a hissing or gurgling sound, stop. Wait a few minutes, then try to slowly unscrew the cap again, stopping if you hear noises. When the cap is off, check the coolant level in the radiator. It should be up to the base of the radiator cap neck. If it isn't, wait another 15 minutes, then add coolant (or water if that's all that's available) until the radiator is full. Install the radiator cap.

If the reservoir level is low, ideally you should add an antifreeze/water mixture, but if you're out on the road, find some clean water. Don't use dirty, funky water from the roadside ditch: it'll clog the cooling system. Pour coolant (or water) into the reservoir until it's up to the FULL line.

If you noticed a coolant leak on the radiator or hoses, fit the radiator cap on the radiator but don't tighten it. This way the system won't pressurize and force the coolant out. If you didn't see any leaks, install the cap and tighten it. Lower the hood, then drive slowly for a while (air conditioner OFF). Keep an eye on the temperature gauge.

Everything seems OK? If you added water only to the radiator, remember to add antifreeze when you get home and the engine is cold. If the coolant level is low again, check the hoses and clamps (Chapter 6, Procedure 2), and do the checks for a leaking head gasket in Section 6.

If the engine overheats again, have Scotty beam you up, or call someone to tow you to the Toyota dealer or a garage and have them pressure test the cooling system (below).

9. Pressure test cooling system and cap: Have the radiator cap and cooling system pressure tested by the Toyota dealer, a garage or radiator shop. It shouldn't cost much.

The cap should hold at least 11 - 15 psi (pounds per square inch) of pressure before the pressure relief valve in the cap opens. If it doesn't, replace it with a new cap.

The cooling system should hold at least 12 psi for two minutes. If it doesn't, check the following items. If you don't have pressure or coolant leaks, skip ahead to the No Pressure Leaks section.

Pressure Leaks: If the cooling system fails the Captain Kirk pressure test, do the following:

Check the seams around the edges of the radiator and where the cooling fins connect to the top and bottom of the radiator. A slow leak will eventually dissolve the black paint and expose the brass radiator and/or form a greenish deposit. If the radiator is leaking, remove it and have it repaired at a reputable radiator repair shop (Chapter 6, Procedure 6).

Check the thermostat housing (that bulbous thing on the engine where the upper radiator hose connects). If it leaks, remove it and replace the gasket (Chapter 6, Procedure 5).

Use a mirror to look at the bottom of the water pump, behind the pulley. There's a little hole back there where coolant will come out if a seal inside the water pump has died. If the water pump leaks, replace it (Chapter 6, Procedure 4).

Check all of the radiator, bypass and heater hoses in the engine compartment. Tighten any loose clamps and replace any leaking hoses (Chapter 6, Procedure 2). See if the heater or heater hoses under the dash are leaking. (Is the carpet or floor mat wet and smelly?) If there's a leak inside the truck, have the Toyota dealer or a garage determine if it's the heater hoses or the heater's core leaking. Let them fix it.

Check the crankcase drain plug on the left side of the engine. If tightening the plug doesn't keep it from leaking, remove the plug and install a new one. If the plug still leaks, you'll need to replace the 17mm fitting that the plug screws into. Chapter 6, Procedure 3, Step 2, tells you where the plug is located and how to remove it.

Check where the intake manifold bolts to the cylinder head. Manifold leaking? Tighten the mounting bolts on the manifold. If that doesn't stop the leak, have the Toyota dealer or a garage replace the intake manifold gasket.

No Pressure Leaks: If the cooling system passed the Captain Kirk pressure test (and there are no signs of coolant leaks) but the engine still overheats, do this:

Look for missing cooling fins on both sides of the radiator. Are there areas where something rubbed against the fins and bent them? If so, have a radiator shop look at it and see if they can straighten them for you.

With the engine off, reach inside the fan shroud and lightly run your fingers over the radiator fins. If they bend or break off easily, the radiator must be recored or replaced (Chapter 6, Procedure 6).

Check the thermostat. Let the engine cool a little if it's hot, then remove the thermostat and check it (Chapter 6, Procedure 5).

A broken temperature sending unit or gauge might lie and tell you the engine is running hot when it's not. Faulty gauges usually show one temperature constantly or the needle moves erratically while the engine is running. If the gauge always indicates an overheating condition, borrow or buy an engine thermometer and take your engine's temperature through the hole for the radiator cap. When the engine is warmed up, the coolant should be between 195° and 208°. If the gauge is showing hot but the thermometer is within the normal range, the temperature sending unit or the temperature gauge is broken. Have the Toyota dealer or a garage check the engine temperature sending unit (temp sender) and the temperature gauge in the dashboard. If it's the temp sender that's screwing up, have them show you where it is, then you can replace it yourself.

To remove the temp sending unit, disconnect the wires, then unscrew it with a deep socket or box end wrench. Have the new sending unit ready to screw in so only a little coolant will be lost. Screw in the new unit and tighten it. Connect the wire(s), start the engine and look for coolant leaks at the sending unit. Does the gauge work now? If not, you'll have to replace the gauge in the dashboard (Chapter 8, Procedure 4, Step 8).

Check the brakes. Put the car in NEUTRAL on level ground, handbrake OFF, and push. The truck should move. If it doesn't, the brakes are stuck, so see the Brake Problems section of this chapter.

Check for slipping clutch. See the Clutch Problems section of this chapter.

Do the 12,000 mile tune-up in Chapter 5. Pay particular attention to ignition timing, valve clearance, engine compression, and carburetor adjustment if your model has a carb. (You'll have to have Toyota or a garage check the mixture adjustment on '81 - '87 models.)

Other things: If you've gone through all the tests and the truck still overheats, here are a few possibilities to try before slashing your wrists.

Change the engine and transmission oil. Maybe they're too thick.

Have the cooling system "back flushed" by a radiator shop. They can also do a flow test to see if the inside of the radiator is clogged and needs to be removed and reconditioned. If necessary, you can remove it and install it yourself (Chapter 6, Procedure 6).

Check the exhaust system for dents that could restrict the flow of exhaust gases (Chapter 10, Procedure 6).

Take the engine apart and check for seizing pistons and bearings. (This is your next-to-last resort.)

Move to a cooler climate or only drive the truck in the wintertime. (This is your last resort.)

4. Engine Doesn't Warm Up.

If it takes longer than you think it should for the engine to warm up, or if the engine never fully warms up, see Chapter 6, Procedure 5, to check the thermostat.

5. Accelerator Pedal Goes to Floor but Engine Speed Doesn't Change.

See Chapter 9, Procedure 3, to check the accelerator linkage and replace it if necessary.

6. Symptoms and Checks for Leaking Head Gaskets.

Some water normally condenses in the engine (especially in cold weather) but after the engine is driven several miles and warmed up, the water boils away and disappears. If after driving several miles you notice any of the symptoms listed below, change the oil and filter (Chapter 5, Procedure 3, Steps 1-5). Drive the truck 50-100 continuous miles and check for the symptoms again. If water is still evident in places where it shouldn't be, have a garage do a "leak-down" test for leaking head gaskets. It shouldn't cost much and is probably worth the money, just to be sure before taking the engine apart.

Here are the symptoms of a leaking head gasket: water or white frothy looking stuff is evident inside the oil filler hole on the valve cover and on the bottom of the oil filler cap; the engine oil becomes a light brown color (like coffee with cream); slimy oil is in the radiator; the engine might run slightly hotter than normal; the compression for two adjacent cylinders is lower than the other cylinders; you have to add coolant frequently.

7. Oil Warning Light Goes On or Oil Pressure Gauge Drops to Zero While Engine Is Running.

A. STOP! Check Oil Level:

Stop the engine as soon as possible and check the engine oil dipstick (Chapter 5, Procedure 2, Step 1). If the oil level is OK, skip down to B to check the oil pressure switch and gauge. If the oil level is low or you can't find any oil on the dipstick, don't drive the truck until you add oil to the full mark. Start the engine to see if the light goes off or the gauge shows you have oil pressure. If the light stays ON, or the gauge remains at 0, turn the engine off immediately and skip down to B: Check Oil Pressure Switch.

If adding oil solved the problem, look under the engine to see if you've developed a sudden oil leak. See the Engine Oil Leaks section that follows to fix any oil leaks you might find. No oil leaks? Slap yourself severely on the wrists, face and the top of your head for letting the oil level get that low—and check the oil level more often from now on!

B. Check Oil Pressure Switch (OPS):

The OPS is screwed into the lower right side of the crankcase just behind the oil filter. It's probably covered with a rubber boot. If you have the rubber boot, gently peel the rubber off the switch and slide it up the wire out of the way.

Models with an oil pressure warning light: Turn the ignition key to ON but don't start the engine. The oil warning light should be on. If it isn't, see Chapter 8, Procedure 4, Step 8, to replace the warning bulb. Warning light is on? Disconnect the wire from the OPS and check the oil warning light on the dash. The light should be off when the wire is disconnected. If it's still on, there's a short in the wire somewhere between the OPS and the gauge. See Chapter 8, Procedure 5. If the light goes off when you disconnect the wire, the problem is either a faulty OPS or the oil pump isn't pumping oil. If you have a volt/ohm meter, here's how to check the OPS:

With the engine OFF, set the VOM to test for continuity (RX1), then touch one probe to the wire terminal sticking out of the OPS and touch the other probe to bare metal (you can use the OPS body). The VOM should read 0. Now start the engine and do the same test again. The VOM needle should be pointing to infinity (∞). If your results are different, replace the OPS. How to do this is in the Oil Leaks section later in this chapter.

Models with an oil pressure gauge: For this test you'll need a Friend, a 12-volt test light and enough wire to reach between the positive battery terminal and one of the wires on your test light. Use your jumper wire or round up a piece of electrical wire with ½" of insulation stripped away from the ends. Attach one end of the wire to one of the test light wires. Connect the other end to the positive terminal on the battery.

With the engine OFF, disconnect the connector from the OPS. It just slides off. Touch the loose end of your test light to the terminal on the OPS. The test light should be off. Have Friend start the engine and let it idle. While Friend watches the oil pressure gauge, touch the loose end of your test light to the OPS terminal again. The test light should flash on and off. Have Friend rev the engine a little and the light should flash more rapidly.

If the test light doesn't flash, either there's a problem with the OPS or there really isn't any oil pressure. Do Step C to check the oil pressure. If the engine has oil pressure, replace the OPS. (How to do it is in the Engine Oil Leaks section of this chapter.) Step C will tell you what to do if there's no oil pressure.

C. Check Oil Pressure:

The best way to see if the oil pump is working is to connect a good oil pressure gauge to the engine. But you probably don't have a spare oil pressure gauge in your tool box. So, here's an alternative method: Place a catch pan under the oil filter, then remove the filter (Chapter 5, Procedure 3, Step 1). Have Friend crank the engine for a few seconds while you watch for oil squirting out of the oil filter mount. When the engine starts, shut it off immediately. If oil squirts out, the pump is working. Install the filter.

If the OPS performed the way it should and oil squirted out the oil filter mount, but the oil gauge still reads 0, have Toyota or a garage check the gauge for you.

If oil doesn't squirt out of the oil filter mount (or just dribbles out), the oil pump parts are worn out or broken, the oil pressure relief valve in the pump is stuck, or the oil screen in the oil pan is plugged. See Chapter 13, Procedure 3, to remove the oil pump and check it for wear. If the oil pump checks out OK, the problem is that either the oil pick-up pipe is broken (unlikely), or the screen covering the end of the pipe is clogged with crud. Is there a big dent in the oil pan that might have broken the pick-up pipe? To see if the screen is clogged, see Chapter 13, Procedure 4, to remove the oil pan and pick-up tube and clean the screen on the end of the tube. Install the pick-up tube and oil pan. Start the engine and see if you have oil pressure now. If not, see the Pros.

8. Alternator Light Goes On in Mid-Flight.

Pull off the road as soon as possible, and do the following:

A. Check Alternator Drive Belt:

Open and prop the hood and check the alternator drive belt (Chapter 8, Procedure 3, Steps 1 and 2). If the belt is broken, whip out your spare belt and install it (Chapter 8, Procedure 3, Step 2). You do have a spare with you, don't you? If not, don't drive the truck because the alternator drive belt also operates the water pump—and without the water pump the engine will overheat quickly.

B. Check Alternator Wire Connections and Battery Voltage:

If the drive belt is OK, do Chapter 8, Procedure 6, Step 1, to check the wire connections on the rear of the alternator. If the wires are connected properly, do Step 2 in that procedure to check the voltage across the battery. You'll be instructed what to do according to the results of the tests. If you don't have the tools to check the voltage, and the drive belt is intact and adjusted properly, you can still drive the truck but the battery will discharge if you try to go too far. Turn off all electrical accessories to minimize the drain on the battery.

9. Leaks.

If you notice ugly spots on the driveway where the truck is normally parked, a quick look at the offending drops can help determine what's leaking.

Black, dark brown or gray spots indicate the engine, manual transmission, differential or transfer case (4WD models) is leaking. The way to determine the difference between engine oil leaks and manual transmission/differential oil leaks is the smell. Open and prop the hood, then remove the engine oil dipstick. Don't wipe the oil off the end. Dip a finger in a fresh spot on the driveway, then compare the aroma of the goo on your finger to the end of the dipstick. If the smells match, it's the engine leaking. See the Engine Oil Leaks section below. If the smells don't match, check the gear oil level in the transmission, differential and transfer case on 4WD models (Chapter 5, Procedure 3, Step 6). The one you have to add oil to is the one that's leaking. Have the Toyota dealer, a garage or transmission shop repair the leak.

Red or pinkish fluid spots are automatic transmission fluid from the automatic transmission or power steering system. Check the fluid levels for both systems frequently so they aren't damaged from lack of the slippery stuff. The leaking system will require fluid frequently. Once you've determined which system is leaking, have it checked by the Toyota dealer or a transmission shop.

Transparent brown or greenish fluid indicates the cooling system is leaking. See Pressure Leaks in the Engine Overheating section in this chapter to check all the places where coolant could be leaking from the engine.

Clear water dripping from under the front of the truck is probably condensation from the air conditioning system. Nothing to worry about.

A. Engine Oil Leaks:

To determine where the oil is leaking you might have to wash the engine (Chapter 5, Procedure 5, Step 2), then crawl under the truck frequently to see where oil first appears.

Here are the most common places for the engine to leak and how to fix them:

1. PCV valve: If the engine seems to be leaking everywhere, check the thumb-size positive crankcase ventilation (PCV) hoses that attach between the valve cover and the air cleaner or intake manifold (Chapter 10, Procedure 1). These hoses relieve pressure that builds up inside the crankcase and if they get clogged with oil and carbon, the pressure will force oil out through the seals and gaskets. To check the hoses, disconnect one end at a time and blow through the hose. You should be able to blow through one end into the valve cover, and into the air cleaner from the other end. I've seen a brand-new rebuilt engine leak badly because the fitting on the air cleaner was clogged. Clean the hoses, valve cover, PCV valve and fittings on the air cleaner and intake manifold if necessary.

2. Valve cover: See Chapter 5 Procedure 8, Step 3, to remove the valve cover. Replace the gasket that fits between the cylinder head and valve cover as well as the rubber coated washers that go on the bolts that attach the valve cover. Be sure there are no pieces of the old gasket stuck to the sealing surface of the cylinder head or valve cover before installing the valve cover. If the engine is warmed up, you might as well adjust the valves while the cover is off (Chapter 5, Procedure 8). Chapter 5, Procedure 8, Step 6 tells you how to install the valve cover.

Oil Tends To Leak Out Around Half Moon Plug

3. Oil pressure switch (OPS): When the oil pressure switch starts leaking, it's like a kid with a runny nose: no matter how often you wipe it, within a few minutes there's big drop hanging down again. If you suspect the OPS is leaking, clean it thoroughly with a rag, then start the engine and watch for the leak.

Before replacing the OPS, be sure the oil isn't running down the side of the engine from a leaking oil filter. Wash the engine (Chapter 5, Procedure 5, Step 2), then after the engine has dried, watch for where oil first appears on the side of the crankcase. If the oil filter is leaking, tighten it a little more or replace it with a new one. If the OPS is leaking, do the following.

The oil pressure switch is screwed into the lower right side of the crankcase just behind the oil filter. On models with an oil pressure light on the dash and no oil pressure gauge, the OPS is slightly larger than a 19mm socket. On models with an oil pressure gauge in the dashboard, the sending unit is round. A wire is attached to the end of the OPS with a push-on or slide-on connector.

If the OPS is leaking, you might be able to reach it through the engine compartment, if there aren't too many accessories in the way. If you can't get to it from the top, you'll need to jack up the front of the truck and put it on jackstands. Remove the skid plate on 4WD models.

If there's a rubber boot covering the OPS, gently peel it off and slide it up the wire out of the way. Disconnect the OPS wire, then use large pliers (models with an oil warning light) or, on models with an oil pressure gauge, use a wrench on the nut located between the crankcase and OPS to gently unscrew the unit *counterclockwise* as viewed from the wire terminal end.

Use a rag to clean the threads for the OPS in the crankcase. Put gasket sealer on the threads of the new OPS, then screw it into the crankcase. Gently tighten it with the large pliers or wrench (depending on your setup). Don't squeeze too hard with the pliers or you might distort the new unit and cause it to leak. The threads on the OPS are tapered so you don't have to get it real tight, just good and snug.

4. Oil pump: The oil pump is on the bottom front of the engine, right behind the crankshaft pulley. Remove the steel skid plate and/or the sheet metal splash pan that covers the bottom front part of the engine. Four 12mm bolts attach the skid plate or splash pan to the truck.

First, be sure it's the oil pump that's leaking. The front crankshaft seal is right in the center of the oil pump. (There's an illustration of the oil pump in Chapter 13, Procedure 3.) If the seal is leaking, oil runs down to the bottom of the oil pump. Use a spray can of carb cleaner and rag to thoroughly clean the oil pump and the crankcase between the oil pump and crankshaft pulley. Start the engine and let it run awhile, then shut it off. Use a flashlight to check the area at the bottom of the crank seal for signs of oil. If oil appears around the crank seal, the crank seal is the culprit. Skip down to the crank seal section. If the area around the crank seal stays dry but oil appears around the edges or on the bottom of the oil pump, the oil pump is leaking.

Once you're sure it's the oil pump that's leaking, use a wrench to see if the five oil pump mounting bolts are tight. They're small bolts, so don't crank on them too hard or they'll break. If the bolts are tight, the rubber O-ring between the oil pump and crankcase has probably become brittle and cracked. See Chapter 13, Procedure 3, to remove the oil pump and install a new O-ring. If the engine has a lot of miles on it, now would be a good time to install a new pump. Shop around for the best price.

5. Front crankshaft seal: How to determine if the front crank seal is leaking is described above in the oil pump section. To replace the crank seal, see Chapter 13, Procedure 2.

6. Rear crank seal: When the rear crank seal starts leaking you'll notice oil dripping from the rear of the engine just in front of the transmission. Oil leaking from the front crank seal, the oil pump, oil filter or the oil pressure switch will end up near the rear of the engine, so be sure they aren't the source of the oil leak.

Just to be sure it's the engine and not the transmission leaking, compare the smell of the oil dripping from the rear of the engine to the oil on the engine dipstick, then to a can of transmission oil, and the automatic transmission fluid dipstick if you have an automatic transmission. (See Chapter 5, Procedure 2, if you aren't sure where the dipsticks are located.) If the dripping oil smells like the transmission oil or automatic transmission fluid, take the truck to a transmission shop and have them check the leak and repair it. If the oil drips smell like engine oil, it's time for some serious contemplation.

Since it's such an expensive or time-consuming job to replace the rear crank seal, weigh the inconveniences and expense of the oil leak (cost of the oil, messy driveway, insecurity about the engine oil level) against the cost and/or effort required to replace the rear seal (see how much a garage would charge to replace the seal and read the transmission removal procedure in Chapter 11 to see if you're up to the task). Now you have to decide whether to live with the leak or fix it. If you want to do it yourself, here's how.

Since the bottom of the truck is probably covered with oil from the leaking seal, do yourself a favor and go to a car wash and wash the bottom of the engine and transmission (Chapter 5, Procedure 5, Step 2). You'll be glad you did, or sorry if you didn't. To replace the rear crank seal, see Chapter 11, Procedure 8, to remove the transmission. You'll be directed to the rear crankshaft seal replacement step. Once the seal is replaced, install the flywheel and clutch assembly. Stick the transmission back in the truck, give it a good tune-up and you're finished. The ordeal is over.

CLUTCH, TRANSMISSION, AXLE AND DRIVESHAFT PROBLEMS

Here's a guide that will direct you to the appropriate procedure to remedy clutch, transmission, axle and driveshaft problems:

1. The Clutch Pedal Goes Down More than ½ Inch Before Any Resistance Is Felt:

Check the clutch pedal adjustment (Chapter 11, Procedure 1) and bleed the hydraulic clutch system (Chapter 11, Procedure 2).

2. The Clutch "Slips" On Hills Or During Acceleration (engine speed increases but the car speed doesn't) and a Smell Like Burning Underwear Wafts Into the Car:

First, check the clutch pedal adjustment (Chapter 11, Procedure 1). If that doesn't solve the problem, the clutch disc, pressure plate or flywheel is worn out. See Chapter 11, Procedure 8, to remove the transmission. How to check the clutch components is also in that procedure.

3. A Squeal Is Heard when the Clutch Pedal Is Pressed (engine running):

The throwout bearing is worn out. See Chapter 11, Procedure 8, to remove the transmission. How to replace the throwout bearing is also in that procedure.

4. It's Difficult to Shift Gears (manual transmission):

The clutch system needs to be bled. See Chapter 11, Procedure 2.

If that doesn't make it easier to shift gears, the clutch master cylinder or slave cylinder is probably leaking fluid because the rubber cups are worn out (check 'em). If one is leaking, see Chapter 11, Procedure 3, to rebuild or replace the clutch master or slave cylinder.

The clutch pressure plate or pilot bearing could be worn out. See Chapter 11, Procedure 8, to remove the transmission and check the clutch components.

The transmission innards might be worn out. The transmission might make a howling noise and jump out of gear frequently. You can remove the transmission, then take it to a garage for repair. See the rap at the beginning of Chapter 11, Procedure 8.

5. There's No Resistance At the Clutch Pedal or the Pedal Is Flat on the Floor:

The clutch fluid reservoir might be empty due to a leaking master cylinder or slave cylinder. See Chapter 5, Procedure 2, Step 6, to check the clutch fluid level. If the clutch master cylinder or slave cylinder is leaking, see Chapter 11, Procedure 3, to repair or replace it.

6. The Truck Jerks Forward Even when the Clutch Is Released Slowly:

The clutch is "grabbing" due to oil on the clutch disc or the clutch disc is worn out. See Chapter 11, Procedure 8, to remove the transmission and check the clutch components.

7. Oil Is Leaking Between Engine And Transmission:

See the Oil Leaks section in this chapter to see where the oil is coming from. If you determine that it's the rear crankshaft seal leaking, see Chapter 11, Procedure 8, to remove the transmission and replace the rear crankshaft oil seal.

8. 4WD Models: You Hear a Knocking Noise when the Truck Is Turned Sharply:

On '79-'85 models, the birfield joint might be worn out or in need of fresh grease. See Chapter 12, Procedure 11, to remove and check the front axle.

On '86-'87 models, the tulip joint and/or constant velocity joint might be worn out. Chapter 12, Procedure 15, tells how to check the joints for wear and replace them if they are worn out.

9. You Hear A Clunk when You Let the Clutch Pedal Up (engage the clutch):

The tulip joint or constant velocity joint (CVJ) on 4WD models, or a U-joint on any model, is worn out. See Chapter 12, Procedure 15, to check the tulips and CVJs on 4WD models or Chapter 11, Procedure 6, Step 2, to check the U-joints on all models.

10. You Hear a Loud Knocking Only when Starting the Engine:

There might be teeth missing from the starter drive gear or from the edge of flywheel. Do Chapter 8, Procedure 10, to remove the starter and check the pinion gears. While the starter is off, peek into the starter mounting hole on the engine to check the teeth on the flywheel. If the flywheel teeth are worn out, see Chapter 11, Procedure 8, to remove the transmission, clutch and flywheel.

11. You Hear a Howl, Squeal, or Whine while Driving:

The transmission and/or differential might be low on oil. Chapter 7, Procedure 2, Steps 2 and 3, and Procedure 3, Step 7, tell how to check the transmission, differential and transfer case oil level. If the oil level is OK, or filling the components doesn't make the annoying noise go away, the bearings or gears in the transmission or differential are worn out. Take the truck to the Toyota dealer or a garage for repair.

12. Truck Shivers and Shakes when Clutch Pedal Is Released (clutch chatter):

The pressure plate, flywheel or clutch disc is worn out or warped, or oil is on the clutch disc. See Chapter 11, Procedure 8, to remove the transmission and check the clutch components.

BRAKE PROBLEMS

All brake shoes, disc pads and rubber seals in the master cylinder and wheel cylinders are mortal, like you and me, and will eventually wear out due to normal use. Keeping the system filled with fresh fluid will prolong the brake system's life (and maybe yours) but sooner or later you'll encounter one or more of the following problems.

Since almost all brake procedures involve jacking up the car, please read the safety precautions in Chapter 2.

1. The Handbrake Handle Comes Up Too High:

The handbrake cables need adjusting (Chapter 7, Procedure 15), the rear brakes need adjusting (Chapter 7, Procedure 7), and/or one of the handbrake cables is broken (Chapter 7, Procedure 16).

2. The Brake Pedal Feels Mushy and You Have to Pump On the Pedal to Stop the Truck:

If the brake pedal feels spongy, mushy, or has to be pumped a few times before any resistance is felt, air is in the hydraulic system. Since air can be easily compressed, the pressure applied to the system by pumping the brake pedal merely causes the air pockets to get smaller (compressed) and thereby undermines the hydraulic fluid's job of forcing the wheel cylinder plungers outward to move the brake shoes or pads.

Air can enter the system if the brake fluid level in the master cylinder reservoir gets too low, when something in the hydraulic system is taken apart for inspection or repair, or when a seal in one of the wheel cylinders wears out. Check the fluid level in the master cylinder reservoir and top it up if necessary (Chapter 5, Procedure 2, Step 5), then bleed the brake system (Chapter 7, Procedure 1).

Always bleed all the wheels, even if the pedal seems firm after bleeding the first wheel or two. It's worth the effort.

3. Brakes Noises:

Squeals, growls, and rumbles coming from the wheels when the brakes are applied mean the asbestos compound has worn through and the metal part of the shoes or pads is contacting the drums or discs. Very bad. This causes scratching or scoring, which can quickly ruin the expensive drums and discs. 1986-'87 2WD models have a wear sensor built into the front pads that squeals at you (a cry for help!) when the pads are almost worn out. If you hear disconcerting noises coming from the wheels, check the front brake pads (Chapter 7, Procedure 3) and rear brake shoes (Chapter 7, Procedure 6).

If the squeal is coming from the front of the truck, and the pads are in good condition, squirting the front brake system with the garden hose when it starts squealing often solves the problem for awhile. This washes away the accumulated brake dust that seems to make the brakes squeal. Don't squirt the brakes while they're hot (within an hour of driving the car) or the discs might warp.

4. Scraping Sound Coming from the Rear when Hauling a Heavy Load:

Check the rear wheel bearings. See Chapter 11, Procedure 4, for all models except '86-'87 Cab and Chassis with dual rear wheels. '86-'87 C&C with dualies should see the Toyota dealer or a garage.

5. The Truck Pulls to One Side when the Brakes Are Applied:

This means the brakes aren't adjusted correctly (or one side is sticking), or there's oil, grease or brake fluid on the brake lining. See Chapter 7, Procedure 3, to check the front brakes, or Chapter 7, Procedure 6, to check the rear brakes.

6. You Have to Add Brake Fluid to the Reservoir Frequently:

Look on the inside of each wheel and around the master cylinder for any signs of wetness (indicating an opening in the system that would let fluid out and air in). But don't do this on a rainy day. If no leaks or wet spots can be found, bleed the system (Chapter 7, Procedure 1). Check the pedal again for firmness. Problem solved? Congratulations!

If no leaks were found and the pedal is still mushy after bleeding the system, adjust the rear brakes (Chapter 7, Procedure 7), then bleed the system again. If the pedal is still spongy, the master cylinder seals are probably incapable of holding pressure in the system. The master cylinder needs to be rebuilt or replaced (Chapter 7, Procedure 12).

If you find a damp-looking area on the inside of a wheel or backing plate, check the smell of the wet spot to see if it's brake fluid. How? Get some of the goo on your finger and compare the aroma to the fluid in the master cylinder. Don't give it a taste test, though, because brake fluid is poison. Smell the same? If so, a wheel cylinder rebuild or replacement is in order (Chapter 7, Procedure 10). On drum brakes, it's best to rebuild or replace the cylinders on both sides even if only one side is leaking. If a front caliper is leaking, take both calipers to Toyota or a garage and have them rebuilt. If the smells don't match, the wet spot could be from a neighborhood dog. Wash your hands and make a note about what to do to that dog the next time you see it.

A leaky master cylinder is easy to spot because it's sticking out of the Master Vac in the engine compartment in plain view. Carefully check all the brake line connections at the master cylinder and the brake line junction block for leaks. The junction block is located somewhere in the engine compartment. Just follow the brake lines from the master cylinder to where they connect to a metal block that has several other lines sprouting from it. Make sure the clamps on the bottom of the brake fluid reservoir(s) are snug and check the reservoir(s) for cracks.

If the master cylinder is leaking, don't try to rebuild it yourself. Take it to an expert! It is vital that the job be done perfectly. Chapter 7, Procedure 12, tells you how to remove and install the master cylinder.

7. The Brake Pedal Goes Down Farther than Normal:

If the brake pedal feels solid, but goes to within two-and-a-half to three inches of the floor before any resistance is felt, the brake pads or shoes aren't making contact against the discs or drums as quickly as they should. Try adjusting the rear brakes (Chapter 7, Procedure 7). If that doesn't help, inspect the shoes and pads for wear (Chapter 7, Procedure 3, for the front pads or Chapter 7, Procedure 6, for rear brake shoes).

8. Dragging Brakes:

Dragging brakes can affect your truck's performance in several ways: decreased gas mileage, engine overheating, and dangerous wheel lock-up when the brakes are applied. To check for dragging brakes, park on level ground with the gearshift in NEUTRAL and the handbrake OFF. You should be able to push the truck without much effort. If you can't, jack up one wheel at a time and check the turning resistance on each wheel. The handbrake must be off to check the rear wheels so be sure and block the front wheels.

If you find a wheel that's harder to turn than the others, jack up the truck at that end and put it on jackstands. If the wheel has drum brakes, remove the brake drum (Chapter 7, Procedure 6, Step 2) and check for broken return springs or linings that have come off the metal part of the shoes. Check the handbrake cable lever to see if it's sticking and holding the brakes on (Chapter 7, Procedure 15). If it's a front wheel, remove the tire and check the brake pads to see if they are free to move in the holder (Chapter 7, Procedure 3).

If all looks well at the brakes, or all the brakes are dragging, the master cylinder might be holding residual pressure after the brake pedal is released. Rebuild or replace the master cylinder (Chapter 7, Procedure 12).

9. More Pressure On The Brake Pedal Is Required to Slow the Truck:

If you have to push on the brake pedal harder to slow the truck, see Chapter 7, Procedure 13, to check the Master Vac (brake booster) unit.

10. Brake Light Problems:

If the brake lights don't light up when you step on the pedal, or they stay on all the time, see Chapter 7, Procedure 14.

NOISES!

If your Toy has developed a noise alerting you that something's amiss, first determine if the noise is related to the *engine*, *drivetrain* (transmission, differential, transfer case on 4WD models, axles, wheels), *suspension system* (shock absorbers, control arms, etc.), or the *steering system* (ball joints, tie rods, steering gearbox, etc.). Here's how to trace some of the sounds:

A. Engine Noises:

If the sound is present when the engine is running but the truck isn't moving, something on the engine is amiss. Here are some clues to tracking it down:

1. Squeals:

If you hear a squeal when you first start the engine then the noise goes away as the engine warms up, check the tension on the drive belt(s) (Chapter 8, Procedure 3), the water pump (see the Overheating section in this chapter) and the distributor shaft for looseness (Chapter 5, Procedure 9, Step 5).

If the squeal changes with the engine speed: If you have a breaker points type distributor, the lobe rider might need a dab of grease (Chapter 5, Procedure 11). Or the alternator bearings might be dry; have the alternator checked out by Toyota or a garage. They might be able to install new bearings if the alternator is otherwise in good condition. If the alternator must be replaced, see Chapter 8, Procedure 7. You can do it yourself.

2. Hissing Sound:

Check all the vacuum hoses in the engine compartment to see that they're connected. Check the spark plugs to be sure they're tight (Chapter 5, Procedure 7). Check the intake manifold and carburetor mounting bolts for tightness (Chapter 9, Procedure 11, Step 11).

3. Clicking Sounds:

A regular clicking sound that changes with engine speed is probably a loose valve. Adjust the valves (Chapter 5, Procedure 8).

If the engine is running rough and you hear a clicking sound, a spark plug wire might have fallen off one of the spark plugs.

A clicking sound that changes with the speed of the car, but not necessarily the engine, may be in the wheel bearings or brakes. Try to determine which corner of the car it's coming from. Then search the Brakes and Suspension sections of this chapter for solutions.

4. Knocking Sounds:

A regular metallic sounding knock when the engine is decelerating is possibly a worn connecting rod bearing. A lower, hollow type sound indicates worn crankshaft main bearings. Another symptom of worn rod and/or main bearings is low oil pressure (the oil warning light comes on at idle or the oil pressure gauge indicates lower than normal pressure). If you suspect worn rod and/or main bearings, I suggest getting a second opinion from the professionals before tearing the engine apart.

Knocking noises from underneath that come and go are often from a loose exhaust system (Chapter 10, Procedure 6) or possibly suspension parts (see the Steering and Suspension section that comes next).

5. Buzzing Sound:

Check the wingnut on top of the air cleaner (20R and 22R models). If the nut is loose, tighten it. If it won't tighten, replace the wing nut.

The large metal heat shield surrounding the exhaust manifold on the left side of the engine is notorious for buzzing at certain engine speeds. Have Friend rev the engine while you press on the heat shield with a screwdriver. If that stops the buzzing, check the mounting bolts on the heat shield for tightness. If the bolts are tight, you might have to remove the shield and install a new gasket between the two halves of the shield. It's a straightforward job if you can get to the shield easily, but if your model has lots of accessories, you might want to have the Toyota dealer deal with it.

B. Steering and Suspension Noises:

You notice clunks, clanks or bangs when you hit bumps or potholes in the road, or the car doesn't handle the way it used to. Chapter 12, Procedure 1, tells you how to check the suspension and steering systems.

Clanks, clunks and bangs when you hit bumps means something is loose. Tracking down some rattles would turn even Sherlock Holmes into a babbling idiot. Usually it's the exhaust system or something rolling around in the cab or bed, but let's check the suspension to be sure.

If the clanks and bangs are coming from the rear, put the truck in gear (or PARK), set the handbrake, chock the wheels, put on your safety glasses, and squeeze under the rear. Don't jack it up.

Grab the bottom end of a rear shock absorber just above the mounting bolt and shake it like you're strangling a cobra. Try and move the shock up and down and side to side. Now grab the shock near the top and strangle that cobra again. Check both rear shocks. Look for looseness in the rubber grommets at the top and bottom of the shock. Check both sides and tighten the shock nuts or bolts if the grommets are loose (Chapter 12, Procedure 2, Step 3). If any of the grommets are AWOL, cracked or can't be tightened, try to round up new or used ones and install them. If you can't find new grommets, the shock will have to be replaced (Chapter 12, Procedure 2). While you're under the rear of the truck, bump the exhaust pipe around a little with your hand (use a rag if the pipe is hot) to see if it's loose and hitting something. Clunks or squeaks? Turn to Chapter 10, Procedure 6, to correct exhaust system problems.

Check the mounting bolts that attach the leaf springs to the frame. If the springs appear to be loose, check the spring shackles, bolts and bushings for wear (Chapter 12, Procedure 14).

If clanks and bangs are coming from the front of the truck, there's a slight possibility one of the front shocks isn't securely bolted to the suspension arm or the mounting bracket. Check them just as you checked the rear shocks (above) and tighten the bolts and nuts, or replace the grommets or shock absorber (Chapter 12, Procedure 3).

'79-'85 4WD models: A thumb-size torque rod with large bushings on each end connects the top left side of the front differential housing to the front of the frame. Grab the torque rod and shake it to see if the bushings are worn out. If you detect looseness in the ends of the torque rod, remove it and replace the bushings (Chapter 12, Procedure 13).

4WD models: A knocking noise when the truck is turned sharply might be a worn tulip joint or constant velocity joint (CVJ). See the driveshaft troubleshooting guide in this chapter.

SMELLS

There are usually two causes for a stinky, smelly engine: The engine is overheating, or oil from the engine or grease from a torn axle boot is on the exhaust system.

1. Engine Overheating:

See the Engine Overheating section in this chapter.

2. Engine Oil on the Exhaust System:

See the Engine Oil Leaks section in this chapter. You'll be instructed where to turn for the solution.

3. Grease on the Exhaust System:

'86-'87 4WD models, see Chapter 12, Procedure 15, Step 2, to check the tulip joint and constant velocity joint boots (CVJ). If a boot is torn, Chapter 12, Procedure 16, tells you how to replace them.

ELECTRICAL PROBLEMS

If you're having trouble with electrical gizmos (such as lights, horn, radio, gauges, heater switch, etc.), see Chapter 8, Procedure 5.

SHAKES, SHIMMIES AND HANDLING PROBLEMS

If the car shakes and/or the steering wheel vibrates at certain speeds on the highway, or the car wanders from one side of the road to the other, see Chapter 12, Procedure 1, to check the steering and suspension systems. If no problem is found, have the front end alignment checked and the tires balanced.

If the car pulls to one side of the road, it's most likely that the air pressure in one of the tires on that side of the car is low. Chapter 5, Procedure 4, Step 15, tells you how to check the air pressure in the tires.

If the truck pulls to one side only when you apply the brakes, you could have a leaking wheel cylinder; see the Brakes section in this chapter for diagnosis and cure.

CHAPTER 5
MAINTENANCE, LUBRICATION AND TUNE-UP

"Translating words into actions is easy when you do it one step at a time. You are not going to intellectualize on these mechanical things, you are going to do them and that's different. The idea to grasp well here is one of Return. You are going to return the car to a position of well-being by adjusting or replacing certain things that have worn, been used up or been bounced out of alignment. As the I Ching says, 'Perseverance Furthers,' and that is your thing. Take your time and do each step completely before you even think about the next."

—John Muir
How to Keep Your VW Alive

This chapter will eventually save you enough money to pay for this book and the tools you've bought, and more. Garages now charge $30 per hour and up, so while you're doing the procedures in this chapter, whistle a happy tune and think about what to do with all that money you save. Is it worth the effort? You bet it is. Buy a present for the mate or a date. If you're into modifying the appearance or performance of your Toy, you'll have the money to buy some of those accessories and goodies you've been drooling over (see Chapter 14: *Modifying Your Toyota*).

This is also the chapter that will keep your Toyota alive! That's what I promised up front and I know we can do it. Even though your Toyota has a strong will to live, and will continue to run fairly well without regular maintenance, doing the procedures in this chapter REGULARLY will keep your truck operating at maximum efficiency and economy. It will also keep you in touch with what it needs right now and what can wait for a while. Often, while doing an oil change, tune-up or massage, you'll notice something that could cause problems if not fixed right away. Things like loose bolts, oil leaks, broken or frayed wires, uneven wear on the tires, etc. If you notice something amiss, turn to the appropriate chapter and follow the repair procedures to remedy the problem as soon as possible. By staying in close touch with your truck you'll probably never have to call a tow truck on a rainy night.

HOW TO USE THIS CHAPTER

Here's how I've organized this chapter for you. It goes by time and mileage. From the top: things you do daily, things you do when you stop for gas, and things you do every 6,000, 12,000, 30,000 and 60,000 miles. Included are such key car maintenance items as oil and filter change and tune-up. You will notice that from the 6,000 mile maintenance on, there's more than one procedure to do at each interval, so allow yourself several hours to do it all, at least the first time through. You may need to set aside most of a Saturday. But, as I said, this is the chapter that's going to keep your Toyota alive—perhaps longer than you ever imagined.

RECORD YOUR EFFORTS

Record all the work you do on your car in the log at the end of this chapter. It's not easy to keep track of the mileage and date you performed maintenance or repair procedures unless it's all in one place and you make a habit of keeping the record current. Also make a list of the little things you want to keep an eye on. When the time comes that you (may) want to sell your truck, your log will very likely impress the buyer and bring you top dollar for your well-maintained Toy.

WARRANTY

If your truck is still under warranty, let the Toyota dealer do the covered repair and maintenance work. You've already paid for it in the purchase price. If your truck is less than five years old, and you don't have a copy of the warranty, ask a Toyota dealer for one. Some emission control equipment is covered for longer than you might have thought, regardless of how many people have owned the truck before you. You might get a pleasant surprise. It never hurts to check.

If a recurring problem isn't fixed to your satisfaction while the car is under warranty, don't wait until the warranty runs out to write a complaint. Later, if something major goes wrong because the original problem was never properly solved by the agency, your written record may help you get it fixed by Toyota at no charge.

BODY MAINTENANCE

Take good care of your body and you'll enjoy life longer! The same applies to your Toyota. Wash it on top and underneath when it gets dirty (weekly, if you live where they salt winter roads) and wax it a couple of times a year. Waxing has been made pretty easy these days, thanks to modern chemicals and our lazy culture. Touch up little nicks and scratches with touch-up paint from Toyota and get fender-bender accidents fixed before rust has a chance to start. It's harder to get motivated to spend time and money on a mechanically sound car if it's filthy and funky looking.

WHY LUBRICATE?

Rub the palms of your hands together real fast for a few seconds and see what happens. Come on, don't be shy. Your palms get hot very quickly, right? Now imagine your hands moving 100 to 1000 times as fast. The heat buildup would be unbearable. Now, if you're really into it, try rubbing your hands together with hand lotion, or even motor oil, on them. Amazingly, there's hardly any heat generated. The same situation goes on in your engine every time you start it. Pistons are moving up and down in cylinders, rods are spinning on the crankshaft, the crankshaft is spinning in the crankcase, etc., etc. As long as there's a thin film of oil between the moving parts, everything goes smoothly. If there's no oil, too little oil, or worn-out oil in the engine, those rapidly moving metal parts overheat, then it's metal against metal. Soon the metal gets so hot it distorts, and very quickly you have a warped, burned mess of Fried Toyota. Preventing heat and wear caused by friction is the main purpose of the oil in your engine. This, my friends, is called lubrication.

MY RAP ON OIL

Oil is truly the lifeblood of your engine. It not only reduces friction and wear,but also helps cool the engine, helps form an airtight seal between the piston rings and cylinder walls, cleanses the internal parts, and counteracts the corrosive by-products of combustion. Therefore, the kind of oil used in your engine plays a major role in how long it will last. Honest Engine!

Like most everything else, oil is made up of molecules. The difference among oils is in the ability of the molecules making up the oil to form and continue to form a lubricating film under pressure and heat. The oil molecules that lubricate the longest are the best and usually the most expensive.

OIL QUALITY

To help sort out the various qualities of oil, the American Petroleum Institute (API) has developed a code which is stamped on the label of oils they have certified. Don't buy any oil that doesn't have the round API certification symbol on the lid or label.

Here's how to read the code: for some reason gasoline engines are designated "S" and diesel engines "C." The S and/or C is followed by the performance level of the oil—A to F for gasoline engines, A to D for diesels. Simply stated, SF is the best for gasoline engines and CD is best for diesels. Some oils are labeled both SF and CC or CD. That's the kind you want, even if your owners manual says "SE or better." So when you buy oil be sure it has API service SF/CC or SF/CD somewhere on the label or lid.

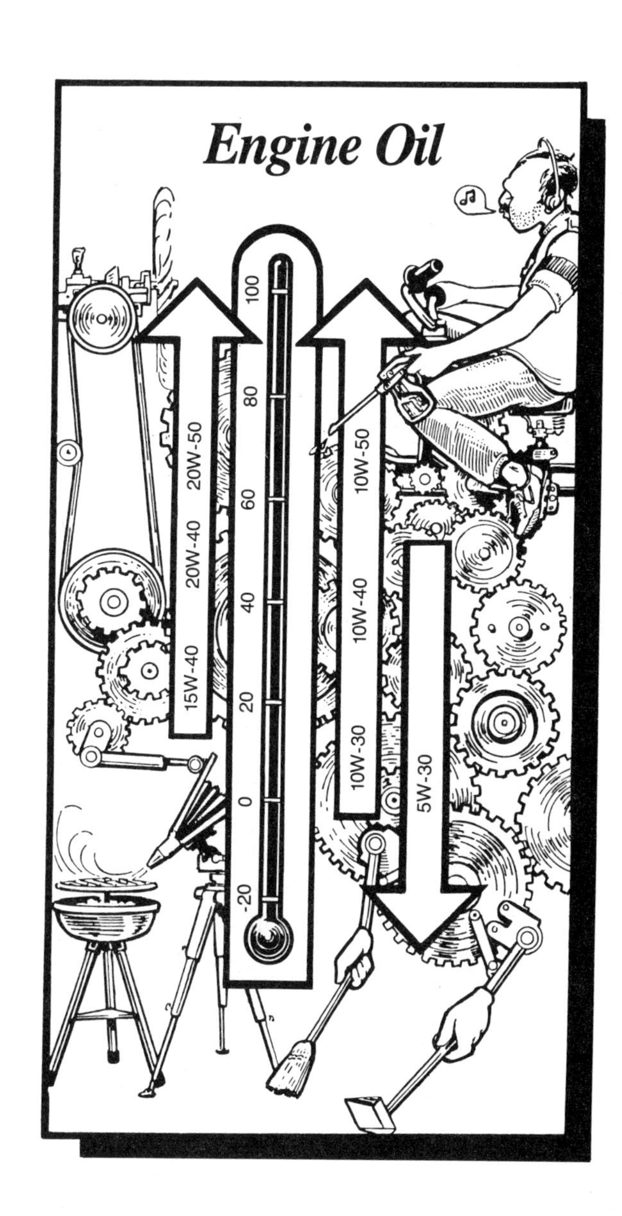

VISCOSITY

Viscosity is a measure of how easily a liquid flows. Oil with high viscosity, such as SAE 50, is thicker and doesn't flow as easily in cold weather. In extreme cold, oil with a high viscosity can get so sluggish it prevents the starter from turning the engine over fast enough to start. On the other hand, high viscosity oil maintains its lubricating ability at high temperatures whereas low viscosity oil becomes too "thin" to do an adequate job as a result of the heat.

If you live in a climate where there are significant changes in temperature, you want an oil that is thin enough to let the engine start easily, yet thick enough to lubricate at high temperatures. Multi-viscosity oils, such as 10W-30, 10W-40 or 20W-50, are ideal for these conditions. Check the chart to determine which grade of oil you should use.

If you happen to live where the temperature is below 0° F (-18° C) and it's difficult to start the engine when it's cold, you can use 5W-30 oil if its service rating is SF. A word of caution, however. This oil is not recommended for sustained high speed driving (especially in Turbo models), so change to one of the oils in the chart as soon as the weather warms up to a balmy 0° F (-18° C).

RECOMMENDATIONS

Most major brands are rated SF and are certified to exceed car manufacturers' specifications. However, *Consumer Report* found that almost one-fourth of the brands they tested didn't live up to their certification. Some of the brands that did, and thus are recommended by *Consumer Report* are:

VISCOSITY	BRANDS
5W-30	Mobil 1 and Pennzoil Multi-Vis
10W-30	Castrol GTX, Pennzoil P-Z-L Turbo Formula and Exxon Uniflo
10W-40	Castrol GTX
20W-50	None were tested.

To read more about the *Consumer Report* tests and to see which brands of oil they recommend NOT using, hotfoot it down to your friendly neighborhood library and look up the February 1987 issue. In that same issue they also report tests on oil filters, oil filter wrenches and tire pressure gauges.

Oil companies use different base oils and additives, so it's best not to mix oils of different brands. If you have to mix brands in an emergency, change the oil and filter as soon as possible. If you choose a brand of oil that is readily available, or carry a spare can or two, you will probably never have to mix brands.

By far the cheapest way to buy oil is when it's on sale by the case. Some hardware stores, discount department stores, and even some drugstores sell oil and filters at about half the price gas stations and auto parts stores usually charge. It's the same oil, so go for the lowest price you can find for the brand you prefer.

I buy oil that comes in plastic screw top containers because it's easier to store partial cans of oil without making a mess, and you can pour the old oil into the containers and haul it to the recycling center.

OIL ADDITIVES AND SUPPLEMENTS

Detergents are put in oils to dissolve burned molecules of oil, carbon and other grunge that forms naturally inside the engine. As the oil is pumped through the engine, some of these contaminants in the oil are trapped in the oil filter while others stay in suspension until the oil and filter are changed. Most modern oils also have additives to retard corrosion and to neutralize acids. (Seems engines get indigestion too.)

When you buy a quart of high grade oil, about 15% of it is additives, carefully blended so the oil will meet the standards of the American Petroleum Institute and the Society of Automotive Engineers. Don't waste your money buying oil supplements that are probably already included. In fact, adding supplements might upset the balance of ingredients in the oil and make it less efficient.

If you just bought a used Toyota, find out what kind of oil the previous owner used. If the truck came off a lot, they might give you the prior owner's name, or you might find the brand of oil used written on a door sticker or in the owner's manual. If a detergent oil was used, you can switch to another brand of detergent oil, if you change both the oil and the filter. Non-detergent oil is rarely used these days, but if that's what is in the engine now, you should wait until after a rebuild to change to a detergent oil. The reason: non-detergent oil doesn't dissolve contaminants as they form. The crud just sticks to the parts on the inside of the engine. Changing to a detergent oil would suddenly get all that stuff in suspension and overload the oil with contaminants. When the mess gets pumped through the engine it could plug oil passages and/or damage bearing surfaces. You can change from detergent oil to non-detergent without ill effect, but don't—there's no reason to.

OTHER OILS

Synthetic "man-made" oils extend the period between oil changes to about 15,000 miles, or one year. Sounds good, but even if the oil molecules maintain their lubricating properties for that long, there's bound to be a buildup of contaminants in the oil.

I've tried synthetic oils and enjoyed the freedom from oil changes. But I found that by not doing an oil change at least every 6,000 miles, the overall maintenance of the car suffered. Things I normally do at oil change time were neglected for too long. Also, I discovered that very slight oil leaks tended to leak a lot more with synthetic oil. At $3.50 a can even a slight oil leak gets very expensive. The cost of the five quarts of synthetic oil was about twice the cost of a year's supply of regular oil so I didn't save any money.

If you decide to use synthetic oil, use one that's readily available, carry a spare can or two, and promise your Toy you won't forget to do the regular maintenance procedures on schedule. Don't use synthetic oil just after an engine rebuild or ring and valve job—the rings won't "seat" properly.

Also available are the "slippery" oils with graphite. These oils are more expensive than regular oil and don't last as long as synthetic, but they are claimed to reduce engine wear. If you abuse your engine it'll need all the help it can get, and slippery oil might be helpful. However, I don't recommend using an oil with graphite in an old engine that's burning a lot of oil because the graphite is a conductor and might foul the spark plugs sooner than a regular oil. Again, don't use slippery oil just after an engine rebuild.

AVOID any oil labeled "Recycled," "Remanufactured," or "New oil blended with 100% recycled oil." The ecological idea is noble, but in reality oil molecules wear out, especially when subjected to high engine temperatures. Recycling or blending can never restore the molecules' lost ability to lubricate properly.

OIL FILTERS

Consumer Report rated Fram PH43 filters as best for filtering harmful grit out of the oil. Fram filters cost about a dollar more than other filters but they are probably worth it. Other filters which were slightly less efficient in the filtering test, but which were comparable in their grit holding capacity before becoming clogged, were Toyota 15601-44011, Lee LF-17HP, Purolator FC0-1 and Sears 45194.

TRANSMISSION AND DIFFERENTIAL OIL (GEAR OIL)

Gear oil for manual transmissions, differentials, and the transfer case on 4WD models with manual transmissions is thick and heavy and isn't exposed to the by-products (contamination) of combustion like engine oil is. Unless a seal breaks and lets contamination in, gear oil stays pretty clean and only needs to be changed every 30,000 miles. I use Castrol Hypoy C 80W/90 gear oil because it's a good multi-viscosity oil and comes in a handy plastic container with a pour spout built into the lid. It's certified to meet the standards for Mack trucks, so I feel safe using it in my Toyota pickup.

Generally, SAE 90 is recommended for the differential(s). For manual transmissions and the transfer case on 4WD models with manual transmissions, SAE 75W-90 or SAE 80W-90 is recommended. Look at your owner's manual to see what grade oil is recommended for your particular year.

Also available through off-road specialty shops is a synthetic gear oil called HPS. It is claimed to make transmissions, differentials and transfer cases last longer and shift smoother. It costs about $12 a can. If you prefer to drive on goat trails and creek beds instead of roads, your truck needs all the help it can get, so the super-stuff might be a worthwhile investment.

AUTOMATIC TRANSMISSION FLUID (ATF)

Like the gear oils, ATF doesn't get contaminated by combustion. But since it's subjected to friction and high temperatures, it should be changed at least every 30,000 miles. As with blood types, there are different types of ATF. Some of these are Type A, Type F, Dexron and Dexron II. '75-'83 model Toyotas are designed to use Type F and '84-'87 models use the Dexron II type. Like blood types, automatic transmission fluid types should not be mixed.

POWER STEERING FLUID

The power steering unit, if your truck has power steering, uses Dexron or Dexron II type ATF. If you have to add more than a quart every 6,000 miles, a seal or gasket is leaking and should be fixed right away.

ANTIFREEZE

Also vital to your engine's health is antifreeze. It keeps the water in the cooling system from freezing and breaking the radiator and/or engine. A mixture of antifreeze and water (called coolant) raises the boiling point of water so that even a very hot engine won't boil away its cooling fluid. Most antifreeze also contains rust and corrosion inhibitors that help keep the innards of the radiator and coolant passages in the engine clean and efficient. Use only an ethylene-glycol-type antifreeze. Don't waste your money on radiator additives or conditioners.

Antifreeze should be changed at least every other year. I recommend replacing it every year. If you live in a climate with severe temperature changes, fresh antifreeze every fall gives you assured protection and peace of mind.

If you live in a very cold climate, either buy an antifreeze tester (cheap ones from Prestone and discount stores will do), or regularly have a service station check the freeze protection level of the coolant. Add more antifreeze if necessary. It's a good idea, although not always possible, to use distilled water when you fill or add water to the radiator. Distilled water doesn't have minerals or other impurities that can form deposits in the water passages.

Using plain water with no antifreeze allows corrosion and rust to form in the water passages of the radiator and engine. The build-up restricts the flow of coolant and thus reduces the efficiency of the cooling system.

Water is more efficient than antifreeze for cooling the engine, so using straight antifreeze isn't as effective as a mixture of the two. The proper mixture is at least 50% antifreeze to 50% water.

Antifreeze can be reused after you've drained it from the engine and radiator. It must be kept clean though, so straining it through a clean rag before pouring it back in is important. It's better to install fresh antifreeze. In Chapter 6 I'll tell you more about the cooling system in your Toyota.

TIRES AND TIRE PRESSURE

If you're planning to keep your Toy for the long run, buying radial tires will save you money. Radial tires cost more, last longer, give you better gas mileage and a better grip on the road, so they're safer than bias ply tires. The only car I have with bias ply tires is my old '53 Chevy Bel Air that only gets driven on special occasions, like to the drive-in movies. I would have gotten radials for it but I couldn't find any wide whitewalls.

I put over 60,000 miles on my last set of Michelin radial tires and they still had a lot of miles left on them when I sold the car. How did I do it? I kept them inflated properly, rotated them regularly and kept the suspension and steering systems in good condition.

I consider the tire pressure listed in the Toyota Owner's Manual to be the minimum allowable pressure for radial tires. You'll find the maximum allowable pressure stamped on the sidewalls of whatever brand of tires you have. Running your tires at the minimum pressure will give you a softer smoother ride, but I've found that by inflating them to the maximum pressure (or near the max) you get increased tire life, better gas mileage and better handling. This is especially true of the metric-size P radials (the letter P will be stamped on the tire just before the tire size). You can experiment between the minimum and maximum pressures until you find the right pressure for you. Just be sure both front tires and both rear tires are inflated to the same pressure. Inflate bias ply (non-radial) tires to the pressures recommended in your Owner's Manual.

Rotate the tires at least every 6,000 miles. The more often the tires are rotated, the more evenly they will wear and the longer they will last. If the tires start wearing in funny patterns (see the illustrations), go through Procedure 1 in Chapter 12 to check for worn steering and suspension parts that could be responsible for the uneven wear.

Have the front end alignment checked and the tires balanced by an alignment shop at least every two years. Do it more often if you do a lot of off-road driving or have a tendency to bash into curbs on the way home from parties.

If you enjoy driving your Toy without the benefit of a road underneath, you might want tubes in your tires so rocks that find their way between the tire and rim won't cause deflated tires and egos. Be sure to use radial tubes with radial tires.

In Chapter 14: *Modifying Your Toyota*, I tell how to read the sticker symbols on new tires telling the tire's load range, heat range, and the mileage you should expect from the tire. There's also a list of companies that sell on and off-road tires that vary in size from almost bicycle size to Mack truck size.

Below are some of the most common symptoms of excessive tire wear and how to remedy the problem. All of the problems will be exaggerated by not rotating the tires regularly.

If your tires start wearing more on the inner and outer edges than in the center of the tread, they are underinflated. If they wear more in the center of the tread than on the edges, they are overinflated. Adjust the tire pressure accordingly.

Rapid wear along the outer edge of the front tires means the camber adjustment is out of whack and should be checked by Toyota or an alignment shop.

Scalloped looking wear spots along the outer edge means some suspension parts are worn out or the front end is out of alignment. See Chapter 12, Procedure 1 to check the suspension parts, then have the front end aligned by Toyota or an alignment shop.

Random spots of excessive wear on the tread indicate that the tire needs to be balanced, or the tire is defective. Have the tires checked and balanced by Toyota or an alignment shop.

MAINTENANCE SCHEDULES

How often should maintenance routines be done on your Toyota? Ask ten different mechanics and you'll probably get ten different answers ranging from a daily 30-minute ritual to "wait until something breaks, then fix it". Well, you won't find me wasting half an hour every day checking out my truck, but you won't find me at the side of the road with my thumb out because I waited for something to break either. Regular preventive maintenance is the key.

How your truck is used greatly affects how often the maintenance procedures should be performed. Therefore "normal" and "severe" maintenance schedules are provided below. Decide which schedule applies to your type of driving and, if there's any doubt, just remember that you can't change your oil too often! If your truck develops engine problems, run through the tune-up procedures in this chapter even if it hasn't been 12,000 miles since the last tune-up.

The maintenance schedule recommended by Toyota has changed from 6,000 miles or six months for an oil and filter change for 1975 models to 10,000 miles or 12 months for 1987 models. Maybe I'm old fashioned, paranoid or slightly crazed, but I'll still change the oil and filter on my Toyotas at least every 6,000 miles (or sooner if it starts looking dirty), regardless of what the factory says. Besides ensuring that the engine oil is clean, performing the lubrication and maintenance procedures every six months keeps me in touch with things like wiper blades, fan belts, radiator hoses, etc., so I don't have to worry about being stranded in the fast lane during rush hour.

Toyota has also extended the recommended maintenance interval on several tune-up procedures such as carburetor and valve adjustment from 12,500 miles to 20,000 and 30,000 miles respectively. Maybe I'm just addicted to having greasy hands because I still adjust my carburetor and valves at every 12,000 mile tune-up. Recommended spark plug replacement has gone from 12,500 miles to 30,000 miles. I still change mine once a year. In other words, I often recommend a more frequent service interval than the factory. If you don't have the need for a grease fix at least twice a year like I do, just use this book to perform the recommended maintenance procedures in the schedule that's in the Toyota Owner's Manual (which should be stashed in your glovebox). You will still be satisfying the Toyota warranty requirements.

So, here's a reasonable, rational maintenance schedule that will keep you in touch with your Toy without making you a slave to it.

NORMAL MAINTENANCE SCHEDULE	MILEAGE OR MONTHS
Gas Stop Fluid Checks	200-400 miles
Oil Change, Lubrication and Minor Massage	6,000 miles or six months (5,000 miles or six months for 22R-TE Turbo engines)
Engine Tune-up and Major Massage	12,000 miles or 12 months
Transmission, Differential Oil Change	30,000 miles or 30 months
Parts Replacement	60,000 miles or 60 months

Severe Maintenance Schedule: The 6,000 mile oil and filter change and lubrication procedures should be done every 3,000 miles (2,000 miles for 22R-TE Turbo engines) if you:

Drive on dusty, muddy or sandy roads;
Tow a trailer;
Make a lot of short trips (ten miles or less) OR
Drive in extremely cold weather (especially if the roads get salted when it snows).

If you're a bona fide off-roader, these are the driving conditions you probably prefer, so this is the schedule for you!

Here's what the procedures for this chapter deal with.

PROCEDURE 1.	DAILY SENSORY CHECK
PROCEDURE 2.	GAS STOP FLUID LEVEL CHECKS
PROCEDURE 3.	6,000 MILE/ 6 MONTH OIL AND FILTER CHANGE, LUBRICATION
PROCEDURE 4.	6,000 MILE/6 MONTH MASSAGE
PROCEDURES 5-13.	12,000 MILE/ 12 MONTH TUNE-UP, FLUID AND PARTS REPLACEMENT
PROCEDURE 14.	12,000 MILE/ 12 MONTH MASSAGE
PROCEDURE 15.	30,000 MILE TRANSMISSION AND DIFFERENTIAL OIL CHANGE, WHEEL BEARING AND AXLE LUBRICATION
PROCEDURE 16.	60,000 MILE PARTS REPLACEMENT

Massaging your Toyota doesn't involve taking it to Madame Noogie's Massage Parlor. By massage I mean going over the whole truck, lubricating things and looking for things that are broken, worn out or will be worn out before the next massage, like windshield wiper blades, light bulbs, rotating the tires, checking the brake system and such.

Make it easy on yourself. Get on a schedule so you do the six- and 12-month maintenance in the spring and fall while the weather is nice. My garage isn't heated or air conditioned. Is yours?

OK, enough verbiage—let's get on with the procedures! Please read through each procedure before doing it so you'll understand what you are going to do and know what tools and materials are needed. Also, arrange for transportation in case you have to make an emergency run to the parts store. Have fun!

PROCEDURE 1: DAILY SENSORY CHECK

Condition: You want to stay in touch with your transportation so it will live a full healthy life.

Tools and Materials: Eyes, ears, nose, skin, brain.

Step 1. Use Your Senses.

Look for oil and water spots on the driveway or garage floor, know how your tires look when properly inflated, listen for new sounds when you start the engine and while you're driving. Be aware of different smells that usually indicate something is overheating, and use the seat of your pants and your hands on the steering wheel to notice new or different vibrations.

Make these simple sensory observations a habit whenever you're in or near your truck. Mechanical problems are like diseases—the sooner they're detected, the easier and cheaper they are to fix.

Step 2. Fix It Now.

If you've found anything that looks, sounds, or smells suspicious, better plan to deal with it pronto. Chapter 4: *Troubleshooting* and the handy index at the end of the book will help you find the right procedure to remedy the situation.

PROCEDURE 2: GAS STOP FLUID LEVEL CHECKS

Checking vital fluid levels when you stop to gas up should become a regular habit. It's also a very good idea to check those vital fluids whenever you suspect you might be low on one or more of them.

Condition: Gas gauge is on or near empty; OR you've noticed drops of fluid on the driveway; OR it's been a quiet week in your hometown and you need something to do.

Tools and Materials: Money, a clean rag or paper towel. You may need: motor oil, ATF (automatic transmission fluid), a funnel, DOT 3 or 4 brake fluid, radiator coolant (water/antifreeze), windshield washer fluid.

Remark: You don't have to take all this stuff to the station every time you go to fill up. Check the levels at home beforehand—or add the fluids when you get home. The important thing is to check them regularly and the gas stop interval will help you remember.

If you notice oil spots on the garage floor or driveway, check all fluid levels immediately—even if you think you still have half a tank of gas. If you have to add oil, fluid or antifreeze at every fill-up or between fill-ups, a seal or gasket is probably leaking and should be fixed right away. Chapter 4: *Troubleshooting* will help you identify the source of the leak, then turn to the appropriate procedure to repair it. Unlike leaks in Washington D.C., oil leaks are pretty easy to fix.

There are three good reasons for filling the tank when you get gas instead of just adding a few gallons: (1) Water condenses in the empty part of the tank when the air temperature changes. The water can rust the tank and dilute the gasoline, causing the engine to run poorly. The fuller the tank, the less area there is for condensation. (2) Fill-ups provide a sensible interval, 200-300 miles, for checking things under the hood. (3) You can keep track of your gas mileage, which lets you know if something mechanical has changed, causing the gas mileage to (usually) get worse. How to determine your gas mileage is explained in Chapter 2 under *Driving Tips*. There's even a snazzy Basic computer program so you can use your home computer to calculate gas mileage—finally a real use (besides games) for your expensive toy.

Also, you should fill up before the needle reaches the thick line next to the letter E on the gas gauge. If the gas level gets too low it could cause the engine to backfire and damage the catalytic converter (an expensive item to replace).

Step 1. Check Engine Oil Level.

Park on level ground with the engine OFF. Open the hood and prop it. If you aren't sure where the various dipsticks and fluid containers are located, look at the fluid levels illustration for your model. (A friend of mine added three quarts of oil too many to the engine while checking the mysteriously unchanging automatic transmission dipstick! Don't get the two mixed up.) Painting the end of the dipstick a bright color makes it easier to spot.

Vital Fluids *20R and 22R*

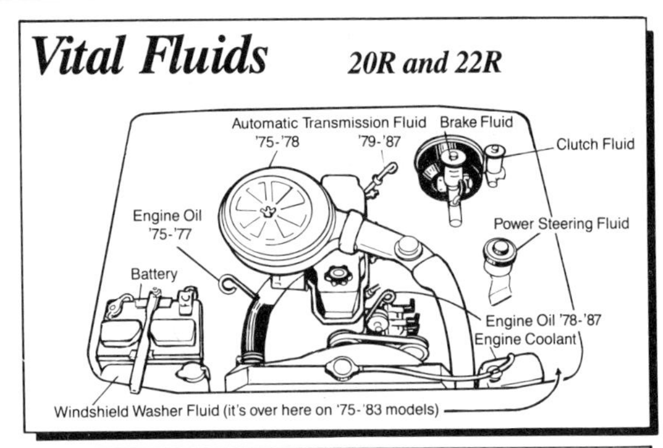

22R-E and 22R-TE

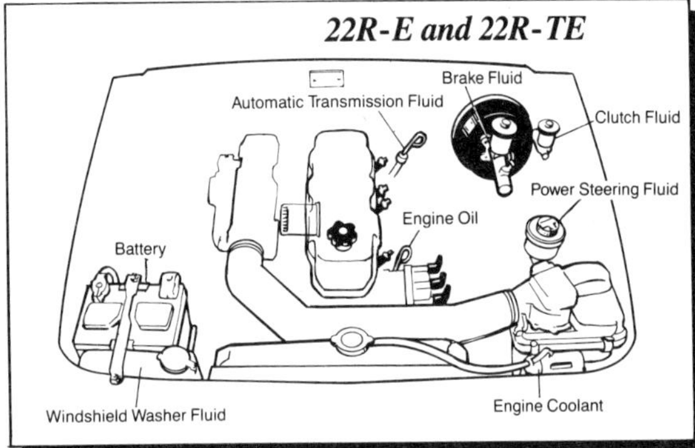

Dipsticks have a wire ring on the top for you to pull on. Pull the **engine oil dipstick** out of its tube and wipe off the bottom end with a clean rag or paper towel. (A pant leg will do if you're wearing funky pants.) Stick the dipstick back into the dipstick tube as far as it will go. On the way in, don't brush it against anything dirty or you'll insert unneeded crud into your engine.

Pull out the dipstick again. The oil on the stick should stop somewhere on the crosshatching that's between the F and L near the bottom end of the dipstick. If the oil level is on or below the L line, add one U.S. quart (0.95 liters) of oil. Use the same kind of oil you already have in your engine. After adding the quart, check the level again.

If the oil level is halfway between the F and L, add ½ quart and check the level again. Be careful not to add too much. If the oil is almost to the F line, don't add any oil.

Oil is added to the engine through an **oil filler hole** on the top front of the engine. The oil filler hole has a black **screw-type cap** that unscrews *counterclockwise*.

Milky looking goo inside the oil filler cap means there's some water inside the engine where it shouldn't be. Water condenses inside the engine because of temperature changes. If you drive five to ten continuous miles every day or so, the moisture boils off and won't cause corrosion problems. Just driving around the block once or twice a week doesn't allow the engine to warm up enough to boil the water out of the oil. If you notice the milky goo even after a long drive, you should consult Chapter 4 and do the tests for a leaking head gasket.

If you don't have an automatic transmission, go on to Step 3.

Step 2. Check Automatic Transmission Fluid (ATF).

Caution: While removing and installing the ATF dipstick, be careful not to touch any of the HOT engine parts with your hand.

For this check the transmission should be warmed up. Driving about ten miles will do it (15 miles if the weather is really cold). Park on level ground, leave the engine running (or start it if you turned it off to do Step 1). Put the handbrake ON, press on the brake pedal and move the gearshift lever into each gear range from P to L, then back to the PARK position. Leave the engine running.

The **automatic transmission dipstick** is on the right rear side of the engine on '75-'78 models or on the left rear side near the brake master cylinder on '79-'87 models. Pull out the dipstick, wipe it off, put it all the way back in, then pull it out again. The level should be between the two little notches on either side of the word HOT on the dipstick if the transmission is warmed up, or between the notches on either side of the word COLD if you didn't warm up the transmission. While you have the dipstick out, take a whiff of the fluid to see if it smells burnt or looks dark. The fluid should smell like oil and be a reddish orange color. If it smells burnt or is dark, the fluid should be changed (Procedure 15).

If the fluid level is low, round up some automatic transmission fluid (Type F for '75-'83 models or Dexron II for '84-'87 models), then use a clean funnel to add a little transmission fluid through the dipstick tube. Add a tablespoon or two of fluid, then check the level again. Be careful not to add too much fluid (it could cause a transmission seal to break). After checking for the last time, you can turn the engine OFF.

Step 3. Check Power Steering Fluid.

If you don't have power steering, go on to Step 4.

Power steering fluid should be checked after the car has been driven a few miles to warm up the fluid. Or you can start the engine and turn the steering wheel as far as it will go in each direction three or four times to warm up the fluid.

Check the level with the engine OFF. The **fluid reservoir** is a soup can-size container located on the driver's side of the engine compartment. Unscrew the reservoir cap *counterclockwise*. The dipstick is attached to the bottom of the cap. Wipe the little dipstick off and screw the cap back on. Remove it again and check the level. The fluid level should stop somewhere in the notch below the word HOT. If the level is low, add about a teaspoon of Dexron or Dexron II automatic transmission fluid, then check the level again. Be careful not to overfill it.

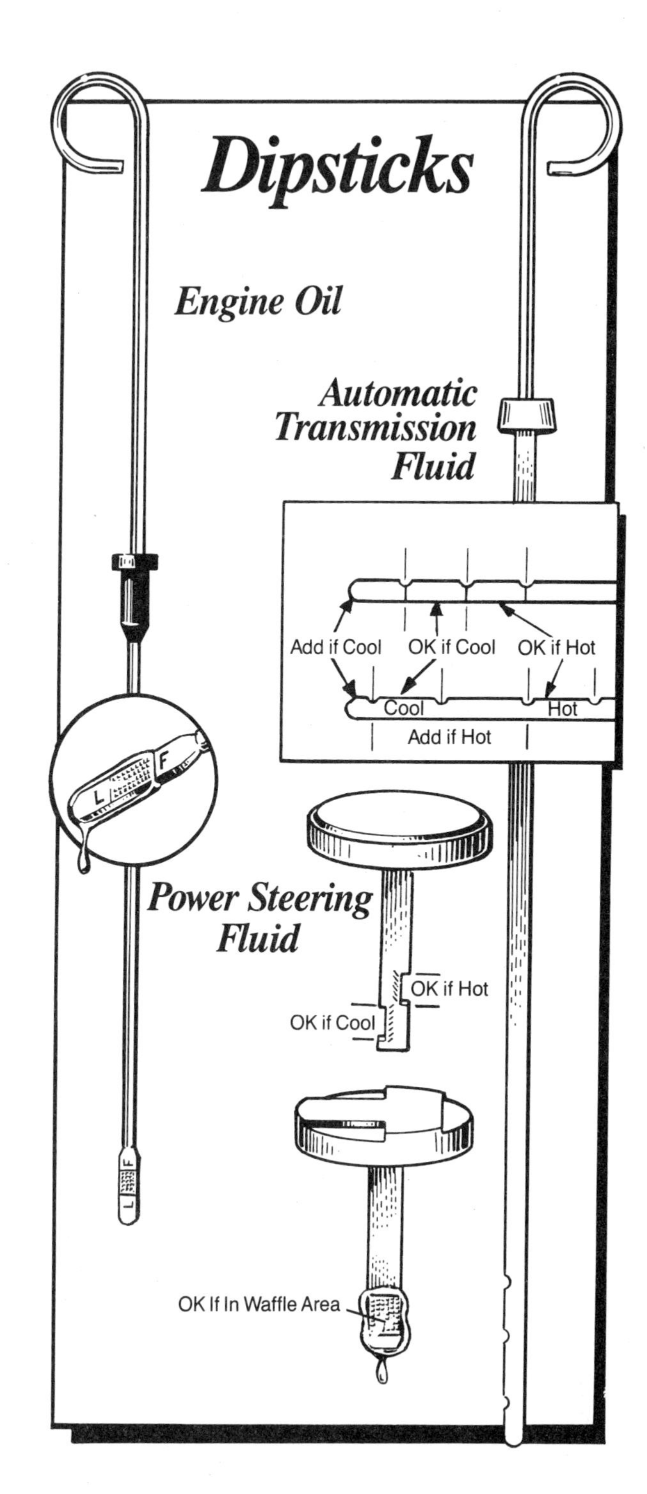

Step 4. Check Drive Belts (fan belt, V-belt).

Caution: Be sure the engine is turned off!

Drive belts look like long pieces of black licorice wrapped around some pulleys on the front of the engine. The drive belts are all turned (driven) by the *crankshaft pulley* at the bottom front center of the engine. The belts then turn the pulleys mounted to various important engine parts. One drive belt, which I'll call the **fan belt**, goes around the *crank pulley*, then around the *alternator pulley* on the driver's side of the engine, then around the *fan pulley* near the top, front, center of the engine.

'75-'80 all models (except Canada 4WD) and '81-'84 California and all Cab and Chassis models: Another drive belt, which I'll call the **air pump drive belt**, goes around the *crank pulley*, then around the *air pump pulley* on the lower right side of the engine. If you have air conditioning, the air pump belt also goes around the *air conditioner compressor pulley* on the top right side of the engine.

'81-'84 non-California (except C&C) models and all '85-'87 models with Air Conditioning: a drive belt goes around the *crankshaft pulley,* an *idler pulley* and a pulley on the *air conditioner compressor,* which is mounted on the top right front corner of the engine.

Models with Power Steering: You have a third drive belt, the **power steering belt**, which goes around the *crank pulley*, the *power steering pump* on the top left side of the engine, and an *idler pulley* near the top front of the engine.

EVERYONE: As the drive belts wear and stretch they become loose on the pulleys and start slipping, which causes them to overheat and wear out even faster. So it's important to check the tension on the drive belts regularly and adjust them if they're loose.

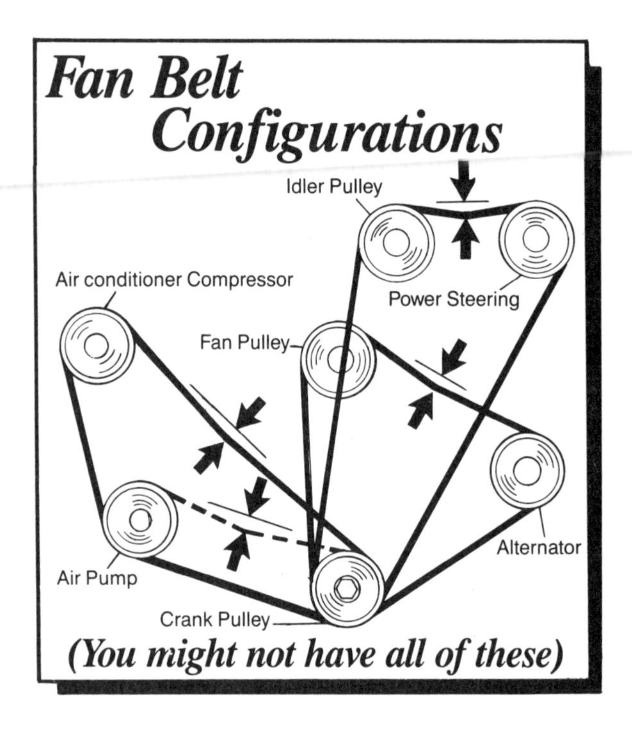

To check the tension on the drive belts, put a finger on each drive belt about halfway between two of the pulleys and give a little push. Use about the same force you would use when pushing on a doorbell button. If the belt moves more than ½" inward, it needs to be tightened. Check both sides of all belts for cracks or frayed edges. Drive belt too loose or worn out? See Chapter 8, Procedure 3, to adjust or replace the drive belt(s).

Step 5. Check Brake Fluid Level.

Cautions: Brake fluid is poison, harmful to your eyes, and can damage painted surfaces!

Don't use brake fluid from a can that has been opened for more than one year, even if the cap has been screwed on tightly. Consider it contaminated and throw it away. The reason: brake fluid is like a magnet to moisture in the air. Contamination decreases the fluid's effectiveness, causing loss of braking power. It also damages the internal parts of the brake system. It's much easier and cheaper to buy fresh brake fluid than to replace the parts of the brake system. I use Castrol GT LMA (low moisture activity) fluid.

Sticking out on the rear wall of the engine compartment, right in front of the driver's seat, is the **brake master cylinder**. '75-'78 models have two small white plastic **brake fluid reservoirs** mounted on top of the master cylinder. On '79-'87 models there is a single white plastic reservoir a little larger than a fist. Look for two lines on the side of the plastic resrvoir(s) marked MIN and MAX. The brake fluid level in the container(s) should be somewhere between the two lines. You can see the fluid through the semi-translucent plastic.

If the level is low, clean the reservoir cap before removing it to be sure no dirt falls into the reservoir. Add fresh DOT3 or 4 brake fluid until the level reaches the dotted line just below the MAX line. Pour the fluid carefully and wipe up any drips.

Check both reservoirs if you have two. Be careful not to get dirt in the reservoirs—dirt plays hell with the little rubber seals inside. If brake fluid has to be added more often than every six months, you probably have a leak in the hydraulic brake system. See the Brake Problems section in Chapter 4: *Troubleshooting*.

Step 6. Check Clutch Fluid Level (Manual Transmission).

The clutch on your truck is activated hydraulically just like the brakes, so use the same kind of fluid for the clutch that you use for the brakes, and be aware of the **Cautions** at the beginning of Step 5.

Hydraulic fluid for the clutch is in a small reservoir located in the far left rear corner of the engine compartment, near the brake master cylinder. The fluid level should be up to the dotted line near the top of the reservoir. If it's low, use a clean rag to wipe off the reservoir and cap, then remove the cap. Add fresh DOT3 or 4 brake fluid until the level reaches the dotted line. Install the reservoir cap. If you have to add fluid frequently, see Chapter 4: *Troubleshooting* to check the hydraulic clutch system for leaks.

Step 7. Check Coolant Level.

Caution: Check the coolant level in the white plastic **coolant reservoir** located in the left front of the engine compartment next to the radiator. DON'T remove the radiator cap on the top of the radiator while the engine is hot.

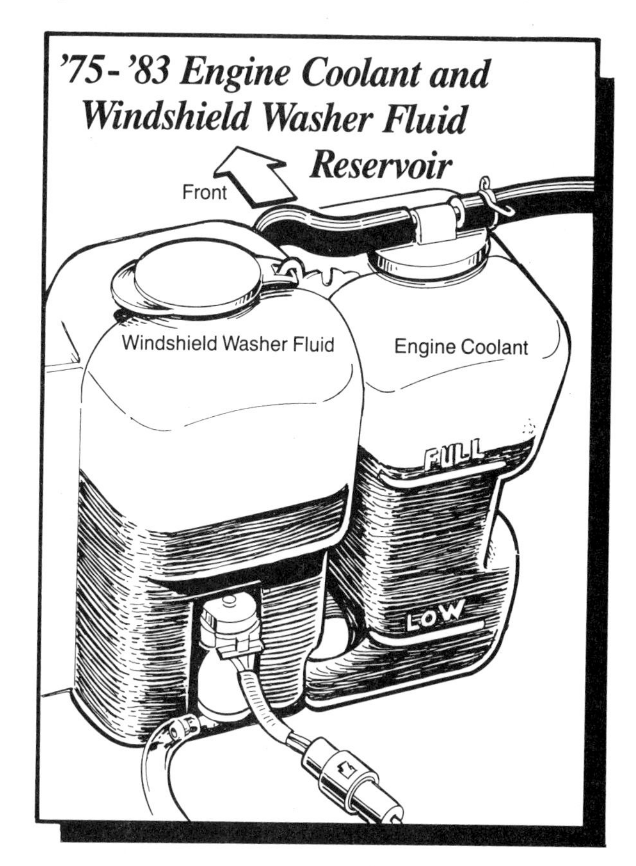

Look at the rear side of the coolant reservoir for two lines marked FULL and LOW. The coolant level will vary with the temperature of the coolant, so don't worry if it isn't all the way up to the full line. If the fluid level is on or below the LOW line, add coolant (50% water and 50% antifreeze) until the level reaches the FULL line.

If you have to add coolant at every gas stop check, there must be a leak in the cooling system somewhere. Chapter 4 covers cooling system diagnosis and Chapter 6 tells you how to make the repairs.

Step 8. Check Windshield Washer Fluid.

Windshield washer fluid is stored in a one- to two-quart white plastic reservoir located in the front of the engine compartment. The reservoir is on the left side of the coolant reservoir on '75-'83 models (don't confuse it with the coolant reservoir). On '84-'87 models it's just in front of the battery on the right side of the engine compartment. The cap might have a little picture of water squirting on the windshield and the wiper blades wiping it off. Add windshield washer fluid and/or water when more than ¼ of the fluid is gone. Don't add plain water if you live where there's a chance it might freeze. Don't use engine antifreeze, either, because it will damage the car's paint.

Step 9. Check Tires.

Finally, eyeball the tires. Check them with your tire gauge at every other fill-up, or any time they look low (Procedure 4, Step 15). If you have to add air to one or more tires at every fill-up, you have a slow leak that could become a fast one very suddenly. Get it fixed right away.

OK, that finishes the gas stop checks. Make a note to take care of anything you weren't able to deal with immediately. After you've done these checks a few times, they'll only take a couple of minutes.

PROCEDURE 3: 3,000 MILE/3 MONTH SEVERE USE OR 6,000 MILE/6 MONTH NORMAL USE LUBRICATION AND MAINTENANCE

Models with 22R-TE engines (Turbocharged) should do this procedure every 5,000 miles or six months of normal use, or every 2,000 miles of severe use.

Now we'll cover the most basic maintenance procedures—ESSENTIAL to the long life of your truck. If this is your first time through, you may find them a little messy, but basically simple.

Here's what you'll be doing: changing the oil and oil filter; checking the gear oil level in the rear differential and the manual transmission (if you have one); and lubricating various suspension, steering and driveshaft parts. On 4WD models you'll also check the gear oil level in the transfer case and front differential.

Also, there's a series of checks and rub-down to do at oil change time that will keep your truck lookin' good and runnin' great. These are all in Procedure 4: *6,000 Mile Massage*.

OK, here we go!

Condition: Routine maintenance according to the maintenance schedule; OR the TV is broken and you're looking for something to do besides clean out your wallet.

Tools and Materials: Depending on the size of your oil drain plug and transmission and differential filler plugs, you'll need a 14mm, 17mm, 19mm or 24mm socket or box end wrench and ratchet.

For the oil and filter change you'll need five quarts of fresh motor oil, a new oil filter, a pan to catch the oil in, an oil filter removal wrench (see Remarks below), an oil can spout or "church key," plastic containers to put the oil in for disposal, lots of rags or paper towels, a few old newspapers, safety goggles. Every fourth time you change the oil you'll need a new drain plug washer.

To check the oil in the transmission, differential(s) and transfer case (4WD), you'll need a 17mm socket and ratchet or box end wrench, a 24mm socket and ratchet or box end wrench or an 8" or larger crescent wrench, maybe some gear oil. To add gear oil to these components, you'll need a clean suction type oil gun or large syringe or refillable oil squirt gun. A large turkey baster would work in a pinch. A short rubber hose attached to the end of the syringe or baster makes it easier to get the gear oil into the hole.

To grease the chassis you'll need a grease gun and molybdenum (moly) or lithium base grease. If grease zerks haven't been installed where they are needed, you'll need four to 12 standard-size grease zerks (depending on the year and model) and a small crescent wrench to install them. Grease zerks are made in three styles; straight, 45°, and 90°. Get several of each type.

To grease the driveshafts on '79-'83 4WD models you'll need the grease gun attachment, which should be in the Toyota tool bag. If you don't have it, get one from the Toyota dealer.

Optional: rubber glove(s).

Remarks: Each step in this procedure involves groveling on the ground. Something to lie on like a large cardboard box flattened out, a sheet of plastic, or a large garbage bag isn't absolutely necessary, but it sure makes sliding around on the ground a lot more comfortable.

The engine oil drain plug and the oil will be warm, even hot, when it comes out of the engine, so wearing a rubber glove while removing the drain plug is a good idea.

Due to limited space around the oil filter, the most convenient kind of oil filter wrench for your truck is the kind that covers the end of the filter. A square hole in the center of the wrench allows you to snap a ratchet on the wrench and unscrew the filter. There are a couple of different sizes of this type wrench available. You need the 95mm size. Band type oil filter wrenches with a handle attached tend to bend and break if the filter is on very tight.

Plastic oil drain pans are very cheap these days and they're also useful for cleaning parts during repair procedures.

If the top or bottom of the engine, transmission or differential(s) is dirty or greasy, you can do yourself a real favor by first driving down to the car wash and hosing the crud off. Procedure 5, Step 2 tells you what things to bring along in case the engine won't start immeidately after its bath. To avoid possible damage to the high tech electrical components, 22R-E and 22R-TE engines shouldn't be washed until they get really dirty. But you can wash off the bottom of the engine, transmission and differential(s) whenever you feel the need.

When you buy a new oil filter, make sure it's the right one for your engine. It's a big disappointment, and an ever bigger nuisance, to discover that the new one won't fit once the old one is off the car. To be sure, get a Fram PH43.

Most people drain the engine oil and then remove the oil filter. I prefer to wrestle the filter off, or at least be sure I can loosen it, before draining the oil. This way if the filter is on too tight to get off, you can drive to a service station or the Toyota dealer and have them loosen it for you. If the engine oil has been drained before you discover the filter is stuck, you'll have to install the new oil and it will get pumped through the old filter, thus dirtying the new oil. So follow this "filter tip" and remove the filter first.

Step 1. Remove the Oil Filter.

Warm up the engine and park the truck on level ground. No level ground? Then park so the front is slightly higher than the rear. Turn the engine off, set the handbrake and block the two rear wheels so the car can't roll. Spread newspapers under the engine to catch stray drops of oil, then spread out a ground cover (cardboard, plastic, whatever) for yourself.

The oil filter is on the right (passenger's) side of the engine, below the intake manifold. It's slightly smaller than an oil can.

2WD models with air conditioning: It's easier to get to the filter from beneath the car. You'll have to thread your arms around some of the suspension

parts to reach the filter. Be sure to wear your safety glasses.

Models without air conditioning: Wrap a rag around the upper radiator hose so your arm won't get burned if you accidentally rub up against the hot hose. You'll probably have to put your left arm down through the space behind the air cleaner to get both hands on the filter.

EVERYONE: Wipe the filter off with a rag so it won't be so slippery. Try loosening it with both hands by turning it *counterclockwise* as viewed from the right side of the car (the top of the filter should turn toward the rear). If the filter won't budge, use an oil filter removal wrench if you have one. (The kind that fits over the end of the filter and has a fitting for a ratchet works best.) Be sure you're turning it the right way. Keep your hand on the filter as it loosens up and starts to come off. If it falls off, it'll make a big mess. When the filter is off, pour the remaining oil in the filter into the drain pan. Toss the old filter in the trash.

If the filter just won't budge even with a filter wrench, drive to a garage or the Toyota dealer and have them loosen the filter for you or, if there's room, use the Desperate or Sadistic Method shown in the nearby illustration.

Step 2. Drain the Oil.

Slide the **oil drain pan** under the engine. Strap on your safety goggles, grab a rag or two and crawl on your back under the front of the car with a 14mm, 17mm, 19mm or 24mm socket and ratchet or box end wrench. A crescent wrench would work in a pinch.

The engine's oil pan is the black, bulbous-looking thing that covers the bottom of the engine. The **oil drain plug** is towards the rear of the oil pan on the bottom rear or side.

Put on your rubber glove (if you have one), then loosen the drain plug *counterclockwise* with the wrench. Remember, the oil that's about to come gushing out will be hot, so be ready to move your hand quickly. Don't worry if the plug and washer fall into the drain pan—you can fish them out after the oil cools off. If your drain plug is on the side or rear of the oil pan, when it first comes out the oil will shoot away from the oil pan slightly. So locate the drain pan accordingly, then move the pan as the stream of oil subsides. If the plug and washer didn't fall into the pan, wipe them off with a rag and put them on the paper or in a place where they won't get dirty or lost.

Step 3. Install the New Filter.

Using a clean rag or paper towel, carefully clean the **mounting surface** on the engine where the filter sits. Remove and discard the **rubber seal** that went with the old oil filter if it's still stuck to the engine. Remove the protective plastic cap from the new filter, if it has one. Squirt a little oil on the new rubber sealing ring and spread it around with a clean finger. If you don't have an oil squirt can, just open a can of fresh motor oil and use some of that.

Screw the new filter *clockwise* onto the threaded pipe on the engine. Make sure that no dirt gets into the filter or on the sealing ring. The filter should go on all the way just by turning it with your hand. If it's hard to twist after the first turn, unscrew it and try again; don't force it. When you're sure it's going on straight, tighten it with your hand until the rubber sealing ring barely touches the smooth mounting surface on the engine. Now follow the directions that came with the filter and tighten it. No directions? Tighten it another ¾ turn with your hand. Don't use the filter removal wrench to tighten it. If the filter gets overtightened the rubber seal will break.

Step 4. Install Oil Drain Plug.

Find the oil drain plug (you might have to fish it out of the drain pan) and clean it with a rag. Every fourth time you change the oil, remove the old **drain plug washer** and install a new one. Check the drain plug for stripped or flattened threads or rounded corners on the head. If it's getting bunged, make a note to get a new one before the next oil change.

Plug and washer OK? Be sure there's a washer on the plug, then screw the plug *clockwise* into the oil pan. Use the wrench to get it good and snug, but not so tight you won't be able to get it off the next time.

Pull the newspapers, drain pan, tools, cardboard and yourself out from under the front of the vehicle.

Step 5. Refill Crankcase with Oil.

Find the **oil filler cap** on the top front center of the engine. Wipe the cap and the area around it off with a rag, then unscrew it *counterclockwise*. Wrap a rag around the oil filler hole, just in case you miss. It does take a little finesse to avoid dribbling oil on the engine. (Are you sure you installed the drain plug?)

If your oil is in cans, wipe off the top of five cans, then open one with your oil spout. No oil spout? Use a clean screwdriver or "church key" to poke two holes on opposite sides of the top. (For you youngsters, church key is what we called a beer can opener before pop tops were invented.) If your oil is in plastic bottles, unscrew the caps.

Pour in four quarts, then screw on the oil filler cap. Start the engine and let it run a few minutes. (The oil light will stay on for a few seconds until the new filter is full of oil.) Turn the engine off, then check the oil level. Add more oil until it reaches the F mark on the dipstick. Be careful not to add too much. Check the drain plug and oil filter for signs of a leak. A leaky filter or drain plug can quickly become a disaster.

If your oil cans don't have screw-top caps, leftover oil can be stored by putting a plastic baggie over the top of the can and securing it with a rubber band, or by using a clean plastic top from a one pound coffee can to keep dust and dirt out of the oil. Stash the can where kids can't get into it.

Step 6: Check Oil Level in Manual Transmission, Differential(s), Transfer Case.

Checking the gear oil in the manual transmission and differential on 2WD models, plus the transfer case and front differentials on 4WD models, involves removing a plug (the **filler plug**), then using your finger as a dipstick to check the oil level. Here's where the filler plugs and drain plugs for the various components are located.

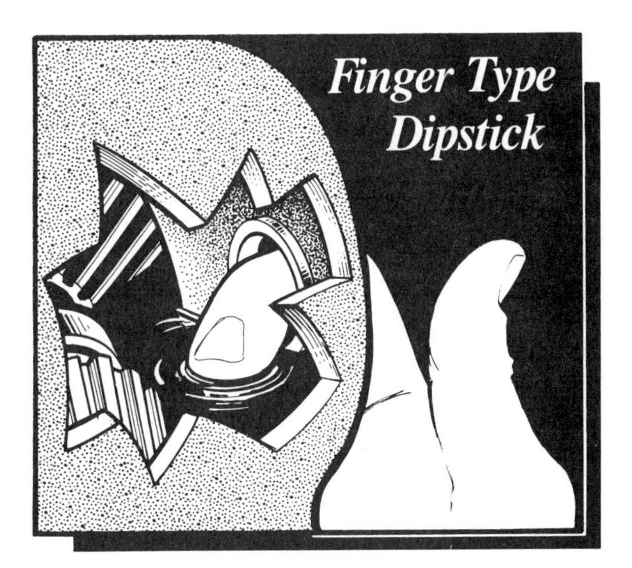

Manual transmissions: Spread out your ground cloth, then crawl under the side of the truck just behind the front wheel. The transmission is in the center of the car bolted to the rear of the engine. The rear end of the transmission is attached to a long, round driveshaft tube. Over the years the **filler plug** has been moved back and forth from the right side to left side depending on the transmission model—so I can't tell you which side it's on. You'll have to find it yourself. Look on the sides of the transmission about five inches up from the bottom for a 17mm hexagonal plug. That's the filler plug where you check the oil level. The transmission **drain plug** is on the bottom. Don't confuse the two plugs.

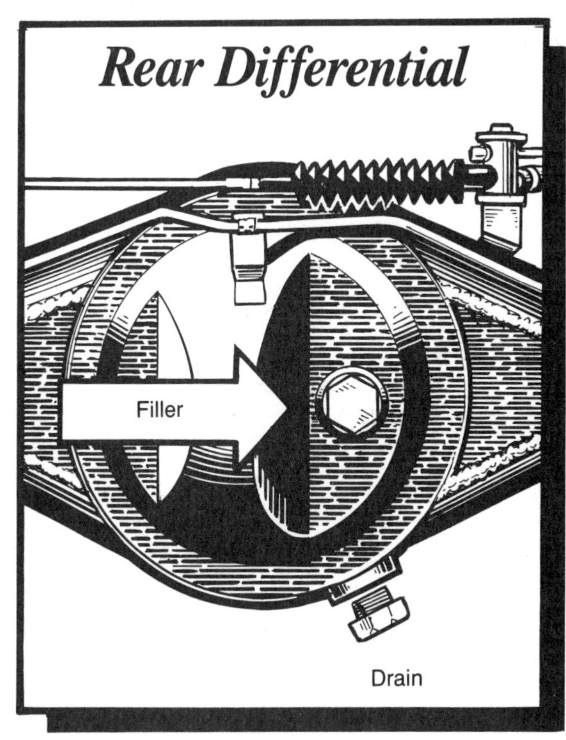

Rear differential: The rear differential (also called the "pumpkin") is halfway between the two rear wheels. The **filler plug** is on the right rear side, about a third of the way up from the bottom. On some models the filler plug is 24mm. No 24mm socket? Use a crescent wrench to remove it. I suggest that you invest in a 24mm socket because the drain plug is also 24mm and you can't use a crescent wrench to remove it. The **drain plug** for draining the oil is near the bottom center.

Transfer case (4WD only): The transfer case is that large clunky-looking thing beneath the truck on the right rear side of the transmission. A short driveshaft connects the front of the transfer case to the front differential. The **filler plug** is on the rear side near the center and about five inches from the bottom. Don't confuse it with the bolts around the outer edge of the case. The **drain plug** is at the very bottom. If you have a skid plate, you might need to remove it to get to the front differential filler plug. 12mm bolts attach the skid plate to the frame.

Front Differential (4WD only): The front differential looks similar to the rear differential, only the pumpkin is offset toward the passenger's side of the car. The filler plug is on the front and the **drain plug** is on the bottom.

OK, to check the oil levels, put your safety glasses on, spread out a piece of cardboard or plastic under the truck next to where the filler plug is located. Grab a 17mm socket and ratchet or box end wrench, a 24mm socket and ratchet or an eight inch or larger crescent wrench and a rag, then crawl under.

First clean the area around the filler plug with the rag so dirt won't fall into the hole when the plug is removed. Put the socket, box end or crescent wrench squarely on the plug and unscrew it *counterclockwise*. It's probably pretty tight so you might have to hit the end of the wrench handle with your hand to pop it loose.

When the plug is out, use a clean pinky as a dipstick and gradually stick it into the hole and feel around inside for signs of oil. If your finger is too big for the hole, don't force it in. It would be a real bummer to get it stuck in there. Go ahead and add oil until it runs out the hole, then install the filler plug. The level should be at or close to the threads at the bottom of the plug hole. If the oil is more than ¼" below the opening, add gear oil until it starts to run out the hole. Look at the oil chart in your Owner's Manual to see what kind of gear oil to add. Remember, 4WD models with automatic transmissions also use automatic transmission fluid in the transfer case.

Getting the gear oil in is a bit of a hassle no matter what you use to install it. You'll need to round up a suction gun with a flexible end, a large syringe (like a cooking baster), or a refillable oil squirt gun to get the oil in. If you're using a syringe, baster or squirt gun, you'll need to fit a flexible hose about 8 to 12 inches long on the end to get the oil into the hole. If you need oil but it's not worth the hassle to

Manual Transmission

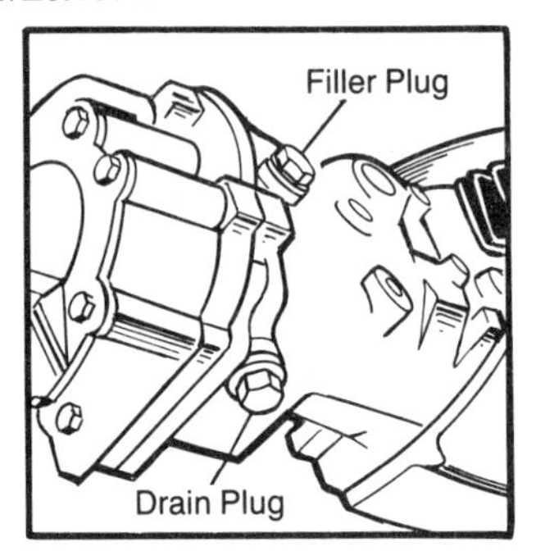

Transfer (manual trans.)

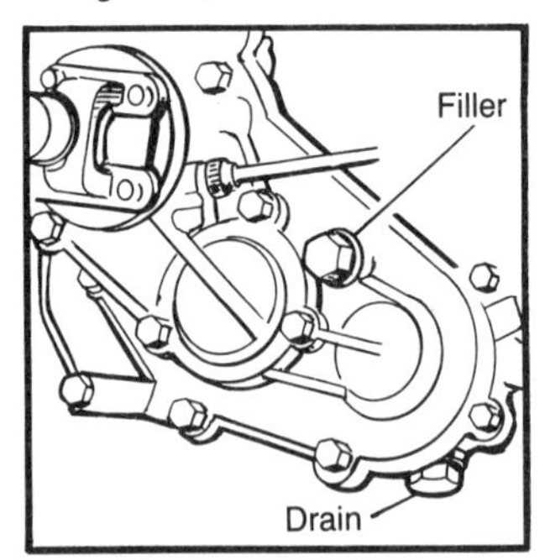

Transfer (Auto. trans.)

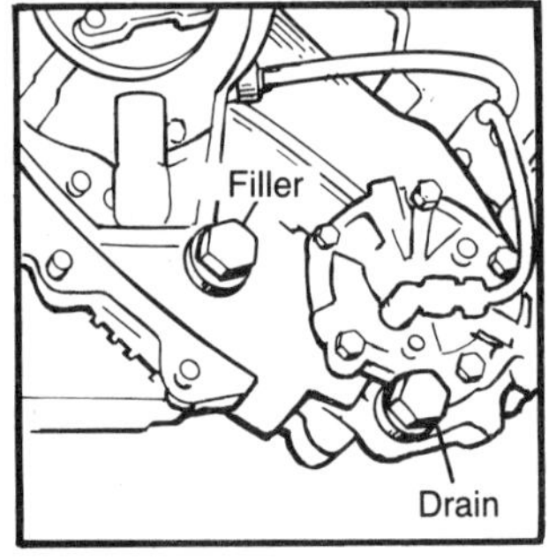

Front Differential ('86-'87)

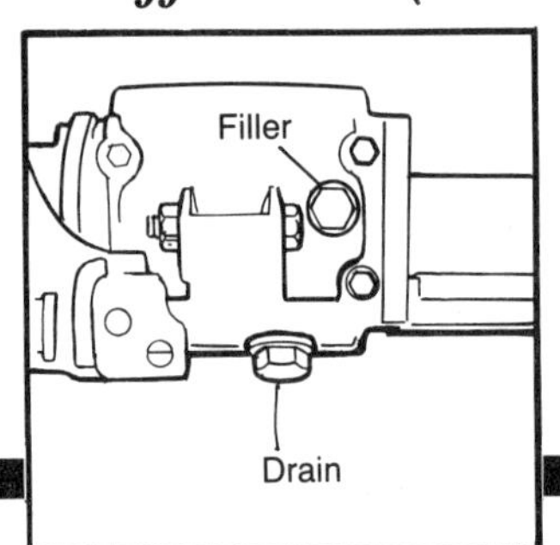

you get to one of these, screw the plug in (see below) and head for the nearest service station to have the oil inserted.

Screw the filler plug back in and tighten it with the wrench, but not tight enough to make the next time you remove it a miserable experience. Then extract the tools, oil can, plastic, cardboard and yourself out from under the car.

Step 7. Lubricate Front Suspension (2WD only).

Remarks: To make this step and Step 8 a little easier, do them when you rotate the tires. If you aren't going to rotate the tires, go ahead and do them now.

'79-'87 models: The Toyota maintenance schedule doesn't mention lubricating the ball joints, probably due to the new high tech fiber bushings built into the joints. However, most Toyota mechanics that I know still take the time to give the ball joints a couple of shots of grease when doing routine maint-tenance. The choice is yours.

EVERYONE: There are **upper** and **lower ball joints** on each side of the truck, just inside the front wheels. On '75-'78 models there are also **suspension arm bushings** to lubricate.

If you are doing this step while rotating the tires, go through this step and Step 8 when the front tires are off to lubricate the front suspension.

If you aren't rotating the tires, turn the front wheels as far to the left as possible. Now the ball joints and front suspension bushings on the left side are readily accessible from the front. With the wheels in this position, the rear suspension bushings on the right side of the truck are also accessible. Look at the illustration to locate the lubrication points on your model.

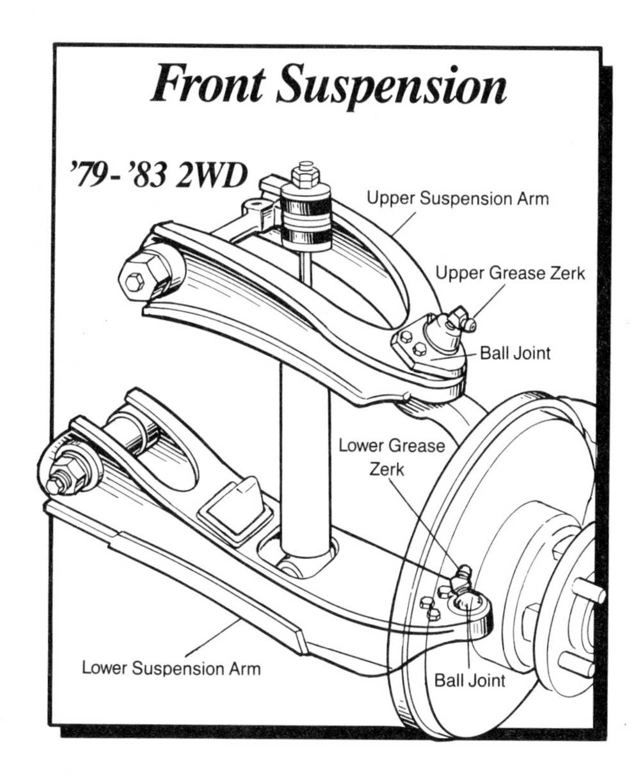

A **screw plug**, which must be replaced with a **grease zerk** before the ball joints and bushings can be lubricated, is installed in each ball joint and suspension arm bushing. If you're lucky, someone has already replaced the plugs with zerks. If the plugs are still there, wipe them off with a rag so dirt won't fall into the joint when you remove the plug. Use a wrench or small crescent wrench to unscrew the plug *counterclockwise,* then install a standard grease zerk in place of each screw plug. Screw the grease zerks in by hand at least two turns to be sure the threads are going in straight before using the

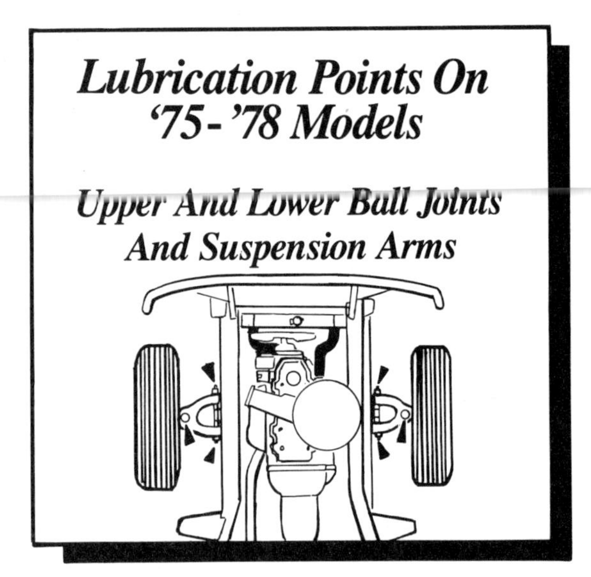

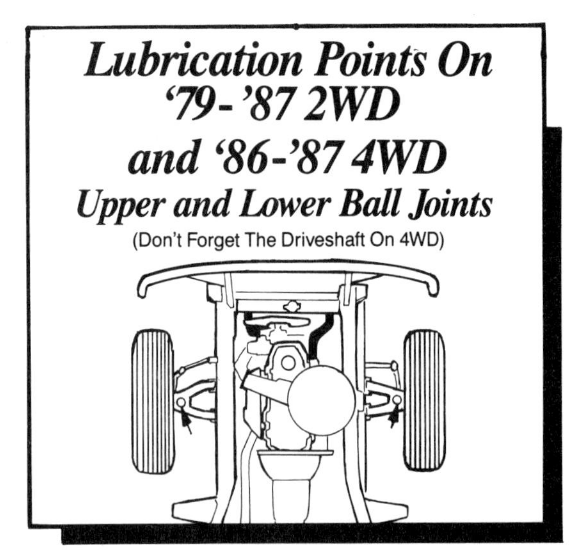

wrench to gently snug them down. Be careful—zerks are fragile dudes and break off easily. If one should happen to break off, see Chapter 15 for tips on how to remove the stub.

Be sure to wipe off the grease gun fitting and the ends of the zerks before fitting the grease gun onto them. You don't want to insert any dirt along with the grease.

While you are installing or cleaning the grease zerks, inspect the rubber dust boots on the ball joints for holes. If you find a broken boot, get a new one from the Toyota Dealer and install it (Chapter 12, Procedure 12). On some ball joints the boot is built into the joint so you have to replace the joint.

When the zerks are installed, fit the end of the grease gun squarely onto the upper ball joint zerk and slowly pump two to four shots of grease into the joint. If you pump too much grease into the joint you run the risk of breaking the rubber dust boot. You'll see the rubber dust boot expand as it fills with grease. Grease the lower ball joint the same way. Use a rag to wipe off the excess grease from the zerk and rubber boot.

If you come across a zerk that is plugged so badly the grease can't get in, remove the old zerk and install a new one.

'75-'78 models: Grease the upper and lower front suspension bushings on the left side, then go to the other side of the truck and grease the upper and lower rear suspension bushings.

EVERYONE: Turn the wheels in the opposite direction, install the grease zerks if necessary, then grease the two ball joints on the right side of the car.

'75-'78 models: Grease the front suspension bushings, then go to the left side of the car and grease the rear suspension bushings.

EVERYONE: Turn the wheels straight ahead. Wipe the grease and crud off the grease gun, then throw the rag in the trash. You'll probably want to clean your hands now. Right?

Step 8. Lubricate Steering Components ('79-'85 4WD only).

In this step you'll be lubricating the **drag link**, the **slide yoke** on the steering shaft, and the **steering knuckles**. Remove the attachment for greasing the U-joints if it's on the grease gun.

If you aren't sure where these parts are located, have Friend rock the steering wheel back and forth while you peek under the front of the truck on the driver's side. Inside the left front wheel, near the front of the truck, you'll see the **steering shaft** rotating just to the rear of the **steering box**. About 12 inches rearward from the box there's a **slide yoke** on the steering shaft with a grease zerk screwed into it. You'll also see a rod attached to the bottom of the steering box moving back and forth as the steering wheel is rocked. That's the **drag link**. As the front wheels are turned back and forth, notice where the wheels are pivoting. Those are the **steering knuckles**. Here's how to grease these parts.

Slide yoke: Turn the steering wheel until you can see the zerk. Use a rag to clean the zerk, then fit the grease gun onto it and pump two shots of grease into the slide yoke.

Drag link ends: Locate the grease zerks on each end of the drag link, wipe them clean with a rag, then slowly pump grease into each zerk until it just begins to ooze out around the rubber seal.

Steering knuckle: Clean around the screw plug near the center of each steering knuckle. Use a crescent wrench to remove the plug and insert the end of the grease gun. Pump a couple of shots of grease into the steering knuckle. Install the plug and tighten it. Wipe the excess grease off the fittings and the grease gun, then toss the rag in the trash.

Step 9. Lubricate Driveshafts.

Not all 2WD models have driveshafts that need to be lubricated. Read the following description of driveshafts and if you can't find grease zerks on the U-joints or slip yokes, skip to the next step.

The **driveshaft** (pilot shaft) is a long round tube that connects the rear end of the transmission to the rear differential. Some models have two driveshafts, one behind the other, supported by a **carrier bearing** (center bearing) where they connect. 4WD models also have a short driveshaft which connects the front of the transfer case to the front differential.

A **universal joint** (U-joint) installed in each end of the driveshaft allows it to rotate smoothly even though

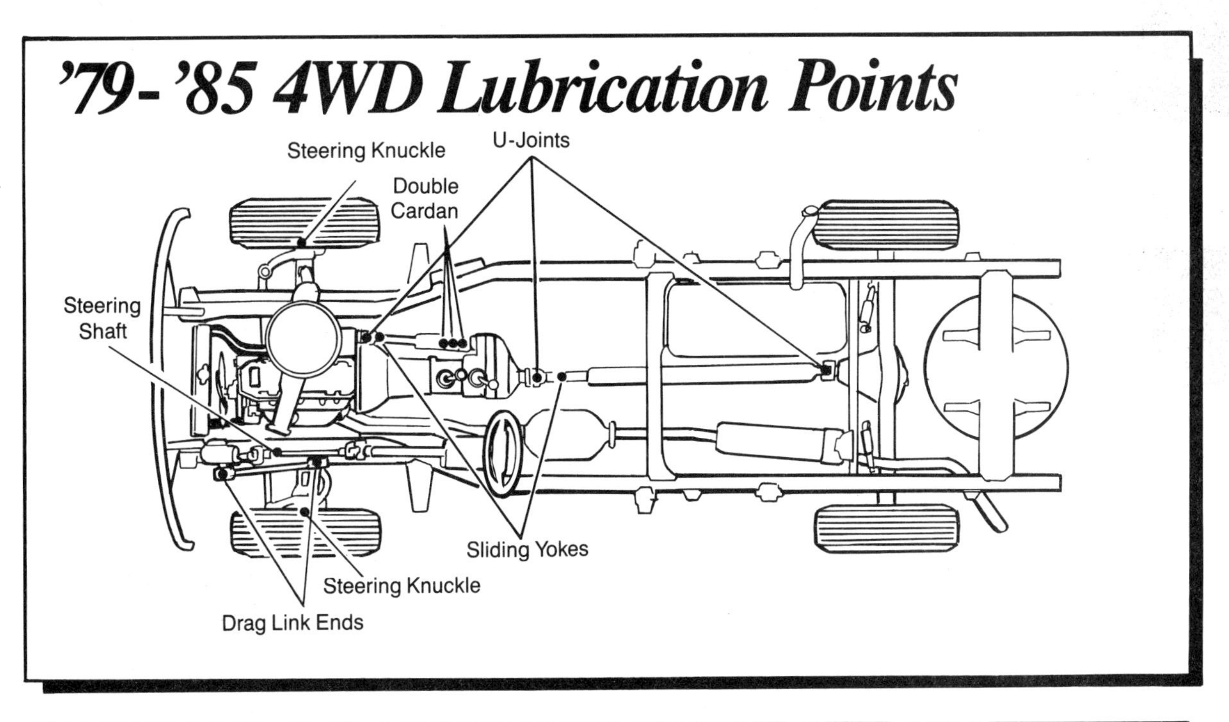

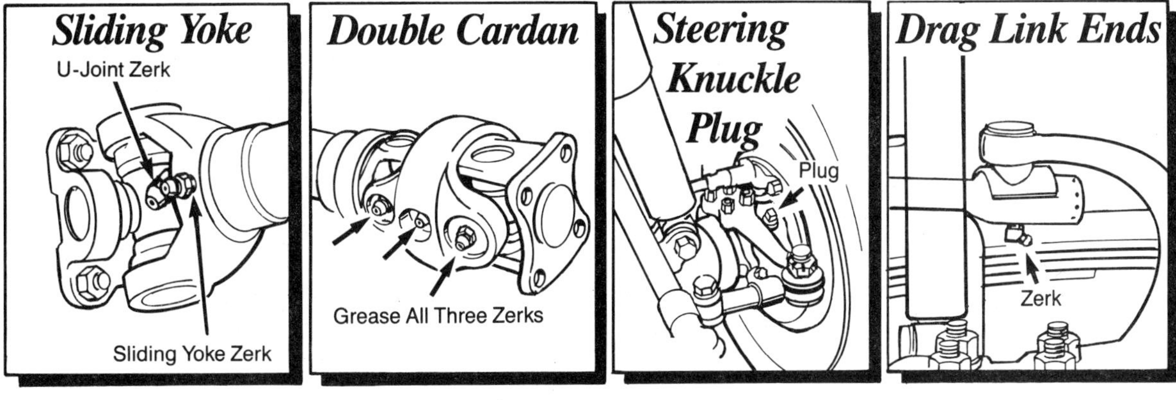

the transmission or transfer case and the differential aren't perfectly aligned. A **slip yoke** (sleeve yoke) installed on one end of the driveshaft allows it to change length as the differential moves up and down following the contour of the road.

The universal joints and slip yokes must be lubricated regularly with grease to prevent excessive wear, especially if you drive through a lot of dust, mud, snow, sand or silly putty. A grease gun attachment for greasing the U-joints on '79-'83 4WD models should be in the Toyota tool bag along with the lug wrench, jack handle extension and jack handle crank. If yours is missing, hotfoot it to a Toyota dealer and buy yourself one. Here's how to grease the driveshafts.

Rear driveshaft: Slide your piece of cardboard or plastic under either side of the truck, just in front of the rear wheels. Grab a rag, a grease gun and the grease gun attachment and slide under. Look just in front of the differential where the driveshaft attaches. You'll see two U-shaped **yokes** connected with an X-shaped cross called a **spider**. In one of the gaps between the two yokes will be a grease fitting called a zerk. Use a rag to wipe the end of the zerk clean.

'79-'83 4WD models: Snap the grease gun attachment onto the grease gun.

EVERYONE: Fit the end of the grease gun squarely onto the zerk. Slowly pump two shots of grease into the U-joint. Stop pumping if grease starts oozing out around the ends of the spider. If the grease gun attachment isn't sitting squarely and firmly on the zerk, grease will ooze out around the fitting and not get into the U-joint. If the zerk is in a position where you can't get the attachment onto it firmly, roll the truck forward or backward until you can get to it.

Grease the front U-joint and the center U-joint on the driveshaft (if your model has one) the same way. After the U-joints are greased, remove the attachment from the end of the grease gun (if you used it). Find the grease zerk on the slip yoke, wipe it clean with a rag, then give it two shots of grease.

Before crawling out from under the truck, wipe the excess grease off the U-joints and slip yoke(s).

Front driveshaft (4WD only): Grease the front U-joint (the one closest to the differential) just like you greased the ones on the rear driveshaft. On '79-'83 models, you'll need to install the attachment onto the grease gun.

On the rear end of the front driveshaft is a **double-Cardan-type U-joint**. It has two U-joints mounted in a heavy steel cage. The zerk for the U-joints is on one end of the spiders. On some models a sheet metal splash protector covers the Cardan joint. Turn the joint so the grease zerks are pointing down. Then you can stick the end of the grease gun through the slot in the splash protector to get to the zerks. If the splash protector prevents the grease gun from fitting squarely on the zerks, unscrew the four 12mm bolts that attach the protector, then remove it.

Pump two shots of grease into the U-joints. Stop pumping if grease oozes out around the spider. Now look through the hole near the center of the steel cage for a grease zerk. It's probably on the same side as the U-joint zerks. When you find it, wipe it clean with a rag, then pump two squirts of grease into it.

Remove the attachment from the grease gun and shoot two globs of grease into the zerk on the slip yoke on the front driveshaft.

Wipe off the end of the grease gun, the attachment, and the excess grease from the U-joints.

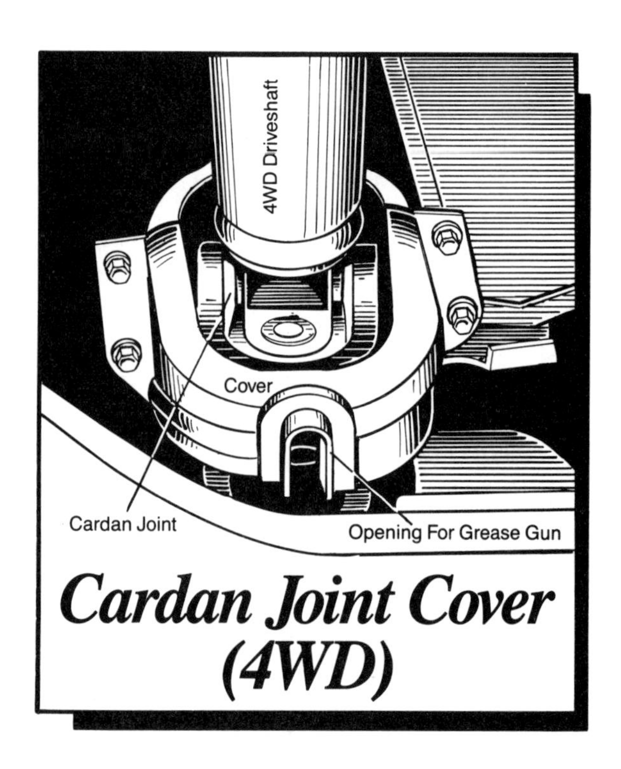

Cardan Joint Cover (4WD)

Throw the rag in the trash so you don't accidentally use it to blow your nose or wipe your brow.

If you removed the splash protector, install it now.

Step 10. Clean Up.

Pour the used motor oil into a plastic water, milk or antifreeze bottle. Some filling stations or recyling plants will accept used motor oil. If this isn't possible, put the capped bottle in the trash. DON'T pour used oil down the drain or toss it over the fence into your neighbor's yard.

The next morning, or after a short drive, look again for oil leaks. If you didn't tighten the oil drain plug or the oil filter enough, there will be a little oil beneath them. Tighten them if need be. If a leak continues after tightening, it's probably due to a bunged-up drain plug washer or oil filter rubber ring. Fix it quick.

Step 11. Keep a Record.

Clean your hands, then record the oil and filter change, transmission and differential checks, transfer case and front differential check on 4WD models, and lubrication, in the log at the end of this chapter.

You're finished with the oil change and lubrication, so let's move right on to Procedure 4 and give the ol' Toy truck a nice massage. The sensuous beast just loves its massage.

PROCEDURE 4: MASSAGE

Condition: Regular maintenance.

Tools and Materials: Friend, tire pressure gauge, light source, safety glasses, maybe some or all of the vital fluids, tape measure or ruler. You may also need: new air filter element, PCV valve, distilled water for the battery.

Remark: Park on level ground, handbrake ON, engine OFF, for these steps.

Step 1. Gas Stop Checks.

Now that you're in your old clothes and your hands have been broken in to the feel of oil, do those Gas Stop Fluid Level Checks you may have been skipping (Procedure 2).

Step 2. Check Battery

Caution: Batteries give off a very explosive gas when the cells are open, so always wear safety glasses and don't smoke anything while you check the battery. Don't connect or disconnect the battery cables while the cell caps are off. A spark could ignite the gas.

Wash your hands after touching anything on the battery. Touching your clothes right after handling battery parts will give them a religious experience—they'll become very holy the next time you wash them.

The battery is located in the right front corner of the engine compartment. If you have two batteries, one is in each front corner of the engine compartment.

EVERYONE: Put on your safety glasses, roll up your sleeves, and wipe off the top of the battery with an old rag so dirt can't fall into the battery cells.

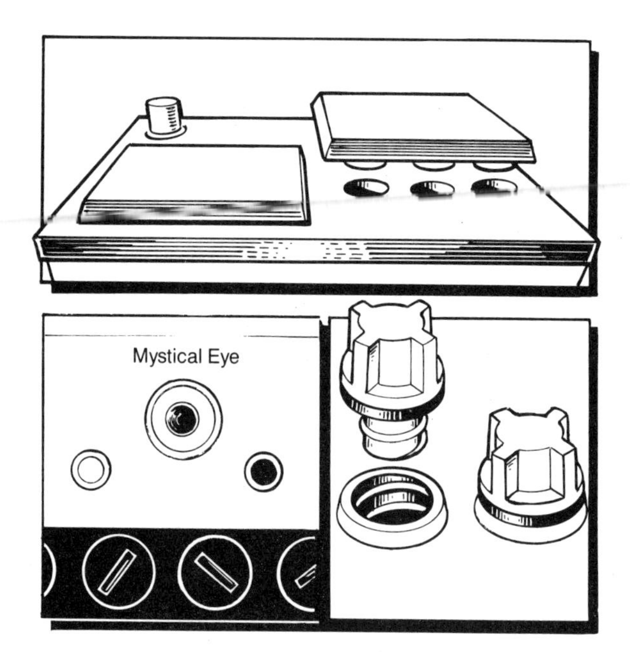

Throw the rag in the trash (don't use it on anything else) and wash your hands.

You have one of the four or so types of modern 12-volt batteries. Some have screw-on plastic caps (plugs), some use snap-off plugs that are often connected with two plastic bars, and some have broad square plastic caps you have to pry off with a screwdriver. Some "maintenance free" batteries have caps you can't remove. On some batteries you'll need to remove the battery bracket lying across the battery to give you access to some of the plugs.

Unscrew the cell plugs in the top of the battery or pop the cell tops up carefully with a screwdriver, depending on battery style. Look into each hole. You should see a fluid (*electrolyte*) in there. The fluid level should be up to the level of the *split ring* (or about ¼" above the metal plates you can see down inside the battery). Check the level in each cell. If the electrolyte level is low, carefully add distilled water a little at a time, keeping your eyes well away from the top of the battery as you pour. A clean plastic funnel is helpful, but don't use a metal one. You can buy distilled water from a drugstore or grocery store—cheap. If none is available, use clean tap water, but don't make a habit of it. Do not add acid or any type of additive to your battery. It's dangerous and unnecessary. Don't overfill the cells. Install the cell caps, then wash your hands again.

If you have one of the new batteries with an *indicator light*, wipe off the sight glass and peer into the mystical eye. There should be something on the top of the battery that tells you what color the eye will be when the battery is fully charged or needs a charge. Some indicator lights even tell you when the electrolyte level is low. Nothing on the battery? Generally the eye is blue if the battery is good. Red or white usually mean the battery is low on water or needs a charge.

Check the **battery cables** where they attach to the two **terminal posts** on the battery. Wiggle each one with your hand to make sure they're on securely. Look for corrosion at the cable ends. Is there white flaky stuff where the cables attach to the terminal posts? If the cables are loose, or there's corrosion on the terminals, look at Chapter 8, Procedure 1, Step 3, to clean and tighten the connections.

Always wash your hands after checking and/or servicing a battery. If any clothing touched the battery or cables, rinse it thoroughly in water right now. I'm serious about the religious experience mentioned at the beginning of this step.

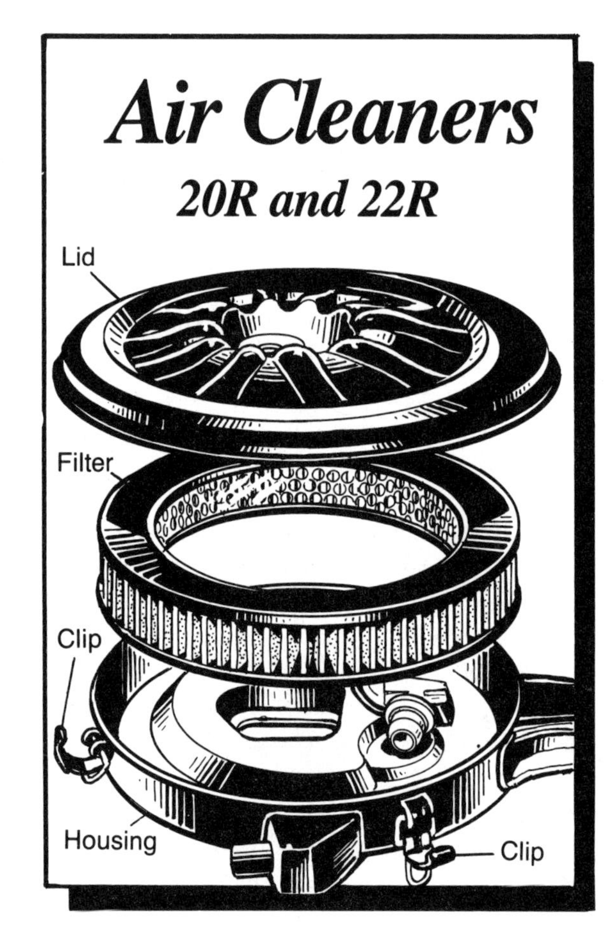

Step 3. Check Air Filter.

Caution: When the air cleaner is open or off the engine, be very careful not to drop anything into the carburetor (20R and 22R), air filter housing, aluminum housing, or large rubber hose (22R-E and 22R-TE). If something accidentally falls in, don't slash your wrists, just be sure and fish it out before starting the engine.

20R and 22R engines: The air cleaner is that large black flat thing sitting on top of the engine. The parts of the air cleaner are the **top** (or lid), a pleated paper **air filter element**, the larger bottom part called the **air filter housing** and a **snout** that sticks out the left side of the housing.

First, take the lid off the housing. Here's how.

A small metal tube on the air cleaner lid connects via a short rubber hose to the valve cover on top of the engine. Squeeze the tabs on the clamp that attaches the rubber hose to the valve cover and pull the hose off the valve cover.

Remove the wingnut in the top center of the lid, then lift up on the bottom of the four clips located around the outer top edge of the lid. Now you can lift the lid off the top of the housing. The pleated paper **air filter element** sits inside, and that lifts right out too.

22R-E and 22R-TE engines: The air cleaner is mounted in the left front corner of the engine compartment. A large round black rubber hose is connected to a squarish aluminum housing (the *air flow metering assembly*). The aluminum housing is mounted to the top of a black rectangular box. To remove the air filter element, pull up on the bottom of the four clips located around the edge of the housing. Lift up on the cover, then slide the flat air filter out of the housing. Don't tip the filter or dirt might fall into the housing.

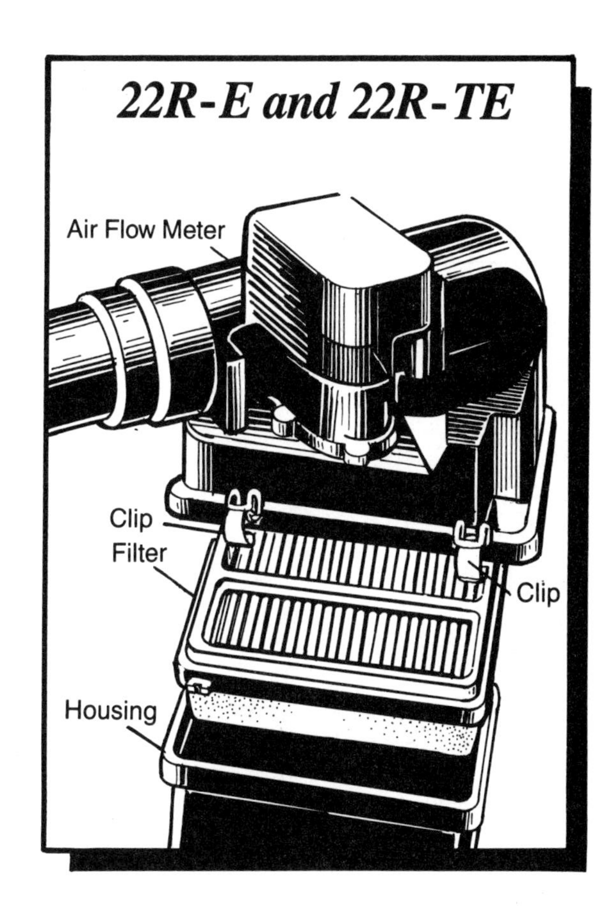

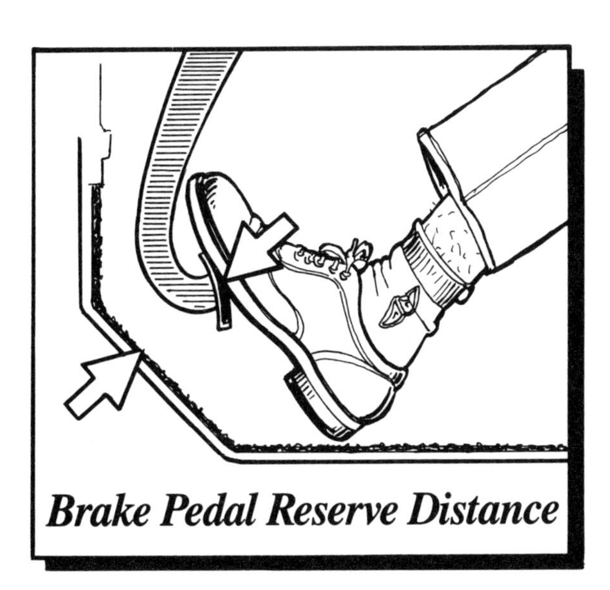

EVERYONE: Tap the filter element gently against a tire or your leg to remove any loose dirt. Lift the filter element up to an unshaded light bulb or nuclear blast, whichever is handiest, and look through the paper pleats. Look for dark areas, indicating dirt or grime, and pinholes of light. The filter should be replaced if you see any holes or cracks in the paper pleats, or if the pleats are clogged with oil or dirt. You can use compressed air to blow on the *inside surface* of the air filter on 20R and 22R models, or on the *top surface* on 22R-E or 22R-TE models to blow the dirt out of the filter. Don't try to wash the filter because it's coated with a special

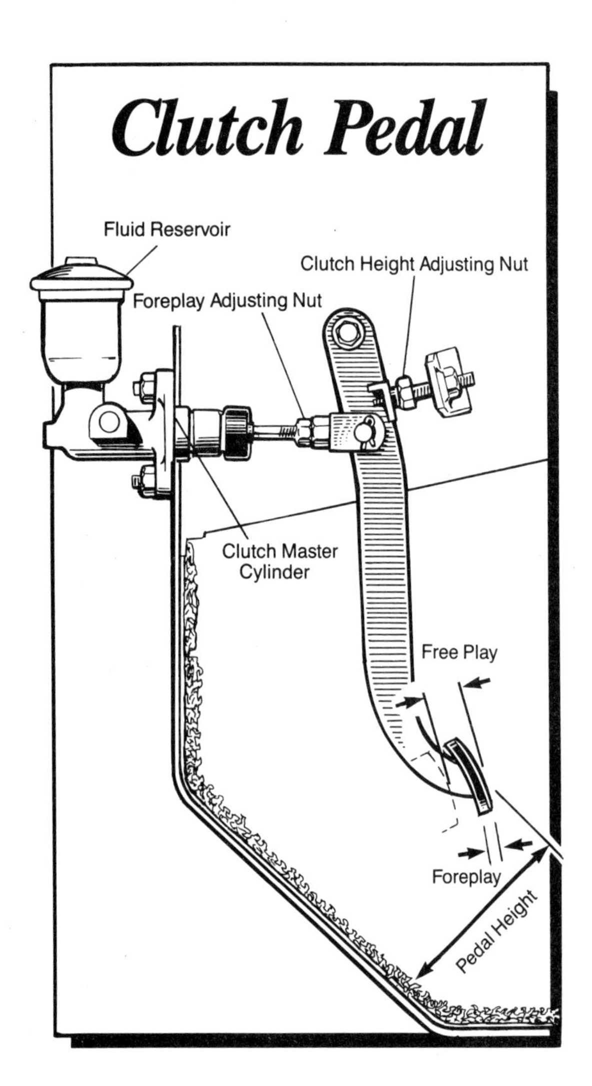

viscous liquid that traps dirt and washing removes this coating.

Wipe out the inside of the air cleaner housing with a clean rag. Set the pleated air filter on the rubber sealing ring. Is the lid clean too? OK, put it back on top of the air filter element.

20R and 22R engines: Align the arrow on the lid with the arrow on the snout, then clamp the lid on with the spring clips. Install the wing nut and snug it down, then reconnect the little rubber hose to the fitting on the valve cover.

22R-E and 22R-TE engines: Clamp the lid on with the four spring clips.

Step 4. Check Clutch and Brake Pedals.

Pedal free play: Checking clutch and brake pedal free play is as easy as eating ice cream. All you need is a tape measure or ruler. Here's how you do it.

Set the end of your ruler or tape measure on the floorboard, perpendicular to the pedal pad. Read the measurement to the surface of the pedal where your foot presses on it, then gently push on the pedal with your hand until you feel a slight resistance. Read the tape again at the pad surface. This difference in the two measurements is called "free play." Find your year and model in the chart below and see if your clutch and brake pedal free play are right on. If they aren't, see Chapter 11, Procedure 1, to adjust the clutch pedal free play, or the *Brake Problems* section in Chapter 4 to do further brake checks and adjustments.

CLUTCH PEDAL FREE PLAY

Year	Model	Inches	Millimete
1975	ALL	1-1¾	25-45
1976-78	ALL	¾-1½	20-40
1979-87	2WD	3/16-5/8	5-15
1979-80	4WD	1-1¾	25-45
1981-87	4WD	3/16-5/8	5-15

BRAKE PEDAL FREE PLAY

Year	Model	Inches	Millimeters
1975-87	ALL	1/8-¼	3-6

Brake pedal reserve distance: This check is to make sure the brake pedal can't hit the floor before the brakes are activated. Turn the engine off if it's running, then press down on the brake pedal several times. If Friend is available, have them press hard on the pedal while you measure the distance from the back of the pedal pad to the carpet or floor mat. This distance is the brake pedal reserve distance. If it's less than the figure for your year and model in the table below, check the front brake pads and rear brake linings for wear (Chapter 7).

MINIMUM BRAKE PEDAL RESERVE DISTANCE

Year	Model	Inches	Millimeters
1975-78	ALL	2 ½	62
1979-81	2WD (exc. C&C)	3 1/8	80
1979-83	4WD	3 3/8	85
1979-81	C&C	3	75
1982-83	2WD	3	75
1984-85	2WD ½ ton	2.6	65
	2WD ¾ ton, 1 ton, C&C	2.2	55
1984-85	4WD	2.4	60
1986-87	2WD 22R-TE	3	75
	2WD 1 ton, C&C	2.2	55
	Other 2WD	2.6	65
1986-87	4WD 22R-TE	2	50
	Other 4WD	2.2	55

Step 5. Check Clutch Fork End Play ('75-'78 2WD and '79-'80 4WD models only).

One other clutch adjustment should be checked. Wiggle under the truck and find the **clutch release cylinder** (slave cylinder). It's attached to the right side of the bell housing (which connects the engine to the transmission). The **release cylinder push rod** sticking out of the release cylinder presses against the end of the **clutch release fork** when you push down on the clutch pedal. This releases the clutch. A spring connected between the clutch release cylinder and the clutch release fork holds the fork against the push rod. If Friend is handy have them pump on the clutch pedal while you watch for movement.

When you've located the release cylinder and fork, disconnect the spring, then gently pull the fork away from the pushrod's spherical seat. The free play should be between .08" and .12" (2-3mm). If there's no free play or too much, turn to Chapter 11, Procedure 1, Step 2, to make the adjustment. If the adjustment is OK, reconnect the spring.

Step 6. Check Handbrake Adjustment.

Grab the handbrake handle and slowly pull it out as far as you can while counting the clicks. If the number of clicks you hear isn't in the specified range in the chart below, see Chapter 7, Procedure 7, to adjust the rear brakes. If the handbrake still makes too many clicks, see Chapter 7, Procedure 15, to check and adjust the handbrake.

HANDBRAKE CLICKS

Year	Model	Clicks
1975-78	ALL	8-12
1979-83	ALL	7-15
1984-87	2WD	10-16
1984-85	4WD	7-15
1986-87	4WD	9-17

Step 7. Check Steering Wheel Free Play.

Turn the steering wheel so the front tires are pointing straight ahead. Grab the rim of the steering wheel between your thumb and forefinger. Watch the front wheel while you gently rock the wheel back and forth until you see the wheel move slightly. The distance the steering wheel moves before the front tires move is the steering wheel free play. If your free play is more than the maximum listed below, see Chapter 12, Procedure 1, to check the suspension and steering systems. Step 6 in that procedure tells you how to adjust the steering box.

MAXIMUM STEERING WHEEL FREE PLAY

Year	Model	Free Play
1975-78	ALL	1 1/8 inches (29mm)
1979-87	ALL	1 3/16 inches (30mm)

Step 8. Check Lights.

Turn the key to ON, but don't start the engine.

Switch the headlights ON, set the handbrake, put the transmission in REVERSE, then walk around the truck to see if the headlights, taillights, rear license plate light and backup lights are all lit up. Switch the headlights from low to high beam and check them again. Is the **high beam indicator light** on the dash working? Do the headlights burn equally brightly on high beam? If not, the dim one's high beam function is kaput.

Turn the lights OFF but leave the key ON. Have Friend get in and pump the brake pedal while you stand behind the car to check the **brake lights**. Brake lights are very important and should be fixed right away if they aren't working.

Push in the **hazard warning light switch** and walk around the vehicle to see if all four turn signal lights are blinking. Turn the hazard switch OFF and check the left and right **turn signals**. Are they blinking, front and rear? Watch the turn signal indicator lights on the dash, too, to make sure they work.

To check the **dashboard lights**, set the headlight switch to the first position (parking lights). Most models have a rheostat that lets you dim the dash lights (so they won't keep you awake while you're driving?). Turn the dimmer switch *counterclockwise* to turn the lights up all the way. Shade the dash or do this check at night so you can tell if any bulbs are burned out. Turn the lights OFF.

The **handbrake warning light** should come on when you pull up on the handbrake lever. The oil and charge light should be on whenever the key is ON but the engine isn't.

If any of the lights don't work, look at Chapter 8, Procedure 4, to check the bulbs. Turn the key OFF.

Step 9. Check Wiper Blades.

You usually don't realize your wiper blades are worn out until you're late for an appointment and caught in the middle of a thunderstorm miles from civilization. Then you notice that annoying blur or streak. Wiper blade refills are very cheap these days, so check them often and change them before they become so worn out they dangerously obscure vision and/or scratch the windshield. According to Murphy (of Murphy's Law fame), the blade on the driver's side always fails first. A good Boy Scout would probably always have a spare blade or two stashed somewhere in the truck.

To check the blades, pull each wiper away from the windshield and feel along the sharp rubber edge for cracks, nicks, torn places or limpness. If they pass this test, thoroughly clean the bugs off the glass, then use the windshield washer to squirt some water on the windshield. Try the wipers to see if they leave streaks or miss some areas completely. Replace the blades if even a few streaks show up—a sign of impending failure. On 4 Runners, don't forget to check the rear washer and wiper if you have one. Windshield washer doesn't work? See Chapter 8, Procedure 5.

When you replace the windshield wiper blades, all you replace is the rubber part. The metal blade holder stays on the car. To replace the wiper blades, lift the wiper mechanism away from the windshield so you can get to the outer end of the rubber blade. Grab the rubber near the end of the blade, then pull the rubber toward the center of the blade until you can slide the ridge on the end of the old wiper out through the hole in the blade holder. Pull the rubber wiper completely out of the holder. Insert one end of the ridge on the back of the new rubber blade into the slot where you removed the old blade and push the blade all the way into the holder, past the hole. Slide the end into the groove on the end of the holder so the hole is covered. That's all there is to it. If you can't figure it out by yourself, or if someone has changed the wiper arms to a style that's different from the one described above, have the nice man at the parts store or an experienced friend show you how to change the blades.

Replacing Wiper Blades

Push Blade Down Past The Wide Slot

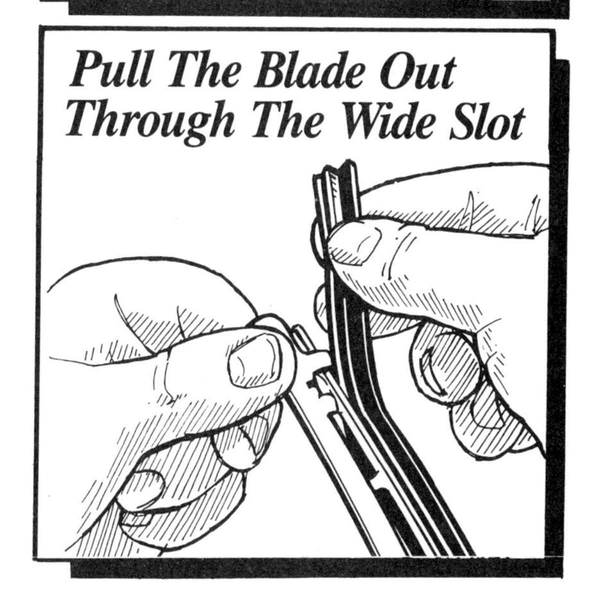

People who live where there's lots of (gasp) smog should check the wipers more frequently because smog attacks and quickly deteriorates rubber. The blades fall apart even if you never use them!

Step 10. Check Front of Radiator for Trash.

Look through the grille to check the front of the radiator for leaves, sticks, paper, bugs and Mopeds. If you see junk in there, carefully brush it off the front of the radiator with a rag. The little vanes that make up the front of the radiator are very thin and fragile, so be gentle, darling.

Step 11. Check Shock Absorbers.

Lower the hood if it's up, then bounce the truck as hard and rapidly as you can by pushing down on a fender or bumper. Do this at all four corners. If the truck continues to bounce more than twice after you let go, the shocks are suspect. Look at Chapter 12, Procedure 1, Step 2, for further shock absorber tests.

Step 12. Rotate Tires.

If 6,000 miles have rolled beneath your truck since the tires were rotated, look at Chapter 2, Procedure 1, to see how to rotate your tires. While the tires are off, check the front brake pads (Step 13). Check the rear brake shoes (Step 14) every 12,000 miles. Be sure to check the tire pressures even if you don't rotate the tires (Step 15).

While you're rotating the tires, examine each tire's sidewalls and treads for cuts, lumps, nails, chunks of glass, armadillo knees or anything (other than dirt or leaves) that isn't rubber. Is the tread getting a little thin? If you find anything irregular, have the tire fixed RIGHT NOW. A high speed blowout can kill you dead.

Also, if you were going to grease the suspension and steering systems while the tires are off, include Procedure 3, Steps 7 and 8, while rotating the tires.

Step 13. Check Front Disc Pads or Brake Shoes.

The front brakes tend to wear out faster than the rear brakes, so it's important to inspect them often. We'll check the rear brake shoes at 12,000 miles. Turn to Chapter 7, Procedure 3, to check the front disc brake pads.

Step 14. Check Rear Brake Linings.

Do this procedure every 12,000 miles (or less). How to check the rear brake shoes is in Chapter 7, Procedure 6.

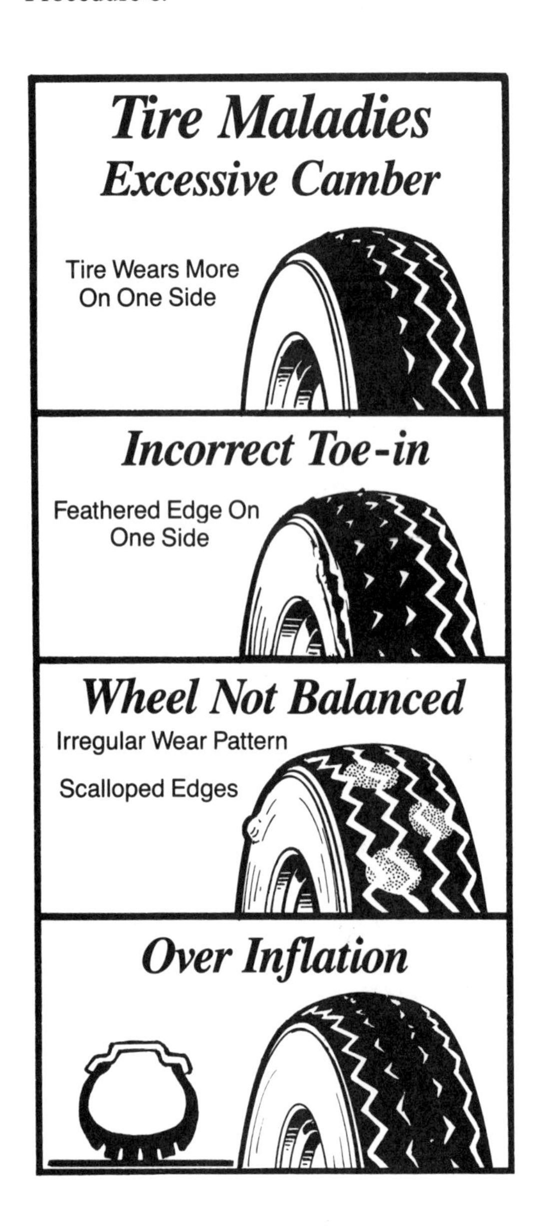

Step 15. Check Tire Pressure

Please read the blurb on Tires and Tire Pressure in the first part of this chapter.

For an accurate reading, check tire pressure when the tires are "cold" (have been sitting still for at least 15 minutes). The warmer the tire, the higher the pressure. If you're parked so one side of the car is facing a hot morning or evening sun and the other side is shaded, the reading on the sunny side might read five to 10 pounds higher than the shady side. Don't let air out to lower the pressure—wait until that side is shaded, then check the pressure again.

To check the pressure, unscrew the **dust cap** from the tip of the **valve stem** (that little black rubber thing sticking out of the edge of the metal wheel). If there's no cap, make a note to get one. Press your tire gauge firmly over the end of the valve and wiggle the gauge around a little until no air escapes. In other words, no hiss. Read the gauge, making sure you get the number right. On some gauges each line counts for 2 psi (pounds per square inch) of air. Pull the gauge off quickly and screw the dust cap back on. Check the air pressure in each tire, including the spare. If you need air in one or more, hop on down and fill 'em up. If you've read my blurb on Tire Pressure, you know how much you want in each tire.

A loss of about 6 psi of pressure between gas stop checks means you have a slow leak that may turn into a fast one rather suddenly. It could be in the valve stem, the valve, the tire, or where the tire seals along the rim of the wheel. Get it fixed.

Step 16. Body Massage.

Rake out the beer cans, dirty diapers and McDooDoo wrappers. Vacuum the interior and clean the dash with a damp rag, then wash and wax the body (Step 17). Your truck will be so happy.

Step 17. Wash and Wax.

Here's the icing on the cake. A clean and shiny truck is a public testimonial to the care and effort you put into maintaining your machine. It also reminds you of the well-maintained, yet unseen, mechanical components.

You'll need: Bucket or large bowl, wash mitt or sponge, light detergent such as dish soap, water hose, chamois or large bath towel, can of wax, lots of clean rags. I recommend buying an artificial chamois so some cute little animal won't have to die just so you can keep your truck lookin' good. The artificial ones work well.

First, let's wash it.

Wash off as much dirt and dried mud as possible with just the hose. Don't forget the inside of the wheel wells.

Soak the mitt or sponge in warm soapy water and wash the top of the truck first. Rinse off the soap before it dries. Work your way from top to bottom doing small enough sections so the soap can't dry before it's rinsed off.

After the entire truck has been soaped and rinsed, dry it off with the chamois or towel. Water that dries on the paint may leave a mineral deposit and make
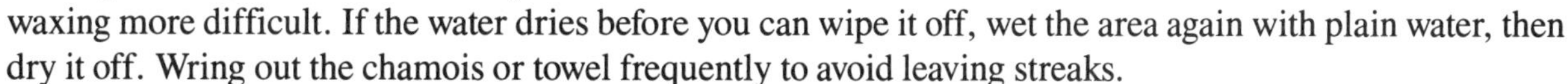
waxing more difficult. If the water dries before you can wipe it off, wet the area again with plain water, then dry it off. Wring out the chamois or towel frequently to avoid leaving streaks.

Now, we'll wax the body.

Unless you love hard labor and aching muscles, don't try to wax the car in direct sunlight on a hot day. The excess wax will be almost impossible to remove, and despite your slave labor it may end up looking blotchy. Park in the garage or under a tree. I prefer to wax my truck on a warm, cloudy day.

Follow the directions on the wax can label for application and removal procedures. Spread the wax on one body panel at a time, then wipe it off when the directions tell you to—usually after the wax becomes chalky looking. Soft terry cloth towels or flannel material work well. The more energy you put into rubbing, the shinier the paint will look. Now, doesn't it look nice?

Step 18. Clean Tape Heads.

Being a devout audiophile, I find it very irritating to try to listen to a tape deck with dirty playing heads. When the tape heads build up a layer of scum, the dynamic output range is narrowed considerably. Those brilliant high frequencies and low rolling bass lines disappear into a muddy sounding mid-range. If the heads aren't cleaned and demagnetized occasionally, they start erasing high and low frequencies from the tape. After playing a tape on a dirty, magnetized tape head a few times, the tape will sound bad even when played on a good, clean tape deck. To protect your tapes, you have to keep your tape heads clean. Here's how.

You'll need: A head cleaning cassette (about $12), or long Q-tips and rubbing or denatured alcohol and a demagnetizing wand or cassette (about $16). See the Stereo rap in Chapter 14 for a source for these cassettes.

Clean the heads: Follow the directions on the head cleaning cassette to clean the tape heads. No head cleaning cassette? Here's how you clean the heads with Q-tips and alcohol.

Shine a flashlight into the tape slot and locate the head(s). You may have to hold the dust flap open with a finger. The head(s) will be either on one side or in the back, depending on where the exposed tape ends up when the cassette is inserted in the slot. The heads look like tiny curved silver boxes with a couple of parallel lines across the surface. Dip a Q-tip in alcohol, then rub it on the heads. Do this about three times. Clean all the levers and tape guides that you can reach with the Q-tip. Let the alcohol dry before playing a tape.

Demagnetize the heads: To demagnetize heads you need a rather expensive demagnetizing wand or a less expensive demagnetizing cassette. If you have a cassette tape deck with your home stereo system, you can rationalize buying a wand because it will work for all cassette tape decks. Instructions for using the wand or cassette should come with it. If not, a stereo shop can tell you how to use it. If you only have a tape player in the car and don't want to spend the money for a demagnetizer, a car stereo shop will probably demagnetize the heads for a couple of bucks. It should be done at least once a year, more often if you use the tape deck frequently.

Step 19. Record All Work in Log.

Turn to the log at the end of this chapter and jot down the **date** and **mileage** for the procedures completed. Make notes about anything that still needs to be done or irregularities that need to be watched closely.

Is the drain plug snug? Are the new filter, oil and oil filler cap installed? Walk around the truck with an eye to any loose ends or unfinished business.

Step 20. Reward Yourself.

Depending on your slant on life—pour a stiff one, open a cool one, roll a fat one, chop a long one, chant a mantra, go for a jog, snuggle up to the mate and. . .? The idea is to do something nice for yourself—you deserve it!

OK, you're finished with the maintenance, lubrication and massage. I hope it was as good for you as it was for your Toy. Now you're probably eager to do a tune-up, right?

PROCEDURE 5: PREP FOR 12,000 MILE TUNE-UP, MAINTENANCE AND MASSAGE

This procedure gets everything ready for you to launch into the tune-up activities (Procedures 6-13). There's nothing like doing a tune-up to give you a sense of mastery over the fate of your machine. Basically, you'll be inspecting, adjusting and replacing various parts on your truck. Some of the old parts might have a few miles left in them, but they probably wouldn't make it to the next 12,000 mile inspection. It's easier to replace nearly worn out parts all at once at home rather than one by one on the side of the road with semi-trucks splashing mud in your face.

The things you normally do at 6,000 miles are also part of the 12,000 mile maintenance, as are a few other checking, cleaning and adjusting items which you'll find in Procedure 14, the 12,000 mile wrap-up.

Some of the tune-up procedures must be done with the engine cold and some after the engine has been warmed up to operating temperature. The first time through the tune-up, follow the procedures in the order they are presented so you'll be doing the cold stuff when the engine is cold and the hot stuff when the engine is warmed up.

Following these directions occasionally entails jumping to another step, procedure, or maybe even a different chapter. While "idiot testing" this chapter for me, a Friend devised a method of flagging the pages during the initial read through. He used a little gummed note pad with the procedure and step number written on it so he could find the next step quickly. When he had to jump to another step, procedure or chapter, he would mark the place he was jumping from with a blank note slip so he could go back just as quickly to his place in the tune-up order.

OK, let's have at it. Remember, if you haven't done these procedures before, it's best to do them in order. Have fun!

Condition: You just bought a used Toyota; OR it's been 12,000 miles since the last tune-up; OR the engine isn't running like it should; OR you're in a horny mood and feel like fondling your Toy truck.

Tools and Materials: Phase 1 tool kit plus the tune-up tools listed in Chapter 3: *Tools*. Materials needed are: five quarts of oil, oil filter, drain pan for the oil, rags or paper towels, valve cover gasket, four new spark plugs, about 12 inches of 4mm inside diameter rubber hose, ½" or wider masking tape, paper, pencil, indelible pen or magic marker. *Optional:* Vacuum hose plugs from a parts store.

The first time you do this procedure you'll need a very small paint brush and small bottle of white paint (model airplane paint will do).

For the 12 month major massage, you'll need the tools and materials listed in Chapter 7, Procedure 1, for changing the hydraulic fluid in the brake and clutch systems, and the tools and materials listed in Chapter 6, Procedure 3, for replacing the antifreeze.

Every 24,000 miles do the regular 12,000 mile tune-up, but instead of inspecting the following parts, replace them with new ones: air filter; fuel filter; ignition points, if your distributor has them; distributor cap and rotor; spark plugs. Therefore, in addition to the materials listed above, you will also need: new air filter, new fuel filter, new distributor cap and rotor. 1975-77 models will also need new breaker points.

Remarks: Here's where you really start being a mechanic! Read through each procedure before you start. Take your time and do each step completely before moving on to the next. The first time through the 12,000 mile procedures could take most of a day. Take your time and enjoy it. After you've done it a few times and become familiar with the procedures, the entire process should only take three to five hours—barring too many interruptions for diaper changes, unwanted insurance salesmen, or phone calls from the White House.

Remember, *right side* means the passenger's side and *left side* means the driver's side. *Rear* means toward the taillights, and *front* means toward the headlights. OK, let's get cracking.

Step 1. The Day Before.

Round up the tools and parts you'll need for these procedures the day before you plan to do the work. They're in the *Tools and Materials* section at the beginning of each procedure.

Engine clean? If you want to make this a clean, warm, caring relationship, give the engine a bath. Step 2 tells you what tools and materials to take to the car wash with you in case the engine doesn't start after its bath. If the engine is clean, skip to Step 3.

Step 2. Wash Engine.

Note: Unless you spring an oil leak or drive on a lot of muddy roads, you shouldn't have to wash the engine more than once a year. To get the engine and transmission really clean top and bottom, you'll probably get covered with water, mud and grease, so wear funky clothes to the car wash. Cover the seats with old towels or blankets to protect the upholstery from your wet, muddy body.

What's happening: The engine looks like it just crawled out of a sewer; OR you're trying to locate the source of an oil leak; Or you want to make the 12,000 mile maintenance a more pleasant experience.

You'll need: Several quarters, four large plastic bags (bread bags work well), tape or rubber bands, screwdriver, clean dry rags or paper towels, safety glasses, an old beach towel or blanket.

Once at the car wash, turn the engine OFF and open the hood. On '75-'78 models put a plastic bag over the end of the air intake snout on the air cleaner and snug it down with tape or rubber bands. If the spark plug wires are marked for position, pull them out of the distributor cap and cover the distributor with a plastic bag also. Secure it with tape or rubber bands. If the wires aren't marked, cover the distributor as much as possible with a plastic bag and tape the edges together. Also wrap a plastic bag around the alternator on the lower left side of the engine and around the coil, which is mounted on top of the wheel well on the driver's side. Secure these bags with tape as well.

Put on your safety goggles and use the water wand to wash the engine and transmission top and bottom, plus the engine compartment, inside the wheel wells, the rear differential, and all the suspension parts you can hit with the hot soapy water. Rinse everything off with plain water, taking special care to remove any grease and crud that might have gotten on the paint.

Remove the plastic bags and, if you removed the spark plug wires, dry off the ends with a dry rag or paper towel and plug them into the distributor cap.

If the engine won't start after its bath, don't run the battery down trying to get it going. It just means a little water is in the ignition system somewhere (usually the distributor). Remove the distributor cap (Procedure 9, Step 2) and thoroughly dry the inside of the cap and distributor with a clean dry rag or paper towel. Some car washes have a hot air blower in or near the engine wash bay just for this purpose. Install the distributor cap and snap the clips securely onto the cap or tighten the screws, depending on your model. Dry the large and small wires connected to the coil. Presto, the engine should start. If it doesn't, check inside the distributor cap again. It doesn't take much water to short the electrical stuff in there and prevent the engine from starting.

Step 3. Paint Crankshaft Pulley and Engine Timing Marks.

You only have to do this once. If you painted the timing marks the first time you did a tune-up on this vehicle, skip ahead to Step 4.

Be sure the handbrake is ON, the wheels are blocked, the gearshift is in NEUTRAL and the ignition key is OFF.

Hood up? Here's how to find the #1 spark plug terminal on the distributor cap. Look at the top of the distributor cap for numbers right next to where the spark plug wires connect. On some models, the distributor cap and/or the spark plug wires have numbers indicating which cylinder they're for. No numbers? Look at the engine and locate the **number one cylinder**. It's the front one. There's the #1 cylinder's **spark plug**, with a wire sprouting from it. Follow the spark plug wire to the **distributor cap** and note its location in relation to the other wires. It's probably the top front one. Use the white paint and small brush to paint a white line on the *distributor* (not the cap) right next to the #1 terminal. On some models the line will end up on the round vacuum advance unit and that's perfectly fine.

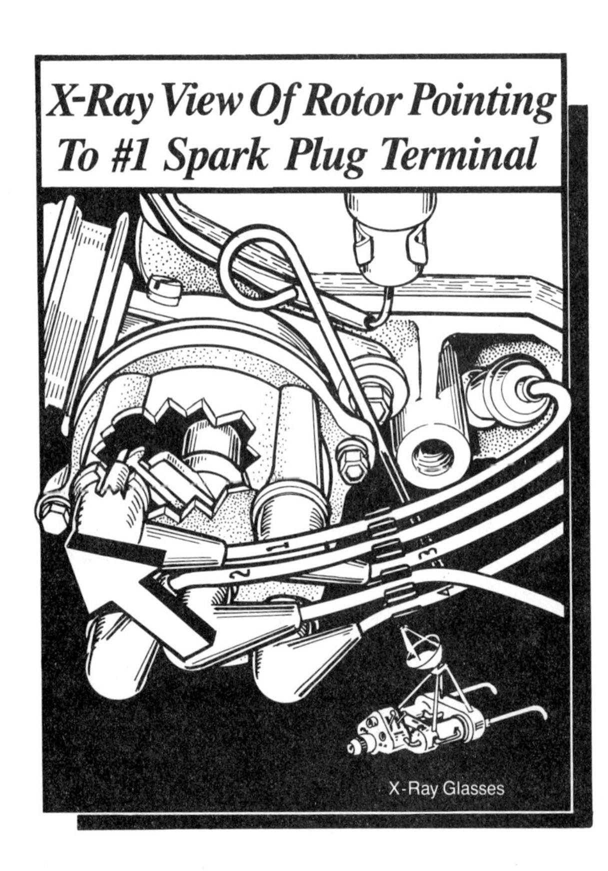

'75-'77 models: Use a medium screwdriver or your thumb to pry the two spring clips off the sides of the distributor cap.

'78-'87 models: Use a phillips or regular screwdriver to loosen the two screws on the sides of the cap.

EVERYONE: Pull the distributor cap away from the distributor and see where the copper tip of the plastic rotor is pointing. It must point to the white line you made, where the #1 cylinder spark plug wire was when the cap was on.

Here's how you do it. Be sure the handbrake is set, the wheels are chocked, and the transmission is in NEUTRAL. Remove the spark plugs. If you don't know how, see Procedure 7, Step 2, then come back here to paint the timing marks.

OK, after the spark plugs are out, put a 19mm socket and ratchet on the bolt in the center of the **crankshaft pulley**. That's right—down there at the front of the engine. See the big bolt head? Be careful not to bang the wrench against the delicate radiator. If you can't get to the crank pulley bolt with the ratchet, use a 22mm socket and ratchet or crescent wrench on the nut on the front of the **alternator pulley** to turn the engine. (You might have to press down on the alternator drive belt with one hand to increase the tension so the belt doesn't slip while you're turning the engine.)

Use the socket and ratchet to rotate the crankshaft or alternator pulley *clockwise* (as viewed from the front). This will turn the **crankshaft** and internal engine parts, including the **distributor shaft**. The rotor will also turn gradually until the brass tip points in the direction of the number one spark plug wire terminal of the distributor cap. Turn the pulley a little, then look at the rotor tip, turn and look again, until the brass tip points to the white line you painted on the distributor body. Got it? Good.

Next look at the front of the engine on the passenger's side, just above the crank pulley. On '75-'77 models you'll see a line; on '78-'87 engines you'll see a small chunk of aluminum with numbers on it. These are the timing marks. There's an illustration of the different timing marks in Procedure 12.

If the rotor is pointing toward the #1 spark plug terminal, there will be a notch in the crank pulley somewhere near the timing marks. You'll see two notches on '75-'77 models. Use a rag to clean the timing marks and the notch(es) on the crankshaft pulley.

Now look at the sticker under the hood for the correct timing for your engine. No sticker? The correct timing is in the illustration for the timing marks.

'75-'77 models: Paint a thin white line over the timing line on the engine. Put a small dab of paint in the center of the two notches on the crank pulley as well.

'78-'87 models: Paint a very thin white line over the line next to the timing number for your engine. Use the socket on the crank pulley bolt or alternator nut to rotate the crank pulley so you can put a dab of paint in the notch on the crank pulley. Remove the socket and ratchet.

Step 4. Do Procedures 3 and 4.

Congratulations! You've completed all the prep steps. Now do the all important 6,000 mile lubrication, maintenance and massage (Procedures 3 and 4). You might want to wait to wash the truck until after the tune-up. When those procedures are finished it's time for what mechanics generally call a tune-up (Procedures 6 through 13). The steps in Procedure 14 are the 12,000 mile massage.

PROCEDURE 6: REMOVE AND INSTALL AIR CLEANER HOUSING (20R AND 22R ENGINES ONLY)

People with 22R-E and 22R-TE engines skip down to Procedure 7.

Condition: Tune-up time; OR you need to get to something beneath the air cleaner housing.

Tools and Materials: 10mm and 12mm wrench, masking tape and indelible marker, maybe pliers.

Caution: While removing the air cleaner (lid, filter and housing) and once it's off, be very careful to not let ANYTHING fall into the opening of the carburetor! Cover it with a clean rag. If anything falls in there, be sure to fish it out before starting the engine.

Step 1. Remove Air Cleaner (20R and 22R engines only).

The **air cleaner** is that big flat round black thing sitting on top of the engine.

If you are going to start the engine with the air cleaner off, use rubber vacuum hose plugs or tape to seal the ends of the small vacuum hoses you disconnect, and in some cases the places on the engine where the small hoses were connected. (Don't worry about the larger thumb-size hose connections.) You can buy inexpensive rubber vacuum line hose plug sets at the parts store. They're handy, but tape will do if you put it on securely.

To remove the air cleaner, first remove the wingnut in the top center of the air cleaner lid, then lift up on the bottom of the four clips located around the outer edge of the housing. Locate the rubber hose that connects the metal tube on the air cleaner lid to the aluminum valve cover on top of the engine, just behind the oil filler cap. Squeeze the two tabs on the hose clamp while you pull the hose off its fitting on the valve cover.

There are several variations of where the hoses from the air cleaner housing can be attached to the engine, depending on which engine and accessories you have, so I can't specifically describe each setup. Luckily the hoses are cut to precise lengths and bent in certain ways so they naturally end up right next to where they're supposed to connect when you set the air cleaner housing back on the carburetor. But you have to be sure to find and reconnect each hose when installing the air cleaner housing. To make it easier, use tape and a marker to label the hoses as you disconnect them so you'll know exactly where they go when installing the housing. The pieces of tape will flag your attention to each hose you disconnected. Also, the hose diagram on the inside of the hood will help (if you have one), or you can draw your own diagram. When removing the hoses, grasp them as close to the end as possible and twist as you pull them off. Don't pull on the middle of the hoses.

Next remove the air cleaner housing. Disconnect the large hose from the small box that's attached to the front of the air cleaner housing. There will be another hose about the same size connected to the bottom right side of the housing. Twist and pull it off. Depending on year and model, these hoses connect the air cleaner housing either to the air pump on the lower right side of the engine, to a bulbous plastic resonator or to a fist-sized aluminum ASV (air suction valve) just below and forward from the carburetor. There might be another large hose or two, or a small hose, to disconnect from the right side of the housing. Label and then disconnect them.

Two hoses, one small and one medium size, connect the bottom of the air cleaner housing to a hexagonal, half-dollar-size, bolt-like thing on the right side of the intake manifold just below the carburetor. The smaller of the two hoses might be attached to a T-fitting an inch or so from the hexagonal thing. It's easier to disconnect these hoses from the engine end rather than from the air cleaner end. The hoses don't have clamps, so just grab them near the end and twist and pull them off. Use tape or vacuum hose plugs to cover the fittings on the hexagonal thing or T-fitting where the hoses were connected.

Don't disconnect the small hose going to the round thing on top of the air snout. It connects to the bottom of the air cleaner housing.

'79-'87 models: Use a phillips screwdriver or 10mm wrench and socket to loosen the clamp screw that attaches the end of the air snout to the oval end of the rubber hose on the left side of the engine compartment. Slide the clamp toward the round part of the hose, then pull the oval end of the hose off the snout. Tuck it below the snout out of the way.

EVERYONE: Remove the two 12mm nuts and washers that attach the snout to the top of the valve cover. Stash the wingnut, nuts and washers where they won't get lost.

Slowly lift the air cleaner off the carburetor while looking for any remaining hoses that need to be disconnected. If you find any, use tape and a marker to label the hose(s), disconnect them, then tape or plug the fitting or hose on the engine.

When the air cleaner is free, lay it on something clean. Don't lay it on the ground, where it might get dirty or stepped on.

If you're here for a tune-up or other engine repairs, leave the air cleaner off while you do your thing (whatever it is). When you're finished, come back here and do Step 2 (below) to install the air cleaner.

Step 2. Install Air Cleaner (20R and 22R engines only).

Use a clean rag to wipe the top of the carburetor where the air cleaner sits. Clean the rubber gasket in the bottom of the air cleaner housing where it fits on the carb. If the rubber is cracked, frayed or missing, replace it with a new one from the Toyota dealer.

Set the air cleaner housing on the carburetor, making sure the large hose on the left side of the engine slides onto its fitting on the air cleaner snouth. Install the two 12mm nuts and washers. Snug them down. Reconnect the two large hoses from the air pump, resonator or ASV to their fittings on the housing. Connect the small and medium size hoses to the hexagonal thing below the right side of the carb. Reconnect any other hoses that were disconnected.

Set the air filter into the housing, then install the air cleaner lid. Align the arrow on the lid with the arrow on the snout, then secure the lid with the four spring clips around the edge. Install and tighten the wingnut in the top center of the lid.

Connect the rubber hose to the fitting on top of the valve cover, squeeze the hose clip and slide it into position near the valve cover end of the hose.

'79-'87 models: Reconnect the rubber hose to the end of the air cleaner snout.

PROCEDURE 7. REMOVE AND INSTALL SPARK PLUGS, DO A COMPRESSION TEST

Since Toyota engines are made of such high quality materials, you probably won't need to do a compression test until the engine has gone at least 60,000 miles. So, unless the engine performance changes for the worse (rough running, excessive oil consumption) and a tune-up won't cure it, I recommend checking the compression at 60,000 miles. Write the numbers in the back of this book every time you do a compression check. If the readings start getting lower, check the compression every 6,000 miles.

I still check the spark plugs every 12,000 miles, regardless of what the Owner's Manual recommends.

Tools and Materials: Spark plug socket, ratchet, three inch to 12 inch extension for the ratchet, light wire brush, spark plug gapper (gauge), anti-seize compound, maybe four new spark plugs. To do a compression test you'll need a compression gauge, paper and pencil, a jumper wire (a piece of insulated wire with alligator clips on each end), safety glasses and a Friend.

Caution! If the engine has been warmed up or if you've just now parked the car, the spark plugs and nearby parts of the engine will be HOT!

Step 1. Warm Up Engine.

If you are going to do a compression check or adjust the valves, the engine should be at normal operating temperature, so warm it up.

20R and 22R engines: If the air cleaner is off, plug the vacuum lines with vacuum hose plugs or put tape over the ends of the hoses.

Step 2. Remove and Inspect Spark Plugs.

First, check the spark plug wires to see if there are numbers indicating which cylinder they are for. If there are no numbers on the wires, number each spark plug wire with masking tape and marker. Spark plug **number 1** is closest to the front of the engine, **number 2** is right behind number 1, **number 3** is behind number two, and **number 4** is closest to the rear of the engine. Twist and pull on the heavy part of the plug wires where they fit over the spark plugs. Don't tug on the middle of the wire.

Use a spray can of carb cleaner, compressed air, or a rag on the end of a small screwdriver to clean around the spark plugs so crud can't fall into the engine when the plugs are removed. At least lean over and blow as hard as you can around each spark plug.

Use the spark plug socket, extension and ratchet to unscrew the spark plugs *counterclockwise*. For quick removal, loosen the plug a few turns with the ratchet, then snap the ratchet off and use your fingers on the extension to turn out the plug. Keep the spark plugs in order as you take them out so you know which cylinder they came from.

If while unscrewing a spark plug it gets harder instead of easier to turn the wrench, stop, squirt some penetrating oil or motor oil around the threads at the bottom of the plug, then screw it back in. Squirt more oil on the base of the plug, then unscrew it again. Do this over and over until the plug comes out fairly easily. Sometimes crud builds up on the end of the spark plug and clogs the threads. Forcing the plug out can tear up the threads in the aluminum head. Oiling the threads often cleans the crud off before it does any damage. If you do remove a spark plug and notice chunks of aluminum in the threads, have the Toyota dealer or a machine shop install a Heli-coil in the hole where the funky plug was installed. Remember, keep the plugs in order as you remove them so you'll know which hole they were in.

The condition of the spark plugs can tell you a lot about the condition of various components of your engine. The **electrodes** consist of a central metal nubbin encircled by a white insulator, and the metal side wire that hooks over the top. The space between the electrodes is the spark plug **gap**. Spark plugs removed from a good, well-tuned engine will have a tan or light gray deposit on the electrodes. A light wire brush, like a battery terminal brush, will easily remove these deposits. Since '75 and later engines run on unleaded gas, the central insulator should be white and the rest of the plug should be free of deposits.

Plugs with rounded center electrodes and tapered side electrodes are just plain worn out. The engine is probably fine.

If the electrode end of the plug is covered with oily residue, the piston rings aren't sealing correctly or a valve guide seal is worn out, allowing excess oil to enter the cylinder. A compression test, Step 3, will check the condition of the rings.

Electrodes that are burned away, with black or gray spots on the central insulator, indicate that either the spark plugs are the wrong heat range (ask Toyota or a parts store), or the engine is overheating (the ignition timing being advanced too far is usually the culprit). We'll check the timing later in the tune-up.

Black sooty deposits on the electrodes tell you the fuel/air mixture is too rich. Procedure 13 will correct the problem on '75-'80 models. All '81-'87 models will have to go to the Toyota dealer or a garage that specializes in Toyotas to have the carb adjusted.

Lots of white/gray deposits mean you buy cheap gas or use Gasoline Helper additives.

Bashed or mangled electrodes mean the plug is too long or there is something inside the cylinder that shouldn't be there. If only one plug is bashed and it has the same number printed on it as the rest of the plugs, there must be something in the cylinder. Get your flashlight and shine it in the spark plug hole while a Friend rotates the engine using the socket-on-the-crank-pulley method. See anything? Bits and pieces? If you do, try and fish 'em out with a magnet or piece of wire. Be sure to do a compression test to see if any damage has been done to the piston or valves.

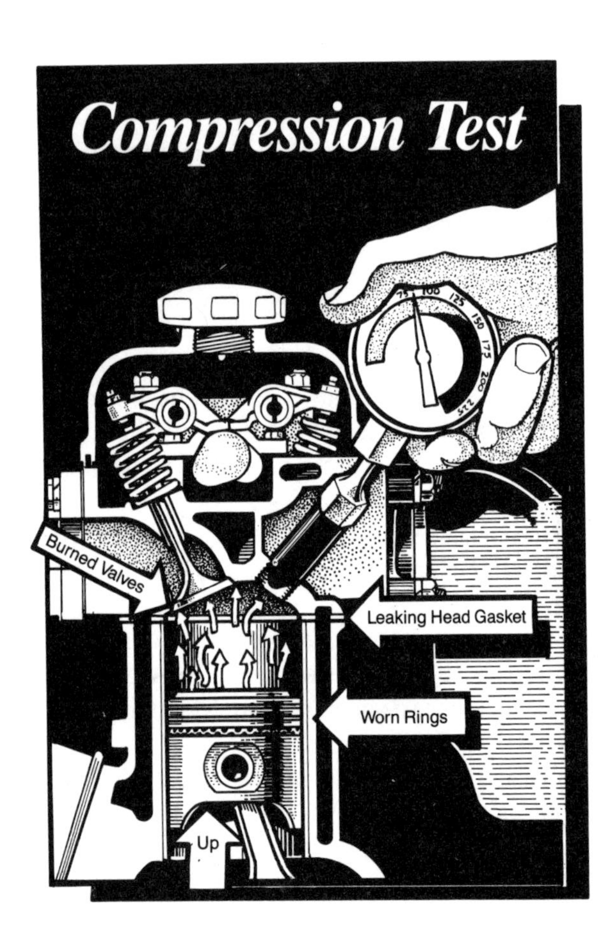

Step 3. Compression Check.

Remove the spark plugs if they are still in the engine (Steps 1 and 2). All four spark plugs must be removed so the starter can spin the engine fast enough to give you an accurate reading. The big wire connected to the center of the distributor cap is the **coil wire**. To avoid getting a shock from the spark plug wires while doing the compression test, pull the coil wire out of the center of the distributor cap. Clip one end of a "jumper" (a piece of insulated wire with alligator clips on each end) to the metal on the end of the coil wire and clip the other end of the jumper to a bolt or bare metal somewhere away from the carburetor. (The engine removal hooks on the front and rear of the engine are good places to clip the wire.) This will ground the coil and keep you shock-free.

22R-E and 22R-TE models: You need to turn the fuel injection system off before doing a compression test so the catalytic converter isn't overburdened and possibly damaged by unburned gasoline. Here's how.

Disconnect Solenoid Resistor: The **solenoid resistor** is a rectangular finned aluminum box mounted near the top center of the right front fender. Wires sprouting from the box go to the two connectors. One has one wire and the other has two wires. Pull the tab away from the connector with the single wire and separate the connector halves. This turns off the fuel injectors.

Disconnect Cold Start Valve: The **air intake chamber** is that long aluminum box mounted on the right side of the engine. EFI or TURBO is probably stamped on top of the chamber. The **cold start valve** is mounted to the left center side of the air intake chamber. A bolt attaches a banjo-type fuel line fitting to the left side of the valve and a rectangular wire connector is connected to the top of the valve. A thin **lock spring** is wrapped around the edge of the rectangular connector. To disconnect the cold start valve, use a small screwdriver or knife blade to pry the spring away from the narrow side of the connector nearest the front. A tab on the valve has to slide under the spring when you wiggle the connector off the valve. Pull on the connector, not on the wires. This turns off the cold start injector valve.

EVERYONE: Get a piece of paper and write the numbers 1, 2, 3 and 4 across the top. Have Friend set the parking brake, put the gearshift in NEUTRAL, press the clutch pedal and gas pedal to the floor and hold them down until the compression test is completed.

Put on your safety glasses and screw the compression gauge into the spark plug hole of #1 cylinder. Only tighten it by twisting on the rubber hose attached to the threaded end. Don't use a wrench. If your gauge doesn't have threads, press the rubber end into the hole as hard as you can and hold it there.

Now crank (or have Friend crank) the engine over by turning the key to START. If the cylinder you're checking has good compression, you'll feel and hear the engine slow down a tad about once every second as the cylinder you're checking goes through its compression stroke. After cranking the engine for about five seconds, or feeling five engine pulses, note where the needle on the gauge stopped. Watch the needle for a few seconds to see if it drops. If it does, drop kick the tester into the trash and buy a good one. Needle stopped? Write the number below the number 1 on the paper. Pull out or unscrew the compression gauge.

Click the gauge back to zero and check each of the other three cylinders just as you did the first. Record the readings you get below the cylinder number on the paper. To keep things straight, do the test in numerical cylinder order.

Step 4. Evaluation.

Look at your figures. These represent the pounds-per-square-inch (psi) of compression each cylinder is developing. If one number is substantially lower than the others (say, 20 psi or more), repeat the compression test for that particular cylinder. Be sure you pushed or threaded the tester fully into the spark plug hole. A hissing sound means the gauge isn't seated properly and you'll get an invalid (low) reading.

Here's what the compression figures should be if you are at sea level:

YEAR	ENGINE	NORMAL	BORDERLINE
'75-'80	20R	128-156	114-128
'81	22R	128-171	114-128
'82-'87	22R	142-171	128-142
'84-'87	22R-E	142-171	128-142
'86-'87	22R-TE	120-149	106-120

Subtract 2 psi for every thousand feet of altitude that you are above sea level. For instance, when I do a compression test in Santa Fe, elevation 7,000 ft., I subtract 14 psi from the normal compression figures. In other words, slightly lower overall readings at high altitudes are OK.

If the readings for all the cylinders fall in the borderline figures, things are still OK for now, but you should do a compression test every time you perform the 6,000 mile maintenance.

If there is a difference of more than 14 psi between the highest and lowest reading, do the compression test again after driving the car a few miles. Sometimes when a spark plug is unscrewed, carbon flakes fall off the plug and get lodged between a valve and valve seat preventing the valve from closing completely. Driving the car will burn the carbon out. Don't forget to remove all four plugs, even when you're just rechecking one cylinder.

If the reading is still low on the later test, something is amiss. Let's see if it's a leaking valve or worn rings. Squirt about a teaspoon of motor oil into the cylinder. (Four shots with an oil can or syringe. Remove the needle first if it's that kind of syringe.) Crank the engine over a few times to spread the oil around inside the cylinder, then do another compression check. If the number goes up by about 10%, chances are a piston ring is worn out or broken, a piston is cracked, or the cylinder wall is scratched, allowing compression to escape into the crankcase. You may need to have a ring and/or valve job done on the engine.

If you don't get an increase in compression by squirting oil into the cylinder, a valve is leaking compression. (Carbon flake, hopefully?) If the reading doesn't improve on a later test, it looks like a valve job is looming over the horizon, so think about doing it before taking off on a long trip.

If the readings for two adjacent cylinders are 20 to 40 psi or more lower than the other cylinders, there is a possibility that the head gasket is leaking between the two low cylinders. Other symptoms of a blown head gasket are: the engine runs hotter than normal, water shows up on the engine dipstick and inside the oil filler cap and valve cover, and oil shows up in the radiator. See Chapter 4: *Troubleshooting* for more information about leaking head gaskets.

If you want a second expert opinion on the internal condition of your engine, go to any well-equipped garage for a "leak-down" test. This checks for leakage between the valves and their seats, the piston rings and the cylinder wall sides or the cylinder head and the crankcase. The test isn't expensive. It's a worthwhile investment, especially if your compression readings are borderline or you suspect a blown head gasket.

Step 4. Clean and Gap Spark Plugs.

If you are going to use the same spark plugs again, clean the electrodes and the threads on the end of each plug with a light wire brush. Scrape off heavy carbon chunks with a knife blade. Be careful not to chip the central insulator. After cleaning the plugs, blow the dust and crud from the space around the central insulator.

Before installing new or used spark plugs, check the gap and adjust it if it isn't .031". The gap is the space between the center straight electrode and the electrode hooked up and over the center of the plug. I have a spark plug gapper, one of those round things with wires all around it, to set mine—but you can do it close enough with any feeler gauge. Adjust the gap so the correct wire or feeler blade slides through the gap with a slight resistance.

The gap is changed by bending the outside electrode toward or away from the center electrode. Most spark plug gappers have a notch for changing the gap. Hook the notch over the outside electrode down close to the threads. Use the gapper as a lever to bend the electrode. If your gapper doesn't have a notch, the gap can be widened with needlenose pliers and narrowed by lightly tapping the electrode end on a piece of hard wood or clean metal. Check and adjust the gap until the proper wire or blade slips through the gap with just slight resistance.

Step 5. Install Spark Plugs.

If you are going to adjust the valves (the next step in the tune-up), leave the spark plugs out so you can turn the engine more easily. Don't forget to install them after the valves are adjusted.

Clean and gap the spark plugs if you haven't already (Step 5). Smear a light coat of anti-seize compound on the threads of each spark plug (don't get any of the goo on the electrodes), then screw each one into the head by hand at least four complete turns. This will eliminate any possibility of getting them cross-threaded. (Incidentally, it makes no difference which plug goes in which hole, even if you're installing the used ones.) Tighten them the rest of the way with the spark plug socket and ratchet. They should be good and snug but not super-tight. The torque is about 15 ft.lbs.

Wipe the spark plug and coil wires off with a clean damp rag. Check each wire for cracks, breaks and melted places where the wire might have touched the exhaust manifold. Replace the wires if you find any abnormalities. Check the ends of the wires for corrosion. If the end of the wire has been eaten away by corrosion, or if it's badly corroded and you can't remove it with a wire brush, replace the wires. Every 24,000 miles check the resistance of the wires (Chapter 8, Procedure 12).

Connect the wires to the appropriate plug—you should feel them click into place. If you forgot to put number tapes on the wires and don't know which goes where, check the illustration.

If you did a compression test, remove the jumper wire and connect the coil wire to the center post on the distributor cap. Push it firmly into place. Oh yes, if your Friend helped you do the compression test they can take their feet off the pedals now.

22R-E and 22R-TE models: Reconnect the solenoid resistor and cold start valve. Be sure the connectors are securely locked in place.

PROCEDURE 8: ADJUST VALVES

Condition: Tune-up time; OR the valves sound noisy. The engine must be warm.

Tools and Materials: You'll need a 12mm box end wrench and a medium screw driver. Also you'll need a feeler gauge with the correct blade sizes for your valve setting (Go-No-Go feeler gauges are easiest to use), ratchet and a 19mm socket, a new valve cover gasket, maybe two half moon valve cover end plugs, and four new rubber washers for the valve cover bolts.

Remark: Remember, the left side of the truck is the driver's side, and the right side is the passenger's side. Front is toward the headlights and rear is toward the taillights.

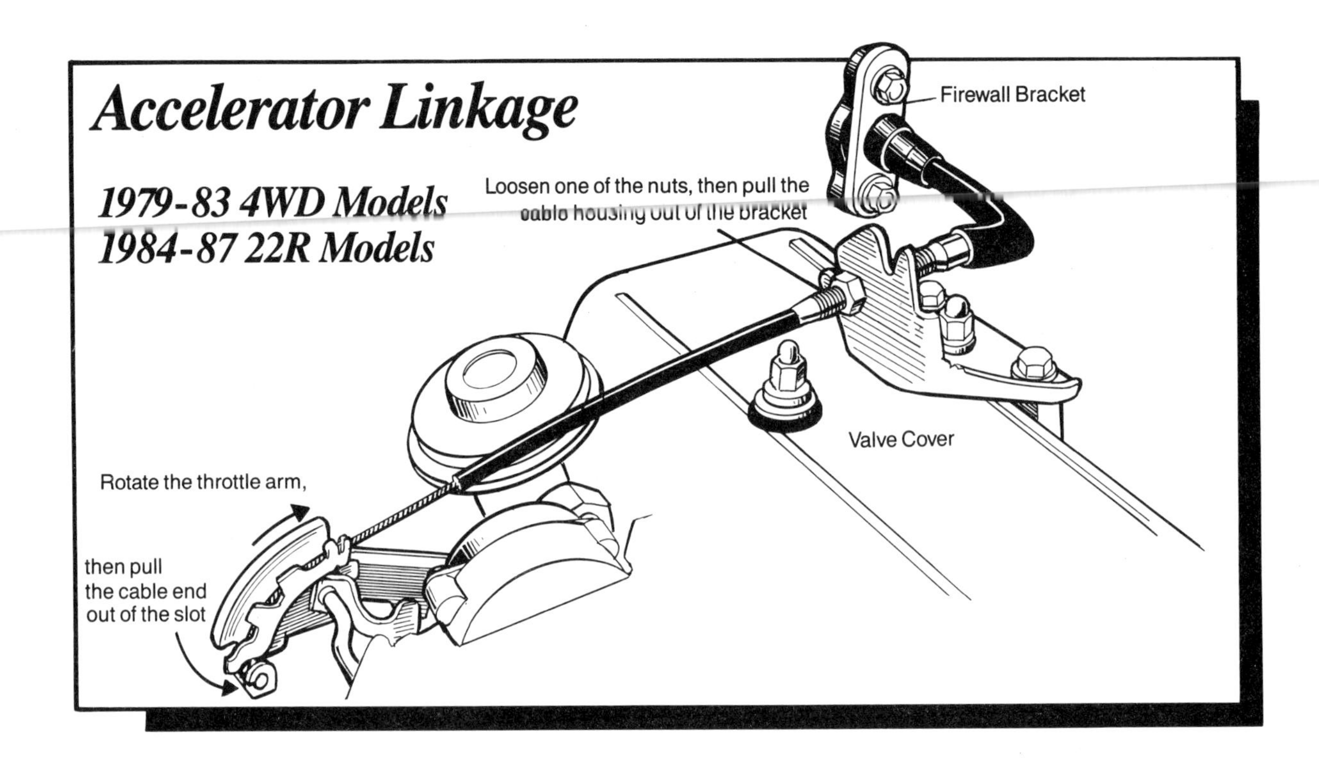

Step 1. Remove the Air Cleaner.
See Procedure 6, Step 1.

Step 2. Mark Crank Pulley and Distributor.
Skip this step if you've already painted white lines on the crank pulley and distributor. If you haven't, do it now (Procedure 5, Step 3).

Step 3. Remove the Valve Cover.
The valve cover is that big chunk of aluminum that covers the top of the engine. It's attached with four 12mm nuts near the four corners. Before removing the nuts, look for other things that might be attached to the valve cover. A plastic wire connector for the distributor might be clipped to a holder on the left front of the valve cover, next to the distributor. If you have the holder, pry the connector out of its holder and tuck the wire away from the valve cover. Also, a gizmo attached to a couple of small hoses might be bolted to the left rear of the valve cover. If so, remove the 12mm bolt, tuck the gizmo out of the way on the right side of the engine, then screw the bolt back into the valve cover so it doesn't get lost. There might be holders for the spark plug wires attached to the top of the valve cover. If so, remove the bolt to free the holder, then screw the bolt back into the valve cover so it won't get lost.

If any hoses or wires are attached to things on opposite sides of the valve cover, you'll need to label and then disconnect the wires or hoses. For example, on some EFI models, the vacuum hose for the Master Vac unit (brake booster) and two hoses for the power steering pump must be disconnected.

There are one or two thumb-size hoses attached to the top of the valve cover. Squeeze the ends of the clamp(s) together and move the clamp(s) away from the ends of the hose(s), then disconnect the hose(s) from the valve cover.

'79-'87 4WD and '84-'87 2WD models with 20R or 22R engines: The accelerator cable is attached to a bracket near the rear of the valve cover. To get it out of the way, follow the cable to the rounded throttle lever near the rear of the carburetor, then rotate the top of the lever toward the valve cover while you align the braided cable with the slot in the lever. Slide the braided cable and the little cylinder on the cable end out of the throttle lever. Next, loosen one of the nuts that attach the cable housing to the bracket on the valve cover, then slide the housing out of the slot in the bracket. Only loosen one of the nuts, and remember which one you loosened, so you don't have to adjust the cable when you reconnect the cable housing to the bracket. Prop the cable on the left side of the engine compartment so it's out of the way.

Look for other things that might be attached to the valve cover. If you find anything, label and then remove it.

EVERYONE: Remove the four 12mm nuts near the top corners of the valve cover. The flat washers under the nuts have rubber bonded to the bottom side which has probably assumed the shape of the bolt threads, so you'll have to unscrew them too. You might need to use pliers initially to help get them loosened.

Once the nuts and washers are off, lift up on the front end of the valve cover to be sure it's free. To remove the valve cover, lift the front and rear ends while you twist and wiggle it out. On some models there's a rubber heater hose attached to the firewall just behind the valve cover. You have to raise the hose slightly to remove the valve cover. A Friend to lift up on the hose is helpful but not absolutely necessary.

'78-'83 2WD models: A thin black accelerator cable housing might be in the way as you remove the valve cover. One end of the cable housing attaches to a bracket near the top center of the firewall and the other end is a plastic fitting that screws into the left center part of the firewall. If you are too rough with the cable housing during valve cover removal, the plastic fitting on the left end of the cable might break. If the plastic fitting breaks, see Chapter 9, Procedure 3, to replace the cable.

EVERYONE: Once the valve cover is off, lay it upside down where it won't get dirty or stepped on. If the rubber valve cover gasket is stuck to the top of the cylinder head, remove it. Now let's adjust the valves.

Step 4. How You Adjust Valves.

The wonders of the **valve train** now lie naked and yearning before you. Slowly pull out your feeler gauge and move toward the wide open hood!

Your **feeler gauge** blades are the keys to successful valve adjustment. You're dealing with a slim gap between the **rocker arm** and **valve stem**. The correct setting for all '75-'87 Toyota truck gasoline engines is .008" (eight thousandths) for the intake valves and .012" (twelve thousandths) for the exhaust valves.

To set a valve to .008" (eight thousandths of an inch), adjust it so an .009: feeler gauge blade won't fit, but a .007" blade will. The same criterion applies for setting one to .012"—adjust it so a .013" blade won't fit but a .011" will. This is where GO-NO-GO feeler gauges help. They combine two sizes on each blade. The tip is one size and the rest of the blade is another. For instance, .007" and .009", or .011" and .013". If the tip fits in the gap but the blade doesn't, the gap is set at whatever number is between the two sizes. They sure make adjusting valves a lot easier.

Whether a valve is too tight or too loose, the procedure for changing the setting is the same: you change the position of the **adjusting bolt** in the rocker arm. Turn the bolt *clockwise* to decrease the distance between the rocker arm and the valve, or *counterclockwise* to increase this clearance.

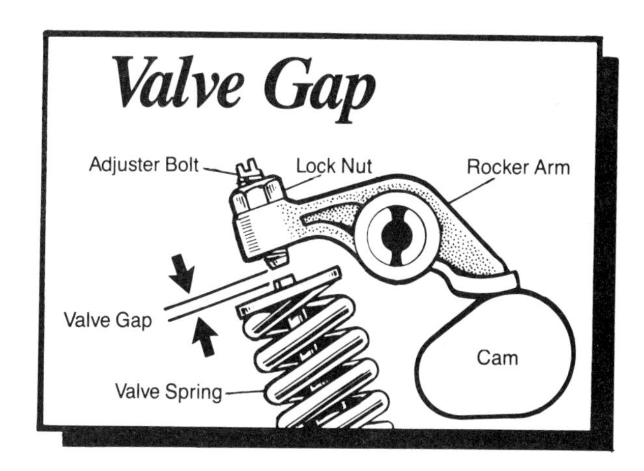

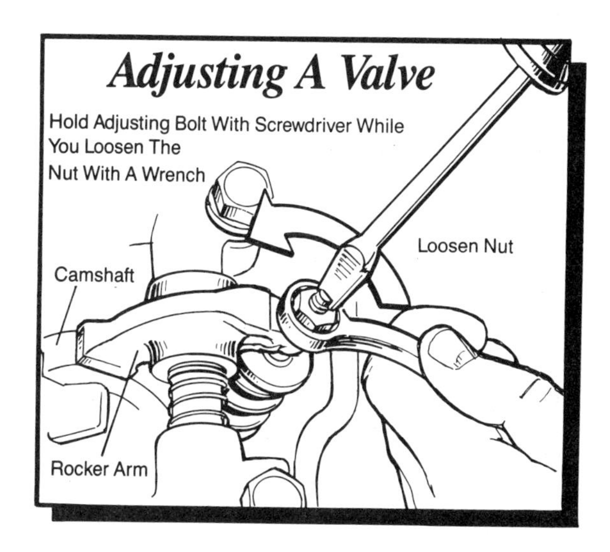

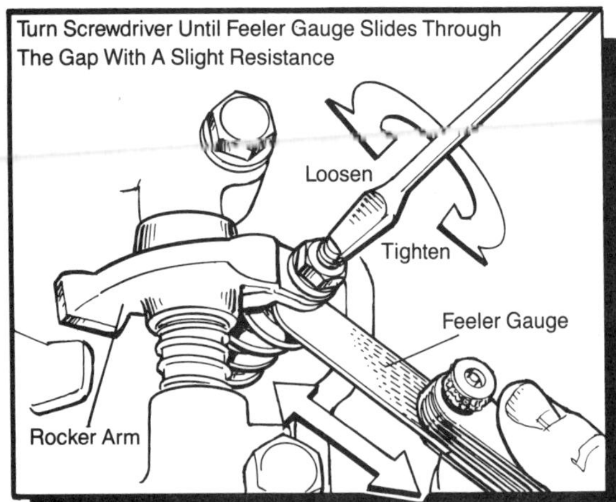

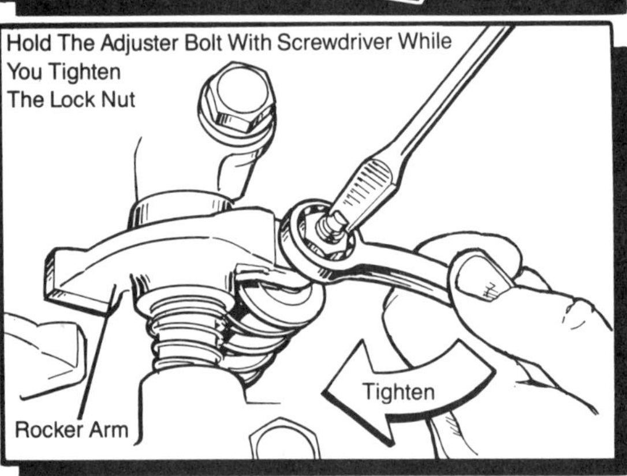

Remember, *clockwise* is less clearance, *counterclockwise* is more clearance.

The adjusting bolt has a **locking nut** to hold it in position after it's been adjusted. The locking nut must be loosened (*counterclockwise*) before you can adjust the bolt to change the gap. You won't have to turn it far. Use your best 12mm box end wrench to loosen the 12mm lock nut. Make sure the wrench is secure on the nut because this is a place where skinned knuckles abound. If the nut doesn't come loose with one hand, use two (watch out for those skinned knuckles). One way to avoid skinned knuckles is to hold the wrench firmly with one hand while you use the free hand to tap (or pound) on the end of the wrench to loosen the lock nut. When the nut is loose, hold it still with the wrench and move the adjusting bolt back and forth in the nut a few times to get the threads in a little better adjusting shape. Use a screwdriver with a good square tip to turn the adjusting bolt. If you use a crummy, worn tapered screwdriver that doesn't fit into the slot snugly, the bolt will turn when you tighten down the locknut and the gap will probably get smaller.

I have two methods for adjusting valve clearances. Which method I use depends on how easily the lock nut moves on the adjusting bolt. If the nut moves easily, I use the "Imprisoned Feeler Blade Method," but if the nut turns hard on the bolt I use the "Memorized Position Method." Sometimes I use a combination of both.

Imprisoned Blade Method: After the lock nut is loose, put the 12mm wrench on the lock nut and the screwdriver blade in the slot on the end of the adjusting bolt. Let the 12mm wrench go and slip the proper feeler blade between the rocker arm and the valve. (If it won't fit, turn the bolt *counterclockwise* a little.) Without putting any downward pressure on the screwdriver, turn the adjusting bolt *clockwise* with the screwdriver until it barely "imprisons" the blade by pinching it between the valve stem and the bolt. The blade can be moved, but offers resistance. Let the blade remain in the gap. Hold the screwdriver in this position, let go of the feeler gauge and tighten the lock nut on the bolt. Try the feeler blade again to see if you got it right. If the blade is too tight, back off on the lock nut, then the adjusting bolt, and do the adjustment again. Be sure you're not letting the screwdriver move at all when you tighten the lock nut.

Memorized Position Method: This method is useful when turning the lock nut tends to turn the adjusting bolt too. The 12mm lock nut is loosened and the 12mm wrench is on the lock nut, right? Let go of the wrench and put the screwdriver on the bolt and the feeler blade in place in the gap and tighten the bolt until the clearance seems right. The blade should be held gently in the gap's grip, as in the Imprisoned Blade Method. Memorize the position of the slot in the end of the adjusting bolt at this point. Slip the feeler blade out. Use the 12mm wrench to turn the lock nut down on the bolt. Just before the lock nut reaches its seat on the rocker arm, loosen (*counterclockwise*) the adjusting bolt with the screwdriver just a little so the lock nut will twist it *clockwise* to the memorized place when you tighten it down. You'll see the blade of the screwdriver turn as you tighten the lock nut. First time through you'll need trial-and-error to determine how far you have to back off the adjusting bolt to get it to return to the memorized position when you snug down the lock nut. Be patient—you'll get it.

In both methods, snug the adjusting nut down tight and check the clearance again with the feeler blade(s). If it's correct, go on to the next valve. If it isn't, you're back where you started, so adjust it again. Remember that a little looser is better than a little tighter. It will take time and patience to get them right, especially the first time. Hang in there. The gaps are important so get them right.

Step 5. Adjust Valves: Stage One

Remove the distributor cap (Procedure 9, Step 2). Turn the crank *clockwise* with the socket on the crank pulley the same as you did when you painted the crank pulley (Procedure 5, Step 3), until the rotor points to the line you painted on the outside of the distributor body, right next to the #1 spark plug terminal.

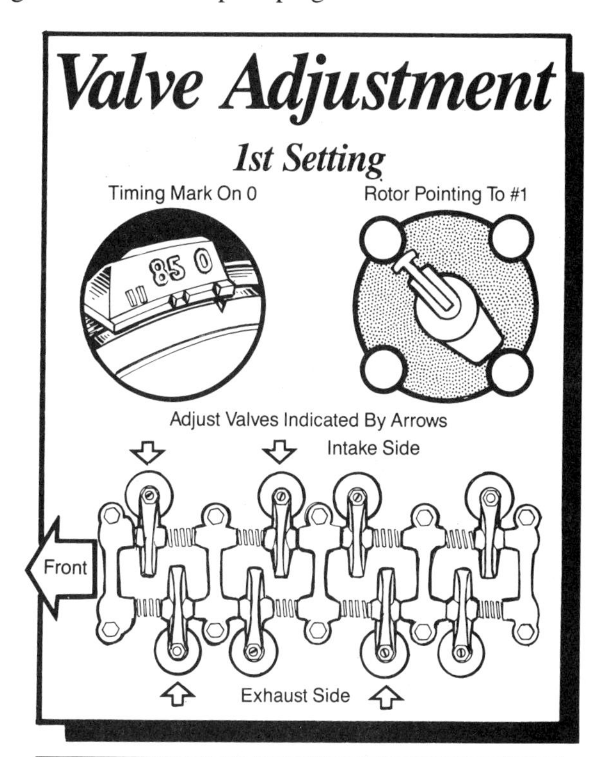

'75-'77 models: Now turn the crank until the 0 notch on the pulley is even with the timing line on the engine.

'78-'87 models: Turn the crank until the notch on the crank pulley is aligned with the 0 line on the engine.

EVERYONE: Be sure the rotor is pointing toward the line you painted on the distributor (the #1 spark plug post), and the notch on the crank pulley is aligned with the proper mark on the engine. The engine is now set at Top Dead Center (TDC) firing position for cylinder #1. Now we're set to adjust the intake and exhaust valves for the #1 cylinder, the intake valve for cylinder #2, and the exhaust valve for cylinder #3.

The intake valves are on the right (passenger's) side and the exhaust valves are on the left (driver's) side. Got it? Good.

The valves for #1 cylinder are the two nearest the front of the engine. The correct valve setting is .008" for intake valves and .012" for the exhaust valves. This is the correct setting for all gasoline Toyota pickup engines from 1975-87.

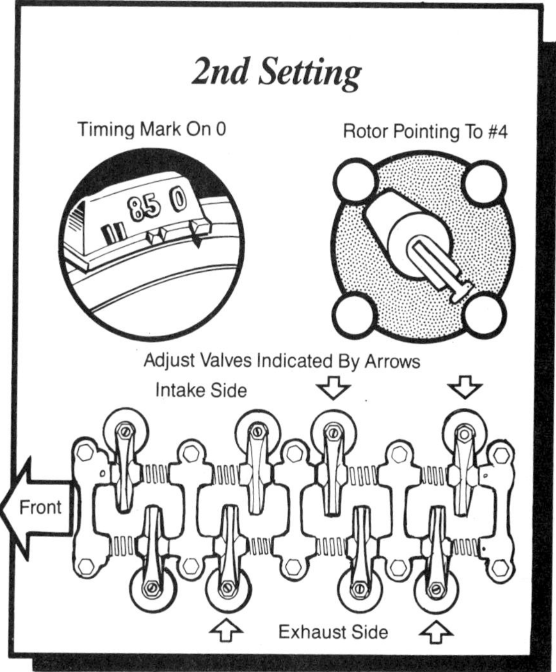

Get out the feeler gauge with the appropriate blades ready for action. Start with the front valve on the right side of the engine. That would be the intake valve for cylinder #1. Slide the .008" feeler gauge blade between the rocker arm and valve stem. Slip it in flat and straight—don't force it. If you're not sure where to stick the blade, push and pull the right end of the rocker arm to see where it hits. It hits the valve stem sticking out of the center of the valve spring. The space between the valve stem and rocker arm is the distance we're checking. It's easiest to arrange the blade so it's going into the gap from the outer edge.

If the .008" blade won't go into the gap, try a .007" blade. If it won't go, you have a tight valve. If an .009" blade falls through the gap, you have a loose valve. If the .008" blade slides through the gap with just a slight resistance to easy sliding, the valve is right. (If it seems OK but you want to make sure, try a .007" and a .009" blade. If the .009" blade won't go through and the .007" will, you know the adjustment is right.) Take your time. You can build up speed later, but right now give yourself all the time you need. It might be useful to have a Friend who's used feeler gauges join you for the first try. Ask him or her to check your first valve and compare notes. You can actually *feel* the blade slipping with a slight pull between the two metal surfaces when the adjustment is correct. If the valve must be adjusted, follow the instructions above to adjust it.

When you're satisfied that the #1 intake valve is adjusted correctly, go on to the exhaust valve. That would be the front valve on the left (driver's) side of the engine. Use the appropriate feeler gauge blade(s) and check and adjust the exhaust valve the same way you adjusted the intake valve. It should be .012". After the exhaust valve is adjusted, take a short break and give your back a rest. After you've been setting your own valves for awhile and are familiar with them, the job will move quickly. Also, you'll find that just one, two or maybe none in the whole engine must be adjusted.

Now you can adjust the intake valve for cylinder #2. That's the second valve back on the right (passenger) side of the engine. Then adjust the exhaust valve for cylinder #3 (third valve back on the driver's side). Look at the illustration again to be sure which is intake and which is exhaust. Be sure you use the right feeler gauge for each. Check and adjust the valves exactly as you did the cylinder #1 valves. Don't hurry.

Step 6. Adjust Valves: Stage Two.

Rotate the crank 360° *clockwise* with the socket and ratchet. The notch on the crank pulley should be aligned with the 0 or line on the engine again just as it was before. Now look at the rotor in the distributor. It should be pointing in the opposite direction from the line you painted on the distributor. If it is still pointing toward the line, you turned the engine around twice—rotate it once more so the rotor points away from cylinder #1 and the notch on the crank pulley is aligned with the 0 timing mark or line on the engine.

Now you're ready to adjust these valves: the exhaust valve for cylinder #2 (the second valve back on the driver's side), the intake valve for cylinder #3 (the third valve back on the passenger's side), and both the intake and exhaust valves for cylinder #4 (the two valves farthest to the rear).

Remember to use the correct feeler gauge blades for the intake and exhaust gaps. Refer to Step 5 of this procedure to do the adjustment, if necessary.

OK, adjust the #2 exhaust valve, then the #3 intake valve. Finally, adjust the rear two valves just as you did the others.

Step 7. Install Valve Cover.

When all of the valves have been adjusted, you're ready to install the valve cover. Feel all the way around the surface on the head where the **valve cover gasket** fits. It must be smooth. Use a knife, putty knife or flat screwdriver to scrape dust, dirt, grease and any remains of the old gasket off the surface. Leaving one little chunk stuck there could cause the gasket to leak and you'd lose oil. Wipe off any crud or gasket parts that fall into the top of the head or get on the valve springs, rocker arms, etc. Wipe the inside of the valve cover clean and check and clean the groove around the edge where the gasket fits.

I recommend replacing the valve cover gasket each time the valve cover is removed, but the old one can be used in an emergency if it isn't broken or too funky. If you have white lithium grease or wheel bearing grease handy, a light coat on both sides of the gasket will help hold it in the valve cover during installation, help it seal better and make it easier to remove the next time.

The gasket is molded to fit into the groove around the bottom of the valve cover. Turn the cover upside down and use a rag to clean the groove. Fit the gasket into the groove, making sure it's seated all the way around.

If you are installing new half moon plugs in the ends of the cylinder head, pull the old plugs out and use a rag and carburetor cleaner or solvent to remove all traces of the old gasket and sealer from the place where the plugs fit. If you're using the old plugs, clean them with a rag, making sure all traces of old gasket sealer material are removed. If the plugs seem hard and brittle, limp, deformed or cracked, replace them with new ones.

To install the plugs, coat the rounded part with high temp gasket sealer (red silicone works well). Fit the plug into its seat on the head being sure the little lip isn't tucked under the plug anywhere. Spread gasket sealer across the top of the plug so it extends about an inch onto the head on each side. Install both plugs.

Hold the gasket in the cover while you wiggle the cover into position on the engine. On some models a heater hose is slightly in the way so you'll have to squeeze the cover under it. Having Friend lift up on the hose is helpful. Once the cover is in place, center the bolts in the holes, then install the rubber coated washers so the fat part fits into the holes in the cover. Use new valve cover washers if the rubber part is broken or missing. If you're using the old washers you'll probably have to screw them onto the bolts. Install the four nuts and snug them down with a 12mm wrench. Get the bolts good and snug but don't crank on them too hard.

Install any other things, like wire and hose holders, that were attached to the valve cover. Reconnect any hoses or wires that you disconnected.

If you released the accelerator cable, fit the cable housing into its slot in the bracket, then tighten the same nut you loosened during disassembly. Rotate the top of the throttle arm toward the valve cover while you thread the braided cable and cylinder into the slot on the arm.

Install the spark plugs now if they are out (Procedure 7, Step 6).

Remove the ratchet and socket from the crankshaft pulley if they are still there. If you're continuing with the tune-up, leave the air cleaner housing and distributor cap off for now (be sure to plug the vacuum lines).

If you've pooped out and are quitting for now, install the distributor cap back on the distributor (Procedure 9, Step 8) and install the air cleaner (Procedure 6, Step 2). Make sure all the wires and hoses are snugly in place. Make sure all tools, rags, etc., are out from under the hood. Did you remove the wrench from the crankshaft pulley bolt? Turn the engine on and warm it up, then check to make sure the valve cover isn't leaking oil anywhere.

Congratulations, you have just completed the most tedious, back-breaking part of the tune-up! Now that the valves are correctly adjusted, only one, two, or maybe none, will have to be changed at the next tune-up. Be sure and check them though. It's going to be easier and easier each time you do this procedure. Your friends will be amazed, your neighbors will applaud, and maybe even David Letterman will call and congratulate you.

Now, on with the tune-up.

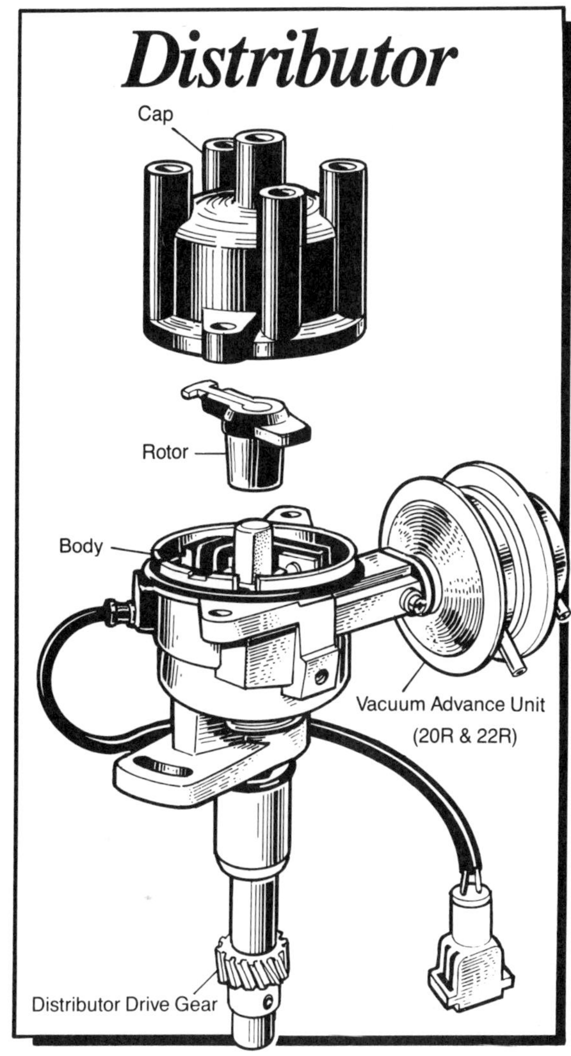

PROCEDURE 9: DISTRIBUTOR CHECKS

Condition: Tune-up time; OR engine is hard to start or running poorly.

Tools and Materials: Medium screwdriver, light wire brush, a clean rag, 12 inch length of 4mm vacuum hose, maybe a new vacuum advance unit, needlenose pliers and small regular and phillips screwdrivers. You may need penetrating oil.

Remark: A faulty distributor cap, rotor, vacuum advance unit, or worn out or loose mechanical advance springs can make the engine backfire, start hard, idle poorly, or have less power.

22R-E and 22RT-E engines: The ignition timing is regulated by a computer rather than by a combination of a vacuum advance unit and mechanical advance weights and springs. So don't freak when you don't find the usual round vacuum advance unit bolted to the side of the distributor.

Step 1. Get Ready.

Engine is turned OFF. Block the wheels, set the handbrake, then put the gearshift in NEUTRAL and open the hood.

Now locate the **distributor**. It sticks out of the front left side of the engine and has five thick wires connected to the cap.

Step 2. Remove Distributor Cap.

If your distributor is wearing a rubber protector, pop the snaps free and remove the rubber.

'75-'78 models: Use your fingers or a medium screwdriver to pry open the two **springy clips** on the sides of the distributor that secure the distributor cap.

'79-'87 models: Loosen the two **screws** on opposite sides of the distributor cap. The screws have long threads so it takes a while to completely unscrew them. They are attached to the cap so you don't have to worry about them falling out.

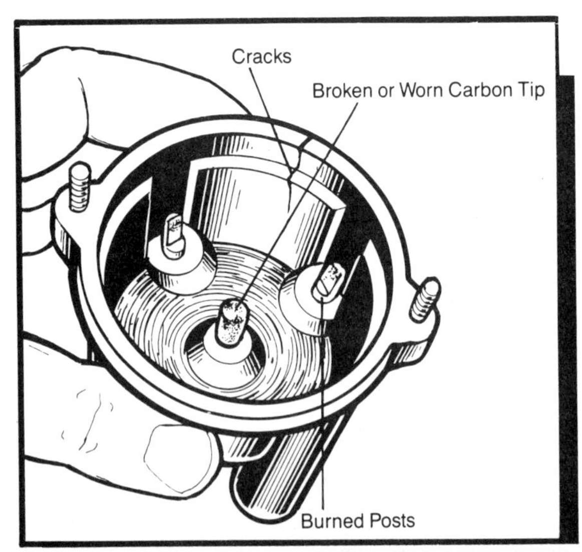

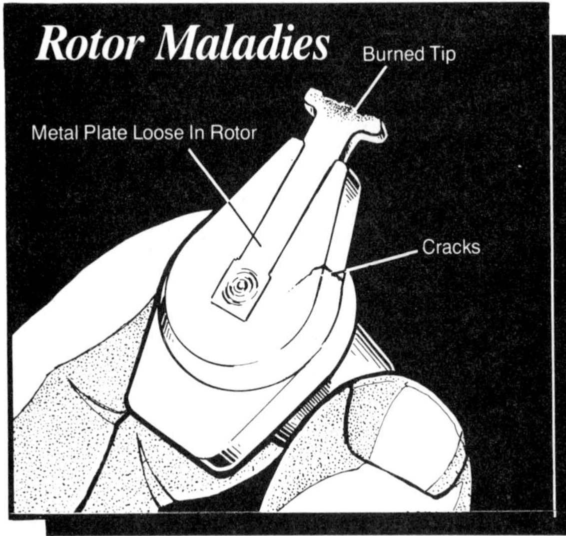

Step 3. Inspect Distributor Cap.

Pull the cap away from the distributor and rotate the bottom so you can peek inside. Leave the wires attached to the cap. Wipe off the outside and inside of the cap with a rag. Eyeball the cap for cracks and chips. A typical crack is a faint jagged line, usually near the little **metal posts** inside the cap. Clean the four metal posts on the inside of the cap with a knife blade or wire brush. Check the little **carbon tip** hanging down inside the center of the cap. The tip should be rounded on the end. It's spring-loaded and should pop back out if you push in on it.

Step 4. Remove and Inspect Rotor.

Now look down into the distributor itself. The **rotor** sits in the center—a plastic thing with a metal tip. To root out the rotor, just pull straight out on it. Check the copper end of the rotor for pitting, carbon tracks and general funk (look at the illustration). If it has deep pits or the copper is burned away on one edge, get a new rotor. Rotors and distributor caps work as a team so if one is replaced, replace the other one too (Step 9).

Step 5. Check Distributor Shaft for Wear.

Grab the **distributor shaft** where the rotor fits and try to move it up-and-down and side-to-side. (You can also do this with the rotor installed, as shown in the illustration.) If the shaft is loose in the distributor housing, the distributor shaft **bushings** might be wearing out. Ask Toyota or a garage for a second opinion. If the bushings are in fact wearing out, see Chapter 13 to remove the distributor, then take it to Toyota or an auto electric shop to have new bushings installed. Chapter 13 also tells you how to install the distributor.

Step 6. Check Mechanical Advance (20R and 22R only).

This step and the next one are only for distributors in 20R and 22R engines. People with 22R-E and 22R-TE engines can skip down to Step 8.

Remove the distributor cap, if it's still on (Step 2). Grab the rotor and turn it clockwise as viewed from the rotor end. The distributor shaft that the rotor is mounted on will turn slightly but should spring back to its original position as soon as you release the rotor. If it does, you can skip down to Step 7.

If the rotor won't rotate clockwise when you turn it with your fingers, or if it doesn't snap back into place when you release it, either the springs in the depths of the distributor are shot or there's junk down there. Do Step 7 in this procedure to see if a **circlip** is loose and jamming the works. If it isn't the circlip that's causing the problem, it's the springs inside the distributor and we can't fix them. They're set very carefully to comply with emission control standards. Have the Toyota dealer or an auto electric shop check and replace the springs if need be.

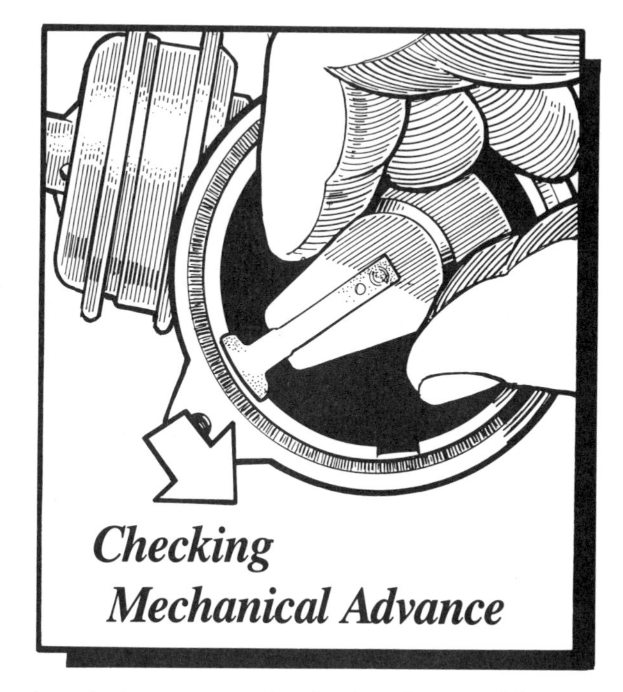
Checking Mechanical Advance

Step 7. Check and Replace Vacuum Advance Unit (20R and 22R only).

People with 22R-E and 22R-TE engines skip down to Step 8.

On 20R and 22R engines a round **vacuum advance unit** is mounted to the side of the distributor. One or two small rubber vacuum hoses are connected to fittings on the unit. The vacuum advance unit is attached to the innards of the distributor by either a slotted tab or an arm. See the descriptions of the two types below to see if you have a "tab-type" or an "arm-type" distributor.

'75-'78 20R engines: The vacuum unit is attached to a **rod** that goes through one side of the distributor and out the top. A knurled knob at the top of the rod is the **octane selector** which allows you to adjust the ignition timing slightly to compensate for the type of gas you use. The octane selector knob is covered by a screw-on clear plastic cap.

A **slotted tab** on the rod is attached to a **pin** on the **distributor plate** inside the distributor. You'll be referred to as "tab-type" for the rest of this step.

'79-'87 20R and 22R engines: A little metal **arm** goes from inside the vacuum unit to a pin on the movable **distributor plate** inside the distributor. You'll be referred to as an "arm-type" for the rest of this step.

EVERYONE: The points or pickup coil are also attached to the **distributor plate**, depending on whether your distributor has points or a pickup coil. For this step it doesn't matter which setup you have because we're only dealing with the vacuum advance unit and distributor plate.

When vacuum is present in the vacuum unit, it pulls on the arm or tab and the distributor plate moves counterclockwise, which advances the ignition timing.

To check the **vacuum unit**, disconnect the hose(s) from the unit. If there are two hoses, label them "front" and "rear" before disconnecting them so you'll know where to reconnect them. Connect one end of a 12 inch to 18 inch long, 4mm inside diameter hose to the hose fitting on the round vacuum advance unit. (If you don't have an extra hose handy, just use the one that is already connected to the vacuum unit. Be sure to reconnect it to whatever it was connected to after checking the vacuum unit.) OK, suck hard on the open end of the hose that's connected to the vacuum unit while watching the inside of the distributor. The vacuum unit should move the distributor plate *counterclockwise* when you suck on the hose. If there are two vacuum hose connections on the unit, check them both. (You might have to suck harder on the rear hose connection.)

If the diaphragms in the vacuum unit are good, you should be able to suck on the hose, then cover the end with your tongue to hold the plate in its advanced position. When you remove your tongue you should hear a little "pop," and the plate should return to its original position. If the diaphragm is broken and leaking, you'll have to keep sucking on the hose to keep the plate in the advanced position and you won't hear a "pop" when you remove your tongue from the hose. Replace the unit if it won't hold vacuum.

If sucking on the hose doesn't move the plate, see if the arm or slotted tab from the vacuum unit is still attached to the pin, or if the pin has broken off the plate. If the arm or slotted tab on the rod is off the pin, here's how you get it back on.

Tab-type: Remove the screw that attaches the vacuum unit to the distributor body. Pull the vacuum unit out of the distributor about one inch. Turn the distributor plate so the pin is toward the slotted tab. Slowly push the vacuum unit back into the distributor, making sure the pin engages in the slotted tab. Install and tighten the vacuum advance mounting screw.

Arm-type: Fit the hole in the arm over the pin. You might have to remove the screw that attaches the vacuum unit to the distributor in order to wiggle the arm over the pin. Look for a loose circlip laying somewhere inside the distributor. If you're remarkably lucky, you'll find it. Examine the circlip. If it looks OK, slip it on the pin so it snaps into the groove on the pin. (Be sure the carburetor is covered so the circlip can't accidentally fly in there while you're trying to install it.) Replace the circlip if it's bent or slides onto the pin too easily. If you removed the vacuum unit mounting screw, install and tighten it.

EVERYONE: If the arm or tab and pin are all OK, try moving the plate by pushing and pulling back and forth on the pin where the vacuum arm attaches. The plate should be free to move about ¼ counterclockwise. Plate stuck? Squirt a little penetrating oil around the outer edge of the plate and let it soak awhile. Try moving the pin again. Sometimes a stuck plate can be loosened by repeatedly using penetrating oil and moving the pin. If the plate just won't loosen enough to move by sucking on the hose, the distributor needs to be rebuilt or replaced (Chapter 13, Procedure 1. If sucking on the hose didn't move the plate, but you could move it easily with your fingers, the vacuum unit is broken).

REPLACE VACUUM UNIT: After the vacuum unit is off, see if the distributor plate moves easily by rotating it with the vacuum arm pin. If it doesn't, squirt some penetrating oil around the edge of the plate and work the plate back and forth until it moves freely. If it's stuck tight and won't loosen up, see Chapter 13, Procedure 1, to remove the distributor. Take it to the Toyota dealer or an auto electric shop for repair. If the distributor plate moves freely, then the vacuum unit is the culprit. Here's how to replace the unit.

Tab-type: Remove the screw that attaches the vacuum unit to the distributor body. Pull the vacuum unit and rod out of the bottom of the distributor housing. See above to check the distributor plate.

Insert the rod on the new vacuum unit into the distributor housing. Engage the slotted tab on the rod with the pin on the distributor plate as you push the vacuum unit all the way into the distributor. Install and tighten the mounting screw. Be sure anything else that was attached with the screw is in place. Set the octane selector knob between the + and −.

Arm-type: remove the screw that attaches it to the distributor body. Spread a clean rag beneath the distributor to catch the circlip if it falls, then carefully pry the circlip from the pin with a small screwdriver. Don't let the clip fall through a hole in the distributor plate. Pull on the vacuum unit until it's almost out of the distributor housing, then wiggle the arm off the pin. See above to check the distributor plate for ease of movement.

To install the new vacuum unit, stick the arm of the new unit into the distributor and hook the arm over the pin. Push the unit into the distributor housing, then carefully snap the circlip into the groove on the pin (if the air cleaner is off, be sure the carburetor is covered with a rag). Install the screw that attaches the unit to the distributor and tighten it.

EVERYONE: Attach the hose(s) to the vacuum unit. If there are two hose connections on yours, be sure to hook them up the same as they were on the old one. Install the rotor and distributor cap now (Step 8), unless you're going to check the points or air gap.

If you're here from the ignition timing procedure because the vacuum advance wasn't working, check the ignition timing again (Procedure 12). The notch on the pulley should move now when you rev the engine.

Step 8. Install Rotor and Cap.

If you're going to check, adjust or replace the points on '75-'77 models (Procedure 11) or check the air gap on '78-'87 models (Procedure 10), leave the cap and rotor off for now. Come back here to install the rotor and cap when you're finished.

Before installing the rotor, first install the round plastic dust shield (if your model has one). Line up the flat spring on the inside of the rotor's hole with the flat spot on the side of the distributor shaft. Push the rotor onto the shaft while wiggling it back and forth until it locks into place.

'75-'78 models: The bottom edge of the distributor cap has a **notch** in it that fits over a **tab** on the rim of the distributor body. When fitting the cap back onto the distributor, rotate the cap until it slips down on the tab. Hold the cap on with one hand while you lift one of the springy clips up to the side of the cap. Press on the rounded middle part of the clip until the top snaps into the groove on the cap. Now fit the other springy clip the same way. If the springy clips won't fit, don't hammer on them—you just haven't lined the cap up properly.

'79-'87 models: Fit the cap onto the distributor so the two screws are aligned with their holes. Use a screwdriver to tighten the screws.

Step 9. Replace Distributor Cap and Rotor.

This step is only for people who are putting in a brand new cap and rotor.

Remove the cap and rotor from the distributor. Leave the five thick wires in the old distributor cap for the moment. If your distributor has a flat plastic dust shield, be sure it's in place before installing the rotor. Install the new rotor as described in Step 8. Push the rotor down on the shaft as far as it will go. It should fit snugly on the shaft.

Fit the new cap on the distributor, lining up the notch on the cap rim with the tab on the rim of the distributor body, if yours has a notch and tab. If your cap has two mounting screws, set the cap on the distributor so the #1 spark plug wire terminal is toward the top front of the distributor. Snap the clips into place, or tighten down the screws.

Now transfer the spark plug wires one at a time from the old cap to the new cap so they don't get out of order. Just grab one close to the cap and twist it back and forth while you pull it straight out. The wires should end up in the same position on the new cap as they were on the old one. If the cap and wires are numbered, you should have no problem. If the cap and wires aren't numbered, think and go slowly, one wire at a time—you don't want to get your wires crossed.

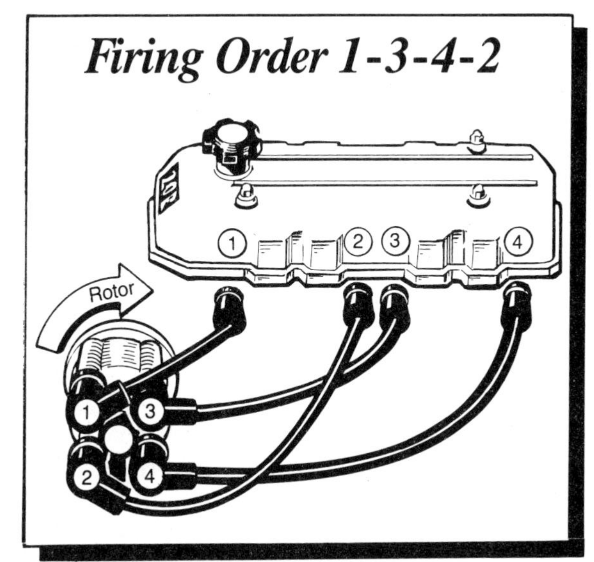

If the ends of spark plug wires or the coil wire are corroded or dirty, use your wire brush to clean the ends before plugging them into the new cap. Replace the wires if the ends are so corroded you can't clean them with the wire brush. Push each one all the way into its hole on the new cap, making sure the **connector boot** is snugly over the nipple on the cap.

If any of the spark plug wires came out of the plastic wire holders (looms) that hold the wires away from hot engine parts, be sure to fit them back in.

PROCEDURE 10. CHECK AND ADJUST BREAKERLESS DISTRIBUTOR (1978-87 MODELS ONLY)

Condition: Tune-up time; OR perhaps you're just curious about what the inside of an electronic breakerless distributor looks like.

Tools and Materials: Brass non-magnetic feeler gauge, medium screwdriver, phillips screwdriver. You may also need your ratchet and 19mm socket.

Remark: Starting in 1978, Toyotas came equipped with electronic "breakerless" distributors. These little jewels are about 40 percent more efficient than the old breaker points type distributors and require a lot less maintenance. Technology triumphs again!

Step 1. Check Distributor Cap and Rotor.

The distributor cap and rotor are essentially the same as those on earlier breaker points type distributors. If you haven't done Procedure 9, Steps 3 to 7 to check the condition of the distributor components, do it now, then come back here. Leave the cap and rotor off so you can proceed to Step 2.

Step 2. Check and Adjust Air Gap.

Remove the opaque plastic dust shield in the distributor, if yours has one. Rotate the engine *clockwise* using a socket on the crank pulley bolt or alternator nut while watching what's going on in the distributor. You did this before in Procedure 5, Step 3. The rotating thing with four short arms you see in there is the **reluctor**. The little black box is known as the **signal generator** (or *pickup coil*). Look at the illustration to see where to put the feeler gauge to check the air gap. Line up a corner of the reluctor with the vertical metal line on the pickup coil. The space between the reluctor and the pickup coil is the air gap.

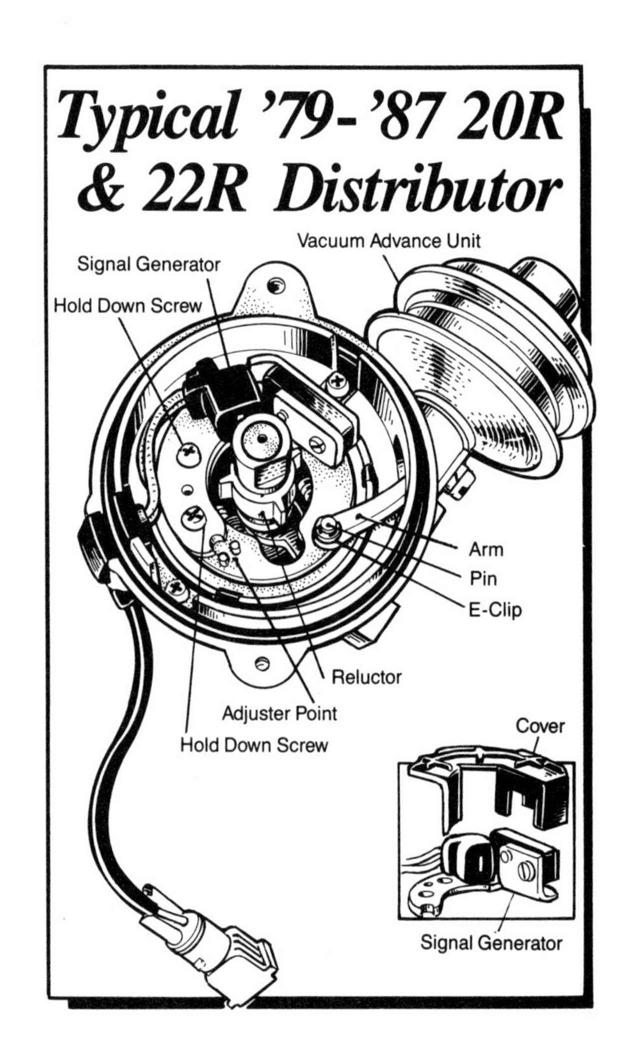

Air gaps are easy to check and adjust because there's so much tolerance (clearance) to work with. To check the air gap, use a BRASS NON-MAGNETIZED FEELER GAUGE and make sure the ignition switch is OFF. The correct range for all Toyota breakerless distributors is .008" to .016".

Whip out your brass feeler gauge set and try different blades between the reluctor and pickup until you find one that slips through with just a little resistance. If that blade thickness is between .008" and .016", everything's cool and no adjustment is necessary. You can advance to Procedure 12. In the unlikely event that the air gap is wider or narrower than it should be, make the adjustment. Here's how.

Slightly loosen the two phillips screws that secure the pickup coil. Put one corner of a screwdriver blade between the two little **nipples** on the distributor plate and the other corner of the screwdriver in the **slot** on the pickup coil plate. Move the pickup coil toward or away from the reluctor by turning the screwdriver a little, then tighten the phillips screws. Check the gap again. When the gap is within the tolerance figures, snug down the phillips screws one last time and you're finished. Easy, isn't it?

Install the dust cover, rotor and distributor cap. Always check the timing after you adjust the air gap (Procedure 12).

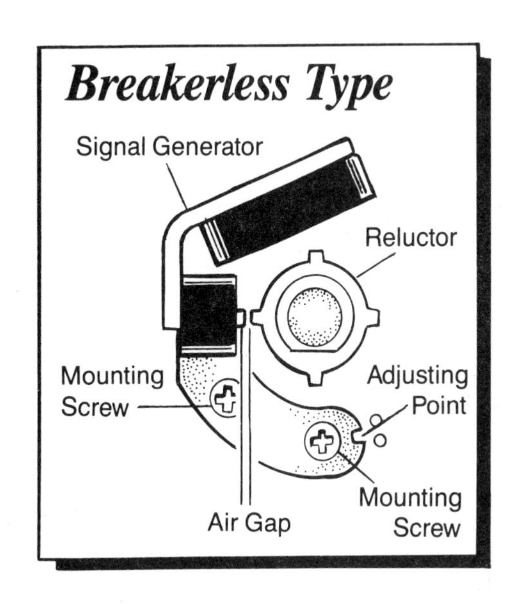

PROCEDURE 11: INSPECT, ADJUST, REPLACE BREAKER POINTS (1975-77 MODELS ONLY)

This procedure is only for 1975-77 models.

Breaker points (usually just called *points*) are mounted to a flat **distributor plate** inside the distributor. As various components of the points wear away, the critical point gap changes, so you must periodically adjust or replace the points set. This very important part of the tune-up ensures easier starting, better performance, improved economy, smoother running and increased longevity.

Condition: It's tune-up time; OR engine is running poorly or not at all.

Tools and Materials: Medium screwdriver, medium phillips head screwdriver, feeler gauge, tach/dwell meter (if you can afford one), 10mm wrench or 10mm socket and ratchet, 19mm socket and ratchet, needlenose pliers.

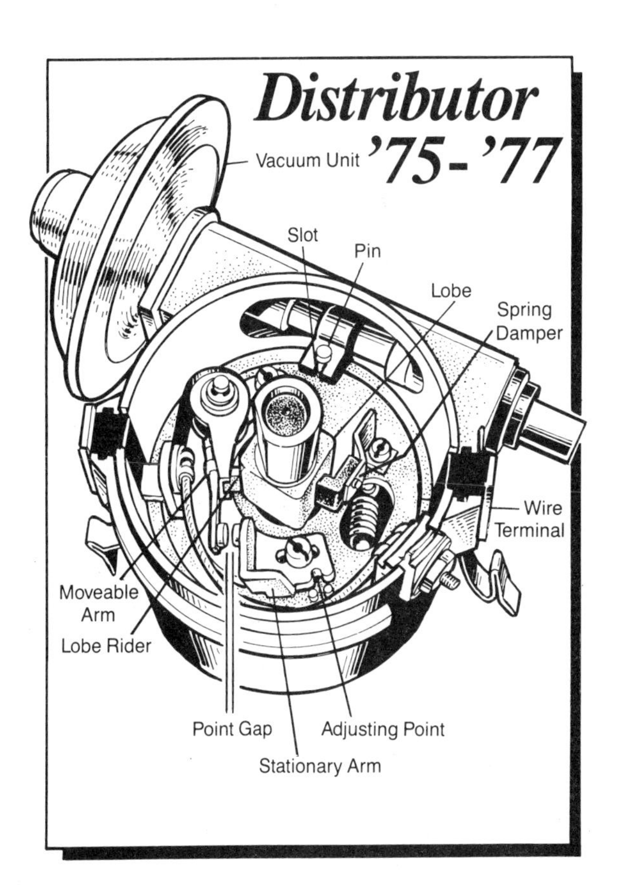

Step 1. Inspect Points.

Block the wheels, set the handbrake, put the gearshift in NEUTRAL. Be sure the ignition key is OFF.

If you're here for a 24,000 mile tune-up, you're going to replace the points set, so skip to Step 5 to install new points.

Release the **distributor cap** (Procedure 9, Step 2) and push it out of the way. The plastic **rotor** sits in the middle of the distributor body. Pull out on the rotor to remove it. If your distributor has an opaque plastic dust cover beneath the rotor, lift it out so you can see the points. Now put the socket and ratchet on the **crankshaft pulley nut** and turn the engine *clockwise*. (See Procedure 5, Step 3 if you need more detail). While rotating the engine with the ratchet, take a look at what's happening in the distributor.

Right next to the distributor shaft is the **points set** (or *points*). There's a movable arm and a stationary arm. The movable arm has a little piece of fiber or plastic that rides on the turning **distributor shaft** (look at the illustration). The points open (spread apart, leaving a gap) as the squarish distributor shaft rotates its corners (called *lobes*) under

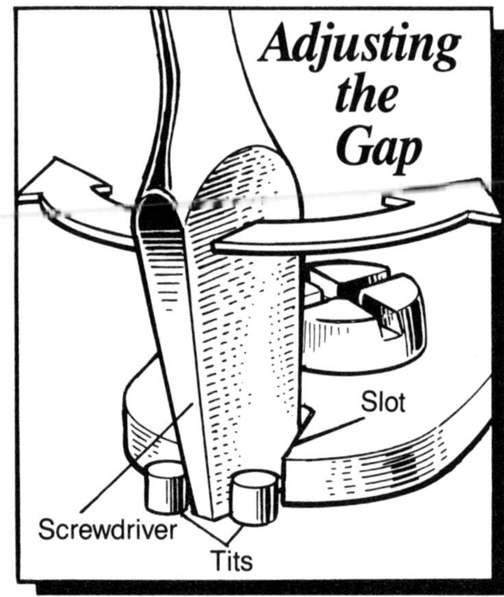

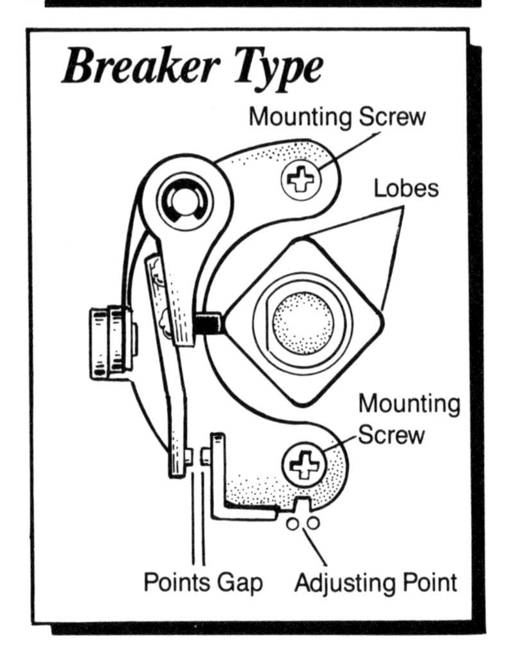

the fiber or plastic block on the moveable point arm. (I call the little fiber block a *lobe rider*.) At the high point of each lobe the points are separated the maximum amount. When a lobe rotates past the lobe rider, the points close. The next lobe opens them again, and so on.

On the opposite side of the distributor shaft from the points set there's a *second* lobe rider mounted on a spring. It's called a **spring damper**. Don't confuse the spring damper with the points.

Using a screwdriver as a lever between the long, moveable arm of the points and the distributor shaft, spread the points and have a look at the two small round **contact surfaces** on the end of the point arms. (This is where the points meet when they are closed.) They should be flat and smooth. Does either of the two surfaces have pits or small white deposits on it? Look closely. If so, they must be replaced. In days gone by, you could file the points smooth and keep using them. Today's points are made of such hard material that filing on them is a waste of time except in an extreme emergency. It's just as quick and easy to replace the points as it is to file them.

Check the condition of the lobe rider for wear. If it's worn unevenly or worn down almost to the metal arm, you need new points. Check the spring damper for wear the same way.

If the points are shot, go to Step 5 to replace them.

Points OK? Do Step 2 to check the gap for the points and spring damper. If you have a dwell meter, check only the spring damper gap, then go to Step 3 to check the points dwell. No dwell meter? Then do Step 2 to adjust the points gap with feeler gauges.

Step 2. Check Point Gap and Spring Damper Gap with Feeler Gauges.

Check spring damper gap: Rotate the engine so the lobe rider on the **spring damper** is next to the flat part of the distributor shaft between two of the lobes. Check the gap between the lobe rider and the distributor shaft with your feeler gauges. It should be between .002" and .016". If it isn't, loosen the phillips screw that attaches it to the distributor plate. Turn the spring damper bracket until the gap is about .008", then tighten the phillips screw. Check the gap again to make sure the spring damper didn't move when you tightened the screw.

To replace the spring damper, remove the phillips mounting screw that holds it in place. Install a new spring damper in place of the old one, then adjust the gap as described above. That's all there is to it.

Check points gap: The points gap is checked by measuring the distance (gap) between the end of the moveable arm and the stationary arm when the lobe rider is on one of the lobes so the points are open as far as they can go. The correct gap is .018". Put the socket and ratchet on the crank pulley bolt and rotate the engine clockwise until the lobe rider is exactly centered on one of the lobes on the distributor shaft.

Whip out the **.018" feeler gauge blade**, wipe it clean, then insert it between the end of the arm that moves and the end of the stationary arm—right between the two contact surfaces. Hold the blade parallel with the stationary arm. If you're lucky, the gauge will just barely fit between the two points without being loose or spreading them farther apart. A very slight resistance when you slip the gauge out means they're right on. If the blade is tight and causes the points to open further, or if it fits with room to spare, the points need to be adjusted (Step 4 in this procedure).

Remove the socket and ratchet from the pulley bolt.

If the points were shot or it's time to replace them anyway, go to Step 5. If the points were good and you have a dwell meter, do Step 3 to set the points dwell. No dwell meter? Don't dwell on it, just do Step 4 to adjust the points gap.

Step 3. Check Point Gap with Dwell Meter (1975-77 models only).

If the points are in good condition, install the opaque plastic dust cover, the rotor, and the distributor cap. Hook up your **dwell meter** according to the instructions that came with it. If the instructions disappeared the day after you got the gauge (mine usually do), try hooking it up this way: if there are two wires coming out of your dwell meter, connect the black wire to the negative (ground) terminal of the battery or to bare metal, and connect the other wire (could be red or green) to the negative (-) side of the **ignition coil**. If your meter has three wires, connect the black one to the negative battery post, the red one to the positive battery post, and the other one (green maybe?) to the (-) side of the coil (see the illustration in Procedure 12). Switch the meter to the *four cylinder position* (eight cylinder position if yours doesn't have a four cylinder position). Make sure the meter is set on the Dwell position (not Tach).

Clear tools, parts, rags and dwell meter wires away from the fan and drive belt(s). Set the meter in a secure position so it won't fall into the works. Remove the socket and ratchet from the crank pulley if they're still there. Be sure all the vacuum lines that were connected to the air cleaner are plugged. Take the rag off the top of the carburetor, then start the engine and let it warm up a few minutes. (Remember, if you want to live to see the grandkids fixing Toyotas of their own, DON'T run the engine in a closed garage.) The dwell meter should read between 50° and 54° on a four cylinder scale or between 25° and 27° on an eight cylinder scale. Since the point gap narrows as various components on the points set wear away, I set my points at the wide end of the range (50°-51°).

If the dwell reading is below 50 degrees (25), the point gap is set too wide. A reading above 54 degrees (27) means the point gap isn't wide enough. Either way it's points adjusting time. Not difficult, but you'll have to take the distributor cap off again. Turn off the engine and proceed to Step 4.

Step 4. Adjust Point Gap (if necessary).

Remark: Be sure and check the ignition timing after adjusting the points.

Remove the distributor cap, rotor, and plastic dust shield. Use a socket and ratchet on the crank pulley to rotate the engine until the lobe rider is on one of the lobes and the points are wide open. The correct point gap is .018".

To adjust the points, loosen the two phillips screws near each end of the points set about ¼ turn each. Insert one corner of a regular screwdriver blade between the two little bumps or "nipples" near the contact points, and the other corner of the blade into the slot in the points plate right next to the nipples. Turn the screwdriver slightly *clockwise* to make the points gap wider. Turn it slightly *counterclockwise* to narrow the gap. If the stationary arm won't budge, loosen the mounting screws a tad more.

Using a feeler gauge: Be sure the lobe rider is on the corner of one of the lobes. Narrow or widen the gap until the correct blade slides between the points with a very slight resistance. Keep the blade straight. When the gap is right, tighten both phillips head mounting screws (tighten the one furthest from the adjusting slot and nipples first), then check the gap again. Sometimes the gap narrows when the mounting screws are tightened. Try again, maybe anticipating a slight narrowing of the gap once the mounting screws are snug. When you're satisfied that the gap is correct, install the plastic dust shield, rotor, and distributor cap. Skip down to the EVERYONE section.

Using a dwell meter: If you're using a dwell meter to set the points, *slightly* widen the gap if your reading was high (above 54°) or narrow the gap if your dwell meter reading was low (below 50°). Now tighten the phillips mounting screws. Tighten the one farthest from the adjusting screwhead first. Put the plastic dust shield, rotor and cap back on the distributor, snap it in place, start the engine and check the dwell meter reading again. Sometimes it takes a few tries. If it's not on the money, turn the engine off, remove the cap, and try again. Be patient and you'll get it.

When you have the point gap set so the dwell reads right on your meter, rev up the engine while watching the dwell meter. Here's how to rev (speed up) the engine without getting in the car and pushing on the gas pedal. Find the end of a thin **rod** on the firewall straight behind the **carburetor**. It's attached to the top of a lever. Push on the top of the lever to rev up the engine.

EVERYONE: OK, now rev the engine while watching the dwell meter. (The above paragraph explains how to rev the engine from the engine compartment.) If the needle wanders more than 10 degrees on the meter, the points are loose or the distributor shaft is worn. Turn the engine off again. Remove the cap and rotor and see if the points are securely mounted to the distributor. Tighten the two phillips mounting screws if they're loose. Try moving the distributor shaft up-and-down and side-to-side. Just grab the end of it and wiggle. If the shaft moves significantly, the distributor needs new bushings or a military funeral. (See Chapter 13 for distributor removal and installation. Take the distributor to the Toyota dealer or an auto electric shop to see if they can install new bushings.)

If the points are good and the point gap has been set to correct specifications with either the feeler gauge or dwell meter, you can move on to Step 6 to lubricate the distributor.

Step 5. Install New Points.

The points are held in place by two phillips head mounting screws. Hold your hand under the distributor to catch the screws as you remove them.

When the screws are out, move the little ground wire that was attached to one of the mounting screws to one side. Loosen, but don't remove, the little nut on the **wire terminal** on the outside of the distributor a few turns. Inside the distributor, pull up on the points wire where it connects to the wire terminal. The points are now liberated.

While the points are out, clean the inside and outside of the distributor with a rag. Clean the contact surfaces of the new points set with alcohol or carb cleaner, or at least wipe them with a clean rag. New points sets are usually coated with oil to prevent corrosion. If not removed, the oil can cause arcing and premature burning of the contact surfaces.

Slide the new points set into position in the distributor. Move the set around until the tab on the bottom goes into its hole on the distributor plate. Fit one of the mounting screws into the terminal on the end of the black ground wire, then install the screw. Install the other mounting screw. Don't tighten the two mounting screws completely until the points have been adjusted, just snug them down a little.

Slip the pronged end of the wire attached to the points onto the terminal on the inside of the distributor. Be sure the plastic insulation block is between the wire and the distributor housing. Tighten the little nut on the wire terminal while pressing a finger or needlenose pliers against the other end of the bolt on the inside of the distributor.

Lubricate the distributor, Step 6, then go to Step 4 to adjust the point gap. Even if you have a dwell meter, you'll have to set the gap with a feeler gauge the first time around.

Step 6. Lubricate Distributor (breaker points type only).

The distributor cap and rotor are off, right? Eyeball the end of the distributor shaft. If there's a **felt wick** in the end of the shaft, squirt four drops of any oil on the felt wick. If you bought new points, there was probably a small packet or capsule of grease in the package. Open the packet and put a small dab of grease on the distributor lobes, and the lobe riders on the points and the spring damper. No grease packet? Use Bosch grease #64139 or High Temp wheel bearing grease. Just a little dab'll do ya—about the size of wooden match head.

Adjust the points (Step 4) if you haven't already, then install the dust shield, rotor and cap. Snap the cap in place with its clips.

If you're doing a tune-up, move ahead to Procedure 12: *Set Ignition Timing*.

PROCEDURE 12. SET IGNITION TIMING

Condition: Tune-up time; OR the points or air gap has been changed; OR the distributor has been removed; OR the engine isn't running right.

Tools and Materials: Stroboscopic timing light, tachometer (see important note below), rubber vacuum line plugs or tape, 12mm wrench. Note: It's best to use an *inductive type timing light* on '78-'87 models with electronic ignition, due to the increased voltage of these systems. *Optional:* A Friend would be handy.

Compare your coil to the ones in the Tach/Dwell Meter Connections illustration. If you have a Type III coil, you'll need a small electrical spade connector to connect the tach/dwell meter to the coil. One might have come with the meter. If not, buy one from an auto parts store.

'85-'87 EFI models will need an insulated wire with about ½" of the insulation stripped from each end. This is a **jumper wire** to bridge across two electric terminals.

Important note: For 1980-87 models, a battery powered tachometer like those shown in the illustration must be used to avoid damaging the ignition system. Be sure to follow the tachometer hook-up instructions for your year model. I use a Sears model 28 2163 Engine Analyzer (about $45).

Remark: Changing the distributor points gap or air gap changes the ignition timing. Make the necessary adjustments to the distributor before checking the timing. Always check the timing after adjusting the points or air gap.

Caution: Keep the wires from the timing light and tachometer away from the front of the engine where they could get caught in the drive belt or fan. Remove the socket and ratchet from the crank pulley and the rag from the top of the carburetor, if they're still there. Be sure all tools are out of the way before starting the engine. If the air cleaner is off, make sure all vacuum lines that were connected to it are plugged (Procedure 6, Step 1).

Step 1. Get Ready.

Warm up the engine to normal operating temperature. Turn the engine OFF and hook up the **tachometer** and **timing light**. Here's how to connect them.

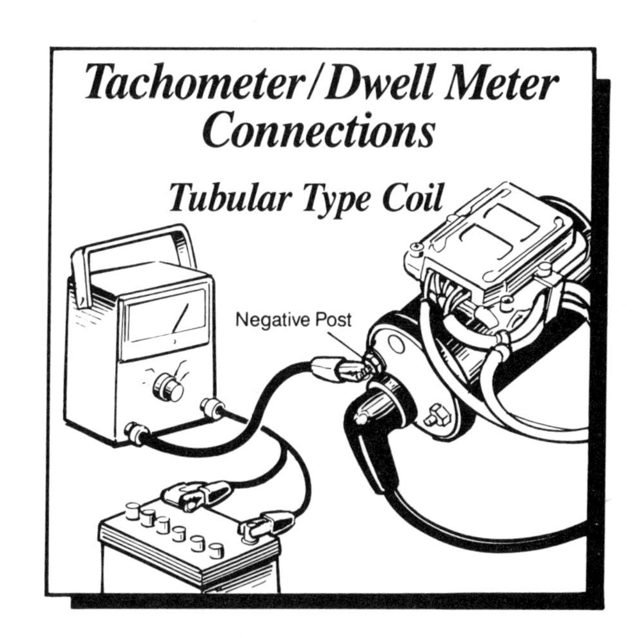

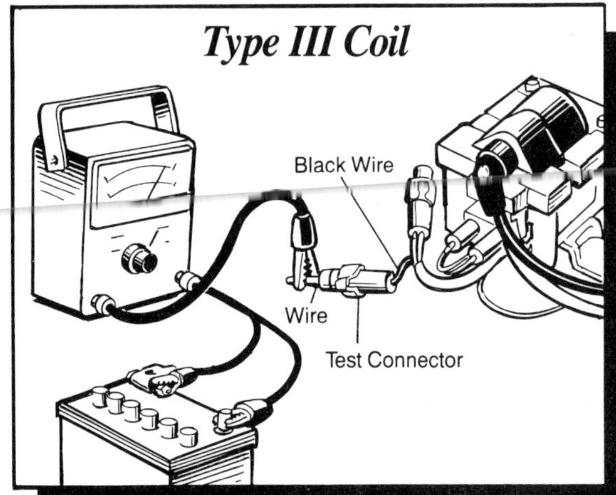

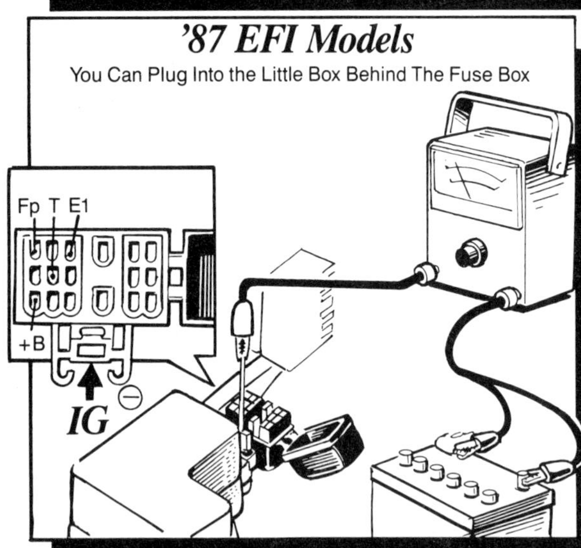

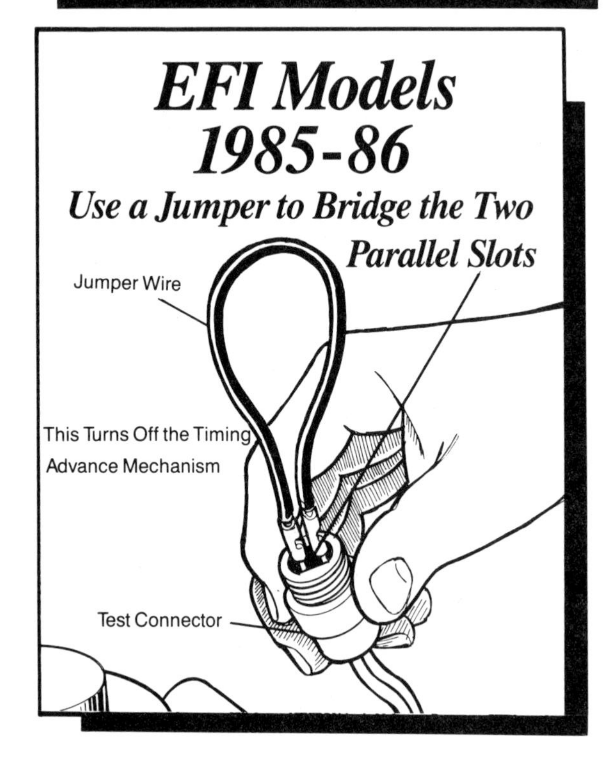

TACHOMETER CONNECTIONS

On some late models there is a plastic protector wrapped around the end of the coil. If your model has a protector, unsnap the little fastener on the side, then remove the protector.

'75-'79 models: Connect the tachometer the same way you connected the dwell gauge in Procedure 11. Step 3. If you have a battery powered tachometer (or tach/dwell meter), use the Tubular Type Coil illustration to hook it up. Skip down to the timing light connection section.

'80-'87 models: Connect the red lead from the meter to the positive (+) battery terminal and the black lead to the negative (-) battery terminal.

Tubular type coils: Connect the third lead to the negative (-) terminal on the coil.

Type III coils: There's a small green connector about the size of your thumb dangling from a black wire near the coil. Remove the little rubber cap from the end of the connector and insert a spade connector in the slot. Attach the third lead from the meter to the end of the spade connector. DON'T connect the third wire directly to the distributor, coil or igniter and DON'T let the wire or spade connector touch bare metal. Wrap it with a rag or paper towel.

TIMING LIGHT CONNECTIONS

Connect the red lead wire from the timing light to the positive (+) battery terminal and the black lead wire to the negative (-) battery terminal. These days most timing lights have an *inductive pickup connection* that clips onto the #1 spark plug wire. If the pickup has an arrow on it, make sure the arrow points *toward* the spark plug.

If your light isn't of the inductive type, pull the spark plug wire off the #1 spark plug. Hook one end of a small spring (usually supplied with the light) to the end of the #1 spark plug. Fit the spark plug wire onto the end of the spring, then clip the third lead from the timing light (usually blue or green) to the spring.

Keep the wires away from the drive belt and fan—make sure they won't fall in there while you're working.

Depending on the year and model, some of the hoses attached to the vacuum advance unit on the distributor might need to be disconnected and plugged before the timing can be checked and adjusted. On 22R-E and 22RT-E engines the ignition advance system must be bypassed. Follow the directions below for your particular truck.

VACUUM LINES

'75-'78 models: If your distributor has a single vacuum advance unit, leave the hose connected to the unit. If your distributor has a double vacuum advance unit, disconnect and plug the vacuum hose from the secondary (inner) diaphragm closest to the distributor.

'79 models: Don't disconnect and plug any hoses from the vacuum advance unit.

'80 models: If you have a California or Cab and Chassis model, don't disconnect and plug any hoses. Everyone else disconnect and plug the vacuum hose from the secondary (inner) diaphragm closest to the distributor.

'81-'87 22R and '84 22R-E models: Disconnect and plug both vacuum hoses from the vacuum advance unit.

20R, 22R and '84 22R-E engines: To remove and plug the vacuum hoses, grab the vacuum hose(s) right where they connect to the round **vacuum advance gizmo** on the side of the distributor. Twist them a few times to break them free from the fitting, then pull them off. If you remove two hoses, mark them so they won't get mixed up when you put them back on. Plug the hose or hoses with rubber vacuum hose plugs or put a piece of tape securely over the end.

ELECTRONIC ADVANCE ON EFI MODELS

Before checking the timing on '85-'87 22R-E and 22R-TE models, the electronic timing advance mechanism must be turned off. This is also how you turn on the EFI self-diagnosing system; if something's amiss with the fuel injection system, the Check Engine light on the dash will blink the trouble code (See Chapter 4). Here's how to turn off the timing advance and turn on the self-diagnosing system.

'85-'86 22R-E and 22R-TE engines: There are two round green test connectors close to the coil near the top of the left front fender. The ends of the connections are either plugged into rubber holders on the fender, or covered with rubber boots. Wiggle the smaller connector out of its holder or remove the rubber cap, then insert the ends of your jumper wire into the two parallel slots in the connector. If

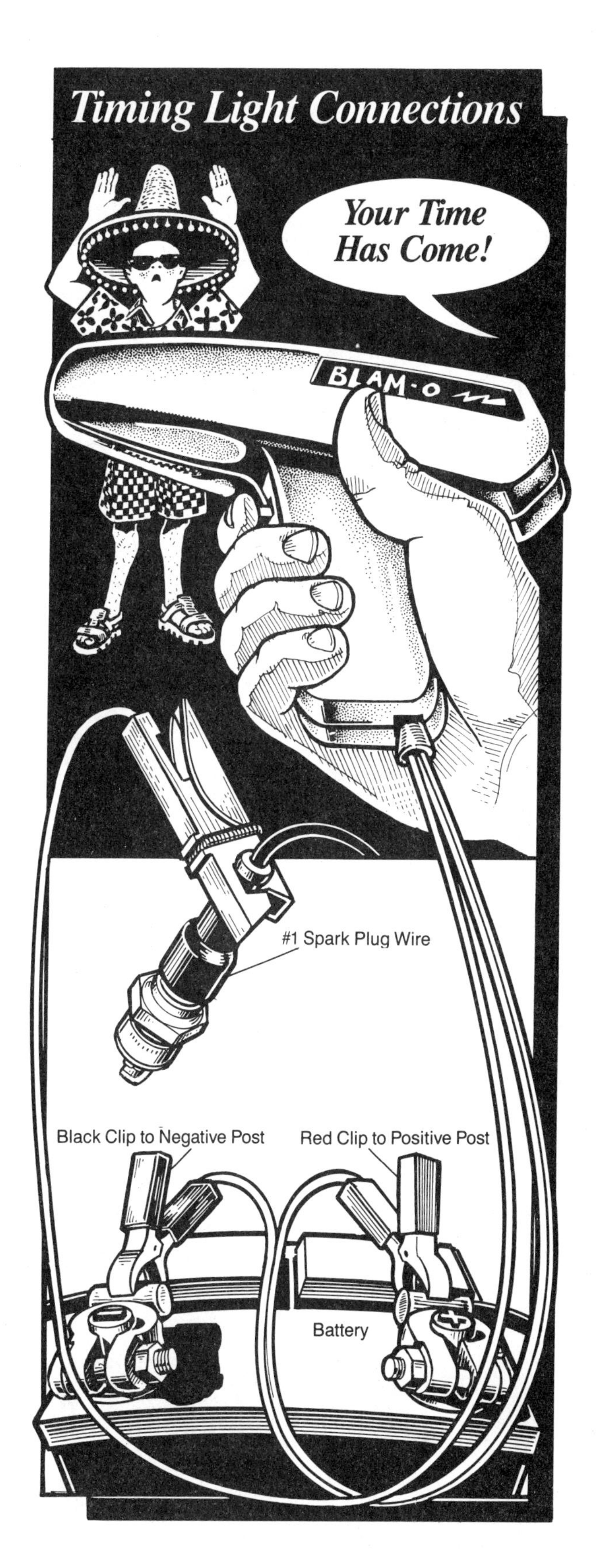

there are several slots, you have the wrong connector. Look at the other one. Don't let the bare wire touch any bare metal. Wrap a rag around the connector to be sure.

'87 22R-E and 22RT-E engines: Remove the cap from the **check connector box** located just to the rear of the fuse box in the engine compartment. Plug one end of your jumper wire into the slot marked 'T' and the other end into the slot marked E1. This bypasses the electronically controlled ignition advance system.

Step 2. Set Idle Speed.

Wipe off the timing plate on the front of the engine. If you haven't painted the timing mark and pulley notch, do Procedure 5, Step 2, before going one step further.

Clear tools, wires, hoses etc., away from the fan and drive belt(s), then start the engine and let it warm up to normal operating temperature.

Do Procedure 13, Step 8, to check and adjust the engine idle speed. After the idle speed is set come back here to time the engine. Don't do Procedure 13, Step 9, to adjust the idle mixture yet.

Step 3. Check and Adjust Timing.

Look at the chart to see what the timing for your engine should be.

With the engine idling at the correct speed, aim the timing light at the **timing plate** and pull the trigger. Amazingly, the crank pulley appears to be standing still while the engine is running!

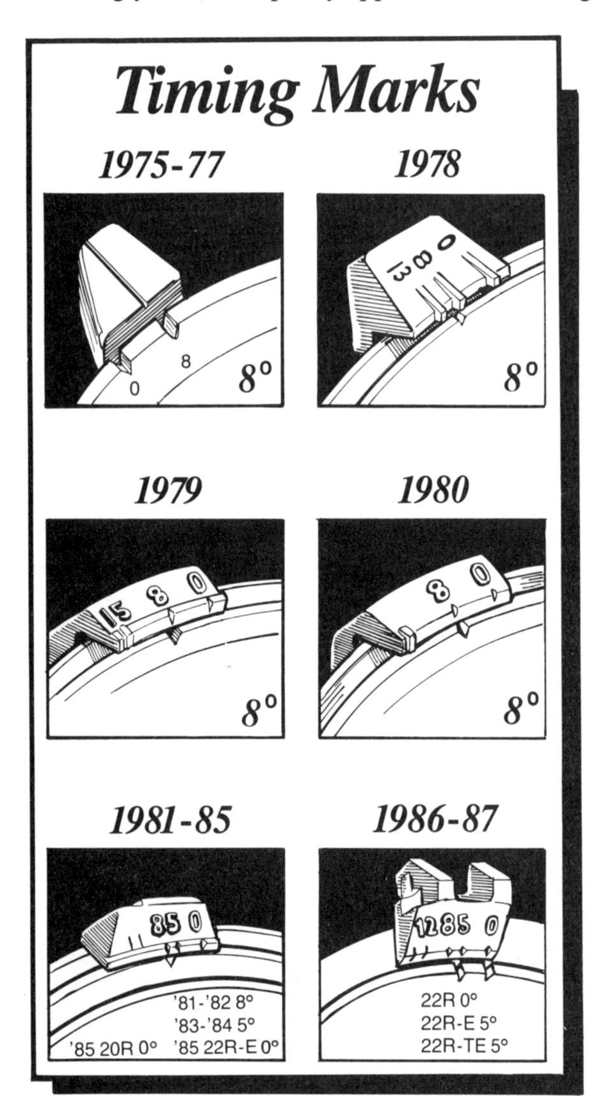

'75-'77 models: If the correct notch on the pulley is aligned with the timing line, the timing is right on so skip down to the next step.

'78-'87 models: If the notch on the crank pulley is aligned with the correct timing line for your engine, the timing is right on. Skip down to the next step.

EVERYONE: If the timing must be adjusted, use a 12mm wrench to slightly loosen the distributor mounting bolt located near the base of the distributor. When turning the distributor to adjust the timing, grab it toward the engine end away from the spark plug wires (less chance of accidentally getting a charge out of this procedure). Watch out for the drive belt(s) and fan. Hold the timing light in your left hand while you turn the distributor with your right hand.

If the notch on the pulley is to the left (your right as you face the engine) side of the correct timing line for your engine, the timing is retarded so rotate the distributor *clockwise* until the notch is even with the correct line. If the notch is on the right (your left as you face the engine) side of the correct timing line, the timing is too far advanced so rotate the distributor *counterclockwise* until it's even with the correct number.

When the notch and appropriate timing marks are lined up (on '75-'77 models the appropriate notch and the timing line), tighten the bolt at the base of the distributor. Put the timing light aside and adjust the engine idle speed if it changed (same as you did in Step 2), then check the timing and adjust it again if need be.

Step 4. Check Ignition Advance Systems.

20R and 22R engines: Have Friend rev the engine up a little while you watch the timing marks with the timing light. If a Friend isn't available, you can rev the engine by rotating the accelerator lever on the rear of the carburetor. As the engine speed increases, the painted timing notch should move to the *right* (your left) toward a higher number if the **mechanical advance mechanism** in the distributor is working properly. If the line doesn't move, the mechanical advance isn't working and needs to be checked (Procedure 9, Step 6).

After the timing is set and the 12mm bolt is tightened, if you removed and plugged any vacuum lines from the **vacuum advance unit** on the distributor, remove the plugs or tape from the vacuum hose(s) and reconnect them to the vacuum advance unit. You can't check the timing with the hoses connected, but you can check the vacuum advance unit. On trucks with double vacuum advance units the notch should be to the right (advanced) side from the correct timing mark. Rev the engine up while watching the timing marks with the timing light. Now the notch on the crank pulley should really move around. If the notch still doesn't move to the right, the vacuum hose(s) are leaking (replace them), OR the hoses aren't connected to the distributor correctly (fix 'em), OR the vacuum unit is broken (check it, Procedure 9, Step 7), OR the movable plate in the distributor is stuck (see Procedure 9, Step 7).

'85-'87 22R-E and 22RT-E engines: After the timing is set and the 12mm bolt is tightened, remove the jumper wire. Check the timing with the timing light again. With the wire removed, the timing should be 10-14°.

EVERYONE: If the notch on the pulley dances around and won't stand still at idle, the shaft and/or bushings in the distributor are probably worn. See Procedure 9, Step 5, to check the shaft and bushings.

Turn the engine off, then unhook the timing light. Leave the tach/dwell meter connected. You'll need the tach to adjust the carburetor.

PROCEDURE 13: ADJUST IDLE SPEED AND IDLE MIXTURE

Condition: Tune-up time; OR the engine is idling too slowly or too fast; OR rough idle; OR poor gas mileage; OR you just rebuilt the carb.

Tools and Materials: Long skinny screwdriver, tachometer, spray can of carb cleaner, rags.

Remark: Before adjusting the idle mixture on '75-'80 models, be sure the point gap or air gap in the distributor is properly adjusted (Procedure 10 or 11), the ignition timing is correct (Procedure 12), and the engine is warmed up to operating temperature.

WARNING! Don't do this procedure in a closed garage! Exhaust fumes will take you off the tax rolls.

Step 1. Check Vacuum Hoses.

20R and 22R models: Remove the air cleaner, if it's on (Procedure 6, Step 1). Be sure to plug all the places on the engine where small vacuum hoses were disconnected.

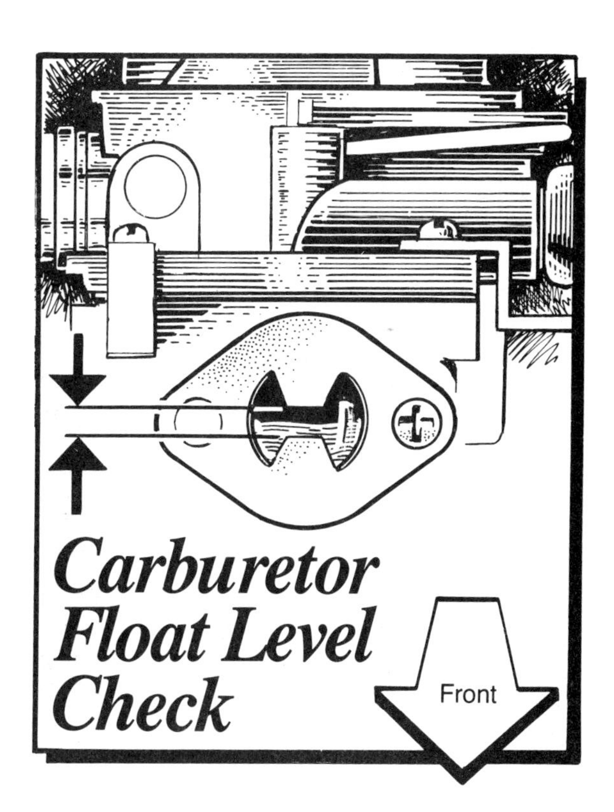

Carburetor Float Level Check

EVERYONE: Inspect all the little rubber hoses in the engine compartment for cracks, holes and loose connections. Replace any hoses that are cracked, stretched at the ends, or slide onto their fittings too easily.

Step 2. Check Float Level (20R and 22R engines only).

Start the engine and let it idle. Locate the little window on the front of the carburetor. The fuel level should be within 1/16" of the dot in the center of the window on '75-'79 models or somewhere in the narrow center part of the window frame on '80-'87 models. If the level is incorrect, have the Toyota dealer or a garage adjust the float level.

Step 3. Check Automatic Choke.

Warm the engine up to normal operating temperature. Look at the two openings in the top of the carburetor. You'll see two flat plates. The plate on the right (passenger's) side is the **choke plate** and should be in the open (vertical) position when the engine is warm. When the engine is cold the choke plate moves to the closed position. The other plate in the top of the carb should be in the closed (horizontal) position and cover the opening on the top left side of the carb. If the choke plate isn't straight up and down when the engine is warm, see Chapter 9, Procedure 9, to check the choke mechanism.

Turn the engine OFF.

Step 4. Clean Carburetor (20R and 22R only).

The engine should be OFF for this step. If the carburetor looks clean inside and out with no traces of dirt or varnish-looking residue anywhere, skip down to the next step.

Break out your spray can of carburetor cleaner. If a little tube came with the can, insert the tube in the hole on the spray head. Use your finger or a screwdriver to hold the flat choke plates in the top part of the carb in a vertical position, then spray the inside of the carb with the cleaner. Let it soak a few minutes, then hit it again. Pay particular attention to the round brass jets and little holes. The inside of the carb should look clean when you're finished.

Use a clean rag or paper towel to cover the opening in the top of the carb, then use the carb cleaner to clean the outside. Mop up the carb cleaner with a rag or paper towel when you're finished.

Step 5. Connect Tachometer.

Follow the instructions in Procedure 12, Step 1, to connect your tachometer or Tach/Dwell meter.

Idle Speed Adjusting Screw On EFI Models

Step 6. Locate Idle Speed, Idle Mixture, and Fast Idle Adjusting Screws.

Look at the illustrations for the location of the adjusting screws.

Idle Speed Adjustment Screw:

20R and 22R engines: The idle speed adjustment screw is on the lower rear side of the carburetor pointing up toward the right front fender at about a 45° angle. Look at the illustration so you don't confuse it with the *idle mixture* or *fast idle* adjusting screws. If there's a little plastic cap on the idle speed adjusting screw, use pliers to crack the cap, then twist it off the screw.

22R-E and 22R-TE engines: To find the idle speed adjustment screw, follow the large air intake hose that runs across the top front of the engine to where it connects to the throttle body on the top right front side of the engine. The idle speed adjustment screw is located on the right side of the throttle body (see the illustration). Some models have a little cap covering the screw. Pop the cap out of the hole while you make the idle speed adjustment, then press it back into the hole when you're finished.

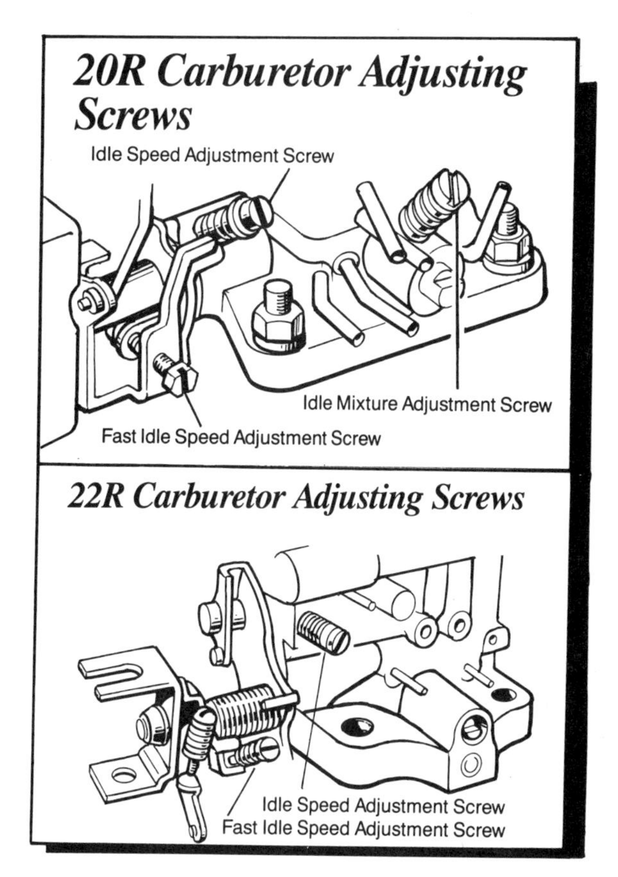

Idle Mixture Adjusting Screw (20R engines only):

'75-'80 models: There's an idle mixture adjustment screw at the bottom center of the right side of the carburetor. If there's a little plastic cap on the mixture adjusting screw, use pliers to crack the cap, then twist it off the screw.

'81-'87 models: Sorry, but you don't have a screw for adjusting the idle mixture. It is set at the factory, then plugged with a pin so you can't adjust it.

Fast Idle Adjusting Screw (20R and 22R engines only):

The fast idle adjusting screw is on the same lever as the idle speed adjustment screw, only lower (see the illustration).

Step 7. Install Air Cleaner (20R and 22R models only).

The air cleaner must be installed before making the final carburetor adjustments. I know it makes getting to the adjusting screws more difficult, but a wise old guru once told me that it is a great way to build character. See Procedure 6, Step 2, to install the air cleaner.

Step 8. Adjust Idle Speed.

EVERYONE: A lot of good tach/dwell gauges have been eaten alive by the moving drive belt or fan, so please keep the wires away from the front of the engine. Block the wheels, set the handbrake, put the gearshift in NEUTRAL, start the engine and let it warm up to normal operating temperature.

22R-E and 22R-TE engines: You need to warm up the O_2 (oxygen) sensor before setting the idle speed. Here's how: Rev the engine to 2,500 rpm for about two minutes after the initial warm-up. Now you can check and adjust the idle speed if necessary.

EVERYONE: Switch the gauge to Tach and read the engine rpm scale. (You might have to double the number on an eight cylinder scale if the gauge doesn't have a four cylinder scale.) Look at the sticker under the hood to see what the idle speed for your engine should be. No sticker? Look up your idle speed in the **Tune-up Specifications Table** at the end of this chapter. If the speed indicated on the Tach matches the rpms on the chart, leave things be. If not, grab the skinny screwdriver and make the adjustment. Put the screwdriver in the slot of the **idle speed adjustment screw** and turn the screw *clockwise* to increase engine speed or *counterclockwise* to slow the engine down.

'81-'87 models: Adjust the screw to the correct idle speed and you're through adjusting the carburetor. Skip down to the next procedure.

Step 9. Adjust Idle Mixture ('75-'80 models only).

Put the screwdriver in the **idle mixture adjustment screw** and slowly turn it *counterclockwise* until the engine rpm just starts to drop. Slowly turn the screw *clockwise* until the engine reaches its highest rpm. You may have to turn the screw in and out a few times until you find the right spot. Got it? Now go back to the **idle speed adjustment screw** and adjust the engine speed to Figure B in the chart below.

Now put your screwdriver in the mixture adjustment screw again and slowly screw it in (*clockwise*) until the engine rpm drops to Figure A in the chart. This is the carburetor *lean drop setting* to keep the carbon monoxide emissions within the legal limits. If the engine idles roughly and you feel you just can't live with it, turn the screw *counterclockwise* slightly to add a little more gas. (You might not pass a smog test if you add the extra gas.)

CARBURETOR LEAN DROP SETTING

YEAR	A	B
1975-76	850	900
1977-80	800 manual	870
	850 automatic	920

If turning the idle mixture screw doesn't affect the engine rpm, check all vacuum lines and connections again for leaks. Turn the engine off and remove the mixture adjustment screw (*counterclockwise*) and look at it. Replace it with a new one if a groove is worn in the tapered needle end of the screw. Squirt some carb cleaner into the mixture screw hole before installing the pointed mixture screw. Are the carburetor mounting nuts tight? Check 'em with a 10mm wrench. Now start the engine and try adjusting the carb again. If you still can't change the rpm with the mixture adjustment screw, some passages in the carb are probably clogged. Try squirting carb cleaner in all the holes inside the carb that you can reach with the nozzle. If you still can't adjust the idle mixture, the carburetor probably needs to be rebuilt. Turn to Chapter 9, Procedure 11, for guidance and inspiration on renovating the carb.

Step 10. Adjust Fast Idle (20R and 22R only).

This is the adjustment that enables the engine to idle while it's cold. If your truck starts and idles OK even on cold mornings, you can skip this step. If the engine won't idle until it warms up, do this step. The engine must be warmed up to make this adjustment.

Turn the engine off if it's running. Remove the air cleaner and plug the fittings on the engine where the small vacuum hoses were attached (Procedure 6, Step 2). Connect the tachometer (see Procedure 12, Step 1, if you need instructions).

Disconnect and plug the small vacuum hose from the top of the round metal EGR valve located on the top right rear of the engine. See the illustration in Chapter 10, Procedure 2, if you aren't sure what the EGR valve looks like.

EVERYONE: Locate the **idle speed adjustment screw** (see Step 6 if you aren't sure where it's located). Pull the idle screw (or the arm it's attached to) toward the right front fender slightly. This is how you open the throttle. You'll need to know this in a minute. Release the screw or arm.

Disconnect and plug the hose(s) from the **vacuum advance unit** on the distributor (Procedure 12, Step 1).

'80 California and '80 C&C: Disconnect and plug the small vacuum hose from the **fast idle cam breaker** (FICB). It's the round gizmo on the right rear side of the carb.

'81-'87 models: Disconnect and plug the small vacuum hose from the round **choke opener diaphragm** on the lower, rear left (driver's) side of the carburetor.

EVERYONE: Hold the throttle open slightly while you close the flat **choke plate** on the right (passenger's side) top of the carburetor. The plate should stay nearly closed when you release the throttle. If not, try again.

Be sure the tachometer wires are clear of the fan and drive belts, then start the engine without touching the gas pedal. If you touch the pedal you'll have to close the choke plate again.

The tachometer should read 2400 rpm for '75-'80 models or 2600 rpm for '81-'87 models. If it's less, use a long skinny screwdriver to slowly turn the fast idle adjustment screw *clockwise* (as viewed from the right side of the engine) until the fast idle speed is correct. Be sure the choke plate hasn't opened before you make the adjustment. If it has, reset it by opening the throttle slightly and closing the choke plate again.

Once the fast idle speed is set, turn the engine OFF. Reconnect the vacuum hoses to the EGR valve, the FICB ('80 Calif. and '80 C&C), the choke opener diaphragm ('81-'87 models), and the vacuum advance unit on the distributor. Disconnect the tachometer, install the air cleaner and you're ready to move on to the massage.

PROCEDURE 14: WRAP-UP (12,000 MILE OR 12 MONTH MAJOR MASSAGE)

Most of the steps in this procedure refer you to other parts of the book. They're all pretty simple, but very important to the long life of your Toyota.

Step 1. Replace Antifreeze and Check Cooling System Hoses.

Condition: You live where the winters are harsh and it's been a year since the antifreeze was changed; OR you live in the banana belt where the livin' is easy, the cotton is high, your daddy's rich, your momma's good lookin', and it's been two years since you replaced the antifreeze.

Before draining the antifreeze, do Chapter 6, Procedure 2, to check the cooling system hoses and replace any that don't meet the "Toyotas 'R Us" standards. Buy all hoses that are needed and replace them when you replace the antifreeze (Chapter 6, Procedure 3).

Step 2. Replace Fuel Filter.

20R and 22R models: Fuel filters get clogged with dirt, rust and water and can eventually cut off the fuel supply to the engine. Turn to Chapter 9, Procedure 2, to check the fuel filter, then come back here and continue.

22R-E and 22R-TE models: You can't check the fuel filter. Just have the Toyota dealer or a garage change the filter every 30,000 miles.

Step 3. Replace Brake and Clutch Fluid.

Don't skip this step or you'll pay for it sooner or later. Brake fluid absorbs moisture, which corrodes the mechanical and hydraulic parts of the brake and clutch systems. Brake fluid is a lot cheaper than master cylinders, wheel cylinders, and disc brake calipers. Changing the fluid regularly will lengthen the life expectancy of your brake and clutch systems and yours too, perhaps. Turn to Chapter 7, Procedure 2, and follow the directions for replacing the brake fluid. Chapter 11, Procedure 2, Step 2, covers replacing the clutch fluid.

Step 4. Check Steering and Suspension Systems.

It only takes about ten minutes to thoroughly check the suspension and steering. Chapter 12, Procedure 1, tells you how. It won't keep you in suspense or steer you wrong.

Step 5. Check Emission Control Systems.

Look at Chapter 10: *Exhaust and Emission Control Systems*, Procedures 1 to 5, to check emission control devices that are capable of being checked at home. Depending on the year and model, you might be checking and cleaning the **exhaust gas recirculation (EGR) Valve**, the **Positive Crankcase Ventilation (PCV) valve**, the **air pump**, the **evaporative canister** and the **hot air control system**.

Yes, there are several more emission control devices on your truck, but checking them requires special tools and training. I recommend making a date with your Toyota dealer every 30,000 miles and have them check the entire emission control system. It shouldn't cost much.

Step 6. Inspect Exhaust System.

Set the handbrake, block the wheels, then start the engine. Get on your hands and knees and crawl along the driver's side of the truck while checking the exhaust pipe, muffler or catalytic converter, and the tailpipe for cracks, dents, holes, and missing rubber cushions which attach the system to the truck. Listen for hissing sounds that tell you there's a leak in the system. Also be sure the heat insulator (a flat sheet of metal) is in place between the muffler or converter and truck body. Replace any components that are leaking, broken, bent or missing (Chapter 10, Procedure 6).

If your truck is equipped with a catalytic converter, check it for dents and replace it if you find any that are more than ¾" (20mm) deep (Chapter 10, Procedure 6).

Step 7. Clean Up.

Put the old oil, antifreeze and brake fluid in plastic containers and take them to a filling station or recycling center. If there isn't one, put the containers in the trash.

Use a rag to wipe off all the tools you used before putting them back in the tool box. Wipe up any oil that spilled on the floor with rags then throw all the oily rags in an outside trash container (they can spontaneously burst into flames). Whew, one more step and we're finished.

Step 8. Record All Work in Log.

Repeat Procedure 4, Step 19, to record your efforts in the maintenance log. This time, include all the extra 12,000 mile things. Your Toy should now be in very fine running condition. Now do Procedure 4, Step 20. See you here next year!

PROCEDURE 15: 30,000 MILE MAINTENANCE

At 30,000 mile intervals, you'll do the regular 6,000 mile maintenance procedures, but don't add any transmission or differential oil—you're going to drain the old oil and replace it with new oil. Look at the oil viscosity charts in your Owner's Manual to see which grade oil you should use.

Condition: You just bought a Toyota with over 30,000 miles on it; OR it's been 30,000 miles since you last performed this maintenance; OR you feel like getting down and getting greasy.

Tools and Materials: You need a catch pan, safety glasses, plastic bottles for disposal of the old oil, plus 17, 19 and 24mm socket and ratchet or box end wrench depending on the size of your drain and filler plugs, phillips screwdriver, new fuel tank cap gasket, lots of rags or paper towels. Funky clothes aren't a bad idea either.

You'll also need a large syringe or a suction-type oil filler to get the oil into the manual transmission, the differential(s), and the transfer case on 4WDs. Automatic transmission models require a funnel with a long skinny neck to get the ATF into the transmission.

Automatic transmissions models: Get three quarts of ATF for the transmission and 3 quarts of gear oil for the rear differential. If you have 4WD you'll need five quarts of ATF for the transmission and transfer case and two more quarts of gear oil for the front differential.

Manual transmission models: It takes five quarts of gear oil to change the oil in the transmission and differential and one new gasket for the drain plug. If you have 4WD, you'll need five additional quarts of gear oil for the front differential and transfer case.

Remark: Always remove the filler plug first to make sure you'll be able to get oil back in after draining the old oil.

Step 1. Go for a Ride.

The transmission and differential should be warmed up to operating temperature before draining the oil. Go for a drive, at least 10 miles, then park the truck on level ground and shut the engine off. Block the wheels.

Step 2. Get Ready.

Spread out your ground cover beneath the truck. Be sure the handbrake is ON and the transmission is in FIRST (manual) or PARK (automatic). Slide the **catch pan** under the truck. Grab 17, 19 and 24mm sockets and ratchet or box end wrenches, and the new drain plug gaskets. Install safety glasses on your face, then squeeze your body under the car.

If you have a clearance problem, perhaps it's time to consider that last piece of cake or six-pack you had. If you just don't fit, jack one side of the truck up a little and put a jackstand under the frame (see Chapter 2, Procedure 1). After removing the drain plug(s), take the truck off the jackstand so the oil can drain completely. Jack it back up and slip the stand into position when you're ready to put the drain plug(s) back in.

You'll be removing the filler and drain plugs in the steps ahead. After the drain plugs are out, come out from under the car and look them over. On most models, magnets are built into the drain plugs to trap tiny metal particles as they wear off the gears. Hopefully, there are no large chunks of metal, which would indicate a chipped gear and potential trouble, stuck to the magnets. Clean the plugs thoroughly with a rag before you attempt to screw them back in. If yours is a standard transmission vehicle, skip ahead to Step 4.

Step 3. Drain and Fill Automatic Transmission Fluid.

The **drain plug** for automatic transmissions is on the bottom front or rear center of the transmission, about 12 to 18 inches behind the engine. One of the three sockets or wrenches fits the plug. Put the correct size wrench on the plug and unscrew it *counterclockwise*. When the plug is loose enough to turn by hand, scoot out from under the truck as far as you can and remove the plug at arm's length. The oil will be hot as it gushes from the drain hole so you don't want any to splash in your face. Don't worry if the drain plug falls into the catch pan; you can fish it out with a magnet or your fingers after the fluid cools off, or retrieve it when you pour the old fluid into the disposal bottles. Let the oil drain for a few minutes.

Install a new drain plug gasket onto the drain plug, then screw the plug into the transmission. Tighten it down with the wrench, but remember who'll have to take it out next time. Then get out from under and find the **dipstick** for the automatic transmission hiding near the rear of the engine compartment. See Procedure 2, Step 2, if you aren't sure where the dipstick is located. Remove the dipstick, wipe it with a clean rag, then put it in a clean place. Stick the small end of the **long, clean funnel** into the dipstick hole. Wipe off the tops of the new ATF cans with a clean rag. Open two cans and pour one quart into the transmission. Keep adding ATF and checking the level with the dipstick until the fluid level is in the "COLD" area of the dipstick. Put the dipstick back in.

Be sure the handbrake is on and the gearshift lever is in the PARK position, then start the engine. Push on the brake pedal while you run the transmission shifter through all the gears and back to the PARK position. Then check the fluid level with the engine running at idle (Procedure 2, Step 2). Add fluid a little at a time until the level reaches the cold area on the dipstick. Be careful not to add too much fluid. Put the dipstick in place and turn off the engine. Check beneath the car for leaks around the drain plug. Empty the drain pan into the disposal bottles, then go on to Step 5, if you have 4WD, or Step 6, if you have 2WD.

Step 4. Drain and Fill Manual Transmission.

Toys with manual transmissions have one drain plug located in the bottom of the transmission case. You shouldn't have to jack the truck up, but if you do, be sure to block the wheels and use jackstands. Put the catch pan beneath the plug. You just warmed up the engine, so watch out for the hot exhaust pipe.

First strap on the safety goggles and remove the oil filler plug on the side of the transmission (Procedure 3, Step 6). Loosen the drain plug with the correct socket or wrench. When you can turn it by hand, scoot out from under the truck and unscrew it the rest of the way at arms length. Don't let the hot oil splash in your face. While the oil drains, wipe off the drain plug with a clean rag and install the new gasket. When the oil is only dripping a couple of drops per minute, screw the plug back into the hole and tighten it with the socket or wrench.

Clean the tops before opening the cans or bottles of gear oil, then use the oil suction gun, syringe or baster to add oil a little at a time until it flows out of the oil filler hole. Relax for a couple of minutes while the oil settles down in the transmission, then check the level with your finger. Add more if necessary, then install and tighten the filler plug. Slide the catch pan and tools out from under. Lower the truck if you jacked it up.

Step 5. Change Transfer Case Oil (4WD only).

Remember, if you have an automatic transmission, put the same kind of automatic transmission fluid in the transfer case that you put in the transmission. If you have a manual transmission, use the grade of gear oil recommended in your Owner's Manual.

First remove the filler plug for the transfer case (Procedure 3, Step 6). Now locate the drain plug near the bottom center of the case. Place the drain pan under the plug, then use your wrench to remove the plug. Remember, the oil might be pretty hot. While the oil is draining, clean and inspect the drain plug. After the oil has all drained out, install and tighten the plug.

Open a couple of fresh cans of gear oil or ATF, depending on your transmission type, then use the oil suction gun, syringe or baster to put it into the transfer case until it starts running out the filler hole. Let the oil settle a few minutes, then check the level with a clean finger. Add some if necessary, then install and tighten the filler plug.

Step 6. Change Differential Oil.

The method is the same for changing the oil in the rear differential on all models and the front differential on 4WD models. Change the oil in both differentials if you have 4WD.

Spread the ground cloth under the truck, then slide the drain pan between the wheels. Get a 24mm socket and ratchet and dive into the underworld. The **rear differential** is that big chunk of metal directly between the two rear axles.

The differential **drain plug** is on the bottom of the differential. The **filler plug** for adding fresh oil is near the center. Clean the area around the plugs with a rag, then use the wrench to unscrew both plugs *counterclockwise* (loosen the filler plug first).

When the oil is dripping out of the bottom hole only a couple of drops per minute, clean the plugs, then screw the one with the magnet on it into the bottom hole and tighten it with the wrench. Pour or pump oil into the top hole until it starts running out. Relax a couple of minutes while the oil settles in the differential, then use a clean finger to check the level. When the differential is full, screw the plug in and tighten it with the wrench. Wipe off any oil on the outside of the housing, then drag all the tools and catch pan from underneath the truck.

Step 7. Clean Up.

Pour the old oil in plastic containers and give it to a service station or the nice people at the recycling center. Record the work you've done in the maintenance log. A shower would probably feel great right about now.

Step 8. Wheel Bearing Lubrication.

Since it's such a hassle, I confess I only get around to greasing my wheel bearings every 50-60,000 miles, or when I have the front brakes off and it's handy to get to everything. However, if you're in the habit of abusing your Toy on mountain goat trails or crossing rivers and streams frequently, check and grease the bearings at least every 30,000 miles.

4WD models will need to do Chapter 12, Procedure 6, to remove the 4WD hubs, then everyone will do Chapter 12, Procedure 5, to remove the front wheels and axle hubs. You'll be instructed where to look for the wheel bearing lubrication.

Step 9. Replace the Fuel Tank Cap Gasket.

If it's been 30,000 miles since the gas cap gasket was replaced, fuel vapors might be escaping. This procedure is easy as toast and helps insure that your truck is as pollution free as possible.

While replacing the gasket inspect the gas cap and replace it if you find cracks or damage.

'75-'78 models: Remove the gas cap and pry the gasket off the bottom. Carefully install the new gasket the same way the old one was installed. Don't use any tools, to avoid damaging the new gasket.

'79-'83 models: Remove the gas cap, turn it upside down and you'll see two or four screws. Use the screwdriver to remove the screws, then carefully remove the round metal locking plate which was attached with the screws.

Now you can pull the old gasket out of the cap. Note which side of the old gasket fits against the cap as you remove it. Use a clean rag to wipe the inside of the cap if it's dirty, then fit the new gasket in place. Be sure the little lips on the inner edge of the gasket are tucked under the metal retainer. Install the locking plate, align the holes, then install and tighten the screws. Fit the gas cap onto the gas tank and you're finished.

'84-'87 models: Unscrew the gas cap from the gas tank and turn it upside down. Use a small screwdriver to pry the rubber gasket from the inside of the gas cap. Fit the new gasket into the cap and use your fingers to press it in until it fits against the cap all the way around. Install the cap on the tank and you're finished.

PROCEDURE 16: 60,000 MILE MAINTENANCE

At 60,000 miles the oxygen sensor should be replaced on all 22R-TE engines and on non-California 22R-E engines, and the power steering fluid should be replaced on models that have power steering.

Condition: 60,000 mile maintenance.

Tools and Materials: To change the oxygen sensor you'll need: a new oxygen sensor, oxygen sensor gasket, 12mm socket, ratchet and short ratchet extension, penetrating oil.

To change the power steering fluid you'll need: Jack, jackstands, Dexron or Dexron II Automatic Transmission Fluid (ATF), small catch pan (coffee can or jar), '84-'87 models require a rubber plug.

Step 1. Remove and Install Oxygen Sensor.

The oxygen sensor is bolted to the exhaust manifold on the driver's side of the engine. On 22R-E engines it points toward the top of the left front fender and on 22R-TE engines it points straight up. It's attached with two 12mm nuts and has a wire sprouting from the end.

Follow the wire from the sensor to a plastic connector. Disconnect the sensor wire. Squirt penetrating oil on the two attaching nuts and let the juice soak in for a few minutes. Use the socket and ratchet to slowly unscrew the nuts *counterclockwise*. If they're tight, douse them with more penetrating oil and screw them back on again. Let the oil do its thing for a few minutes, then try and unscrew them again. Do this over and over until the nuts come off easily. It pays to have patience here, otherwise the studs might break.

When the nuts are off, wiggle the old sensor out of the manifold, then use a knife blade or razor to scrape the old gasket off the manifold. Fit the new gasket onto the new sensor and install it in the manifold, aligning the holes with the studs. Install the nuts and snug them down. The torque is only 14 ft.lbs. so don't over tighten them.

Connect the wire from the new sensor to the wiring connector and you're finished.

Step 2. Replace Power Steering Fluid.

Park on level ground, block the rear wheels, set the handbrake and put the gearshift in NEUTRAL. Jack up the front of the car and put it on jackstands (Chapter 2, Procedure 1).

The power steering reservoir is a small round can mounted on the inside of the fender on the driver's side. Two rubber hoses are connected to the reservoir: a fluid supply hose on the bottom and a fluid return hose on the side.

Place a catch pan beneath the reservoir, then disconnect the fluid return hose from the side of the reservoir and let the fluid drain. When the reservoir is empty, stick the end of the hose into the catch pan and start the engine and let it idle. Be sure the catch pan is clear of the fan belts. Turn the steering wheel as far as it will go in each direction (lock to lock) about four times, then turn the engine off. This drains the fluid from the system. Reconnect the return hose to the reservoir, then add fresh Dexron or Dexron II ATF until it reaches the "HOT" area on the dipstick.

'79-'83 models: Turn the steering wheel lock to lock two or three times, then check the fluid level in the reservoir. Add fluid if necessary.

Start the engine and run it at 1000 rpm (if you don't have a tachometer, run it slightly faster than idle speed). Turn the steering wheel lock to lock two or three times.

'84-'87 models: Disconnect the return hose from the reservoir again and plug the fitting on the reservoir with a rubber plug.

Start the engine and run it at 1000 rpm until fluid comes out of the return hose (probably only a second or two), then check the fluid level again. Do this four or five times until no air bubbles are seen in the fluid coming out of the hose. Connect the return hose to the reservoir.

EVERYONE: Now we need to bleed the air out of the power steering system. Here's how.

Turn the engine off, then lower the front of the truck off the jackstands. Be sure the handbrake is set, the gearshift is in NEUTRAL and the wheels are blocked. Start the engine again and run it at 1000 rpm while turning the steering wheel lock to lock several times. Center the steering wheel so the front tires are pointed straight ahead, check the fluid level in the reservoir, then turn the engine off. Check the fluid level in the reservoir again.

The bleeding is complete if the fluid level in the reservoir hasn't risen more than .2" (a little less than ¼") when the engine is turned off and no sign of foam can be seen in the fluid. If the fluid level rose more than .2" when you turned the engine off, or you see foam in the reservoir, run the engine at 1000 rpm while slowly turning the steering wheel lock to lock several more times. Eventually the foam should disappear and the fluid level should remain constant. If not, it's time to have the power steering checked by the Toyota dealer or a garage.

TUNE-UP SPECIFICATIONS 1975-1987 TOYOTA PICKUPS AND 4 RUNNERS

POINTS GAP
(1975-77): .018in (.45mm)

POINTS DWELL
(1975-77): .50-54 degrees

AIR GAP
(1978-88): .008-.016in (.2-.4mm)

SPARK PLUG GAP: .031in (.8mm)

VALVE SETTING (HOT)
INTAKE: .008in (.2mm)
EXHAUST: .012in (.3mm)

IGNITION TIMING

1975-76	8° @ 850 rpm
1977-78	
Manual	8° @ 800 rpm
Automatic	8° @ 850 rpm
High altitude	
Below 4,000 ft.	8° @ 700-900 rpm
Above 4,000 ft.	13° @ 700-900 rpm
1979-82	8° @ 950 rpm or less
1983-84 (all)	5° @ 950 rpm or less
1985-87 22R	0° @ 950 rpm or less
1985-87	
22R-E	5° @ 750 rpm
22R-TE	5° @ 800 rpm

IDLE SPEED (RPM)

1975-76	850 (automatic in NEUTRAL)
1977	
Manual	800 rpm
Automatic	850 rpm in NEUTRAL
1978-80	
Manual	800 rpm
Automatic	850 rpm
1981	
Manual and Non-Calif. 4-speed A/T	700 rpm
Calif. 4-speed A/T and Non-Calif. 3-speed A/T	750 rpm
1982-87	
22R Manual	700 rpm
22R Automatic	750 rpm
22R-E (all)	750 rpm
22R-TE (all)	800 rpm

FAST IDLE SPEED (20R and 22R)

1975-78	2,200-2,600 rpm
1979-80	2,400 rpm
1981-87	2,600 rpm

MAINTENANCE LOG

6,000 MILE INTERVAL

MILEAGE																		
GAS STOP CHECKS																		
CHANGE OIL & FILTER																		
CHECK OIL LEVELS:																		
REAR DIFFERENTIAL																		
MANUAL TRANSMISSION																		
TRANSFER CASE (4WD)																		
FRONT DIFFERENTIAL (4WD)																		
LUBRICATE:																		
SUSPENSION																		
DRIVESHAFT(S)																		
STEERING (4WD)																		
CHECK:																		
BATTERY																		
AIR FILTER																		
CLUTCH & BRAKE PEDALS																		
STEERING FREE PLAY																		
LIGHTS																		
WIPER BLADES																		
TIRE PRESSURE																		
FRONT BRAKE PADS																		
REAR BRAKE SHOES																		
ROTATE TIRES																		
BODY MASSAGE																		
CLEAN TAPE DECK																		
REWARD YOURSELF																		

NOTES:

MILEAGE																		
12,000 MILE INTERVAL																		
CLEAN & GAP SPARK PLUGS																		
ADJUST VALVES																		
DISTRIBUTOR CHECKS																		
CHECK & SET IGNITION TIMING																		
CHECK & ADJUST CARBURETOR																		
CHECK:																		
COOLING SYSTEM																		
SUSPENSION & STEERING																		
EMISSION CONTROLS																		
EXHAUST SYSTEM																		
REPLACE:																		
FUEL FILTER																		
ANTIFREEZE																		
BRAKE FLUID																		
CLUTCH FLUID																		
30,000 MILE INTERVAL																		
REPLACE OIL OR FLUID IN:																		
MANUAL TRANSMISSION																		
DIFFERENTIAL(S)																		
AUTOMATIC TRANSMISSION																		
TRANSFER CASE (4WD)																		
LUBRICATE WHEEL BEARINGS																		
REPLACE FUEL TANK CAP GASKET																		
60,000 MILE INTERVAL																		
CHECK COMPRESSION																		
REPLACE																		
OXYGEN SENSOR (22R-TE)																		
POWER STEERING FLUID																		

VITAL STATISTICS FOR MY TOYOTA (MY SPECS)

ENGINE TYPE:
ENGINE NUMBER:
BODY NUMBER:
PRODUCTION DATE:
ENGINE OIL
  BRAND:
  WEIGHT:
OIL FILTER:
  (BRAND AND #)
MANUAL TRANS./DIFF. OIL
  BRAND:
  WEIGHT:
AUTOMATIC TRANS. FLUID
  BRAND:

POINTS GAP (1975-77):	.018" (.45MM)
POINTS DWELL (1975-77):	50-54 DEGREES
AIR GAP (1978-88):	.008-.016" (.2-.4MM)
SPARK PLUG GAP:	.031" (.8MM)
VALVE SETTING (HOT)	
INTAKE:	.008" (.2MM)
EXHAUST:	.012" (.3MM)

IGNITION TIMING:
IDLE SPEED:
PARTS NUMBERS
SPARK PLUGS:
DISTRIBUTOR CAP:
ROTOR:
POINTS SET:
AIR FILTER:
FUEL FILTER:
PCV VALVE:
BRAKE FLUID (DOT3 or 4)
TIRE PRESSURE
FRONT:
REAR:
SPARE:

CHAPTER 6

COOLING AND HEATING SYSTEMS

Since the engine runs by burning a fuel/air mixture, it's logical that heat is generated. In fact, when the engine is running at normal operating temperature, each of the four combustion chambers reaches temperatures of over 4,000° F (2,222° C). To prevent the engine from self-destructing, some of the heat is carried away by the exhaust system, some by the lubricating oil, and some is radiated directly into the surrounding air, but mainly the engine temperature is controlled by the **cooling system**. In cold weather, some of the heat generated by the engine is used to warm the passenger compartment.

COOLING SYSTEM

Here's how the cooling system works: Narrow passages called **water jackets** surround the cylinders in the crankcase and the combustion chambers in the cylinder head. A mixture of water and antifreeze (called **coolant**) is pumped through the water jackets by a **water pump**. The pump is turned by a **drive belt**, which is driven by a pulley on the end of the engine **crankshaft**. Most of the heat generated in the combustion chambers is absorbed by the coolant as it flows through the water jackets. The heated coolant is pumped from the engine through the **upper radiator hose** to the top right side of the **radiator**. The coolant radiates the absorbed heat to the outside air as it is pumped through small finned tubes to the bottom of the radiator. Since the radiator is in the front of the vehicle it receives a constant flow of onrushing air to carry the heat away. The cooled coolant then flows through the **lower radiator hose** on the bottom, left side of the radiator to the water pump, where it is pumped through the engine water jackets again to absorb more heat.

The cooling system on your truck is a closed system. This simply means that a small white translucent plastic

reservoir mounted just to the left of the radiator stores surplus coolant. When the coolant level in the radiator drops, coolant is sucked out of the reservoir through a tube that connects to the radiator, just below the radiator cap. When the amount of coolant in the radiator is excessive, coolant is returned to the reservoir through the same tube. Coolant is normally added to the engine by removing the **reservoir cap** on the reservoir. Only when the radiator or engine block have been drained will you need to remove the **radiator cap** on top of the radiator to add coolant.

There is one exception to the normal flow of coolant through the engine. When the engine is cold, a **thermostat** closes the passageway between the engine and upper radiator hose, thus restricting the coolant from flowing to the radiator. Once the coolant temperature in the engine is around 185° F (85° C) the thermostat opens and the coolant flows normally. The reason for the thermostat is that a lot of wear occurs while the engine is cold, so it's best to get it up to operating temperature quickly.

When the truck isn't moving, or is moving slowly, a **fan** on the front of the engine draws air through the radiator to help dissipate the heat. The fan is mounted to a **fluid coupling** (fan clutch) which disengages the fan at high engine speed, conserving energy. The same drive belt that turns the water pump and alternator also turns the fan on the engine.

Here are some fascinating facts about coolant:

The freezing point of plain water is 32° F (0° C), and the boiling point is 212° F (100° C). Plain water allows rust and corrosion to form inside the cooling system. A 50/50 solution of antifreeze and water lowers the freezing point to about -32° F (-35° C), raises the boiling point to about 220° F (105° C), and inhibits the formation of rust and corrosion. So it's logical that straight water should not be used in a cooling system. Straight antifreeze shouldn't be used either because water dissipates heat better than antifreeze. Antifreeze wears out with use so it should be replaced at least every two years (yearly in severe weather). The use of distilled or bottled water in the cooling system is preferred (but not always available) in order to prevent mineral deposits from building up inside the system.

Like Capt. Kirk, the cooling system is more efficient when under pressure. For instance, the boiling temperature of coolant at sea level is around 220° F (105° C). Add 15 pounds of pressure and the boiling point rises to about 265° F (130° C). Since the normal operating temperature is near 200° F (94° C), it is essential that the cooling system be pressurized for the engine to keep its cool under strain when more heat is generated, as when cruising at higher speeds or hauling heavy loads.

The amount of pressure in the cooling system is regulated by the **radiator cap** on top of the radiator. That's why you should never remove the radiator cap when the engine is hot—the coolant may be hotter than its normal boiling temperature, but doesn't boil because it's under pressure. When the radiator cap is removed quickly, the pressure drops, and the boiling point suddenly falls well below the temperature of the coolant. The result: a dangerous geyser of super-hot liquid.

HEATER SYSTEM

Although it sounds strange, the heater system is also part of the cooling system. Located under the dashboard behind the radio are the **heater fan** and **heater core**, which look like a small square radiator. When the heater control lever on the dashboard is set to the HOT position, coolant from the engine flows through **heater hoses** to the heater core, then back to the engine. When the engine is warm, turning the fan switch to ON blows air over the hot water filled heater core and into the passenger compartment. 4 Runners have a second heater core and fan mounted between the front seats. The fan blows hot air toward the rear seats.

Following is a list of diagnostic, maintenance and repair procedures that will keep your Toyota cool even under the most sadistic conditions. If they are performed at appropriate intervals, you'll never be caught with the hood up, the radiator bellowing clouds of steam, and your thumb out trying to hitch a ride. To keep a cool engine (and temper), go through Procedures 1-3 when you do the 12,000 mile or 12 month tune-up and massage.

PROCEDURE 1: CHECK COOLANT LEVEL

Condition: Regular maintenance; OR engine overheating; OR replacing coolant.

Tools and Materials: Coolant (50/50 antifreeze/distilled water mix), rag. Distilled or bottled water is preferred but not essential.

Remark: The coolant level is checked by looking at the fluid level in the white plastic coolant reservoir beside the radiator, not by removing the radiator cap on top of the radiator. If for some reason you need to remove the radiator cap, see the caution below.

Caution! If the engine is hot, wait for at least five minutes before removing the radiator cap.

Step 1. Locate Coolant Reservoir.

The coolant reservoir is on the left (driver's) side of the radiator. The words FULL and LOW are stamped on the rear side of the reservoir. COOLANT might even be stamped across the top. The plastic cap has two hoses attached; one attaches the cap to the top center of the radiator, just below the radiator cap. The other hose is a short overflow hose and just hangs down on the side of the reservoir.

On some models the reservoir for the windshield washer fluid is also on the left side of the radiator. It's on the left side of the coolant reservoir. Don't confuse the two. The windshield washer reservoir doesn't have LOW and FULL stamped on the rear side. The windshield washer fluid reservoir cap probably has a little picture of the wiper blades cleaning the windshield or the word WASHER stamped on it.

Step 2. Check Coolant Level.

Once you've found the reservoir, look on the rear side for two lines marked LOW and FULL. If necessary, clean the reservoir with a damp rag so you can see the lines. You should be able to see the coolant through the translucent plastic. If you can't see it, either the reservoir is empty (add coolant) or the coolant is so weak it's mostly water (replace the coolant).

If the fluid level is between the FULL and LOW lines, don't add anything. If it's below the LOW line, lift up on the tab on the reservoir cap to remove the cap, then add coolant until the level reaches the FULL line. Install the cap by hooking the rear edge of the cap over the rim, then push down on the front of the cap. You should feel it snap into place.

PROCEDURE 2: CHECK AND REPLACE HOSES AND CLAMPS

Condition: Regular maintenance; OR you have to add coolant to the radiator frequently; OR a hose or clamp is broken; OR the engine is overheating.

Tools and Materials: To check hoses—safety glasses, at least one good eyeball, one hand with a few good fingers and a thumb. To replace hoses—new hose(s), regular and/or phillips screwdriver, maybe a 10mm wrench, knife, wire brush and/or emery cloth, maybe new hose clamps.

Remark: First, a word about the various types of **hose clamps** you might encounter on your truck.

Wire Type: These consist of a piece of wire twisted so it goes around the hose twice, a screw, a tiny washer that fits on the end of the screw, and a flat piece of metal (screw plate) with three holes in it for the screw and the two hooked ends of the wire. The clamps are loosened and tightened with a phillips screwdriver. They won't work without the little washer on the end of the screw because the screw is small enough to slide through the wire ear, so be careful not to lose the little devil.

Band Type: These are flat bands of steel. Slots cut into the band engage in a worm-type gear built into the screw part of the clamp. Depending on the screw head, a regular or phillips screwdriver, or sometimes a 10mm wrench is used to loosen and tighten the clamp. This is usually the easiest kind of clamp to work with. Why aren't they all like this?

Clamp Type: These are flat pieces of spring steel bent into a circle. To loosen the clamp, use pliers to squeeze the two ends of the clamp together. When replacing these clamps I suggest substituting the band type.

Cotter Key Type: A short fat cotter key is wound up in a flat band of metal. To remove the clamp use pliers to grab the head of the cotter key and turn it counterclockwise several turns. It's like opening a can of Spam. Once the cotter key is loose wiggle the band away from the end of the hose. Replace it with a band-type hose clamp.

A hose clamp is worn out if the wire or band is broken, the screw is rusted to the screw plate, or the head of the screw touches the screw plate without clamping the hose sufficiently. You can replace any of the clamp types with band-type hose clamps, available in parts stores. Be sure the new clamp is the same size as the old one. I prefer using hose clamps that can be removed with either a screwdriver or a 10mm wrench so no matter how the clamp is oriented on the hose you can get to it with one tool or the other.

Now, how tight is tight? Overtightened clamps will cut into the rubber and can cause the hose to leak. A

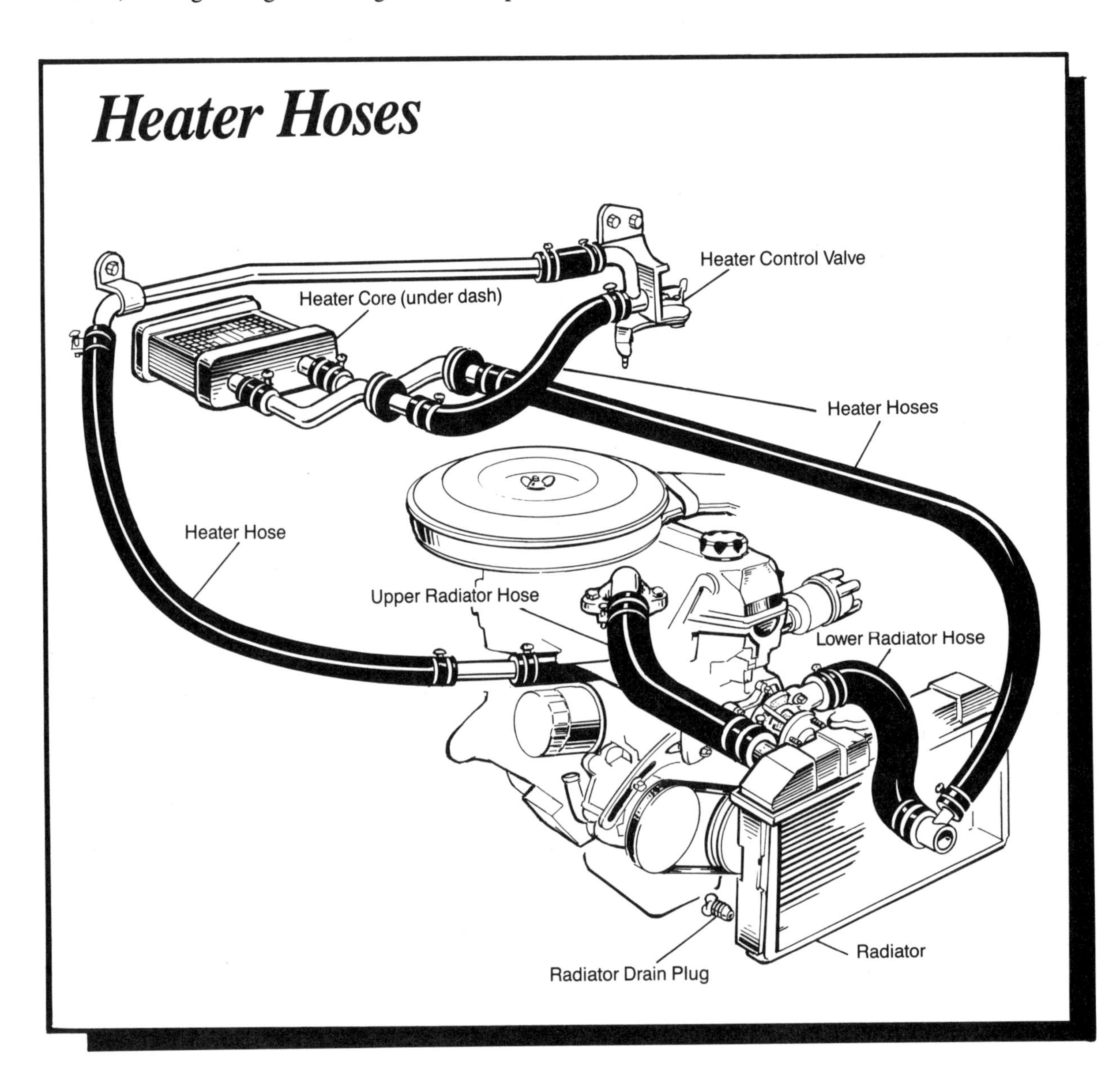

correctly tightened clamp will indent the rubber slightly without cutting it. If there's crud or corrosion between the hose and fitting that it's attached to, the hose will leak no matter how much you tighten the clamp. So be sure and clean all fittings before installing the hoses.

Step 1. Check Radiator Hoses.

Locate the large upper radiator hose that's attached to the top right corner of the radiator and the large lower radiator hose attached to the lower left side. On 4WD models the lower hose connects to a U-shaped metal pipe that curves up around the rear of the alternator. A second radiator hose connects the metal pipe to the water pump.

Put your safety glasses on. Squeeze the hoses and look for cracks, pinholes, soft mushy spots, bulging spots (especially near the hose clamps), and hard, stiff areas that feel brittle. Replace the hose (Steps 2 and 3) if any abnormalities are found.

The lower radiator hose should feel firm. Some even have a steel spring inside. The reason is that at high engine rpms the hose can collapse due to suction from the water pump. Replace the lower radiator hose if it feels flabby.

White crud at the end of a hose or around the clamp means the hose has been leaking. If the hose seems good otherwise, try tightening the screw in the clamp (clockwise) a little to stop the leak. You might have to remove the hose and clean the inside of the hose and its fitting. Replace the clamp if it's broken or already tightened as far as it can go.

Step 2. Remove Radiator Hoses.

Replacing the upper radiator hose is easy. The lower hose, especially on 4WD and models with power steering, is a bit more difficult.

First, drain the radiator into a clean catch pan (Procedure 3, Step 1).

4WD models: When replacing the part of the lower radiator hose that's attached to the radiator, remove the skid plate. It's easier to get to the hose from beneath the truck.

When replacing the part of the lower radiator hose that's attached to the water pump, cover the alternator with a plastic bag so it doesn't get an antifreeze bath when you remove the hose. Look for a heater hose that might be attached to a T-fitting on the hose. If you find one, loosen the clamp that attaches the heater hose to the fitting, then twist and pull the heater hose off its fitting.

Models with power steering: The power steering pump is just above the fitting where the lower radiator hose connects to the water pump. In other words, it's right in the way, making the clamp difficult to remove. Use a long screwdriver or 10mm socket on the end of a long extension to reach it. When installing the hose, orient the clamp so the screw is in the most accessible position.

EVERYONE: Completely loosen the hose clamps on each end of the hose you're removing and slide them away from the ends. Hold the hose tightly near one of it's ends and give it a few good twists to break it loose from the fitting. Do the same on the other end, then pull and wiggle the hose off. If you're replacing the hose and it won't come off easily, cut the hose off with a sharp knife. Don't use a screwdriver to lever a hose off, especially if it's stuck hard onto the radiator. You may damage the radiator (it's made of soft stuff). Save the clamps if they're good.

Step 3. Install Radiator Hoses.

When the old hose is off, clean the fittings with a wire brush or emery cloth until they're smooth. Slip the hose clamps onto the center of the new hose. Put them on so you can get to the screw with a screwdriver or wrench when they're in the installed position. Moisten the inside of the hose with water or antifreeze and slide the hose onto its fittings. There's probably a small lump of metal that will stop the hose when it's on far enough. Push the clamps into place past the raised bead on the fitting, but not closer than 1/8" to the end of the hose. Tighten the clamps with your screwdriver or wrench.

4WD models: If you removed the lower radiator hose and the heater hose was attached to it, fit the heater hose onto its fitting, then position and tighten the clamp. Also remove the plastic "shower cap" if you covered the alternator.

EVERYONE: If you drained the radiator and/or engine block, tighten the radiator and/or the engine block **drain valve(s)**, then install the coolant (Procedure 3, Step 3). Run the engine for a few minutes with the radiator cap off to allow trapped air to escape, then add more coolant if necessary. Install the radiator cap and run the engine while you check for leaks. Look for coolant oozing out around the ends of the hose. Check the coolant level again after driving a few miles.

Step 4. Locate and Check Heater Hoses.

Don't confuse the heater hoses with the similar sized hose that connects the intake manifold to the large round black Master Vac (brake booster) located near the left rear corner of the engine compartment, just behind the brake master cylinder. Also, if you have air conditioning, don't confuse the two heater hoses with one or two air conditioning hoses that go from the right side of the firewall to the air conditioning compressor on the right front of the engine. Be sure and check all of the heater hoses.

'75-'78 models: A short heater hose attached to a fitting on the firewall near the right rear corner of the engine connects to a fitting on the intake manifold. A long heater hose is attached to a fitting on the firewall right next to the brake booster. The other end of the hose connects to a fitting on the lower left side of the radiator next to the lower radiator hose.

'79-'87 models: Locate the **heater control valve** on the firewall just above the rear of the engine. The valve is either brass or grey plastic. A short hose goes from the valve to a fitting on the firewall just to the right of the valve.

Follow the other hose attached to the valve to where it connects to a pipe mounted horizontally on the firewall (earlier models) or to a pipe on the left side of the engine (later models). *Earlier models*: follow the pipe toward the right side of the engine to where it connects to a short hose. The other end of the short hose connects to yet another pipe which is connected to the right rear side of the water pump. *Later models*: the pipe curves around the rear of the engine then runs up the right side of the engine beneath the intake manifold to where it connects to the rear of the water pump. On EFI models there might be a smaller hose or two connecting the pipe to the intake manifold.

Another heater hose is attached to a fitting on the firewall near the heater control valve. The other end of the hose connects either to the lower rear side of the radiator, right next to where the lower radiator hose connects, or to a fitting on the lower radiator hose, or to a pipe near the left rear corner of the engine.

To check the heater hoses, start at the firewall and squeeze each hose every inch or so. The hoses should be firm, yet flexible, and not feel like they're cracking as you squeeze them. If they feel harder and more brittle in places, they need a fix.

Step 5. Repair or Replace Heater Hoses.

To replace the heater hoses, first you'll need to drain the radiator (Procedure 3, Step 1).

Next, loosen the clamps at each end of the hose you're replacing, then wiggle or cut the hose off the fittings. If possible, get new hoses from Toyota because they're curved in just the right places so they won't rub against anything in the engine compartment. If a Toyota dealer isn't handy, take the hoses to a parts store and get replacement hoses of the same inside diameter and length as the old ones.

Use a wire brush or emery cloth to clean the metal tubes (fittings) where the hoses connect. Slip the clamps onto the new hose, push the hose onto the fittings (use water or antifreeze to make them slide on easier), then position and tighten the hose clamps.

If you drained the radiator, tighten the drain plug, then fill the radiator and reservoir with coolant (Procedure 3, Step 3). Start the engine and let it run for a few minutes with the radiator cap off so air trapped in the system can escape. Then screw on the cap and let the engine run while you check for leaks. After driving a few miles, top up the coolant level in the reservoir if need be.

Step 6. Check and Replace Bypass Hoses.

When the engine is cold and the thermostat is closed, small **bypass hoses** allow the coolant to circulate through the water jackets in the crankcase and intake manifold so the engine warms up quicker.

'75-'80 models: You have two water hoses connected to the automatic choke mechanism on the rear of the carburetor. A short hose on the driver's side of the carb connects the choke to a fitting on the intake manifold and a longer hose on the passenger's side of the carb connects the choke to a pipe below the intake manifold. Check both hoses.

EVERYONE: Some models have a hose directly under the intake manifold that connects a pipe on the rear of the water pump to another pipe which is connected to one of the heater hoses. It's a hassle, but try to feel the hose to see if it's brittle, spongy or damp from a slow leak.

Check the hoses the same way you checked the radiator and heater hoses. Some of the small ones are difficult to get to, but check them anyway and replace them *now* if they are cracked, bulging in spots, or appear to have one foot in the grave. It's a lot easier to do it now than at the side of the road with trucks splashing mud in your face. If possible, get the hoses from Toyota; they're curved in the right places so they won't rub against hot engine parts.

Need to replace them? OK, drain the radiator (Procedure 3, Step 1), then loosen the hose clamps. Twist and pull the hose off the fittings. Round up new hose clamps if yours are funky, and a new hose the same length and inside diameter as the old one. Clean the metal fittings with a wire brush or emery paper, then lubricate the inside of the hose with water or antifreeze. Slide the hose clamps onto the new hose, then slide the end of the new hose onto the fitting. Move the clamp to the end of the hose, then tighten it with a regular or phillips screwdriver.

Close the radiator drain valve, then fill the radiator with coolant (Procedure 3, Step 3). Start the engine and let it run for a few minutes with the radiator cap off. Top up the coolant, then install and tighten the radiator cap. Start the engine and check for leaks. After driving a few miles, check and add coolant to the reservoir if necessary.

PROCEDURE 3: DRAIN AND INSTALL COOLANT, FLUSH SYSTEM

Conditions: Regular maintenance; OR you just bought the car; OR the engine is overheating; OR you need to replace hoses; OR you're removing the radiator or cylinder head or engine.

Tools and Materials: Catch pan, funnel, five quarts of ethylene-glycol antifreeze, one gallon of distilled water, screw top plastic containers for disposal of the old antifreeze. Park the car so you can reach the filler neck on the radiator with a garden hose. *Optional*: On some models there's a little tube on the bottom of the radiator drain valve. If you put a 12" or longer piece of 3/16" or 1/4" inside diameter hose on the tube, you can drain the coolant into the catch pan without making a mess. Some models already have the tube.

Caution! Sweet-tasting ethylene glycol is lethal to cats, dogs, kids and other crawling things. Don't let it stand in the open; cap the old coolant and discard it. It can also stain your driveway, so be neat when draining the radiator and/or crankcase.

Don't drain the radiator or engine block while the engine is hot; the block or cylinder head might warp, or you might get burned by the hot coolant.

Step 1. Drain Radiator.

Pull the handbrake on, set the heater control to HOT, block the rear wheels, then remove the radiator cap. If the engine is hot, wait until it cools off before removing the cap or draining the coolant.

Locate the radiator **drain valve bolt**. It's a flat little plastic gizmo that sticks out toward the engine on the lower right rear corner of the radiator.

If there is a short tube pointing down between the drain valve and radiator, attach one end of a 3/16" or ¼" inside diameter hose to the tube and stick the other end in the drain pan—less mess this way. There might already be a hose there on later models. If you don't have the right size hose or there's no tube on your drain valve, just slide the catch pan under the valve and catch as much coolant as possible when you open the valve.

Unscrew the drain valve *counterclockwise* as viewed from the rear of the truck. If you can't move it with your fingers, use pliers, but don't force it. The drain valve is a plastic bolt with a slot in it. The more you unscrew it the faster the coolant will drain. If you don't have a plastic hose fitting on the drain plug, you can loosen it a few turns to get a steady flow, then set the bolt so the stream is aimed at the drain pan. If you're not trying to catch or save the coolant, you can remove the bolt completely. Be careful not to lose the rubber washer that fits between the bolt and radiator. Peel it off the radiator if it's stuck there. After the radiator has drained, pour the old coolant in screw top plastic containers and put them in the trash. Don't pour it down the drain.

If you aren't going to drain the crankcase, skip down to Step 3.

Step 2. Drain Engine Crankcase and Flush System.

The engine is cool, right? Remove the cap from the top of the radiator.

The brass 14mm crankcase drain plug is located on the left rear side of the engine, beneath the exhaust manifold. It's screwed into a 17mm brass fitting which is screwed into the engine block. To get to it you have to either crawl under the truck or reach it through the left front wheel well. (Lift up on the little rubber flap between the body and frame to see it.)

Use a 14mm socket, extension and ratchet to remove the plug. If the larger part of the fitting instead of the plug starts unscrewing, hold it with a 17mm wrench while you remove the plug. Let the coolant drain.

If you're replacing the antifreeze, what's left of the old coolant should be flushed out of the radiator, crankcase and reservoir. Here's how: Stick the garden hose into the radiator and turn the water on enough to keep the radiator full while washing the crud out of the engine. Water should be coming out of the crankcase and radiator drain valves. Use a screwdriver or piece of wire to open the drain holes if they get plugged with crud that's on the way out.

When the water flowing out of the drain valves is clear, turn the hose off and let the water drain from the radiator and crankcase. When the flow stops, install and tighten the drain plug in the crankcase. Install and tighten the plastic radiator drain bolt and rubber washer.

If you're flushing the system, use a baster or syringe to suck the old coolant out of the plastic reservoir. No baster or syringe? Remove the bolt(s) that attach the reservoir to the body. If your coolant reservoir is attached to the windshield washer reservoir, disconnect the wires to the washer. Remove the lid on the coolant reservoir, then pour the old fluid into the catch pan. Use a clean rag on the end of a screwdriver to remove any crud in the bottom of the reservoir. Install the reservoir(s) if you removed it/them, then reconnect the wires to the washer, if you disconnected them.

Step 3 covers filling the system with fresh coolant.

Step 3. Install Coolant.

Install and tighten the radiator and crankcase drain plug bolts. Drain plugs tight?

I recommend using fresh antifreeze every time the radiator and/or engine block is drained. However, if you're short on bucks and must use the same coolant again, it's a good idea to filter it through a fine screen as you pour it into the radiator. At least fish out the big chunks of grease, sticks, leaves, $100 bills, etc. Put a clean funnel in the filler neck on top of the radiator, then pour the coolant in. Add fresh coolant until the fluid level reaches the top of the radiator. If necessary, add coolant to the reservoir until the level is between the FULL and LOW lines.

If you're changing to new antifreeze, pour five quarts of fresh antifreeze into the radiator, then fill the radiator with distilled water.

IMPORTANT! After draining and refilling the radiator and/or crankcase, start the engine and let it run a few minutes before installing the radiator cap. This allows air trapped in the system to escape. When you're satisfied no air is left in the system, fill the radiator with coolant, then install and tighten the radiator cap. Fill the reservoir halfway with antifreeze, then fill it to the FULL line with water. Install the reservoir cap.

After driving a few miles, let the engine cool off and check for leaks. Check the coolant level in the radiator and reservoir. Add some if need be (Procedure 1). Record the antifreeze change in the maintenance log at the end of Chapter 5.

PROCEDURE 4: REPLACE WATER PUMP

Symptoms of a worn out water pump are: (1) squeals up front when you first start the car in the morning; (2) the pulley on the water pump can be wiggled up and down or side to side by hand; (3) coolant leaking from the water pump. To be sure it's the pump leaking, use a small mirror to peek behind the bottom of the water pump pulley. There's a little hole in the water pump housing where coolant will leak if the seals in the water pump are worn out. You'll see drips or other signs of water residue at the hole.

Conditions: Water pump leaks; OR the pulley on the water pump feels loose, indicating worn out bearings; OR the pump squeaks and squeals when you first start the engine in the morning, then gets quieter after a few moments; as time goes by, the squeak will last longer, and longer, and longer. . .

Tools and Materials: 10mm and 12mm socket and ratchet, a short extension for the ratchet, 10mm open end wrench, regular and/or phillips screwdriver, a new or rebuilt water pump, a water-pump-to-engine mounting gasket, silicone gasket sealer. 22R-TE models will need a new air tube mounting gasket for the turbocharger.

Remark: People used to rebuild their own water pumps, but in this disposable age we just replace them with new or factory rebuilt ones.

Step 1. Drain Radiator and Crankcase.
(Procedure 3, Steps 1 and 2.)

Step 2. Remove Drive Belt(s), Fan, Fluid Coupling, Pulley.

The fan is mounted to the front of the finned, aluminum **fluid coupling**, mounted to the water pump pulley on the front of the water pump.

If you have a skid plate, remove it. Four 12mm bolts attach it to the chassis.

Models with air conditioning: Locate two metal clips located at about 4 o'clock and 8 o'clock on the rear edge of the fan shroud. Pull the outer side of the clip away from the shroud while you wiggle the clips off toward the rear. Next, find a tab sticking into a slot at the bottom of the shroud. Wiggle the tab out and the lower half of the fan shroud will pop off in your hand. Stash it where it won't get stepped on.

22R-E models: Remove the large tube across the front of the engine that connects the throttle body to the air cleaner. Just loosen the two large hose clamps, slide the hose off the throttle body, then pull the hose off the air cleaner. Cover the openings in the throttle body and air cleaner with a clean rag or paper towel and secure it with tape or rubber bands.

22R-TE models: Remove the large metal tube across the top front of the engine that connects the throttle body to the turbocharger. First disconnect the small rubber hoses from the small pipes that are attached to the large pipe. One connects to the top of the valve cover, one to the top rear side of the radiator, and the third to a small pipe on the turbocharger. Remove the two nuts that attach the tube to the left side of the turbocharger, then use a phillips screwdriver to loosen the large hose clamp on the throttle body end of the tube. Pull the hose off the throttle body, then remove the tube from the turbocharger.

22R-E and 22R-TE models: Remove the upper radiator hose from the radiator, then remove the four 10mm bolts that attach the fan shroud to the rear of the radiator. Lift the fan shroud straight up until it clears the radiator. Lay it someplace where it won't get stepped on. Now you have more room to get to the water pump.

Models with power steering: Remove the power steering drive belt (Chapter 8, Procedure 3, Step 5).

Models with air conditioning: Remove the air conditioning drive belt (Chapter 8, Procedure 3, Step 4).

EVERYONE: Remove the four 10mm nuts that attach the rear flange of the fluid coupling to the water pump

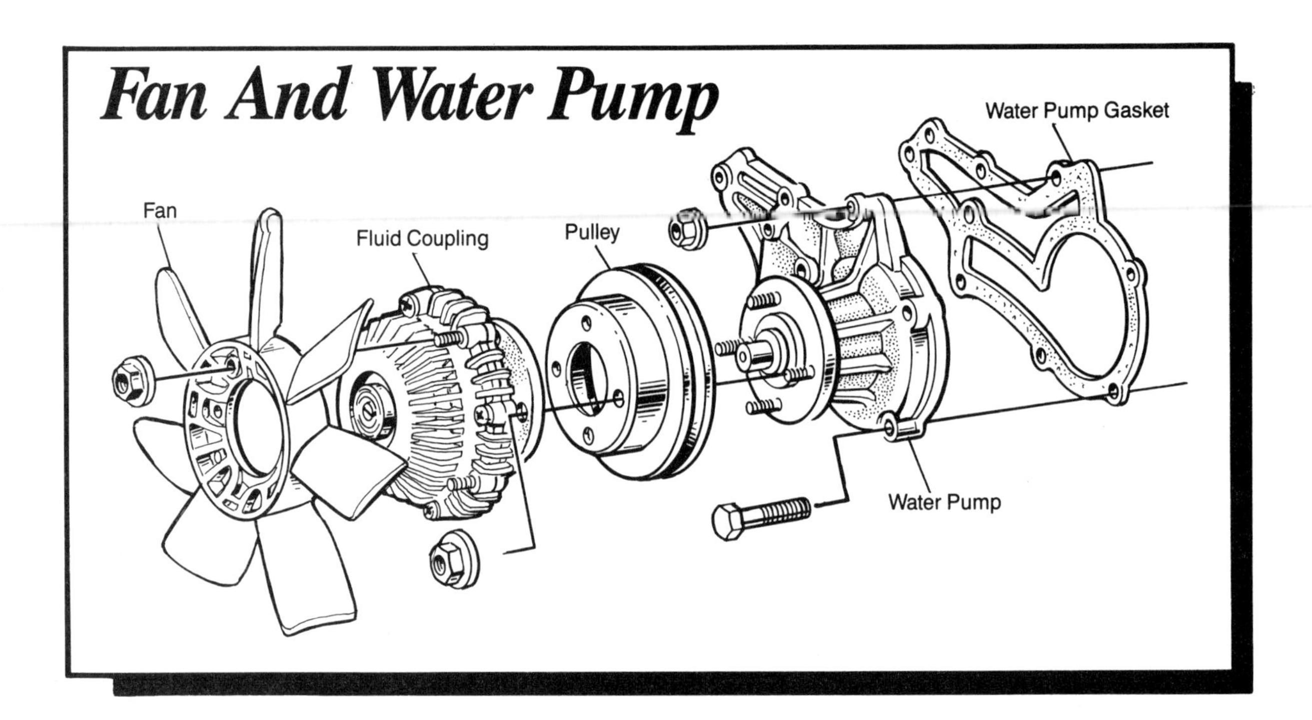

pulley. Stash the nuts someplace safe. Carefully pull the fan forward until the flange is off the studs on the water pump. Don't hit the radiator. Wiggle the fan and fluid coupling up and out of the engine compartment. You might need to disconnect the vacuum hoses from the vacuum unit on the distributor (if you have them) to make more room. Lay the fan where it won't get stepped on.

Step 3. Unbolt Water Pump.

Pull the bottom of the water pump pulley forward. This will release the tension on the drive belt. Pull the pulley off the water pump, then prop the drive belt out of the way. Unscrew the nine 10mm or 12mm bolts and nuts around the edge of the water pump. If the water pump doesn't fall off in your hand when the bolts are removed, use a hammer to gently tap on the rear of the pulley flange. Don't use a screwdriver between the water pump and block to pry the pump off. The mating surfaces might get damaged. When the pump breaks free, carefully pull the water pump off the studs. Be careful not to bang the pump against the delicate radiator.

Use a wire brush, putty knife, emery paper, dull knife blade, or whatever works, to clean the gasket surface on the engine where the water pump fits. It's the size and shape of the water pump. Be sure the gasket surface is absolutely clean and smooth. Clean the threads on the mounting bolts and studs with a wire brush, then give them a light coat of anti-seize compound or oil.

If you're installing a used water pump, clean the gasket surface on the rear of the pump the same way you cleaned the mounting surface on the engine.

Step 4. Install Water Pump.

Whether you're installing a new or used water pump, rotate the shaft sticking out of the pump to be sure it turns smoothly and quietly. Try to move the shaft side to side and in and out to check for looseness. If the shaft doesn't turn smoothly, makes noise or feels loose, have the professionals check it for you.

All's well? Put a thin even coating of silicone gasket sealer on the mating (gasket) surface of the water pump. Lay the new gasket in position on the pump, then coat the exposed side of the gasket with gasket sealer.

Fit the gasket, then the water pump, into position over the mounting studs on the engine. Install and tighten all the bolts and nuts finger tight. Put your hand on the head of the ratchet and tighten the bolts and nuts a little at a time in a crisscross pattern until they are all snug. They are small bolts, so be careful to not overtighten them.

Grab the fan and fluid coupling and give them a quick inspection. Look for cracks in the plastic fan blades and rotate the fan on the coupling to see that it turns smoothly with moderate resistance. If the fan spins freely, is loose and wobbly, or makes noises, replace the fluid coupling. If the fan is cracked or broken, replace the fan. Four 10mm nuts attach the fan to the coupling. All's well? Wiggle the fan and coupling down behind the radiator. The fan end goes toward the front. Just set them at the bottom of the radiator while you install the water pump pulley and drive belt.

Here's the quick and easy way to install the water pump pulley and drive belt. Fit the drive belt into groove on the crank pulley, the alternator pulley, and finally onto the water pump pulley. Be sure the belt is seated in the grooves of all the pulleys. Turn the water pump flange so one of the bolts is at top center. Hold the water pump pulley so a bolt hole is at top center. Tilt the top of the pulley toward the engine and slide the pulley onto the stud. You'll have to pull up on the pulley while slipping it onto the stud. It might take a few tries to get it on.

Hold the water pump pulley in place while you pick up the fan and coupling and fit the flange on the fluid coupling onto the top water pump pulley stud. Install a nut on the stud and screw it on a few turns. Push the bottom of the water pump pulley toward the engine and install the other three nuts. Use a 10mm wrench to tighten them in a crisscross pattern until they are all snug. Check the belt tension and adjust it if necessary (Chapter 8, Procedure 3, Step 2). Fit the vacuum hoses onto the vacuum unit on the distributor, if you removed them.

If you can't get the pulley on, see Chapter 8, Procedure 3, Step 2, to loosen the two alternator adjusting bolts, then push the alternator toward the engine to loosen the fan belt. Install the water pump pulley, then wiggle the fan and fluid coupling into position and slip it onto the water pump pulley. Install and tighten the four mounting nuts. You'll need to adjust the drive belt (Chapter 8, Procedure 3, Step 2). Install the vacuum hoses onto the vacuum unit on the distributor if you removed them.

Step 5. Finish the Job.

Close the radiator drain valve and install the crankcase drain plug.

If you have an air pump and/or air conditioning and/or power steering, see Chapter 8, Procedure 3, to install and adjust the drive belts.

If you removed the fan shroud, slide it into position and secure it with the four 10mm bolts. If you removed the lower part of the fan shroud, fit the tab on the bottom into the slot on the fan shroud, then wiggle the two metal clips forward until they lock into place. If you disconnected the upper radiator hose slip it onto its fitting, then position and tighten the clamp (if it's the kind you tighten).

Pour the coolant back into the radiator if it looks clean. Replace it with fresh coolant if it's over a year old, rusty brown, or has chunks of dirt, grease or a nuclear submarine floating in it (Procedure 3). Add fresh coolant until the radiator is full, then start the engine and let it run for a few minutes to let trapped air escape. Add more coolant to the radiator if necessary, then install and tighten the radiator cap. Add coolant to the reservoir if necessary.

Start the engine and check for leaks. After driving the truck a few miles, let the engine cool off, then remove the radiator cap and check the coolant level in the radiator and reservoir. Add more coolant if needed.

PROCEDURE 5: REMOVE, CHECK AND INSTALL THERMOSTAT

Condition 1: Engine overheats. The thermostat is sticking or stuck in the closed position.

Condition 2: Engine underheats. It takes a long time for the engine to warm up to normal operating temperature and the interior heater output is poor. The thermostat is AWOL or stuck in the open position.

Tools and Materials: 12mm socket, ratchet, an extension at least 4" long for the ratchet, new thermostat housing gasket, silicone gasket sealer, wire brush, rags or paper towels, knife, emery cloth, maybe a new thermostat. To test the thermostat you'll need a cooking pot and the kitchen stove.

Remark: Some coolant will be lost when you remove the thermostat housing, but not enough to warrant draining the radiator. On some models, hoses or wires across the top of the thermostat housing must be disconnected and moved aside so you can get to the housing. To avoid confusion during reassembly, use masking tape and a marker to label the hoses and wires, and whatever they are connected to before disconnecting them.

Thermostat Closed

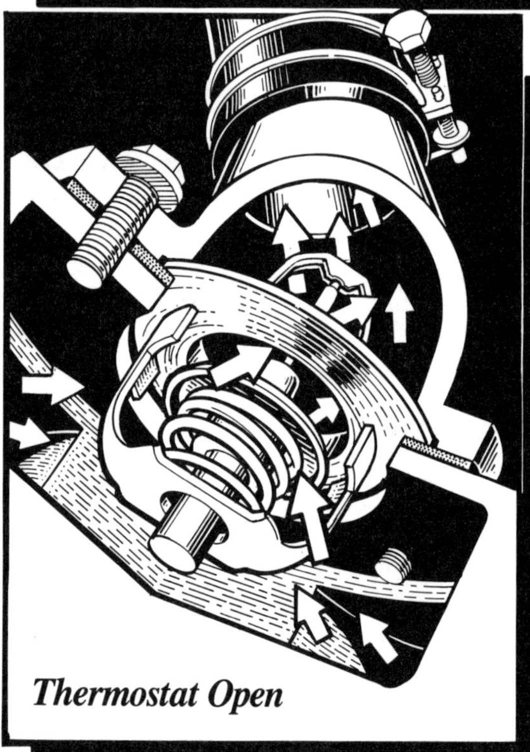

Thermostat Open

Step 1. Remove Thermostat Housing.

20R and 22R engines: Remove the **air cleaner** (Chapter 5, Procedure 6, Step 1), then cover the carburetor with a clean rag.

EVERYONE: To find the thermostat housing, follow the upper radiator hose from the top right side of the radiator to where it connects to the **intake manifold** on the engine. That rounded bulbous thing at the end of the hose is the **thermostat housing**.

There might be one or two thermosensors screwed into the top of the thermostat housing. If you have any, label the wires attached to them, "front" or "rear," then disconnect the wire(s).

If any hoses or wires connected to the intake manifold are in the way, use masking tape and marker to label them "hose 1," "hose 2," etc., and whatever they're connected to "hose fitting 1," "hose fitting 2," etc. Then disconnect them.

Loosen the hose clamps that attach the upper radiator hose to the thermostat housing and the radiator. Pull the hose off the fitting on the thermostat housing (Procedure 2). Twist the radiator end of the hose so the thermostat end of the hose is pointing up to prevent coolant from running out of the radiator.

Locate two 12mm bolts that secure the thermostat housing to the intake manifold. Make a note if other things are held in place by the bolts, then unscrew the bolts *counterclockwise*. Tap up on the hose fitting on the housing to break it free from the intake manifold. Remove the housing and gasket. The **thermostat** is that brass thing sitting in the intake manifold. Just pull it out of the manifold.

No thermostat? Some jerk left it out thinking the engine would run cooler. That's why you've been stuck with slow warmups and a weak heater. Buy a new thermostat and skip to Step 3 to install it.

Step 2. Check Thermostat.

Condition 1 (engine overheats): The thermostat may not be opening. Here's how to check it:

Put the thermostat in a cooking pot of water, put the pot on the stove and turn the heat on low. If you have a thermometer capable of checking temperatures up to 220° F (105° C), use it to monitor the water temperature. Watch the thermostat as the water heats up. The round center valve part of the thermostat should start moving toward the spring end when the water is 180-190° F (82-88° C) or as the water approaches the boiling point. This allows water to flow through the center of the thermostat (see illustration). The thermostat valve should be open about 5/16" (8mm) when the temperature reaches 203-212° F (95-100°C) or a full boiling condition. If the center valve doesn't open before the water boils, or is rusted or locked to the outer part, buy a new thermostat and install it (Step 3).

Fish the thermostat out of the cooking pot, then wash the cooking pot thoroughly with soap and water before anyone has a chance to cook in it. Antifreeze is an additive you definitely don't want in your food.

Condition 2 (engine underheats): If the engine takes a long time to warm up and the interior heater doesn't warm your toes the way it should, see if the thermostat is stuck in the open position. If the round center valve part doesn't seat against the larger round part (see illustration) when the thermostat is cool, the thermostat is broken. Buy a new thermostat and install it (Step 3).

If you live in Eskimo type country, where the temperature stays below zero frequently, you might have to cover the grille with something like cardboard, plastic or blankets to block the flow of frigid air through the radiator. If you do this, check the temperature gauge frequently to be sure the engine isn't overheating. It's easy to overcompensate.

Step 3. Install Thermostat.

Clean the gasket mating surfaces on the intake manifold and thermostat housing with a knife and emery cloth. Clean the bolt threads with a wire brush and give them a light coat of anti-seize compound or oil. Use a knife, wire brush or emery cloth to clean the hose fitting on the thermostat housing. Clean up any dirt and gasket material that might have fallen into the intake manifold. Twist the end of a rag or paper towel into a point and clean the bolt holes in the manifold. Be sure there's no antifreeze or water in the bolt holes or you won't be able to screw the bolts in all the way.

Install the thermostat in the intake manifold so the spring end is inside the manifold. Coat both sides of the new gasket with silicone gasket sealer. Be sure the gasket surface on the manifold is dry before installing the new gasket. Put the gasket on the manifold, then install the housing. Lightly coat the threads of the two 12mm bolts with anti-seize compound, then install them. Be sure any other things held by the bolts are in place, then tighten them. Install the radiator hose and tighten its clamp.

Reconnect any other hoses or wires you disconnected, then install the air cleaner if you removed it (Chapter 5, Procedure 6, Step 2).

Use water to wash off the top of the engine where coolant spilled when the hoses were disconnected. Dry the water off with rags or paper towels. Remove the radiator cap and check the coolant level. Add some if necessary.

Start the engine and let it warm up, then check for leaks. After driving a few miles, let the engine cool off and check the coolant level in the radiator. Add coolant if the level is low (Procedure 1, Step 2).

PROCEDURE 7: REMOVE AND INSTALL RADIATOR

Condition: Radiator leaks; OR you suspect the radiator is clogged; OR you're removing the engine.

Tools and Materials: 10mm and 12mm sockets, ratchet, small ratchet extension, regular and/or phillips screwdriver, catch pan. If you have an automatic transmission, you'll need a couple of baggies and rubber bands, and a can or jar. If it's time to replace the coolant, you'll need five quarts of fresh ethylene glycol antifreeze and one gallon of distilled water.

Remark: Radiators are delicate dudes, so avoid close encounters with sharp objects.

If you suspect the radiator is worn out, call radiator shops to see what recoring the radiator will cost. Also call the Toyota dealer and a few parts stores to see how much new and rebuilt radiators cost.

Step 1. Drain the Radiator.

See Procedure 3, Step 1.

Step 2. Disconnect Radiator Hoses.

See Procedure 2, Step 2.

Disconnect the upper and lower radiator hoses and prop them away from the radiator so they're out of the way.

If a heater hose is attached to the lower hose fitting on the radiator, loosen the clamp, then pull the heater hose off the fitting.

Also disconnect the small overflow hose that attaches just below the radiator cap. It's the one that connects the radiator to the coolant reservoir.

Step 3. Automatic Transmission Vehicles Only.

Two hoses from the transmission connect to the left side of the radiator. These hoses carry automatic transmission fluid from the transmission to a tank built into the radiator. The fluid is cooled in the tank, then pumped back to the transmission.

Loosen the two small hose clamps on the left side of the radiator. Use a can or jar to catch the automatic transmission fluid that will come out of the hoses and radiator. To keep dirt out of the hoses, put tape over the hose ends and secure it with rubber bands. Stick the ends of the hoses in baggies and secure them with tape or rubber bands.

Step 4. Remove Fan Shroud.

Remove the 10mm bolts that attach the fan shroud to the rear of the radiator, then set the fan shroud over the fan away from the radiator.

Step 5. Haul Out the Radiator.

Two 12mm bolts on each side of the radiator attach it to the body. Hold the top of the radiator so it can't fall against the engine while you remove the bolts *counterclockwise*. Carefully lift straight up on the radiator to remove it. It ain't heavy, brother. Don't bump it on anything.

There are **rubber pads** that fit between the radiator and body and between the radiator and mounting bolt heads. If the pads are stuck to the radiator, remove them and stash them with the mounting bolts for the fan shroud and radiator. If the pads are cracked, squished or missing, replace them with new ones.

Stash the radiator somewhere safe if you're not hauling it away to be repaired. A flattened cardboard box will protect the delicate fins and tubes during storage or transit. See ya later, radiator!

Step 6. Install Radiator.

Fit a rubber pad onto each of the four mounting bolts, then stick the bolts through their holes in the radiator. Fit four more rubber pads over the bolts. Remove the string or wire holding the air conditioner condensor if you tied it up.

Carefully lower the radiator into position and screw all four bolts in as far as you can with your fingers. Be sure all of the rubber pads are in place. Use a wrench to tighten the 12mm bolts.

Fit the **fan shroud** onto the radiator, then install and tighten the 10mm bolts.

Install the upper and lower radiator hoses, and the heater hose (if you removed it), and reconnect the small overflow hose to the radiator.

Automatic Transmission people: Connect the two hoses to the left side of the radiator. Tighten the clamps.

EVERYONE: Tighten the radiator drain plug, then fill the radiator with fresh coolant (Procedure 3, Step 3). Start the engine and let it warm up to operating temperature while you check for leaks. Check the coolant level in the radiator after the engine has warmed up and then cooled off. Add coolant if necessary. Check the level again after driving a few miles.

Automatic Transmission people: Check the automatic transmission fluid level after driving a few miles (Chapter 5, Procedure 2, Step 2).

CHAPTER 7
BRAKES

"The ability to stop is often more important than any other capability—humans, cars, what-have-yous. Do a good slow solid job on your brakes."

—John Muir

Caution! Warning! Wear a dust mask or respirator while working on the brakes and don't breathe any of the black brake dust. It can cause cancer if inhaled too often. Before removing brake drums or calipers, spread newspapers under the wheel to catch the accumulated dust. As you remove brake drums, dump the dust onto the newspaper then fold the newspaper so the dust is safely wrapped inside. Secure it with a rubber band or piece of string and put it in the trash, then put a fresh newspaper under the wheel. After handling brake parts, wash your hands before eating or smoking anything.

DON'T press on the brake pedal while a brake drum or the front pads are removed: the pistons might shoot out of the wheel cylinders like cannonballs and you'll have a nasty mess to clean up!

HOW THEY WORK

Your Toyota has two brake systems that work independently of each other—a **hydraulic system** and a **mechanical system**. The hydraulic system is operated by applying pressure on the brake pedal with your foot. As Archimedes says, the pressure in an interconnected fluid system is the same in all parts of the system, so the pressure you put on the pedal is transmitted equally to the brakes on all four wheels. The mechanical system is operated by pulling on the "emergency" **handbrake lever** located below the dashboard. Only the rear brakes are activated by the mechanical handbrake system.

Let's go through the hydraulic system first. When you push on the brake pedal with your foot (ear, nose or whatever), a rod attached to the pedal is moved into the **master cylinder** bolted to the firewall in the engine compartment. The rod pushes against two **pistons** located inside the master cylinder. The pistons are fitted with rubber seals that form an air/fluid-tight seal against the smooth walls of the master cylinder. When the plungers are forced forward by the rod attached to the brake pedal, pressure is created in the hydraulic fluid inside the master cylinder. It's like a hypodermic syringe—a plunger forces fluid into a hollow metal tube. The **brake lines** are hollow metal tubes that carry the hydraulic pressure to **wheel cylinders** at each of the four wheels. These wheel (or "slave") cylinders are bolted to brackets near the end of each axle. A short rubber **brake hose** takes the place of the metal lines near each wheel, allowing the wheels to move up and down and the front wheels to turn right and left.

The master cylinder on your truck is called a tandem master cylinder because there are two separate hydraulic circuits in the master cylinder body. The primary circuit operates the front brakes and the secondary circuit operates the rear brakes. If a seal in the master cylinder or wheel cylinder of one of the circuits breaks, the other circuit still provides 50 percent of the normal braking action—you just have to press harder on the pedal. It's like having a safety net.

A **Master Vac** unit is located between the brake pedal and the master cylinder. The pretentiously named Master Vac uses vacuum from the engine's intake manifold to reduce the amount of brake pedal pressure needed to stop the car.

1979-83 4WD, ¾ ton and C&C models, and all '84-'87 models have a **load sensing valve** that senses the weight of the load in the truck, then proportions the braking pressure to the front and rear wheels so they engage with maximum efficiency. Testing the load sensing valve requires special equipment, so if your front and rear

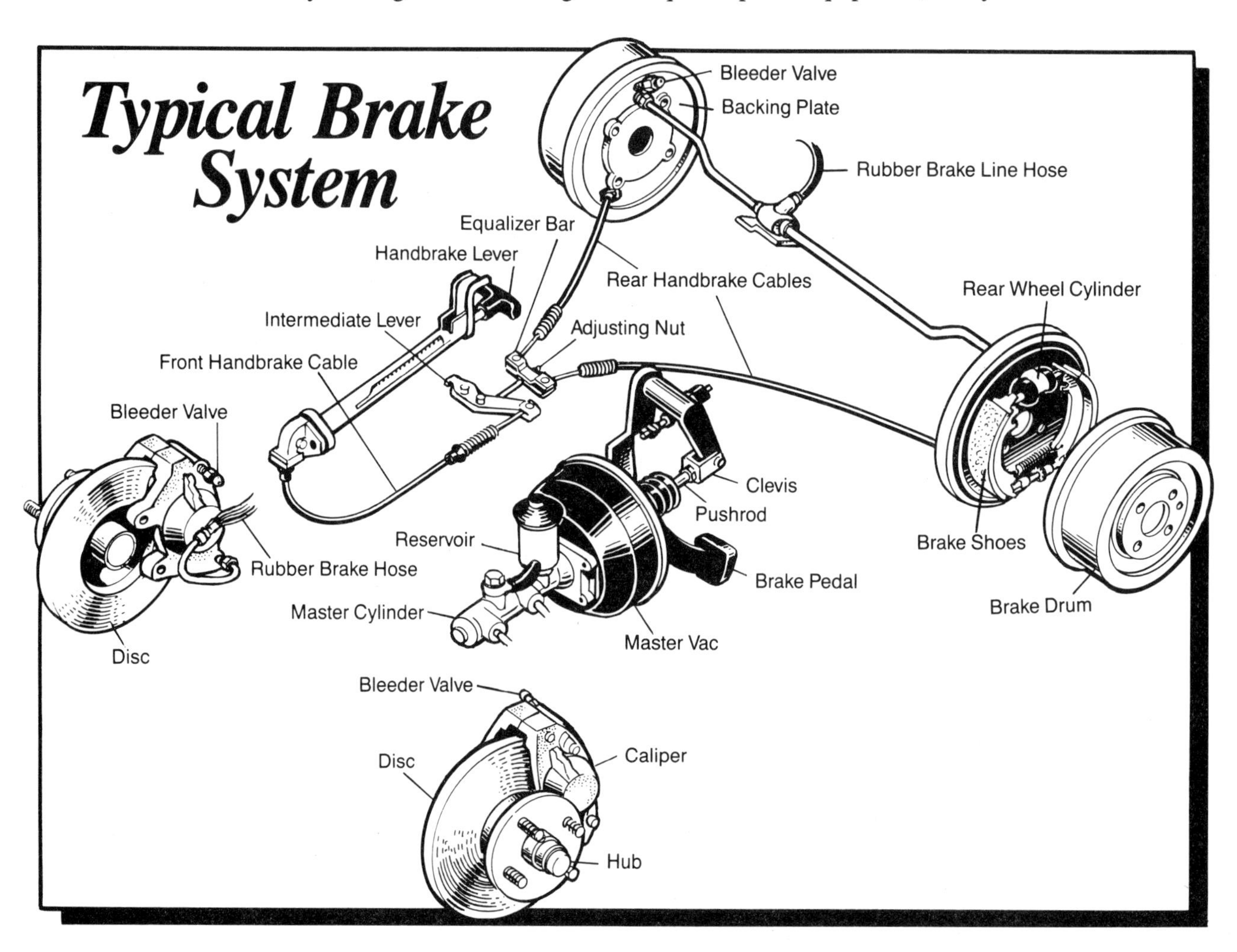

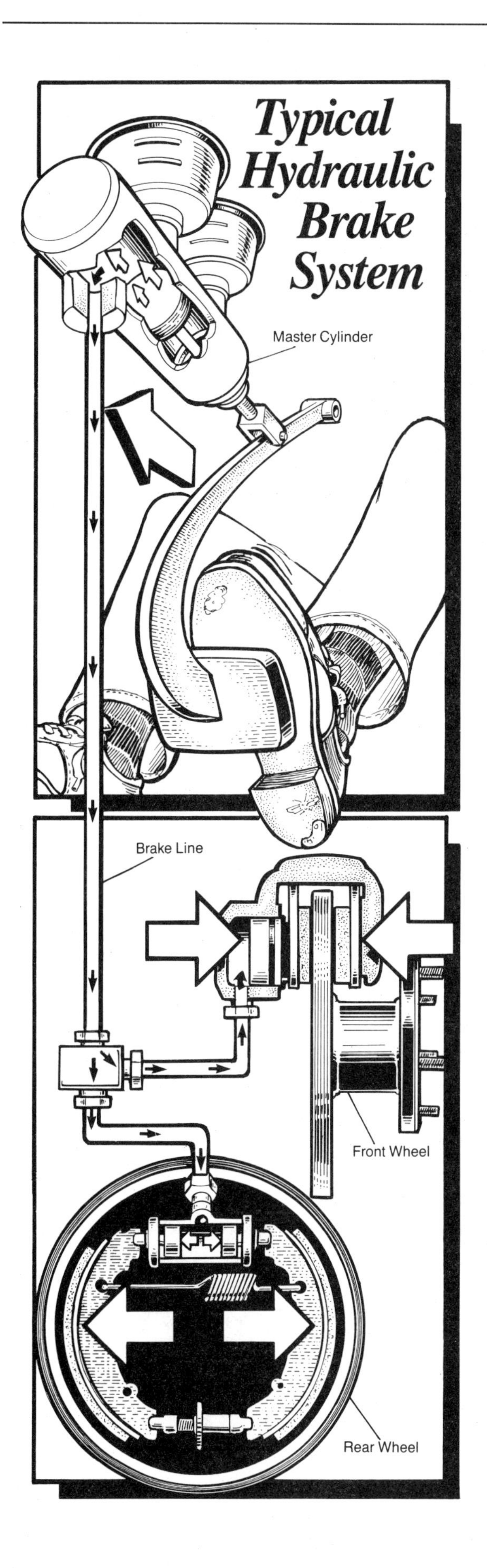

brakes don't grab at the same time, take the truck to the Toyota dealer and have them test the valve and replace it if necessary.

On '75-'78 models **brake failure switches** are incorporated into the brake system. When the pressure in one of the hydraulic circuits is less than the pressure in the other circuit, a red light on the dash lights up. The same light reminds you that the handbrake is on. In 1979 Toyota changed to a **low brake fluid warning** system. The brake fluid reservoir cap has a switch that lights the brake warning light on the dash if the fluid level is low.

Here's how your outside **brake lights** work. A switch for the brake lights is mounted to a bracket near the top of the brake pedal. When the pedal is pushed away from the switch, the rear brake lights light up.

When there's friction, there's also wear and tear. Naturally it's best to have one surface (the cheaper one) wear out before the other. That's why replaceable *asbestos compound* brake pads and brake shoe linings are softer than the metal discs and drums they rub against. Eventually the brake pad and shoe linings wear thin and must be replaced.

For the brake system to operate at maximum efficiency, the brake shoes and pads must ride as close to the drums and discs as possible. The brakes, be they drum or disc, are self-adjusting so no manual adjustment is necessary (except when the rear brake shoes are replaced). Nice for us lazy people.

The front brakes on your truck do most of the stopping for you, so the front pads wear out faster than the rear shoes. I tend to go through two or three sets of front pads before I need a new set of rear shoes.

There are two types of hydraulic brake system used on Toyotas—**drum brakes** on the rear wheels and **disc brakes** on the front. I'll describe the drum-type first.

Drum Brakes: When the hydraulic pressure reaches a rear wheel cylinder, it forces two plungers inside the wheel cylinder to move outward against the tops of two **brake shoes**. The plungers in the wheel cylinders are fitted with rubber seals to form an air/fluid-tight seal, just like the master cylinder. The shoes are hinged at the bottom and secured to a **backing plate** by a pin. The brake shoes move outward and contact a heavy steel **brake drum** bolted to the wheel. Friction created by the brake shoe rubbing against the rotating brake drum makes it harder for the wheel to turn, thus slowing the car. This happens at all four wheels at the same time. **Brake springs** attached between the two brake shoes pull the shoes back away from the brake drum when the pressure is released from the brake pedal.

There are two different types of rear brakes on Toyota trucks; **duo-servo** and **leading/trailing**. Both work essentially the same way—brake fluid pressure in the wheel cylinder forces the shoes outward against the brake drums to slow the vehicle. However, the various components within the two types are quite different, so be sure you're following the directions for your particular year and model.

You'll find duo-servo brakes on all '75-'78 models, '79-'85 4WD, and '79-'87 Cab and Chassis (C&C) models. Due to special tools and expertise required, replacing and repairing the rear brakes on '86-'87 Cab and Chassis models with dual rear wheels is not covered in this manual.

Leading/trailing rear brakes are fitted on all '79-'87 2WD models except Cab and Chassis models (they have the duo-servo type), and on '86-'87 4WD models.

Disc Brakes: With disc brakes, the wheel is bolted to a heavy steel **disc**. Together they rotate on roller bearings on the axle. Bolted to each axle is a brake **caliper**. Depending on the year and model, each caliper has one, two or four **wheel cylinders** and two **brake pads**. The calipers are designed so the brake pads are on opposite sides of the disc.

Models with one wheel cylinder in each caliper are called "floating calipers." Here's how they work. When hydraulic pressure from the master cylinder reaches a front wheel cylinder, it presses the pad next to the wheel cylinder against the rotating steel disc. The pressure of the pad against the disc causes the caliper to move slightly ("'float") so the pad on the opposite side is pulled against the disc. If the wheel is turning, friction results as the disc is squeezed between the two pads. It's like clamping a phonograph record in a vise. The friction, or drag, slows the car.

On models with two or four wheel cylinders in the calipers, the caliper is attached solidly to a mounting bracket. The wheel cylinders are opposite and facing each other with the disc pads and disc between them. Hydraulic pressure from the master cylinder forces the pistons in the wheel cylinders toward each other, thus squeezing the disc between the pads.

On most models, changing the brake pads and removing the caliper for repair or replacement is as easy as making toast. On the other models it's as easy as making French toast. Rebuilding the calipers is very tedious and difficult and should be left to the professionals.

THE HANDBRAKE SYSTEM

The **mechanical handbrake system** (also called the emergency or parking brake) works when you pull on the **handbrake lever** beneath the dash. The handbrake lever is held up (brake ON) by a notched locking arrangement: pawl teeth fall into notches on the top side of the lever. When the handbrake lever is pulled, the lever pulls on a **cable** that is attached to an equalizer bar beneath the truck. Cables attached to the equalizer bar are attached directly to the rear brake shoes and apply those brakes.

The handbrake usually needs to be adjusted (tightened) after the brake drums have been "turned" at a machine shop. Installing new brake drums might necessitate loosening the handbrake cables a little.

When you park, set the handbrake before releasing the clutch (manual transmission cars) or before putting the automatic shift lever in PARK. This way no strain is put on the drivetrain and things last longer. If you're ever cruising down the road and (gulp!) the brake pedal goes to the floor when you press on it, DON'T PANIC. Just gently use the handbrake lever to slow you down. It's unlikely this will ever happen to you, thanks to the dual master cylinder.

Since almost every brake procedure involves jacking up the car, please read the safety precautions in Chapter 2.

PROCEDURE 1: BLEED BRAKES

The purpose of bleeding the hydraulic system is to eliminate all air bubbles and air pockets in the system. This is accomplished by forcing brake fluid into the system from the master cylinder and forcing air and water out through the **bleeder valves** located on the wheel cylinders. Seems like blood should squirt out but it never does.

Check the fluid level in the master cylinder reservoir(s) frequently while you're bleeding the brakes. Never let the fluid go below the MIN line. If the level gets too low, air will get pumped into the system and you'll have to start all over.

Bleed the brakes in this order: Start with the right rear wheel, then bleed the left rear wheel. Move to the front of the truck and bleed the right front, then the left front. On '79-'83 4WD, ¾ ton and C&C models, and all '84-87 models, after the wheel cylinders have been bled, see Step 7 to bleed the load sensing proportioning valve (LSPV).

If you're replacing the brake fluid (Procedure 2), keep bleeding each wheel cylinder until the fluid flowing through the plastic tube is clear and has no bubbles in it. Don't forget to check the reservoir frequently to be sure it doesn't run dry.

Read all the way through the brake bleeding steps before you do them. They go too fast to thumb through while you're under the car.

Condition: The brake pedal feels spongy or mushy and it takes a few pumps on the pedal before any braking action occurs; OR some part of the hydraulic system has been opened for inspection or repair; OR you are replacing the brake fluid.

Tools and Materials: Pint of DOT3 or 4 brake fluid, small glass jar with lid, at least 18 inches of 3/16in inside diameter clear plastic hose (old suction tubing from a hospital works well), 10mm box end wrench, safety glasses, jack, jackstands, a Friend who can hear and is willing to follow your instructions. My son has been helping me bleed brakes since he was three years old.

Remarks: Wear safety glasses while you bleed the brakes and be careful not to get any brake fluid in your mouth—it's extremely poisonous. Use the glass jar to catch the used brake fluid, then properly dispose of it. Brake fluid also ruins paint; if any gets on the car, wipe it off immediately and wash the spot with warm soapy water.

Caution! Brake fluid is like a magnet for moisture in the air. On a humid day an open can of brake fluid can become contaminated within a few minutes, so keep the can of brake fluid tightly sealed and the reservoir caps on except when adding fluid.

Don't reuse fluid pumped out during the bleeding process. It's become aerated (full of tiny bubbles) and thus useless.

If you're stuck on the road, you can bleed the brakes without the glass jar or plastic hose. Hold a rag over the end of the bleeding nipple to keep the fluid off the tires and out of your eyes. Do it this way only in a real pinch.

Step 1. Chock, Jack, Block, Remove Wheels.

Raising the vehicle usually isn't necessary just to bleed the brakes. However, if this is your first time through this procedure it might make things a little easier. So, if you are going to remove the wheels, park on level ground, put the gearshift lever in FIRST (manual) or PARK (automatics) and chock the wheels on the opposite end. Loosen the lug nuts a little, then jack up the end you are getting ready to bleed. Lower the truck onto jackstands, then remove the wheels.

Step 2. Bleed Master Cylinder.

You only need to do this step if you've disconnected brake lines from the master cylinder, or if the brake fluid reservoir has become completely empty.

Everyone except '85-'87 ½ ton and 4WD models with 22R-TE engines: To bleed the master cylinder, first bleed the right front, then the left front wheel cylinder (Steps 4-6). Then bleed all four brakes in the normal brake bleeding sequence.

'85-'87 ½ ton and 4WD models with 22R-TE engines: Fit a flare nut wrench onto one of the brake line fittings on the side of the master cylinder. Leave the wrench on the fitting while you wrap a rag around the fitting. Have Friend push down on the brake pedal while you loosen the fitting about half a turn. When Friend's foot reaches the floor, tighten the fitting. Repeat this four times, then tighten the fitting. Bleed the other brake line fitting on the master cylinder the same way.

Toss the rag in the trash and use warm soapy water to wash off any brake fluid that dripped on the paint. You'll be sorry if you don't.

Step 3. Adjust Rear Brakes.

If you've installed new rear brake shoes, adjust the rear brakes before bleeding the brake system (Procedure 7).

Step 4. Check Brake Fluid Level.

The **brake fluid reservoir(s)** are on top of the master cylinder. To keep dirt out of the brake fluid, clean the cap(s) and reservoir(s) with a clean rag before removing the cap(s). Lay the cap(s) somewhere clean and cover them with a clean rag or paper towel. Look for two lines on the side of each reservoir marked MIN (minimum) and MAX (maximum). Fill the master cylinder reservoir(s) to the MAX line with fresh DOT3 or 4 brake fluid, then put the reservoir cap(s) on.

Step 5. Locate Bleeder Valves.

Bleeder valves look like hollow bolts that screw into the wheel cylinders. They are usually covered with a rubber cap and tend to be rather fragile, so be sure you use a box end wrench when loosening and tightening them. Open end wrenches quickly round off the corners and leave you unable to bleed!

The bleeder valves for the rear drum brakes are at the top of the brake backing plate and rather difficult to reach.

On disc brakes the bleeder valves are located near the top on the inboard side of the calipers. They can be reached by turning the wheels in the opposite direction from the side of the car you're working on. However, it's easier to reach the bleeder with the wheel off—especially the first time.

Step 6. Bleed 'em.

If the master cylinder has been replaced or the reservoir(s) have become completely empty of fluid, first do Step 2 to bleed the master cylinder. If the master cylinder hasn't been replaced or run out of fluid, start here and bleed all four wheel cylinders.

Put on your safety glasses. Find the bleeder valve on the right rear wheel and peel off the **rubber cap**, if there is one. Position the box end of a 10mm wrench over the bleeder valve so the valve can be opened *counterclockwise* at least a quarter turn, but don't open it yet. Slip one end of the clear plastic hose over the end of the bleeder valve nipple and stick the other end of the hose into the glass jar. Pour about one inch of fresh brake fluid into the jar and check to see that the end of the tube is submerged in the fluid.

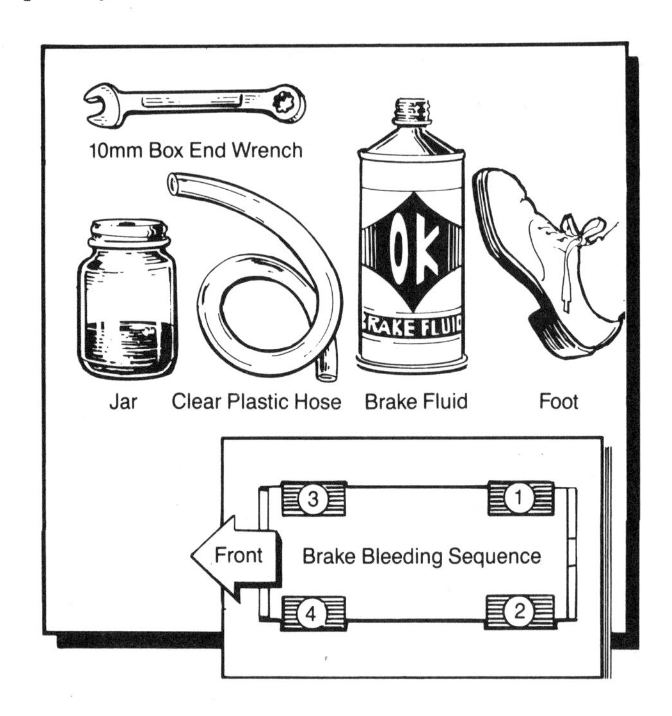

Bleeding the brakes is a team sport, so you and your Friend should read and practice the next five

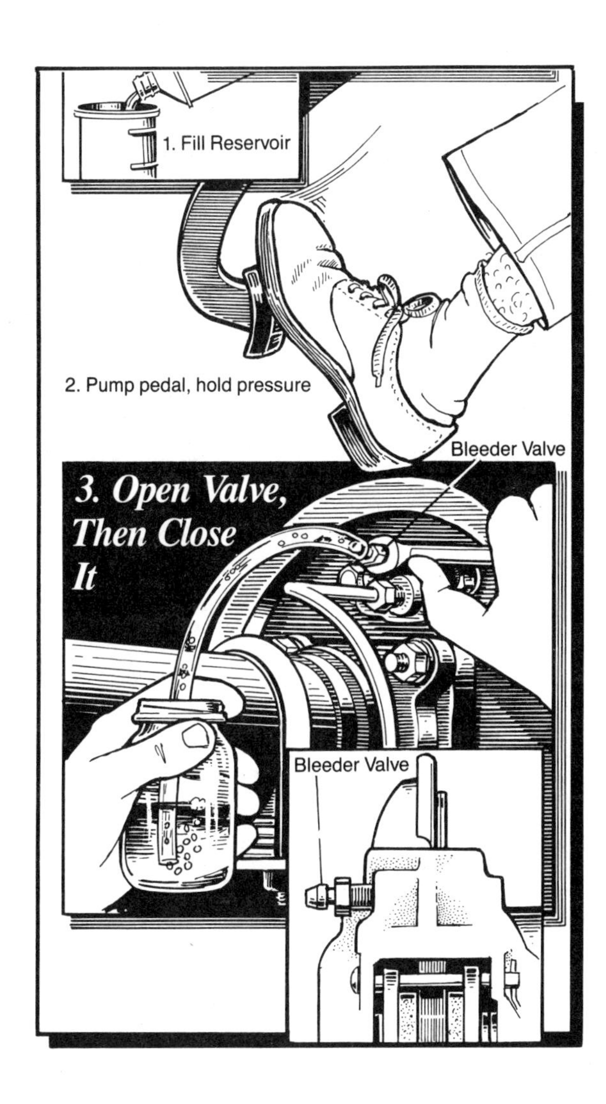

sub-steps at least once before bleeding the brakes for real.

A. Friend slowly pumps the brake pedal about ten times, then, while holding his or her foot firmly on the pedal, yells, "READY!"

B. When you yell, "DOWN," Friend presses on the brake pedal while you open the bleed valve at least a quarter turn (*counterclockwise*). You'll watch fluid and maybe some air bubbles coming out of the bleeder valve as Friend's foot forces the pedal to the floor and HOLDS IT DOWN. When it hits the floor Friend yells, "IT'S DOWN."

C. When Friend yells, "IT'S DOWN," you quickly close the bleeder valve by tightening it (*clockwise*). When the valve is closed, yell, "UP," at friend.

D. Friend slowly lets the pedal come up to its normal position, then yells, "IT'S UP." If the pedal is released while the bleeder valve is open, air or used fluid will be sucked into the system. Don't panic, just repeat A through E.

E. Have Friend check the fluid level in the reservoir after you've done B, C and D three or four times. Fill it to the MAX line, then repeat steps B through E until no bubbles can be seen coming out of the bleeder valve. It might only take two times, or it could take several.

When you're sure all the bubbles are gone (and the fluid is clear if you're here from Procedure 2 to replace it), make sure the bleeder valve is closed tight. Install the little rubber cap if there was one and wipe up any fluid that might have spilled. Move on to the next wheel and try not to think about how silly you and your friend sound to the neighbors. Bleed all four wheel cylinders.

Step 7. Bleed Load Sensing Valve.

'79-'83 4WD, ¾ ton and C&C models, and all '84-'87 models: After all four wheel cylinders have been bled, bleed the load sensing valve (LSV). The way to find the LSV is to follow the brake lines from the rear wheels to where the rubber brake line attaches to the LSV.

2WD models: You'll see a bleeder valve similar to those on the wheel cylinders. Bleed the valve just like the wheel cylinders.

4WD models: The bleeder bolt looks like an ordinary bolt and is located just below the nipple where you attach the hose. Attach the clear plastic tube to the bleeder nipple just above the bleeder bolt and bleed the valve until no air bubbles can be seen.

Step 8. Do This and That.

Fill the reservoir(s) to the MAX line (or to the dotted line just below the MAX line, if you have it) with fresh brake fluid, then install the cap(s). If there are wires attached to the cap(s), reconnect them securely to the wiring harness.

If you removed any wheels, install them and snug down the lug nuts. Lower the car and torque the lug nuts to 65-87 ft.lbs. Lower the hood and be sure it's latched securely. If you changed the brake fluid, record it in the log at the end of Chapter 5. Thanks.

Step 9. Clean Up.

Put the lid on the jar of old brake fluid and throw it away—never reuse brake fluid. And never store anything but brake fluid in a brake fluid can, or someone might accidentally use it thinking it's brake fluid, with bad to fatal results. Keep spare cans of brake fluid tightly sealed so the fluid can't be contaminated by moisture in the air.

PROCEDURE 2: CHANGE HYDRAULIC BRAKE FLUID

Condition: You just bought the truck; OR you're doing the 12,000 mile maintenance.

Tools and Materials: Same as for bleeding the brakes (Procedure 1) except three pints of brake fluid will be needed, plus something like a syringe or turkey baster to suck the fluid out of the brake fluid reservoir(s). If you can't find a sucking tool, you can dip clean paper towels or rags into the reservoir(s) to sop up the brake fluid.

Remarks: This procedure is usually performed in shops with a machine called a *pressure bleeder*, but we can do it without one. Read Procedure 1 before performing this procedure.

Brake fluid absorbs water, which hastens the demise of the wheel cylinders and master cylinder. Changing the brake fluid regularly will save you money in the long run and make your car safer to drive—a nice combination.

Step 1. Drain Master Cylinder Reservoirs.

If there is a wire attached to the top of the reservoir cap, follow the wire to a connector located a few inches from the reservoir and disconnect the wires.

Clean each master cylinder reservoir cap to prevent dirt from falling into the reservoir, then remove the cap and the little *strainer basket* that's inside the reservoir. There might also be round rubber floats in the reservoir(s). Store the cap(s), strainer(s) and float(s) in a clean, safe location while you change the brake fluid.

Use a clean syringe or turkey baster to suck the fluid out of the reservoir(s) until the fluid level reaches the aluminum part at the bottom of the master cylinder. Be sure to leave a little fluid in the master cylinder. No syringe? It's a little messy, but you can use clean paper towels or rags to soak up the fluid. Be sure to leave a little fluid in the reservoir. Toss the towels or rags in the trash. Wash off any brake fluid that drips on the paint.

Use a clean rag to clean the inside of the reservoir(s), the strainer(s), and the floats if you have them. Install the strainers in the reservoir(s), then drop in the floats if you have them. Fill the reservoir(s) to the MAX line with fresh brake fluid, then do Step 2 below.

Step 2. Bleed Wheel Cylinders.

Bleed each wheel cylinder in the sequence described in Procedure 1. Start with fluid in the master cylinder reservoir at the MAX line and bleed each wheel cylinder until the fluid is at the MIN line. Keep filling the reservoir and bleeding the wheel cylinder until the brake fluid flowing through the plastic hose is nice and clear. It will probably take two to three reservoirs of fluid for each rear wheel and one or two reservoirs for front wheels. Be sure to tighten the bleeder valves and install the rubber dust caps when you're through bleeding.

Do Procedure 1, Steps 8 and 9 to finish the job.

PROCEDURE 3: CHECK FRONT BRAKES FOR WEAR

Condition: 6,000 mile maintenance; OR you just bought the truck; OR the front brakes are squealing like a ruptured pig.

Tools and Materials: Safety glasses, dust mask, small tape measure or ruler, jack, jackstands.

Caution: Avoid getting grease, brake fluid, or anything but water or brake cleaner on the disc and brake pads.

Remark: After doing this procedure a couple of times you'll know what the disc brake pads and the wear grooves (if your pads have them) look like, so at 6,000 miles you can probably check the pads without removing the wheels. Just turn the wheels toward the opposite side of the truck from the side you're checking, then peek around the rear edge of the tire to check the pads. I recommend removing the wheels so you can thoroughly check the disc, calipers and brake hoses at least every 12,000 miles.

Step 1. Chock, Jack, Block and Remove Front Wheels.

Turn the ignition key to *unlock* the steering wheel, then turn the front wheels in the *opposite* direction from the side you're going to check, then turn the key to OFF. In other words, turn them so you have access to the rear of the wheel. Block the rear wheels, set the handbrake, put the gearshift in FIRST (manual) or PARK (automatics), then loosen the front lug nuts a little. Jack the truck up and put it on jackstands (Chapter 2), then remove the wheels.

Step 2. Identify Disc Brake Components.

Rotate the disc by using the lug bolts to turn it. It should turn fairly easily by hand. The big flat shiny surface that rotates with the axle is the *disc* (sometimes called the rotor). The large lumpy looking hunk of metal the disc passes through is the *caliper*.

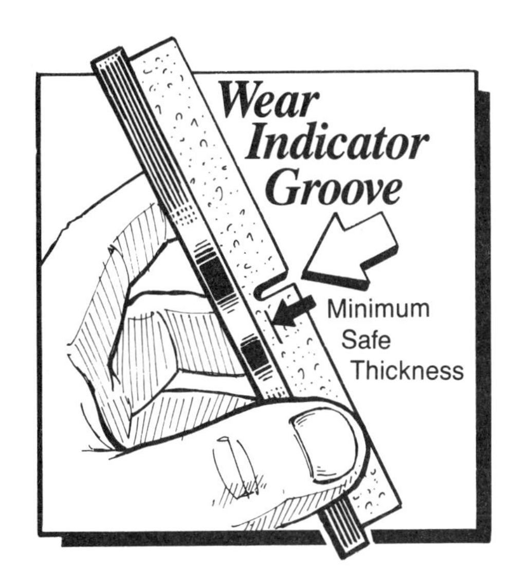

Step 3. Measure Pad Thickness.

The caliper has an *inspection hole* in the rear for checking pad wear. Look through the hole while rotating the axle so you can see which part is the moving disc. On either side of the disc is a brake pad. Most pads have a slot in the middle that serves as a *wear indicator*. When the pads wear to the bottom of the slot it's time to change pads. If your pads don't have wear indicator slots, cut a strip of paper 1/16" wide to measure the pad thickness. Look at the illustration to see where to measure pad thickness. DON'T include the metal backing plate in your measurement. If the pad thickness is less than 1/16" (1.5mm), it's time for new pads (Procedure 4). Just to be safe, I change my pads when they're down to 1/8".

Step 4. Check Disc.

Run a clean fingernail over the disc surface to check for grooves. Does your nail hang up on ridges and scoring? If so, the disc should be removed and machined ("turned") to make it smooth again (Procedure 5).

Step 5. Examine Brake Hoses.

Inspect the rubber brake hoses attached somewhere between the body and the calipers. Replace the hoses if they are hard, cracked, split, or bulging in places (Procedure 11).

Step 6. Check Brakes on Opposite Side.

Turn the ignition key so the steering wheel is unlocked, then turn the front wheels in the opposite direction. Turn the key off. Check the front brakes on the other side of the car. If the pads need replacing, do Procedure 4.

Step 7. Put It All Back Together.

If everything is OK, put the wheel back on, lower the truck, torque the lug nuts to 65-87 ft.lbs., then install the hubcap if you removed it.

PROCEDURE 4: CHANGE FRONT DISC BRAKE PADS

Read the **Caution! Warning!** in the introduction to this chapter.

ABOUT BRAKE PADS (Read Before You Begin!)

When buying replacement pads for disc brakes, you can often choose between *regular pads* that are quieter but wear out faster, or harder *semi-metallic pads* that tend to squeal more but last longer. The semi-metallic pads also seem to wear out the disc faster than the regular pads. The regular pads are fine for normal driving, but if you're a leadfoot or do a lot of high speed freeway cruising or mountain driving, the semi-metallic pads might be best for you. The choice is yours.

To be sure you're getting the right pads, have your chassis number and production date with you when you trek to the parts department. Before installing the pads, carefully compare the length, width and dimensions of the tabs and holes or slots on the ends of the new pads to those on the old pads. The new pads should be free to slip into the caliper holder without binding. They shouldn't be loose enough to rattle either. A nice, lightly snug fit is just right. If the pads are too tight, return them for some that fit. Pads from the Toyota dealer usually fit the first time around.

For '84-'87 2WD trucks, I urge you to always get pad kits from the Toyota dealer. The kits come complete with new pads, new spring clips, packets of grease and installation instructions. The price of the kit is comparable to parts store prices.

When installing new pads, always replace the pads on both left and right wheels. It's the law in some states. Do one side first, so you have the other side as a reference for the proper location and placement of the pads, shims and clips. Also, if the pads on both sides of the truck are removed, the pistons on the opposite side might pop out when you press the pistons into the caliper.

Condition: Brake pads are worn out; OR brake fluid or grease has gotten on the pads; OR the brakes must be removed so you can remove the disc or steering knuckle.

Tools and Materials: Phase 1 tool kit, new brake pads for both front wheels, safety glasses, dust mask, needlenose and regular pliers, large screwdriver, small wire brush, high-temp disc brake grease, alcohol or spray can of brake cleaner. For 1984-87 2WD and all Cab and Chassis models you'll need a piece of wire, small rope or heavy string at least 18 inches long, clean rags.

ORIENTATION: The kind of calipers you have depends on the year and model Toyota you have. Do Step 1, then go to the step that applies to your year and model. Here's where to find the step for replacing your front brake pads.

Year and Model	Brake Type	See Step
2WD except C&C		
1975-83	S16	2A
1984-87	FS17	2B
Cab and Chassis		
'79-'83	K-type	2C
'85-'87	PD 60	2B
4WD models		
1979-87	S12+8	2A

Step 1. Chock, Jack, Block and Remove Front Wheels.

Do Procedure 3, Step 1, to get the front of the truck jacked up and the wheels off. If your model has FS17, K-type or PD 60 brakes, tie one end of a piece of wire, rope or string to the upper suspension arm. Let the other end hang down for now. You'll need it to hang the caliper from later.

Step 2A. Remove and Install Brake Pads on 1975-83 2WD Pickups (except C & C) and All 4WD Models.

This step is for S16 and S12+8 type calipers.

REMOVE BRAKE PADS

1975-78 2WD models: Use needlenose pliers to remove the two tiny hairpin clips in the retaining pins. They're located between the outer edge of the pad and the caliper.

1979-83 2WD: Use needlenose pliers to remove the wire clip that secures the two retaining pins. Just grab the wire near the center and pull on it. The ends will pop out of the pins.

4WD models: Unhook the wire clip from the hole in the side of the caliper, then pull the clip out of the holes in the pins.

EVERYONE: Carefully note where the top ends of the anti-rattle spring are hooked into the inner side of the brake pads. Notice how the lower retaining pin fits through the bottom of the anti-rattle spring.

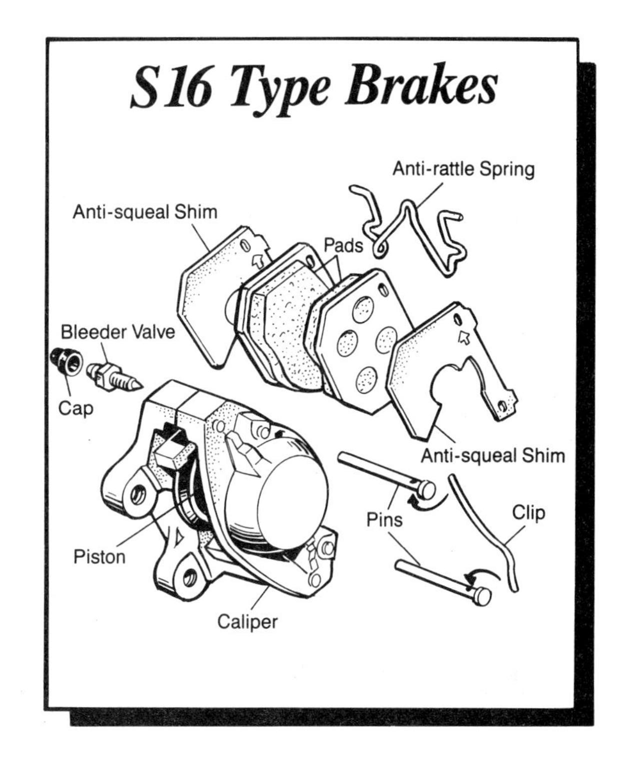

Use the end of a screwdriver to push or tap against the inner end of the two retaining pins. This will move the head of the pins away from the caliper far enough so you can grab the head with pliers. Pull the top pin straight out of the caliper. Hold the anti-rattle spring with one hand while you pull the lower pin out. Squeeze the top ends of the anti-rattle spring together and pull the spring out of the caliper. Retaining pin(s) stuck? You'll need to use a hammer and small punch or nail to tap the pin out of the caliper from the inner end.

Use pliers to grab the tabs on the pads and wiggle them straight out of the caliper. 2WD models have thin anti-squeal shims on the outside of each pad. They slip right off.

Accumulated brake dust and maybe a little rust might make the pad slightly difficult to pull out. If so, move the pad in and out a few times to clear away the crud and be sure you're pulling straight out.

If you are going to use the pads again they must be installed in the same place. Use paint or chalk to mark them "inner" and "outer" so you'll know where they go.

If you are here to remove the calipers, see Procedure 5. Come back here when you are ready to install the brake pads.

Now see Step 3 to inspect the pads, calipers and rotors. If you are installing new brake pads, also see Step 4 to push the pistons into the calipers.

INSTALL BRAKE PADS

Before putting the brakes back together, clean and then carefully examine the retaining pins, retaining pin clips, anti-rattle spring, and the anti-squeal shims (2WD). Are there thin spots or grooves worn in any of the parts? If so, replace them with new ones from Toyota.

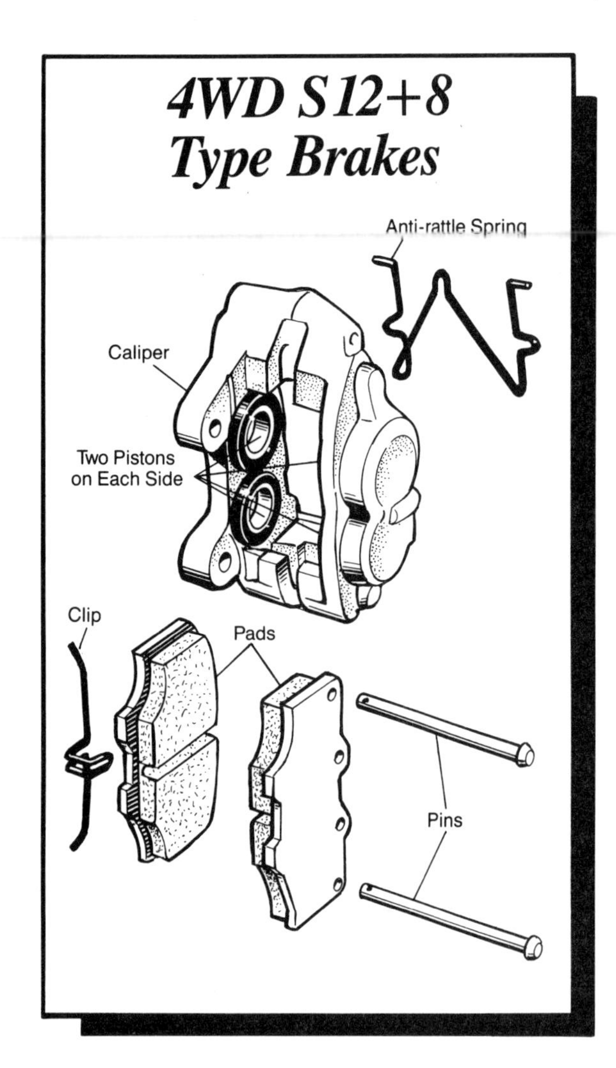

If you're installing the old pads, wipe the metal part with a clean rag to remove the accumulated brake dust. If you have a can of brake cleaner, use that to clean them. Use a wire brush or rag and brake cleaner, if you have it, to clean the calipers where the brake pads fit.

Grab the pads and smear a light coat of brake grease, high temperature wheel bearing grease or antiseize compound along the top and bottom edges of the metal parts of the shoes. Don't get any grease on the pads. On 2WD models, smear a little grease on the outer part of the pads where the anti-squeal shims fit.

OK, to install the pads, just slide them into the slots so the friction surfaces are facing the disc and the tabs are toward the rear. If you're reusing the old pads, be sure and install them in their original position.

2WD models: Slip the anti-squeal shims into position between the pad and caliper. The arrow should be pointing up and the little tabs on the shim should hook over the metal part of the pads.

EVERYONE: Wiggle the *upper* retaining pin into its hole through the caliper, brake pads and anti-squeal shims (2WD).

Position the anti-rattle spring in the caliper so the lower retaining pin can slip through the hoops. Now install the lower retaining pin, making sure it's going through the hoops in the anti-rattle spring. Hook the upper ends of the anti-rattle spring in the holes in the pads. If you've forgotten where they go, look at the caliper on the other side of the truck.

To install the retaining pin clips, use pliers to turn the pins so you can see the holes for the clips. You might need to press the outer pad toward the disc in order to see the holes.

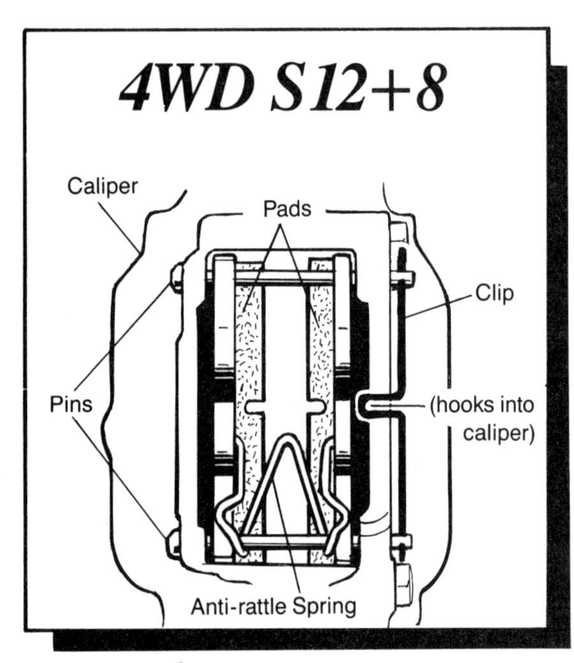

1975-78 models: Use needlenose pliers to fit the two small hairpin clips into their holes in the pins. If the clips slide onto the pins too easily, remove them and use pliers to squeeze on the rounded end so the open ends are closer together. If the clips are still loose after squeezing the ends together, buy new ones from the Toyota dealer.

1979-83 2WD and all 4WD models: Fit the crooked end of the clip into the hole in the top retaining pin, then hold the center of the spring with pliers while you use your finger to guide the straight lower end of the clip into its hole in the lower retaining pin. Wiggle it all the way into the hole.

4WD models: Fit the hook on the side of the clip into its hole on the caliper.

EVERYONE: Go to Step 5 to adjust the brakes.

Step 2B. Remove and Install Brake Pads on 1984-87 2WD Pickups and 1985-87 Cab and Chassis Models.

This step is for FS17 and PD60 type calipers.

To get to the brake pads, you must move the calipers out of the way, so tie a piece of wire, string or rope to the upper suspension arm to support the caliper once it's released from the torque plate (caliper holder).

REMOVE BRAKE PADS

The caliper is attached with two bolts to a bracket called a **torque plate**. To remove the brake pads, look at the lower inboard side of the caliper and locate the lower bolt. Use a 17mm socket and ratchet to remove the bolt *counterclockwise* until you can pull it out with your fingers. There's a little rubber **boot**, which you may need to hold in place with a finger while unscrewing the bolt so it won't twist and tear.

FS17 type: Pull up on the bottom of the caliper and it will rotate up and away from the disc. Use the wire or string to tie the bottom end of the caliper up so it's out of your way.

Wiggle the inner and outer pads out of the torque plate: just grab them with your fingers and pull them away from the disc. Mark them "inner" and "outer" if you're going to reuse them. As you remove the pads, notice the position of the top and bottom support plates (clips) in the torque plate where the pads fit.

You'll notice that the outer pad has a flat anti-squeal shim clipped over the outer surface. Remove the shim from the pad.

PD60 type: Remove the upper caliper bolt the same way you removed the lower bolt, then pull the caliper straight off the torque plate. Suspend the caliper using the string or wire that you tied to the upper suspension arm. Tie it up so no strain is on the rubber brake hose.

Remove the two **anti-squeal springs**, then wiggle the brake pads out of the torque plate. Remove the **anti-squeal shim** from the outside of the outer pad. There's also a round anti-squeal shim clipped into the brake piston in the caliper. Use a small screwdriver to carefully pry it out. Inspect the shims for damage; replace them if they are broken, bent or rusty.

EVERYONE: Step 3 tells you how to check the brake pads, caliper and rotor for wear and damage. If you are installing new brake pads, see Step 4 to press the pistons into the calipers.

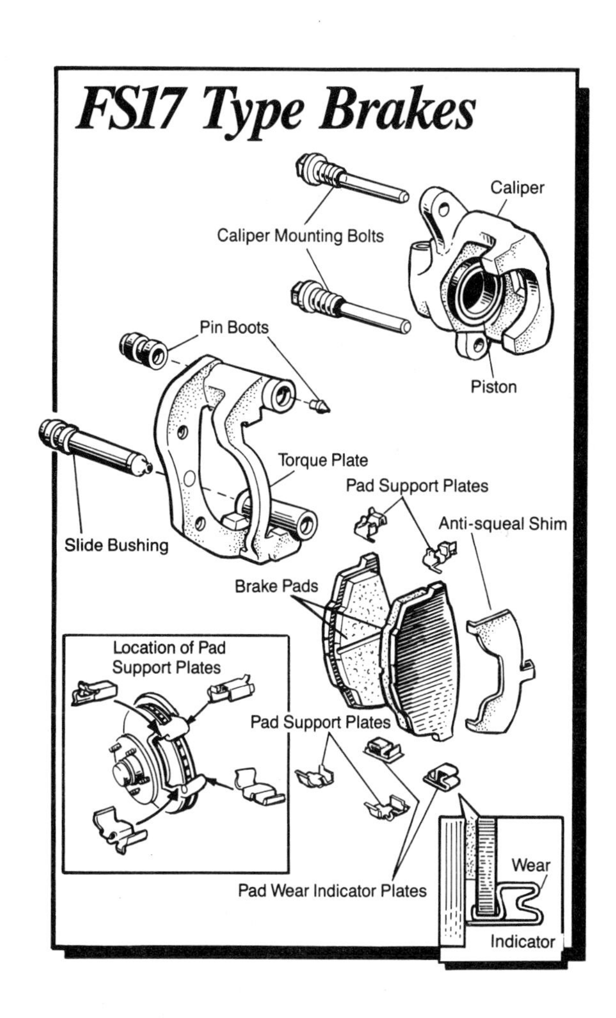

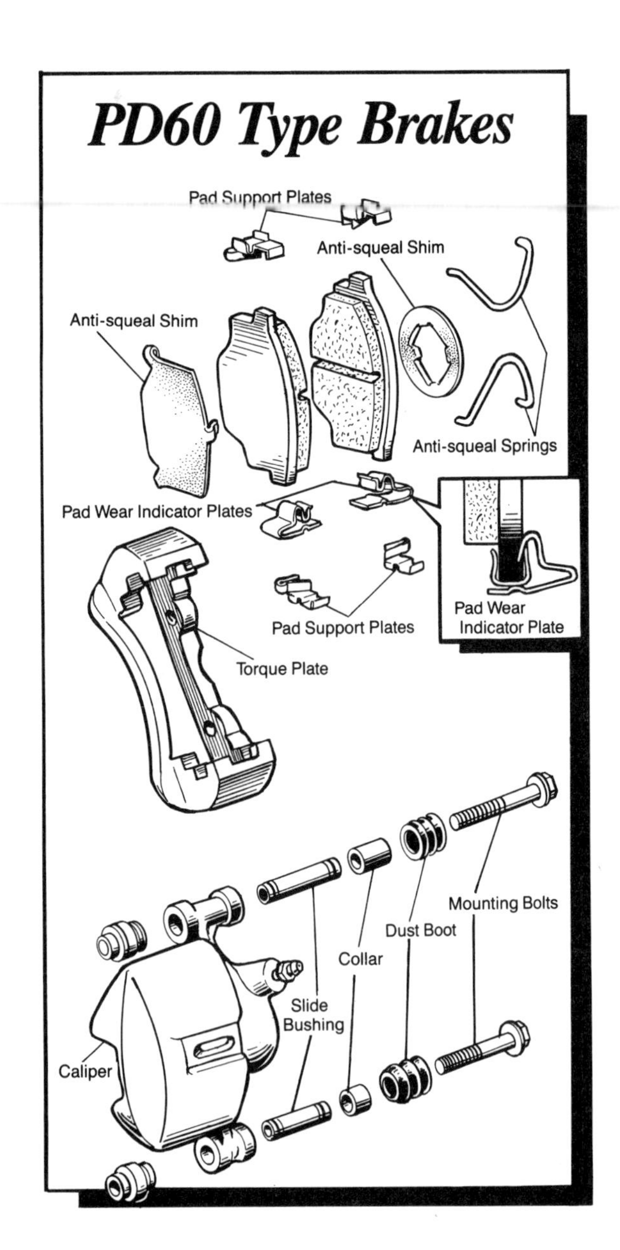

INSTALL BRAKE PADS

If you are installing new brake pads and the kit has new pad support plates and/or anti-squeal shims, by all means use them. Remove the old support plates one at a time from the torque plate and install the new ones. Be sure and install the new ones exactly the same way as the old ones. If you get confused, you can look at the brake setup on the other side of the truck. If you have new pad wear indicator plates, slip them onto the bottom of the new pads so the little tangs fit into the holes on the pads. The looped part of the wear indicator goes toward the outside metal part of the pads (see the illustration). If you don't have new wear indicator plates, get some or remove the ones from the old pads and use them.

If you aren't replacing the pads, use a wire brush or emery cloth to clean the **pad support plates** in the torque plate. Check them for cracks and worn areas that might prevent the pads from sliding smoothly; replace any pad support plates that are broken, bent or questionable.

Smear a little disc brake grease on the pad support plates, on the tabs on the top ends of the brake pads, on the bottom of the wear indicator plates, on the outer surface of the pads where the anti-squeal shims fit and on the side of the anti-squeal shims that touch the pads. Be careful to not get any of the grease on the friction surface of the pads or the disc.

PD60 type: Install the large anti-squeal shim on the outer pad and the smaller round anti-squeal shim into the piston in the caliper. If the shims fit loosely, use pliers to bend the tabs a little so they fit tighter. Install the pads into the torque plate so the tabs on the ends of the pads fit into the pad support plates. The pads should fit flush against the disc. Install the anti-squeal springs.

Untie the caliper and fit it over the brake pads and torque plate. If the caliper won't fit over the pads, see Step 4 to press the pistons further into the caliper. Straighten the little dust boots if necessary so the two mounting bolts can be installed. Install and tighten the mounting bolts to 29 ft.lbs.

Now skip to Step 5 to adjust the brakes.

FS17 type: If you are installing new pads, install the wear indicator plates if your model has them on the bottom of the pads. See the illustration.

Install outer pad: Smear disc brake grease on the outside of the pad and the inside of the pad shim (see illustration), then install the shim on the metal side of the pad. If necessary, bend the little tabs slightly to make the shim snug. Fit the tabs on the ends of the pad into the outer pad support plates so the friction side of the pad is toward the disc.

Install inner pad: Slip the brake pad into the torque plate so the tabs on the top and bottom of the pad fit into the inner pad support plates.

Both pads should be flat against the disc and feel securely in place. Sometimes you have to wiggle them until they seat properly in the pad support plates. Do a final visual inspection of the setup before moving ahead.

Release the caliper from the wire or string and carefully let it rotate down and over the brake pads. If the caliper won't fit over the pads, see Step 4 to press the pistons into the caliper. Be sure the rubber dust boots don't get pinched and torn. Straighten the rubber boot between the caliper and torque plate so the mounting bolt can be installed. Clean the slide mounting bolt, then lightly coat the smooth part with disc brake grease. Install the bolt into the caliper and torque plate and torque it to 65 ft.lbs. If the little boot twists as you turn the bolt, hold it in place with a finger.

Air trapped in the mounting bolt hole can keep the caliper from seating properly. This causes the outer pad to drag, and that's a drag. To relieve the pressure, pull the rubber boot away from the bolt so the trapped air can escape.

Recheck the position of the shims, pads, and clips, and recheck the bolt tightness. Your life depends on these parts. If everything looks good, go to Step 5 to adjust the brakes.

Step 2C. Remove and Install Brake Pads on 1979-83 Cab and Chassis Models.

This step is for Cab and Chassis models with K-type calipers. On these models the caliper must be removed before the brake pads can be replaced. Here's how.

REMOVE BRAKE PADS

The calipers are attached to a **torque plate** with two bolts: one at the top and one at the bottom. As you remove the caliper, keep the parts for the top separate from the ones for the bottom and pay attention to how the parts are oriented on the caliper as you remove them. It will make reassembly easier.

Remove the lower bolt, the **cylinder guide plate**, the **cylinder guide spring** and the **pad support plate**. Next, remove the same parts from the upper end of the caliper. Stash the parts somewhere safe.

Now you can pull the caliper off the holder. The outer pad will come off with the caliper and the inner pad will remain in the torque plate. Hang the caliper from the wire or string that you attached to the upper suspension arm. Don't let the caliper dangle by the rubber brake hose.

To remove the outer pad, use pliers to pull one end of the anti-rattle spring away from the caliper until you can slide it over the lump that holds it in place. Do the same to the other end of the spring, then slide the spring out from under the hook on the pad. Remove the outer pad and C-shaped anti-squeal shim.

To remove the inner pad, just wiggle the pad and anti-squeal shim away from the disc and out of the torque plate.

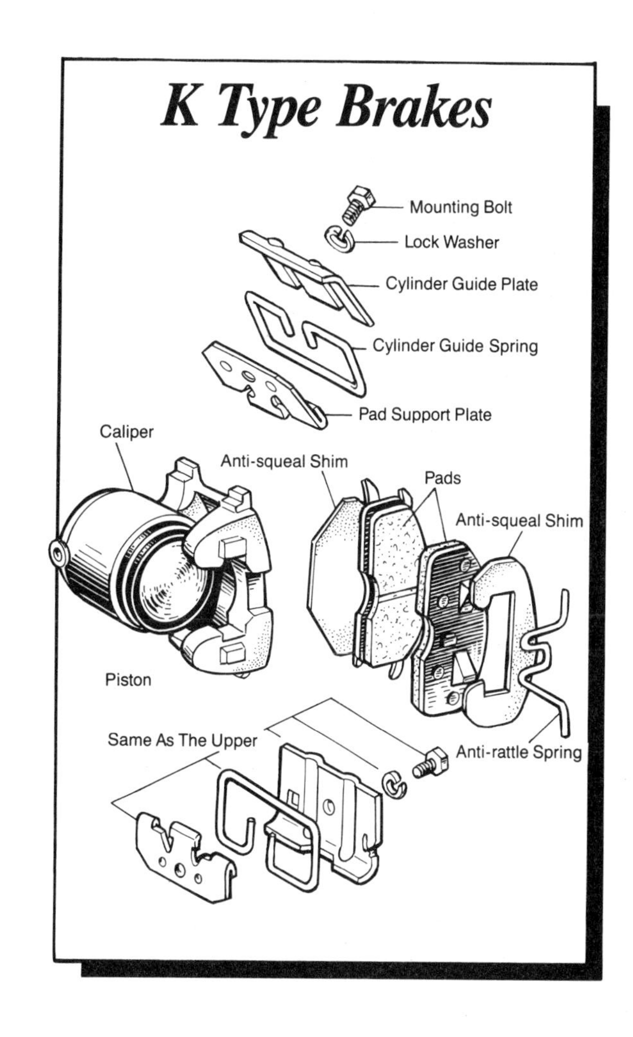

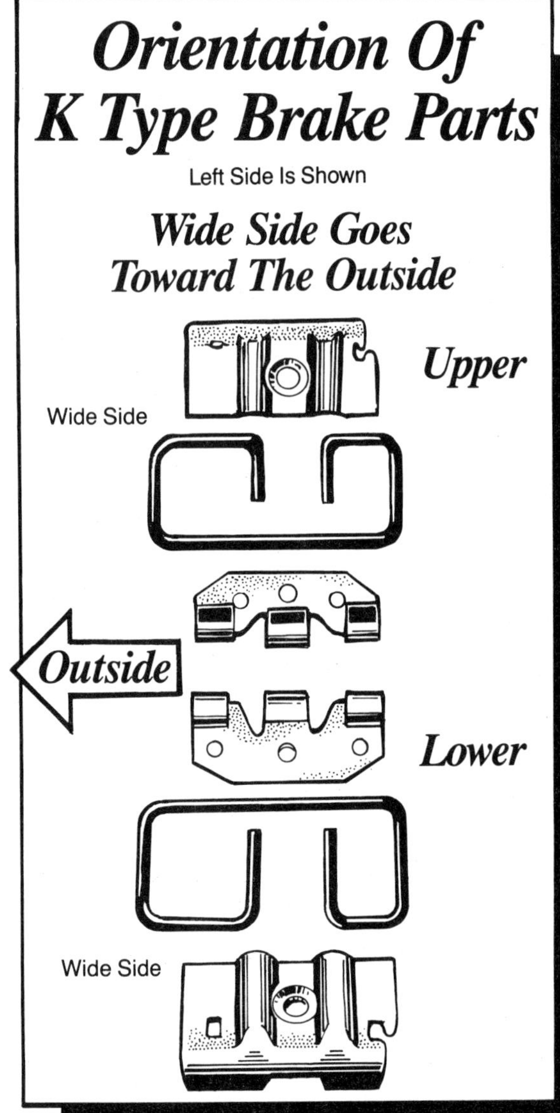

Now see Step 3 to inspect the pads, disc, and wheel cylinder. If you're installing new pads, also see Step 4 to press the pistons into the calipers. When it's all ready to go back together, come back here.

INSTALL BRAKE PADS

Smear a light coat of disc brake grease along the edges of the torque plate where the caliper makes contact. Don't use too much. Put a little grease on the edge of the brake pad tabs—the part that fits into the notches on the caliper or torque plate and on the metal part where the anti-squeal shims fit. Don't get any grease on the friction part of the pads.

To install the pads, fit the inner pad into the torque plate so the tabs on the ends fit into the notches in the torque plate. Fit the anti-squeal shim onto the metal part of the pad. The pad should evenly contact the disc.

Put the C-shaped anti-squeal shim on the metal side of the outer pad. Fit the outer pad and shim into the caliper so the little hook on the pad is centered in the caliper. Fit the center part of the anti-rattle spring under the hook on the pad, then use pliers to hook the ends of the spring over the bumps on the caliper.

Untie the caliper from the wire or string and fit it into place on the holder. The grooves in the top and bottom of the caliper mesh with the grooves on the torque plate. Be sure the caliper fits the same at the top and bottom.

To attach the caliper, fit the upper pad support plate onto the top of the caliper so the hook on one edge is at the bottom and facing away from the caliper. Fit the long edge of the cylinder guide spring into the support plate so it is engaged in the hook. The larger side of the spring goes toward the outside of the caliper. Next, fit the cylinder guide plate over the guide spring so the curved edge covers the upper edge of the spring. Check that the spring fits into the grooves in the support plate and guide plate.

Install and tighten the bolt and lockwasher to 29-44 ft.lbs. Install the lower pad support plate with the hooked edge at the top. Fit the long part of the spring into the hook so the larger side of the spring is toward the outside. Fit the guide plate over the spring so the curved edge covers the lower edge of the spring. Be sure the spring is in the grooves in the support plate and guide plate. Install and tighten the bolt and lockwasher to 29-44 ft.lbs. Now go to Step 5 to adjust the brakes.

Step 3. Inspect Brake Pads, Caliper and Disc.

Examine the pads for scoring or uneven wear. If they are worn down to the metal, I'll bet the disc is scratched and scored and needs to be resurfaced. If the pads have worn down evenly, and haven't reached the metal, the disc is probably OK. But check it for grooves, uneven wear, and dark blotchy looking areas anyway. Remove the disc and have it machined smooth if it's rough, uneven, or has dark "hot spots" on it (Procedure 5).

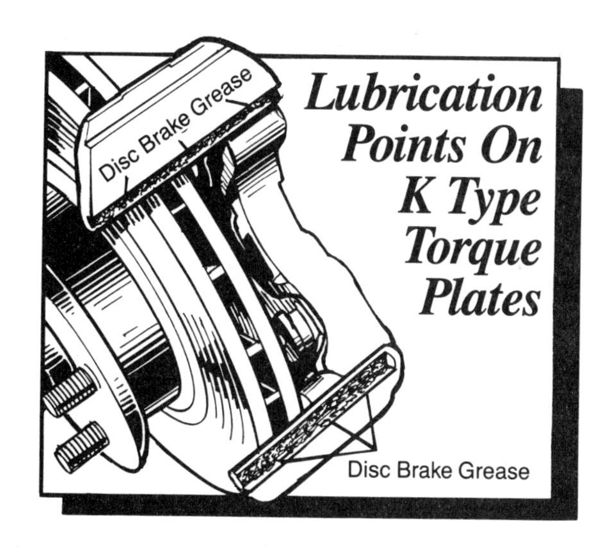

Is there any brake fluid on or around the pads or any part of the brake mechanisms? Yes? Then the brake cylinder will have to be rebuilt. Even if only one side is leaking, rebuild both front calipers/cylinders at the same time. See Procedure 5 to remove the calipers.

Carefully examine the rubber boot around the wheel cylinder piston. If the boot is torn, you should remove it, clean the piston with a clean rag, then install a new boot.

All looks well? Proceed . . .

If you aren't installing new brake pads, go back to Step 2A, 2B or 2C to install the old pads.

If you are installing new pads, do Step 4 to press the pistons into the calipers.

Step 4. Press Brake Piston Into Caliper.

If you're installing new pads, the pistons must be pushed back into the caliper. If you're using the old pads again, the pistons can probably stay where they are. However, if you have difficulty installing the old pads, you might have to press the pistons in slightly.

While pushing the pistons in, some of the brake fluid in the cylinders will flow back to the master cylinder reservoir. Check the reservoir frequently and, if necessary, use a syringe or clean paper towel to remove some of the fluid to be sure it doesn't overflow.

If the pistons refuse to move into the caliper, attach a hose to the bleeder valve on the caliper and stick the other end into a can or jar to catch the fluid. Open the bleeder valve a little and try pushing the pistons in again. They should slide in easily now. Once the pistons are in, be absolutely certain that you tighten the bleeder valve, then remove the hose and install the little rubber dust cap.

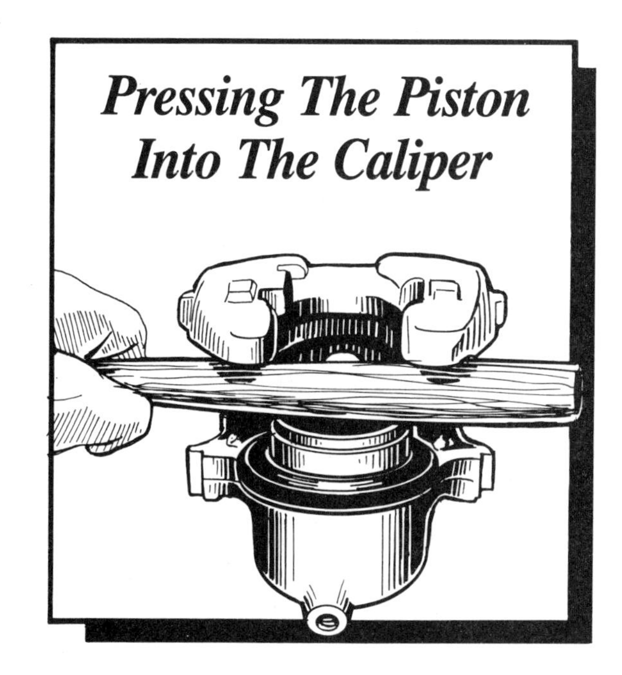

S16 and S12+8 type calipers: To push the pistons in, place the tip of a large screwdriver, thin hammer handle or piece of wood against the front edge of the piston and use the disc as the lever point to force the piston back into the caliper. You'll feel resistance as the piston moves inward. Don't rush it—just keep a steady pressure on the piston until the edge is flush with the caliper. When the pistons on one side of the caliper are pressed in, install the brake pad on that side. Otherwise, pushing the pistons in on the other side might make them slide out again.

If you can't get the pistons pushed in even by opening the bleeder valve, remove the caliper (Procedure 5) and take it to Toyota or a garage to have the pistons pressed in.

FS17, PD60 and K-type calipers: Support the caliper with one hand while using something like a wooden hammer handle or strong piece of wood for a lever to press the piston into the caliper. Place the tip of the lever against the edge of the piston and use the opposite side of the caliper as a pivot point. You'll feel resistance as the piston moves inward. Don't rush it—just keep a steady pressure on the piston until the edge is flush with the caliper.

If you can't get the piston pushed in even after opening the bleeder valve, remove the caliper (Procedure 5) and take it to Toyota or a garage to have the piston pressed in.

Step 5. Adjust Front Brakes.

Check the brake fluid level and add fluid if necessary. After the pads and calipers on both sides are installed, pump the brake pedal a few times to adjust the brakes, then check the brake fluid level and add some if necessary. At first the pedal might go all the way to the floor and feel mushy. Keep pumping until the pedal feels solid. If you loosened the bleeder valve(s) to press the pistons into the caliper, bleed the front brakes (Procedure 1). This would be a good time to flush the entire brake system if the brake fluid hasn't been changed recently (Procedure 2).

Do Step 6 to finish up.

Step 6. Do This and That.

Put the wheels on and snug down the lug nuts. Remove the jack stands, lower the car to the ground, and torque the lug nuts to 65-87 ft.lbs. Throw old brake pads and the dust mask in the trash and clean up all traces of black brake dust. Clean your hands before eating or smoking anything. It's a good idea to blow your nose to remove any brake dust. This isn't intended to be funny—the stuff is dangerous. Now take your truck for a slow and easy drive around the block to test the operation of the brakes.

PROCEDURE 5: REMOVE AND INSTALL CALIPER AND BRAKE DISC

Read the **Caution! Warning!** at the start of this chapter.

Condition: You weren't able to press the brake piston into the caliper when installing new pads; OR you found a fluid leak in one or both of the brake cylinders; OR the pads have worn to the metal and gouged the discs so they need to be removed and turned or replaced; OR you're removing the brakes in order to remove the steering knuckle.

Tools and Materials: Phase 1 tool kit, disc brake grease, two cans or jars to catch the brake fluid when the brake hoses are disconnected, two pints of fresh DOT3 or 4 brake fluid, dust mask, baggies and rubber bands.

Remarks: Please don't try to remove the calipers when they are hot. Also, always remove the caliper and torque plate, if you have one, before trying to remove the disc. See the Orientation section of Procedure 4 if you aren't sure which type brakes you have.

Step 1. Chock, Jack, Block and Remove Front Wheels.

Chock the rear wheels, set the handbrake, loosen the lug nuts a little, jack the front of the truck up, lower it onto jackstands or blocks, then remove the front wheels. (See Chapter 2 if you need details.)

Step 2. Remove Brake Pads.

Depending on the year and model you have, see Procedure 4, Step 2A, 2B, or 2C to remove the pads.

Step 3. Disconnect Brake lines.

FS17 and PD60 type brakes: If you are removing the caliper just so you can remove the disc or steering knuckle, you don't need to disconnect the brake line. If you are removing the caliper from the truck, disconnect the brake line.

EVERYONE: Use a 10mm flare nut wrench to carefully unscrew the brake line from the rear inboard side of the caliper. When it's unscrewed, remove the little rubber cap from the brake bleeder valve at the top of the caliper. Gently pull the brake line away from the caliper just far enough to stick the rubber cap over the end. This will help prevent the brake fluid from draining out of the master cylinder. If you have baggies handy, slip one over the end of the brake line and secure it with tape or a rubber band.

Step 4A. Remove and Install Calipers on 1975-83 2WD models (except Cab and Chassis) and all 4WD models.

This step is for people with S-16 and S12+8 type brakes.

There are several bolts on the inboard side of the caliper. Two or four 14mm bolts hold the two halves of the caliper together (don't mess with these), and two 17mm bolts attach the caliper to the steering knuckle—these are the two bolts you need to remove. Use a 17mm socket and long handled ratchet (they're on pretty tight) to remove the bolts. The caliper can now be lifted away from the disc. If the calipers need to be rebuilt, remove the one from the other side and take both of them to Toyota or a garage.

Before hauling the caliper away to be rebuilt or replaced, inspect the rubber brake line hoses and replace them if they are hard, stiff, cracked, or bulging in places (Procedure 11).

If you need to remove the disc, turn to Chapter 12, Procedure 5 to remove the wheel hubs and discs. Come back here when you are ready to install the caliper and brake pads.

Fit the caliper over the disc and install the two 17mm mounting bolts. Tighten the bolts to the following specifications:

'75-'83 2WD models	68-86 ft.lbs.
'79-'85 4WD models	55-75 ft.lbs.
'86-'87 4WD models	90 ft.lbs.

Press the pistons into the caliper (Procedure 4, Step 4), then Install the brake pads (Procedure 4, Step 2A), then skip down to Step 5 to reconnect the brake line to the caliper.

Step 4B. Remove and Install Calipers on 1984-86 2WD and '85-'87 C&C models.

This step is for people with FS17 and PD60 type brakes.

If you are removing the caliper from the truck, see if the brake line bracket is attached to the inboard side of the caliper. If it is, remove the two bolts that attach it to the caliper. Next remove the two 17mm bolts that attach the caliper to the torque plate. Pull the caliper off the torque plate. Before hauling the caliper away to be rebuilt or replaced, inspect the rubber brake line hoses and replace them if they are worn, stiff, cracked, or bulging in places (Procedure 11).

If you are only removing the caliper so you can remove the disc, tie a piece of string or wire at least 18" long to the upper suspension arm, then remove the two 17mm bolts on the inboard side of the caliper. Lift the caliper away from the torque plate and tie it up out of the way with the string or wire. If you need to remove the disc, locate the two 17mm bolts that attach the torque plate to the inboard side of the steering knuckle, slightly forward from the inside brake pad slot. Unscrew the two bolts *counterclockwise*, then pull the torque plate away from the disc.

Now skip to Chapter 12, Procedure 5 to remove the wheel hub and disc. Come back here to install the caliper and brake pads.

To install the caliper, fit it onto the torque plate and install the two mounting bolts. If necessary, straighten the rubber boots so the bolts can fit into the holes. Torque the bolts to the following specifications:

'84-'87 2WD with FS17-type brakes	65 ft.lbs.
'85-'87 C&C with PD60-type brakes	29 ft.lbs.

Now see Step 5 to reconnect the brake line to the caliper.

Step 4C. Remove and Install K-Type Caliper.

If the caliper is in good condition and you are here only to remove the disc, see Procedure 4, Step 2C to remove the brake pads. Don't disconnect the brake lines. Once the caliper is off the torque plate and hanging by a string or wire, skip to Chapter 12, Procedure 5 to remove the wheel hub and disc. Come back here to install the caliper and brake pads.

If you are here because the calipers need to be rebuilt, see Procedure 11, Step 2 to disconnect the end of the rubber brake line hose that's attached to a bracket mounted to the frame of the truck. Then disconnect the brake line from the caliper. Remove the two bolts that attach the caliper to the torque plate. They are the same two bolts you remove when removing the brake pads (Procedure 4, Step 2C). The caliper is now liberated.

To install the caliper, follow the instructions in Procedure 4, Step 2C to install the brake pads and mount the caliper to the torque plate. Once the pads are installed, see Step 5 to connect the brake line to the caliper. Be careful not to get any brake fluid on the pads. Now reconnect the brake lines at the bracket on the frame. See Procedure 11 if you aren't sure how to connect the brake lines.

Step 5. Connect Brake Line.

Inspect the rubber brake hose. Replace it if it's stiff, cracked, split, or bulging in places (Procedure 11).

Hose OK? Carefully insert the brake line fitting into its hole on the caliper. Wiggle the brake line a little while you screw the fitting in with your fingers until you're dead certain that it isn't cross-threaded. Use the flare nut wrench to tighten the fitting. The torque is only about 11 ft.lbs., so it doesn't have to be super tight. If your model has a brake line bracket that attaches to the inboard side of the caliper, install and tighten the two bracket mounting bolts.

K-type: See Procedure 11 to attach the brake line hose to the bracket on the frame.

Step 6. Finish the Job.

If the brake lines were removed from the calipers and all the brake fluid drained out of the master cylinder, go to Procedure 1 and bleed the master cylinder, then bleed the entire brake system. If there is still fluid in the master cylinder, you'll need to bleed the front brakes, then follow the bleeding sequence in Procedure 1 and bleed all four wheels.

Put the wheels back on, lower the truck and torque the lug nuts to 65-87 ft.lbs. Install the hubcap.

PROCEDURE 6: CHECK REAR BRAKE SHOES

Read the **Caution! Warning!** at the beginning of this chapter.

Condition: You just bought the truck; OR you're doing the 12,000 mile maintenance; OR strange noises are coming from the rear when the brakes are applied.

Tools and Materials: Everyone will need the following tools: Safety glasses, a dust mask or respirator to protect you from the nasty carcinogenic brake dust. '75-'86 2WD and '79-'85 4WD models will need a ruler or small tape measure, jack, lug wrench, jackstand(s), good medium-size screwdriver, rags or paper towels and newspapers. You might need two 8x1.25mm bolts.

'86 4WD and all '87 models will need a screwdriver and a flashlight or drop light.

Step 1. Check Brake Shoes on '86 4WD and all '87 models.

This step is only for some '86 4WD and all '87 models. If your model doesn't have the little inspection hole in the brake backing plate, skip down to Step 2.

Park on level ground, put the gearshift in FIRST (manual) or PARK (automatics), put chocks in front of and behind the front wheels.

Slip into your safety glasses and put a dust mask on your face, then grab a flashlight and screwdriver and crawl under the rear of your truck.

Locate the round rubber plug about the size of a quarter near the outer edge of the brake backing plate. Use the screwdriver to gently pry the plug out of its hole, then shine the flashlight into the hole so you can see the brake shoe. Look at the illustrations to see what a good brake shoe and a worn out brake shoe look like. The minimum safe brake shoe thickness is 1mm (about 1/16"). I replace my brake shoes when they wear down to 1/8". If the lining is getting thin, cut a 1/8" strip of paper and stick it in the hole. Compare the width of the brake shoe to the strip of paper. If the shoe is the width of the paper or less, replace the brake shoes (Procedure 9). Wiggle the rubber plug back into its hole.

While you're under there, check the backing plate for signs of wetness. If a wheel cylinder is leaking, the top of the backing plate will be damp (see Procedure 10 to fix it), or if the rear axle seal is leaking it will be damp around the center where the backing plate attaches to the axle (see Chapter 11 to fix it).

Check the rubber **brake hose** to the rear brakes for cracks, worn, split or bulging spots. To find the rubber hose, follow the brake line from the top of either backing plate to where it connects to a rubber hose. There it is. Replace the hose if any of the aforementioned abnormalities exists (Procedure 11).

Check the brake shoe on the other rear wheel. Then, depending on your reason for being here, go back to your place in Chapter 5 to continue the massage, to Procedure 9 to replace the rear brake shoes, or back to whatever you were doing when overcome by the urge to check your rear brake shoes.

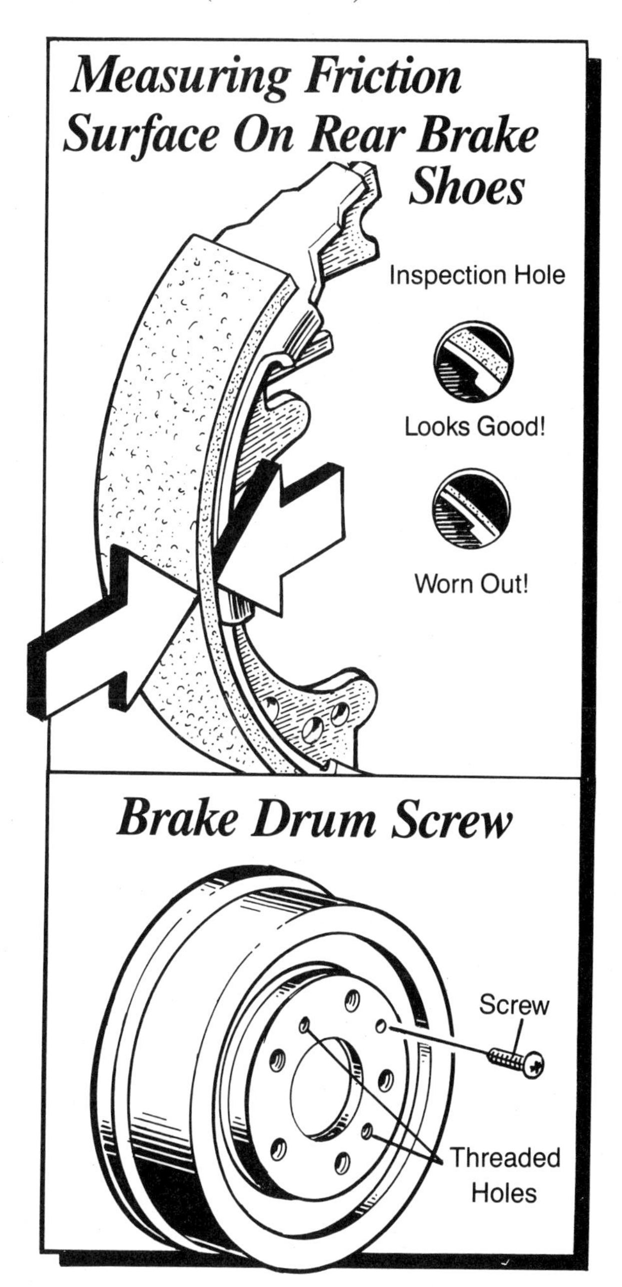

Step 2. Remove Brake Drum.

Park on level ground, put the gearshift in FIRST (manual) or PARK (automatics), put chocks in front of and behind the front wheels. Release the handbrake (OFF).

Remove the rear hubcaps if you have them, then loosen the lug nuts counterclockwise about one turn. Jack the rear end up and put it on jackstands, then remove the wheels.

On some models the brake drum is attached to the axle with a large screw. If you find a screw on the outboard surface of the drum, use a good large phillips screwdriver to remove it. Stash it where it won't get lost, then pull straight out on the drum to remove it. If the drum slides off easily, skip down to Step 3 to inspect the brakes, or go back to whatever procedure you were doing when sent here to remove the brake drum.

If the drum is stuck, look for two threaded holes in the outboard side of the drum. If you have these holes, round up two 8mm bolts with a 1.25 thread pitch. Screw the bolts into the holes evenly to force the drum off the axle. If you don't have the two threaded holes or if the drum is hanging up on the brake shoes, see Procedure 7 to back the brake shoes off a little.

Step 3. Inspect Brake Shoes, Wheel Cylinder and Brake Drum.

OK, now that the brake drum is off, check the **brake shoes** and the **wheel cylinder** at the top of the backing plate for any signs of wetness—an indication that the wheel cylinder is leaking fluid. A slight leak will make the brake dust darker right around the cylinder. A bad leak will coat everything with brake fluid. If any fluid is present, the wheel cylinder must be rebuilt or replaced (Procedure 10). Replace the brake shoes if any brake fluid or grease is on the linings.

Use a ruler or tape measure to measure the brake lining where it looks the thinnest—don't include the metal part of the shoe. If the lining of the shoes is 1/16" or less, the shoes should be replaced.

Use a clean, non-oily finger to check the surface of the brake lining and the contact area inside the brake drum. Both surfaces should feel almost smooth with no large ridges or grooves worn in them. If the linings and drum are real groovy, the shoes should be replaced and the drums turned (machined).

Check the rubber **brake hose** for cracks, worn, split or bulging spots. To find the rubber hose, follow the brake line from the top of the backing plate to where it connects to a rubber hose. There it is. Replace the hoses if any of the aforementioned abnormalities exist (Procedure 11).

Check the brake shoes on the other side of the truck the same way. If the shoes, drums, and wheel cylinders on both sides of the truck are OK, go on to Step 4 and install the drums.

Step 4. Install Brake Drums.

Hold the drum so your fingers won't get squished between the drum and backing plate—ouch! If your brake drum was secured with a screw, line up the hole in the drum for the screw with the hole in the axle and carefully slide the drum onto the axle. Install the screw and tighten it as tight as you can with the screwdriver. No screw? Push the drum onto the axle as far as you can. It helps to wiggle the drum slightly while pushing on it.

Then install the wheel and snug the lug nuts. If you backed the brake shoes off to remove the drums, adjust the rear brakes (Procedure 7). Lower the truck and torque the lug nuts to 65-87 ft.lbs. Look at the illustration in Chapter 2 for the tightening sequence. Install the hubcaps (if you have them) and you're finished!

Depending on your reason for being here, go back to your place in Chapter 5 to continue the massage or to Procedure 8 or 9 to replace the rear brake shoes.

PROCEDURE 7: ADJUST REAR BRAKES

Condition: You just removed and installed the brake shoes; OR your truck doesn't stop as well as it used to; OR the pedal goes almost to the floor before resistance is felt; OR you're tired of dragging your foot out the door to stop the truck.

Tools and Materials: Safety glasses, jack, jackstands, blocks for the wheels, one small and one medium screwdriver. If you need to back off (loosen) the brakes so that you can remove the brake drum, you might also need a small hook (you can make one out of a paper clip).

Step 1. Chock, Jack and Block.

Park on level ground, put the truck in FIRST (manual) or PARK (automatics). Set the handbrake and put chocks in front of and behind the front wheels. Place the jack under the jack point on the rear axle (Toyota jack) or under the rear differential (floor jack) and raise the truck until the wheel is off the ground. Block the car up with jackstands in case your jack fails (Chapter 2, Procedure 1). Put the gearshift lever in NEUTRAL, then release the handbrake.

Step 2. Orientation.

Put on your safety glasses and crawl under the rear of the truck. Look behind the wheel at the round brake backing plate attached to the outer end of the rear axle. The backing plate serves as a bracket for the brake components and prevents dust and moisture from entering the mechanisms.

You'll see a horizontal, oblong hole on the backing plate. The hole is covered with a rubber plug. Depending on the year and model, the hole will be near the top or the bottom of the backing plate. Find the hole, then pry the rubber plug out of the hole so you can get to the adjusting mechanism.

Peek into the hole and you'll see a small toothed wheel and a small flat lever resting against one side of the wheel. The lever is the part of the automatic adjusting mechanism that turns the wheel to tighten the brake shoes as they wear away. To adjust the brake shoes, you rotate the little wheel one direction to tighten the shoes and turn it in the opposite direction to loosen the shoes.

The easiest way to tell which direction to turn the adjusting wheel to tighten or loosen the brakes is to stick a screwdriver through the hole in the backing plate and try to move the wheel in both directions. The only way the wheel will move without pulling or pushing on the adjuster arm is in the tightening direction. Once you figure out which way to turn the wheel to tighten the shoes, you can push or pull on the adjuster arm and turn the wheel in the opposite direction to loosen them.

Tighten the shoes: Basically here's what you'll be doing. First you will turn the little wheel on the adjustment mechanism to tighten the brake shoes until you can just barely hear the brake shoes rubbing against the brake drum. If you tighten them too much so the rubbing sound is easily heard (and the tire is probably harder to turn), then you'll turn the little wheel in the opposite direction to loosen (back off) the shoes.

Back off (loosen) the brake shoes: On all '79-'87 2WD models (except C&C) you have to use a small hook or screwdriver to *pull* the automatic adjuster arm toward you while you turn the adjuster wheel to back off the shoes. On all other models you have to use a second screwdriver to *push* the arm on the automatic adjuster mechanism away from the toothed wheel when you back off the shoes.

Here's another way to figure out which direction to move the adjuster lever. If the lever is between you and the wheel, you'll have to pull it toward you while turning the adjusting wheel to loosen the shoes. If the adjusting wheel is between you and the little lever, push the lever away from the wheel while you loosen the shoes.

'79-'83 2WD Rear Brake Adjustment

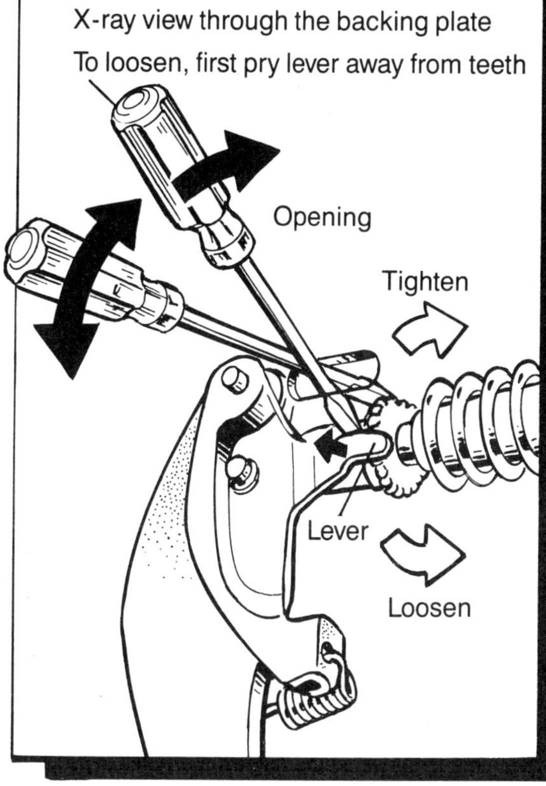

Step 3. Adjust Rear Brake Shoes.

Look at the illustration to see where to place the screwdriver to tighten the shoes. Slip the end of the screwdriver into the hole and engage the tip with the teeth on the adjuster.

To adjust the brake shoes, turn the adjusting wheel in the tightening direction while rotating the tire until you hear the shoes just begin to rub the brake drums. That's when you stop tightening. If you tighten them too much, there's a noticeable rubbing sound and the tire becomes harder to turn. Pull or push the adjusting lever away from the adjusting wheel while you turn the wheel in the opposite direction.

Once the brake is adjusted, wiggle the little rubber plug into the brake adjusting hole.

Repeat this step to adjust the other rear brake.

PROCEDURE 8: REPLACE DUO-SERVO TYPE REAR BRAKE SHOES

Please read the **Caution! Warning!** at the beginning of this chapter. Thanks.

This procedure is only for '75-'78 models, '79-'85 4WD and '79-'87 Cab and Chassis models. If you have a '79-'87 2WD (except Cab and Chassis) or '86-'87 4WD model, go to Procedure 9.

How to repair or replace the rear brakes on '86-'87 Cab and Chassis models with dual rear wheels is not covered in this manual. Why? Because it is a very complicated procedure and too many special tools are required to make it feasible to do at home.

Condition: Groans, growls or squeals come from the rear of the truck when the brakes are applied; OR the brake linings are 1/16" or less; OR a wheel cylinder has taken a leak on the brake linings; OR the drum and shoes have to come off so you can replace the handbrake cable or remove the axle or wheel bearing housing.

Tools and Materials: Phase 1 tool kit, maybe new brake shoes, two new horseshoe clips (if you're replacing the shoes), safety glasses, dust mask or respirator, needlenose pliers, channel lock pliers or Vise Grips, medium screwdriver, catch pan, can of brake cleaner or solvent, stiff cleaning brush, rags, old newspapers, brake grease or high temperature wheel bearing grease or antiseize compound.

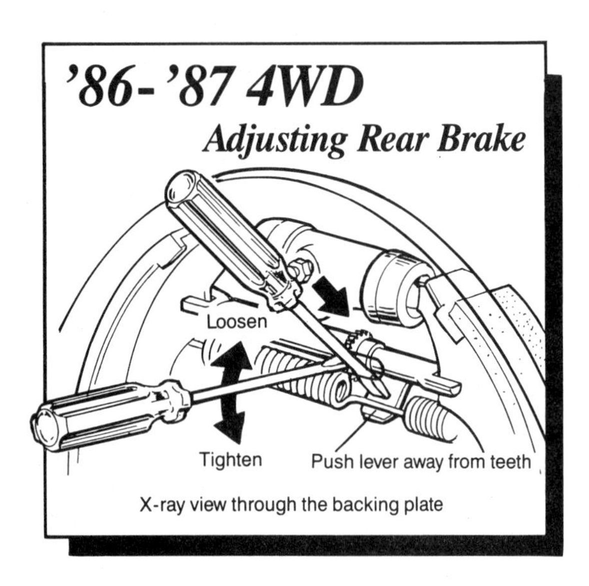

Remarks: Take your time on this procedure—brakes are very important! Remove and replace the brake shoes on one wheel at a time so you can use the other side for reference when assembling the shoes.

You can buy new brake shoes from Toyota or rebuilt ones from auto parts stores. The rebuilt units seem to work as well and last as long as new ones, so call around for prices and go for the best deal.

Step 1. Remove Rear Brake Drums.

Wear your safety glasses and respirator!

See Procedure 6, Step 2, to get the rear end jacked up and the wheels and brake drums off.

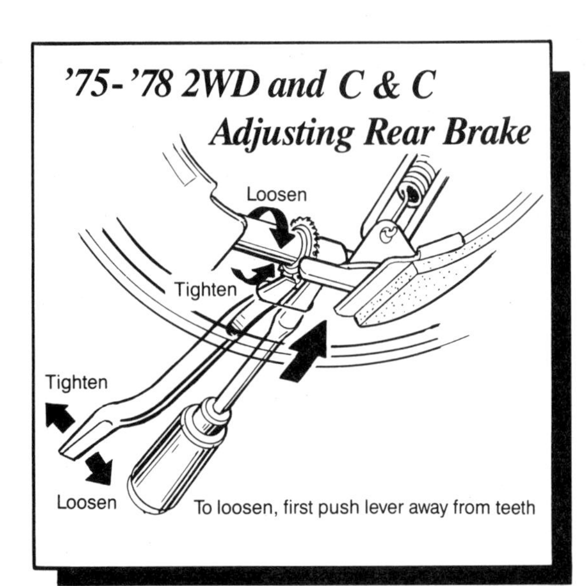

Step 2. Identify Rear Brake Components.

The brake shoe closest to the front of the car is called the **primary shoe**. The brake shoe closest to the rear of the car is the **secondary shoe**. Remember this.

The top of the brake shoes fit against a **metal post** that is attached firmly to the brake backing plate. Two heavy **return springs** attached between the brake shoes and the metal post keep the shoes away from the drum until the brakes are applied. Just below the metal post is the **wheel cylinder**. Short **horns** on the brake shoes rest in slots in the ends of the **plungers** on each end of the wheel cylinder. A **handbrake lever** pivots on a pin on the upper end of the primary shoe (4WD models) or the secondary shoe (2WD models). The lower end of the lever is attached to the **handbrake cable**. Just below the wheel cylinder is a horizontal **strut** that activates the brakes when the handbrake is applied.

The bottom of the brake shoes fit into slots on each end of an automatic **adjuster rod**. A **brake return spring** attached between the bottoms of the two shoes holds the shoes away from the drum until the brake pedal is pressed. Some models have another **small spring** attached between the bottom of the secondary shoe and a tab on the backing plate. **Spring clips** located near the center of the brake shoes hold the shoes against the backing plate.

The automatic adjusting mechanism consists of a **lever** that pivots on a metal **pin** located on the lower end of the secondary brake shoe. One end of the lever contacts the teeth on the brake adjusting rod and adjusts the clearance as the brake linings wear away. The other end of the lever is attached to one end of a **spring cage**. The spring cage is connected to a cable that goes up the inside of the secondary brake shoe, around a **cable guide**, and hooks to the metal post at the top of the backing plate. The automatic adjuster operates when the brakes are applied while the car is moving backwards.

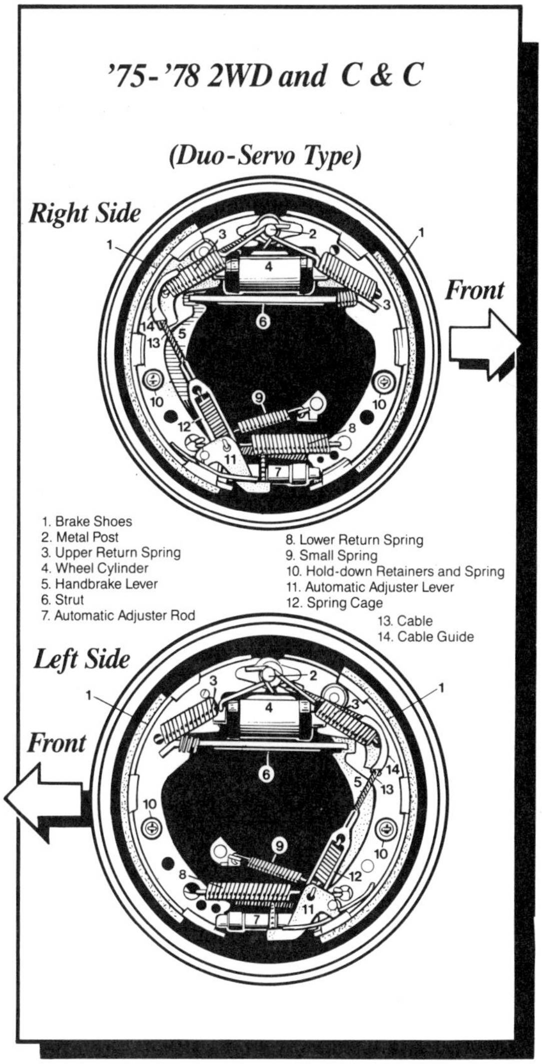

'75-'78 2WD and C & C

(Duo-Servo Type)

Right Side — *Front*

1. Brake Shoes
2. Metal Post
3. Upper Return Spring
4. Wheel Cylinder
5. Handbrake Lever
6. Strut
7. Automatic Adjuster Rod
8. Lower Return Spring
9. Small Spring
10. Hold-down Retainers and Spring
11. Automatic Adjuster Lever
12. Spring Cage
13. Cable
14. Cable Guide

Left Side — *Front*

Step 3. Remove Brake Shoes.

It's best to replace the brake shoes on one side of the truck at a time so you can use the other side for reference. Some of the brake parts will only work on one side, so if you do remove both sides at once, keep the parts for the left and right side separated and put them back on the side they came from.

Locate the spring that hooks over the automatic brake adjuster lever on the lower end of the secondary brake shoe. Lift up on the wire with a screwdriver or pliers and pull toward you to unhook the spring from the lever. Wiggle the lever until it's free of the brake shoe pin. Unhook the lever from the spring cage. Let the spring cage dangle by the cable. Slide the spring that held the automatic adjuster lever off the brake shoe pin.

Use pliers to remove the smaller of the two lower shoe return springs. Not all models have this smaller second spring. If you have it, one end is attached to the secondary shoe and the other end is attached to a little arm fastened to the backing plate. Don't grab it on the coiled part of the spring. Use the pliers to remove the other, larger, lower return spring. Grab the straight part of the spring and pull the spring toward the secondary brake shoe, then push or pull the hook of the spring through the hole in the shoe. When it's free, unhook the other end of the spring.

Now you can remove the **automatic adjusting bar** located between the bottoms of the brake shoes. The bar is different on each side of the small toothed wheel near the center of the bar. Note which end goes toward the front, then pull the bottoms of the shoes apart while you remove the bar.

Determine which of the top return springs is outermost on the metal anchor pin. Use your big channel lock

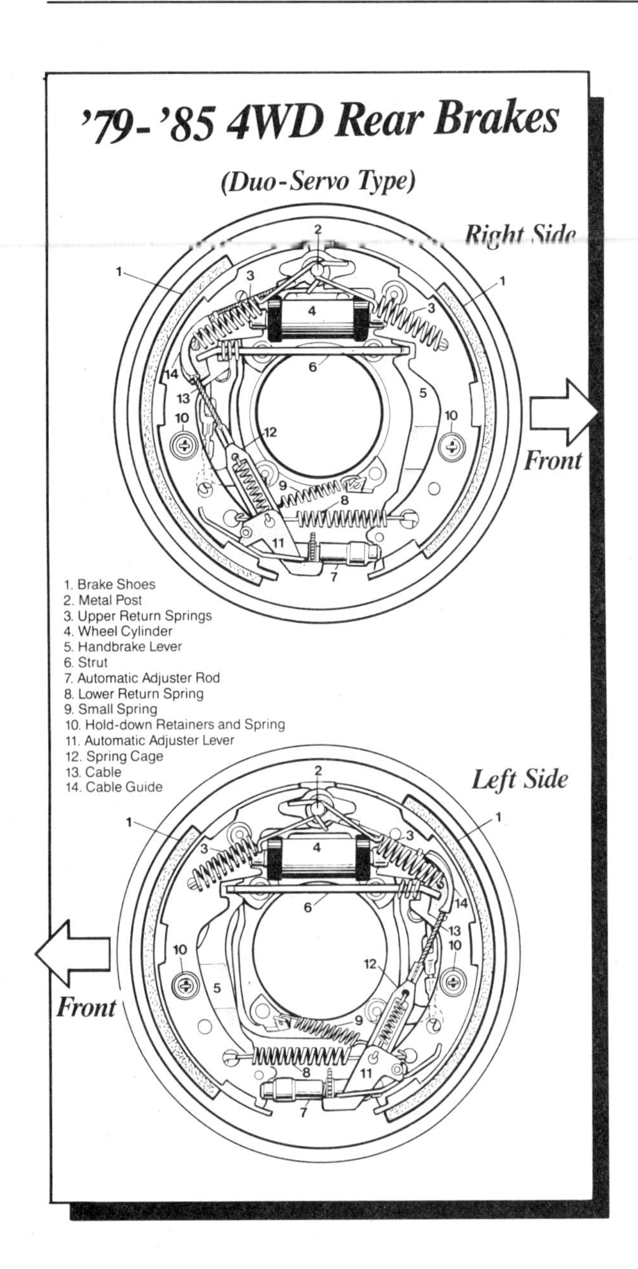

pliers or Vise Grips to pull that spring toward the post until the spring can be unhooked. It takes a fair amount of muscle—squeeze hard on the pliers! Note how the end of the spring fits into the hole in the brake shoe. Remove the other top spring the same way.

Take the round washer on the end of the automatic adjuster cable off the post, then remove the diamond-shaped **brake shoe holder** from the post.

Locate the round **hold-down spring and retainer assembly** near the center of each shoe. Hold the round spring retainer on the primary brake shoe with regular pliers and turn the flat end of the pin 90 degrees with needlenose pliers. Remove the outer spring retainer, spring, and inner spring retainer. The primary brake shoe can be removed now.

4WD models: The handbrake cable is hooked into the bottom of the handbrake lever that's attached to the brake shoe. Slide the cable forward until you can slip it out of the slot in the lever.

EVERYONE: Note the **strut** that goes between the shoes just above the axle. It should have a **spring** wrapped around the front end on 2WD models or around the rear end on 4WDs. Note where your spring is located. The strut is slightly curved so it can clear the axle housing. Remember how it goes when you install the shoes. Pull the strut forward and it will slide out.

Remove the round hold-down spring and retainer from the secondary brake shoe, same as you did with the front retainer assembly.

2WD models: Pull the secondary shoe out until you can see where the handbrake cable attaches to the bottom of a movable lever mounted to the top of the shoe. Hold the lever in one hand and grab the emergency brake cable spring with your other hand. Pull the spring toward the backing plate while twisting the lever so the cable can slide out of the slot.

EVERYONE: The shoes are now liberated. If you're here to install new brake shoes, do the next step. If you're not here to install new shoes, but only need to replace the handbrake cable, wheel cylinder or whatever, now's the time to do it—don't do the next step.

Step 4. Remove Emergency Brake Lever from Brake Shoe.

Locate the **pin** that attaches the emergency brake lever to the brake shoe. The pin is held in place by a **horseshoe clip**. Pry the end of the clip open with a screwdriver, then pull the pin and lever away from the shoe. Save the washer that's behind the clip.

Step 5. Clean, Inspect and Lubricate Brake Parts.

Look at the backing plate around the wheel cylinder for wetness. If you see any sign of fluid, the wheel cylinder is leaking and should be rebuilt or replaced (Procedure 10) before installing the brake shoes.

If you're installing new shoes, put the old shoes in a sack to return to the parts store for $$. They'll send them off to a rebuild factory for new linings for someone else—and their cycle of life goes 'round again.

Caution: Stash the brake shoes somewhere clean and safe until your hands are clean and you're ready to install them. Keep the right and left side brake parts separated.

Put a catch pan or large rag under the backing plate. Use brake cleaner or solvent and a stiff brush to clean the backing plate, brake drum, and all the parts you removed (except the shoes). Remove the ends of the adjuster bar and clean the parts inside and out. Use a wire brush to clean the threads on the bar. If you're using solvent, wipe the parts off with clean rags. Replace any broken springs, clips, anchor pins, etc., with new ones. Check the little adjuster wheel and replace it if any teeth are missing or worn.

Lightly lubricate the following parts with brake grease, high temperature wheel bearing grease or antiseize compound. Don't use regular multipurpose grease because it might melt and get on the brake shoes. Smear a light coat on the threads of the automatic adjuster bar, then screw it all the way into its holder. Lube the other end of the bar, then slide the thin brass washer (if yours has one) and the slotted shoe holder onto the bar. Use a small screwdriver to lube the slots on the ends of the adjuster bar where the brake shoes fit. Lube the post at the top of the backing plate where the top of the shoes rub. Smear a very light coat of the grease on the six bumps on the backing plate where the shoes rub—one on each side of the metal post, one near each anchor pin hole, and two near the bottom of the backing plate. Wipe excess grease off the parts and backing plate with a rag.

If a groove has worn in some of the bumps on the backing plate, try to smooth them with a file. A groove there can cause the shoe to hang up and not operate properly. Replace the backing plate if the grooves are too deep to file smooth (Chapter 11).

Step 6. Install Brake Shoes.

Clean your hands before fondling the new brake shoes and clean up around the wheels if it's a disaster area. Spread fresh newspapers under each wheel and lay out the new and cleaned parts in their relative positions.

Find a new brake shoe that has a pin sticking out near one end. This will be a secondary brake shoe. Hold the shoe up to the backing plate in its installed position so the pin is at the bottom. If the pin isn't on the outside of the shoe, try the other new shoe that has a pin. Be sure you have one new shoe with a pin correctly installed as the secondary shoe for each side of the car. Sometimes one of the pins is installed wrong. If this is the case, either take the shoes back to the parts store or tap the pin out of the shoe with a hammer and reverse it. Be sure the pin is in tight.

If you're installing new shoes, fit the pin on the handbrake cable lever through the hole on the brake shoe from the back side of the shoe (primary shoe on 4WD, secondary shoe 2WD). Install the washer and then the new horseshoe clip. Locate the clip in the groove of the pin and squeeze the ends of the clip together with pliers.

2WD models: Hold the secondary brake shoe (with the handbrake cable lever attached) up to the backing plate to see which way the brake cable goes through the slot. Got it? Grab the cable spring near the end with one hand and hold the brake lever with other hand. Slide the spring as far as you can away from the cable end. Slide the cable through the slot on the brake lever, then release the spring. This may take a few tries.

4WD models: Fit the handbrake cable into the slot on the brake lever. Be sure the other end is hooked on the lower end of the bell crank.

EVERYONE: Grab the shoe that has the handbrake lever attached and put the top of the shoe against the metal post on the backing plate. Fit the little *horn* on the shoe into the slot on the *wheel cylinder plunger*. Push the *anchor pin* through the hole in the brake shoe. With one hand, hold the pin from behind the backing plate with your fingers while pressing the brake shoe against the backing plate with your thumb. Slide one of the retaining clips onto the pin (the fat side goes toward the spring), then hang the spring on the pin while you get the other clip. The fat side of the outer clip fits into the spring. If you're strong you can push the outer retainer clip on and turn it 90 degrees with your hand. Otherwise, grasp the clip in the end of your pliers and press it over the pin, then turn it 90 degrees to lock it securely in place. Be sure the end of the anchor pin is perpendicular to the slot.

Slide the spring onto the end of the *handbrake (horizontal) strut*. If you don't remember which end it goes on, compare the strut on the brakes on the other side of the truck. Slide the strut over the bearing housing and engage the notched end with the notch on the handbrake cable lever.

Put the top of the other shoe against the metal post. Be sure the little horn fits into the slot in the wheel cylinder plunger. A notch in the shoe should fit into the slot on the end of the handbrake strut. Push the anchor pin through the hole in the shoe and install the bottom clip, spring, and outer clip the way you did on the other shoe.

Slide the diamond-shaped *shoe holder* over the metal post and move it around until it fits over the shoulder of the post. Hold it in place while you put the big washer on the end of the automatic adjuster cable on the post. Point the cable toward the secondary shoe.

Find the hole in the primary brake shoe that is closest to the horizontal strut notch. Hook the short end of one of the heavy *upper shoe return springs* into the hole and turn it so the big hook is next to the post. Use the big pliers to hook the spring over the post.

Put the *cable guide* into the upper spring hole on the secondary shoe. Slide it around until it seats in the hole. Hold it there while you hook the short end of the other upper return spring in the hole. Twist the spring until the hook is close to the post. Be sure the diamond-shaped shoe holder is seated on the post correctly or there won't be enough room on the post for both springs. Put the adjuster cable over the cable guide, then use the big pliers to hook the spring end over the post.

Check the horizontal strut to see that its notches are engaged in the notch of the brake shoe and the notch of the handbrake lever.

Put the *adjuster bar* between the bottom end of the shoes. Remember which end is which? If not, look at the brakes on the other side of the truck. See that the shoes fit snugly into the slots.

Slide the long wire end of the lower return spring behind the secondary brake shoe, then turn it until the hook comes through the hole just above the pin near the bottom of the brake shoe. Use pliers to hook the other end of the spring into the hole on the front brake shoe. Use the same method to install the small spring (if you have one) from the shoe return spring hole of the secondary shoe to the tab on the backing plate.

Slide the automatic adjuster spring over the pin on the bottom of the secondary shoe. The hook hangs over the end of the shoe and points toward the backing plate.

Thread the automatic adjuster cable over the cable guide and pull it toward the bottom of the secondary shoe. Hook the adjuster lever to the bottom of the spring in the spring cage. Insert the notch in the lever into the groove on the pin on the brake shoe. Use pliers to hook the adjuster spring over the lever arm.

To check the automatic adjuster, push on the cable just above the spring cage toward the rear of the car—the lever should engage a tooth of the adjuster bar and turn the wheel. If the lever slides by the adjuster without engaging it, the cable is too short. Check the cable to be sure it goes over the cable guide. Use a screwdriver to slide the washer on the end of the cable toward the rear as far as it will go. It will look off-center on the post but that's OK. Try pushing on the cable again. The lever should turn the adjuster wheel. If it doesn't, look at the brakes on the other side of the car to be sure everything is installed correctly.

Now the shoes need to be adjusted so they are almost touching the drums. Garages do this preliminary brake shoe adjustment with large measuring calipers that you (and I) don't have. We can do it with a trial and adjust method:

Trial and adjust brake shoes: Slide the brake drum onto the axle and over the shoes. It should slide on easily since the adjuster bar is screwed all the way in. Drum won't fit over the shoes? See that the top of the shoes are seated on the post at the top of the backing plate. Wiggle them around until they do. Drum slides on easily? Slide it off the axle, then turn the little adjustment ratchet gear one full turn *counterclockwise* (as viewed from the front of the car) if you're working on the left side, or *clockwise* (as viewed from the front of the car) if you're working on the right side. Got that? You'll hear the teeth click past the automatic adjuster as you turn. If the gear won't turn, you're turning it the wrong direction. Try putting the drum on again. Still slide on easily? If it does, take it off and turn the adjuster gear another round. Do this over and over until the drum rubs against the shoe linings. Now we need to center the brake shoes.

Center the brake shoes: Install both brake drums if you removed them, then pump the brake pedal a few times. This centers the shoes.

If you're here to install new brake shoes, install the new shoes on the opposite side of the truck, then do Procedure 7 to adjust the rear shoes.

Step 7. Install Brake Drum and Wheel.

Fit the brake drum onto the lug nuts so the screw hole is aligned with the hole in the axle. Install the brake drum screw and tighten it with a screwdriver. Install the wheel and snug down the lug nuts, then lower the car off the jackstands and tighten the lug nuts to 65 to 87 ft.lbs.

If you disconnected any brake lines, check the fluid level in the master cylinder reservoir and add fluid if necessary (Chapter 5, Procedure 2, Step 5), then bleed the brake system (Procedure 1 in this chapter). This would be a good time to change the hydraulic fluid if it hasn't been changed recently (Procedure 2).

Step 8. Final Brake Adjustment.

After installing the brake drum and wheel, but before hitting the road, clear the tricycles, bicycles, kids and pets from behind the car, then drive in and out of the driveway a few times applying the brakes every two or three feet while going backwards. This does the final brake adjustment.

PROCEDURE 9: REMOVE AND INSTALL LEADING/TRAILING TYPE REAR BRAKE SHOES

This procedure is only for '79-'87 2WD (except C&C) and '86-'87 4WD models. Please read the **Caution! Warning!** at the beginning of this chapter. Thanks.

Condition: Groans, growls or squeals come from the rear of the car when the brakes are applied; OR the brake linings are 1/16" or less; OR a wheel cylinder has taken a leak on the brake linings; OR the drum and shoes have to come off so you can repair or replace the wheel cylinder, replace the handbrake cable or remove the axle.

Tools and Materials: Phase 1 tool kit, safety glasses, dust mask or respirator, needlenose pliers, regular pliers, medium screwdriver, catch pan, can of brake cleaner or solvent, stiff cleaning brush, rags, old newspapers, brake grease or high temp wheel bearing grease or antiseize compound. If you are installing new shoes, you'll need new brake shoes, two new horseshoe-shaped C-clips, and two E-ring clips.

Remarks: Take your time on this procedure—brakes are very important! Remove and replace the brake shoes on one wheel at a time so you can use the other side for reference when assembling the shoes.

You can buy new brake shoes from Toyota or rebuilt ones from auto parts stores. The rebuilt units seem to work as well and last as long as new ones, so call around for prices and go for the best deal.

Step 1. Chock, Jack, Block, Remove Rear Wheels.

See Procedure 6, Step 2 to get the rear end of the truck jacked up and on safety stands and the rear wheels removed.

Step 2. Remove Rear Brake Drums.

Safety glasses and respirator on? Remove the large phillips screw on the outboard side of the brake drum, then pull the brake drum off the end of the axle. If it doesn't come off easily, see Procedure 6, Step 2.

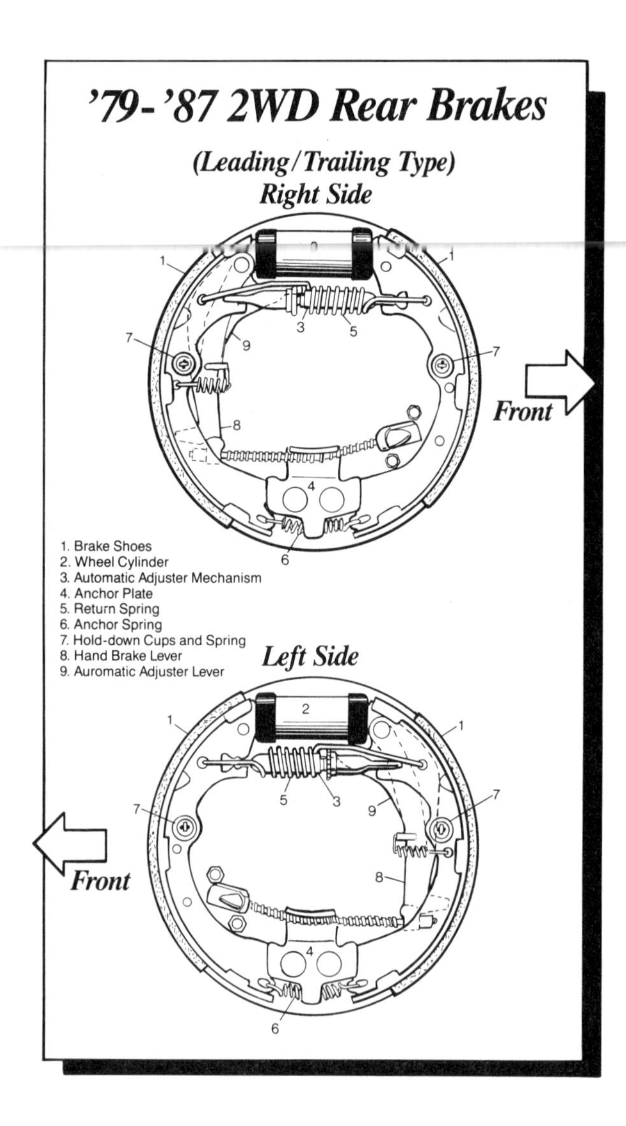

Step 3. Identify Rear Brake Components.

The top ends of the brake shoes fit into rubber boots on each end of the **wheel cylinder**. An **automatic adjuster mechanism** fits between the shoes just below the wheel cylinder. The bottoms of the shoes fit against a block of metal called an **anchor plate** attached to the brake backing plate. A long, heavy **return spring** attached between the shoes near the top and a short **anchor spring** at the bottom keep the shoes pulled away from the drums until the brakes are applied. On 2WD models the large upper return spring is wrapped around the automatic adjuster mechanism. On 4WD models the large upper return spring is just below the automatic adjuster mechanism. An **anchor pin** sticking through the backing plate and the center of each shoe is held in place by hold-down cups and a hold-down spring.

2WD models: Two levers located between the rear brake shoe and backing plate are attached to the upper end of the shoe. The longer lever is the **parking brake lever**. When the parking brake is applied, the parking brake cable pulls on the bottom end of the lever, which forces the brake shoes against the brake drum and locks the rear wheels. The shorter lever, the **automatic brake adjuster lever**, has a tab that wraps around the center of the parking brake lever.

4WD models: A **parking brake lever** and **automatic adjuster lever** are mounted on a post near the top end of the front brake shoe. A cable attaches the bottom of the parking brake lever to a **bellcrank lever** bolted to the backing plate. A tab on the bottom of the automatic adjuster lever wraps around the center of the parking brake lever. A small spring is attached between the tab on the automatic adjuster lever and the inboard side of the brake shoe.

EVERYONE: An **arm** at the top of the adjuster lever engages a small **toothed wheel** when the parking brake is applied and adjusts the brakes so the shoes are the correct distance from the brake drum.

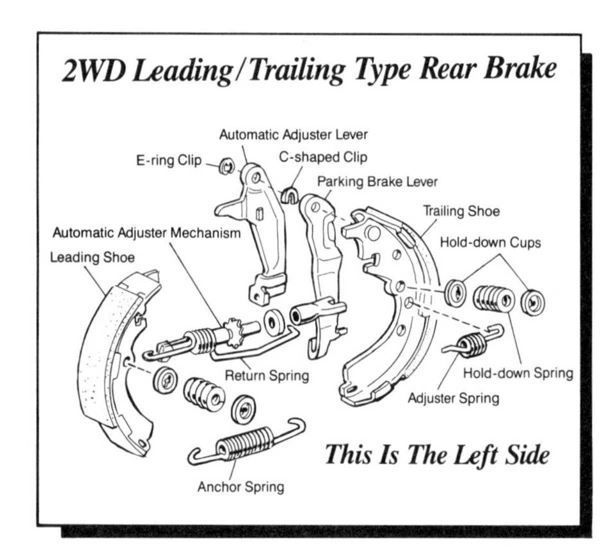

Step 4. Remove Rear Brake Shoes.

Safety glasses and respirator on? Place your catch pan beneath the wheel you're working on. If you have a spray can of brake cleaner, use it and a brush or rag to wash the accumulated brake dust off the shoes, wheel cylinder, springs, levers, etc. It will make removing the shoes a lot more pleasant. When the brakes are clean, or if you don't have brake cleaner spread out some newspapers under the side you're working on.

2WD: Use pliers or a brake spring tool to unhook the large upper spring from the front brake shoe. If you're using pliers, grab the straight part of the spring, then pull the spring forward until you can pull the hook on the end of the spring out of its hole in the brake shoe.

4WD: Use large pliers to unhook the end of the large spring from the hole in the top of the rear brake shoe.

EVERYONE: Locate the hold-down cup half way between the top and bottom of the front shoe (2WD) or rear shoe (4WD). Grab the little flattened anchor pin sticking out of the cup with needlenose pliers. Hold the round cup with your fingers while you turn the pin 90 degrees in either direction so the flat part of the pin lines up with the slot in the cup. The cup will pop off when the pin is aligned. Remove the cup, spring and inner cup next to the brake shoe. Lay them aside, then push the pin through the hole in the brake shoe. Now you can remove the front shoe (2WD) or rear shoe (4WD). Just wiggle it away from the backing plate. Disconnect the anchor spring from the bottom of the shoe.

To remove the rear shoe (2WD) or front shoe (4WD), remove the hold-down cups and spring located near the center of the shoe the same way you removed them from the other shoe. Wiggle the shoe away from the backing plate. It is still attached to the parking brake cable at the bottom of the parking brake lever.

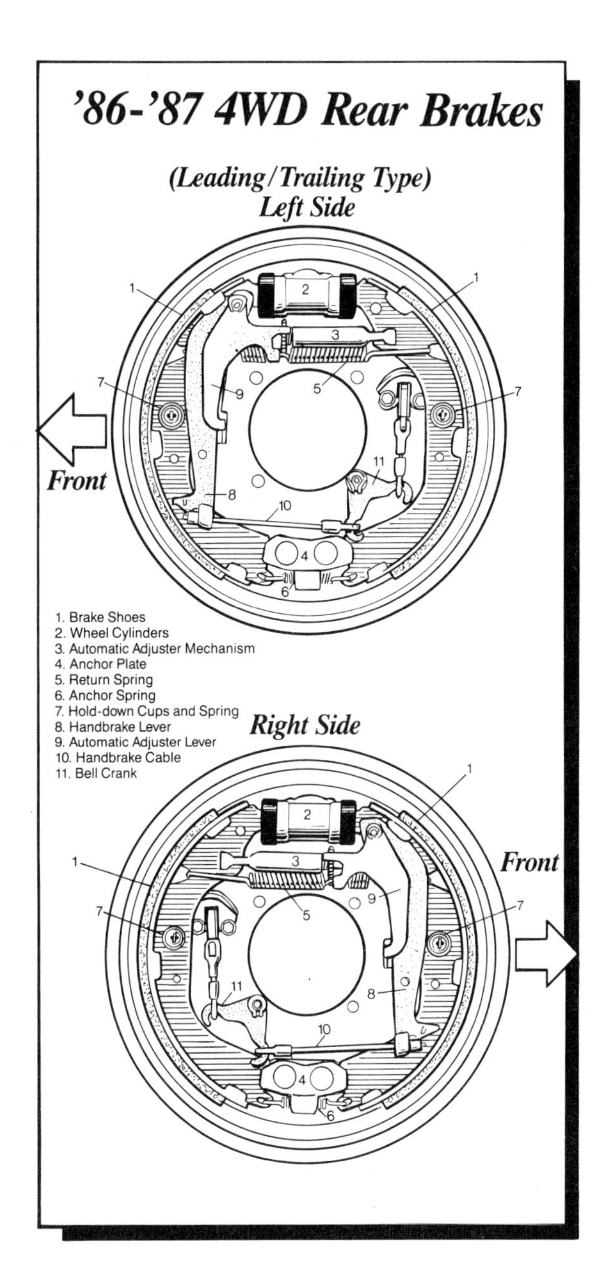

Look at the two levers attached to the brake shoe. The one closest to the shoe is the parking brake lever and the other, shorter one is the automatic adjusting lever. A tab at the bottom of the adjusting lever wraps around the parking brake lever. Use pliers to remove the short adjusting spring that connects the brake shoe to the tab on the adjusting lever. Remove the brake shoe end of the spring first. Note where and how the adjusting spring is attached to the brake shoe and the tab on the adjusting lever.

2WD: Now you can disconnect the end of the large spring that's wrapped around the automatic adjusting mechanism from the brake shoe. Wiggle the large spring and automatic adjuster off the brake shoe.

To disconnect the parking brake cable from the bottom of the parking brake lever, use pliers to grab and pull on the knob on the end of the cable. Push the parking brake lever away from the knob until the cable can slip out of the slot in the lever. The shoes are now liberated.

4WD: Now you can pull the shoe and adjuster mechanism away from the backing plate. Wiggle the automatic adjuster mechanism from between the levers. Locate the cable attached between the bottom of the bellcrank and the bottom of the parking brake lever. Pull the cable forward far enough to lift it out of the slot on the parking brake lever. Unhook the other end from the bellcrank. The shoes are now liberated.

EVERYONE: See Step 5 to clean and inspect the springs, levers, brake drums, and so on.

Step 5. Clean, Inspect, Lubricate Brake Parts.

If you are replacing the shoes because the wheel cylinder leaked on them, rebuild or replace the wheel cylinder (Procedure 10) before installing the new shoes.

Inspect the brake parts and replace any springs, levers and cups that are broken, bent or worn thin. Check the little teeth on the wheel part of the automatic adjuster mechanism. Replace the mechanism if any teeth are rounded or missing.

Put a catch pan or rags under the backing plate and use brake cleaner, or a rag or stiff brush soaked in solvent to clean the backing plate and the inside of the brake drum. If you're using solvent, dry everything off with a clean rag.

Put a very light coat of brake grease, wheel bearing grease or antiseize compound on the *six bumps* on the backing plate where the shoes rub. Two are near the wheel cylinder at the top, two are near the bottom, and one is next to each anchor pin hole. Use a small screwdriver to smear a little grease or antiseize compound in the slots on the adjuster. Wipe off excess grease with a rag.

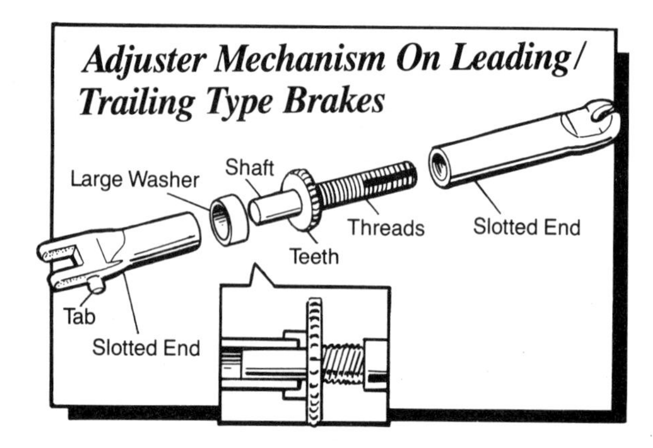

Unscrew the wheel on the automatic adjuster mechanism several turns so you can apply a thin coat of high temp grease to the threaded part. The screw on the left side of the car will be lefthanded so you screw it *clockwise* to unscrew it and *counter-clockwise* to screw it into the adjuster. Screw the adjuster back together as far as it will go. Pull the slotted end and large washer off the rear end of the adjuster mechanism. Clean and then lightly grease the shaft where the slotted end fits. Install the large washer on the shaft with its open part toward the end of the shaft. Next install the slotted end. Wipe off any excess grease. Put dabs of grease into the notches on both ends of the adjuster.

Here's how to check the brake drums: if the friction surfaces on the inside of the brake drums have grooves, scores or ridges, you should get them smoothed out by having them "turned" by a machine shop, parts store, garage or Toyota dealer. If the grooves are too deep, the drum must be replaced. You might find a good used one at a junkyard and save some money.

If you are installing new brake shoes, do Step 6 to install the levers on the new shoes. If you aren't installing new brake shoes, go to Step 7 to install the old brake shoes.

Step 6: Assemble New Brake Shoes

This step is for people who are installing new brake shoes. If you are installing the old shoes and haven't removed the parking brake lever and automatic adjuster lever from the brake shoe, skip down to Step 7 to install the shoes.

Clean and dry your hands, then break out the new shoes and compare them to the old ones. If the shape of the metal part of the new shoes doesn't match the old, the parts store gave you the wrong shoes. Put the old shoes in a paper sack and take them, along with the new shoes, back to the store.

Shoes match? Good. First we'll install the parking brake and automatic adjusting levers on the new brake shoe. Grab the old shoe that has the levers attached and note how the levers are oriented so you can install them on the new shoe in exactly the same way. Use a very small screwdriver to remove the E-ring clip from the end of the shaft that the levers are mounted on. While removing the E-ring, hold it with one hand so it can't fly off and get lost. Wiggle the automatic adjusting lever off the shaft. Use a medium screwdriver to spread the ends of the little C-shaped clip that attaches the parking brake lever to the old brake shoe. Wiggle the lever off.

Clean the levers if they are dirty, then install the parking brake lever onto the shaft on the new shoe that has a post. Fit a new C-shaped clip onto the groove on the shaft, then use pliers to squeeze the ends together. Be sure the clip locks the lever onto the shaft. Fit the automatic adjuster lever onto the shaft and install a new E-ring into the thin groove near the end of the shaft. Check that it is securely in the groove.

Step 7. Install Brake Shoes

OK, the brake parts have been cleaned, inspected and lubricated. And if you're installing new shoes, the levers have been transferred from the old shoes to the new shoes. Spread the clean brake parts on a clean sheet of newspaper.

2WD: Now it's time to connect the parking brake cable to the parking brake lever on the rear shoe. Use your fingers to push the spring away from the knob on the end of the cable just far enough to slip the tips of needlenose pliers between the spring and knob. Hold the knob on the end of the cable with pliers while you use the needlenose pliers to push the spring on the cable about an inch away from the knob. Squeeze on the needlenose pliers to hold the spring there while you slip the cable into its groove on the backside of the parking brake lever. When the cable is in the slot, remove the needlenose pliers.

Fit the slot on the rear end of the automatic adjuster mechanism into the notch on the rear brake shoe. Be sure the large spring is on the outboard side of the brake shoe. Engage the tab on the side of the automatic adjuster mechanism into the hole on the adjusting lever. Hold the adjusting mechanism in place while you check that the tab at the bottom of the adjusting lever is wrapped around the parking brake lever. Install the short adjusting lever spring into the tab on the adjuster lever, then hook the other end into the hole in the rear brake shoe. Next connect the large upper return spring to the rear brake shoe.

Wiggle the rear brake shoe upright so the top end fits into the wheel cylinder and the bottom end fits into the anchor plate.

Retrieve the rear anchor pin if it's fallen out of the backing plate, then push it toward you through the holes in the backing plate and brake shoe. Hold the pin from behind the backing plate while putting one of the round hold-down cups on the pin. Install the cup so the flat side is toward the shoe and the fat side is away from the brake shoe. Fit the shoe hold-down spring onto the anchor pin. Grab the other cup and install it so the fat side fits into the hold-down spring. Align the slot in the cup with the flat end of the pin. Use your fingers or pliers to press against the cup until the pin sticks through the hole. Push and turn the cup 90 degrees so the end of the pin fits securely in the groove of the clip.

Grab the front shoe and install the short anchor spring between the bottom ends of the brake shoes. Install the front shoe so the upper end fits into the wheel cylinder and the lower end fits into the anchor plate. The anchor spring should be across the bottom of the anchor plate. Install the shoe hold-down cups and spring on the front shoe just as you did on the rear shoe.

Use pliers or a brake spring tool to hook the large return spring into its hole on the front shoe. This is the hard part, so you'll have to squeeze hard on the pliers while pulling the end of the spring forward. Be sure the end of the spring is hooked securely into its hole.

4WD: Fit the slot on the front end of the automatic adjuster mechanism into the notch on the front brake shoe. Engage the tab on the side of the mechanism into the hole on the adjusting lever. Hold the adjusting mechanism in place while you check that the tab at the bottom of the adjusting lever is wrapped around the parking brake lever. Install the short adjusting lever spring into the tab on the adjuster lever, then hook the other end into the hole in the brake shoe. Wiggle the front brake shoe upright so the top end fits into the wheel cylinder and the bottom end fits into the anchor plate. Hook the end of the large return spring in its hole on the front brake shoe.

Hold the front shoe in position against the brake backing plate so the top end of the shoe is inserted into the wheel cylinder and the bottom end is in the anchor plate. The adjuster mechanism and large return spring should be laying across top of the axle housing.

Retrieve the front anchor pin if it's fallen out of the backing plate, then push it toward you through the holes in the backing plate and brake shoe. Hold the pin from behind the backing plate while putting one of the round hold-down cups on the pin. Install the cup so the flat side is toward the brake shoe and the fat side is away from the shoe. Fit the shoe hold-down spring onto the anchor pin. Grab the other cup and install it so the fat side fits into the hold-down spring. Align the slot in the cup with the flat end of the pin. Press against the cup until the pin sticks through the hole. Push and turn the cup 90 degrees so the end of the pin fits securely in the groove of the clip.

Now it's time to connect the parking brake cable to the parking brake lever on the front shoe. Slip the end of the cable with the knob into its groove on the parking brake lever, then hook the other end to the bellcrank lever.

Grab the rear shoe and install the short anchor spring between the bottom ends of the brake shoes. Install the rear shoe so the upper end fits into the wheel cylinder and the lower end fits into the anchor plate. Check that the slot on the rear end of the automatic adjuster mechanism is engaged in the notch on the rear shoe. The anchor spring should be across the bottom of the anchor plate. Now install the shoe hold-down cups and spring on the rear shoe just as you did on the front shoe.

Use pliers or a brake spring tool to hook the large return spring into its hole on the rear shoe. This is the hard part, so you'll have to squeeze hard on the pliers while pulling the end of the spring rearward. Be sure the end of the spring is hooked securely into its hole.

EVERYONE: Before installing the brake drum, check the automatic adjuster to see if it's working. Here's how. Grab the bottom of the parking brake lever and pull it forward. On 2WD models you might need to use a screwdriver to push against the lever if you can't get to it your fingers. As you pull on the lever, the adjusting bolt in the little toothed wheel on the automatic adjuster mechanism should turn slightly. Push on the lever several times. If the wheel doesn't turn, read through the brake shoe installation step again while checking the shoes, levers and springs to be sure everything is assembled correctly. Make any changes that are necessary. If the adjuster is working correctly, push (2WD) or pull (4WD) the automatic adjuster lever away from the little wheel to disengage it while you screw the wheel in so the adjuster mechanism is the shortest possible length.

Install the brakes on the other rear wheel, if you haven't done so already.

Slide the drums onto the axles and over the brake shoes. Watch those fingers—if they get caught between the brake drum and backing plate you'll most likely say a bunch of naughty words! Once the brake drums are on, install and tighten the brake drum screw, if your model has one.

See Step 8 to adjust the rear brakes.

Step 8: Adjust Rear Brakes, Finish the Job.

To adjust the rear brakes, get in the cab and pull out on the parking brake lever as far as it will go, then release it. Repeat this several times. Keep the handle twisted *clockwise* while you pull and release so it won't make the clicking sound. Listen for clicks coming from the rear brakes. That's the automatic adjuster lever turning the little toothed wheel. Keep pulling the handbrake lever out and releasing it until you no longer hear clicks coming from the rear brakes. That's all there is to it.

This would be a good time to change the hydraulic brake fluid if it hasn't been changed recently (Procedure 2).

Install the wheels and snug the lug nuts. Lower the truck off the jackstands, then torque the lug nuts to 65-87 ft.lbs.

Before heading out into heavy traffic, go for a leisurely drive around the block to see that the brakes are working properly.

PROCEDURE 10. REBUILD OR REPLACE REAR WHEEL CYLINDERS

The wheel cylinders on all models are very similar. They consist of a metal cylinder, a short spring in the center of the cylinder, a rubber cup on each side of the spring, and a wheel cylinder piston on the outside of the rubber cups. A rubber wheel cylinder boot with a hole in the center covers each end of the cylinder. On some models a slotted rod fits in the boot.

Condition: Rear wheel cylinders are leaking.

Tools and Materials: Phase 1 tool kit, new wheel cylinder(s) or wheel cylinder repair kit(s), 10mm flare nut wrench, fine steel wool and alcohol, at least three pints of DOT3 or 4 brake fluid, safety glasses.

Remark: The wheel cylinders force the brake shoes into contact with the brake drum. If they're leaking fluid or admitting air, they won't do their job properly, so you risk a dent in your fender at the very least. There are two ways to go. You can buy new wheel cylinders from Toyota or a foreign car parts store (they don't cost much), or you can rebuild the existing cylinder for about half the cost. Go for the new ones if you can afford it.

If you decide to rebuild the old wheel cylinders, but when you get the thing apart you find that the inside of the wheel cylinder is rusted, scored or nicked at all, don't try to save money by installing a rebuild kit. The cylinder won't work properly and may contribute to your demise. Buy a new cylinder. If you can't decide whether to replace or repair, take the cylinder to someone who knows. If one of the mounting bolts or the bleeder nipple breaks off the cylinder, you have no choice but to replace the cylinder with a new one.

Step 1. Remove Rear Wheels, Brake Drums and Shoes.

Duo-Servo rear brakes: '75-'78 models, '79-'87 C & C (except '86-'87 with dual rear wheels) and '79-'85 4WD models see Procedure 8.

Leading/Trailing rear brakes: '79-'87 2WD (except C & C) and '86-'87 4WD models: see Procedure 9.

Step 2. Remove Wheel Cylinder Components.

Locate the bleeder valve on the inboard side of the backing plate. If there's a rubber cap on the bleeder valve, remove it, then use a 10mm box end wrench to loosen the bleeder valve about one full turn.

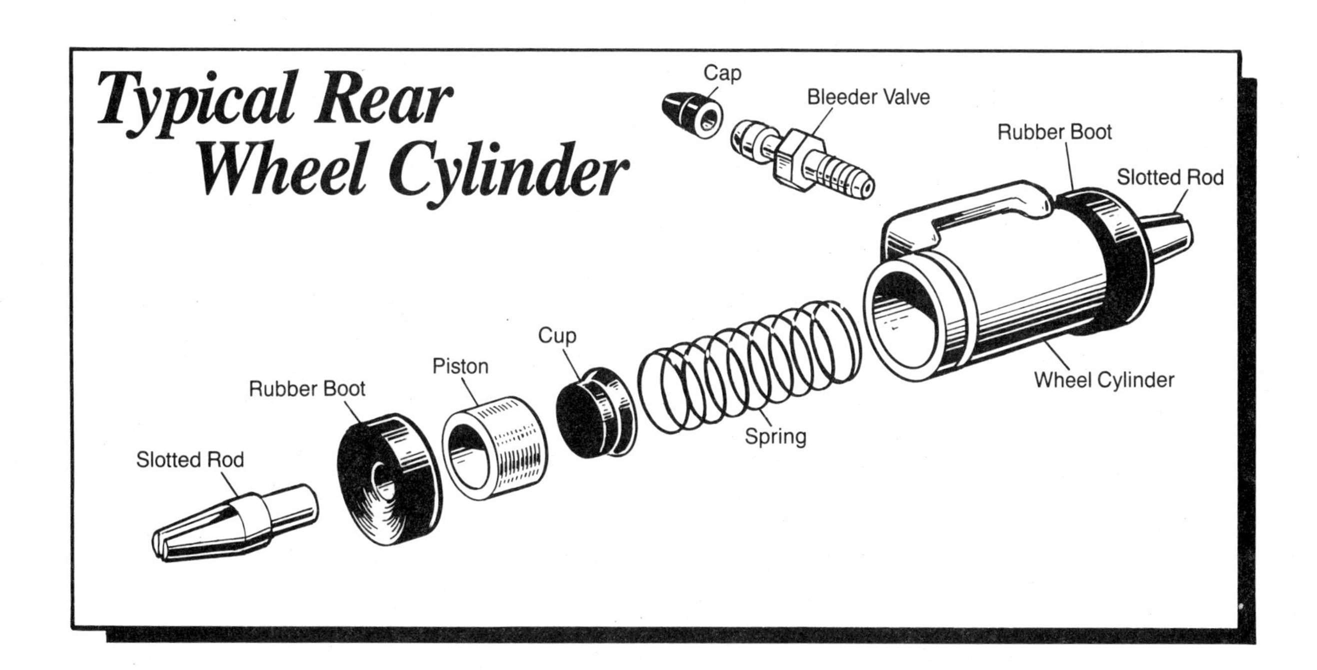

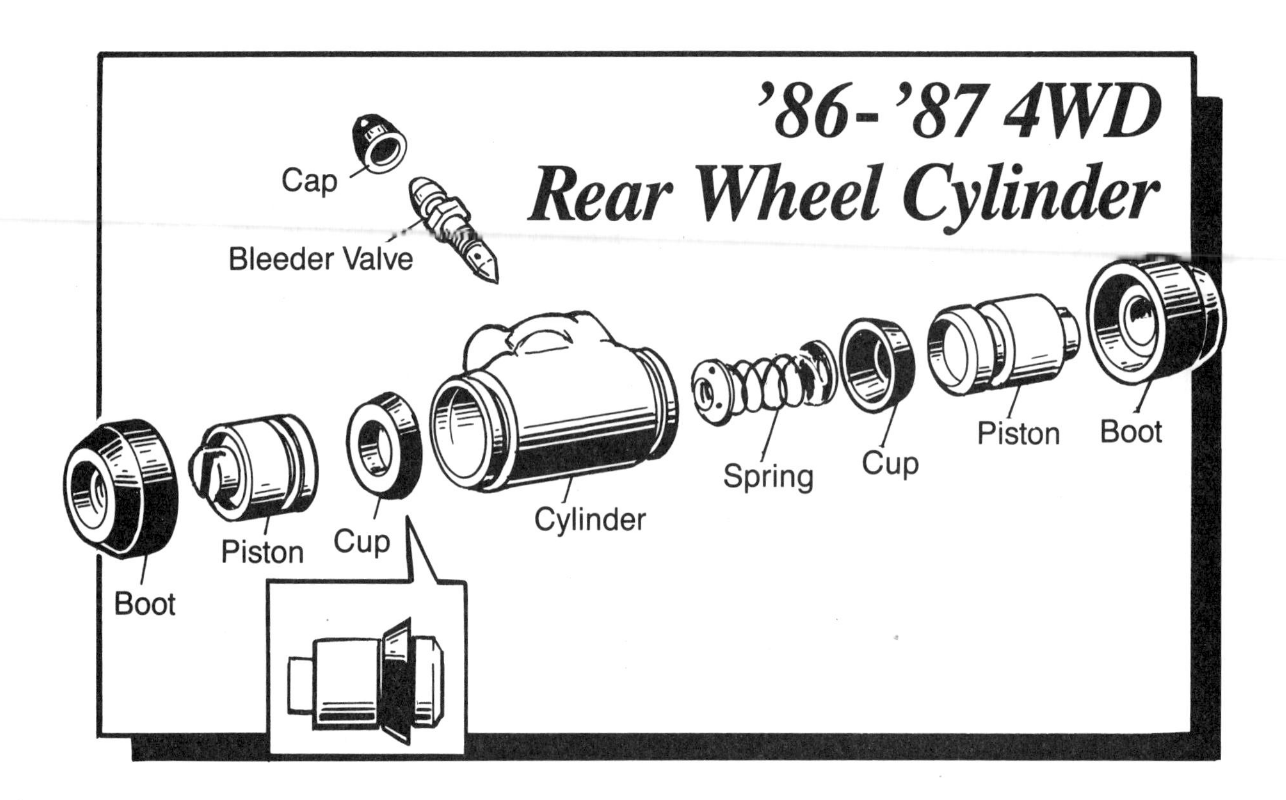

All models except '86-'87 4WD: Pull the **rubber boots** from each end of the wheel cylinder. On models with Duo-Servo brakes, a **slotted rod** will come off with the rubber boot. Use your finger to push on the plunger in either end of the wheel cylinder to force the pistons, rubber cups and spring out of the cylinder. Note how the rubber cups are oriented as they come out of the cylinder.

'86 and '87 4WD models: Pull the rubber boots off the ends of the wheel cylinder. A **piston** with a **rubber cup** attached to the end will come out when you remove each rubber boot. If the boot comes off the piston, just grab the end of the piston and pull it out. Remove the short spring from the cylinder.

Note how the rubber cups are oriented on the ends of the pistons. The large flange on the cup faces toward the center of the wheel cylinder.

Step 3. Clean and Inspect Inside of Wheel Cylinder.

Once the pistons, cups and spring are out, dip a piece of steel wool in alcohol and push it into the wheel cylinder. Stick a screwdriver into the center of the steel wool and twist it around and around so the steel wool tangles with the blade—but don't let the blade touch the side of the cylinder. Put a good shine on the inside of the cylinder. Don't push the steel wool backward and forward—only 'round and 'round until the cylinder bore is nice and smooth. You can stick another screwdriver into the steel wool from the other end of the cylinder for better action.

When the inside of the cylinder is clean, inspect it for grooves and corrosion pits. If the inside of the cylinder is nice and smooth, you can rebuild the cylinder (Step 4).

Dark spots near the center of the bore are indications that the surface of the cylinder has been etched by water and crud in the brake fluid. Play dentist for a minute and gently probe the spots with a small screwdriver to see if they are indeed "cavities." If they are, that's probably the reason you're doing this procedure. If there's any doubt, replace the cylinder with a new one (Step 5). New wheel cylinders are a lot cheaper than hospital bills.

Step 4. Rebuild Wheel Cylinder.

If you are going to replace the wheel cylinders, skip to Step 5.

'86-'87 4WD models: If the cups fit into grooves on the piston, remove the old, tired rubber cups from the ends of the pistons. Pry them off with a small screwdriver, being careful to avoid scratching the piston.

EVERYONE: Clean the pistons with the steel wool and alcohol. Dry the pistons with a clean rag to remove any traces of the steel wool.

Wash your hands thoroughly to remove any traces of grease. Break out your can of brake fluid and pour a little into a clean container. Dip a corner of a clean rag or your forefinger into the brake fluid and thoroughly swab out the inside of the wheel cylinder.

Take the wheel cylinder rebuild kit out of the box and put the two round cups and the clean pistons and spring in the container with brake fluid. Don't soak the two large end boots.

EVERYONE (except '86-'87 4WD models that have grooves in the piston for the cups): Take one of the rubber cups and gently insert the larger side into one end of the wheel cylinder until the flat side of the cup is flush with the end of the cylinder. Be sure the lip of the cup isn't flipped over backward. Use one of the pistons to push the cup into the cylinder until the end of the piston is flush with the edge of the cylinder.

Now insert the short spring into the other end of the cylinder. Fit the other cup and piston into the cylinder just as you did before.

Fit the slotted rods into the rubber boots, then fit the boots onto the ends of the wheel cylinder. Turn the slotted rods so the slot is vertical. Skip down to the EVERYONE section.

'86-'87 4WD models with grooves in the pistons for the cups: Take one of the pistons and one of the rubber cups and slip the cup into the groove of the piston. The large shoulder of the cup should be closest to the end of the piston that fits against the spring. Slide one of the rubber end boots into the groove on the other end of the piston. Assemble the other piston, cup and boot the same way.

Next, push and wiggle one of the pistons into one end of the wheel cylinder, rubber cup end first. Snap the end of the boot over the groove on the end of the wheel cylinder so the piston won't fall out. Slip the short spring into the other end of the cylinder, then wiggle the other piston into the end of the wheel cylinder. Don't push so hard you pop the other piston out. Turn the pistons so the slots are vertical, as shown in the illustration. Slip the new dust cap on the bleeder valve. See Step 6 to finish up.

Step 5. Replace Wheel Cylinder.

If you've done Step 4, you can ignore this step; it's only for people who discovered they need a new wheel cylinder.

Remark: There are three easily avoided hazards to removing and replacing wheel cylinders:

1. The nut that attaches the brake line to the wheel cylinder gets rounded off because a 10mm flare nut wrench wasn't used. If this happens, and you can't unscrew the nut, cut the metal brake line with a hacksaw and replace the line with a new one (Procedure 11). Use a flare nut wrench!

2. The attaching bolts for the wheel cylinder break off when you try to unscrew the nuts, thus ruining the cylinder. This is common no matter how careful you are, or how much holy water (penetrating oil) you put on the nuts. If you're replacing the cylinder anyway, so what if they break?

3. The threads on the brake line nut get cross-threaded when they are screwed into the wheel cylinder, ruining both the cylinder and the brake line. Cross-threaded means the threads on the nut aren't aligned with the threads in the cylinder. When this happens the nut goes in at an angle, tearing up the threads and preventing the nut from going into the cylinder far enough to make a good seal. To avoid this catastrophe, move the brake line as little as possible and don't even think about using a wrench on the nut until it's screwed into the cylinder at least half-way by hand.

Now, on with the show.

Use a 10mm flare nut wrench to unscrew the brake line nut from the back of the wheel cylinder. Unscrew it but don't pull it away from its hole. You want to keep the brake line aligned with the hole and also avoid bending it.

Soak the two 10mm nuts on each side of the brake line connection with penetrating oil. Let them soak in for a few minutes, then unscrew the two nuts with a 10mm box end wrench. Pull the cylinder off the backing plate, being careful not to kink the brake line.

When installing a wheel cylinder, don't let any dirt, dust, or dung fall into the bleeder hole or brake line connection hole. Be sure the end of the brake line is clean and uncontaminated before you screw it in.

Wheel cylinders for the right and left side are slightly different, so be sure you are installing the correct wheel cylinder.

To install the wheel cylinder, slip the wheel cylinder bolts into their holes in the backing plate while guiding the brake line nut into its hole. Tighten the brake line nut with your fingers until you are absolutely positively sure it's not cross-threaded. It helps to wiggle the wheel cylinder a little while screwing in the brake line nut. Screw it in as far as you can with your fingers. Install the lockwashers and 10mm nuts and tighten them with the box end wrench. Tighten the brake line nut with the 10mm flare nut wrench.

Step 6. Finish the Job.

Install the brake shoes (Procedure 8 for Duo-Servo or Procedure 9 for Leading/Trailing), then install the brake drums. Install the wheels and snug the lug nuts. Lower the car and torque the lug nuts to 65-87 ft.lbs. After both sides are rebuilt or replaced, change the brake fluid (Procedure 2). I mean it—it's tedious but very important.

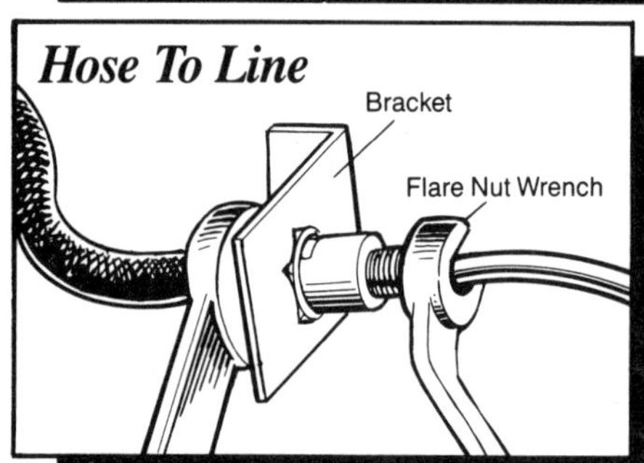

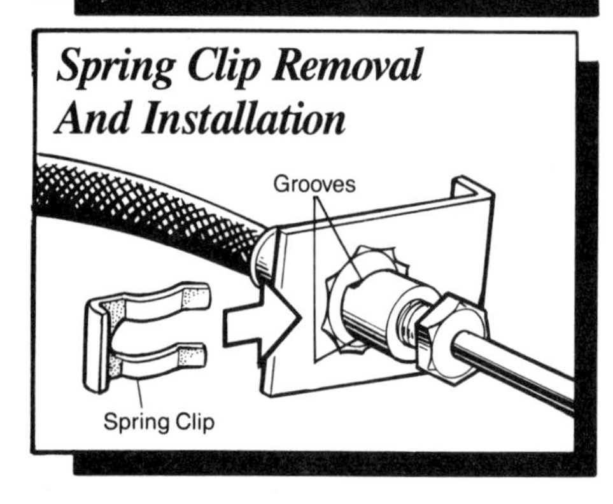

PROCEDURE 11: REPLACE RUBBER BRAKE HOSES

Condition: The hoses are worn, cracked, split or bulging in places.

Tools and Materials: Phase 1 tool kit, 10mm flare nut wrench, new hoses, three cans of DOT3 or 4 brake fluid.

Remarks: If one brake hose is worn out, the others are probably nearing the end of the trail too. Check them carefully. When you buy a new hose, compare the length of the new against the old.

Some models have two rubber hoses under each front fender. Be sure to check both of them.

To locate the rubber brake hose for the rear wheels, follow the metal brake lines from the top of the brake backing plates until you come to the rubber hose.

Step 1. Chock, Jack and Block.

Chock the wheels, loosen the lug nuts a little, jack up the car and put it on jackstands or blocks. Remove the lug nuts, then the wheel.

You don't want any dirt to get into the metal brake line or caliper when you divorce. . . I mean, separate the brake lines, so clean the connections on both ends of the rubber brake hose before removing it.

Step 2. Remove and Install Brake Hose.

Use a rag to catch the brake fluid that's sure to run out of the line. Use a 17mm open end wrench to keep the nut at the end of the rubber brake hose from turning as you use a 10mm flare nut wrench to unscrew the nut on the metal brake line. When the nut is completely unscrewed, use pliers to remove the **spring clip** that attaches the rubber brake hose to the **brake line bracket**. Pull the rubber hose away from the bracket. *DON'T* pull the metal brake line away from the bracket. If it gets bent, even slightly, it will be hard to screw the nut into the new brake hose. Remove the other end of the hose the same way.

To install the hose, stick the end of the brake hose through the mounting bracket hole. Screw the nut on the metal brake line into the hose by hand until you're sure the threads have started correctly. Position the hose so there are no kinks and so the hose can't rub against anything. Secure the hose to the bracket with a spring clip. Use a 17mm wrench on the brake hose nut to keep the hose from twisting while you tighten the 10mm nut with a flare nut wrench. Make it tight.

Step 3. Bleed.

After replacing the worn out hoses, bleed the brake system (Procedure 1). When the brakes have been bled, have someone press the brake pedal a few times while you watch the hose connections for leaks. Don't forget to replace the dust caps on the bleeding nipples. That's it.

PROCEDURE 12: REMOVE AND INSTALL MASTER CYLINDER

The master cylinder sticks out from the left side of the firewall and has one large or two small semi-opaque white plastic hydraulic **fluid reservoirs** on top. The master cylinder is mounted on the front of a black cylindrical "Master Vac" brake booster.

A special tool is required to set the clearance between the master cylinder pushrod and the Master Vac unit. You'll need to buy or borrow the tool before replacing the master cylinder. If you can't get the tool, have the Toyota dealer replace or rebuild the master cylinder for you.

Condition: Master cylinder is leaking; OR no matter how much you bleed the brakes the pedal is still spongy; OR you have to bleed the brakes frequently; OR the Master Vac needs to be removed.

Tools and Materials: Special Toyota Tool #09737-00010, phase 1 tool kit, 10mm flare nut wrench, three pints of fresh DOT3 or 4 brake fluid, brake bleeding hose and jar (Procedure 1), two baggies, rags. *Optional:* syringe or eye dropper.

Remarks: If you've determined that the master cylinder isn't performing the way it should, call a few garages to see how much they'll charge to rebuild your old one. Then call Toyota and a few parts stores to see what a new or rebuilt one costs. If the prices are close, go for a new or rebuilt one. They usually come with new reservoirs and sometimes even have new reservoir caps.

Step 1. Unplug Wires, Drain Master Cylinder.

Place a large rag under the master cylinder to catch stray drops of brake fluid. Brake fluid is harmful to eyes and paint, so be careful!

If there are wires coming from the reservoir cap or caps, trace the wires to a connector located about 3" from the master cylinder. Disconnect the wires by pulling the connector apart.

Pull off the reservoir **cap(s)** and remove the little plastic **strainers** (if you have them) and put them somewhere clean and safe. If there are round rubber floats in the reservoirs, remove them too.

Use something like an eye dropper or syringe to empty the brake fluid out of the reservoir(s). Don't suck the stuff out yourself—POISON! As an alternative, use clean rags or paper towels to soak the fluid out.

Step 2. Remove Master Cylinder.

Remove the two brake line nuts from the master cylinder with a 10mm flare nut wrench. Pull the lines just slightly clear of their fittings, but don't kink the lines! Put a baggie over the end of each line to keep it clean.

Remove the four 12mm nuts that connect the master cylinder to the Master Vac unit. Make a note of other things attached with the mounting bolts, then carefully pull the master cylinder and its gasket forward and free. Pour any brake fluid remaining in the master cylinder into a suitable container. Stuff a clean rag into the hole left by the departed master cylinder. Clean the outside of the master cylinder if you're going to take it to a brake specialist for rebuilding.

Step 3. Adjust Push Rod.

Here's where you use that special Toyota tool.

Install the master cylinder gasket on the firewall end of the master cylinder. Set the gauge on the master cylinder so the legs of the gauge are squarely on the gasket and the gauge pin is pointed toward the master cylinder. Gently push the pin into the master cylinder until it touches lightly. Remove the gauge without moving the gauge pin.

Set the gauge on the end of the Master Vac unit so the legs are against the body and the knob on the end of the pin is toward the **booster push rod** that's sticking out of the Master Vac. You'll probably need to hold the push rod in the center of the hole. The end of the rod should lightly touch the knob on the end of the gauge pin. If the rod is too short and doesn't touch the knob, or if it's too long and pushes the pin into the gauge, the booster push rod must be adjusted. If the rod lightly touches the knob, everything is OK so you can skip down to Step 4 to install the master cylinder.

Here's how to adjust the booster push rod. Use pliers to hold the rod while you screw the nut on the end of the rod in or out until the push rod lightly touches the knob on the gauge. Set the gauge in the master cylinder again to set the gauge pin, then check the booster push rod again to be sure it's set right. Adjust the rod again if necessary.

Step 4. Install Master Cylinder.

Fit the gasket onto the studs on the Master Vac unit. Guide the booster push rod into the end of the master cylinder as you slide the master cylinder onto the mounting studs. Don't put the nuts on yet. Remove the plastic baggies and put the two brake lines into their respective holes in the master cylinder. Get the threads on both lines started by hand. Please make sure they're not cross-threaded. Install other things that are attached with the master cylinder mounting nuts and washers, then install and tighten the nuts. Next tighten the two brake line nuts with a 10mm flare nut wrench.

Step 5. Prepare Master Cylinder for Action.

Clean each brake fluid strainer and/or rubber float with a clean rag, then insert it into the reservoir. Replace any that are torn, broken or greasy. Fill the reservoir(s) with fresh clean brake fluid to the MAX line. Slowly pump the brake pedal five times, then check the fluid level. If necessary, add more fluid to keep the level at the MAX line. Pump and add, pump and add until the fluid level doesn't drop.

Bleed the master cylinder (Procedure 1, Step 2), then bleed all four wheels (Procedure 1). After replacing the master cylinder, it will take more bleeding than usual to get the air out of the lines. Be patient and persevere. When you're finished bleeding, fill the reservoir to the dotted line below the MAX line. Clean each reservoir cap and round white **fluid level indicator** (if your cap has one) with a clean rag, then put the cap on the reservoir. Reconnect the electrical wires for the fluid level indicator (if you have them).

PROCEDURE 13: CHECK, REMOVE, REPLACE MASTER VAC UNIT

The Master Vac unit is attached via a rubber hose to the engine's intake manifold. When the engine is running, a vacuum is created in the intake manifold as the pistons suck air and fuel into the cylinders. The Master Vac utilizes this vacuum to reduce the amount of pressure required on the brake pedal to stop the car. A check valve in the rubber hose prevents the vacuum from flowing back to the manifold.

Condition: Everything in the brake system checks out OK, but extra force must be applied to the brake pedal before braking action occurs.

Tools and Materials: Phase 1 tool kit, 10mm flare nut wrench, big baggie.

Remark: If it almost takes both feet on the brake pedal to slow the car, run through the Master Vac check (Step 1). If the tests indicate the unit is faulty, have a Toyota dealer check the old unit with gauges before replacing it with a new one. They're expensive, so be sure the old one is dead before replacing it.

Step 1. Check Master Vac Operation.

Be sure the handbrake is on.

Operation Check: Before starting the engine, pump the brake pedal a few times using the same pressure. After a few pumps the pedal height shouldn't vary with each pump of the pedal. Hold the pedal down and start the engine. When the engine starts the brake pedal should move toward the floor slightly. If the pedal doesn't drop a little, do Step 2.

Loaded Air Tightness Check: Hold the brake pedal down while the engine is running, then turn the engine off. Hold the pedal down for 30 seconds. If the pedal height stays the same, the Master Vac is OK. If the pedal moves up away from the floor, the Master Vac has a problem; do Step 2.

Air Tightness Check: Start the engine and let it run for a few minutes, then turn it off. Push on the brake pedal a few times with the same force you usually use to stop the car. If the Master Vac is working properly, the pedal should go further toward the floor the first time you press on it and stop further away from the floor with each following stroke. If there is no change in the distance the pedal travels, check the **check valve** and rubber **vacuum hose** (Step 2).

Step 2. Test Check Valve and Vacuum Hose.

Check the large black hose that connects the Master Vac to the intake manifold on the engine. Look for cracks, splits and/or loose connections. Replace any hoses that are suspect.

Somewhere along the big black vacuum hose between the Master Vac and the intake manifold on the engine you'll find a brass or plastic **check valve** that's about the same diameter as the vacuum hose. On some models the check valve is almost hidden beneath a clamp or clip. If it's under a clamp, remove the phillips screw, then the clamp. If it's under a clip, just pop the valve out of the clip. Notice that the ends of the valve are different; one end might be slightly tapered or grooved. Make a note or draw a picture of your valve so you can install it in the same position later.

Use pliers to squeeze the little tabs on the spring clamps next to the check valve, then slide the clamps up the hose, away from the valve. Twist and pull the hose off each end of the check valve. The valve is now free.

Hold the valve while you blow into each end. Air should only flow through the valve in one direction—from the Master Vac end toward the engine end. If air passes both ways, replace the valve with a new one and test the Master Vac again.

Install the check valve back on the hoses. Use your note or drawing to orient the valve. Slide the clamps into place on each end of the valve, then secure the valve in the clamp or clip. If the Master Vac still doesn't work, here's how to replace it.

Step 3. Remove and Install Master Vac.

Remove the master cylinder (Procedure 12). Put it in a clean baggie and stash it somewhere clean and safe.

Use pliers to squeeze the clamp on the end of the large black vacuum hose where it attaches to the Master Vac. Slide the clamp up the hose a few inches, then twist and pull the hose off the Master Vac.

Look at the brake pedal inside the car. About 6" above the foot pad is a **clevis** (a U-shaped thing), with a round **clevis pin** going through it and the **brake lever**. Attached to the clevis is the **brake pushrod** that goes through the firewall and into the Master Vac unit. Use needlenose pliers to remove the little **cotter key** or **snap pin** on the end of the clevis pin. Just tap the clevis pin out of the clevis.

Still under the dash, remove the four 12mm nuts around the hole where the brake pushrod goes through the firewall. Now the Master Vac can be removed from the car. Go back under the hood and carefully pull the unit away from the firewall without bending the master cylinder brake lines.

Note the number and location of the gaskets and/or brackets that fit between the Master Vac and firewall. You'll need to install them in the same position during reassembly.

To install the Master Vac, install the gaskets and/or brackets onto the firewall side of the Master Vac. Carefully slide the unit over the brake lines, then push the four mounting bolts into the holes on the firewall. From under the dash, screw on and tighten the four 12mm mounting washers and nuts. Slide the clevis over the brake lever and install the clevis pin. Install the cotter key or snap pin in the end of the clevis pin. If you have a cotter pin, bend the end of the cotter pin around the clevis pin.

Connect the black vacuum hose to the Master Vac unit in the engine compartment, then use pliers to slide the clamp back over the connection to secure it.

Install the master cylinder (Procedure 12). Bleed the master cylinder and then the whole brake system (Procedure 1).

Go through Step 1 to see that the Master Vac is operating properly before you hit the road.

PROCEDURE 14: CHECK, REMOVE, INSTALL BRAKE LIGHT SWITCH

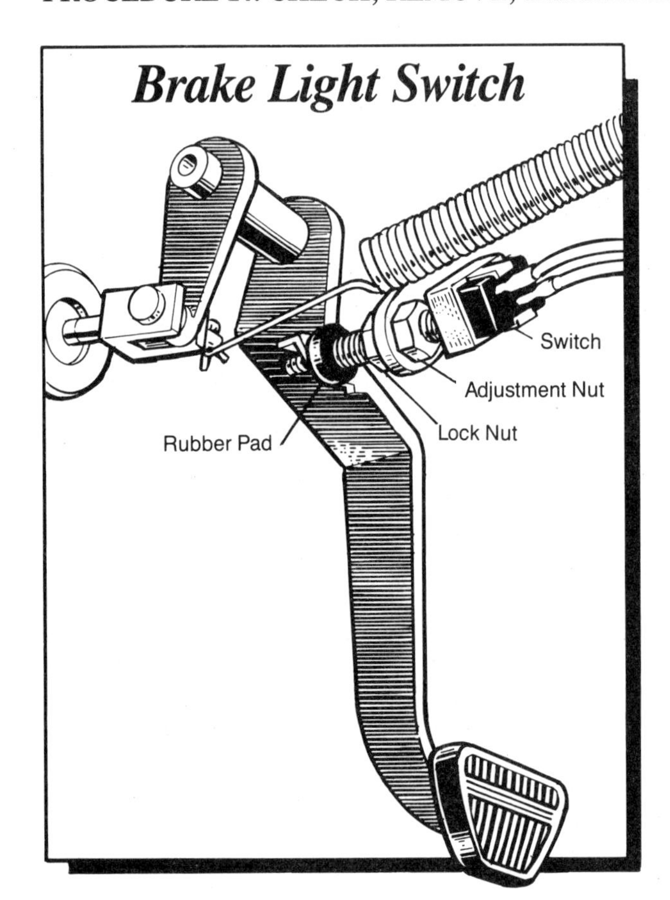

Condition 1: The brake lights stay on all the time. Do Steps 1 and 2.

Condition 2: Brake lights don't light up when the brake pedal is pressed. Do steps 1, 3, 4, and 5 (omit Step 2).

Remark: If Condition 2 is your problem, check the brake light *bulbs* and *fuse* (Chapter 8) before testing the brake light switch.

Tools and Materials: Step 2 requires a new rubber brake pedal stopper, Step 3 may require some penetrating oil, Step 4 requires a 12-volt test light and a short piece of insulated wire and Step 5 requires a 14mm open end wrench, a new brake light switch, a small ruler (either inches or centimeters is OK) and Friend.

Step 1. Locate Brake Light Switch.

Look up under the dash while pumping the brake pedal with your hand. When you release the pedal, a **rubber pad** on the brake lever pushes a plunger into a little round **switch**. See it?

Step 2. Replace Rubber Brake Pad.

If the rubber pad is missing, the brake lights will stay on all the time. Buy a new pad from Toyota and press it into the hole. The brakes lights should go off now when the pedal is released.

Step 3. Check Plunger.

While holding the brake pedal down, push on the end of the switch with your finger to see if the plunger moves freely. If it's stuck in the switch, spray some penetrating oil on it and try to move it in and out until it slides easily. If you can't get it unstuck, you need to replace the switch (Step 5).

Step 4. Test Electrical Source.

Follow the wires from the switch to a plastic *connector*. Pull the connector apart.

Use a 12-volt test light to check for electricity in the two *slots* of the connector that the brake light switch wires plug into. On models with cruise control there will be four slots; the two larger perpendicular slots are the ones you want. Stick one of the test light wires (or the metal probe on the test light) into one of the slots on the connector and touch the other wire to an unpainted piece of metal or screw head that's attached to the car. Try both slots. One of the slots should light the tester.

If no electricity is getting to the connector, the wire must be broken or shorted somewhere between the switch and the fuse box. You did check the fuse, didn't you? Look at Chapter 8, Procedure 5, to track down the broken wire.

If the test light goes on, there's "juice" at the terminal. Find a short piece of spare insulated electrical wire and strip about ¼" of insulation from each end of the wire. Stick one end of the wire into each of the terminal slots (larger ones if you have cruise control) in the connector end that's attached to the wiring harness. Check the rear brake lights. If the brake lights are on, the brake light switch is bad. Replace it (Step 5). Still no lights? Either a wire is broken between the switch and brake light bulb, or the brake light system isn't grounded properly. See Chapter 8, Procedure 5.

Bypassing the Brake Light Switch

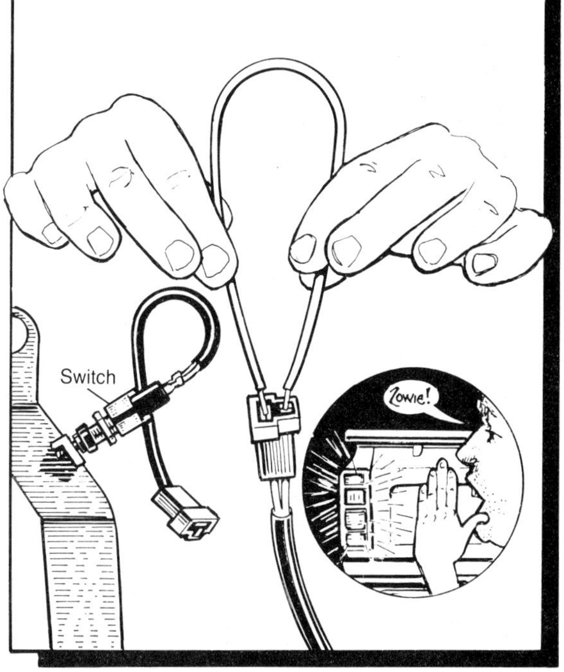

Step 5. Replace Brake Light Switch.

Disconnect the wires from the switch at the plastic connector if you haven't already. Unscrew the 14mm nut that's on the opposite end of the switch from the wires. You may have to be patient; it isn't particularly easy to get to. Slide the switch out of its holder. Remove the other nut from the switch.

Screw one of the nuts about halfway onto the new switch. Slide the switch into the holder with the plunger end pointed toward the brake lever. Hold the brake pedal down while you screw the other nut onto the switch. Don't tighten it yet.

Adjust the brake pedal height so there is .20in-.43in (5mm-11mm) free play. *Free play* is the distance the pedal travels before encountering any resistance (see illustration). A little free play is important; otherwise, you could have the brake switch putting pressure on the brakes without help from your right foot. Screw the two nuts further onto the switch to decrease the amount of free play, or further toward the end of the switch to increase the free play. When the free play is right, tighten the 14mm nut that's closest to the plunger end of the switch, *clockwise* against the mounting holder. Then reconnect the wires to the plastic connector.

Finally, test the light by pressing on the brake pedal a few times while Friend looks for the lights to turn on and off at the back of the car.

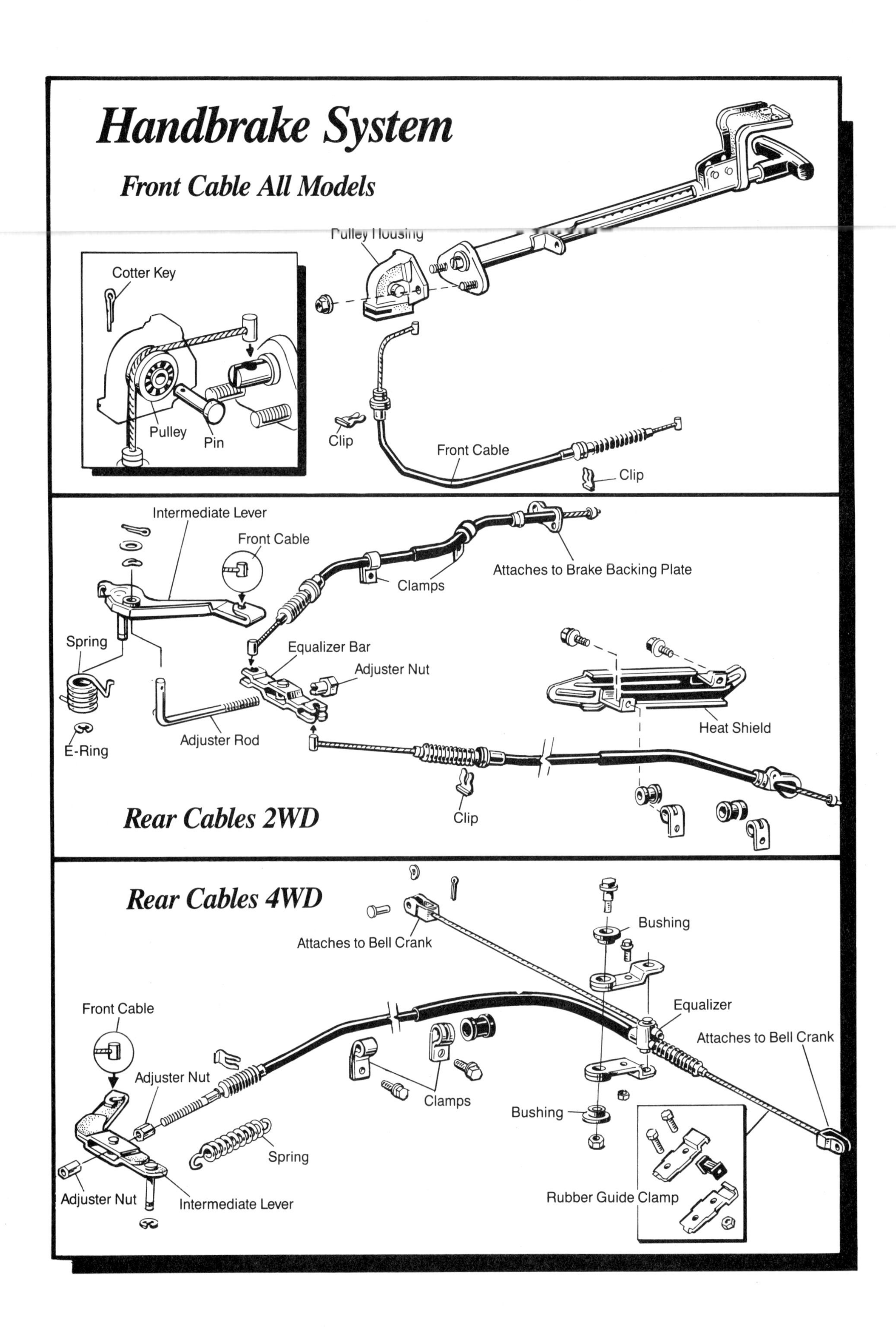
Handbrake System
Front Cable All Models
Pulley Housing
Cotter Key
Pulley
Pin
Clip
Front Cable
Clip
Intermediate Lever
Front Cable
Attaches to Brake Backing Plate
Clamps
Spring
Equalizer Bar
Adjuster Nut
Heat Shield
E-Ring
Adjuster Rod
Clip
Rear Cables 2WD
Rear Cables 4WD
Bushing
Attaches to Bell Crank
Front Cable
Equalizer
Attaches to Bell Crank
Adjuster Nut
Clamps
Bushing
Spring
Rubber Guide Clamp
Adjuster Nut
Intermediate Lever

PROCEDURE 15: ADJUST HANDBRAKE

Condition: Handbrake lever goes up 12 or more notches (clicks) on '75-'78 models; 17 or more notches (clicks) on '79-'87 models. If your handbrake won't keep your truck from rolling on a slope, adjust it now.

Tools and Materials: 12mm wrench, 10mm wrench, pliers, maybe some penetrating oil.

Caution: Be sure the transmission is in FIRST (manual) or PARK (automatic) and the wheels are blocked.

Step 1. Adjust Handbrake.

The handbrake lever pulls on a cable that is connected to one end of a short **intermediate lever** underneath the truck. The opposite end of the lever is attached to the frame with a pin which allows the lever to rotate. If you can't find the intermediate lever, have Friend pull and release the handbrake while you watch for movement beneath the truck.

2WD models: An L-shaped **threaded rod** connects the intermediate lever to the center of a short **equalizer bar** which is free to pivot on the end of the rod. The nut that attaches the equalizer bar to the rod is where you make the handbrake adjustment. Two cables connect the equalizer bar to the rear brake shoes. Thus the force applied to the center of the equalizer bar is transmitted equally to both rear brakes.

To adjust the handbrake, locate the 12mm nut on the rear end of the threaded rod at the rear center of the equalizer bar. Use your wrench to turn the nut *clockwise* to tighten the cable or *counterclockwise* to loosen the cable. Put the handbrake handle in the OFF position (down). Turn the 12mm nut toward the equalizer bar with your fingers until you can only lift the handbrake lever eight to 12 clicks on '75-'78 models, or ten to 15 clicks on '79-'87 models.

4WD models: Crawl under the rear of the truck and locate a **bellcrank lever** attached to the inboard side of the brake backing plate. The end of the handbrake cable will be attached to the upper end of the bellcrank. Also near the upper end you'll see a bolt (called a **stopper screw**) screwed into the bellcrank, pointing toward the backing plate. A 10mm nut on the stopper screw locks it to the bellcrank.

With the handbrake off, use a 10mm wrench to loosen the locknuts on the stopper screws. Slowly screw the stopper screws clockwise until there's no play in the bellcrank. Loosen the stopper screw one turn, then tighten the lock nut.

Crawl under the middle of the truck and locate the intermediate lever. Loosen the 12mm nuts that attach the threaded rod to the intermediate lever. Screw the two nuts toward the rear of the truck to tighten the cable, or toward the front of the truck to loosen it. Pull on the handbrake and count the number of clicks; too many clicks means the cable is too loose and too few clicks means the cable is too tight.

Once the cable is adjusted to the right number of clicks, tighten the nut on the front end of the threaded rod against the intermediate lever. Count the handbrake clicks again. Everything OK? Release the handbrake and crawl under the rear of the truck again to look at the bellcrank stopper screws. They should be touching the backing plates.

PROCEDURE 16: REPLACE HANDBRAKE CABLE

Condition: The handbrake handle comes up with no resistance and the parking brakes don't function. Adjustment (Procedure 15) does nothing. Conclusion: One of the handbrake cables has broken.

Tools and Materials: 12mm wrench, 12mm socket, ratchet, short extension for the ratchet, regular pliers, new handbrake cable, maybe needlenose and channel lock pliers, maybe penetrating oil.

Step 1. Find Broken Cable.

Remember, you are here because the handbrake isn't working. Before crawling under the truck, be sure and put the transmission in FIRST (manual) or PARK (automatics) and chock the wheels so the truck can't roll in either direction.

Crawl under the truck and locate the intermediate lever (see Procedure 15). Pull on the cables attached to the lever. A broken cable will have more slack than the others and probably slide right out of the cable sheath. If the broken cable goes toward the front of the truck and connects the intermediate lever to the handbrake lever, see Step 2 to replace the front cable. If one of the cables that runs toward the rear of the truck is broken, see Step 3 for 2WD models, or Step 4 for 4WD trucks, to replace the rear cable.

4WD models: If both cables attached to the intermediate lever appear to be OK, crawl under the rear of the truck and check where the cables attach to the bellcrank levers on the inboard side of the brake backing plates. Also check the equalizer bar that's bolted to top of the differential housing. If one of the cables is broken, see Step 4 to replace it. If the equalizer is broken, remove the bolt that attaches it to the rear differential, then remove the nut and bolt that hold the two halves together. Replace the bushings that the equalizer is mounted in if they are cracked, broken or missing. If the equalizer bars are bent or broken, replace them too.

Step 2. Replace Front Handbrake Cable.

Look under the dash and locate the parking brake warning light switch mounted on the driver's side of the handbrake lever. A small pin on the side of the lever pushes on the end of the switch when the handbrake is released. You need to remove the warning switch.

Pull the handbrake lever so the pin is away from the switch. Use a 12mm box end wrench to remove the nut that attaches the switch to the handbrake lever. If the nut is so tight that the switch bracket starts bending when you try to loosen the nut, use channel lock pliers to hold the switch while you unscrew the nut. Once the nut is off, pull the switch out of the bracket and let it dangle by the wires.

Look for two small metal pawls sticking up on the top side of the handbrake lever, near the handle. Release the handbrake lever and push it in as far as possible. Push the top end of the two pawls toward the front of the truck while pushing forward on the handbrake handle. This allows the lever to move forward another ¼", which is critical.

Open the hood and find a rounded pulley bracket bolted to the firewall. A cable attached to the bottom of the bracket disappears underneath the truck. Use a 12mm socket, short extension and ratchet to remove the two 12mm nuts that attach the bracket to the firewall. Make a note of other things attached with the two nuts.

Pull the bracket away from the firewall and you'll see a small barrel-shaped thing on the end of the cable sitting in a hole in the end of the handbrake lever. Lift the barrel thing out of the lever.

Use regular or needlenose pliers to remove the cotter pin on the side of the pulley bracket. Push the pulley pin through the bracket, then remove the pulley. Use pliers to remove the spring clip that attaches the cable to the bottom of the pulley bracket. The cable is now liberated from the bracket.

Crawl under the truck and pull the cable toward the rear while pushing forward on the cable end of the intermediate lever until you can slip the cable up through the slot in the top of the lever. Follow the cable forward to where it's attached to the frame with a spring clip. Use pliers to remove the spring clip. The cable might also be attached to the body with little tabs. If you find any, just bend the tabs away from the cable. Remove the old broken cable from the truck.

To install the new cable, slide the end with the long rubber boot through the bracket in the frame and install the spring clip. Don't attach the rear end of the cable to the intermediate lever yet. Thread the front end of the cable up into the engine compartment. Bend the tabs on the body over the cable to hold it in place.

Working in the engine compartment, pull the cable out of its housing as far as possible. Lay the cable in the pulley bracket, then fit the pulley into the bracket and slip the pin through the pulley. Use pliers to straighten the cotter pin, then insert it into the pulley pin. Spread the ends of the cotter pin so it can't fall out. Now install the spring clip that attaches the cable to the bottom of the pulley bracket.

Fit the little barrel on the end of the cable into the hole in the end of the handbrake lever. Hold it there while you slide the pulley bracket onto the two mounting studs. Fit anything else that was attached with the mounting nuts onto the studs. Install and tighten the two 12mm pulley bracket nuts.

Crawl under the truck and push the cable end of the intermediate lever forward while you slip the barrel on the end of the cable into its hole. Slide the cable down through the slot and release the lever. If there's not enough slack in the cable, loosen the adjusting nut a little.

Go to the cab and pull on the handbrake lever. Install the handbrake warning light switch and tighten the 12mm nut.

Check the handbrake adjustment (Chapter 5, Procedure 4, Step 6) and adjust it if necessary (Procedure 15 in this chapter).

Step 3. Replace Rear Brake Cable (2WD).

Chock the wheels, put the gearshift in FIRST (manual) or PARK (automatic). Release the handbrake if it's on.

Pull the broken cable forward and twist the end so the cable can slip up and out of the slot in the top of the equalizer bar. Loosen the adjusting nut if necessary.

Follow the cable rearward to where it is attached to the frame with a spring clip. Use pliers to remove the clip. The clip on the left side might be covered with a small metal shield. If so, remove the 12mm nut that attaches the shield to the top of the frame.

Follow the cable further toward the rear, removing the 12mm bolts that attach cable clamps to the frame. The clamps that attach the left cable probably also attach a heat shield to the frame, right next to the muffler.

Now the fun begins. Do Procedure 8 or 9, depending on your year and model, to remove the wheel, brake drum and brake shoes on the side with the broken cable. Once the cable is released from the handbrake lever on the brake shoe, remove the 12mm bolt that attaches the handbrake cable to the brake backing plate. Slide the cable out of the backing plate.

To install the new cable, attach the rear end to the backing plate with the 12mm bolt. Install the brake shoes, brake drum and wheel. Lower the truck and torque the wheel nuts. How to do all this is in Procedure 8 or 9, depending on your year and model.

Working from the rear toward the front, attach the cable clamps to the frame with the 12mm nuts. Make sure anything else attached with the bolts (like heat shields) is in place. Slide the front end of the cable through the bracket on the frame, then install the spring clip.

Fit the barrel and cable through the slot in the top of the equalizer bar. Check the handbrake adjustment (Chapter 5, Procedure 4, Step 6), and adjust it if necessary (Procedure 15). That's all there is to it.

Step 4. Replace Rear Cable (4WD).

Remove the front adjusting nut on the threaded rod that goes through the intermediate lever. Follow the cable rearward to where it is attached to the frame with a spring clip. Use pliers to remove the spring clip. Continue following the cable rearward, removing the clamps that attach it to the frame.

The cable is attached to an equalizer bar on the rear axle housing (differential). Remove the equalizer from the differential, then remove the smaller bolt from the center of the equalizer. Separate the two halves of the equalizer to free the cable. There's one more cable guide near the left rear wheel that must be removed from the axle. Remove the clamp from the axle, then remove the bolt and nut that hold the clamp together. Separate the clamp halves and the two rubber cable guides to free the cable.

The cable splits at the equalizer and goes to each of the rear wheels, where it attaches to bellcrank levers on the inboard side of the brake backing plates. On each cable end is a U-shaped clevis and clevis pin. Use pliers to remove the cotter pins that secure the clevis pins, then pull the clevis pin out of the clevis. The rear cable is now liberated.

To install the rear cable, attach the two clevis units to the ends to the bellcrank levers with the clevis pins and cotter pins. Wrap the ends of the cotter pins around the clevis pins so they can't come out. Fit the cable into the rubber cable guide, then bolt the cable clamp together. Attach the cable guide to the rear axle with its bolt.

Assemble the equalizer so the ends of the fitting at the cable junction fit into the holes at the ends of the equalizer halves. Bolt the two halves together with the bolt and nut. Now attach the equalizer to the rear differential. Be sure there's a bushing on each side of the equalizer bar.

Thread the cable forward and attach it to the frame with the clamps that were on the old cable. Push the end of the cable through the hole in the frame just to the rear of the intermediate lever. Install one of the adjusting nuts onto the threaded end of the cable, then guide it into its hole in the center of the lever. Secure the cable to the frame with the spring clip. Install the other adjusting nut onto the end of the cable. Now adjust the handbrake (Procedure 15)

CHAPTER 8
THE ELECTRICAL SYSTEM

This high-charged chapter is about your truck's electrical system. Electricity is used to start the engine, to ignite the fuel/air mixture to make the engine run, and to operate accessory gizmos like lights, wipers, and the radio. An alternator "generates" electricity when the engine is running to keep the battery fully charged so it can supply electrical energy to the various electrical gizmos even if the engine isn't running.

I freely admit that I don't completely fathom the theory that electrons dancing merrily from one atom to another along a wire is what makes a light bulb light, a horn beep, or an electric motor turn. It's been explained to me in countless high school and college courses over the years and I could always pass the tests, even if I didn't really "grok" it. The theory is relatively simple, but if something's invisible, I'm skeptical. I just consider electricity as a first water mystery and relate to it as "controllable magic." This is as reasonable to me as dancing electrons.

Furthermore, I think the reason most people, including electricians, refer to electricity as "juice" is because they, too, have trouble relating to the dancing electron theory. Imagining something *tangible* flowing through the wires is psychologically easier to digest, so throughout this chapter I'll be calling electricity "juice."

Anyway, I've found over the years that you don't need to know anything about electrons (or believe in them) to keep your car's electrical system working. All you need to grasp is the concept that electricity must make a complete circle starting and ending at the battery to make electrical components work: if the circle is broken, they don't work. Just think of a circle whenever a circuit is mentioned and you won't have much trouble understanding the electrical wonders of your truck. Simple enough? OK, with a circle in mind, I'll elaborate.

WHAT ARE THE NECESSARY ELEMENTS IN AN ELECTRICAL CIRCUIT?

Four elements are necessary for an **electrical circuit** to work: (1) a source of juice like a **charged battery**; (2) a **"hot" wire** to carry juice from the **positive battery post** to the component; (3) a **component**—such as a light bulb, horn, electric motor, etc.—in the circle that resists (slows) the flow of juice; and (4) a **"ground" wire** to carry juice from the component back to the **negative battery post** to complete the circuit. Why do you need the resisting component? Without the resistance to the flow of juice, the juice would flow too fast and overheat the battery and the wires in the circuit.

Now let's add a **switch** to break the flow of juice in the circuit when we want to turn the component off (in other words, break the circle). And let's add a **fuse** to protect the wires, components and battery in case of a problem (such as a **"short,"** which happens when the resistance is bypassed, or an **overloaded circuit**). Now we have a complete circuit, just like all the ones in your truck.

What follows is an explanation of the two most common electrical problems—"shorts" and overloaded circuits.

SHORTS AND OVERLOADED CIRCUITS

If the juice takes a short cut from the positive battery post back to the negative post without going through a component to slow the juice, it's called a "short." Shorts cause the battery and wires to overheat, melt, and maybe start a fire. The battery might even explode. Nasty.

Circuits can occasionally be overloaded by turning on too many components at the same time. The wires are designed to handle the load, but once in a while there's just too much going on. Again, the wires may overheat, or damage may be done to the battery.

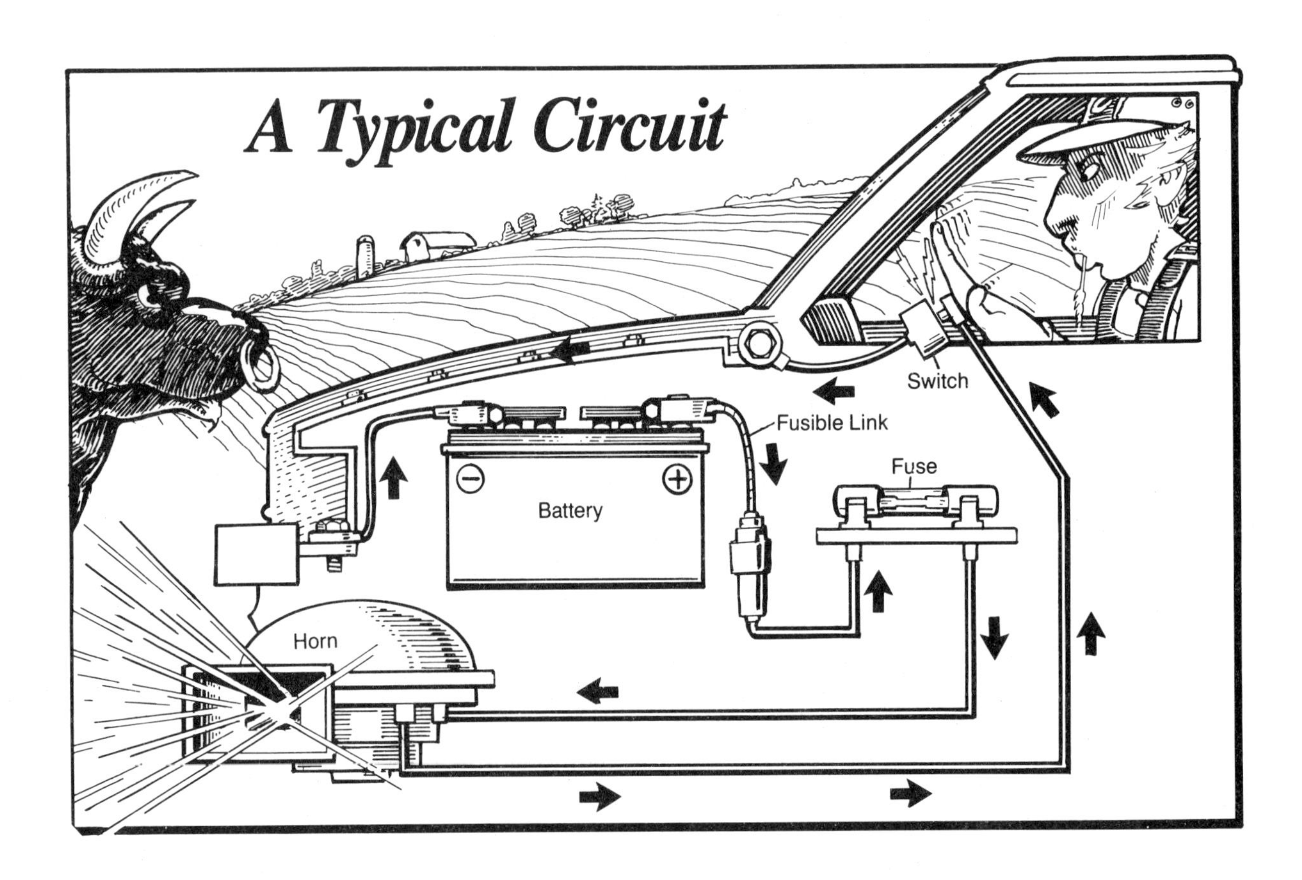

FUSES AND FUSIBLE LINKS

To protect the wires, components and battery when a short or overload condition occurs, **fuses**, and **fusible links** are installed in each circuit. (One exception: the cranking circuit.) Fuses and fusible links are made of lighter, more fragile material than the wires and components in the circle. They're designed to melt and break if more juice is flowing through the circuit than the wires or components can handle.

CIRCUIT BREAKERS

1982-87 models also have one or two circuit breakers mounted in the main fuse box. The circuit breaker on '82 and '83 models is for the heater fan motor. On '84 and '85 models there's a circuit breaker for the power window system (if you have power windows), and for '86 and '87 models there are two circuit breakers; one is for the power door locks (if you have them), and the other breaker is for power windows on models with power windows, and for the power rear window, rear window wiper and washer on 4 Runners.

A TYPICAL CIRCUIT

Let's follow the juice all the way around a circuit (circle) to see how it works. Using the horn as an example, we'll and start and end the circle at the battery.

Starting at the positive (+) battery post, juice flows through a "hot" wire to the fusible links and then to the fuse box. From the fuse box, the juice goes through a wire to a wire terminal on one side of the horn mechanism. A wire attached to a wire terminal on the other side of the horn mechanism carries the juice to the steering wheel. At the steering wheel the end of the wire is bare and is mounted a fraction of an inch from a metal plate attached to the horn button. The horn button is connected to the body of the car with a "ground" wire. Thus the only open place in the circle is the small gap between the hot wire and the horn button, so the horn button is the switch in the horn circuit.

When you press on the horn button, the metal plate touches the hot wire and completes the circle so the juice can squeeze through the horn mechanism, causing a beep. Now, here's a nifty part. The juice still has to get back to the battery to complete the circle, but instead of using another wire to carry the juice all the way from the steering wheel back to the battery, the car body is used to do it. This is called a **"ground"** ("earth" in England), and all circuits work this way on their return run to the battery. The juice flows through the metal body, finally meeting the point where the negative battery cable is attached to the body (and/or engine). It flows through the cable to the negative battery post, and thereby completes the circuit (circle).

With all that electricity in the body, how come you don't get zapped when you touch the car? Because the voltage is so low (12 volts) and it's in the form of **Direct Current** (DC), you can touch both posts of the battery at the same time and not even feel the full 12 volts of DC current coursing through your body. The coil and spark plug wires, however, should be left alone when the engine is running because the ignition coil hops the 12 volts up to about 30,000 volts!

ELECTRICAL SYSTEMS IN YOUR TRUCK

Your truck has four separate electrical systems with four distinct jobs; the **charging system**, the **ignition system**, the **cranking system**, and the **accessory** (everything else) **system**. The four systems have one important common component: the battery. They also share the battery cables and the "ground" (body), so they are interrelated. Let's take it from the top and go through them one by one.

CHARGING SYSTEM

The main parts of the charging system are the **battery**, the **alternator**, the **voltage regulator**, and the wires that connect them.

You know the battery: it's the big box with two posts sticking out of the top and plastic **filler caps** on top so you can add water (except on maintenance free batteries). The battery stores electricity so you can start the engine, play the radio or tape deck while parked in Lovers' Lane, and operate any of the other electrical gizmos even if the engine isn't running.

The battery chemically stores electricity through the interaction of lead plates and electrolyte (a fluid consisting of sulfuric acid and water). Sounds pretty mysterious and magical to me. Anyway, suffice it to say that as long as the lead plates and electrolyte are in good condition the battery stores electricity.

When the engine is running, a **drive belt** from the **crank pulley** turns the **alternator**, which then "generates" electricity, very much like the generators at a power plant like Hoover Dam or Three Mile Island. The fresh juice travels through a wire to the **voltage regulator**, then to the battery, and on to supply the electrical needs of the engine and accessories. Excess electricity is stored in the battery for use when the engine isn't running.

Why the voltage regulator? The alternator is capable of generating more electrical volts than the battery can handle. Limiting the excess is the job of the voltage regulator. When the battery is fully charged (has taken on all the juice it can handle), the voltage regulator shuts off the juice supply from the alternator until more is needed. When the supply in the battery drops, the regulator allows more to come through from the alternator.

CRANKING SYSTEM

The only function of the cranking system is to spin the engine fast enough for it to start. Here's how it's done: The **positive battery cable** is attached directly to a part on the starter called the **starter solenoid** that's mounted on an electric **starter motor**. When you turn the **ignition key** all the way over, juice is sent from the battery to the *ignition system* (for the spark plugs) and to the solenoid on the starter motor. When the solenoid is energized by juice from the battery, it does two things: it pushes the **starter gear** on the end of the **starter motor shaft** into teeth on the outside of the **flywheel** (drive plate on automatics) of the engine, and also starts the starter motor spinning. The starter motor thus turns the flywheel, and the flywheel turns the engine to get it started.

IGNITION SYSTEM

The **ignition system** provides a large spark to each **spark plug** at just the right time to ignite the fuel/air mixture in the cylinders. The main components of the ignition system are the **ignition switch**, **coil**, **distributor**, **spark plugs**, and the wires that connect them. When the ignition key is turned on, 12 volts of juice go from the battery to the coil. The coil boosts the 12 volts up to about 30,000 volts (WOW!), then sends the super-juice through a **high tension wire** to the center of the **distributor cap**. Inside the distributor, **breaker points** on earlier models, or a **reluctor** and **pickup coil** on later models, act as switches to turn the juice on and off. This happens quickly: it goes on each time a spark plug is supposed to fire. The rotor sequentially directs the hopped-up electrical charge to the right spark plug through **high tension spark plug wires**.

THE ACCESSORY SYSTEM

The accessory system includes the **battery**, **ignition switch**, **lights**, **heater**, **horn**, etc.—and the wires that connect the battery to these components. This system includes everything electrical that isn't related to the cranking, charging, or ignition systems, with the exception of the battery and ignition key switch, which all the systems share.

LET'S GET ON WITH IT

The following procedures cover maintenance, diagnostic, and repair of the electrical things on your truck. When special tools or expertise are required, I'll refer you to your local Toyota dealer or an auto electric shop for the repair.

CAUTIONS!

In order to avoid expensive accidents, please disconnect the negative battery terminal when I tell you to.

Never connect the battery cables in reverse; the negative battery terminal always connects to the engine or body and the positive cable always connects to the starter.

Never disconnect the battery cables while the engine is running.

Always disconnect both battery cables when charging the battery.

Never spray water directly into the alternator. When washing the engine, cover the alternator with a plastic bag.

Thanks.

PROCEDURE 1: BATTERY MAINTENANCE, CHECK AND REPLACEMENT

Condition: Routine maintenance; OR you've been referred here from another chapter; OR you need to replace your dead battery.

Tools and Materials: Safety glasses, 10mm or 12mm wrench depending on your battery clamps, distilled water, battery terminal cleaning brush or something abrasive like emery cloth or sandpaper, maybe a large screwdriver or battery terminal puller, maybe a box of baking soda, maybe a new battery.

To check the battery condition you'll need a 12-volt test light or a Volt/Ohm meter (VOM) and a hydrometer. To charge the battery you'll need a battery charger (I recommend a 4 to 6 amp "trickle" charger). Depending on the problem you may also need: a new battery hold-down bracket, battery tray, bracket rods, battery cables, new battery, rags, jumper cables.

Caution: The electrolyte fluid in batteries is mostly sulfuric acid, which can do a bad number on your eyes, clothes or any cuts or scratches you might have on your hands. Wear safety glasses and don't get any of the fluid or white flaky stuff from the battery on your clothes (they'll end up full of holes the next time you wash them). Wipe off tools you've used on the battery before putting them away. Throw rags used for cleaning the battery or tools in the trash so you can't accidentally grab one to wipe your brow or blow your nose. *Always* wash your hands after messing with the battery or its cables.

Remark: With proper maintenance a good battery should last at least three to five years. I've had batteries that lasted eight years!

Step 1. Check and Add Battery Fluid.

Safety glasses on? Lift the hood and look at Chapter 5, Procedure 4, Step 2, to check the fluid level in the battery and add some if necessary.

Step 2. Clean Battery.

If the battery is dirty or has white flaky stuff around the posts where the cables connect (*terminals*), use a solution of baking soda and water and an old rag to remove the crud. Be sure the caps are on snugly when you do this, so as not to contaminate the electrolyte. The baking soda neutralizes acid around the battery so it isn't so caustic. When the battery's clean, be sure and rinse the battery and the area around it with lots of fresh water. Throw the rag in the trash immediately.

Step 3. Disconnect and Clean Battery Terminals.

'75-'78 models: The *negative* (-) *battery terminal* is the one closest to the engine and the *positive* (+) *battery terminal* is the one closest to the right front fender.

'79-'87 models: The *negative* (-) *battery terminal* is the one closest to the right front fender and the *positive*

(+) *terminal* is closest to the engine.

EVERYONE: To be sure, look for a + or-stamped on or near the round battery posts, or on top of the battery. There's a picture of a battery somewhere nearby.

Use a 10mm or 12mm wrench (depending on your clamps) to loosen the nut on the end of the bolt sticking through the end of the **battery cable clamps**. On some models the positive terminal is covered with a molded piece of rubber. If yours is covered, carefully pry the rubber away from the sides where the clamp bolt and nut are located. Remove the negative (-) clamp from the battery first, then the positive (+) clamp.

If the clamps are stuck, gently twist them side to side, and/or put a large screwdriver in the slot where the bolt goes through and twist it to spread apart the end of the clamp. *Don't pry up on the clamp or twist it hard to remove it because the post might pop out of the battery.* If the clamp still refuses to budge, you'll need a battery terminal puller. But patience and the above method will usually do the trick.

Once the clamps are off, use a battery terminal brush, sandpaper, emery cloth, wire brush or a knife to clean the two posts on the battery and the inside of the cable clamps until they're bright and shiny. If the clamp bolts are funky or the inside of the clamps won't clean up, you can either replace the clamp on the end of the cable or replace the entire cable (Step 4).

When you're done, place the clamp back on the correct post, wiggle it down until it's snug, then tighten the nut on the clamp bolt with your wrench. Put the positive (+) clamp on first, then the negative (-) one. Don't force them. If one won't go on, check that you're connecting the cable clamp to the correct battery post—the negative post is slightly smaller than the positive. If everything is correct, spread the ends of the clamp apart a little more as you slip it onto the post.

Step 4. Clean or Replace Battery Cables.

If you're here because the battery checked out OK but the starter still doesn't crank the engine very fast, or the lights don't shine as bright as they should, check both ends of both battery cables for looseness, funk and corrosion. Replace the cables if the clamps are funky and can't be cleaned, or if the clamp bolts are broken, stripped or mangled, or if the cable itself is corroded where it attaches to the ends.

Negative cable: First, disconnect the negative (-) battery clamp from the battery (Step 3). The negative cable goes from the negative battery post to the truck body and/or engine, where it's attached with a bolt.

To clean or replace the negative (-) battery cable, detach the cable from the battery post and follow it to where it bolts to the body and/or engine. Make a note if other things are attached with the same bolt. Remove the bolt(s) (probably 12mm). If it's a clean-up job, clean both sides of the cable end(s) and the bolt(s) with a wire brush, sandpaper or knife blade. Clean the battery terminal post if you haven't already done so.

If the cable is terminally funky and you're going to replace it, remove it now and install the new one. Connect the cable end(s) to the body and/or engine with the bolt(s), then torque the bolt(s) to 15 ft.lbs. Don't connect the clamp to the battery until after you've cleaned or replaced the positive cable.

Positive cable: The positive cable goes from the positive battery post to a terminal post on the *starter solenoid*. The little wire(s) attached to the positive cable clamp go to the *fusible links*, then to the fuse box.

If you're replacing the positive cable, be sure the new clamp has the same arrangement as the old cable for attaching the small wires.

To remove the positive (+), disconnect the negative (-) cable clamp from the battery post if you haven't already. Now follow the cable from the positive battery terminal to where it connects to the solenoid on the starter motor. It's down there on the lower right rear side of the engine and rather difficult to get to. On some models you might need to jack up the front of the truck and put it on jackstands, then crawl underneath to get to the terminal.

Once you're in position, peel back the **rubber boot** covering the cable end, then remove the 12mm nut and washer that secure the cable to the solenoid. Clean the cable end with a wire brush or sandpaper, and the threaded post on the starter solenoid with a wire brush.

Disconnect the positive battery clamp from the battery post, then clean the battery post and cable clamp (unless you're replacing the cable). Step 3 tells you how. If you're here to replace the cable, disconnect the small wire(s) attached to the cable near the battery. Now you can pull the old cable out and install the new one.

Slip the cable end onto the starter solenoid post, then install and tighten the washer and nut. Pull the rubber boot over the starter solenoid post. If you replaced the cable, attach the small wire(s) to the cable clamp. Wiggle the positive cable clamp onto the positive battery post, then tighten the clamp bolt with the 10mm or 12mm wrench. Attach the negative clamp to the battery (Step 3).

Step 5. Check Battery Condition.

If your battery seems tired, if it has to be charged frequently, or if the engine sounds like it's struggling to turn just fast enough to start—don't rush out to buy a new battery before you check the old one. The problem might not be the battery.

First, check the fluid level in the battery and add some if need be (Step 1), then clean and check the battery terminals (Steps 3 and 4). Try driving the car to see if the battery will charge up now. If the battery still struggles to crank the engine, further tests are necessary. If you have a **hydrometer** and/or a **volt/ohm meter** you can do the following two tests yourself. If you don't have the tools and don't want to buy them, take your Toy to the friendly local Toyota dealer or to an auto electric garage and have them check the specific gravity of the battery fluid, the voltage and amperage of the battery, and do a "load test" to see how much reserve cranking power the battery has. These tests only take a couple of minutes and shouldn't cost much.

Check specific gravity: If yours is a maintenance-free battery with no caps to remove, you can't check the specific gravity, so skip down to the Volt/Ohm meter test.

You can buy a cheap battery test hydrometer from any auto parts store or large discount house. Put on your safety glasses and remove the top or tops from the battery. The electrolyte (water-acid mix) in each battery cell is of a certain specific gravity which we measure to find out a battery's condition. The hydrometer has an inner float with numbers on it. Squeeze the ball on the end of the hydrometer, then put the tip into the first battery cell. Slowly release your grip, and electrolyte will be sucked into the hydrometer. The float will sink or float inside the electrolyte, and your job is to read the number on the float which corresponds with the top level of the electrolyte. If the syringe sucked up too much electrolyte so the float hits the top of the instrument, squeeze a little back into the cell.

At 68° F (20° C) a fully charged cell will read 1.260 on the float scale. A half-charged cell in reasonable condition will read 1.160 to 1.20. A discharged cell or one in poor condition reads around 1.060. Anything below that means the battery's deceased. The battery needs recharging if the reading in any cell is between 1.060 and 1.160 (see Step 6). Check each cell the same way.

Battery voltage test: If you have a **Volt/Ohm meter** (VOM), set the meter to 15 DC volts. Touch the *red* (+) probe from the meter to the *positive* (+) battery terminal and the *black* (-) probe from the meter to the *negative* (-) battery terminal. The meter should read about 12 volts with the engine off. If it's less than 12 volts, either the battery is discharged or worn out, or the alternator isn't charging it the way it should. Do Procedure 6 to see if the battery is getting a charge from the alternator. If the charging system checks out OK, come back here and finish this step.

If you don't have a Volt/Ohm meter, or if you checked the battery and charging system with a VOM and everything checked out OK, check the *cranking system* (Procedure 9). You don't need a VOM to check the cranking system.

If the cranking system is good, take the car to an auto electric shop or garage and have them check the *specific gravity* of the battery fluid, the *voltage* and *amperage* of the battery, and do a "load test" to see how much reserve cranking power the battery has. If the battery, charging and cranking systems all check out OK, you should run through Procedure 5, Step 3, to check for electrical shorts.

Step 6. Charge the Battery.

Naturally, you'll need a battery charger to do this step. Small ones are usually available at reasonable prices from auto parts stores or department stores.

Before charging the battery, disconnect both cables from the battery posts (Step 3) to protect the various components in the charging system. This is especially critical on EFI models, to protect the delicate electronic fuel injection system. Check the fluid level in the battery and add some *distilled water* if need be (Chapter 5,

Procedure 4, Step 2). Leave the filler caps loose while the battery is being charged and cover the top of the battery with a clean rag.

It's best for the battery to charge for 5 to 8 hours with a 4-6 amp "trickle" charger, rather than giving it a one- to two-hour "quick" or "booster" charge at 8-15 amps. Never charge the battery with more than 10 amps. Follow the instructions that come with the charger to give your battery a full charge. Set the switch on the charger (if yours has one) to the 12-volt position. Do not plug in the charger or turn it on until *after* you hook it up to the battery. Attach the red clamp to the positive (+) battery post and the black clamp to the negative (-) battery post. When you're ready to disconnect, turn the charger off (or unplug it) before detaching the clips to the battery.

After the battery is charged, tighten the filler caps, then reconnect the cable clamps. Tighten the clamp nuts with your 10mm or 12mm wrench.

If the battery becomes weak again within a few days, do the battery check (Step 5), the charging system check (Procedure 6), and the cranking system tests (Procedure 9) before buying a new battery.

Step 7. Remove and Install the Battery.

If you're installing a new battery, to give it its best shot at a long and happy life, replace the battery **hold-down bracket**, **battery tray**, **cables** and/or **clamps** if they're corroded and funky.

Remove the negative and positive cable clamps from the battery posts (Step 3). Remember that the negative cable should come off first.

Loosen the 12mm nut on the rear of the horizontal rod that's across the top of the battery. Remove the 12mm bolt that attaches the front end of the rod to the body. Now you can unhook the bottom of the vertical rod at the rear of the battery from its bracket in the body and lift off the hold-down bracket.

Carefully lift the battery out of the engine compartment keeping it level so the acid (electrolyte) can't spill. Hold it away from your clothes as you lift it out. Don't set the battery on the fender or anything you don't want full of holes. If the battery hold-down bracket is corroded and funky, replace it with a new one from Toyota. Clean the old one if it's still in good condition. A solution of baking soda (Arm & Hammer soda bicarb) and water really does a good number on corrosion. Use the solution to wash the plastic battery tray (if there is one) and the shelf where the battery sits. Rinse them with lots of fresh water and old rags. Toss the rags in the trash.

Set the plastic tray (if yours has one) on the battery shelf in the engine compartment with the arrow pointing toward the front, if yours has an arrow. Set the battery on the shelf so the negative (-) and positive (+) posts are in the same position as they were on the old battery. Hook the bottom end of the vertical rod into its hole behind the battery, then fit the hold-down bracket on the battery top. Install the washers and 12mm bolts, nuts or wingnuts and tighten them. Clean, then reconnect, the positive and lastly the negative cable clamps to the battery posts (Step 3). Snug the clamp nuts with your wrench.

Step 8. How to Use Jumper Cables to Get a Jump Start.

You'll need a set of **jumper cables** for this step. Avoid cheap ones that will come apart or fail you when you need them most. Good ones have a solid, heavy feel to them.

If your battery is too weak to start the engine, or you're being a good samaritan and helping someone else start their car, follow this sequence to safely connect and disconnect the jumper cables:

Park the running car close enough so the jumper cables can easily reach from the "live" battery terminals to the "dead" battery terminals. If you have to stretch the cables, there's a good chance one of the cable ends will touch something you don't want it to touch. Be sure the car bodies (or bumpers) aren't touching. And don't lean over the batteries when connecting the jumper cables.

To help reduce the danger of an explosion, if either or both of the batteries have removable filler caps, remove the caps and cover the tops of the batteries with rags.

One of the jumper cables will be *red* and one *black*, or at least the handles will be red or black. First, connect one end of the red jumper cable to the positive (+) terminal of the dead battery, then connect the other end of the red cable to the positive (+) terminal of the live battery. Next connect one end of the black cable to the negative (-) terminal of the alive car and the other end to bare metal on the dead car. The metal hook on the top front of the engine is a good place to connect the black cable. The reason you don't connect the black cable to the negative battery terminal is because of the sparks that usually fly when the last connection is made. Since batteries are known to give off an explosive gas, you sure don't want to take a chance of igniting any gas that might be lurking around the top of the battery.

Start the car that has the live battery and rev it up to about 2000 rpm. Turn off all accessories in both vehicles, then attempt to start the car with the dead battery. If it doesn't crank strongly, either the jumper cables are a little loose (wiggle them where they connect), or a clamp on one of the dead car's battery cables is loose or corroded, which could be your problem in the first place. When the dead car starts, run it at a fast idle speed for several minutes. Carefully disconnect the black cable first, then the red cable.

Thank the chap who helped you. Buy him (or her) a brew, if camaraderie has developed over the cables—and it usually does. If it was your truck that needed the jump start and there was no apparent cause for the dead battery (like leaving the lights on), turn to Procedure 1, Step 5 to check the battery when you get home.

PROCEDURE 2: CHECK AND REPLACE FUSES, FUSIBLE LINKS AND CIRCUIT BREAKERS

Condition: An electrical component (lights, heater, etc.) isn't working. If several components aren't working, start by checking the fusible links (Step 3). If nothing electrical is working, check the battery, battery cables and clamps (Procedure 1).

Tools and Materials: Maybe new fuses and or fusible links, maybe a 12-volt test light or Volt/Ohm meter (VOM), and maybe a 10mm wrench, 12mm wrench, wire brush and/or needlenose pliers.

Remark: The proper fuse amperage and a list of each fuse circuit are stamped on the fuse box cover. A list of the components in each circuit is in the Specification Section of your owner's manual. If you're missing the cover or manual, get a new one from Toyota.

Find the circuit on the list for the component that's not working. Remove the fuse for that circuit from the holder and insert a new one. (You probably have a new fuse stashed in the box somewhere.) Turn on and check the component to see if it works now. If it does, throw the old fuse away and go merrily on your way. Replace the spare fuse you used with a new spare as soon as possible. If the component still doesn't work, do Step 2. If the new fuse blows immediately after inserting it, do Procedure 5 to check for shorts.

It's a good idea to always have an extra couple of fuses and fusible links of each amperage stashed in the glove box. You can check fuses with a VOM to see if they're good (Chapter 15, Procedure 2).

If a fuse for the engine (EGI, Engine, Ignition) blows and you don't have a new fuse, borrow one from a component like the radio, dome light, heater or something that isn't necessary to run the engine. Again, always use a fuse of the same or less amp rating and replace it with the correct fuse as soon as possible.

Caution: The correct fuse amperage (10, 15, 25, etc.) for the different electrical circuits is stamped on the fuse box cover and listed in the Specification Section in the back of the owner's manual. When replacing fuses, always use new ones that are of the correct amp rating. You'll find the amp rating stamped on the fuse. In an emergency you can replace a burned fuse with one of a less amperage rating—just be sure and replace it with the correct fuse as soon as possible. *Don't* substitute tinfoil for a fuse because expensive electrical components could be damaged very quickly! It's dangerous, too.

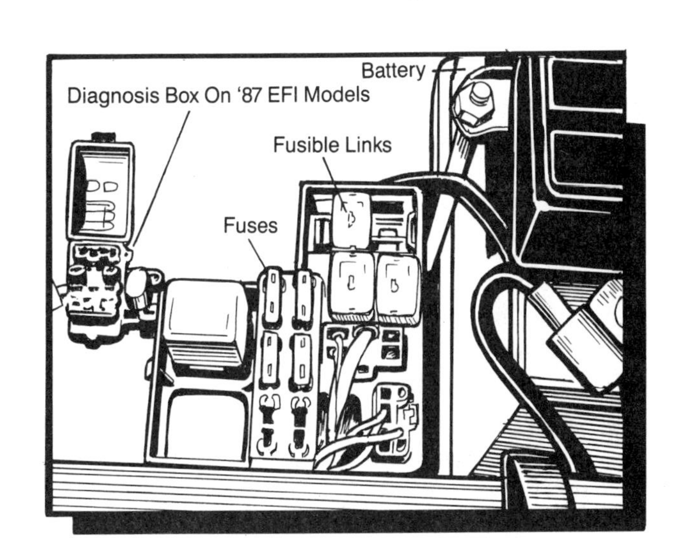

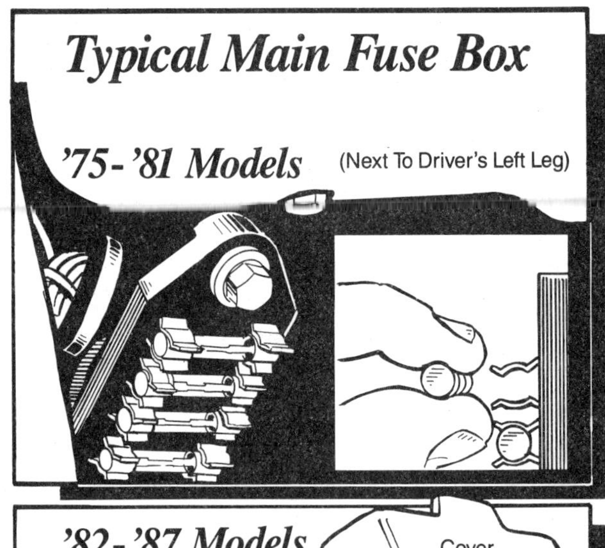

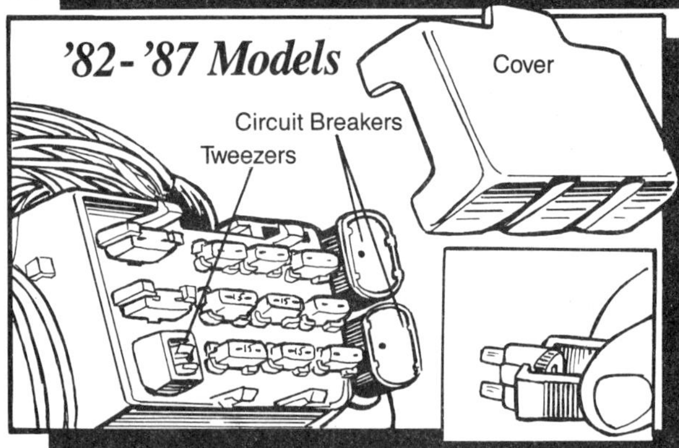

Step 1. Locate and Check Fuses and Circuit Breakers in Fuse Box(es).

Main fuse box: On all models the main fuse box is under the dash near your left knee as you sit in the driver's seat. Some models also have circuit breakers and other fuse boxes. Here's where to find 'em.

'82-'83 models: There is a circuit breaker for the heater blower in the main fuse box.

'84-'87 models: Round circuit breakers for power windows and power door locks are mounted just forward of the main fuse box.

A fuse box just behind the battery in the engine compartment contains fuses for the headlights, charging system, hazard lights and horn. The fusible links are also in this box.

A fuse box behind the glovebox contains fuses for the air conditioner and heater systems.

How to Open the Fuse Box

'75-'78 models: Press in on the ends of the cover while pulling it away from the box. The tabs on the ends of the cover are different sizes so the cover can only fit on the box one way. There's a little clip in each end of the cover to hold spare fuses.

'79-'81 models: The latch for the fuse box cover is on the rear of the fuse box where you can't see it. Just put your fingers behind the box and pull the tab away from the box and the top will pop right off.

'82-'87 models: Push down on the tab on the fuse box lid and the lid will pop off.

Replace Fuse(s)

'75-'81 models: The barrel-type fuses are held in place by metal clamps on each end. To remove them, use your finger or the end of a pencil or ball point pen to pry one end of the fuse out of the clamp, then grab the fuse and pull the other end out. Don't use a screwdriver or anything metal to pry on the fuse because it might cause a short. Don't grab the glass part of the fuse with pliers either—the glass will shatter easily.

Once the old fuse is out, hold a new fuse so the metal ends are against the metal clips, then push on the ends of the fuse until it pops into place.

You can't always tell whether a barrel-type fuse is good or bad just by looking at it. The little flat wire you can see in the glass part of the fuse might look perfect, but be burned or broken near the end where you can't see it. Also, the wire in the fuse tends to warp with age, then break due to vibration, so while you're in the fuse box, take a quick look at all the other fuses. Replace any fuses whose wire inside looks warped.

'82-'87 models: There are rows of colored fuses and a tweezer-like fuse puller/installer inside the main fuse box (see illustration). To change a fuse, pull the tweezer thing out and use it to remove and install the fuses in the holder.

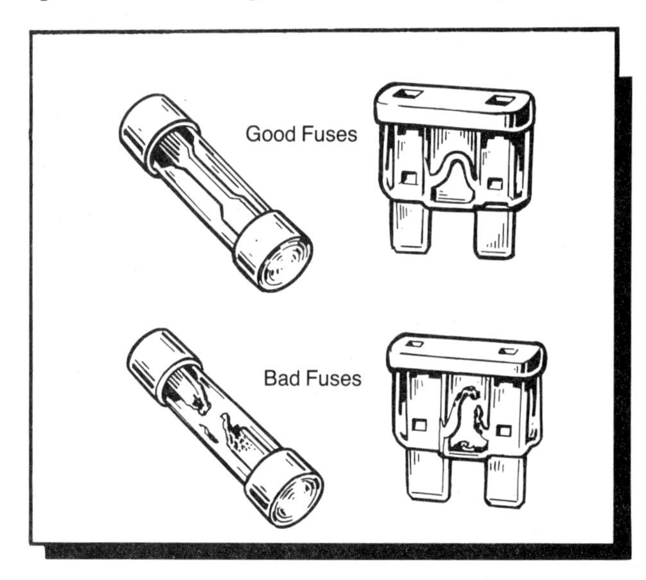

Step 2. Check Fuse Holder for Juice.

If the component still doesn't work after installing a new fuse, check the fusible links (Step 3). Still doesn't work? You'll need a 12-volt test light or a VOM to see if juice is getting to the fuse box.

If you have a VOM, set it to 15 DC volts. Turn both the *ignition key* and the *component* you're checking ON and touch the red (+) probe of the VOM to one of the two clips that holds the fuse ('75-'81 models) or to one of the tiny slots near the end of the fuse ('82-'87 models). Ground the other probe by touching it to bare metal (not the other fuse clips).

Test both fuse clips or both slots depending on your setup. The test light should light or the VOM should register about 12 volts on one of the clips. If the fuse is good, you should get juice on both ends of the fuse. If you do, the fuse is good and the component is getting juice—so the problem is either in the component itself or in the wire between the fuse box and the component. See Procedure 5 to check the various components. If you get juice only on one side of the fuse, the fuse isn't carrying the juice. Try another fuse.

If there's no juice to the fuse box, there's a problem in the wire between the battery and fuse box (see Procedure 5), or the fusible link is burned (see Step 3). Turn the ignition switch OFF now.

Step 3. Check and Replace Fusible Links.

A fusible link is really just a high-tech fuse. There are two links on '75-'78 models, *three* links on '79-'83 models and three or four links on '84-'87 models. Except for the juice for the starter motor, all current flowing from the battery goes through the fusible links. If the current flowing through one of the wires in the link is higher than it should be, the fusible metal in the wire melts and breaks the circuit to protect the wires and electrical components on that circuit—just like a fuse.

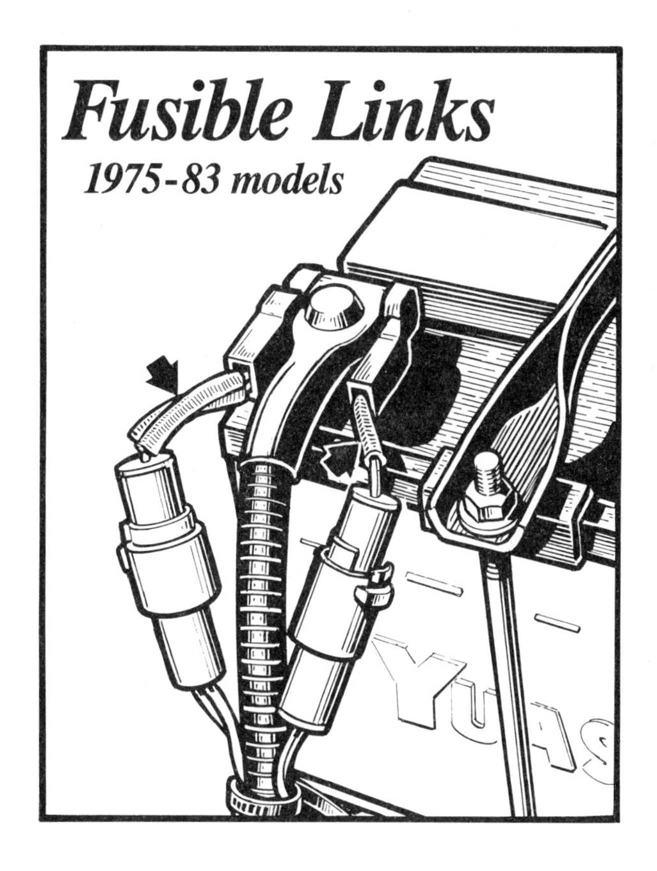

'75-'83 models: The fusible links are small wires attached to the positive (+) battery terminal clamp on one end and to a plastic connector on the other end. The links consists of an insulated wire covered with a loose-fitting piece of cloth. To check the wires in the link, feel along the cloth on each wire to see if the wire is still intact. Sometimes the cloth will be burned and black at the point where the wire melted. Some fusible links are paired, so if one of the wires is burned or broken you have to replace them both. Be sure the new links have the proper rating for your year and model.

Replace Fusible Links

Connector end: Locate a little tab on the side of the connector. Lift up on the tab while pulling the two halves of the connector in opposite directions. Align the bump on the new connector with the tab on the other part of the connector, then wiggle the two halves together until the tab locks them together.

Battery end:

'75-'78 models: The battery end of the links is secured to the positive cable clamp with a 10mm or 12mm nut and washer. Use a wrench to remove the nut and washer, then pull the end of the old link off the post. Use a wire brush to clean the post and top of the cable clamp. Fit the end of the new link onto the post, install the washer and nut, and snug the nut down with a wrench. Careful—it's a small bolt, so don't overtighten it or the bolt might break.

'79-'83 models: The battery end of the fusible links consist of a plastic connector that fits over a flat "spade connector" attached to the positive cable clamp. To release the link, spread the ends of the connector apart while pulling the plastic end off the spade connector.

'84-'87 models: The fusible links are in a little plastic box just to the rear of the battery. To get to the links, pull forward on the tab on the bottom front of the box while lifting up on the box, then wiggle the lid off the box. The links are flat plastic rectangles with a thin piece of wire visible in the center. Use your fingers or needlenose pliers to gently pull the links out of the box. You can see the thin piece of wire through the tiny window in the side of the link. If you find a break in the wire, the link is broken. Buy a new one with the same rating as the old one and insert it in the slot.

EVERYONE: If the new link blows (breaks) right away, there's a problem in one of the components in the circuit controlled by that link. Procedure 5 tells you how to trace faulty components.

Step 4. Check and Reset Circuit Breaker.

Circuit breakers are in the heater blower motor circuit on '82 and '83 models. On '84-'87 models, circuit breakers are in the circuits for the power windows and/or power door locks, if you have these options. 4 Runners also have a circuit breaker for the power rear window and the rear window wiper and washer.

The circuit breakers are located in the front part of the main fuse box. Circuit breakers are switches that turn off automatically when too much juice is flowing through the circuit.

To reset (turn on) the circuit breaker, turn the ignition switch OFF, then stick something thin and pointed, like a toothpick, needle, ice pick, or the end of your 12-volt test light, into the small hole in the face of the circuit breaker. You'll hear a click when the breaker is reset.

Try the component now. If the circuit breaker clicks off again it means there's a short in the circuit. See Procedure 5. If the component still doesn't operate, and the fuses and fusible links are good, the component is probably broken.

PROCEDURE 3: CHECK, REPLACE AND/OR ADJUST DRIVE BELT(S)

Condition: Drive belt(s) are too loose, too tight, worn out, or broken; OR the drive belt(s) must be removed in order to remove the crankshaft pulley, alternator, water pump, air pump, air conditioner compressor, or power steering pump.

Tools and Materials: One 12mm and two 14mm wrenches. For tightening the alternator belt or air pump belt (on some models without air conditioning), you'll need a large screwdriver (or broom handle, long ratchet handle, etc.) to use as a lever.

Remarks: After three or so years of use, drive belts can break suddenly regardless of how good they look. I recommend that you make a habit of replacing the drive belt(s) every three years, or at least carry spare belts and the tools to replace them.

Models with air conditioning and/or power steering: If you need to replace the alternator drive belt, you'll have to remove the air conditioning (A/C) and/or power steering (P/S) drive belts before you can replace the alternator drive belt.

Caution: Be sure the engine is off when you deal with the belts. Everyone should do Step 1, then go to the specific belt step that concerns you.

Step 1. Check Condition and Tension of Drive Belts.

All drive belts are located on the front of the engine. So, with the engine turned off, open the hood and peer down there.

Look at the outer edges of the drive belt(s) for signs of fraying (little threads of material will be unraveling from the belt). Twist the belt 180° so you can see the inner side of the belt. Look for cracks, tears, or missing chunks. If you see any of these maladies, the belt should be replaced now.

To check the belt tension, push down on the belt midway between two of the pulleys. (It's best to check it between the two pulleys that are farthest apart.) Toyota says to use 22 lbs. of pressure. You'll have to guess how hard you're pushing (or maybe use a fisherman's spring scale and pull on the belt with 22 lbs. of force) while you measure the distance the belt deflects. To make things simple, use two fingers and push a bit harder than you push a doorbell. A new belt should deflect about ½" and a used belt about 9/16".

Loose belts tend to squeal and don't turn the components (such as the alternator) as fast and efficiently as they're supposed to. Belts which are overtightened are hard on the bearings inside the components and can cause them to fail prematurely. Just a little too loose is better than a little too tight. When you install a new belt, always check the tension again after running the engine for about 15 minutes, to see if the new belt stretched a little.

Step 2. Replace and/or Adjust Alternator Drive Belt.

The alternator is attached to the engine by two brackets. Locate an "ear" on the top front of the alternator. The 12mm bolt screwed into the ear is the **drive belt tension adjustment bolt**. Notice how the adjustment bolt goes through a long, curved **slotted bracket**. A 14mm bolt on the bottom of the alternator allows the alternator to pivot in the **mounting bracket**.

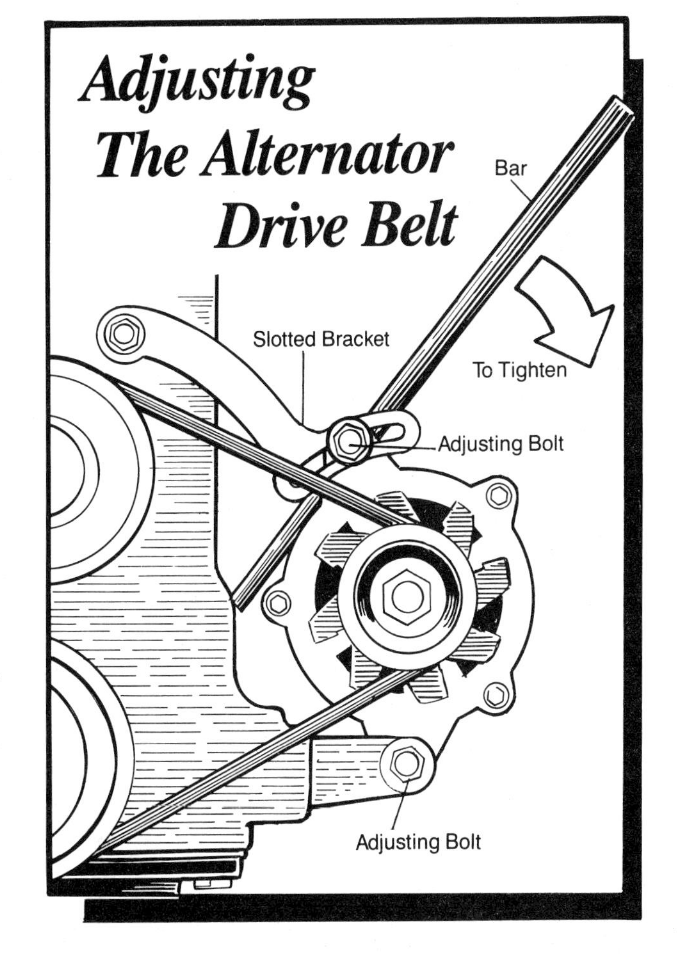

Replace Drive Belt: If your engine has an air pump or air conditioning, you'll need to remove the drive belt for those components before you can replace the alternator drive belt (Step 3 and/or 4).

Loosen but don't remove the 12mm bolt that attaches the top of the alternator to the slotted bracket on the engine.

From under the front of the truck, remove the skid plate (if you have one) and the large flat sheet metal splash pan beneath the front of the engine, if it's in your way. Working underneath the front of the truck, loosen the 14mm pivot bolt at the bottom of the alternator.

Push the top of the alternator toward the engine until the adjusting bolt hits the inner end of the slotted bracket. Slip the belt off the alternator pulley, fan pulley and crankshaft pulley. Wiggle the belt over the front of the fan to remove it.

Slide the new drive belt over the front of the fan, then fit it around the crank, fan and alternator pulleys. Pull the top of the alternator away from the engine with your hand to hold tension on the belt while you lightly snug down the adjuster bolt with the wrench. Adjust the belt to the proper tension (see below). If the old belt still looks pretty good, stash it somewhere for emergency service.

Adjust Alternator Drive Belt: Working from the engine compartment, slightly loosen the 12mm tension adjusting bolt at the top of the alternator. From beneath the truck, loosen the 14mm pivot bolt at the bottom of the alternator. If you have a skid plate and/or splash pan, you'll need to remove it/them to get to the bolt.

Slide a large screwdriver, broom handle, ratchet handle, long ratchet extension, or whatever you're using for a lever, between the alternator and engine. Be sure you're not smashing any hoses, tubes or wires with the end of the lever. Pull the top of the lever away from the engine to tighten the drive belt. Loosen the adjuster bolt a little if it's too tight. Pull on the lever with one hand while you check the tension on the belt with your other hand. Get the tension so the belt will deflect about 9/16" (used belt) or ½" (new belt) when you push on it midway between two of the pulleys. Step 1 tells you exactly how to check belt tension. When the belt is tight enough, keep the pressure on the lever while you tighten the adjuster bolt with a 12mm wrench. Now tighten the 14mm bolt on the bottom of the alternator. You'll probably have to hold the bolt head with one 14mm wrench while tightening the nut with another 14mm wrench.

To loosen a too-tight belt, you can usually just push down on the belt between two of the pulleys after you loosen the two bolts. This will pivot the alternator toward the engine slightly.

Check the belt tension again (see the illustration) and tighten or loosen it if necessary. When the tension is right, tighten the pivot bolt(s). New belts quickly stretch a little, so if you installed a new belt, run the engine for about five minutes, turn the engine off and check the tension. Tighten the belt if need be.

Step 3. Replace or Adjust Air Pump Drive Belt.

If you're replacing the air pump drive belt and your truck has power steering, you'll need to remove the power steering drive belt in order to remove the air pump drive belt. See Step 5.

Models without air conditioning: Just loosen the 12mm bolt that attaches the top of the air pump to its bracket on the engine. Also loosen the 14mm pivot bolt at the bottom of the pump.

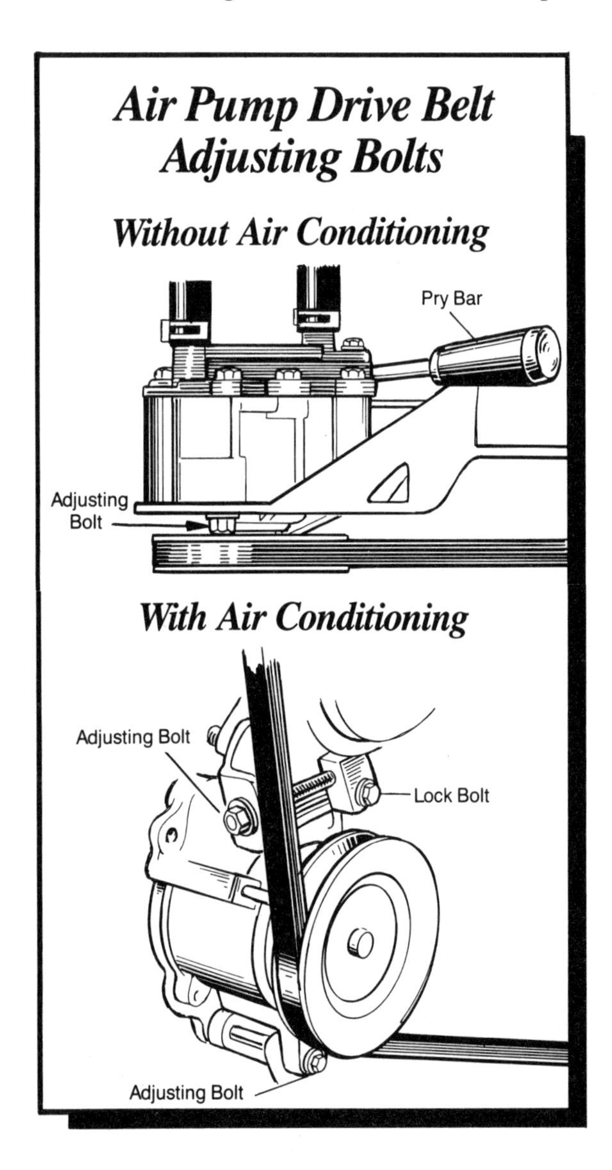

To replace the belt, push the top of the air pump toward the engine, then remove the belt. Fit the new belt around the crank pulley and air pump pulley, then pull the top of the air pump away from the engine to hold tension on the belt.

To adjust the belt, use a large screwdriver as a lever between the engine and the rear of the air pump to pry the pump away from the engine. Don't pry on the aluminum body of the air pump because it might crack or become distorted. Check the belt tension while pulling on the lever. When the tension is correct, tighten the 12mm bolt at the top, then the 14mm bolt at the bottom. Check the tension again and adjust it if necessary.

Models with air conditioning: There's a 14mm adjusting bolt in the bracket about halfway between the A/C compressor and the air pump. The head of the bolt is to the right side of the bracket. A 12mm or 14mm lock bolt is on the front side of the bracket, near the inboard end of the adjusting bolt.

To remove the drive belt, loosen the lock bolt (*counterclockwise*), then the adjusting bolt until the belt can slip off the pulleys. Fit the new belt over the crank, air pump and A/C compressor pulleys.

To adjust the drive belt, tighten the adjusting bolt until the tension is correct, then tighten the lock bolt. Easy, eh?

Step 4. Replace or Adjust Air Conditioner Drive Belt.

You'll see that the A/C drive belt goes around the **crank pulley** and the **A/C compressor pulley**. On models with an air pump mounted to the lower right side of the engine, the A/C belt also goes around a pulley on the front of the air pump. Models without an air pump have a small **idler pulley** mounted to the engine beneath the A/C compressor. The small idler pulley can be moved to tighten or loosen the drive belt.

Models with air pump: See Step 3 above to adjust or replace the belt.

Models without an air pump: Remove the skid plate if you have one. Crawl under the front of the truck and locate a small pulley just to the right of the crank pulley. Just behind the bottom of the pulley you'll see a 14mm bolt screwed almost vertically into the pulley bracket and another bolt in the center of the pulley. Loosen the bolt in the center of the pulley, then turn the vertical bolt head *clockwise* to tighten the belt or *counterclockwise* to loosen it. If you're replacing the belt, loosen the vertical bolt far enough so you can slip the belt off the pulleys, then install the new belt. Tighten the vertical bolt until the tension is correct, then tighten the bolt in the center of the pulley. Check the tension again after running the engine for about 15 minutes. Why aren't all belts this easy to adjust?

Step 5. Replace and/or Adjust Power Steering Drive Belt.

The drive belt for power steering (P/S) goes around the crankshaft pulley, the pulley for the **P/S pump** located on the top front left side of the engine, and around a small **idler pulley** mounted on a **bracket** near the top front of the engine. A bolt for adjusting the belt tension is on the top right side of the idler pulley bracket. The bolt in the center of the idler pulley locks the pulley in place after the belt is adjusted. The belt tension is adjusted by loosening the bolt in the pulley, then screwing the adjustment bolt *clockwise* to tighten the belt or *counterclockwise* to loosen it. Don't forget to tighten the bolt in the center of the idler pulley.

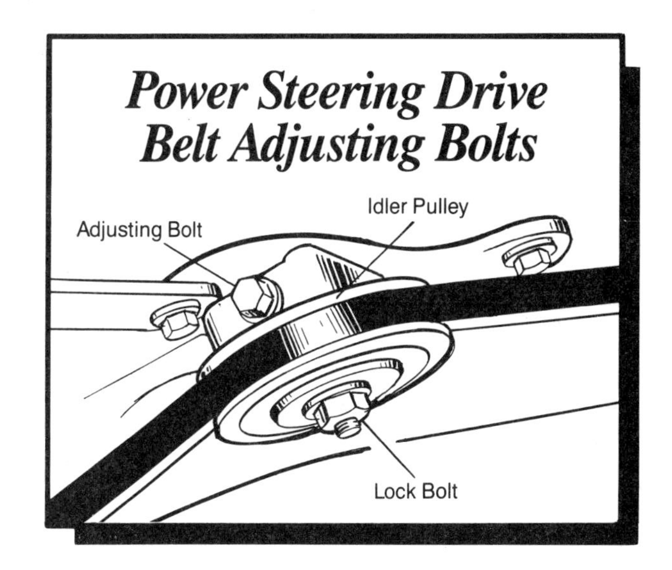

If you're replacing the belt, loosen the bolt in the center of the idler pulley, then turn the adjusting bolt *counterclockwise* until you can pull the belt off the pulley. If the belt doesn't loosen, use a hammer or screwdriver handle to tap the head of the bolt toward the bracket.

Remove the old belt from the pulleys. Slip a new belt over the crank pulley, then over the power steering pump pulley, then over the small idler pulley.

To adjust the belt tension, turn the adjusting bolt *clockwise* until there's about ½" to ¾" deflection when you press on the belt halfway between the adjusting pulley and the pulley on the power steering pump. When the deflection is correct, tighten the bolt in the center of the idler pulley. If you just installed a new belt, check the belt adjustment again after the engine has run for about five minutes.

PROCEDURE 4: REPLACE LIGHT BULBS

This procedure covers all kinds of light bulbs. If a headlight is your problem, do only Step 1. If it's one of the other light bulbs, read Step 2, then go to the step that deals with your particular bulb. Turn the ignition key and light switch OFF when replacing bulbs. If the hazard (emergency) or turn signal lights and the indicator light on the dashboard light up but don't flash, see Step 10 to replace the flasher unit(s).

Condition: One or more of the lights aren't working; OR the turn signals or hazard lights won't flash.

Tools and Materials: Phillips screwdriver. Maybe new bulb(s), new flasher unit, a wire brush, two small screwrivers and a flashlight.

Remarks: If lights on both sides of the car are out, check the fuses before changing the bulbs (Procedure 2, Step 1). The little owner's manual for your truck shows the locations of all the bulbs and tells you how to replace them, kind of.

Step 1. Replace Headlight.

Before buying a new headlight, check the fuses (Procedure 2, Step 1). Most parts stores won't let you return electrical parts even if you bring them back in virginal condition.

You might want to take the time to pull out and install the headlight from the other side of the car in place of the non-working one to see for sure if it's the light, the fuse, or the wiring.

To change a headlight bulb, either the grille or a piece of plastic molding around the headlight(s) must be removed. This is done from the front of the car. It's easy because they're held on only by phillips screws or plastic clips. Here's how.

Remove Grille

'75-'78 models: The grille has a left and right half. If you are here to replace the horn, only remove the right half of the grille. If you're replacing a headlight, the half on the side with the burned out headlight must be removed so you can get to the headlight retaining screws.

One screw is near the top outer corner of the grille, one is between the headlight bulbs at the bottom of the grille, one is along the top edge of the grille about halfway between the inner headlight and the grille emblem, a screw is at the top and bottom of the grille emblem, and one screw attaches a horizontal tab on the top of the grille to the body. Remove the six phillips screws, then remove the grille half.

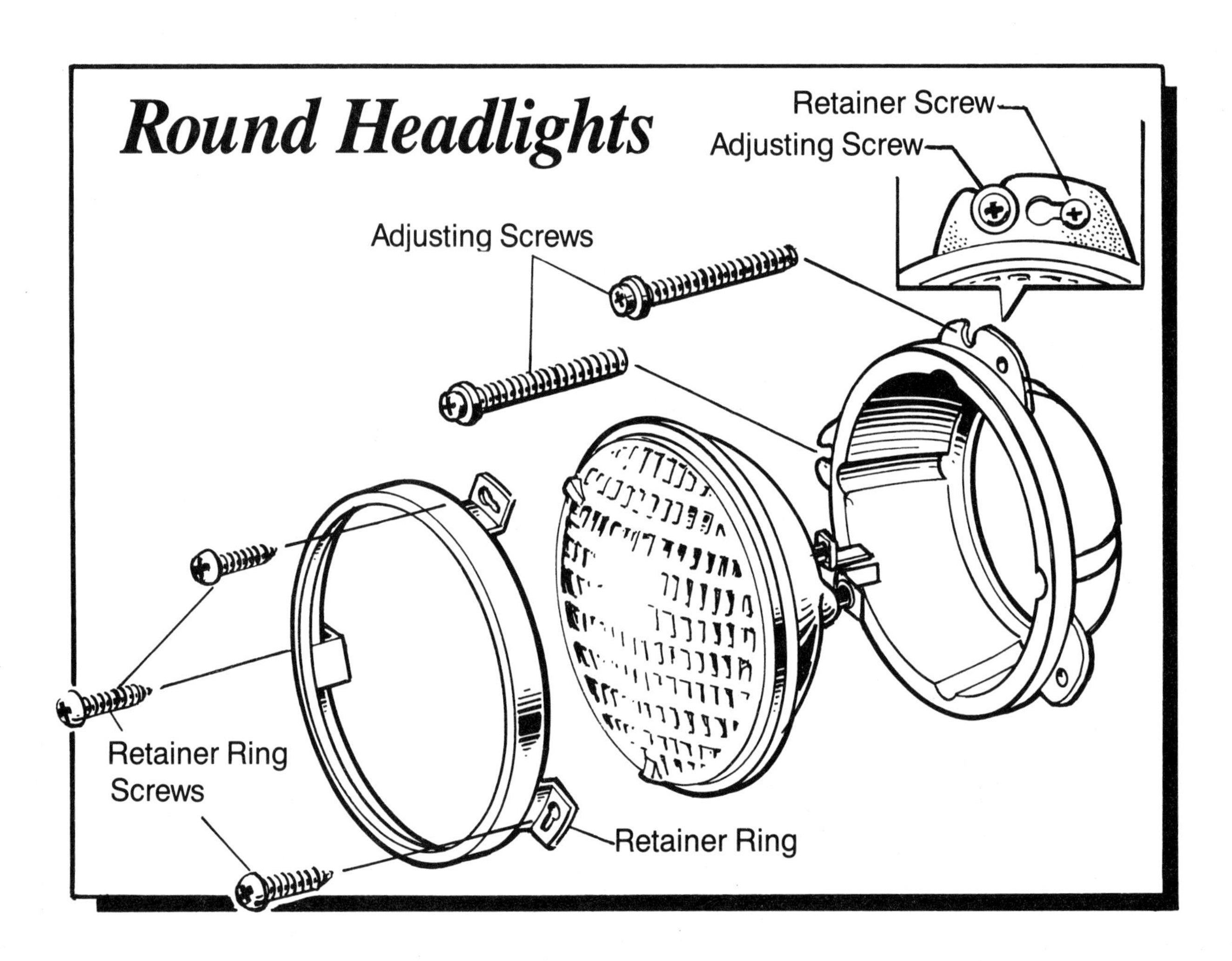

'79-'83 models: If you're replacing the headlight, you only have to remove the plastic molding that's around the headlight. Here's how: remove the screws on the corners of the molding (three screws on '79-'81 models or four screws on '82-'83 models), then pull the molding off.

If you're removing the grille to get to the horn, follow the instructions below for '84-'87 models.

'84-'87 models: The entire grille must be removed to get to the headlight retaining screws. It's easy because the grille is held in place by only two screws and nine plastic clips around the outer edge. Remove the two screws and stash them where they won't get lost. To release the plastic clips, stick a medium screwdriver into the slot of the clips, then twist the screwdriver handle clockwise. Pull the grille away from each clip as it's released.

EVERYONE: Now that the decorations are off, you'll see several phillips screws around the edge of the headlight. Two of the screw heads will be larger than the others. Don't mess with the two larger screws, they're adjusters used only for aiming the headlight. The headlight **retainer ring** is held in place by three smaller screws on round headlights or four smaller screws on square headlights.

Round headlights: Loosen the three small screws just enough so you can rotate the chrome retainer ring clockwise until the heads of the screws will fit through the round holes in the ring. Pull the retainer ring and headlight bulb away from the **headlight cradle**.

Square headlights: Remove the four smaller screws and pull the metal retainer ring and headlight out of the **headlight cradle** (socket). The headlight will lift right out into your hands.

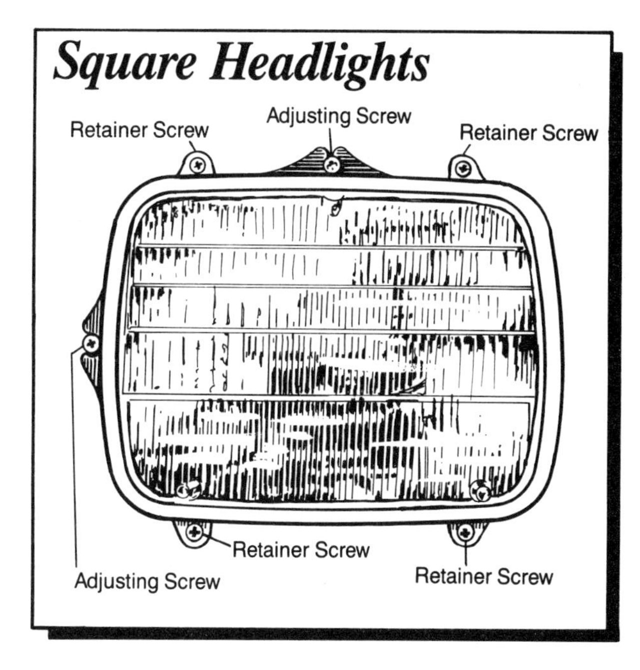

EVERYONE: Wiggle the **electrical connector** off the back of the old headlight. It just pulls straight out. (Grab it by the plastic connector so you don't put too much tension on the wires.) Then plug the electrical connector onto the new headlight.

Look for TOP stamped on the front of the new headlight. Insert the bulb into the cradle so TOP is, you guessed it, at the top. On square headlights there might be three bumps on the front of the bulb. If so, install the bulb so the single bump is at the top. The bump(s) on the back of the light fit into the slot(s) on the cradle. If the front of the new bulb isn't marked TOP and doesn't have bumps, orient the light so the bump(s) on the back of the bulb fit into the slot(s) in the cradle.

Square headlights: Hold the headlight in place with one hand while you install the metal retainer ring and tighten the four small phillips screws. Remember, don't touch the two adjusting screw heads.

Round headlights: Slip the retainer ring over the bulb, aligning the big part of the slots over the mounting screws. Turn the ring *counterclockwise* so that the narrow part of the slots tucks under the screw heads. Then tighten the mounting screws. Don't touch the two larger adjusting screws.

Install Grille

'75-'78 models: Fit the grille half back in place and install the retaining screws.

'79-'83 models: Headlight replacers install the plastic molding around the headlight with the phillips screws. Horn replacers follow the instructions below for '84-'87 models.

'84-'87 models: Fit the grille in place with all the plastic clips aligned with the holes. Press on the grille close to each clip to be sure it locked. When you are sure they're all locked, install and tighten the two phillips screws.

EVERYONE: If you accidentally messed with one or both of the larger phillips screw-heads that aim the headlights, or you don't think the headlights are aimed correctly, have the Toyota dealer or a garage adjust the headlights. It's fastest and easiest to let them to do it.

Here's how the headlight aim is adjusted, in case you're desperate and have to do it yourself. Screw the large phillips screwhead on the side of the headlight *clockwise* to aim the headlight more toward whichever side the screwhead is on. Turn it *counterclockwise* to aim the light more in the opposite direction from the side with the screw. If there's a large phillips screwhead above the headlight, turn it *clockwise* to aim the headlight higher, or *counterclockwise* to lower the aim. If the large screwhead is below the headlight, screw it *clockwise* to lower the beam, or *counterclockwise* to raise the beam.

Step 2. How to Replace Light Bulbs (except headlights).

The rest of the steps in this procedure (2 through 9) tell you how to get to the different bulbs by removing the **lenses** or the **bulb holders**. This step explains how to replace the bulb after you've gotten to it. So find the step below that relates to your particular dead bulb, then return here to replace the bulb.

Once the lens is off or the bulb holder is removed, you'll see either a **small round bulb**, a **tiny oblong bulb** or a tubular **double ended bulb**. Here's how you replace the different kinds of bulbs.

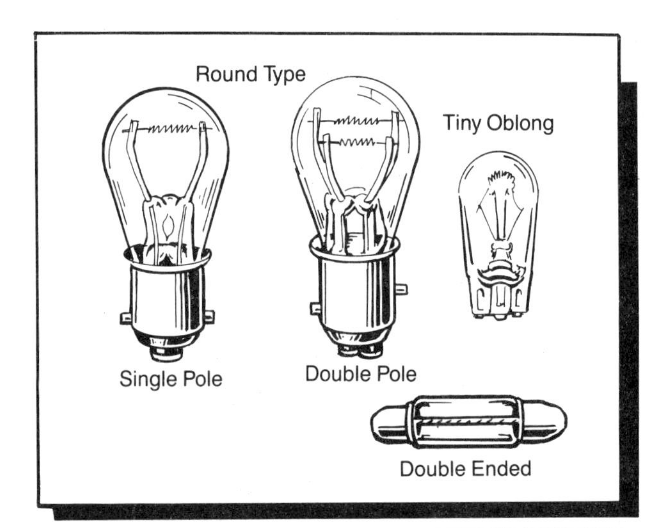

Replace Round Bulbs: Taillights, brake lights, turn signals, parking lights and backup lights are typical of the round-bulb style. To remove a round light bulb, push in on the bulb and gently turn it *counterclockwise* until it stops, then pull it out of the bulb socket. It should come out easily. If it won't, push and turn again—you may not have turned it far enough.

To install a new round bulb, align the two little bumps on the sides of the metal part of the bulb with the little grooves in the bulb socket. Push in on the bulb until it touches bottom, then hold pressure on it and turn it *clockwise* to lock it into place. Bulbs with two filament wires must be installed in a certain position because one of the bumps on the side is further from the end than the other. Try the bulb one way and if it won't go into the socket all the way, pull it out, rotate it around 180° and insert it again. It'll turn and lock into place this time.

Round-Type Bulb Installation

Replace Tiny Oblong Bulbs: The front and rear side marker lights on '79-'87 models, and the parking lights on '84-'87 models are of the tiny oblong type. To remove a tiny oblong bulb, just wiggle it out of its holder.

To install a new tiny oblong bulb, align its flat bottom with the slot in the socket, then wiggle it in.

Replace Tubular Double Ended Bulb: This strange type of bulb is usually found lurking in the interior light fixture(s). The pointed metal ends are held in place either with clamps, which wrap around the metal part of the ends, or the pointed ends fit into holes in the springy clips on each end of the bulb.

To remove the bulb if it's held with metal clamps, pry one end out of the metal clip, then pull the other end out of its clamp. To install the bulb, just press the metallic ends into the metal clamps.

If the pointed ends are sticking into holes in the clips, push the bulb toward one of the clips while you pry the clip on the other end away from the bulb. The bulb will drop right out. To install the bulb, fit one pointed end into its hole in the clip, then push the bulb toward that clip while you push the other end into its hole on the other clip. That's it.

EVERYONE: After replacing a bulb, test the light with the switch to see if it works. If the light still doesn't work, see Procedure 5.

If you removed a lens to replace the bulb, clean the inside of the lens, as well as the shiny reflector behind the bulb, with a rag. Then carefully fit the rubber gasket (if you have one) and lens in place and secure them with the phillips screws.

Step 3. Front Turn Signal and Parking Lights

1975-78 models: *front turn signal and parking lights:* These are small round bulbs of the double filament variety—one bulb does the work of two. To get to the bulb remove the four small phillips screws at the corners of the lens, then pull the lens off. When you remove the bulb (Step 2), note where the two little bumps are located on the sides of the round metal bulb base. One bump will be closer to the end than the other. The new bulb must be installed with the bumps in the same position.

1979-87 models: *turn signal bulbs:* The turn signals are mounted in the front bumper. The front lenses are easy to remove; just unscrew and remove the two phillips screws and carefully pull the lens off. (You want to be careful so as not to tear up the rubber gasket that may be between the lens and the bumper.) Changing the bulb is explained in Step 2. Be sure and clean the inside of the lens and the reflector.

Parking lights: The parking light bulbs are behind the lenses next to the headlights. Depending on the year, there are two or three phillips screws to remove in order to remove the lens. Once the lens is off, see Step 2 to replace the bulb. On '79-'83 models it's the small round bulb type and on '84-'87 models it's the tiny oblong type.

EVERYONE: Try the lights to see if they work now. If not, see Procedure 5.

Step 4. Bulbs in Side Marker Lights.

The **side marker lights** are mounted on the sides of the body near the front or rear: yellow in the front, red in the rear.

'84-'87 models: The rear side marker bulbs are mounted in the side of the rear combination light assembly, so see Step 6 to replace them.

EVERYONE: To remove the side marker lens, unscrew the two phillips screws in the lens, then pull the lens off the car, being careful not to damage the rubber gasket. Replacing the bulb is explained in Step 2.

Install the lens with the two phillips screws, then try the light switch to be sure the light works. If it still doesn't work, see Procedure 5.

Step 5. Brake Lights.

If the brake lights aren't working, check the **fuse** (Procedure 2, Step 1) and the **bulbs** (Step 6 in this procedure). If the lights still won't work when you step on the pedal, look at Chapter 7: **Brakes**, Procedure 14, to check the **brake light switch**.

Step 6. Rear Lights.

The bulbs for the brake lights, taillights, rear turn signals, backup lights and, on '84-'87 models, the side marker lights are all in what's called a **rear combination light assembly**.

The lens for the rear combination light assembly is held in place by phillips screws through the lens itself.

Remove the phillips screws, then carefully pry the lens away from the combination light assembly and lay it aside. Now you can replace the bulb (Step 2). Check the bulb to see that it works. Before putting everything back together, clean the inside of the lens and the reflector. Be sure the rubber gasket for the lens is in place, then fit the lens on the assembly and install and tighten the screws.

Step 7. Replace Rear License Plate Bulbs.

'75-'83 models and all 4 Runners have two license plate lights. '84-'87 models (except 4 Runners) have only one. The method for changing the bulbs is the same. Whenever the headlights are on, the license plate light(s) should also go on. In some places the cops may stop you if it's not working.

There are two phillips screws in the license plate lens holder. Remove the screws and pull the lens holder off to expose the bulb. Step 2 tells you how to change the bulb.

When the new bulb is installed, switch on the lights to see if it works. Yes? Install the lens holder. If not, see Procedure 5.

Step 8. Dash, Warning and Indicator Light Bulbs.

This step is for instrument panel illumination bulbs and the bulbs for the **warning lights** (brake, oil, charge, etc.) and **indicator lights** (high beam, turn signals, 4WD, etc.). See the *Other Dash Lights* section later in this step to replace bulbs not located behind the instrument panel.

If all of the dash lights are out, the problem is probably a blown fuse, a broken headlight switch or a faulty ignition switch. Rotate the dash light dimmer switch knob *counterclockwise* to check if the dash lights aren't just dimmed all the way down. If some of the dash lights work, you probably have one or more burned-out bulbs.

There are two ways to replace the bulbs in the instrument panel: by reaching up under the dashboard, or by removing the instrument cluster. The first way is quicker but more uncomfortable; the second way takes longer but is almost a necessity on later models that have lots of stuff packed under the dash. I suggest that you peek up under the dash to see if it looks like the front of the instrument cluster is accessible. If it's too congested back there and/or you don't feel like twisting your body into a pretzel to replace the bulbs, remove the instrument cluster.

Replace bulbs without removing instrument cluster: With a flashlight in hand, wiggle into a position, probably uncomfortable, so you can peek under the dash and at the back of the instrument panel. Through the wires you'll see several short knobs. Determine which knob is closest to the unlit area of the instrument panel or to the non-functioning warning or indicator light. Grasp the little knob and turn it *counterclockwise* (as viewed from the end of the knob), then pull it out. With this little unit in hand, crawl out from under the dash.

Remove instrument panel: First, disconnect the negative battery cable (Procedure 1, Step 3). Here's how you remove the instrument panel trim.

'75-'78 models: Find a clamp on the bottom of the dash that attaches the steering column to the dash. Loosen, but don't remove, the two bolts in the ends of the clamp. Then remove the three phillips screws that attach the instrument cluster trim to the dash. One screw is in the center, just above the turn signal indicators. The other two are on the lower outside corners of the two instruments. Pull the instruments away from the dash slightly so you can disconnect the speedometer cable and wiring connectors. The instrument panel is now liberated. Skip down to the EVERYONE section.

'79-'87 models: Remove the phillips screws just above the instrument panel. They are screwed up into the dash where it runs across the top of the instrument cluster. Remove the phillips screws on each side of the steering column that attach the trim across the bottom of the cluster to the dashboard. On '84-'87 models there's a screw to remove on the left end of the dash. Remove the screws, then wiggle the trim off the face of the instrument cluster.

Locate four phillips screws that attach the instrument cluster to the dash (two on the top, two on the bottom). Remove the screws and pull the cluster away from the dash just far enough so you can reach behind it and disconnect the large plastic electrical connectors. Squeeze the lever on the side of the round speedometer cable fitting and disconnect the speedometer cable. Now you can remove the instrument cluster from the dash. Find the short knob close to the burned out bulb, then turn it *counterclockwise* to remove it.

EVERYONE: Wiggle the small bulb out of the knob. If it doesn't look burned out, you may have pulled out the wrong knob and bulb. Take the bulb with you when you buy a new bulb. Some of the bulbs are small and some are downright tiny. Insert the new bulb into the knob, then stick it in the hole and rotate it until you feel the tabs on the knob fit into the notches on the instrument panel. Push in on the knob while twisting it clockwise to lock it into place.

Install instrument cluster: Once the bulb is replaced, hold the instrument cluster up to the dash and reconnect the plastic electrical connectors. They are shaped differently so you can't get them mixed up. Reconnect the speedometer cable.

Now install the instrument cluster with the phillips screws. On '79-'87 models you'll need to install the trim panel with the phillips screws.

Other Dash Lights: On some models there is a little light mounted just above the heater/vent/air conditioner/fan control. To replace this bulb, remove the two phillips screws, pull the bulb holder down, then replace the bulb (Step 2).

On other models the heater control panel light is behind the control panel. To get to it first pull the knobs off the control levers and fan switch. If there's a nut behind the fan switch knob, remove it. Now use a small screwdriver to pry the right end of the panel away from the dashboard. Replace the light bulb. To get it all back together, snap the control panel in position in the dashboard. Install the lever knobs and the nut (if you have one) and knob on the fan switch.

Step 9. Other Light Bulbs.

Dome Light: The interior dome light on the ceiling is covered by an opaque plastic lens. To remove the lens, use a screwdriver in the switch slot to gently pry the lens off its holder. The bulb is tube-shaped with pointed metal ends that fit into two springy clips. To remove the bulb, pry one end out of the clip, then pull the bulb out of the other clip.

To install the new bulb, just press the metal ends into the clips. See if the light works, then wiggle the lens into place.

Personal light (map light): This is the airplane-type overhead light found in some '84-'87 models. It's mounted just to the rear of the rear view mirror. Use two small screwdrivers in the small notches on the front edge of the lens to gently pry the lens off the holder. See Step 2 to replace the tubular double end bulb.

Door courtesy light ('85-'87 models), deck light (some pickups) and luggage compartment light (4 Runner): Remove the two phillips screws that attach the lens to the holder. The bulb is the tubular double ended type. See Step 2 to replace it.

Step 10. Check Turn Signal and Hazard Light Flasher Unit.

Flasher units seldom wear out, so let's eliminate other possibilities. If the turn signals flash faster for one side of the car than for the other side, a bulb is probably burned out. Check the bulbs (Chapter 5, Procedure 4, Step 8). If none of the turn signals and/or emergency lights work, check the fuses and fusible links (Procedure 2).

If the turn signals work on one side of the car, but neither the lights nor the indicator light on the dashboard work for the other side, the turn signal switch might be broken. See Procedure 14 to replace the switch.

The symptoms of a defective flasher unit are: The turn signal lights go on when the turn signal lever or hazard switch is turned on, but the lights flash very slowly, very quickly, or not at all. It's a good idea to buy the new flasher unit before digging around under the dash so you'll know what you're looking for.

The flasher unit is a small box-like gizmo with a plastic three-wire connector attached to it. The unit either attaches with a screw to the body or slips onto a tab mounted to the body. "Flasher" might even be stamped on the unit. On '75-'78 models the unit is mounted in front of the center part of the dashboard. On '79-'87 models the unit is mounted to the left or right kick panel (wall), just forward of the doors.

Peek up under the dash and locate your flasher unit. Remove the screw that secures the unit or slip the unit off the tab. Release the tabs on the wire connector, then pull the connector off the unit. Fit it onto the new flasher unit. It will only fit one way. Attach it with the mounting screw or slide it onto the tab. Turn the ignition key to ON (don't start the engine), then try the turn signals or hazard lights to see if the problem is solved. If everything's working properly, turn the key OFF. If there's still a problem, see Procedure 5 or seek professional help.

PROCEDURE 5: HOW TO DIAGNOSE NON-ENGINE ELECTRICAL PROBLEMS

This deals with electrical failures or gremlins not related to the way the engine starts or runs. If the engine has cranking or charging problems, see Procedure 6 or Procedure 9 in this chapter.

Condition: An electrical component isn't working; OR the battery loses its charge, OR a fuse keeps blowing (breaking); OR anything amiss that seems like it may have an electrical source.

Tools and Materials: A 12-volt test light or Volt/Ohm meter (VOM), safety glasses, maybe new fuses, fusible links, light bulbs, or whatever component you're checking, maybe a 10mm or 12mm wrench to disconnect the negative battery terminal. Depending on the problem you might also need: wire brush, sandpaper or knife for cleaning contacts, a piece of insulated wire about 12 inches long for testing "ground," some extra fuses to help locate shorts, electrical tape for patching shorts.

Remarks: Most problems with the electrical system are due to a blown fuse, a poor wire connection, or a worn-out component (bulb, switch, etc.). Very seldom is a broken wire the problem.

If you've never used a Volt/Ohm meter (VOM), or need a refresher course, see Chapter 15, Procedure 2.

Step 1. Check Fuses.

Start by locating the fuse box and the fuse for the component that isn't working (see Procedure 2). Replace the fuse for that component with a new fuse, then try the component to see if it works. Don't forget to turn the ignition key to ON if the component is switched by the ignition system. If the new fuse doesn't blow but the component still doesn't work, see Step 2. If the new fuse blows within a few seconds after installation, see Step 3.

Is yours a headlight problem? Some models have three fuses, a fusible link, and a relay unit which affect the headlights: one fuse for the high beams or right headlights, a separate fuse for the low beams or left headlights, and a master fuse that controls all the headlights and a few other lights. There's also a relay switch for the headlights. If the bulbs, fuses and fusible links are all good but the lights still won't work, have the Toyota dealer or a garage check the relay and headlight switch.

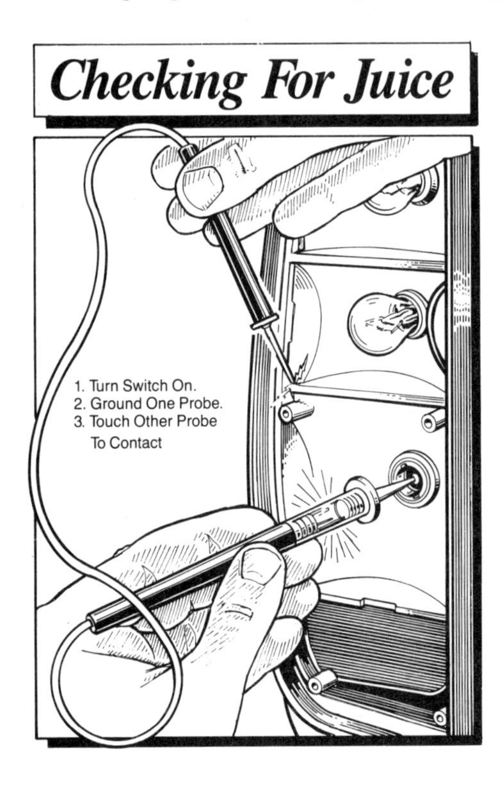

Step 2. Check for Juice and Ground at Component.

All electrical components receive their supply of electrical energy from the **positive** (+) terminal of the battery. The electrical energy (juice) arrives at the component through an insulated wire, passes through the component to make it light, beep, pump, or whatever the component was designed to do, then returns to the **negative** terminal of the battery through the car body and frame (the "ground"). This circuit must be completed for electrical things to work. Here's how to see if juice is getting from the battery to the component through a wire, and if there's a good ground connection so the juice can get back to the battery.

Light Bulbs: Remove the lens and bulb (Procedure 4), then come back here to check for juice and ground connection.

The juice for light bulbs gets to the filament inside the bulb through small brass or aluminum contact(s) inside the bulb socket which touch a metal contact (or contacts) on the bottom of the bulb. The contacts inside the socket and on the bottom of the bulb must be clean and free of crud and corrosion for the bulb to work properly. Be sure the ignition key and light switch are OFF, then use sandpaper, a knife, or a small screwdriver to clean the contact points in the bulb socket and on the end of the bulb. Try the bulb again. On small round bulb setups, also clean the metal walls of the socket. If the light still doesn't work, see if there's juice to the contact(s) in the socket and if the socket is grounded. (See "Check for Juice" and "Check for Ground," just ahead.)

On some lights, the bulb socket and/or its mounting screw(s) touch the car body and act as the ground to return the juice to the battery. Other light sockets have a wire (usually black) running from the socket to a part of the body to provide the ground. Check to see that the socket is grounded or that the wire is firmly attached at both ends.

Other Components: There's usually a wire connection on or near the electrical component (windshield washer motor, windshield wiper motor, etc.), which supplies the current to make the thing work. To complete the circuit, either there's a wire connecting the component to the body or the component itself is mounted to the body to provide the ground directly. Get out your test light or VOM.

Check for juice: Turn the ignition switch and the component's switch ON. If you have a VOM, set it to 15 DC volts. Disconnect the wire that supplies current to the component. Touch one probe of the test light or the red (+) probe of the VOM to the wire and touch the other probe to bare metal. If you're checking a bulb socket, touch the probe to the little metal contact point in the bottom of the socket (without touching the sides of the socket) and touch the other probe to bare metal (like the bumper). Test both contacts if there are two.

If none of the wires or contact points for the component lights the test light or moves the VOM needle, it means no juice is getting to the component. If the fuses are good, the problem is likely in the switch or the relay, if that component has a relay. Have the Toyota dealer or a garage check the switch and relay (if there is one). If it's the switch that's bad, see Procedure 14 to replace the switch.

If more than one wire goes to the component and one of the wires has juice but the other one is black and doesn't have juice, check the black wire to see if it's a ground wire. Its other end will attach to bare body metal somewhere. Here's more about grounding.

Check for ground: If there's juice to the component but it still won't work, maybe the component isn't grounded properly. Again, first turn the ignition and the component switch ON. You'll need a VOM or piece of wire to test the ground. Set the VOM to RX 10, then touch one probe to the component's metal body or to the black ground wire that didn't have juice in it. Touch the other probe to bare metal. DON'T touch the wires or contact points for the bulbs! The needle should swing over to 0 ohms if the component is properly grounded. No VOM? Install the bulb if it's a light you're checking. Check again that the component is switched on. Touch one end of a piece of wire to the metal part of the bulb socket, or to the metal body of whatever thing you're checking. Touch the other end of the wire to bare metal. If the bulb lights up or the component works, the thing itself is good but it isn't properly grounded.

If that's the case, turn off the switch and remove the mounting nuts, bolts, or screws that attach it to the car body, or follow the black wire from the component to where it attaches to the body and detach it. Use sandpaper or a wire brush to clean the place where the screw, nut, bolt, wire and/or socket touches the body. Make it shiny. Now attach the light socket or component to the body, turn on the switch, and see if the problem is solved.

If the component is getting juice and is grounded properly but still doesn't work, the component is probably bad. Seek a professional second opinion or replace the component with a new one.

If the component isn't getting juice and you're sure the fuses and fusible links are good, have the professionals check the switch and relay for the component (if there is a relay).

Step 3. Checking for Shorts.

A short means the juice is taking a short cut back to the battery before going through the component. How? A break in the insulation (the wire's plastic sheath) allows the wire to contact the body or frame of the car and this completes the circuit. Without the resistance in the component to slow the flow of juice, the juice flows so fast it overheats the wires and blows the fuse for the circuit. If new fuses blow within a few seconds after you install them, you have a major short for sure. A minor short can slowly drain the battery over a period of a few days without blowing the fuse.

Check for a minor short: Put on your safety glasses, then disconnect the negative (-) battery cable from the body and/or engine. Don't disconnect the cable from the terminal of the battery. Turn the ignition switch and all electrical components OFF (close the doors so the interior light is off), then gently touch the negative battery cable end to clean bare metal while watching for a very small spark. You can also use a Volt/Ohm meter between the body and the disconnected end of the negative battery cable to see if juice is flowing when it shouldn't be. If you see a spark or the Volt/Ohm meter shows juice flowing, you have a short in one of the circuits. On '79-'87 models with a clock, the clock might draw enough juice to indicate a short. To be sure, remove the fuse for the clock then do the test again.

Now to find the short if the above test indicates you have one. Go to the fuse box (see Procedure 2, Step 1, to locate it) and pull out one of the fuses, then try the battery-cable-to-bare-metal test or use the VOM again. Still sparks? Put the fuse back in and try another fuse. Try each fuse like that until you find the circuit that *doesn't* cause a spark or register current on the VOM when the fuse is removed. The short is in that circuit. Put the fuse back in, then read the Identify Faulty Component section, which comes next.

Identify Faulty Component: If you have a major short, the fuse will blow immediately or very soon after the faulty component is turned on. You can use spare fuses to find the short. It might take several fuses to locate the problem so be sure you have several new ones handy.

Disconnect the components on the problem circuit one at a time (they're listed in Section 8 of your Owner's Manual). Then do the spark check (for minor short) or install a new fuse (for major short). Keep disconnecting components, then testing one at a time. When you find the component that doesn't cause a spark or blow a fuse when it's disconnected, the short is in that component or the wiring to that component. Note the color of the wire(s) to the component, then follow that wire until it disappears into a large bundle of wires taped or wrapped together (the **wire harness**). If you find a bare place in the wire, tape it with plastic tape. Look for a wire running from the fuse box that's the same color (**color code**) as the one to the component and check it for bare places. Reconnect the component and try the ground-clamp-to-negative-post spark test, or install another new fuse, to see if the short is eliminated.

If you can't find a break or bare place in the wire, the short is either in the component itself or in the wiring where you can't find it. If the wiring appears to be in good condition and hasn't been messed with by a demented electronics freak, buy a new component and install it. If that doesn't solve the problem or if the wiring is funky, it's time to seek professional assistance.

PROCEDURE 6: CHECK CHARGING SYSTEM (BATTERY, ALTERNATOR, VOLTAGE REGULATOR)

The **red alternator (charge) light** on your dashboard is the key to checking your charging system. If the battery is completely dead it won't go on—you'll have to first charge the battery or jump-start the car with jumper cables. When you turn the ignition key ON, the alternator light turns on, so you know the bulb's OK. As soon as the engine starts it turns OFF and should stay off if the charging system is OK. If the bulb stays off when the engine is off and the ignition key is on, check the fuses (Step 1 in this procedure). If the fuses are OK, check the bulb (Procedure 4). Be sure the warning light is functioning correctly.

The charging system operates everything electrical while the engine's running, and keeps the battery full of juice to run accessories while the engine is off and to start your truck in the morning.

'75-'84 models: Two types of alternator/voltage regulator setups have been used. Look in your engine compartment for a small black box mounted to the inside of the left front fender, near the ignition coil. It probably has "Regulator" printed on it. If you find the box, you have an externally mounted Tirrill regulator. No box? You have an IC regulator which is built into the alternator itself.

'85-'87 models: Your alternator has an IC regulator built into the alternator.

Condition: The red alternator light stays ON while the engine is running; OR the battery needs recharging every few days.

Tools and Materials: Volt/Ohm meter (VOM) or 12-volt test light, maybe a volt meter, ammeter, tachometer, three jumper wires and a 10mm wrench.

Remark: If the red charge light goes OFF when the engine is running, but the battery needs frequent recharging, do Procedure 5, Step 3, to see if it's a *minor short* that's draining the battery.

Step 1. Check Electrical Connections.

Start by checking the fuses. The charging system is protected by the circuit in the fuse box under the following labels. '84 and later models have more than one fuse to check.

YEAR	CIRCUIT	FUSE	LOCATION
'75-'76	TURN/ GEN.	15 Amp	MAIN FUSE BOX
'77-'85	ENGINE	15 Amp	MAIN FUSE BOX
'86-87	IGN	7.5 Amp	MAIN FUSE BOX
'84-87	CHARGE	7.5 Amp	ENGINE COMPARTMENT

If the fuses are all good, check the connections on both ends of the battery cables to be sure they're clean and tight (Procedure 1, Steps 3 and 4). Check the alternator drive belt for tightness (Procedure 3, Step 1). Check the electrical connections on the alternator (Procedure 7, Step 4) and voltage regulator if you have one (Procedure 8, Step 3). Disconnect the wire connections, clean them with a wire brush, then reconnect them. Now see if the red alternator light on the dash goes out with the engine running. If there's a voltmeter in the dash, the needle should go to about 14 volts when the engine is revved above idle. Still a problem? Read on.

Step 2. Check Voltage Across Battery.

To see if the alternator is supplying voltage to the battery you'll need a Volt/Ohm meter (VOM) or at least a 12-volt test light.

Start with the engine off. Set the VOM at 15 DC volts. Touch the *red* probe to the *positive* (+) battery terminal, and the *black* probe to the *negative* (-) battery terminal (or touch the probes of the test light to the battery terminals). The VOM should read about 12 volts or the test light should light up. Start the engine and read the meter again. If the battery is too weak to start the engine, use jumper cables to fire it up (Procedure 1, Step 8).

Evaluation: With the engine revved above idle the VOM should read about 13.8 to 14.8 volts, or the test light should glow brighter than at idle. In other words, there should be a slight increase in voltage when you rev the engine a little above idle.

If the voltage is slightly higher (up to 14.8 volts), the battery is probably the problem since the alternator and voltage regulator are supplying the proper voltage.

If the voltage is too high (above 14.8), the voltage regulator isn't functioning properly and the battery cells in the battery might be burned out due to constant overcharging. Replace the voltage regulator (Procedure 8) and have the battery checked.

If the voltage is too low, there's obviously a problem with the alternator and/or the voltage regulator, but it's difficult to determine which one is bad. You need an **ammeter** to test the amperage output and a volt meter to test the voltage output of the alternator. Since it's probably cheaper to have the alternator/voltage regulator checked by a garage than to buy a good ammeter and volt meter, I suggest you have a garage determine which component is bad. You can replace either of them yourself and save some money (Procedure 7 to replace the alternator or Procedure 8 to replace the regulator). If you want to check them yourself, see Step 3 below.

Step 3. Check Alternator and Voltage Regulator.

For this test you'll need a volt meter, an ammeter, and three jumper wires to connect the meters to the alternator. A tachometer is also handy but not essential.

First, disconnect the negative (-) battery terminal. Locate the B terminal on the rear of the alternator.

'75-'84 models: The B terminal is on the rear, near the top along the outer edge, just above a plastic connector that is plugged into the rear of the alternator.

'85-'87 models: The B terminal is on the top rear of the alternator body.

EVERYONE: Pry the rubber cap off the B terminal and you'll see a wire attached to the alternator with a 10mm nut. Remove the 10mm nut and disconnect the wire from the alternator. Attach the wire you just disconnected from the alternator to the negative (-) terminal of the ammeter. Use a jumper wire to connect the positive terminal of the ammeter to the B terminal on the alternator. Now connect the positive (+) terminal of the volt meter to the B terminal on the alternator. Connect a jumper between the negative terminal on the volt meter to a clean, unpainted metal surface (ground).

Caution! Be sure the jumper wire clips are touching nothing but the terminals they are connected to. If they touch any other bare metal the alternator and/or regulator could be damaged.

When you're sure the wires are connected properly, reconnect the negative battery terminal. Connect your tachometer if you have one (Chapter 5, Procedure 12, Step 1). Check that the jumper wires are clear of the fan, fan belts and pulleys, and that they aren't laying on the exhaust manifold. Start the engine. While doing this test don't rev the engine much above 2,000 rpm. Electrical components could be damaged.

NO LOAD TEST: With the engine running at about 2,000 rpm, the ammeter reading should be less than 10 amps.

'75-'84 models: The volt meter reading should read between 13.8 and 14.8 for alternators with Tirrill (separate) voltage regulators or between 14 and 14.7 volts if you have an IC voltage regulator built into the alternator.

'85-'87 models: The voltage reading should be between 13.5 and 15.1 volts.

LOAD TEST: Now turn the high beam headlights on and the heater fan motor switch to the high position. With the engine running at about 2,000 rpm, the ammeter reading should be over 30 amps for '75-'80 and '85-'87 models, or over 20 amps for '81-'84 models.

Turn the headlights, fan motor and engine off.

EVALUATION: If the voltage reading is higher than normal, the voltage regulator is shot. The battery might also be damaged from being constantly overcharged. If you have an external Tirrill regulator you can replace it (Procedure 8). If you have an IC regulator built into the alternator, have Toyota or a garage replace it for you.

Slightly lower than normal amp readings in either test could be due to a fully charged battery, which just can't hold any more juice. To discharge the battery a little, disconnect the coil wire from the distributor and use a jumper wire to ground it to bare metal so the engine can't start. Crank the engine for about ten seconds, then reconnect the coil wire, start the engine and do the two tests again quickly. If the ammeter readings are still low, the alternator isn't putting out as much juice as it should. Remove the alternator (Procedure 7) and take it to the Toyota dealer or an auto electric shop for further tests. If the problem is something minor, like worn out brushes, they can be replaced fairly cheaply. If major parts within the alternator are worn out, the alternator must be replaced. It would be a good idea to get a second opinion before forking over the money for a new or rebuilt one.

PROCEDURE 7: REMOVE AND INSTALL ALTERNATOR

Condition: Alternator needs replacing; OR you need to remove the alternator for engine rebuild or some other repair procedure.

Tools and Materials: 10mm, 12mm and two 14mm wrenches, masking tape and pen. Maybe a new or rebuilt alternator, if your old one has died. You'll also need a large screwdriver (or lever) to tighten the drive belt after installing the alternator. '85-'87 models will also need a catch pan for draining the radiator.

Remarks: Brand new alternators from the manufacturer are pricey. Fortunately for you, rebuilt alternators can be found at parts stores and are generally about as reliable as new ones. They usually cost about half as much as replacement ones from the factory.

Step 1. Disconnect Electrical Wires.

Disconnect the clamp from the negative (-) battery post on the battery (Procedure 1, Step 3).

Carefully peel the rubber covers away from the wire connections on the alternator. To disconnect the plastic wire connector plugged into the rear of the alternator, pry the plastic arms away from the connector, then wiggle it out. Now remove the 10mm nut and washer that attaches the single wire to the alternator. Remove the wire, then stash the nut and washer so they won't get lost.

Step 2. Remove Alternator.

Loosen the **drive belt** (Procedure 3, Step 2), then remove the **belt adjustment bolt** from the **slotted bracket**. Stash the bolt and washer where they won't get lost. Crawl under the front of the car and remove the bolts that attach a large piece of thin sheet metal to the body below the radiator. Also, if you have a skid plate, remove it.

'85-'87 2WD models: Drain the radiator into a clean catch pan (Chapter 6, Procedure 3, Step 1). Locate a piece of pipe attached between the lower radiator hose and the engine. Remove the two bolts that attach the water pipe to the engine. Disconnect the water hose on the engine end of the water pipe and pull the pipe away from the engine so you can get to the pivot bolt on the bottom of the alternator.

4WD models: The lower radiator hose and heater hose are right in the way for removing the alternator. To clear them out, drain the radiator into a clean catch pan (Chapter 6, Procedure 3, Step 1), then disconnect the lower radiator hose from the engine. Push the hoses away from the alternator so you can get to the mounting bolts.

EVERYONE: Unscrew the 14mm nut from the rear end of the **pivot bolt** on the bottom of the alternator while holding the bolt head with another 14mm wrench. When the nut is off, support the bottom of the alternator with one hand while you remove the pivot bolt. Now you can lift the alternator away from the engine. Stash the pivot bolt, nut and washers with the adjustment bolt and washers.

Step 3. Install Alternator.

Position the alternator on the mounting bracket so the pulley end is toward the front of the car. From the front, slide the pivot bolt through the alternator ears and the bracket holes. Slide the washer onto the bolt, then screw the nut on until it's lightly snug. Fit the drive belt onto the alternator pulley. Be sure it's also in the grooves on the crank pulley and fan pulley. Pull the alternator away from the engine so there's enough tension on the belt to hold it in the pulleys. Be sure there's a flat washer on the adjustment bolt. Fit it through the slotted bracket and into the ear on the alternator, then screw it in. See Procedure 3, Step 2 to adjust the drive belt tension.

If you disconnected the lower radiator hose and/or a water pipe from the engine, install them and tighten the clamps (Chapter 6, Procedure 2, Step 3).

'85-'87 2WD models: Attach the water pipe to the engine with the two bolts.

EVERYONE: Install the piece of sheet metal below the radiator and/or the skid plate. If you drained the radiator, tighten the drain valve, then fill the radiator with coolant (Chapter 6, Procedure 3, Step 3).

Step 4. Attach Wires.

Plug the plastic wire connector into the rear of the alternator. Finally, attach the wire to the terminal with the nut. Slip the wire, washer and nut over the stud and snug it down with your wrench. Fit the rubber caps over the wire terminals, then connect the negative battery cable clamp to the negative post on the battery.

PROCEDURE 8: REPLACE VOLTAGE REGULATOR (MODELS WITH TIRRILL REGULATOR ONLY)

The Tirrill regulator, if you have one, is a black box approximately two inches by two inches mounted to the inside of the left front fender, near the ignition coil. If you don't have one you'll need to remove the alternator to have the voltage regulator repaired or replaced.

Condition: You or your garage has determined the voltage regulator has reached the end of a long, high-charged life.

Tools and Materials: New voltage regulator; phillips screwdriver or 10mm wrench depending on your setup; 10mm or 12mm wrench depending on your battery clamp nut.

Remark: Voltage regulators tend to outlive the car, so be sure yours is bad before replacing it (Procedure 6).

Step 1. Disconnect Battery.
Disconnect the negative (-) battery cable from the battery (Procedure 1, Step 3).

Step 2. Remove Regulator.
Follow the bundle of wires from the regulator to a plastic connector. You have to pry on a tab that's in a slot on the connector so it can slip over a bump to separate the connector. Remove the two 12mm bolts that attach the voltage regulator to the body. Make a note if other wires are attached with the mounting bolts.

Step 3. Install New Regulator.
Position the new regulator the same as the old one was. Attach the new regulator to the car with the bolts and tighten them. Be sure any other wires which were attached with the bolts are in place. Align the fastening clips on the two halves of the connector, then press them together (be sure it's tight). Connect the negative battery clamp, tighten its bolt, and you're finished.

PROCEDURE 9: CHECK CRANKING SYSTEM (STARTER MOTOR, SOLENOID, IGNITION SWITCH)

The starter is bolted to the lower right rear side of the engine and rather difficult to get to. For some of the tests the starter must be removed from the truck.

The starter **solenoid** (also called the *magnetic switch*) is mounted to the **starter motor**. For simplicity's sake, when referring to the entire unit I'll just call it "the starter." The cable from the positive (+) battery terminal mounts to a post on the solenoid. The function of the solenoid is to engage a little gear on the starter motor with teeth on the flywheel of the engine. Thus engaged, the starter motor cranks the engine around to get it started.

Two basic types of starters are used on '75-'80 model Toyota trucks: a "conventional" direct drive starter and a "reduction" gear driven starter. The two types operate in basically the same way, the major difference being that the reduction starters utilize a three-gear reduction set rather than the starter motor itself to rotate the engine. All '81-'87 models are equipped with the reduction type.

Conventional starters are 1.0kw and the reduction types are either 1.0kw (1.34hp) or 1.4kw (1.87hp). Although the conventional and reduction starters are interchangeable, the reduction type works best in cold climates where the engine is liable to be more sluggish.

Condition: The engine won't turn over when the ignition switch is turned to START; OR you can hear the starter engage but it won't turn the engine; OR the engine turns over too slowly to start.

Tools and Materials: Depending on how far the tests take you in tracking down the problem, you might need the battery cleaning tools and materials listed in Procedure 1, 12-volt test light, phase 1 tool set, jack and jackstands, jumper cables, jumper wires, an ammeter, and maybe a new starter.

Remark: Except for the first three steps in this procedure, the starter must be removed from the truck in order to do the tests.

Step 1. Check Battery.

First, let's be sure the battery is delivering a good supply of juice to the starter. Turn the headlights on and see if they shine brightly. If not, check the battery connections (Procedure 1, Steps 3 and 4) and fusible links (Procedure 2, Step 3). If that doesn't make the headlights bright, check the battery (Procedure 1, Step 5). Now try to start the car. If you still have problems, move on to Step 2.

Step 2. See If Starter Is Hung Up in the Flywheel.

If the starter motor turns the engine, skip this step.

Check both starter motor mounting nuts and tighten them if they're loose. A loose starter can easily get hung up in the flywheel.

Manual Transmission models: Caution: If you happen to be stuck on a hill, either have a Friend sit in the car with one foot ready to stomp on the brake, or do the automatic transmission routine below. To keep from getting run over by your own truck, don't stand on the downhill end while you rock it back and forth.

Open and prop the hood. Put the gearshift in FOURTH, take your foot off the clutch pedal, then release the handbrake. Push on the truck to rock it back and forth while watching the engine drive belts. If the engine (belts) turns a little, the starter isn't hung up, so you can skip down to Step 3.

If the engine doesn't turn, rock the car a little harder while listening for a satisfying clunk. A clunk means the starter just broke free and the engine should turn now. No clunk? Then you'll have to remove the starter (Procedure 10). Be sure and read the EVERYONE section of this step.

Automatic Transmission models: Set the handbrake, then put the gearshift lever in NEUTRAL. Use a socket on the crankshaft pulley nut to turn the engine *clockwise* (Chapter 5, Procedure 5, Step 3, tells you how). If the engine turns a little, the starter isn't hung up, so you can skip down to Step 3.

If the engine won't turn, remove the starter (Procedure 10), then try to turn the engine again. Read on.

EVERYONE (who has removed their starter): Once the starter is off, try to turn the engine with whatever method you were using (car rocking in gear or socket on the crankshaft pulley). If the engine still won't turn, the GOOD news is that the starter is probably OK. The BAD news is that something inside the engine is locked up so an engine rebuild or replacement seems imminent. And, brethren, that is bad news.

If the engine turns after the starter is removed, the starter is probably bad. Either perform the following diagnostic steps or take it to the Toyota dealer or an auto electric shop to see if they can salvage it. If you have to buy a new or rebuilt starter, shop around because the price can vary radically from store to store.

Step 3. Check Ignition Switch Wire to Starter.

The battery and cables are in good shape, right? Follow the positive (+) cable from the battery to a **terminal post** on the starter solenoid. Right next to the terminal post, there's a **small wire** from the ignition switch attached to the starter with a push-on connector. Wiggle the ignition wire off the starter. It should be tight. If the wire was off and just dangling there, or if it came off easily, use pliers to gently squeeze the little grippers on the sides of the connector so it will fit tightly on the starter. Put the wire back on the starter and see if your problem is solved. If it is, consider yourself lucky.

Problem still not solved? Pull the small wire from the ignition switch off the starter again. Attach a 12-volt test light to the connector on the end of the wire and ground the other end of the test light to clean, bare, unpainted metal. Have Friend turn the ignition switch to START while you watch the test light. If the light doesn't light up, no juice is getting to the starter from the ignition switch. Check the fuses again (Procedure 2). If the fuses are good, the problem is probably the switch. Have the Toyota dealer or a garage check the switch. If it's bad, see Procedure 14, Step 3, to replace it.

If the test light lights up when the ignition switch is in the START position, the switch is good so the problem must be in the starter. The starter must be removed to do the following tests (Procedure 10). Once it's off the car, come back here to check it.

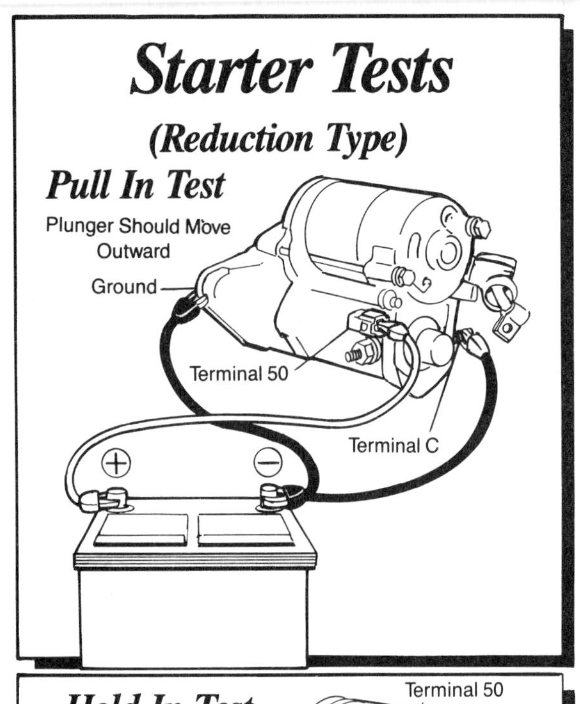

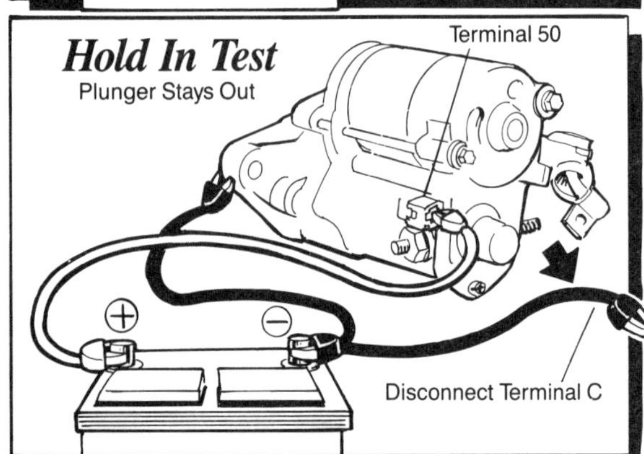

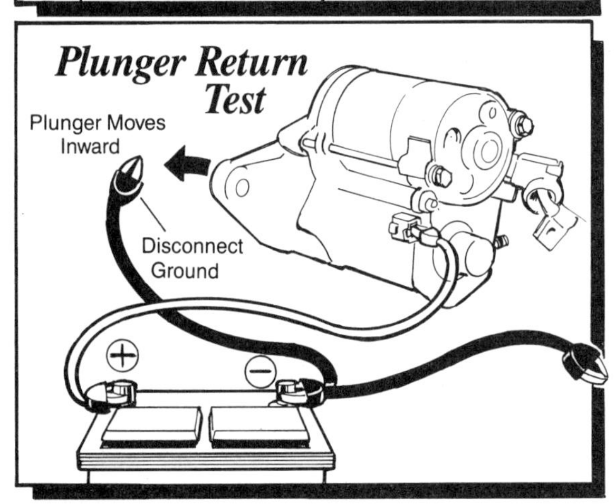

Step 4. Starter Orientation.

Regardless of which type of starter you have (conventional or reduction) the large terminal post on the starter where the cable from the positive battery terminal was connected is called **terminal 30**. The small spade-type terminal where the small wire from the ignition switch was connected is **terminal 50**. Terminal 50 is always right next to terminal 30.

There's one more large terminal post on the solenoid. It connects the solenoid to the motor and is called **terminal C**. A wire attached to terminal C disappears into the starter motor. On conventional starters terminal C is on the end of the solenoid right next to terminal 30. The nut and post are the same size as terminal 30. On reduction type starters terminal C is on the opposite side of the solenoid from terminal 30 and is covered with a rubber boot.

Cautions! When performing the following tests be sure and connect the battery to the starter exactly as shown in the illustrations. Read through the tests before actually doing them so you can do them within three to five seconds to avoid damage to the starter.

When the starter is activated it might jump due to the torque of the motor. So if possible, clamp the starter in a soft-jaw vise or have Friend put a foot on it to hold it on the floor.

Keep fingers away from the **plunger** (small gear) in the end of the starter while doing the tests. It jumps out with great force.

Step 5. Solenoid Tests.

These tests check that the solenoid is operating properly. Look for a small pinion gear on one end of the starter. A plunger inside the solenoid should cause the plunger to jump away from the starter when the proper electrical connections are made. Keep your fingers away from the pinion gear while doing the tests.

Pull-in test: Disconnect the wire from terminal C on the solenoid. Wrap the end with tape or a rag so it can't make connection with the starter or jumper cable.

Connect a jumper cable from the negative battery terminal to terminal C. Connect a jumper wire from the negative battery cable to the body of the starter. The mounting bolt brackets are a good place for this connection.

Now connect a jumper wire from the positive battery terminal post to terminal 50 (the little spade connector on the starter where the ignition switch wire connects). The gear on the end of the starter should jump outward. If it doesn't, the solenoid isn't working and must be replaced.

Hold-in test: Quickly disconnect the jumper wire from terminal C. The gear should remain out. If it moves back toward the starter, the solenoid is kaput and must be replaced.

Pinion return test: Now disconnect the jumper from the negative battery terminal to the starter body. The gear should retract toward the starter. If it doesn't, the solenoid must be replaced.

Now that we know the condition of the solenoid, let's check the condition of the starter motor.

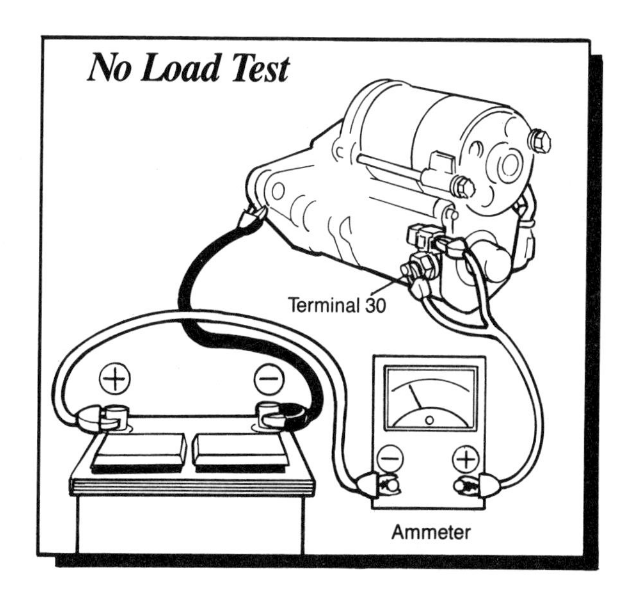

Step 6. Starter Motor Tests.

Reconnect the wire from the starter motor to terminal C on the solenoid, if you disconnected it. Connect a jumper from the negative battery terminal to the body of the starter (the mounting bracket is a good place). Connect a jumper from the positive battery terminal to the negative terminal on an ammeter. Connect the positive terminal on the ammeter to terminal 30 on the solenoid. Now use a jumper wire to connect terminal 30 to terminal 50 and check the ammeter reading. It should be less than 50 amps for conventional type starters or less than 90 amps for reduction starters.

If the starter motor didn't whir when you made the connections and/or the amp reading was higher than normal, the motor is kaput.

Step 7. Replace Starter Motor or Solenoid.

If you've determined which part is the culprit and want to replace just that part instead of the entire starter, here's how.

Conventional starter models: Note on which side of the solenoid terminal 50 (the little flat connector) is located so you can be sure it's on the same side during reassembly. Disconnect the wire from the starter motor to the solenoid (terminal C). It's right next to terminal 30, which is for the positive battery cable. Next remove the two phillips screws from the terminal end of the solenoid. They are long screws that go completely through the solenoid. When the screws are out, tilt the terminal end of the solenoid away from the motor to release the hook on the opposite end.

To install a new solenoid on the old motor or the old solenoid on a new motor, tilt the terminal end of the solenoid away from the motor while you engage the hook on the end of the solenoid with the lever spring in the housing. Lower the solenoid toward the starter. Be sure terminal 50 is on the correct side, then install and tighten the phillips screws that attach the solenoid to the motor. Fit the wire from the starter motor onto terminal C on the solenoid, then install and tighten the nut. Install the starter (Procedure 10).

Reduction starter models: Note on which side of the solenoid the wire from the motor is attached (terminal C) so you can reconnect it the same way. Pry the rubber boot off the end of the wire, then remove the nut which secures the wire.

The motor is attached to the solenoid with two long bolts on opposite sides of the motor. The bolt heads are near the terminal end of the solenoid on some models and on the gear end of the solenoid on the rest. Remove the two bolts, then pull the motor away from the solenoid. Look for a felt washer on the motor shaft. If it's stuck in the solenoid, pry it out. Some models also have a large rubber O-ring between the outer edge of the motor and where it fits into the solenoid. If you have the O-ring, check it for cracks and breaks.

To reassemble the motor and solenoid, fit the felt washer onto the motor shaft. If your model has a rubber O-ring, fit the O-ring into the recessed groove on the solenoid. Now look for a small protrusion on the motor and a notch on the solenoid. No protrusion and notch? Look for a small squarish patch of metal on the motor and solenoid near the edge where they attach. The protrusion and notch or patches of metal must be aligned in order for the motor to fit into the solenoid. Once you've found the marks, fit the motor into the solenoid, install the bolts and tighten them, then reconnect the wire from the motor to terminal C on the solenoid. Tighten the nut, then fit the rubber boot over the nut. Install the starter (Procedure 10).

PROCEDURE 10: REMOVE AND INSTALL STARTER (MOTOR AND SOLENOID)

The starter can usually be replaced with a quality rebuilt one for much less than it would cost for a new one. Call Toyota and several parts stores for starter prices, then call an auto electric shop to see how much it would cost to rebuild your old one. Sometimes you can trade your old starter in on a new or rebuilt one and save some money. Be sure and ask.

Condition: Starter appears to be dead; OR you wish to examine your starter at close range.

Tools and Materials: Jack, jackstands, 10mm, 12mm, 14mm and 17mm wrenches, 17mm socket, long extension, ratchet, and maybe a new or rebuilt starter.

Step 1. Get Ready.

Disconnect the negative (-) battery terminal (Procedure 1, Step 3). Remove the air cleaner on 20R and 22R engines (Chapter 5, Procedure 6, Step 1). Cover the top of the carburetor with a rag.

Chock the rear wheels and set the handbrake. Jack up the front of the vehicle and put it on jackstands (Chapter 2, Procedure 1).

Step 2. Disconnect Wires from Starter.

The starter is mounted to the lower right rear corner of the engine. Wiggle the small ignition switch wire off its post on the starter. Peel the rubber boot away from where the battery cable attaches to the starter. Remove the 12mm nut and washer, then lift the cable end off the post. Tuck it out of the way. Stash the nut and washer where they won't get lost.

Step 3. Remove Starter.

The starter is attached with a 17mm nut and lockwasher on the top and a 14mm or 17mm bolt, nut and lockwasher toward the bottom. It's easiest to remove the top bolt by reaching down through the engine compartment even though you have to wiggle your arm into a very uncomfortable position around the rear of the intake manifold. Remove the bottom bolt from beneath the car with a socket, long extension, and ratchet. You'll have to hold the nut on the end of the bolt with a wrench while unscrewing the bolt.

Remove the mounting nuts and bolt, then wiggle the starter toward the front of the car. Thread the starter down through the lines, wires and suspension parts to remove it. Kind of heavy, isn't it?

Step 4. Install Starter.

Thread the starter into position on the flywheel housing. Fit the starter over the mounting stud, then push the bolt through the starter and flywheel housing. Put it through the same way it came out. Install the two lockwashers and nuts and tighten them. Sometimes a liberal amount of patience is required to get the top nut on and tightened.

Step 5. Connect Wires and Finish.

Connect the battery cable to the starter terminal post with the nut and lockwasher and slip the rubber boot over the connection. Then fit the ignition switch wire snugly onto the small post. Be sure the cable and wire are on tight.

Lower the truck off the jackstands, then install the air cleaner if you removed it (Chapter 5, Procedure 6, Step 2). Reconnect the negative (-) battery terminal and tighten the clamp nut. Start the engine to see that everything is working properly.

PROCEDURE 11: CHECK AND REPLACE IGNITION COIL AND SIGNAL GENERATOR (PICKUP COIL)

The **ignition coil** is located in the engine compartment on the left fender. Two distinct types have been used over the years. One type is a long black tubular coil which I'll call a "tubular type." Mounted piggy-back on top of tubular coils there might be a white ceramic gizmo (an external resistor) and/or a small box (the igniter).

The other kind of coil consists of a short, round coil mounted in the top of a square aluminum bracket that houses the igniter. These square-looking coils and igniters are called "Type III."

Regardless of which type coil you have, a thick wire connects one end of the coil to the center of the distributor cap. At least two small wires are attached to the coil either at metal wire terminals (tubular type) or with a plastic connector (type III).

The **signal generator** (also called the *pickup coil*) is located inside the distributor on '78-'87 models. '75-'77 models don't have signal generators.

The following steps will check the condition of the ignition coil and signal generator. If the coil and signal generator check out OK but there's still no spark to the distributor, have Toyota or a garage check the condition of the igniter.

Condition: 12,000 mile tune-up; OR you're here from Chapter 4.

Tools and Materials: To quick-check the coil: Friend, insulated pliers or a wooden spring-type clothes pin or thick rag, maybe a 12-volt test light.

To thoroughly test the coil and signal generator you'll need a Volt/Ohm meter.

To replace the coil: phillips screwdriver, maybe 8mm, 10mm and 12mm wrenches.

To replace the signal generator: phillips screwdriver, brass feeler gauges, 19mm socket and ratchet.

Step 1. Check Coil.

Quick coil check: Engine OFF. Pull the thick center wire (the coil wire) from the center of the distributor cap. Inspect the end of the wire and its socket in the cap for crud, rust and/or cracks. Replace the cap and/or wire if they're corroded or funky and can't be cleaned with a wire brush.

Roll the rubber boot away from the end, then hold the wire with insulated pliers, a wooden clothes pin or a thick rag. Don't use your bare hands; the results could be painfully shocking. (In an emergency you can use two plastic handled screwdrivers like chopsticks to hold the wire.) Have Friend put the transmission in neutral and turn the engine over with the key while you hold the metal end of the coil wire about ¼"-½" (6mm-13mm) away from any *bare* metal surface **except the carburetor or fuel pump!** Don't crank the engine for more than two seconds at a time. A hot blue-white spark should jump from the tip of the wire to the bare metal (the ground). If the spark is a weak sickly orange, the coil is shot and must be replaced. A strong, but yellow spark that can jump the gap indicates the coil and/or the igniter control unit for the electronic ignition is going around the bend toward old age, but will last a while yet.

If there's no spark at all, check the two small wires attached to the coil. On models with a type III coil, the wires are attached with a plastic connector. On models with tubular coils, the wires are attached to two wire terminal posts. Are the small wires securely attached to the coil? Wiggle them to be sure. To be sure the coil is getting juice do the following checks.

Tubular type coil: Turn the ignition key to ON, then touch one end of a 12-volt test light to the positive (+) wire post on the coil. There's a small + next to the terminal. On '81 and newer models the wire attached to the positive post is brown. Touch the other end of the test light to bare metal.

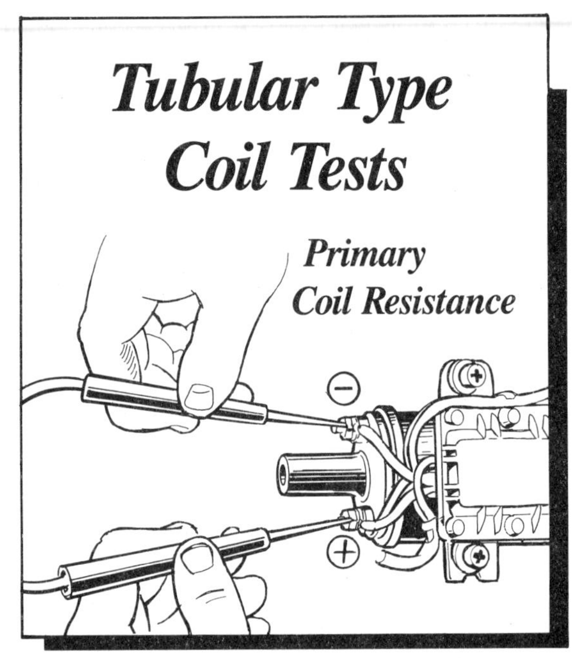

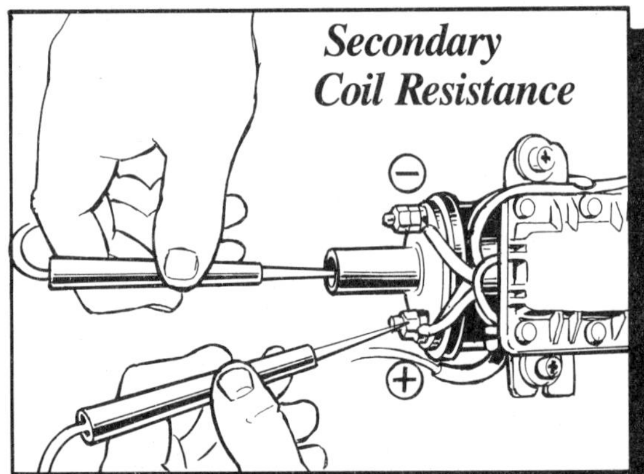

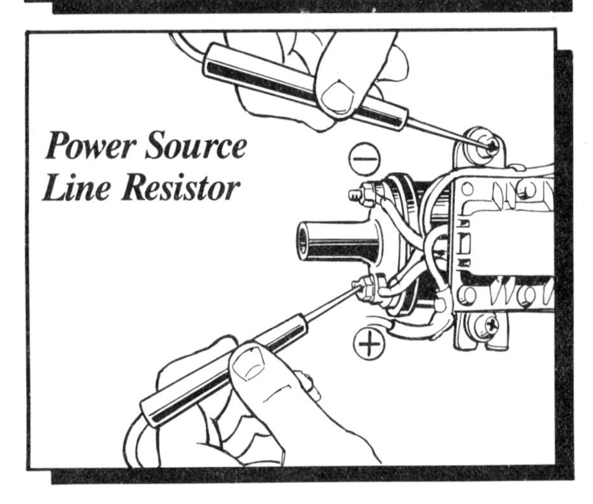

Type III coil: Find the green connector just to the rear of the coil with brown wires attached to each half of the connector. Pry up on the little tab while you separate the connector. One of the brown wires connects to the coil and the other connects to the wiring harness. Turn the ignition key ON, then touch one end of the test light to the brown wire attached to the wiring harness and the other end of the test light to bare metal.

EVERYONE: The test light will light up if the coil is getting juice. No juice? The ignition circuit isn't being supplied with electricity. Check the fusible links and the ignition fuse (usually marked IGN) in the fuse box (Procedure 2). If the fuses and links are good but no juice is getting to the coil, the ignition switch is suspect. Have the Toyota dealer or a garage check the ignition switch for you. Procedure 14 tells how to replace the switch.

If the coil is getting juice but a spark didn't jump the gap from the coil wire to ground, pull the coil wire out of the end of the coil and check the wire and its socket for corrosion. Use a wire brush to clean them if need be. Is the socket on the coil cracked or chipped? If so, replace the coil. If you have a VOM, check the large coil wire between the coil and distributor for resistance to see if it's broken (Procedure 12).

Check coil with VOM: If you have a Volt/Ohm meter (VOM), here's how to measure the resistance in the primary and secondary circuits of the coil. If you get different readings from those in the table, the coil is probably worn out.

Check to be sure the ignition switch is in the OFF position, then remove the large coil wire from the end of the coil.

Tubular type coil: Label and then remove the wires attached to the positive and negative terminals on the coil.

Type III coil: The two wires are attached to the coil with a plastic connector. The black wire goes to the negative terminal and the brown wire goes to the positive terminal. You might have to peek under a loose cloth around the wire to check the color. Use a tiny screwdriver to pry the tabs on the sides away from the connector while you pull the connector off the coil.

EVERYONE:

Measure primary coil resistance: Look at the Primary Coil Resistance chart below to see what the resistance of your coil should be. If it's less than 1, set the VOM to RX1. If it's more than 1, set the VOM to RX10. Zero the meter, then touch one VOM probe to the negative terminal on the coil and the other probe to the positive terminal. Compare the meter reading to the figure for your model.

PRIMARY COIL RESISTANCE

YEAR AND MODEL	RESISTANCE
1975-76	1.30-1.50 ohms
1977	
California	1.35-1.61 ohms
Federal and Canada	1.30-1.50 ohms
1978-79	1.3-1.7 ohms
1980	
Calif., Canada and C&C	0.8-1.0 ohms
Federal except C&C	1.3-1.7 ohms
1981-82	0.4-0.5 ohms
1983-84	
Tubular-type coil	0.8-1.1 ohms
Type III coil	0.4-0.5 ohms
1985-87	
22R	0.4-0.5 ohms
22R-E and 22R-TE	0.5-0.7 ohms

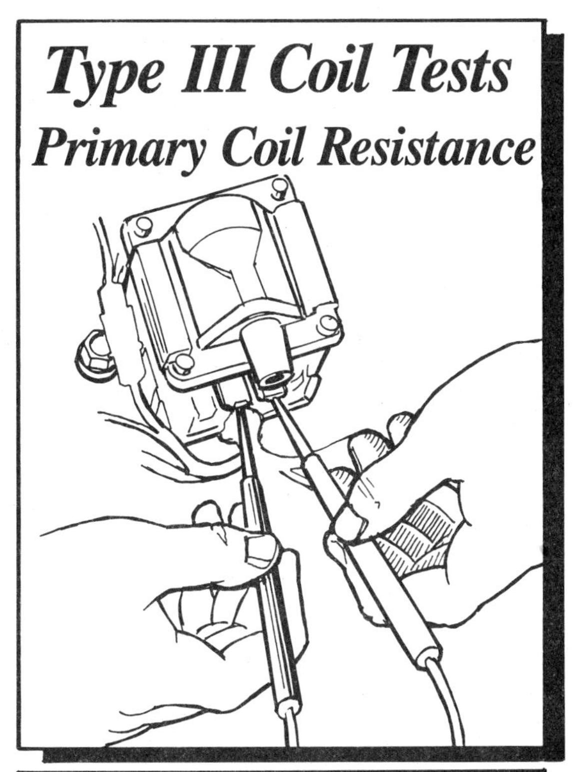
Type III Coil Tests
Primary Coil Resistance

Measure secondary coil resistance: Set the VOM to RX1K (RX1000), zero the meter, then touch one probe to the positive coil terminal and stick the other probe into the socket for the large coil wire so it makes contact with the metal inside. Use a screwdriver or nail as a contact if your tester probe is too big. Check the chart to see what the resistance should be.

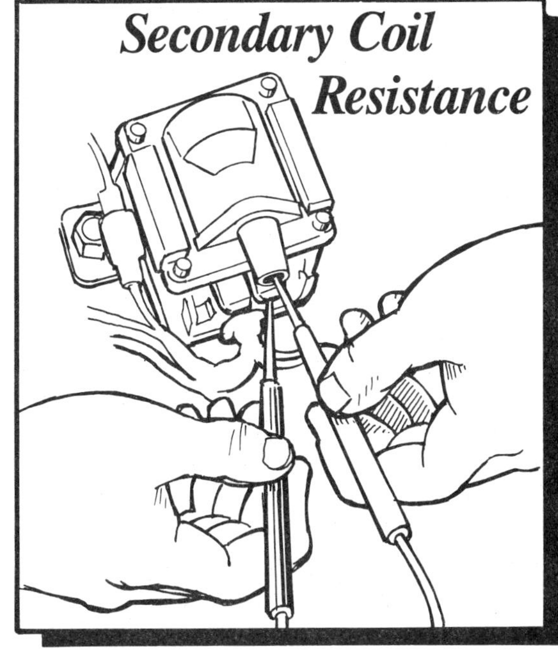
Secondary Coil Resistance

SECONDARY COIL RESISTANCE

YEAR AND MODEL	RESISTANCE
1975-76	6.5-10.5 kohms
1977	
California	12.8-15.2 kohms
Non-California and Canada	6.5-105 kohms
1978-79	12.0-16.0 kohms
1980	
Federal except C&C	12.0-16.0 kohms

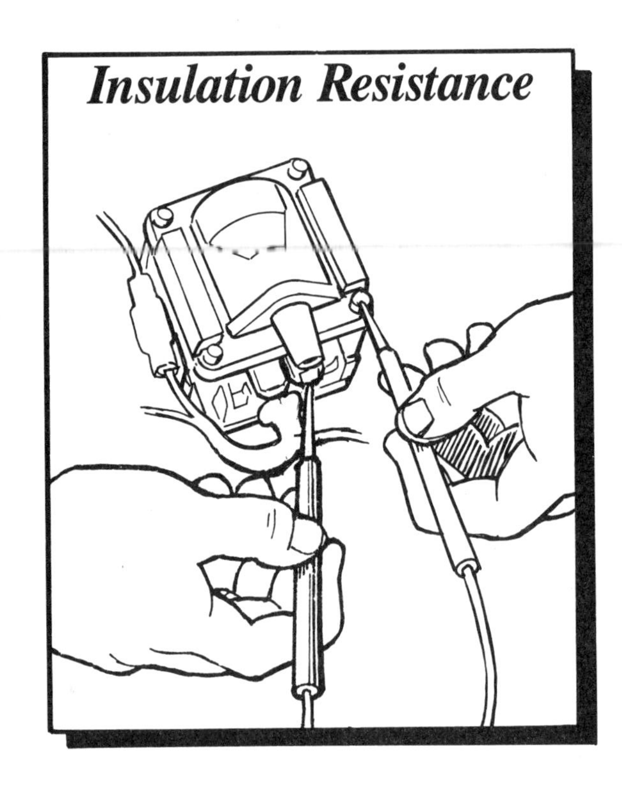

Insulation Resistance

Calif., Canada and C&C	11.5-15.5 kohms
1981-82	8.5-11.5 kohms
1983-84	
Tubular-type coil	10.7-14.5 kohms
Type III coil	8.5-11.5 kohms
1985-87	
22R	8.5-11.5 kohms
22R-E and 22R-TE	11.4-15.6 kohms

Evaluation: If the primary or secondary resistance is much different from those in the chart, the coil should be replaced. Step 2 tells you how to do it. If the readings were as they should be, reconnect the small wires to the coil terminals and plug the large coil wire into its socket on the coil. Then test the signal generator (pickup coil) in the distributor (Step 3).

Step 2. Replace Coil.

Disconnect the clamp from the negative (-) battery post (Procedure 1, Step 3). Twist the coil wire out of its socket on the coil.

Tubular type coil: Label the wires attached to the terminal posts + or -, then disconnect them from the coil. Make a note of any wires attached to the mounting bolts on either side of the coil. Remove the two 12mm bolts that attach the coil to the fender.

A large flat clamp around the center of the coil holds it in place. Use a phillips screwdriver and maybe pliers to loosen the long thin bolt going through the clamp. Note where the positive and negative terminals are positioned, then slide the old coil out of the clamp. Insert the new coil so the positive and negative terminals are in the same position as they were on the old coil, then tighten the phillips clamp screw while holding the nut with pliers.

Mount the new coil to the fender with the two 12mm bolts. Be sure anything attached with the bolts is in place, then tighten the two bolts.

Attach the wires to the new coil the same as they were on the old coil.

Type III coil: Disconnect the plastic wire connector from the coil. Remove the four phillips screws on top of the aluminum frame that holds the coil, then lift the coil away from the aluminum frame. Set the new coil in position on the frame the same as the old coil, then install and tighten the four phillips screws. Be sure anything else held in place by the screws is securely attached. Reconnect the plastic wire connector to the coil.

EVERYONE: Install the large coil wire in its socket on the new coil. Reattach and tighten the clamp on the negative (-) battery post. Do the spark jump test again to see what a good spark looks like. Fit the coil wire back into the center of the distributor.

Step 3. Check Signal Generator (pickup coil) in Distributor.

This step is only for '78-'87 models.

Turn the ignition switch OFF if it's on. Near the distributor, locate the plastic connector that connects the distributor to the coil or igniter. Pry the tab away from the connector while you separate the two halves.

Set the VOM to RX1, zero the meter, then touch the probes to the two metal ends in the connector half that's attached to the distributor. The VOM reading should be between 130 and 190 ohms for '78-'81 or between 140 and 180 ohms for '82-'87 models. If the reading is different, the signal generator is shot and should be replaced (Step 4).

If the signal generator readings are within the normal range and you've determined that the coil is good but still there's no spark to the spark plugs, check the spark plug wires and coil wire (Procedure 12). If the wires are OK, it's time to seek professional help for your ignition system problem.

Step 4. Replace Signal Generator.

Be sure the ignition switch is in the OFF position. Remove the distributor cap, rotor and dust shield (if you have one) from the distributor. Carefully pry the rubber sealing ring off the outer edge of the distributor. Note where the chunks of rubber fit into notches. Follow the small wires from the distributor to a plastic connector. Pry the tab away from the connector while separating the two halves.

20R and 22R models: Remove the vacuum advance unit from the distributor (Chapter 5, Procedure 9, Step 7).

EVERYONE: Use a phillips screwdriver to remove the two phillips head screws that attach the signal generator to the distributor plate in the distributor.

Fit the new signal generator in place in the distributor the same way the old one was, then install the two phillips screws but don't tighten them yet. Adjust the air gap (Chapter 5, Procedure 10, Step 2). Inspect the rubber sealing ring for cracks and torn spots and replace it with a new one if you find any. Install the rubber sealing ring on the distributor.

20R and 22R models: Install the vacuum advance unit on the distributor (Chapter 5, Procedure 9, Step 7).

EVERYONE: Install the rotor, dust shield (if you have one) and distributor cap. Reconnect the small wires from the distributor to the plastic connector, then snap the connector into its holder (if it has one). Be certain the coil wire and all the spark plug wires are firmly seated on the distributor cap, coil and spark plugs.

PROCEDURE 12: CHECK AND REPLACE SPARK PLUG AND COIL WIRES

Eventually the insulation in the spark plug wires wears out, the wires break, or the connections on the ends get broken. It's an easy and satisfying job to check and replace them if necessary.

Condition: Routine maintenance; OR you suspect that the spark plug and/or coil wires are worn out or broken.

Tools and Materials: To check the wires: a Volt/Ohm meter. To replace the wires: new set of wires; tape and marking pen.

Remark: If the wires need to be replaced, try to buy a set designed for Toyotas. (NGK makes nice Toyota spark plug wires.) The wires in generic "one size fits all" four cylinder replacement sets are generally much longer than necessary. When installed they look awful and are frequently in the way while working on the engine.

Step 1. Check Spark Plug Wires.

Set up your VOM to check for resistance (See Chapter 15, Procedure 2, if you need instructions). The knob should be set at RX1K. Remove the distributor cap (Chapter 5, Procedure 9, Step 2).

Disconnect the #1 spark plug wire from the #1 spark plug. Stick one of the VOM probes into the *spark plug end* of the wire so it touches the metal end. Now touch the other probe to the *metal post* inside the distributor cap that corresponds to the #1 spark plug wire. The needle on the meter should move toward the zero end of the scale. If your Toy has *resistor spark plug wires* (and most of them do these days) the needle will stop at around 4 or 5 on the scale. Multiply the number on the scale by 1000 (RX1K) to see how much resistance is in the wire and distributor cap. With resistor wires you should have about 4,000 to 5,000 ohms resistance. If the resistance is more than 25,000 ohms or the needle doesn't move (wiggle the probes around to be sure), the wire is shot. Non-resistor wires should have 0 (zero) resistance. Check all four spark plug wires and the coil wire the same way.

If any wires appear to be defective, disconnect them from the distributor cap and check them again. If the wires test OK now, the distributor cap is shot and should be replaced (Chapter 5, Procedure 9, Step 9). If there's no change in the VOM reading, the wire is dead for sure. If any spark plug wires are defective, replace all of them (see Remarks). Step 2 tells you how. Install the distributor cap (Chapter 5, Procedure 9, Step 8).

Step 2. Replace Spark Plug Wires.

Arrange the new spark plug wires according to length. Use the shortest wire to replace the wire for cylinder #1, the next shortest for cylinder #2, the next to longest for cylinder #3, and the longest for cylinder #4. Replace the wires one at a time so they don't get mixed up. Be sure the wires are securely fastened in the plastic holders (looms) on the engine. This would be a good time to use tape and an indelible marking pen to label each end of the wires with the appropriate cylinder number, if they aren't marked or labeled already. A new coil wire usually comes with spark plug wire sets, so install it if you have it. Note that the ends are different so it will only fit one way.

PROCEDURE 13: FIX HORN

The horn is an electromagnetic noise-making device. Here's how it works: A "hot" wire from the positive (+) battery post goes through the fuse box to a wire terminal on the horn. The ground wire, to complete the circuit, runs from another wire terminal on the horn up through the hollow steering rod to the horn button. Pushing on the horn button touches the end of the ground wire to bare metal completing the circuit and the horn goes BEEP. If your horn ever starts to blow without your consent and keeps blowing, the ground wire is shorting out somewhere between the horn and button. To stop the racket, remove the horn fuse so you don't have to listen to it while you're removing the grille to disconnect the two wires from the horn. Be sure to reinstall the fuse after disconnecting the wires because other electrical things are probably also on the horn circuit.

Toyota horns are about the size and shape of small pancakes. They're round (about 4 inches in diameter), thin, and have two wires attached with plastic connectors. The horn is mounted just behind the grille next to the right headlight.

Condition: Horn doesn't work.

Tools and Materials: Depending on the problem you might need some or all of the following: phillips screwdriver, small screwdriver, sandpaper or wire brush, new horn fuse, 12-volt test light or VOM, two lengths of wire, Friend, new (or used) horn.

Remarks: You can probably find a used horn in a salvage yard and save some money.

Step 1. Check Fuse, Wire Connections and Mounting Nut.

Check the fuse for the horn (Procedure 2, Step 1) and replace it if necessary. Try the horn now. Still not working? Remove the grille (Procedure 4, Step 1) and set it where it won't get stepped on.

Locate the horn and disconnect the wire connector. Use a small screwdriver to pry the sides away from the connector while pulling the two halves apart. Use sandpaper or a wire brush to clean the wire terminals. Reconnect the wires, then try the horn again. Still not working? Tap the horn with a small hammer or screwdriver handle. Sometimes the plate, which vibrates inside the horn to make the noise, gets stuck, and the tapping just might free it. Try the horn again. Still won't beep? Remove the mounting bolt which attaches the horn to the body. Use sandpaper or a wire brush to clean the mounting surface so the horn mounting bracket can make a good metal to metal contact. Install the horn and tighten the bolt. Horn still doesn't work? Have friend repeatedly push and release the horn button while you touch the horn. If the horn is getting juice, you'll feel and probably hear a click. If the horn clicks, you can skip down to Step 3 to hot-wire the horn. No click? Do Step 2.

Step 2. Check for Juice at Horn.

Use a 12-volt test light or VOM (set at 15 volts DC) to check the two wires from the wiring harness that attach to the horn (Procedure 5, Step 2). One of the wires should light up the test light or show about 12 volts on the VOM. If there's juice in one of the wires, skip down to Step 3. No juice? Check the fuse holder for the horn fuse to see if there's juice on both sides of the fuse (Procedure 2, Step 2). If there's no juice at the fuse holder, the wire between the battery (or fusible links) and fuse box is broken. If there's juice on both sides of the fuse holder when the fuse is installed but there's no juice at the horn connection, the wire between the fuse box and horn is broken. Procedure 5, Step 3 tells you how to trace wires in search of a short. If you can't locate the problem, have the Toyota dealer or a garage deal with it.

Step 3. "Hot Wire" Horn.

The is the final check to see whether the horn is broken or there's a problem in the wiring.

Strip about ½" of insulation from the ends of two pieces of wire that are long enough to reach from the battery to the plastic connector attached to the horn. Connect one end of one of the wires to bare metal on the car body or engine and stick the other end into one of the slots in the connector attached to the horn. Stick one end of the other wire into the other slot in the connector, then touch the other end of that wire to the positive battery terminal. The horn should blast. If there's no sound, try reversing the two wires in the wire connector of the horn. Still no sound? The horn is shot and must be replaced (Step 4). If hot-wiring the horn made it toot, the horn is OK but the wiring from the horn to the button on the steering wheel or the horn button itself is defective. Go through Steps 1 and 2 again, or take the car to Toyota or a garage.

Step 4. Replace Horn.

Remove the phillips screws around the edge of the grille, then use a small screwdriver in the slots of the plastic clips to release them. Lift the grille off. Set it where it won't get stepped on.

The horn is attached to a flat metal strap that is bolted to the car body. Disconnect the wires from the wire connector near the horn, then use a 12mm wrench to remove the bolt from the flat metal strap. The horn is now liberated.

Position the new (or used) horn the same as the old one, then install and tighten the mounting bolt. Attach the wire for the horn. Push the horn button to be sure it's working. BEEP! BEEP!

PROCEDURE 14: REPLACE SWITCHES

This procedure is about replacing the ignition switch, headlight switch, turn signal switch, windshield wiper switch, horn switch and heater switch. To replace some of these switches the steering wheel must be removed.

Condition: One or more of the switches isn't working.

Tools and Materials: Small and medium phillips and regular screwdrivers. Maybe a tiny screwdriver, hammer, 19mm socket and ratchet, needlenose pliers, 10mm wrench, flat-nose expanders.

To remove the steering wheel you'll need a small bar-type puller and two 8x1.25 bolts about three inches long. 8mm is the bolt size (not the bolt head size) and 1.25 is the pitch of the threads. Be sure you're using the correct size bolts. You'll also need a crescent wrench or whatever size wrench it takes to operate the puller.

You'll need several baggies or a cupcake pan, masking tape and an indelible pen to bag and mark the various sets of screws as they are removed. This will make reassembly much easier. No baggies or pan? At least try to keep the screws separated into groups to avoid reassembly insanity.

To remove the switches located on the dashboard on '75-'78 models you might need a special Toyota tool #09810-25010. Try using the small screwdriver and hammer method described in the step before running out to buy the special tool. It usually works for me.

Step 1 covers replacing switches located on the dashboard. Steps 2 - 10 cover replacing switches mounted on the steering column, next to the steering wheel.

Remark: Before replacing switches, or any electrical component, first disconnect the negative battery terminal cable (Procedure 1, Step 3).

Step 1. Remove and Install Headlight, Windshield Wiper, Heater, Emergency Flasher Switches on '75 - '78 Models.

Disconnect the negative battery terminal cable.

Remove switch: Peek under the dashboard and locate the wire or wires that are attached to the switch you are replacing. Follow the wires to a plastic connector and separate the two connector halves.

Look around the sides of the switch knob for a tiny screw. Use a tiny screwdriver to remove the tiny screw. Remove the knob from the switch by unscrewing it *counterclockwise*.

Now you'll see a washer with a groove on opposite sides of the shaft where the knob was attached. Use a small screwdriver and hammer to tap, not pound, in the outer edge of one of the grooves so the washer is forced to turn *counterclockwise*. Try both grooves. Once the washer starts turning, keep tapping until you can remove the washer with your fingers. While tapping be careful not to bung up the threads on the switch or the removal will be more difficult. Once the slotted washer is off, you can pull the switch out of the dashboard.

If the screwdriver/hammer method didn't work, you can use a piece of tubing approximately the size of the slotted washer. Just file the end of the tube so two small tabs are left on opposite sides. Fit the tubing over the shaft so the tabs are in the grooves, then use pliers or Vise Grips to turn the tube *counterclockwise*. If neither of these methods works you'll have to buy the special tool from Toyota.

Install switch: Slip the switch into the hole from behind the dashboard. It will only fit one way. Hold the switch with one hand while you install the slotted washer with the other. Use whatever method you used to remove the slotted washer to tighten it. It doesn't have to be real tight, just good and snug.

Connect the wire(s) from the switch to the wiring connector under the dash. Screw the knob onto the switch shaft, then install and tighten the tiny screw in the side of the knob.

Reconnect the negative battery terminal, then check the switch to be sure whatever it controls is working now.

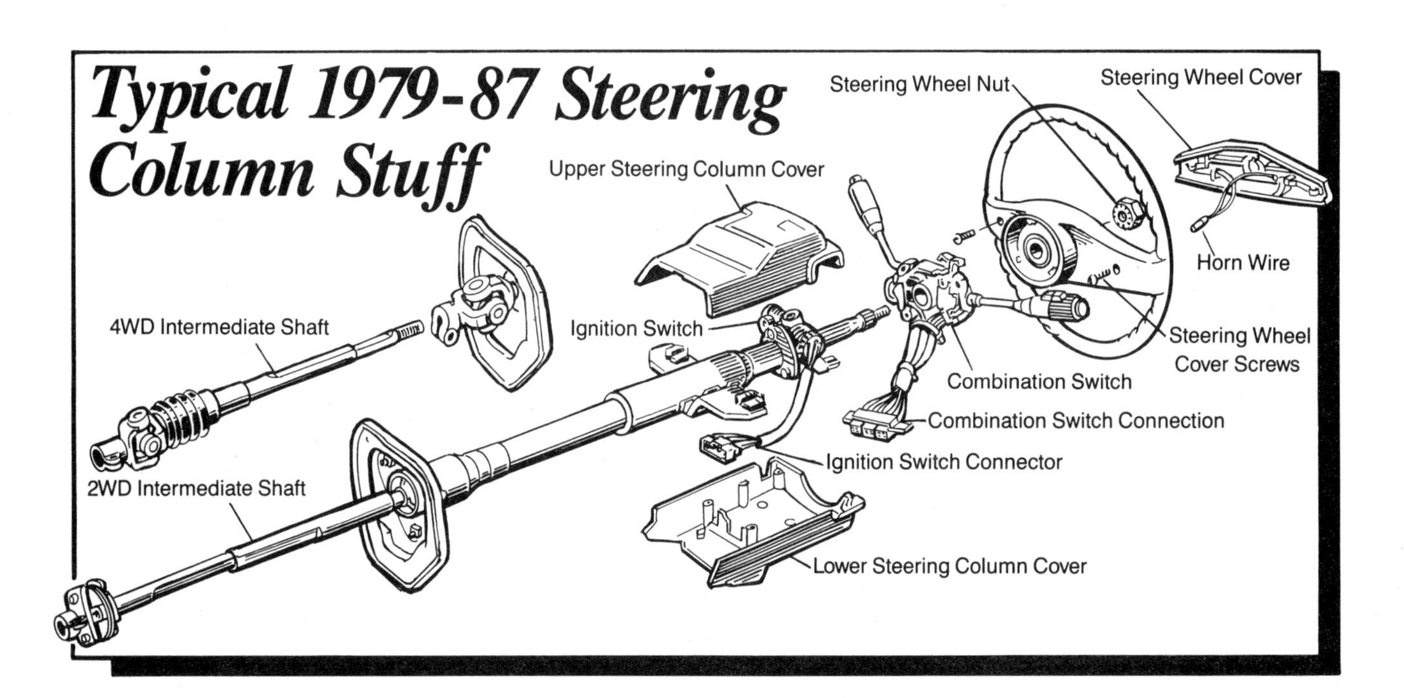

Step 2. Remove and Install Steering Column Covers.

To get to the various switches mounted on the steering column you must first remove the steering column covers. Except for replacing the ignition switch, you must also remove the steering wheel (Step 4).

Remove steering column covers: The steering column covers consist of two pieces of molded plastic secured with phillips screws through holes on the bottom. To remove the covers use a long medium-size phillips screwdriver to unscrew the screws (*counterclockwise* as viewed from the bottom). The screws on the right and left sides attach the two halves together while the screws near the center attach the cover to the steering column. Some models have two screws near the bottom center which attach the wiring connector to the lower half of the cover. Remove the screws and stash them where they won't get lost.

Remove the key if it's in the ignition switch, then wiggle the upper and lower covers off the steering column. Now you can replace the ignition switch if that's your problem (Step 3). If you're here to replace any of the other switches you'll also need to remove the steering wheel (Step 4).

Install steering column covers: Remove the ignition key if it's in the switch. Install the upper and lower steering column covers. The smaller screws go nearer to the center of the bottom cover and attach the cover itself to the ignition switch bracket, and on some models they attach the wiring connector to the cover. The larger sheet metal screws attach the two halves of the cover together. Install and tighten the screws.

Step 3. Remove and Install Ignition Switch.

There are two parts to the ignition switch: a mechanical part operated by the ignition key, and an electrical part operated by the mechanical part. The two parts can be replaced separately. If you are just having trouble turning the key in the switch or if the key is broken off, you probably only need to replace the mechanical part. If the ignition key is working smoothly but the car won't start (and you've checked the battery and cranking system already) then the electrical part has pooped out. Either part is easy to replace. Here's how:

To replace the *mechanical* part, insert the key in the switch and turn it to the accessory (ACC) position. Insert the tip of a ball point pen into the hole on the side of the switch, right next to the LOCK position. Push the pen into the hole while trying to pull the key out of the switch. The mechanical part will slide right out of the bracket.

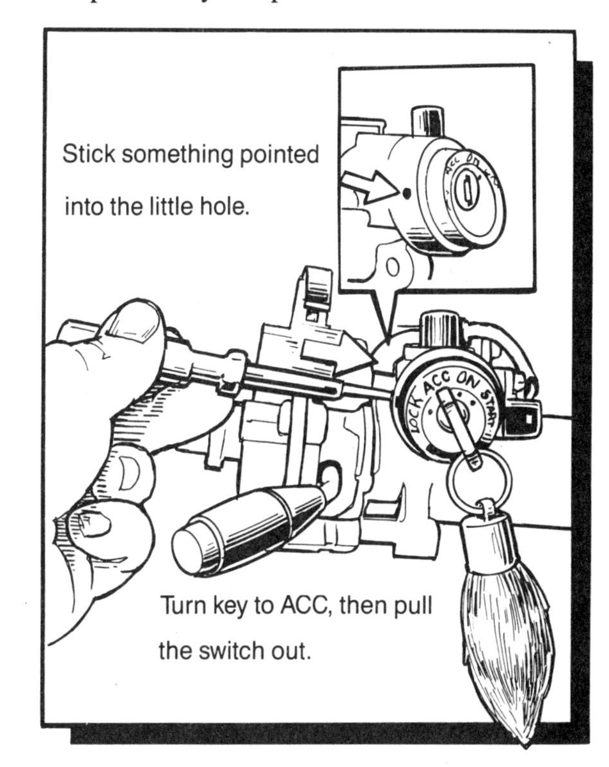

To install the *mechanical* part, align the small pin on the side of the switch with the small hole in the bracket. Be sure the key is inserted in the switch and turned to the ACC position. Push the switch in until the pin locks it in place. Install the steering column covers (Step 2).

To remove the *electrical* part of the switch, follow the wires from the left side of the switch to a plastic connector under the dash. Disconnect the connector.

Now find a small phillips screw on the left end of the switch. Remove the screw, then pull the switch out of the bracket. On '82-'87 models there is also a key lock warning switch mounted to the bracket on the dashboard side of the mechanical part of the switch. Use a short phillips screwdriver to remove the two screws securing the switch and the screw on the wire clamp, then remove the key warning switch.

To install the *electrical* part of the switch, align the slot in the end of the switch with the tab located in the bracket. Use a small screwdriver to turn the slot or the key in the ignition to turn the tab. Fit the switch into the housing. Don't force it if it won't go in all the way. Just gently press the switch into the bracket while turning the ignition key until the switch is in all the way. Install and tighten the screw that attaches the switch to the bracket. If you had a key lock warning switch, install it on the bracket and tighten the screws. Install and tighten the screw with the wire clamp. Reconnect the wires to the harness under the dash. Install the steering column covers (Step 2).

Using a Puller To Remove The Steering Wheel

Step 4. Remove and Install Steering Wheel.

Caution! Don't do this step while cruising down the road.

Remove steering wheel: Remove the phillips screws on the dashboard side of the steering wheel. Lift the center cover off the wheel, being careful not to pull the horn wire off its connection. Lay the cover on top of the steering column. Hold the steering wheel with one hand while you use a 19mm socket and ratchet to remove the nut in the center of the wheel (*counterclockwise*).

Use a punch and hammer or an indelible marker to make a mark on the steering shaft and one right next to it on the steering wheel. This will insure that the steering wheel is straight when you reinstall it.

Now set up a puller (look at the illustration). You'll need two 8x1.25 bolts to screw into the threaded holes in the steering wheel. Be sure the bolts go into the threads several turns. Tighten the center bolt on the puller and the wheel will suddenly pop loose. Hold the steering wheel cover with one hand while you pull the wheel off the shaft. Lay them aside.

Install steering wheel: Fit the steering wheel onto the steering shaft so the match marks you made during disassembly are aligned. Check it carefully because being off just one spline will make the steering wheel seem crooked even while driving in a straight line. Install the 19mm nut and tighten it. Fit the steering wheel cover in place, making sure the horn wires are neatly tucked inside. Install and tighten the two screws from the dashboard side of the steering wheel.

Step 5. Remove and Install Combination Switch.

You've removed the steering column covers and steering wheel, right? Now you are face to face with the combination switch. You must remove the combination switch from the steering column in order to replace the individual switches which are attached to it.

Remove combination switch: The wires from the various switches are attached to one or more plastic connectors near the bottom of the dash. Follow the bundle of wires from the switches to the connectors, and push on the tabs on the sides of the connectors while you separate the connector halves. Each connector is a different size and shape so it's impossible to screw up when reconnecting them.

Remove the screws that attach the combination switch to the aluminum bracket on the steering column. On '75-'78 models there are three screws (two at the bottom, one at the top center). '79-'87 models have four screws located at the four corners of the combination switch. Pull the entire unit off the steering shaft.

'75-'78 models: If you are here to replace the turn signal/dimmer switch, skip down to the Install combination switch section. If you're here to remove the ignition switch bracket, skip down to Step 11.

'79-'87 models: Turn the combination switch over so you are looking at the front (dashboard) side. The wiper/washer switch is now on the left side and the headlight/turn signal/dimmer switch is on the right.

To replace any of the switches, first you must disconnect the wires for the old switch from the plastic connector and plug in the wires for the new switch. A metal pin with little tabs locks the end of each wire into the plastic connector. The wires are color coded and the wires from the new switch must go in exactly the same place as the same colored wire from the old switch. To avoid confusion, remove one wire at a time from the connector

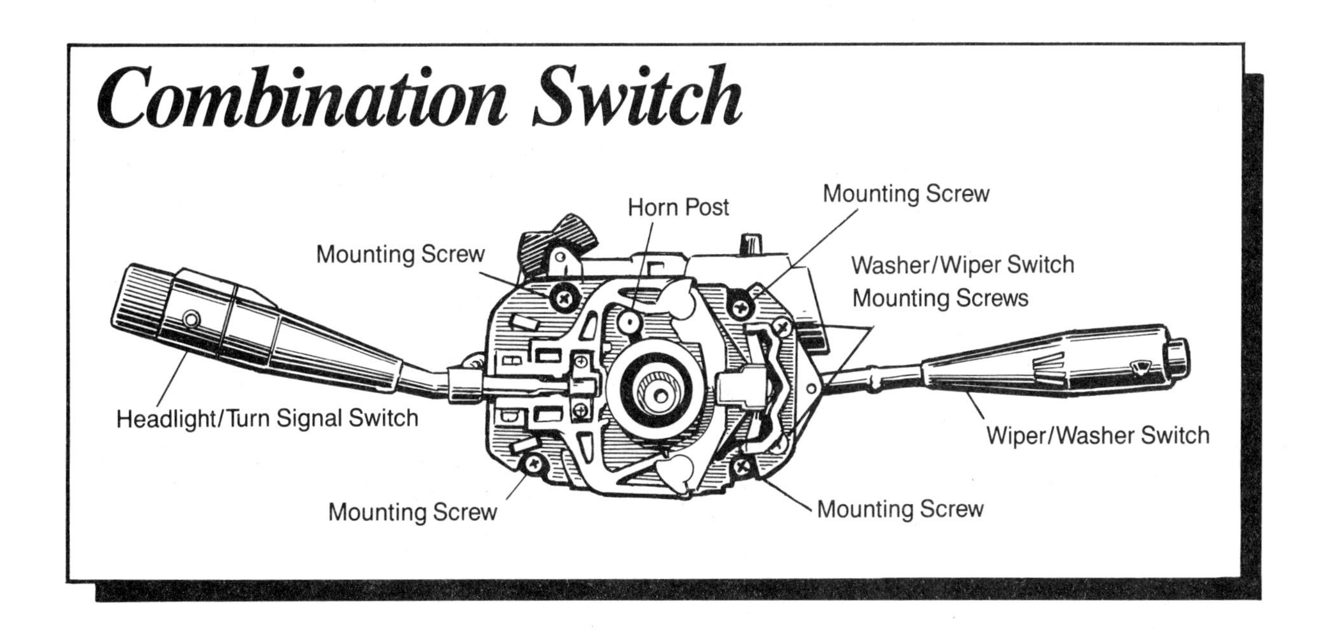

and insert the same color wire for the new switch. Look into the end of the plastic connector and I'll tell you how to release the pins:

'79-'81 models: You'll see two tiny tabs, one on each side of each pin. To release the pin use something pointed (like an ice pick, heavy paper clip, whatever) to press the tabs toward the pin while you pull the wire out of the connector. Push the pin on the new wire into the connector until the two tabs lock the pin in place.

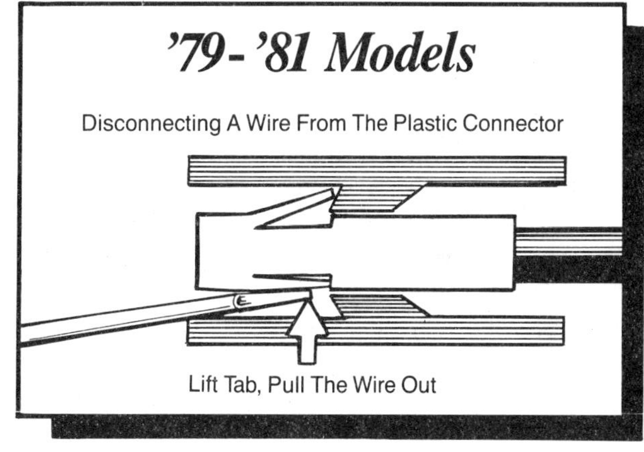

'82-'87 models: You'll see two little plastic tabs between the pins. Use something like an ice pick or a very tiny screwdriver to pry the tab away from the pin you want to remove while pulling the wire out of the connector. Push the pin with the same color wire for the new switch into the hole until it locks into place.

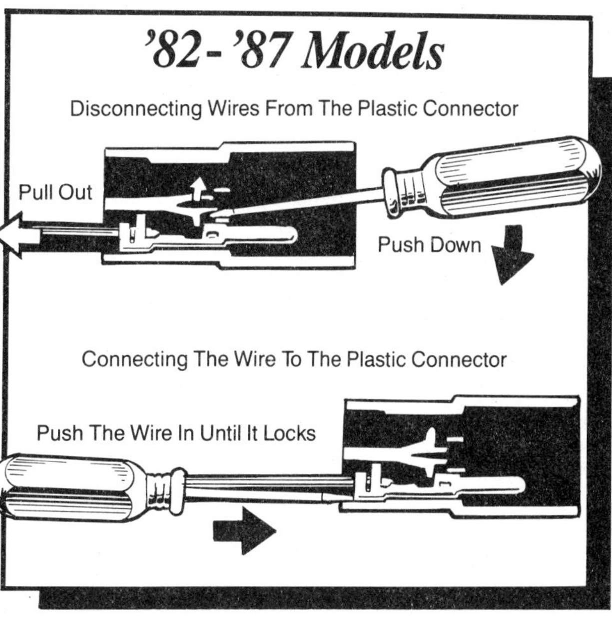

EVERYONE: OK, now find the step below that covers the switch you're replacing. After the switch is replaced come back here to install the combination switch.

Install combination switch: Fit the combination switch onto the steering shaft and align the mounting holes with the holes in the ignition switch bracket. Install the three or four screws and tighten them.

If you removed the ignition switch, install it now.

Reconnect the plastic wire connectors that you disconnected. Be sure they are locked together. See Step 2 to install the steering column covers and Step 4 to install the steering wheel.

Step 6. Replace Windshield Wiper/Washer Switch.

Remove the two screws from the steering wheel side of the wiper/washer switch. Fit the new switch in place, then install and tighten the screws. Switch the wires in the plastic connector if you haven't already. See Step 12 to put everything back together.

Step 7. Replace Turn Signal Switch.

If the turn signal lever is loose and/or doesn't lock into place, skip down to Step 10. If the lever seems to be working OK, the switch is probably the problem.

The turn signal switch is on the outer edge of the combination switch and has about six wires soldered to it. To remove it, remove the two screws from the dashboard side of the switch. The lower screw probably has a plastic wire clamp on it. Pull the turn signal switch off the combination switch.

The new switch has a tab on one side that fits into a groove in the combination switch. Position the turn signal lever in the center position, move the tab on the switch to the center of its groove, then fit the new switch into place. If your emergency/hazard switch button is mounted on top of the steering column cover, be sure the lever sticking out of the top of the turn signal switch is engaged in the button. Install the two mounting screws for the turn signal switch and tighten them, making sure the wires are neatly tucked under the plastic wire clamp. Replace the wires in the plastic connector if you haven't done so already. See Step 12 to finish the job.

Step 8. Replace Headlight Dimmer/Flasher Switch.

The dimmer/flasher switch is next to the turn signal switch. It probably has a clear plastic cover. First remove the turn signal switch from the combination switch (Step 7) but don't disconnect the wires. Next remove the three screws that secure the dimmer/flasher switch to the combination switch body.

Fit the new switch into position so the spring and plunger sticking out of the switch fits into the hole in the combination switch body. Install and tighten the three screws, install the turn signal switch (Step 7), then install the wires in the plastic connector, if you haven't done so already. See Step 12 to finish the job.

Step 9. Replace Horn Switch Post.

The horn switch post sticks out of the steering wheel side of the combination switch. It's a small, round brass post that rubs against a round plate mounted on the front side of the steering wheel. If the post is worn away so it doesn't rub against the plate, it must be replaced.

To replace the post, use needlenose pliers to remove the wire terminal from the dashboard end of the post. Push on the post from the steering wheel side while you use a small screwdriver to remove the E-ring clamp and spring from the dashboard side of the post. Once the clamp is off, you can push the post out of the combination switch.

To install a new post, push the thinner end into the hole from the steering wheel side. Fit the spring onto the post, then push on the steering wheel side of the post while you install the E-ring clamp into its groove. Once the clamp is on, push the wire terminal onto the end of the post. See Step 12 to finish the job.

Step 10. Replace Headlight Switch/Turn Signal Lever.

The lever is attached to the combination switch with a small pivot screw through the lever itself. A small metal clamp is attached across the inner end of the lever with two small screws. To remove the lever, remove the two screws which secure the clamp, but don't remove the clamp yet. Remove the pivot screw that goes through the lever. Now lift the lever and clamp off the combination switch and slide the pivot screw back into its hole in the lever. A tiny metal ball is between the clamp and the end of the lever which you don't want to lose. Look for it as you lift the clamp away from the lever. Stash the ball with the screws. There's a tiny spring inside the lever, which you'll probably have to remove with a small pointed object like a needle, toothpick or the tip of a ball point pen.

If you're here because the turn signal lever was loose and floppy, examine the small ball and spring. If the ball is missing and/or the spring is broken, or the pivot bolt is broken, get new ones from Toyota and skip down to the next paragraph. If the headlight switch is broken, get a new switch/lever assembly from Toyota and go on to the next paragraph.

To put the headlight switch/turn signal lever back together, fit the lever into the slot on the combination switch so the writing on the lever is on the steering wheel side of the combination switch. Install the pivot screw through the lever and snug the screw down. It doesn't have to be real tight. Now tilt the lever so you can fit the spring into the inner end. Install the spring, then put the ball on the end of the lever (use a dab of grease to hold it in place). Next pivot the lever to its normal position. Fit the clamp over the end of the lever and wiggle it down into its slot in the combination switch. Install and tighten the two screws for the clamp. Replace the wires for the headlight switch in the plastic connector, if you're replacing the headlight switch. Check that the lever works properly in the left and right turn signal positions. See Step 12 to finish up.

Step 11. Remove and Install Ignition Switch Bracket and Steering Shaft Bearing.

Remove the steering wheel and combination switch if you haven't done so already.

Remove the three screws that attach a triangular bearing retainer to the steering wheel side of the aluminum ignition switch bracket. Pull out on the steering shaft while you use flat-nose expanders to remove the lock ring from the steering shaft. Then remove the three 10mm bolts from the rear of the bracket. Wiggle the bracket off the steering shaft.

If you're here to replace the bearing in the bracket, use a screwdriver and hammer to tap the old bearing out of the housing from the dashboard side. Set a new bearing on the bracket and gently tap around the outer edge of the bearing with a small hammer. Don't hit the inner part of the bearing. Tap lightly until you're sure the bearing is going in straight. Keep tapping around the outer edge until the bearing is flush with the housing. Check that the bearing turns freely.

If you're here because the steering lock mechanism doesn't work, or perhaps works too well and won't release no matter which position the key is in, you'll have to get a new bracket from Toyota. If the new bracket doesn't have a bearing installed, remove the bearing from the old bracket and install it in the new one (see above).

To install the bracket, slide it onto the steering shaft. Wiggle the steering shaft around to center the ignition bracket so it can slide into the steering column. It should end up touching the mounting bracket on the steering column. Align the bolt holes in the two brackets, then install and tighten the three 10mm bolts. Use the expander pliers to slide the lock ring onto the steering shaft. You'll have to pull the steering shaft out from the

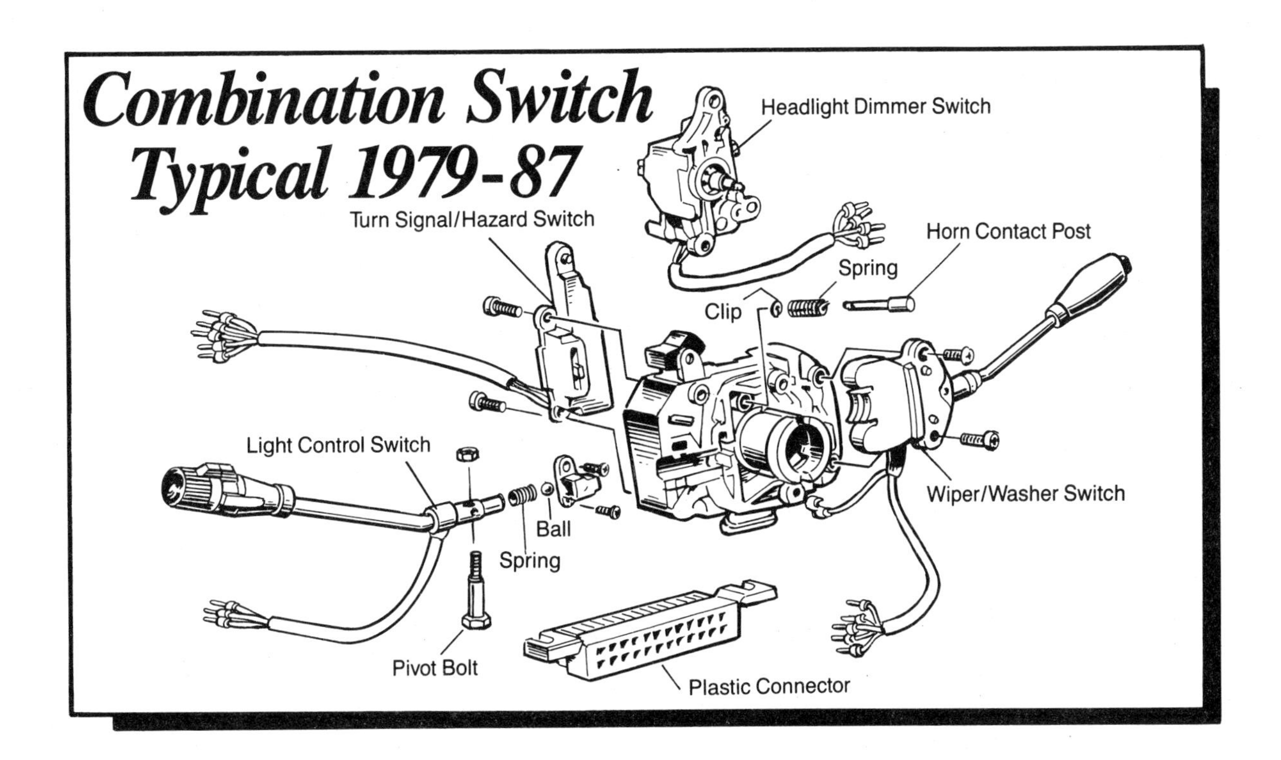

bracket far enough for the lock ring to fit into its groove on the shaft. A Friend to pull on the shaft while you deal with the lock ring would be handy. Once the lock ring is seated in the shaft, install the triangular bearing retainer and tighten the three screws.

Step 12. Finish Up.

Now install the ignition switch (Step 3), the combination switch (Step 5), the steering wheel (Step 4) and the steering column covers (Step 2).

CHAPTER 9
FUEL SYSTEMS

CAUTION! FIRE WARNING: Don't light any matches, rub two Boy Scouts together, think about former lovers or do anything that could create a spark while working on the fuel system.

A spark could turn your truck into a large black ugly mess so when I tell you to disconnect the battery, please do so. This will eliminate sparks made by accidentally touching live wires to metal. Please read Chapter 2 and keep a fire extinguisher handy.

If your water heater is in the garage like mine, turn the pilot light off until you're finished working on the gas tank. The pilot light could ignite the fumes—just don't forget to relight the pilot when the fumes have cleared or your next shower will be quite shocking.

THE FUEL SYSTEM

The gasoline in the **tank** is pumped to the engine through metal and rubber **fuel lines** by either an **electric** or **mechanical fuel pump**. On its way to the engine, the gas passes through a **fuel filter** to remove rust, bugs and other debris that could clog the system.

The liquid gasoline pumped to the engine is flammable and will burn easily and quickly, but just being flammable won't make the engine run. The stored energy in the gasoline must be mixed with the air drawn in through the **air cleaner** in a precise ratio to create an **EXPLOSIVE** mixture. On models with 20R or 22R engines, the **carburetor** accomplishes this feat. Models with 22R-E and 22R-TE engines have an **electronic fuel injection** system (EFI) that mixes the fuel and air.

Your carburetor (carb for short) or fuel injection system is very delicate and sensitive, yet it can work well for many years, forever maybe, if proper maintenance procedures are followed. Besides things like a five-pound sledge hammer, dirt and rust are their two main enemies. Dirty air and/or fuel can clog the tiny passages inside the carburetor or injection system and cause the fuel/air ratio to get out of whack so the truck won't run well, or won't run at all. By inspecting the air and fuel filters frequently, and replacing them when they become contaminated, you can extend the life of your fuel system indefinitely.

ORIENTATION: WHICH SETUP DO YOU HAVE?

All '75-'87 Toyota trucks with 20R or 22R engines have carburetors. A large round black air cleaner sits directly on top of the carb. '84-'87 trucks with 22R-E engines have fuel injection, and models with 22R-TE engines have fuel injection plus a turbocharger. Look at the sticker on the top front of the engine or the sticker on the underside of the hood to see which engine you have.

CARBURETORS

There are two vertical holes, called **barrels**, going through the carburetor, one right beside the other. Since there are two barrels, you have what's called a *two-barrel carb*. The slightly smaller barrel closest to the right side of the truck is the *primary system* (sometimes called the first stage). It operates when you start the engine and while you're driving under light to moderate conditions. When you push the gas pedal more than halfway to the floor (or "put the pedal to the metal") the other, larger, barrel, called the *secondary system* (second stage) of the carb comes into action. This allows you to drive economically on the smaller primary system until you need the power to pass a car, drive up a steep hill, race a Porsche, etc., when more power (fuel and air) is needed.

CARBURETOR PROBLEMS

If your truck starts misbehaving suddenly, or dies and won't start no matter how much you beg and plead with it (or cuss at it), follow the troubleshooting chart in Chapter 4. You will be referred back here at the appropriate time.

The fuel system is easy to check, so before tearing into the carburetor because the engine doesn't run right, go through Procedures 1, 2, 4-7, 9 and 10, to do some simple tests to locate the problem. Do a carburetor rebuild or replace the carburetor only as a last resort.

Procedure 10 tells you how to do a "quicky" carb clean. If you're broken down in the boonies and determine the carburetor is the problem, Procedure 10 also tells you how to tap on the top of the carb to free a sticking **needle valve and seat** (the most likely cause of your problem).

If you're looking for more power, see Chapter 14, *Modifying Your Toyota*.

If you determine that the carburetor is faulty, the carburetor can be removed and rebuilt or replaced with a new or factory rebuilt unit. Procedure 11 tells you how to remove and install the carb.

Rebuilding your carb will require relaxed determination and attention to detail. It'll take at least a full day counting mental health breaks. Don't try to rebuild the thing the night before a Monte Carlo rally; wait until you have peace and quiet. . .and time. The work is really more like fine watch repair than car repair, and you'll need an uncluttered, clean place in which to work.

How to rebuild your carburetor is not included in this manual because Toyota carbs tend to be very durable and cause few problems. Most carb problems can be remedied by checking the connections for the electrical devices attached to the carb or by doing what I call a quicky carb clean (Procedure 10). If you determine that your carb needs to be rebuilt, buy a carb rebuild kit and follow the instructions in the kit. Procedure 11 tells you how to remove and install the carb.

FUEL INJECTION SYSTEM

I'll describe how the fuel injection system works even though how to repair it isn't covered in this manual.

The fuel injection system is controlled by several sensors on the engine and exhaust system. The sensors transmit electrical signals to a microcomputer called the Electronic Controlled Unit (ECU) which analyzes the signals relative to engine speed, temperature, throttle position, etc., then sends signals to the injectors to tell them how much fuel to squirt into the cylinders.

Fuel Injection Problems

Most problems with the fuel injection system can be traced to faulty fuses or fusible links, or to air leaks on the engine. Fuses related to the EFI system are listed in Procedure 6, Step 1.

The air flow meter located on top of the air cleaner housing measures the volume and temperature of air being drawn into the engine through the air cleaner and sends the information to the ECU. The ECU in turn tells the injectors how much fuel to squirt into the cylinders. If air enters the system anywhere other than the air cleaner, the delicate fuel to air ratio will be upset and the engine will run poorly.

Some common places where unmeasured air can enter the system are the oil filler cap, the engine oil dipstick, PCV valve hoses, a loose valve cover or broken valve cover gasket, or a loose or broken air intake hose between the air cleaner and engine. You can check the condition and tightness of these components and most likely solve the problem.

I have included a section on the self-diagnosing capabilities of '84-'87 models in Chapter 4, so if the "Check Engine" light on the dash comes on and you're curious about what's going on you can decipher the code. If you suspect something is wrong with the turbo or fuel injection system, take the truck to the Toyota dealer or a garage that specializes in Toyotas.

TURBOCHARGER

The turbocharger unit (turbo) is driven by the engine's exhaust gas. Basically what a turbocharger does is force the fuel and air mixture into the cylinders (" pack" it), rather than relying on atmospheric pressure and vacuum created by the pistons to fill the cylinders.

Here's how the turbo works. On its way to the exhaust pipe, the exhaust gas passes through a **turbine housing** causing a windmill-like **turbine wheel** to spin. The turbine wheel is attached via a shaft to an **impeller** wheel located in a separate **compressor housing**. The impeller wheel sucks air through the air cleaner and forces it through the **throttle body** and into the cylinders. As engine speed increases, more exhaust gas is created so the turbine automatically turns faster to meet the engine's demands. The turbine wheel/compressor impeller speed varies between approximately 20,000 and 130,000 revolutions per minute! Servicing the turbo unit should be left to the professionals because a misadjusted turbo can quickly ruin the engine.

PROCEDURE 1: CHECK AND REPLACE AIR FILTER

Condition: Regular maintenance; OR you just went through a Texas-type dust storm; OR your engine seems sluggish and the gas mileage has taken a nosedive.

Tools and Materials: 10mm and 12mm wrenches, phillips screwdriver, maybe a new air filter element.

Step 1. Do It.

Turn to Chapter 5, Procedure 4, Step 3, to check and/or replace the air filter element.

PROCEDURE 2: CHECK AND REPLACE FUEL FILTER

The Toyota manuals don't mention any maintenance for the fuel filters on 22R-E and 22R-TE models. I have included instructions for changing the filter, but since the job is extremely difficult and slightly dangerous (the fuel system is under high pressure), I recommend that you have the Toyota dealer mess with the fuel filter when you take your EFI truck in for emission control checkups every 30,000 miles or so.

Condition: Regular 12,000 mile maintenance; OR fuel isn't getting to the carburetor; OR the fuel in the gas tank is contaminated.

Tools and Materials: Depending on the clamps, you will need either a regular or phillips screwdriver, pliers, a rag or two and maybe a new fuel filter. And safety glasses.

'82-'87 22R models: You might need a jack and jackstand.

22R-E and 22R-TE models: You will also need four new gaskets for the banjo fittings on the fuel pump, a 12mm socket, ratchet and ratchet extension, 17mm and 19mm open end wrenches, a can to catch gasoline in, plastic baggies and a new fuel filter.

Remark: On 20R and 22R models, if you are here from the 12,000 mile maintenance procedure, don't bother checking the filter. Replace it.

CAUTION: The smoking lamp is OUT. Keep smokers busy making sandwiches or something while you replace the fuel filter.

Always remove the gas tank filler cap to relieve pressure or vacuum in the tank before disconnecting any hoses from the fuel filter.

Step 1. Locate and Check Fuel Filter.

Look at the fuel filter illustrations so you'll know what you are looking for. Be sure the ignition key is OFF.

'75-'81 models: The fuel filter can be found in the engine compartment mounted on the right fender.

'82-'87 22R models: The fuel filter is located beneath the truck in front of the right rear wheel.

20R and 22R models: To check the fuel filter, look through the plastic for signs of dirt and crud, especially on the bottom. Little blobs in the bottom mean there is water in the gas. If necessary, pull the filter out of its clip-type holder so you can see into it. If you see any dark residue, blobs or little chunks of stuff in the filter, replace it (Step 2). If the filter is clean, snap it back into the holder.

If someone has installed a metal fuel filter, you can't check it—just replace it every 12,000 miles, or sooner if you suspect it's dirty. You can replace the metal filters with plastic filters.

22R-E and 22R-TE models: The fuel filter is beneath the intake manifold. It's made of metal so you can't check it the way you check plastic filters—just replace it every 30,000 miles or so.

Step 2. Replace Fuel Filter.

First, remove the gas tank filler cap to relieve any pressure or vacuum in the tank. The pressure or vacuum can cause fuel to gush out of the fuel lines when you disconnect them.

20R and 22R models: Before removing the old filter, make a mental note or draw a picture of which hose connects to the *outlet* end of the filter. You'll see an *arrow* pointing to the outlet tube. The hoses must connect to the same places on the new filter. Have some rags handy to mop up any spilled gas. After replacing the filter, start the engine and check for gas leaks. Tighten or replace the clamps or hoses if they're cracked, leaky or broken.

'75-'81 models: The fuel filter is in the engine compartment near the right fender. Depending on your type of hose clamps, loosen them with a regular or phillips screwdriver or pliers. Just do the two clamps right next to the filter. On the wire type where you need pliers, just squeeze on the two tabs and slide 'em back with the pliers. Slide the clamps away from the filter a few inches. Hold the filter while you twist one of the hoses off its connection. Fit the hose onto the new filter. Remove the other hose from the old filter and install it on the new one. Be sure the arrow is pointing toward the hose that runs to the fuel pump or carburetor, then slide the clamps to the end of the hoses where they used to be, and tighten them if they're the screw type. Tighten them snug but not so tight you risk breaking the clamps. Push the filter into the holder clips. Start the engine and check for leaks.

'82-'87 22R models: The fuel filter is under the truck, so put the gearshift in FIRST (manual) or PARK (automatic), set the handbrake and put chocks in front of and behind the front wheels.

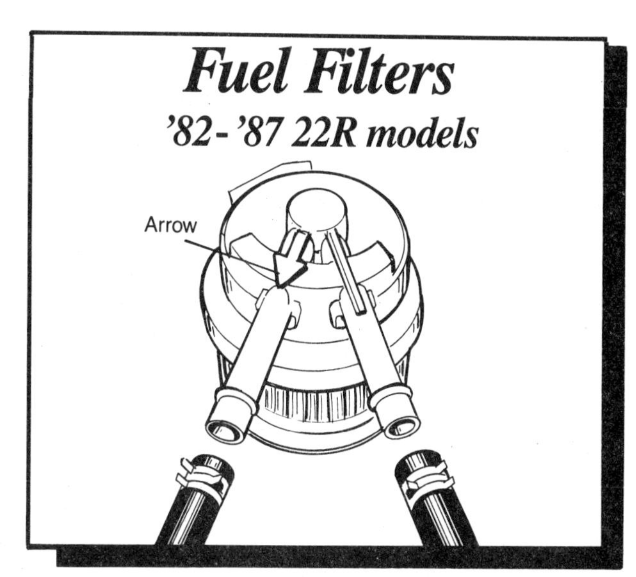

The first time you replace the filter you might want to jack up the rear end of the truck and put it on jackstands. After you've changed the filter and are familiar with the process you probably won't need to put the truck on jackstands. Don't forget to remove the gas cap.

Tie strips of rags around your wrists so gasoline can't run down your arm when you remove the fuel filter. You'll be sorry if you don't. Put your safety glasses on, grab the new filter and several rags, then lie down just in front of the right rear wheel. The filter is mounted in a clamp that's bolted to the frame. Wiggle the filter out of its holder and look at the top. Note which hose is attached to the fitting marked with an arrow.

Locate your body so your face isn't under the fuel filter. Gasoline in the eyes, ears or mouth is a major league bummer, so work at arm's length. Loosen the two hose clamps at the filter and slide them away from the filter a couple of inches. Twist one of the hoses off the old filter and fit it onto the same fitting on the new filter. Now remove the other hose from the old filter and install it on the new filter. Slide the clamps into position and tighten them if they have screws.

Wipe up any gas that spilled, slide out from under the truck, then lower it to the ground if you jacked it up. Start the engine and check for leaks around the filter and where you clamped the hose.

22R-E and 22R-TE models: Be sure the ignition switch is OFF. Remove the key from the ignition so no one can turn the switch on while the fuel pump is disconnected.

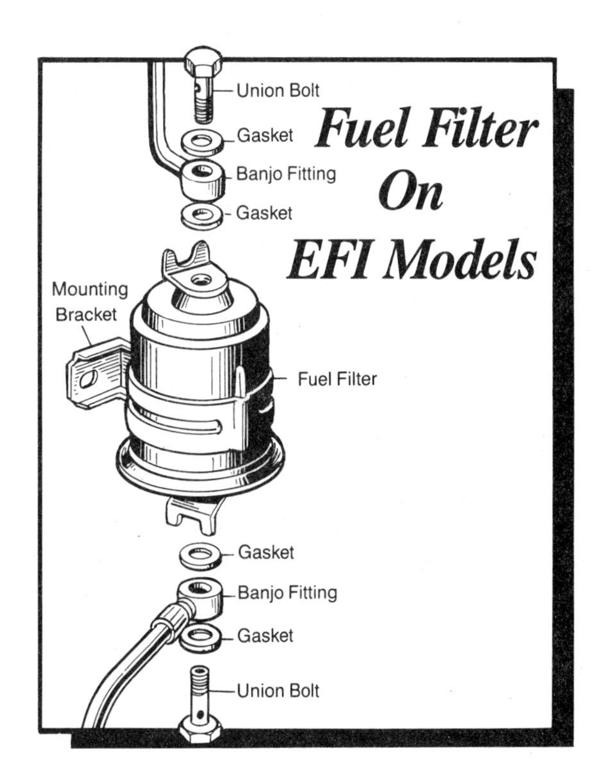

Fuel filters for EFI models are expensive but very important to the long life of the fuel injection system. If you neglect the filter, you'll pay for it later in injectors.

Since the fuel system is under high pressure on EFI models, you must release the pressure before removing the fuel filter hoses. If the hoses are getting funky, replace them with new ones while you're changing the filter. Be sure to get *high pressure* fuel line hoses.

Before removing the fuel filter, put on your safety glasses. The fuel pump, shaped like a short tube of sausage, is bolted to the right rear side of the engine, just beneath the intake manifold where it's very difficult to see. You have to stick your arms down through the engine compartment and remove the filter by feel.

Place the can, pan, pot or whatever you can get below the filter to catch the fuel that will come out of the fuel lines. Use a 17mm box end wrench to slowly loosen the **union bolt** on one end of the filter. Just loosen it until you hear the hiss of the pressure being relieved. When the hiss stops, remove the union bolts on each end of the filter. Pull the union bolt out of the round **banjo fittings** that's on the end of the fuel line. Fit plastic baggies over the ends of the fuel lines to keep dirt out. Remove the two or three 12 mmm bolts that attach the filter to the engine.

To install the filter, lightly oil the gaskets for the banjo fitting. If you don't have an oil gun handy, use some oil off the dipstick. Hold a new gasket on each side of one of the banjo fittings while you insert the union bolt. Fit the banjo fitting onto the end of the filter so the metal tube fits into the notch on the small bracket. Screw the union bolt into the banjo fitting on the other hose and tighten it with your fingers. Use new gaskets. Fit the filter onto the engine, then install the mounting bolts. The correct torque for the mounting bolts and union bolts is 22 ft.lbs., but since you can't get a torque wrench in there you'll have to guess. Get the bolts good and snug, but don't crank on them as hard as you can or the bolts will break.

Start the engine and check for fuel leaks around the filter.

PROCEDURE 3: CHECK AND REPLACE ACCELERATOR LINKAGE

The accelerator linkage is the vital connection between your right foot and the engine. On '75-'78 models the cable is actually a series of metal **linkage rods** connected with ball and socket type fasteners. Step 2 tells you how to disconnect and replace the various parts.

On 1979-87 models, the accelerator cable consists of a woven *wire cable* inside a thicker black *cable housing*—the whole works is usually just called the accelerator cable. The woven cable rarely wears out, but the plastic cable housing sometimes get broken where it attaches to the firewall during valve cover removal. Steps 2 through 7 tell how to replace the cable and housing.

Condition: Engine will start and idle, but won't speed up normally when you step on the gas pedal.

Tools and Materials: Friend, maybe a new accelerator rod or cable, grease, 10mm open end wrench, 10mm and 12mm socket, ratchet, ratchet extension, medium phillips screwdriver, regular pliers, and a flashlight.

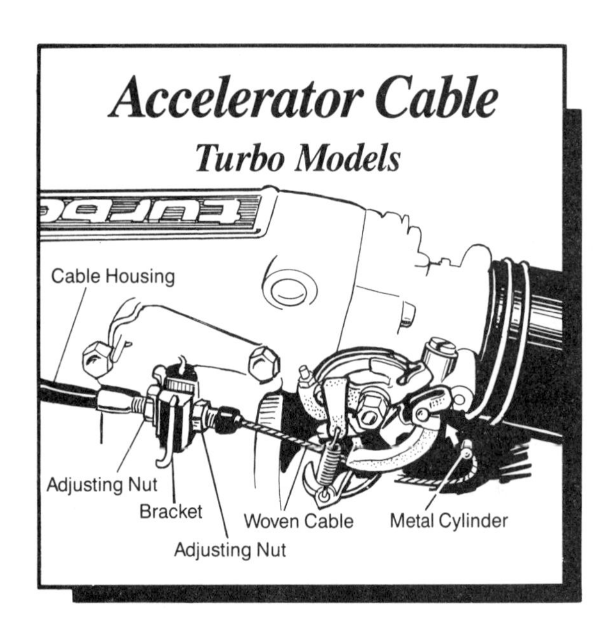

Remark: Before buying a new cable, check the old one to see if it's broken or if one end has just come loose. Or maybe the cable housing is just loose in its bracket. If it's loose, we can probably reconnect and/or tighten it. If it's broken, remove it and take it with you to the Toyota parts department when you buy a new one.

Step 1. Check Accelerator Linkage.

20R and 22R models: Remove the air cleaner (Chapter 5, Procedure 6, Step 1).

EVERYONE: Have Friend pump the gas pedal a few times while you watch for action in the engine compartment.

20R and 22R models: You should see the throttle arm bracket moving on the lower rear side of the carb.

22R-E and 22R-TE models: You should see

the rounded throttle arm rotating near the right front of the engine.

EVERYONE: If you don't witness the thrilling movements mentioned above, follow the linkage from the throttle arm to where it disappears through the firewall. Check the clamps along the cable and tighten them if they are loose. (See Step 6 to adjust the cable tension). Check the cable where it attaches to the firewall. Is the cable housing broken? If the woven wire, cable housing, linkage rods, or connection on the end of the cable or rod is broken, replace the cable or rod.

If you don't find the problem in the engine compartment, look at the lever at the top of the accelerator pedal, inside the truck. A linkage rod or cable end should be connected to the lever. If the rod or cable is broken, replace it. If it has just come loose, see Step 3 to reconnect it.

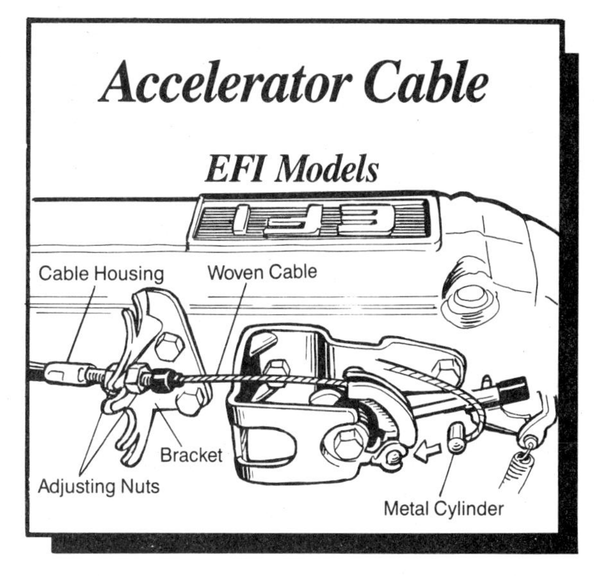

Step 2. Remove Accelerator Linkage Rods or Cable and Housing.

'79-'87 models: Look for the end of the cable inside the truck under the dashboard. A flashlight helps. It's at the top end of the metal lever part of the gas pedal. Two different arrangements have been used to connect the cable to the lever. The first type I describe is used on earlier models and the second type is used on later models. You'll have to determine which type you have.

Early type: Push the lever toward the firewall while you pull on the cable. Align the wire cable with the slot in the left side of the lever, then slide the metal cylinder tip out of the lever.

Later type: Pull the small round chunk of aluminum on the end of the cable toward the rear while you press the lever toward the firewall. You'll see a small white piece of plastic where the cable goes through the lever. Pop the plastic toward you, out of the lever. Slide the cable through the slot on the side of the lever.

EVERYONE: From the engine compartment, follow the cable from the firewall toward the engine looking for clamps that attach it to the firewall or engine.

'79-'83 2WD models: The cable housing is bolted to a bracket near the center of the firewall. Remove the screw or bolt that clamps the housing to the bracket. Follow the cable housing to the end where the woven cable is attached to a movable lever. Wiggle the cable end off the ball on the lever. You might have to twist on the cable end while you pull because the connection is supposed to be tight.

'79-'83 4WD and '84-'87 22R models: The cable housing is attached to a bracket on the valve cover.

22R-E and 22R-TE models: The cable housing is bolted to a bracket on the engine a few inches behind the throttle arm.

'84-'87 models: Hold the metal part of the housing with pliers while you unscrew one of the 10mm nuts on either side of the bracket until the housing is loose enough to pull out of the slot in the bracket.

Unless you are replacing the cable, only loosen one of the nuts. If you move both nuts you'll need to adjust the cable tension after you install the cable. Sometimes one of the nuts is glued to the shaft, so if the first nut you try to loosen is difficult to turn, try the other nut.

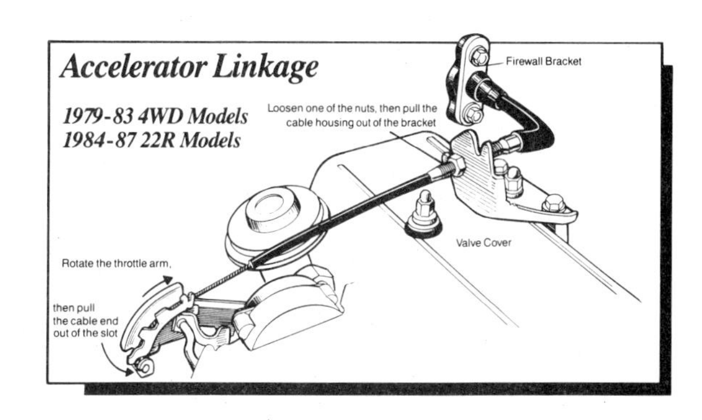

The end of the cable connects to the throttle arm on the front of the engine. Rotate the top of the throttle arm toward the cable housing and hold it there while you align the wire cable with the slot in the side of the throttle arm. Slide the little metal cylinder on the end of the cable out of the throttle arm.

'79-'87 models: The cable housing is attached to the firewall in one of three ways: two bolts in the engine compartment attach the housing to the firewall, or two bolts attach the housing to the firewall from the passenger compartment side, or the cable housing has a threaded end that screws into the firewall from the engine side. A quick look at where the cable passes through the firewall will determine which setup you have. Remove the bolts or unscrew the housing to release it from the firewall. Pull the cable housing through the firewall.

The cable and housing are liberated. See Step 3 to install a new cable and housing.

'75-'78 models: The linkage rods are connected to levers with a ball and socket type fastener; a ball on the lever fits into a socket on the end of the rod. To replace the linkage rods, grab one end and pop the socket off the ball. They are on pretty tight sometimes, so you might have to twist the socket back and forth while pulling it off the ball.

To install the linkage rod(s), put a small dab of grease into the socket, then wiggle it onto the ball. If the socket fits too loosely on the ball, check the ball for wear; it should be round. If it's worn away, replace the lever it's attached to. If the socket is elongated and not perfectly round, replace the rod. Once the rod(s) have been connected, try the accelerator pedal to see that everything is working smoothly. That's all there is to it.

Step 3. Attach Cable End to Gas Pedal Lever and Cable Housing to Firewall.

Caution! Don't kink or bend the new cable and housing during installation. A bent cable will bind in the housing, causing premature wear and a scary sticking accelerator.

From the engine compartment, push the cable end through the hole in the firewall. If your cable housing is the kind that screws into the firewall, screw it in now. If your cable housing attaches with two bolts, install and tighten them now.

Early models: To attach the cable end to the gas pedal lever, align the wire cable with the slot in the pedal lever and insert the metal cylinder cable tip into its hole on the lever. Pull the cable toward the front of the car.

Later models: Pull the little white plastic clip toward the round metal ball on the end of the cable. Fit the cable through the slot in the lever, then push the little round white thing into the hole in the lever. Pull the cable toward the front of the truck. Check that the white thing is locked into place.

Step 4. Attach Accelerator Cable Housing to Bracket.

'79-'87 20R and 22R models: Thread the cable to the bracket on the engine or firewall so there are no sharp bends.

'79-'83 2WD models: Fit the metal end of the housing onto the bracket the way the old cable was attached. Install the clamp on the housing, then install the screw or bolt but don't tighten it yet.

'79-'83 4WD and all '84-'87 models: Thread the cable housing to the bracket so there are no sharp bends. If you are installing a new cable and there are no 10mm nuts on the end, use the ones from the old cable. Install two 10mm nuts onto the threaded part of the cable housing, then slide the housing into the slot in the bracket.

Step 5. Attach Accelerator Cable to Carburetor Linkage.

'79-'83 2WD models: Reconnect the end of the cable to the throttle linkage the way the old cable was connected. Put a dab of grease into the socket, then fit the end onto the ball.

'79-'84 4WD and all '84-'87 models: Rotate the top of the throttle arm while you thread the cable into the groove. Align the cable with the slot in the arm, then slide the little metal cylinder on the end of the cable into the hole on the throttle arm. Let the throttle arm rotate to the idle position. Be sure the cable stayed in the groove. Reconnect the throttle return spring if you unhooked it.

Step 6. Adjust Accelerator Cable Tension.

When properly adjusted, the cable should have about ¼ - ½" of slack (" give") when you push lightly on the woven cable.

'79-'87 20R and 22R models: Before adjusting the cable tension, set the choke plate in the top of the carb to the OFF (vertical) position. If it flips back to the ON (horizontal) position while adjusting the cable tension, reset it to the OFF position. Here's how:

Rotate the top of the throttle bracket on the rear of the carb toward the left side of the truck and hold it there. Reach into the top of the carb with a finger and push down on the right edge of the flat **choke plate** that covers the right half of the opening. Hold the plate in a vertical position while you let go of the throttle bracket. The choke plate will stay in the vertical position unless you move the bracket. If the choke plate flips closed while you're adjusting the cable, repeat this paragraph to set it in the horizontal position again.

'79-'83 2WD models: The cable should be attached loosely to the bracket on the firewall. Slide the end of the cable housing toward the driver's side of the truck to remove slack from the cable. Move it toward the passenger's side to increase the slack in the cable. When the cable tension is correct, tighten the screw or bolt in the clamp.

'79-'83 4WD and all '84-'87 models: The adjustment is made with the two 10mm nuts on the end of the cable housing. Screw the nut on the cable housing side of the bracket toward the bracket to tighten the cable and remove slack, OR screw the nut closest to the end of the housing toward the bracket to loosen the cable and add slack.

To adjust the slack, first decide whether the cable is too loose or too tight and which nut you need to move to make the adjustment. Screw the other nut a few turns away from the bracket and out of your way. Hold the smooth unthreaded metal part of the cable housing with pliers while you turn the nuts—you don't want the housing to get twisted. When the slack is correct, tighten the other nut against the bracket.

Step 7. Do This and That.

'79-'87 20R and 22R models: Plug the small vacuum hoses and lines that were connected to the air cleaner (don't worry about the large ones).

EVERYONE: Start the engine and let it warm up. Press the gas pedal a few times to be sure it operates smoothly. If it sticks, the housing is kinked or the wire cable is bent inside the housing. Can you see the problem? If the gas pedal sticks, remove the cable and install it again.

Check the idle speed and adjust it if need be (Chapter 5, Procedure 13, Steps 5 and 6). If the engine won't idle slow enough by adjusting the idle speed adjustment screw, give the cable a little more slack (Step 6), then set the idle speed.

20R and 22R models: Install the air cleaner if you haven't already (Chapter 5, Procedure 6, Step 2).

PROCEDURE 4: CHECK FUEL SUPPLY ON 20R AND 22R MODELS

Condition: You were sent here from Chapter 4 because your truck won't start, or starts but runs poorly.

Tools and Materials: Friend, 10mm and 12mm wrenches, pliers, rag, maybe a regular screwdriver or phillips screwdriver depending on the kind of fuel line hose clamps you have, a jumper wire (a piece of insulated wire with alligator clips on each end), 12 ounce beer or soft drink can with the top removed, small tape measure or ruler.

Remark: You are absolutely certain there is an adequate amount of gasoline in the tank? I've seen several people do a lot of unnecessary work trying to get their cars or motorcycles to run with an empty gas tank.

Caution: Before disconnecting any fuel lines, remove the gas cap to relieve the pressure or vacuum in the gas tank. There is a possibility that some gasoline will run out of the fuel lines when you disconnect them, so place a can or rag under the connection to catch the gas. *NO SMOKING!*

Step 1. Remove Air Cleaner.

See Chapter 5, Procedure 6, Step 1.

Step 2. Check Float Bowl for Fuel.

Wipe off the little round *sight glass* on the front of the carb and check the fuel level in the bowl. If fuel is in the bowl, you'll see a horizontal line indicating the level. No fuel? Start the engine if possible, or crank it with the starter for about ten seconds. Turn the key to OFF. The fuel pump should fill the *float bowl* to the center of the sight glass. Still no fuel? Go to Step 3. If you can see fuel in the float bowl, the line should be very close to the center of the sight glass. If the fuel level is more than 1/16" (1.5mm) above or below the center, the float level needs to be adjusted (take the truck to the Toyota dealer or a garage). If the fuel is at the proper level, let's see if the fuel pump is supplying a sufficient amount when the engine is running.

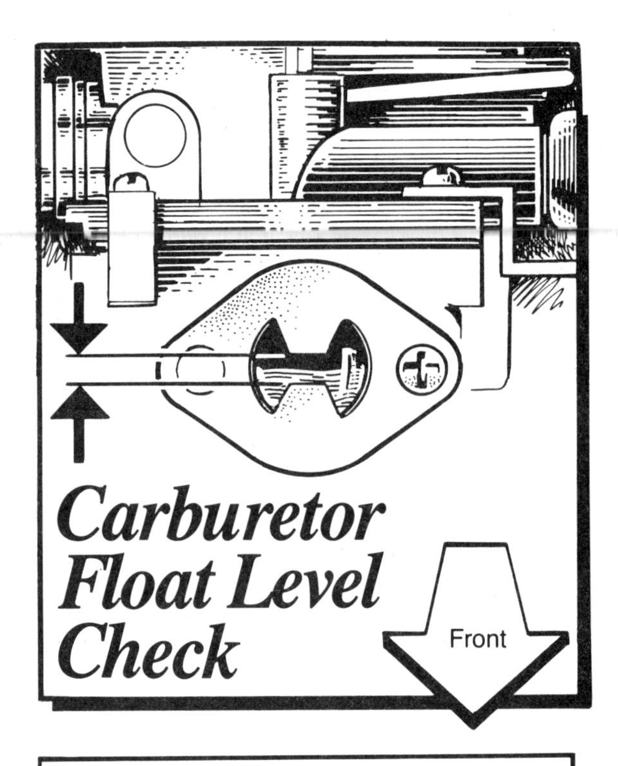

Step 3. Test Fuel Supply At Carb.

Caution! A spark near an open container of gasoline can cause a fire. While doing this test, hold the pop or beer can as far away from the engine as possible. Disconnect the coil wire from the center of the distributor cap, clip one end of a jumper wire to the metal tip of the coil wire and clip the other end to bare metal away from the can. Remove the gas cap from the gas tank filler to relieve pressure in the tank.

The **fuel supply hose** connects to the top front of the carb. Put a rag under the fitting to catch any gas that might dribble out of the hose.

Disconnect the fuel supply hose from the carb. It's attached with a clamp that you unscrew with a regular or phillips screwdriver, or a clip that you squeeze with pliers. Loosen the clip or clamp and slide it away from the carb. Grab the hose close to the fitting on the carb and twist and pull it off. Cut the top off of a 12 ounce beer or pop can and stick the hose into the can.

Have Friend pull the handbrake ON and put the transmission in PARK or NEUTRAL. Hold the hose in the can while Friend turns the key ON and cranks the engine for ten seconds (time it with your digital watch). Have Friend turn the key to OFF. Measure the gasoline in the can. There should be between one and two inches of gas in the can. If there is, the fuel supply is sufficient so the problem isn't the fuel pump. Skip to Procedure 7.

If the fuel pump pumped less than 1 inch of gas into the can, not enough fuel is being pumped to the carb. Check the fuel filter (Procedure 2). If the filter

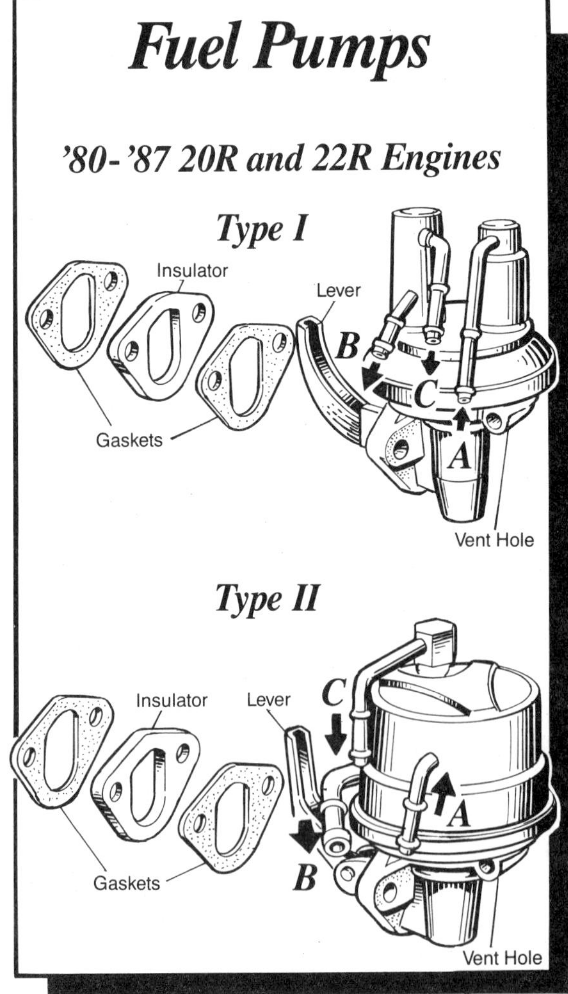

appears to be OK, check the fuel pump (Procedure 5 or 6). Remove the jumper wire and reconnect the coil wire to the distributor cap. Reconnect the fuel hose to the carb, then slide the clamp back to its original position over the fitting and tighten it (if it's the kind you tighten). Install the air cleaner if you removed it (Chapter 5, Procedure 6, Step 2).

PROCEDURE 5: REMOVE, CHECK AND INSTALL FUEL PUMP ON '80-'87 20R AND 22R MODELS.

Condition: Your tests indicate the fuel pump is not pumping an adequate supply of gas to the carburetor.

Tools and Materials: 12mm socket, ratchet, extension for the ratchet, two new fuel pump gaskets, clean catch pan, masking tape, marker, gasket sealer, maybe a new fuel pump, maybe one gallon each of fresh antifreeze and distilled water.

Remark: You'll need to drain the radiator and remove the upper radiator hose so you can get to the fuel pump. This would be a good time to replace the coolant (Chapter 6, Procedure 3).

Step 1. Drain the Radiator, Disconnect the Upper Radiator Hose.

See Chapter 6, Procedure 3, Step 1, to drain the coolant into a catch pan. When the coolant stops draining, install and tighten the drain plug. If you are going to replace the antifreeze, do Chapter 6, Procedure 3, Step 2, to drain the crankcase and flush the system.

Now disconnect the upper radiator hose from the thermostat housing on the engine (Chapter 6, Procedure 2, Step 2).

Step 2. Remove Fuel Pump.

The fuel pump is bolted to the right front corner of the cylinder head. Three rubber hoses are connected to it.

Look at the fuel pump illustration. Use masking tape and a marker to label the three hoses connected to the fuel pump "A," "B" and "C" to match the fittings in the illustration. Or draw a simple sketch so you'll know where the hoses go when you install the fuel pump.

Loosen the clamps for the hoses and slide them away from the fuel pump. Grab the hoses near the fuel pump and give them a good twist to break them free. Wiggle the hoses off the fuel pump.

Use a 12mm socket and ratchet with a ratchet extension to remove the two nuts that attach the fuel pump to the cylinder head. Pull the fuel pump off the mounting studs. Also remove the thick insulating plate that fits between the fuel pump and cylinder head.

Step 3. Check Fuel Pump.

Look at the illustration to see if you have a Type 1 or Type II fuel pump. Notice that one of the hose fittings is labeled "A," another "B" and the third one "C." Fitting A connects to the hose that delivers gas from the tank to the fuel pump. Fitting B connects to the hose that delivers the fuel to the carburetor, and fitting C connects to the hose that carries excess fuel back to the gas tank.

Initial test: Round up a small amount of gasoline. Hold the pump upside down while you squirt or pour it into fitting A. Hold the pump in one hand so fitting A is at the top. Push on the fuel pump lever a few times to get a feel for how much pressure is required to operate the pump and how far the lever moves. You'll need to remember these things for the tests that follow.

Test inlet valve: Cover fittings B and C with your fingers, then operate the pump lever. It should be easier to move the lever, and the lever should travel farther than in the initial test.

Test outlet valve: Cover fitting A with your finger, then operate the lever using the same amount of force you used in the initial test. The lever should not move.

Test the diaphragm: Cover all three fittings with your fingers, then operate the lever using no more force than you used in the initial test. The lever should not move.

Test the oil seal: Locate the small vent hole in the lower half of the rounded part of the pump body (not the big hole for the lever). Cover the small hole with a finger, then operate the lever using no more force than you used in the initial test. The lever should not move.

Evaluation: If the results of any of the preceding tests were other than what I said they should be, the fuel pump has reached the end of a long and useful life. Buy a new fuel pump, then go bury the old one behind the tool shed.

If the pump performed as it should in every test, yet not enough fuel is reaching the carburetor, the problem has to be a clogged fuel filter or fuel line, or the filter screen in the gas tank is clogged. Replace the filter (Procedure 2). If there's still a problem, remove the fuel tank and clean the filter screen and inside of the tank (Procedure 8).

Step 4. Install Fuel Pump.

Clean the mounting surfaces on the cylinder head, fuel pump and both sides of the insulator plate.

Spread a light coat of gasket sealer on both sides of the insulator plate, then fit a new gasket on each side so it matches the shape of the plate. Smear a light coat of gasket sealer on the exposed sides of the gaskets, then fit the insulator plate and gaskets on the two mounting studs.

Guide the fuel pump lever into the cylinder head as you slip the pump onto the mounting studs. Install the washers and nuts and torque the nuts to 11 - 15 ft.lbs.

If any of the hose clamps were broken, rusted or weak, replace them with new ones. Install the hoses onto the proper fittings on the fuel pump, then position and tighten the clamps.

Reconnect the upper radiator hose to the thermostat housing (Chapter 6, Procedure 2, Step 3), then fill the radiator with coolant (Chapter 6, Procedure 3, Step 3).

Start the engine and check for leaks at the fuel pump hose connections. Tighten or replace the clamps as necessary.

PROCEDURE 6: CHECK FUEL PUMP OPERATION ON '75-'79 MODELS AND 22R-E AND 22R-TE ENGINES

Condition: Fuel supply is insufficient; OR, the fuel pump isn't working; OR loud clacking noises come from the rear of the truck when the engine is running.

Tools and Materials: Regular or phillips screwdriver, or pliers, depending on the type of fuel hose clamps you have; maybe a new fuel pump.

To replace the pump you will need the tools listed in Procedure 8 to remove the fuel tank.

'84-'87 22R-E and 22R-TE models: To test the pump you'll need a short piece of insulated wire with about ½" of insulation stripped from each end.

Remark: Be certain there is an adequate amount of gasoline in the tank. I've seen several people nearly go nuts trying to get their cars or motorcycles to run with a dry gas tank.

Toyota fuel pumps tend to outlive the car, so be sure the fuel pump is dead before replacing it.

Step 1. Check Electrical Stuff ('75-'79, 22R-E and 22R-TE models).

See Chapter 8, Procedure 2, to check the **fusible links** and the following **fuse(s)**.

MODEL	FUSES TO CHECK	FUSE AMPERAGE
1975	HEATER/GAUGE	20
	IGNITION	
	COIL	15
1976-78	HEATER	20
1979-80	GAUGES	10
	ENGINE	15
1984-87	ENGINE	15
	EFI	15
	STOP	10
	IGNITION	7.5

If all is well in Fuseville, let's see if the fuel pump is pumping.

Step 2. Check Fuel Pump on '75-'79 models.

Chock the front wheels, pull the handbrake on and put the transmission in FIRST (manuals) or PARK (automatics).

The fuel pump and oil pressure sender are electrically interrelated, so when there is no oil pressure the fuel pump won't work. Great idea!

To check the fuel pump, you must first disconnect the wire from the oil pressure sending unit mounted on the right side of the engine crankcase next to the oil filter. Find the wire and slide the connector off the sending unit.

Turn the ignition switch to ON, then go to the right side of the truck and kneel down just in front of the rear tire. Listen for a whirring sound that would indicate the fuel pump is working. Hear it? Does it sound like the pump is turning smoothly? If so, the fuel pump is probably OK. However, if the pump sounds good but no gas squirts out of the hose when you check the fuel supply (Procedure 4, Step 3), the filter screen on the pump might be clogged. Remove the gas tank (Procedure 8), then remove the pump and check the screen (also in Procedure 8).

If no sounds are coming from the tank, the fuel pump isn't working. There are two electrical gizmos—a resistor and a relay—involved in the fuel pump scenario. You'll have to have the Toyota dealer or a garage check them for you. If the resistor and relay are OK, do Procedure 8 to remove the fuel tank and install a new fuel pump.

If you hear clacking, rumbling or other unusual noises, the pump is probably worn out. Remove the gas tank (Procedure 8), then the fuel pump (Procedure 8, Step 5).

Don't forget to turn the key OFF and reconnect the wire for the oil pressure sender.

Step 3. Check Fuel Pump on 22R-E and 22R-TE models.

The fuel pump is mounted inside the gas tank, which is located below the right side of the truck bed.

The air cleaner is mounted in the left front corner of the engine compartment. A large round black rubber hose is connected to a squarish aluminum housing (the air flow metering assembly). The aluminum housing is mounted to the top of a black rectangular box (the air filter housing). To release the air flow meter from the air filter housing, pull up on the bottom of the four clips located around the edge of the housing.

To see if the fuel pump is working, turn the ignition key to ON (don't start the engine), then wiggle your hand up into the air flow meter. Feel around until you find an opening with a little flap. Slip your fingers through the opening and push on the little flap. Listen for a soft purring or pumping sound coming from the right rear side of the engine. Hear it? If you do, the fuel pump is pumping, so there doesn't seem to be a problem with it. Fit the air flow meter onto the air filter housing and secure it with the four clips. You've done all the checking you can do at home. Drag the truck to the Toyota dealer for further tests.

No sound? Either the fuel pump or the air flow meter isn't working. Fit the air flow meter onto the air cleaner housing and snap the clips in place. Let's do some more checking.

'84-'86 models: Locate a green T-shaped test connector on the inside of the left front fender. It's near the top and connected to a brown wire and a green wire. Be sure you get the connector with the wire sockets perpendicular to each other.

Turn the ignition switch to ON but don't start the engine. Insert one end of your jumper wire into each of the two slots. This turns on the fuel pump.

'87 models: Locate the small black box just to the rear of the fuse box in the engine compartment. Open the little box and look at the labels inside the cover. Find the **Fp** and **+B**. The letters relate to the openings in the little box.

Turn the ignition switch to ON but don't start the engine. Place one end of your jumper into the Fp slot (right rear corner) and the other jumper end into the +B slot (right front corner). This turns on the fuel pump.

EVERYONE: Listen for a soft purring or pumping sound on the right rear corner of the engine. If you hear the sound the fuel pump is working. No sound? Locate the fuel hose to the cold start injector. It's beneath the intake manifold connected to the front end of the fuel filter. The hose snakes its way out toward the right front tire. Squeeze the hose to see if there is pressure in it. When you squeeze the hose you should hear a sound at the right rear corner of the engine. The sound is made by fuel returning to the gas tank. If there is pressure in the hose and you hear the sound, the fuel pump seems to be working properly.

If you don't feel pressure in the hose and don't hear the fuel returning to the tank, the fuel pump is suspect. I recommend that you get a second opinion; then, if necessary, remove the gas tank and replace the fuel pump (Procedure 8).

If the fuel pump is working now but wasn't working when you opened the flap in the air flow meter, it means the air flow meter isn't working properly. Have the Toyota dealer check it for you.

If the fuel pump is working but you still don't have an adequate supply of gasoline to the engine, you've checked all that you can check at home. You'll have to have the Toyota dealer or a garage diagnose your problem.

Turn the ignition switch off and remove the jumper wire.

PROCEDURE 7: CHECK FOR WATER IN THE GAS TANK

Condition: The truck sputters and flutters. You've already checked the ignition system and fuel supply, and everything else seems OK; AND/OR you've noticed water in the fuel filter.

Tools and Materials: Clear glass jar, two long thin strips of rags, 17mm wrench, safety glasses.

Remark: There are commercial products called "fuel conditioners" available that you pour into the gas tank to remove small traces of water. You might want to try a can of the stuff before doing this procedure. If the fuel conditioner doesn't work, do this procedure to drain some gas from the bottom of the tank.

Caution! Fire Hazard! Remember the warning at the start of this chapter?

Step 1. Get a Gas Tank Specimen.

Put the transmission in FIRST (manual) or PARK (automatic). Set the handbrake and put chocks in front of and behind the front wheels.

Look under the truck on the bottom right side for a large, black, contoured sheet metal tank. The drain bolt is in the lowest section of the tank.

On some 4WD models a steel fuel tank protector covers the bottom of the tank. Remove the bolts at the front and rear of the protector and lower it to the ground.

Tie strips of rags around your wrists so gasoline can't run down your arm and into your armpit when you remove the plug. Seriously, gasoline irritates delicate bare skin so wash your hands, arms and any place touched by gasoline with soap and water after obtaining your specimen. Put on your safety goggles.

Crawl under the right side of the truck and clean the area around the drain bolt with a rag. Loosen the drain bolt with the wrench while holding the jar under the drain bolt to catch the gas. You don't need to completely remove the plug. When you have a couple of inches of gas in the jar, quickly tighten the drain plug. Crawl out from under the truck without spilling the gas.

Step 2. Diagnosis Please, Doctor.

Clean gasoline is normally a transparent reddish-orange color. Water in the gas will turn it a milky off-white color, or form round beads or blobs in the bottom of the jar. Remember that water is heavier than gas, so it will be on the bottom. See anything besides clean fresh gas? If not, be sure the drain plug is tight, then lower the truck if it's on stands.

If the gas is milky-looking or has blobs in the bottom of the jar, replace the *fuel filter* (Procedure 2). Check the fuel filter frequently and if you see more dirt and crud right away, the gas tank should be removed and cleaned (Procedure 8).

Install the gas tank protector (if you have it) and tighten the bolts to 14 ft.lbs.

PROCEDURE 8: REMOVE AND INSTALL GAS TANK

Condition: You found water, rust or other crud in the gas tank; OR your fuel pump is mounted inside the gas tank and you need to remove it.

Tools and Materials: Depending on how full the gas tank is, you'll need several metal gas cans to drain the gas into, 12mm socket, ratchet, one long extension or several short ones that equal at least six inches, masking tape, marking pen, rags, maybe new hoses or clamps for the fuel filter or fuel lines attached to the tank, solvent, brush, Friend.

If you remove the fuel pump or the fuel pick-up from the tank, you'll need new mounting gaskets.

Remark: Carefully label the hoses and wires as you disconnect them. If they get reconnected to the wrong fitting, the following problems might develop: insufficient fuel supply to the engine, the fuel tank might collapse, or gas fumes in the system could be vented improperly.

If you find lots of rust and crud on the inside of the tank, take it to the Toyota dealer or a garage that can steam clean it. Some specialty shops can coat the inside of the tank with a rust and corrosion preventing compound.

Caution: Let me reiterate that gasoline fumes are highly explosive. Don't light any matches, and check that there is nothing in the area that could ignite the fumes—things like heaters, water heaters, electric motors, or cigarette smokers.

Step 1. Disconnect Negative Battery Cable.

See Chapter 8, Procedure 1, Step 3, to disconnect the cable clamp from the negative battery terminal.

Step 2. Drain Gas Tank.

First, remove the gas cap. If your tank has a steel gas tank protector that covers the entire tank or just protects the front of the tank, remove the bolts that attach it to the truck. Lower it to the ground and slide it out of the way.

Tie strips of rags around your wrists to keep gasoline out of your armpits (unless burning 'pits turns you on), then remove the drain plug in the gas tank and drain the gasoline into a catch pan or metal gas cans.

Step 3. Chock, Jack and Block.

Put chocks in front of and behind the front wheels. Raise the rear of the truck and put it on jackstands (Chapter 2, Step 1).

If you have a 4WD or a lift kit, you might be able to remove the gas tank without jacking up the truck.

Step 4. Remove Gas Tank.

Look through the wheel well so you can see the top of the gas tank. Locate the wires sprouting from the tank and follow them to a wiring connector. It's probably near the fuel filler hose. Disconnect the wiring connector.

Wiggle into a position so you can follow the small hoses from the tank forward through a hole in the frame to where they connect to metal fuel lines. Label the hoses "right," "left," "center," etc., or paint one line on a hose and the metal line it connects to, two lines on another hose and line, etc. until all the hoses and lines are marked. Disconnect the hoses from the metal gas lines. Have a rag handy in case gas runs out of the lines. Leave the hoses connected to the tank.

Working through the wheel well, loosen the clamps that attach the large fuel filler hose and the medium size vent hose to the neck of the tank. Unfortunately the screw heads might be in a difficult position to get to. Remember, Perseverance Furthers. Wiggle the hoses off the fittings.

If you have a hydraulic floor jack, put a block of wood on the end and raise it under the fuel tank so the tank won't crash to the floor when you remove the mounting bolts. No jack? Have Friend hold the tank while you remove the mounting bolts. No Friend? Pile rags, blankets or whatever under the tank and try to support it when you remove the mounting bolts. OK, remove the six bolts at the front and rear of the gas tank and gently lower it to the ground. Guide the hoses out of the frame as you lower it.

If you removed the tank because it was full of crud, haul it away to be steam cleaned, boiled or whatever it takes to clean it.

Step 5. Remove Fuel Pick-Up Tube or Electric Fuel Pump.

If you removed the tank to get to the fuel pick-up or fuel pump (on models with electric fuel pumps), locate the large round flange on top of the tank where the hoses connect. Use chalk or paint to mark the flange and tank so you'll know which way the flange goes during reassembly. If your tank has a smaller flange with wires connected to it, that's the gas gauge sending unit.

Now remove the small screws, bolts and/or nuts around the edge of the large flange. Pull the fuel pick-up tube or the fuel pump bracket out of the tank.

If you are removing the pick-up tube to clean the filter, use solvent and a brush to thoroughly clean the wire screen on the end of the tube. If the screen is loaded with crud, the inside of the tank should also be cleaned (see the Remarks section). When everything is clean, skip down to Step 6 to put everything back together.

If you have an electric fuel pump, make a note of which wire connects where on the pump, then remove the two small nuts that attach the electrical wires to the pump. Pull the bottom of the pump out of the rubber cushion at the bottom of the bracket.

The top of the fuel pump is connected to the metal fuel line with a rubber hose. Squeeze the ears on the clamp next to the fuel pump while you wiggle the fitting off the hose. Remove the small clip that attaches the filter screen to the bottom of the fuel pump.

Now you can clean the filter screen or replace the fuel pump. When you are ready, see Step 6 to put everything back together.

Step 6. Put It All Back Together.

Models with electric fuel pumps: Fit the fuel pump filter screen onto the bottom of the fuel pump and install the little clip.

Wiggle the fitting at the top of the fuel pump into the hose on the bracket. Squeeze the ears of the hose clamp while you slide it into position near the end of the hose. Push the bottom of the pump into the rubber cushion at the bottom of the bracket. Reconnect the wires to the pump, then install and tighten the two little nuts.

EVERYONE: Fit a new gasket onto the fuel tank, then install the fuel pump or pick-up tube into the tank so the marks you made are aligned. Install the mounting screws, nuts and/or bolts for the flange, then snug them down. Don't overtighten the little devils. If there were little rubber cushions between the tank and frame, be sure the cushions are in place before installing the tank.

Now comes the teamwork. Use your hydraulic jack or Friend to raise the tank while you guide the small hoses through the frame and fit the larger hoses onto their fittings. Hold the tank in position while you install the six mounting bolts. Torque the bolts to 14 ft.lbs.

Reconnect the large and small hoses to the filler neck, then tighten the clamps. Reconnect the smaller hoses to the metal fuel lines, using the labels you made during disassembly to get the hoses connected correctly.

Reconnect the electrical wires, being certain the connectors lock into place.

Finally, install the drain plug and snug it down. The proper torque is only 4½ ft.lbs., so don't overtighten it.

Install the gas tank protector and tighten the bolts to 14 ft.lbs.

Lower the truck off the jackstands if you raised it, then reconnect the negative battery cable clamp.

Pour fresh gas into the tank and check for leaks. Tighten the clamps if you find any leaks.

PROCEDURE 9: CHECK AUTOMATIC CHOKE (20R AND 22R ONLY)

Start this procedure when the engine is cool.

Read Chapter 2: *Driving Tips* for an explanation of how the automatic choke works.

Condition: It's hard to start the engine on cold mornings; OR the engine starts but won't idle; OR the engine starts easily but runs poorly and the gas mileage is down.

Tools and Materials: 12mm wrench, phillips screwdriver, pliers.

Step 1. Remove Air Cleaner Lid.

See Chapter 5, Procedure 4, Step 3, to remove the top of the air cleaner. The large air cleaner housing can remain on the engine.

Step 2. Check Position of Choke Plate.

With the engine off and cold, push the accelerator pedal to the floor one time and release it. This should set the choke to its horizontal ON position.

Now look in the top of the carb. The **choke plate** (butterfly valve) should be covering the right half of the opening in the top of the carb. If it is, skip to Step 3.

If the choke plate isn't covering the opening, the choke isn't working. See if you can move it with your fingers or a screwdriver. If it's stuck, squirt a little penetrating oil on each end of the choke plate shaft inside the carb opening, then squirt some on the shaft that connects the choke plate and the round choke housing on the rear side of the carb.

Push the accelerator pedal down again and release it. If the choke works now, your problem is solved. Do Step 3 to see if the choke opens automatically.

If the choke still doesn't work, read on.

'75-'80 models: If the choke plate is stuck or doesn't open and close properly, see Step 4 to check the choke mechanism.

'81-'87 models: If you can't free the choke plate, you'll need to seek professional assistance to remove and check the choke mechanism.

Step 3. See if Choke Opens.

Clear tools, rags, etc. away from the drive belts and fan. Be sure any disconnected vacuum lines are plugged, then start the engine. As the engine warms up, the engine speed will increase. Tap the accelerator pedal occasionally and see if the engine slows to idle. It should.

The choke plate should gradually open to a vertical position as the engine warms up. If it doesn't, feel the round *choke housing* on the rear of the carb. It should be warm.

'75-'80 models: If the choke housing is warm but the choke plate didn't change to a vertical position, look for small lines on top of the round choke cover and the choke housing on the carb. The two longest lines should be aligned. If not, slightly loosen the three phillips screws around the outer edge of the choke cover, then move the cover so the lines are aligned. Tighten the phillips screws. If this opened the choke plate to a vertical position, your problem is most likely solved.

If the marks are aligned and the choke plate didn't move, feel the two small water hoses connected to the bottom of the choke housing. If the hoses are warm but the choke plate doesn't open to a vertical position, the choke mechanism must be broken or worn out. See Step 4 to replace the automatic choke element.

If the hoses aren't warm, something is preventing the coolant from flowing through the choke housing. You'll need to remove the two hoses to see if they are clogged (Chapter 6, Procedure 2, Step 6).

Once the problem is remedied, install the air cleaner (Chapter 5, Procedure 6, Step 2).

'81-'87 models: If the choke housing isn't warm, see if the *electrical wire* to the choke is connected. Wire OK? Use a test light to see if there's juice in the wire at the connection to the choke (Chapter 8, Procedure 5, Step 2). If juice is getting to the choke wire but the choke housing doesn't warm up, the little *heater wire* or *spring* inside the choke cover is probably kaput. Unfortunately, the choke mechanism is riveted to the carb so you'll have to take it to the pros to have it replaced or repaired. The carburetor top might even have to be replaced.

EVERYONE: Install the air cleaner (Chapter 5, Procedure 6, Step 2).

Step 4. Remove, Check and Install Choke Cover ('75-'80 models only).

The round *choke cover* is attached to the *choke housing* on the rear of the carburetor. Two small rubber hoses connect to fittings on the bottom corners of the choke cover.

Disconnect the two small water hoses from the choke cover. Remove the three screws around the perimeter of the round choke cover and their little washers. Don't remove the bolt in the center of the choke cover.

Lift off the cover to see if the spring inside is broken or bent. The *flat spiral-shaped spring* should be wound evenly around the center post. If the spring looks good, try to move the choke plate again. If it moves now or if the spring is distorted and weird, get a new choke cover. If the choke plate is still stuck, have Toyota or a garage check it for you.

Before installing the choke cover, be sure there is a gasket on the choke housing body on the carb.

To install the choke cover, hold it in the installed position next to the choke housing. The hose fittings should be toward the bottom. Turn the cover until the hook on the end of the spring is aligned with the little lever inside the choke housing. Turn the choke cover slightly *clockwise* (as viewed from the rear of the carb) to be sure the spring hooks the little lever, then fit the cover onto the housing. Rotate it *counterclockwise* until the mark (line) on the cover is aligned with the larger center mark on the housing. Hold the choke cover in this position while you install and the tighten the three mounting screws.

Repeat Steps 2 and 3 to see if the choke is working now. Install the air cleaner (Chapter 5, Procedure 6, Step 2).

PROCEDURE 10: EMERGENCY! OR QUICKY CARB CLEAN

Carburetor problems can often be cured without a full-scale carb rebuild. Step 1 or 2 might solve your problem. If all this fails, you'll have to remove the carb and rebuild it or install a new or rebuilt one.

In Step 1 you'll be removing the air cleaner lid, then cleaning the accessible jets with carburetor cleaner. In Step 2 you'll remove the air cleaner housing and tap on the top of the carb to hopefully free a stuck needle valve.

Condition: You're stranded on the side of the road and suspect the carburetor is the culprit—gas is pouring out around the top of the carb, or there's no gas visible in the sight glass on the front of the carb; OR the engine isn't running right and you want to do a quicky carb clean.

Tools and Materials: For Step 1 you'll need a spray can of carburetor cleaner, rags and maybe some pliers to remove the air cleaner lid.

For Step 2 you'll need 10mm and 12mm wrenches, phillips screwdriver, and pliers. Some clean rags (handkerchief, tie, socks, etc.) would be helpful. If you just happen to have a spray can of carb cleaner, you are truly blessed.

Caution: Be careful not to drop anything into the carb while you're working on it. If something does drop into it, try to fish the part out with a magnet, or remove the carb if you can't get it out otherwise.

Remark: One day on the way home from work, my truck decided it would run only at idle or full throttle with nothing in between. What a frantic ten miles of driving just to get home! All the way I was thinking for sure I'd be up late that night rebuilding the carb instead of going to a beach party I had been looking forward to for weeks. In desperation I yanked off the air cleaner lid and sprayed the inside of the carb with carb cleaner. I must have used half a can of the stuff. When I started the engine it coughed, sputtered, belched a cloud of blue smoke that nearly brought out the fire department, then smoothed out and purred like a kitten. My evening wasn't ruined after all, thanks to the "mechanic in a can." Maybe you'll be just as lucky. There's only one way to find out.

Step 1. Quicky Carb Clean.

If you don't have a spray can of carb cleaner, skip down to Step 2.

Remove the *air cleaner lid* (Chapter 5, Procedure 4, Step 3).

Put the little tube that comes with the carb cleaner can in the nozzle and spray the inside of the carburetor. Use your finger or a screwdriver to hold the flat plates in the top of the carb in a vertical position so you can get a good shot at everything inside the carb. Let the cleaner soak a few minutes, then spray it some more. Stick the tube into the holes in the top of the carb and give them a good shot. Look for small round brass screws to squirt. If you have a clean rag handy, use it to wipe away as much crud as possible from inside the carb.

Now try to start the engine. If it starts, it'll probably belch a huge cloud of blue smoke. That's the carb cleaner burning, so don't worry. Just be sure you aren't in a closed garage. Try revving the engine with the gas pedal. Is your problem solved? If so, install the air cleaner lid (Chapter 5, Procedure 4, Step 3). Go for a test drive to be sure you've eliminated the problem. If your truck still doesn't run right, let's dig a little deeper for the solution.

Step 2. Tap Carb Top to Free Needle Valve.

Remove the air cleaner housing (Chapter 5, Procedure 6, Step 1).

Look at the sight glass on the front of the carb. If the fuel level line in the glass is near the top or bottom of the glass, or gasoline is flooding out around the top of the carb, use a wrench or the handle of a screwdriver or hammer to tap on the top of the carb near the fuel inlet. Tap, don't bash! The tapping might free the *needle valve* if it's stuck. Tap the carb a few times, then start the engine if possible. You'll need to plug the small vacuum lines that were connected to the air cleaner. If the fuel level returns to the center of the sight glass, you may have solved the problem. Have the needle valve replaced as soon as possible to avoid future emergency situations (and possible ulcers).

If there doesn't appear to be any gas in the float bowl after tapping the carb top, check the fuel supply (Procedure 4). If fuel is getting to the carb and tapping the top didn't solve the problem, you need to rebuild or replace the carb (Procedure 11).

PROCEDURE 11: REMOVE AND INSTALL CARBURETOR (20R AND 22R ENGINES ONLY)

Condition: You've done the 12,000 mile tune-up and checked all the things in Chapter 4: *Troubleshooting*, gotten a second opinion from the Toyota dealer or garage, and come to the conclusion your carburetor needs to be rebuilt or replaced.

Tools and Materials: 10mm socket, ratchet, ratchet extension, phillips and/or regular screwdriver, regular and needlenose pliers, notebook and pencil, masking tape, indelible pen, rags, knife or razor blade or putty knife, mounting gaskets. You'll need a tachometer to adjust the carb once it's back on the engine.

Remarks: If you decide to buy a rebuilt carb from a parts store or the Toyota dealer, be sure the rebuilt carburetor has the same part number stamped on the tag on the top of your old carb.

Shop around for the best deal; prices can vary radically from store to store. If you're replacing the carburetor, you might want to consider installing a high performance Weber carb (see Chapter 14).

If your engine compartment is dirty, nasty, greasy and filthy, give it a bath (Chapter 5, Procedure 5, Step 2). You don't want any junk to get into the intake manifold when the carburetor is off. Always cover the hole in the manifold left by the departed carb with a clean rag or paper towels.

Before removing the carb, draw a simple diagram of the vacuum hose(s) and electrical wire connection(s) for your setup. As you disconnect the hoses and wires, label them and whatever they were connected to "A," "C"", "B," and so on, with masking tape and indelible pen. *This is important!* It's impossible for me to describe what goes where for every year and model. This is something you can (and must) do yourself. If you have a camera, take pictures of the carb from several different views before disconnecting anything.

Now, with masking tape, notebook and pen at hand, you can begin to remove the carburetor.

Step 1. Disconnect Negative (-) Battery Terminal.

See Chapter 8, Procedure 1, Step 3, to disconnect the negative battery cable from the battery.

Step 2. Drain Coolant from Radiator ('75-'80 20R models only).

Look at Chapter 6, Procedure 3, Step 1, to drain the radiator. When the coolant has stopped draining, install and tighten the drain plug.

Step 3. Remove Air Cleaner.

See Chapter 5, Procedure 6, Step 1.

Step 4. Remove Fuel Inlet Hose.

Remove the gas tank cap to relieve pressure or vacuum in the gas tank. Locate the rubber **fuel line hose** on the top front left side of the carburetor. Put a rag below where the hose connects to the carb, loosen the clamp and slide it back, then pull the hose off the carburetor fitting.

Step 5. Disconnect Wires from Carb.

Follow the wires attached to the carburetor to large plastic connectors. On some connectors you have to push on tabs on the sides of the connector to separate the two halves. On other connectors you have to pry a little tab away from the connector while you separate the two halves.

Since the connectors are different sizes and shapes, the halves will only fit together when you have them matched correctly, so you shouldn't have any trouble getting things back together correctly when you install the carb.

Step 6. Disconnect Hoses.

There are several hoses attached to the carb that go to the *intake manifold* and/or to small metal pipes near the intake manifold. Label all the hoses connected to the carb and whatever they are connected to on the carb. Pull the hoses off the carb fittings but leave them attached to the manifold and/or metal pipes. Be sure and label each hose as you disconnect it. Draw a simple picture of your hoses if necessary.

Step 7. Disconnect Water Hoses for Choke ('75-'80 models).

Disconnect the two small water hoses from the choke housing on the rear of the carb.

Step 8. Disconnect Accelerator Linkage.

The accelerator linkage at the carb is an L-shaped rod, running front to rear, that fits into a bracket on the lower rear side of the carb. The short end of the L-shaped rod fits into a slot at the top of the bracket and a hole at the bottom. A spring clip attaches the bottom of the rod to the bracket.

Rotate the rod *clockwise* (as viewed from the front of the truck) so you can see the bottom. Use pliers to pull the clip off the bottom of the rod. If the clip gets bent or broken, make a note to get a new one.

Automatic transmission models: If there is a cable attached to the throttle bracket, rotate the bracket so you can slide the cable out of the slot.

Step 9. Disconnect Other Stuff.

You may have some other hoses and wires to disconnect from the carb. Check the carb carefully and label each hose or wire you disconnect.

Step 10. Remove Carburetor.

Check all around your carburetor to see if there's anything else hooked to it that would prevent lifting it off. All clear? Proceed.

Unscrew (*counterclockwise*) the four 10mm bolts or nuts at the bottom of the carb. Two are on the left side and two are on the right. You might have to pull a round plastic gizmo out of its holder to get to the nuts on the right side.

When the nuts and/or bolts are removed, lift the carb straight up to remove it. Watch for any wires or hoses still connected. Once the carb is off, hold it over a can and tilt it so the fuel in the float bowl can drain out the *fuel inlet fitting*. Cover the holes in the intake manifold with a clean rag or paper towel.

If you are going to rebuild the carb yourself, follow the instructions in the rebuild kit or Toyota Repair Manual. Take your time, and if your carb doesn't exactly match the ones in the illustrations, make notes and draw pictures during disassembly so you'll know where everything goes when it's time to put it all back together. Remember that when it comes to carburetor rebuilding, cleanliness is next to godliness.

Step 11. Install Carburetor.

You are now ready to install a new or rebuilt carb. Stuff a clean rag or paper towel into the hole in the manifold where the carburetor fits so pieces of the old gasket can't fall into the engine, then use a knife, putty knife, or razor blade to scrape all traces of the old carburetor mounting gasket off the intake manifold. If there is a thick insulator plate on the manifold, pull it off and remove the gaskets. Be sure the mounting surfaces on the intake manifold, insulator plate and bottom of the carb are absolutely smooth. A little solvent will help remove the last of the crud. Remove the rag or paper towel from the hole. Remove any traces of dirt or gasket that might have fallen into the manifold.

Find a new mounting gasket that matches the old one. It takes two if you have an insulator plate. Fit a gasket over the four studs sticking up on the manifold, making sure the holes match perfectly. If you have an insulator plate, install it so the holes (if any) are aligned, then install another gasket so the holes are aligned.

Set the carb onto the four mounting studs. Remember, the adjusting screws are on the right side and the round choke housing on the top of the carburetor goes toward the rear of the truck. Guide the accelerator rod into its slot and hole on the rear of the carb as you fit it onto the mounting studs.

Put a lockwasher (and whatever was under the nuts) and a 10mm nut on each stud, then screw the nuts down as far as you can with your fingers. Use a 10mm wrench to tighten them evenly in a diagonal pattern (first one corner, then the far opposite corner, then back to the other side, etc.). Go around a few times until all four nuts are snug.

Step 12. Connect Vacuum Hoses and Wires to Carb.

Connect the vacuum hoses and wires to the carb. Refer to the labels and/or your sketch or photos to be sure. There may also be a diagram under your hood. You'll need all the help you can get. Persevere. If you are installing a new or rebuilt carb you might need to transfer hoses from the old carb to the new carb.

Connect the *fuel inlet hose* to the fitting on the top of the carb, then position and tighten the clamp.

'75-'80 models: Reconnect the two small *water hoses* to the automatic choke housing on the rear of the carb. Position the clamps, then tighten them.

Reconnect the wires on the carb to the wiring harness connectors.

EVERYONE: Be sure the vacuum hoses are securely attached to the intake manifold, metal pipes or whatever. Check for any loose hoses or wires; reconnect them if you find any. It's like a puzzle: it's not done till the last piece is in place.

Step 13. Do This and That.

Check that the L-shaped accelerator rod is in the slot at the top of the accelerator bracket and in the hole at the bottom. Rotate the rod clockwise (as viewed from the front of the truck), then use pliers to install the clip onto the bottom of the rod.

Reconnect the negative (-) battery cable clamp (Chapter 8, Procedure 1, Step 3).

'75-'80 models: Add coolant to the radiator and be sure to check the coolant level again after the engine has warmed up and then cooled down (Chapter 6, Procedure 3, Step 3).

Step 14. Adjust Carb.

'75-'79 models: See Chapter 5, Procedure 13, Step 6, to locate the idle mixture adjustment screw. Gently turn the screw *clockwise* into the carb until it stops. Don't force it. Now turn the screw 2½ turns *counterclockwise*. This is the preliminary setting. You'll do the final adjustment with the engine running.

EVERYONE: Plug the open vacuum lines or hoses on the engine that connect to the air cleaner, then start the engine. It will take a few seconds for the fuel pump to fill the float bowl, so don't panic. You might have to screw the *idle speed adjustment screw* in (*clockwise*) a little to keep the engine running at first (Chapter 5, Procedure 13, Step 6).

Once the engine will idle, check the *fuel level* in the sight glass on the front of the carb. It should be within 1/16" above or below the center.

Fuel level is right on? OK, let the engine warm up to normal operating temperature, then adjust the *idle speed* on all models and the *idle mixture* on '75-'79 models (Chapter 5, Procedure 13, Steps 5-10).

Install the *air cleaner* if you haven't already (Chapter 5, Procedure 6, Step 2).

'75-'80 models: Check the coolant level after the engine has cooled off and add some if it's needed (Chapter 6, Procedure 1).

EVERYONE: Go for a test drive. Does the truck accelerate properly, idle as it should, etc.? Sit back and wallow in the pride of your accomplishment.

CHAPTER 10
EXHAUST AND EMISSION CONTROL SYSTEMS

This chapter is about *waste*: what to do with the left-overs after the good stuff has been removed. It's a problem which has always plagued humanity—from human waste to nuclear waste. When it's carelessly or improperly dealt with, we all suffer from the resulting pollution. Other than furtive protestations, you and I can't do much about nuclear waste, but we can help reduce air pollution by keeping our cars well-tuned, and the *emission control system* in good working order.

Automotive exhaust fumes contain *hydrocarbons* (HC), *carbon monoxide* (CO) and *nitrous oxides* (NOx) that react chemically in sunlight. These chemicals form inside the engine when gasoline is burned, then get pumped through the *exhaust system* and into the air. Since the '60s, car manufacturers (under pressure from environmentalists and the government) have been using a trial and error process to develop ways to reduce these harmful exhaust emissions. The first steps were rather simple, but in recent years they've developed into complex computer controlled electrical and vacuum devices. The good news is that since emission control laws went into effect, the amount of pollution pumped out of exhaust pipes has dropped significantly. Here's how the miracle is accomplished.

EMISSION CONTROL SYSTEMS

Some mechanics (and would-be mechanics) blame emission control devices for poor gas mileage, decreased power, premature engine failure, acne, hemorrhoids, famine and floods. The truth is, emission control devices rarely cause the problems they're frequently blamed for. A good thorough tune-up (which includes some emission control maintenance) will remedy most engine performance problems.

If the engine still runs poorly after a tune-up, or there's a sudden decrease in gas mileage, first check all vacuum hose and wiring connections under the hood. A poor connection is the most frequent cause of problems. When disconnecting hoses, pull on the end, not the middle of the hose. When disconnecting wires, pull on the connector, not on the wire. Label all hoses and electrical connections before disconnecting them and double check that they're reconnected correctly when the job is finished. Even factory trained Toyota mechanics label and recheck, due to the multitude of variations from year to year and model to model. Use the sticker under the hood, if you have one, for reference.

Your truck uses the following three systems to make it one of the cleanest running machines on the road; **Positive Crankcase Ventilation** (PCV) system, **Fuel Evaporative Emission Control** (EVAP) system and **Exhaust Emission Control** system. I'll tell you which components of the three systems you can easily check at home. The rest require special tools or expertise to maintain, diagnose or replace.

Here are a few precautions to follow to avoid damaging some of the emission control devices. Only use unleaded fuel in models with catalytic converters. (You'll see "Unleaded Fuel Only" stickers on or near the gas cap and maybe on the dash.) Avoid coasting with the car in gear and the ignition off. (The unburned fuel being sucked through the engine will coat the catalyst and ruin it.) Be careful to not bang against electrical devices while working on the engine.

Leaving the engine running for more than 20 minutes at regular idle or more than ten minutes at fast idle can overheat and possibly damage the exhaust system—maybe even start a fire.

POSITIVE CRANKCASE EMISSION CONTROL (PCV) SYSTEM

When the fuel is ignited in the cylinders, some of the burned gas (called *blow-by gas*) squeezes past the piston rings into the crankcase. As the engine runs, the blow-by gas builds up pressure inside the crankcase. The pressure must be relieved or it will break the engine seals and gaskets. In the old days, the pressure was released through a pipe directly into the air. Nowadays a hose connected to the top of the valve cover allows the blow-by gas to be sucked into the intake manifold so it can be burned again. A gizmo called a **positive crankcase ventilation (PCV) valve** allows fresh air from the air cleaner to be sucked into the crankcase to mix with the blow-by gas before it's burned again.

The PCV valve fits into a rubber grommet near the top center of the valve cover. A small hose attached to the PCV valve connects it to the intake manifold. The hoses attached to the top of the valve cover and the PCV valve need to be checked and cleaned periodically. Procedure 1 tells you how.

EVAPORATIVE EMISSION CONTROL SYSTEM

Unburned gasoline is very volatile and causes pollution if allowed to evaporate into the air. The **evaporative emission control** system on your truck captures the gas fumes before they have a chance to evaporate, then sends them back either to the gas tank (where they condense into liquid again) or to the carburetor to be burned. A coffee can sized black **canister** in the engine compartment serves as a holding place for the vapors until they're sent to the gas tank or carburetor.

The evaporative emission control system is mainly composed of rubber and metal lines to carry the vapors from the engine to the gas tank or canister, and from the canister to the engine. A few check valves are in the lines to prevent the vapors from flowing in the wrong direction. There's not really much that can go wrong with the system, so checking the rubber hoses periodically is the only maintenance required. Procedure 4 tells you how to replace the canister.

If you've ever wondered why the gas pump nozzles in California are so weird, it's because they capture the vapors that are displaced by the gas as you fill the tank. The vapors go through a separate hose to the station's tanks where they condense to a liquid again. Hmmm.

EXHAUST EMISSION CONTROL SYSTEMS

Depending on the year and model, the **exhaust emission control** system utilizes a computer and vacuum and electrical devices to reduce the by-products of combustion (pollutants) that are pumped out of the exhaust pipe. Some of the devices are temperature sensors, revolution counters, timers, thermovacuum valves and thermoswitches. The interval recommended by Toyota for checking some of these systems varies from year to year, but generally it's every 30 months (2½ years) or 30,000 miles. Since the maintenance and repair of most of these devices require professional expertise, I suggest that you look in your owner's manual to see when emission control service is recommended for your year and model. Then when the time comes, make a date with your local Toyota dealer to have them check the emission system. It shouldn't cost much.

Here are some components of the exhaust emission control system that you can check and repair at home.

Hot Air Intake (HAI) System (20R and 22R models only).

To promote efficient combustion and minimize hydrocarbon exhaust emissions, the temperature of the air drawn into the carburetor should be between 86° and 113°. Drawing warm air into the carb in cold weather also shortens engine warm up time and helps prevent carburetor icing. Controlling the temperature of the air that enters the carburetor is what the **Hot Air Intake (HAI)** system is all about.

There are two ways for air to enter the air cleaner housing; cool air can enter through the end of the **air cleaner snout**, or hot air can enter through the large **hot air intake hose** connected to the bottom of the snout. The other end of the hot air intake hose is connected to an **air stove** on the exhaust manifold.

When the air temperature in the engine compartment is below 86° F, a flap in the snout closes the opening so hot air is sucked into the air cleaner through the **hot air intake hose**. When the temperature is above 113° F the flap opens so cool air only is sucked into the air cleaner.

There are two simple gizmos involved in the hot air intake system: an **HAI diaphragm (vacuum motor)** and a **Thermo Valve (temperature sensor)** that controls the vacuum motor.

The hot air control system is easy to check and should be inspected at every 12,000 mile/12 month tune-up. You probably wouldn't notice a malfunction of the system in hot weather, but in cold weather the engine might use more gas, lose power, stall easily, or hesitate when you want to accelerate. Procedure 5 covers maintenance and repair of the hot air intake system.

Air Injection System

The **air injection (AI)** system utilizes an **air pump** to blow compressed air into the exhaust ports to mix with the hot exhaust gases which promotes burning of unburned hydrocarbons and carbon monoxide. The air pump is controlled by several temperature and vacuum valves that we can't check at home. The air pump, however, is easy to check and replace if it's broken (Procedure 3).

Oxygen Sensor

An **oxygen (O_2) sensor** screwed into the exhaust manifold monitors the ratio of oxygen in the air compared to the oxygen in the exhaust gases and tells the computer to tell the carburetor to make the fuel/air mixture richer or leaner. The oxygen sensor should be replaced periodically and Chapter 5, Procedure 16, Step 1, tells you how to do it.

Catalysts

Starting in 1976 on California models, 1977 on High Altitude models, 1980 on C&C models, and 1981 on all models except Canadian 4WD models, a **catalyst (cat)** was added to the exhaust system to help reduce noxious exhaust emissions.

Two kinds of catalysts are used on Toyota trucks. On some models a **catalytic converter** is added to the exhaust system to reduce hydrocarbon (HC) and carbon monoxide (CO) emissions. On other models a **three-way catalyst** is used to reduce HC, CO, and nitrous oxides (NOx) emissions. Some models don't have a catalyst. For simplicity I'm going to call both the catalytic converter and three way catalyst "the catalyst."

The catalyst consists of granular alumina carrier, coated with a compound of platinum (Pt) and rhodium (Rh), filled into a steel case. The catalyst permits simultaneous *oxidation* and *reduction* to convert the noxious gases to harmless carbon dioxide (CO_2). (See your high school chemistry book for an explanation of oxidation and reduction.) Models with a cat must use unleaded fuel because lead coats the special metals and renders them ineffective.

THE EXHAUST SYSTEM

The exhaust system serves two basic functions: silence and safety. It stifles the noises made by all those little explosions in the cylinders, and carries the burned gases from the engine to the rear of the car so they don't go into the passenger compartment. A noisy, leaky, worn-out exhaust system is not only embarrassing and irritating, it's downright *dangerous*. One of the by-products of burning gasoline is carbon monoxide. This is an odorless gas that first makes you sleepy, then as you doze off it kills you. Dead. It's a method of choice for those bent on suicide, but I presume you're not one of them. The lethal potential of carbon monoxide poisoning is the main reason it's wise to keep your exhaust system in shape.

The exhaust system on all trucks is essentially the same. The exhaust gases created in the cylinders rush past the exhaust valves into the **exhaust manifold**, which is bolted to the left side of the cylinder head. An **exhaust pipe** carries the exhaust gas rearward to the catalytic converter on models so equipped, then to the **muffler/tailpipe assembly**, then into the air (and everybody's lungs).

On Turbo models, the turbocharger is bolted to the bottom of the exhaust manifold and the exhaust pipe is bolted to the bottom rear of the turbocharger. The rest of the exhaust system is the same as non-Turbo models.

Metal and asbestos **gaskets** fit between exhaust system components to prevent leaks. The rear end of the exhaust pipe assembly is securely bolted to an **exhaust pipe bracket** that's bolted to the rear of the engine. On all models, the catalytic converter (when present) and the muffler/tailpipe assembly are attached to the body with **rubber cushions** which dampen vibrations and hopefully prevent rattles.

Replacing most exhaust system components is relatively straightforward. Procedure 6 tells you how to do it.

PROCEDURE 1: CHECK AND CLEAN PCV (POSITIVE CRANKCASE VENTILATION) VALVE.

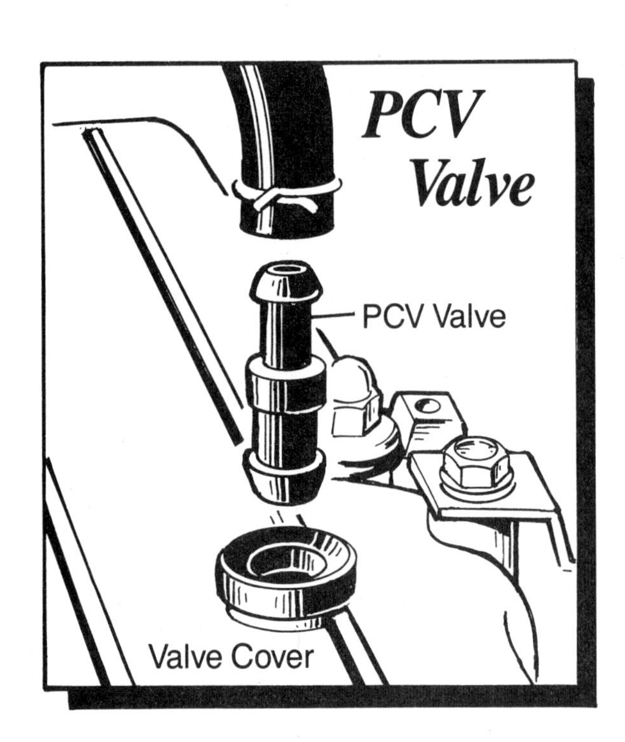

Condition: Routine maintenance; OR you were sent here from Chapter 4.

Tools and Materials: To check the valve: a finger, maybe a Friend. To clean the valve: a spray can of carb cleaner and a rag.

Step 1. Remove, Clean and Install PCV Valve and Hoses.

The **PCV valve** fits into a rubber grommet near the top center of the **valve cover**. A black rubber **hose** from the intake manifold connects to the top of the valve. Just pull the hose off the PCV valve. Don't confuse the PCV hose with the hose that attaches near the front of the valve cover, just behind the oil filler cap.

Remove the hose attached to the PCV valve if you haven't already (Step 1). Wiggle the valve out of the grommet in the valve cover. When the valve is out, shake it to see if it rattles. If it doesn't rattle, replace it with a new one (they're pretty cheap). If the valve rattles, spray carb cleaner into it, then cover both ends and shake it. Do this several times to remove the built-up sludge inside the valve.

To install the valve, wiggle the larger end of the valve into its grommet on the valve cover, then fit the hose from the intake manifold onto the valve. That's all there is to it.

Step 2. Check Other Parts of the PCV System.

The *oil filler cap* is also an integral part of the PCV system. Unscrew the cap and check it for cracks. Replace it if it's cracked or broken.

Check the hose near the top front of the valve cover that connects to the air cleaner (20R and 22R) or intake manifold (22R-E and 22R-TE). Blow through one end of the hose to be sure it isn't clogged. Replace the hose if it's cracked or if the ends have stretched and fit loosely.

Check around the edge of the valve cover for oil leaks. If you find leaks, try tightening the four 12mm nuts that attach the valve cover to the cylinder head. Don't overtighten them—just good and snug, then check the valve cover for leaks the next couple of times you gas up. If there's still a leak, replace the valve cover gasket (Chapter 5, Procedure 8, Steps 3 and 6). You might as well do the whole procedure and adjust the valves while the valve cover is removed.

Pull out the engine oil dipstick and check the little rubber gasket on the upper end. Replace it if it's broken or missing, or if oil appears to be escaping around the dipstick.

Crawl under the front of the truck and check for oil leaks around the edge of the oil pan. If it appears to be leaking, use a socket and ratchet to gently tighten as many of the bolts as you can reach. Overtightening the bolts can break the gasket. If tightening the bolts doesn't stop the leak, do Chapter 13, Procedure 4, to replace the oil pan gasket.

PROCEDURE 2: CHECK EGR VALVE

Condition: Routine maintenance.

Tools and Materials: An 18 inch long piece of 5/32" (4mm) inside diameter vacuum hose, 12mm wrench, phillips screwdriver, vacuum line plugs or tape. If you remove the EGR valve you'll need two new gaskets for the valve and a crescent wrench or Channel Lock pliers to remove it.

Remark: The most common problem with the EGR system is the passages in the valve and cylinder head becoming clogged with carbon. Step 1 tells how to see if the passages are open. The vacuum modulator and bimetal vacuum switching valve (BVSV) rarely cause problems.

Caution: Don't soak the EGR valve in solvent or degreaser because it will damage the diaphragm.

Step 1. Check EGR Valve.

Remove the air cleaner, if it's on, and plug the vacuum lines on the engine (Chapter 5, Procedure 6, Step 1).

The round brass-colored EGR valve is mounted on the top right rear corner of the engine. On most '78-'87 models a round **vacuum modulator** is mounted just above the EGR valve.

To check the EGR valve, disconnect the rubber vacuum hose attached to the top of the valve, then connect one end of a 5/32" (4mm) inside diameter

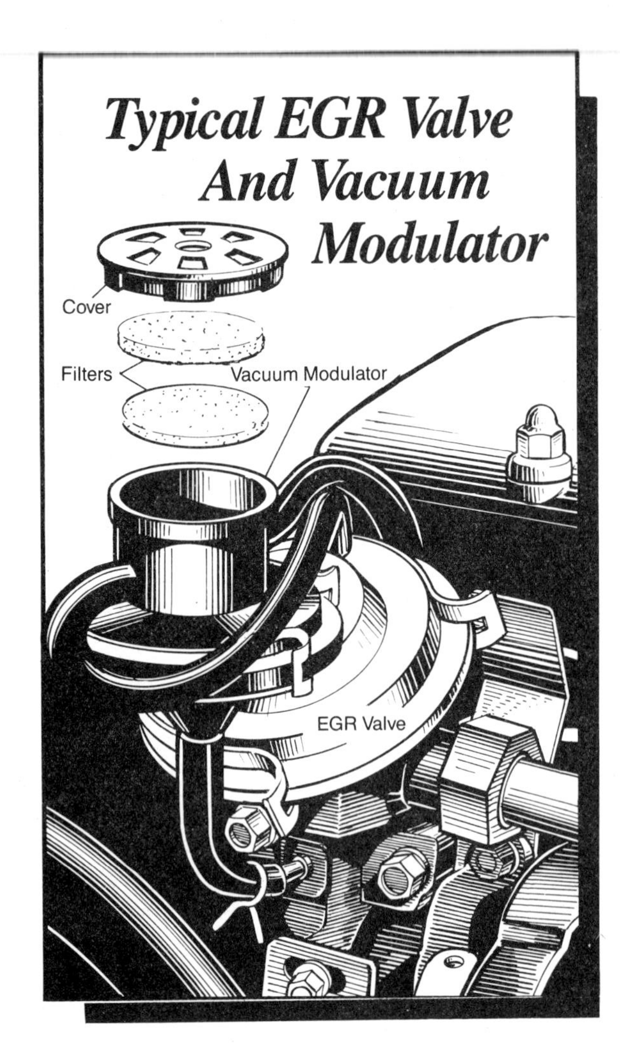

test hose to the fitting on the valve. Don't disconnect any hoses from the vacuum modulator.

Start the engine and let it idle. Suck on the open end of the test hose that's connected to the EGR valve. If, when you suck on the hose, the engine begins to idle roughly or dies, you know the passages are open and the EGR valve is working properly. Sucking on the hose opens the valve and allows exhaust gas to be sucked into the combustion chambers. At idle speed the engine can't handle the high concentration of exhaust gases, so it stumbles or dies.

If the valve is working properly, remove the test hose and reconnect the rubber vacuum hose. If you are here from the tune-up procedure, go back to your place in Chapter 5. Otherwise, install the air cleaner (Chapter 5, Procedure 6, Step 2).

If there's no change when you suck on the hose, either there's a problem with the EGR valve or the EGR passage in the cylinder head is clogged. You'll need to remove the valve to check the valve diaphragm and clean the passages in the valve, cylinder head and intake manifold.

Step 2. Remove and Check EGR Valve, Clean EGR Passages.

Remove the 12mm bolts and nuts that attach the valve to the cylinder head. Follow the large pipe on the bottom of the valve to where it attaches to the intake manifold and remove the two mounting bolts. Pull the valve and pipe off the cylinder head. Use a crescent wrench or Channel Lock pliers to loosen the large nut on the pipe.

Connect the test hose to the valve and suck on the open end. From the underneath side of the round part of the valve you should be able to see the diaphragm move when you suck on the hose. If it doesn't move, replace the EGR valve.

If the diaphragm is good, check inside the valve, the pipe and the passages in the cylinder head and intake manifold for carbon and crud. Use a sharp screwdriver to clear the passages. Blow into the passages to remove any loose crud.

Step 3. Install EGR Valve.

To install the EGR valve, attach the pipe to the valve but don't tighten the large nut. Just screw it on part way. Clean the mating surfaces of the valve, cylinder head, intake manifold and the fitting on the end of the pipe. Install new gaskets on the cylinder head and intake manifold, then install and tighten the mounting bolts and nuts. Now tighten the large nut on the pipe. Reconnect the vacuum hose to the EGR valve. Check the EGR again (Step 1). If everything's OK now, go back to your place in Chapter 5 to continue the tune-up, or install the air cleaner (Chapter 5, Procedure 6, Step 2).

PROCEDURE 3: CHECK AND REPLACE AIR PUMP

This procedure is for '75-'78 models, '79 models except California 4WD, and '80-'84 California and C&C models only.

Condition: Routine maintenance; OR you've determined that the air pump is shot.

Tools and Materials: Phase 1 tool kit, maybe a new or used air pump.

Step 1. Check Air Pump.

The **air pump** is located on the lower right side of the engine. Two hoses are connected to the rear; one goes to the air cleaner and one goes to an aluminum, fist-sized **air control valve (ACV)**. Be sure the drive belt for the air pump is properly adjusted before do the following test.

To check the pump, disconnect the hose from the air pump where it connects to the ACV. Start the engine and rev it up while feeling the open end of the hose for discharge pressure. If you can feel air coming out of the air pump, everything's cool so you can reconnect the hose to the ACV. No air coming out of the hose? Replace the air pump (Step 2).

Step 2. Replace Air Pump.

New air pumps cost big bucks now, so it would be worth your time to look around for a used one. To remove the air pump, disconnect the hoses from the rear of the air pump, then remove the drive belt (Chapter 8, Procedure 3, Step 3). Remove the bolts that attach the air pump to the bracket on the engine.

To install the air pump, wiggle it into position on the bracket, then insert the mounting bolts. Tighten the pump mounting bolts but not the drive belt adjusting bolt. Now install and adjust the air pump drive belt (Chapter 8, Procedure 3, Step 3). Attach the hoses to the rear of the air pump and tighten the clamps and you're finished.

PROCEDURE 4: INSPECT AND REPLACE EVAPORATIVE CANISTER

Condition: Regular maintenance; OR you smell gasoline but can't find a leak.

Tools and Materials: 10mm wrench, a phillips screwdriver or pliers depending on the type of clamps on the canister hoses (some of the hoses don't have clamps), masking tape, and pen to mark the hoses, maybe a new canister.

Remark: Some models have one, two or three canisters located on the right side of the engine compartment. Check them all.

Step 1. Inspect and Replace EVAP Canister.

The **canister**(s) for the evaporative emission system is/are black and about the size of a coffee can. Each canister has two or three hoses connected to the top and one hose connected to the bottom. Label the hoses on the canister, then pull them off. Loosen the bolt or screw in the bracket holding the canister, then pull the canister out of its holder and out of the engine compartment.

Inspect the canister and replace it if it's cracked. Check the rubber hoses that attach to the top and bottom of the canister. Replace any that are cracked or stretched so much they fit loosely on the fitting.

To clean the canister you'll need to take it someplace that has an air compressor. Set the air pressure to 43 psi, then blow air into each of the fittings on top of the canister while holding a finger over the other fittings on top. Don't cover the fitting on the bottom. When you blow on one of the fittings, air should come out the bottom of the canister. If when you blow into the top fittings no air comes out the bottom, or if charcoal comes out the bottom, replace the canister with a new one.

Fit the canister into its holder and tighten the clamp. Inspect the hoses that attach to the canister for cracks and replace any that are loose or funky. Attach the hoses to the canister with the clamps, and you're finished.

PROCEDURE 5: CHECK AND REPAIR HOT AIR CONTROL SYSTEM (20R AND 22R ENGINES ONLY)

Condition: Periodic maintenance; OR the carburetor has been icing up; OR the truck runs poorly and balks during cold weather.

Tools and Materials: To check the system, you'll need a flashlight. '79-'87 models need a phillips or regular screwdriver to remove the rubber hose attached to the air cleaner snout. If there's a problem with the system you'll need an 18 inch to 24 inch piece of 5/32" (4mm) inside diameter vacuum hose to check the HAI diaphragm, maybe a new hot air intake hose, HAI diaphragm or thermo valve.

Step 1. Inspect, Replace Hot Air Intake Hose.

Check both ends of the hot air intake hose that connects the bottom of the air cleaner snout to the air stove on the exhaust manifold. If the hose is torn, crushed or missing, replace it with a new one while the engine is cool.

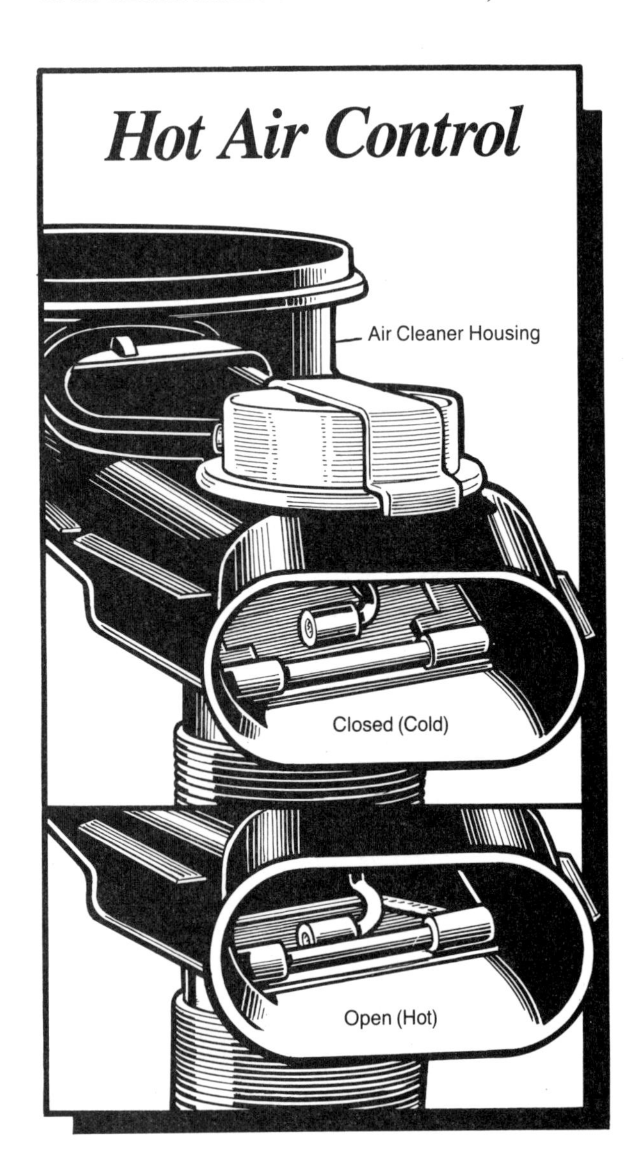

To remove the hose, you must first remove the air cleaner (Chapter 5, Procedure 6, Step 1). When the air cleaner is off, grab the hose as close to the end as possible (over its fitting) and gently twist until it's loose, then pull the hose off the fitting. Remove both ends the same way.

Before installing the hose, carefully enlarge the ends a little with your fingers. It's made of heavy tinfoil, so it bends easily. Align one end of the hose with the fitting and gently slide it on while rotating it slightly back and forth. If the end of the hose gets crimped or caught on the tube and messed up, remove it and straighten it with your fingers.

Step 2. Check Vacuum Hoses.

It's easiest to check the hoses while the air cleaner is off. If you're here from the tune-up chapter, the air cleaner is already off. If the air cleaner is still on, remove it (Chapter 5, Procedure 6, Step 1).

A rubber vacuum hose connects the round HAI diaphragm on top of the air cleaner snout to a thermo valve fitting on the bottom of the air cleaner housing. Another vacuum hose on the thermo valve connects it to the intake manifold or to a T-fitting in another vacuum line. Check both hoses for cracks and breaks and see if they fit tightly on the fittings. Replace them if they're damaged or fit loosely.

Install the air cleaner (Chapter 5, Procedure 6, Step 2).

Step 3. Check HAI Diaphragm.

Do this step when the engine is cool.

Use your flashlight to look into the end of the air cleaner snout. A flap should be covering the hole in the bottom of the snout where the hot air intake hose connects. This is the **cool air** position.

Now start the engine and let it idle while you check the position of the flap. It should have moved to a vertical position, covering the passageway in the snout. This is the **hot air** position. As the engine warms up, the flap should gradually move back to its horizontal (cool air) position. If you're here from the tune-up, see if the flap is in the cool air position, then check the flap after the engine is tuned, everything's back together and you've gone for a test drive. Depending on the air temperature, it might take up to 20 minutes to change, so don't waste your time waiting for it.

If the flap isn't working the way it should, see the next step.

Step 4. Check HAI Diaphragm and Thermo Valve.

Disconnect the rubber vacuum hose from the round vacuum motor on top of the snout. Attach a piece of 5/32" (4mm) inside diameter vacuum hose to the motor, then suck on the open end of the hose.

Sucking on the hose should raise the flap away from the hole in the bottom of the snout to the vertical **hot air position**.

If the flap doesn't return to the cool air position when there's no vacuum applied to the vacuum motor, the flap is stuck. If sucking on the hose didn't change the position of the flap from the cool air position to the hot air position, the diaphragm in the vacuum motor is broken or the flap is stuck in the hot position.

If the flap moved to the hot air position when you sucked on the hose, suck on it again and hold vacuum in the hose while you quickly cover the end of the hose with your tongue. The flap should stay in the hot air position for at least 30 seconds. If it doesn't, there's a leak in the vacuum motor diaphragm. Step 5 tells you how to see if the flap is stuck and how to replace the vacuum motor if it's shot.

If the flap doesn't move to the cool air position, and the vacuum motor and hoses are all in good condition and connected properly (you checked them in Steps 2 and 3 didn't you?), there's a problem in the thermo valve (see Step 6).

Step 5. Replace HAI Diaphragm.

The HAI diaphragm is attached to the air cleaner snout with a **flat strap**. The shaft sticking out the bottom of the diaphragm hooks into a slot on the flap to move it.

Disconnect the vacuum hose from the diaphragm, then remove the phillips screw on top of the air cleaner snout. Hold the diaphragm down while you gently lift up on the screw end of the flat strap until it clears the motor. Lift the strap out of the slot on the snout and set it aside.

Look into the snout while you wiggle and tilt the diaphragm to disengage the shaft from the flap. When the diaphragm is out, notice that the hole in the snout and the matching one on the bottom of the vacuum motor are square.

While the diaphragm is out, check the flap with your finger to see if it moves freely. If it sticks, the snout is bent or the flap shaft is bent. If you can't straighten things so the flap moves smoothly, you'll have to replace the air cleaner housing. Look for a used one and check the diaphragm (Step 4) before buying it.

To install the diaphragm, hold it so the hook on the shaft is pointed toward the rear of the round tab on the flap. Insert the shaft into the snout and fit the hook into the round tab on the flap. Gently push and pull on the diaphragm while watching the flap to be sure the shaft is engaged. When you're sure, wiggle the diaphragm down so it fits into the square hole on the snout. Hold it there while you insert the end of the strap into the slot on the snout. Press the strap over the diaphragm, then install and tighten the screw. Reconnect the vacuum hose. If you're replacing the thermo valve, go on to Step 6. Otherwise, install the air cleaner, if it's off (Chapter 5, Procedure 6, Step 2).

Step 6. Replace Thermo Valve.

Remove the air cleaner lid and the air filter. Look inside the air cleaner for a small plastic gizmo on the snout side of the carburetor. That's the **thermo valve**. Make a note of how it's oriented so you can install the new one the same way. Now look at Chapter 5, Procedure 6, Step 1 to remove the air cleaner housing.

Follow the hose from the HAI diaphragm to where it connects to the thermo valve on the bottom of the air cleaner. There's another hose connected right next to the hose from the diaphragm. Make a note about which hose goes where, then disconnect both hoses. You might have to use a small screwdriver to pry the metal clips away from the hoses as you remove them. The thermo valve is held in place by the clip around the two metal *vacuum tubes*. Pull outward on the two clip arms to release the clip, then slide the clip off the metal tubes. Pull the thermo valve out of the air cleaner. There might be a rubber gasket between the sensor and the air cleaner. If it's stuck to the air cleaner, leave it there; if it's torn or funky, replace it.

Install the new thermo valve into the air cleaner housing so it's oriented the same as the old one. Be sure the rubber gasket is in place. Hold the valve in place with one hand while you fit the clip over the vacuum tubes on the bottom of the air cleaner. When the clip is on as far as you can get it with your fingers, press on the sides of the clip with a screwdriver until the valve is held tightly in place. Reconnect the vacuum hoses to the valve, then install the air cleaner housing, air filter and lid (Chapter 5, Procedure 6, Step 2).

PROCEDURE 6: REPLACE EXHAUST SYSTEM COMPONENTS

Condition: Your truck sounds like an angry semi and you're getting hostile stares from fellow motorists; OR holes may be visible in the exhaust pipe, catalytic converter or muffler/tailpipe assembly.

Tools and Materials: Safety glasses, penetrating oil, 12mm and 14mm wrenches and sockets, ratchet (a long extension for the ratchet is sometimes handy), medium screwdriver, sandpaper or emery cloth, new exhaust gaskets, a block of wood, maybe a new exhaust manifold, exhaust pipe, catalytic converter or muffler/tailpipe assembly. I recommend using new nuts, bolts, lockwashers and flat washers when replacing exhaust components. At least have a few handy because, due to the heat and rust they're subjected to, exhaust nuts and bolts tend to break easily when you remove them. You might even need a hacksaw to remove some of the rusted bolts.

Remark: Replacing the exhaust system components reminds me of when, as a teenager in the '50s, I was changing the mufflers on my old Chevy almost every weekend in search of the perfect loud, mean and powerful sound. Mufflers were cheap then (about ten bucks) but a real pain to replace due to the way the pipes fit together. Replacing exhaust system components nowadays is a cinch. Why couldn't it have been that easy when I was a teenager?

If you're planning to keep the truck for several more years, check out the muffler shops that give a lifetime guarantee on their mufflers. The slightly higher price may save you money in the long run.

Caution: Don't try to work on the exhaust system while it's hot. Let things cool down for 20 minutes after you shut off the engine.

Step 1. Chock, Jack and Block.

Depending on the location of the component you're replacing, you might need to jack up the front or rear. See Chapter 2 to do it safely. Be sure to use jackstands! 4WD models, especially ones with lift kits or oversize tires, probably won't need to be jacked up, but be sure the wheels are chocked, the handbrake is ON and the gearshift is in PARK (automatics) or FIRST (manual).

Step 2. Replace Exhaust Pipe and/or the Gasket between the Exhaust Manifold and Exhaust Pipe.

If you're only replacing the gasket between the manifold and exhaust pipe, you won't need to disconnect the exhaust pipe from the catalytic converter or muffler/tailpipe assembly. You will, however, need to remove the bolt and clamp that attaches the exhaust pipe to the exhaust pipe bracket.

OK, to remove the exhaust pipe from the exhaust manifold or turbocharger, squirt liberal quantities of "holy water" (penetrating oil) on the three nuts that connect the front end of the exhaust pipe to the bottom of the exhaust manifold or turbo. Also squirt holy water on the bolt that attaches the exhaust pipe to the exhaust pipe bracket. The bracket is attached to the rear end of the engine, where it connects to the transmission. If you're removing the exhaust pipe, also soak the threaded parts of the two bolts that attach the rear end of the exhaust pipe to the catalytic converter or muffler/tailpipe assembly. Let the juice soak in for a few minutes.

Remove the 12mm bolt that attaches the exhaust pipe to the exhaust pipe bracket.

If you are removing the exhaust pipe, use a 14mm socket and ratchet to remove the two bolts that attach the rear end of the exhaust pipe to the front end of the cat or muffler assembly, then unhook the rubber hangers that support the cat or muffler from their brackets on the body. Pry the exhaust pipe away from the cat or muffler just far enough to break the bond between the two.

Remove the three nuts from the front end of the exhaust pipe. Use a box end wrench or socket and ratchet on the nuts, because open end wrenches round the corners off and make the nuts impossible to remove. It's usually easiest to remove the three nuts from beneath the truck using a socket on a long ratchet extension. Once the nuts are off, pry the exhaust pipe down and off the studs in the exhaust manifold or turbocharger. If you are replacing the exhaust pipe, pull it out from under the truck.

Before installing the exhaust pipe, pull the old gasket off the exhaust manifold or turbocharger, if it's there, then use a knife, chisel or screwdriver to scrape the mating surfaces free of gasket debris. Smooth the mating surface on the manifold with sandpaper or emery cloth, then fit a new gasket onto the three studs. It will only fit one way. Gasket sealer isn't necessary. If you are reusing the old exhaust pipe, clean the mating surface the same way you cleaned the manifold. Also clean the rear mating surface of the exhaust pipe and the front end of the cat or muffler if you disconnected them.

To install the exhaust pipe, hold the new gasket in place while you fit the pipe onto the three studs. It helps to have Friend raise the rear end of the pipe. Install the lockwashers and nuts but don't tighten the nuts yet. Crawl under the truck and attach the exhaust pipe to the exhaust pipe bracket with the 12mm bolt but don't tighten the bolt yet.

Tighten the nuts where the exhaust pipe attaches to the exhaust manifold or turbo, then tighten the exhaust pipe bracket bolt. If you disconnected the exhaust pipe from the cat or muffler, check that the bracket for the rubber hangers is in place, then fit a new gasket between the exhaust pipe and the cat or muffler. Install and tighten the two bolts and nuts. Install the rubber hangers that support the exhaust system.

Lower the truck off the jackstands, if you jacked it up. Start the engine and check for exhaust leaks. Tighten the bolts and/or nuts if you hear leaks.

Step 3. Replace Catalyst and/or Muffler/Tailpipe Assembly.

Chock, jack and block the rear end of the truck (Step 1).

Catalyst: Check the cat to see if there's a temperature sensor with a wire sprouting from it bolted to the right rear corner of the cat. Find one? No? Skip down to the next paragraph to remove the cat. Yes? If you are going to use the same cat again, follow the wire from the sensor to a plastic connector that's probably under the driver's seat. Separate the connector, then use a screwdriver to pry the rubber grommet out of the body so you can pull the wire and connector half through the body.

To remove the catalytic converter, just remove the two 14mm bolts on each end that attach it to the rear end of the exhaust pipe assembly and the front end of the muffler/tailpipe assembly. Unhook the **rubber hangers** from the brackets on each end of the cat and gently lower it to the ground.

If you are replacing the cat, remove the bolts that attach the sensor to the cat. Once the bolts are removed, pull the sensor out of the cat. If the bolts are tight they will probably break off during removal—and that's OK, because you should use new bolts when you install the sensor in the new cat.

To install the cat, use a knife, putty knife or large screwdriver to scrape the old gasket material from the mating surfaces of the exhaust pipe, muffler/tailpipe assembly, and the cat if you're installing the old one. Use sandpaper or emery cloth to make the mating surfaces smooth. Check the brackets and rubber hangers that support the cat and replace them if they are broken, badly rusted or bent.

If you are installing a new cat and your old one had a temperature sensor, place a new gasket on the sensor, then fit the sensor into the plastic-lined hole in the new cat. Install two new bolts and gently tighten them. They are small bolts so just get them snug.

To install the cat, fit a new gasket between the cat and exhaust pipe and hold it in position while you install the mounting bolts. Next, fit a new gasket between the rear end of the cat and the muffler/tailpipe assembly and install the bolts. Tighten all of the mounting bolts to 32 ft.lbs.

Muffler/Tailpipe Assembly: The muffler and tailpipe are welded together so they must be removed and replaced as a unit. To remove them, just remove the two 14mm bolts that attach the front end of the assembly to the catalytic converter or exhaust pipe, then remove the rubber rings that support the unit. There might be a rubber tailpipe hanger that slides off a round pin mounted to the body. Pull the muffler/tailpipe assembly forward over the rear differential to remove it. Inspect the rubber rings and tailpipe hanger (if you have one) and replace them if they're cracked, funky or missing.

To install the new muffler/tailpipe assembly, thread the rear end of the tailpipe over the differential housing. If you have a rubber tailpipe hanger, fit it onto the round pin on the tailpipe, then onto the pin mounted on the body. Next fit the rubber rings over the hooks on the muffler, then fit them onto the hooks on the body. Install a new gasket between the exhaust pipe or catalytic converter and the pipe on the front end of the muffler/tailpipe assembly. Install and tighten the bolts to 32 ft.lbs. Lower the truck, start the engine and check for leaks around the gaskets. Do this outside, where exhaust fumes won't zap you. Tighten the bolts a little more if necessary.

CHAPTER 11
CLUTCH, TRANSMISSION, DIFFERENTIAL, DRIVESHAFTS AND REAR AXLE

CLUTCH

If your Toyota has a manual transmission (also called a *standard transmission* or *stick shift*), it has a **clutch assembly** that links the engine to the transmission. Without the clutch, the engine would be mechanically connected to the rear wheels all the time, making it impossible to stop the car without turning the engine off, and also making shifting the gears next to impossible.

The parts of the clutch assembly are: the engine **flywheel**, which is bolted to the rear end of the crankshaft; a spring loaded **pressure plate** (also called a *clutch cover*), which is bolted to the outer edge of the rear surface of the flywheel; a **clutch disc** with friction surfaces on both sides that's sandwiched between the flywheel and pressure plate, and a **throwout bearing** (clutch release bearing), which pushes on the pressure plate when the clutch pedal is pressed down. The clutch disc is attached to the transmission via the splined **transmission mainshaft**. A small **pilot bearing** in the flywheel supports the front end of the transmission shaft.

As long as the clutch pedal inside the car is up, the engine is connected to the transmission: the clutch disc and transmission shaft will turn with the flywheel because it's squeezed tightly against the flywheel by the pressure plate.

The clutch mechanism is operated by a hydraulic **clutch master cylinder**, much like the brake master cylinder. When you press down on the clutch pedal, hydraulic pressure created in the master cylinder travels through a metal tube to a **clutch slave cylinder** bolted to the side of the transmission **bell housing**. The hydraulic pressure in the slave cylinder pushes a **push rod** sticking out of the slave cylinder against the outer end of the **clutch release fork**. This causes the fork to pivot like a teeter-totter on a ball attached to the inside of the bell housing. The inner end of the release fork pushes the **throwout bearing** against the pressure plate, compressing its springs. When the springs in the pressure plate are compressed, the pressure of the plate against the clutch disc is released. This allows the engine to run without turning the clutch disc and transmission shaft.

Repairing or replacing the clutch master cylinder and slave cylinder can be done without removing the transmission and is, in fact, fairly simple.

To replace the clutch disc, pressure plate, flywheel, throwout bearing and pilot bearing, the transmission must be removed. Since the transmission is a very heavy, unwieldy unit (especially on 4WD and automatic transmission models), removing it is pretty difficult without a hoist to lift the truck off the ground. It's not an impossible task, but not a particularly pleasant experience either. Instructions for removal and installation of manual transmissions is in Procedure 8. I consider it a Phase 2 procedure, which means it's more difficult than most procedures in this manual, so be sure to read through the entire procedure before attempting it.

AUTOMATIC TRANSMISSION

Trucks with automatic transmissions have a fluid-filled **torque converter** linking the engine to the transmission. The fluid, rather than mechanical, connection is the key to the torque converter's magical ability to let the engine idle while the transmission is in gear. The torque converter is like a large donut filled with transmission fluid. Inside, a "shell" with vanes like a windmill turns around, forcing the fluid to operate another shell with vanes. (Blow against a child's pinwheel with an electric fan, and you'll get the idea.) The outer shell of the torque converter is attached to the engine crankshaft via a **torque plate**, and the inner part of the torque converter is connected to a splined **transmission shaft**. When the engine speed increases, the fluid around the vanes of the outer shell of the torque converter moves, causing the inner part to turn the transmission gears.

Due to critical adjustments required on automatic transmissions, I haven't included their removal and installation in this manual. Take it to the Toyota dealer or an automatic transmission shop.

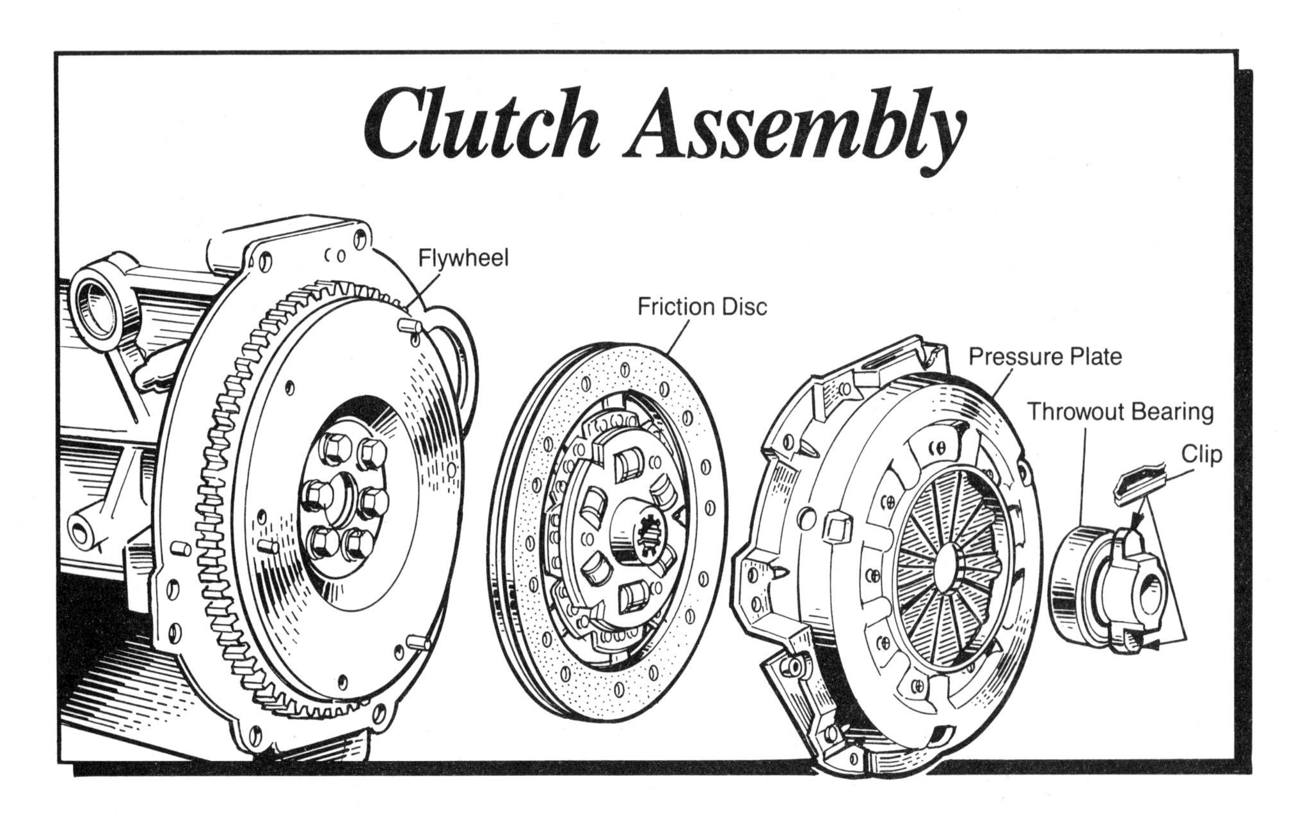

MANUAL TRANSMISSION

I'm not going to go into the complexities of transmissions in this book. Suffice it to say, you've got a number of movable gears in there of different sizes. When you move the shift lever, you engage gears of different sizes. You convert the revolutions of the engine into different ratios of speed (five in a five-speed, plus reverse) depending on the power and speed needs of the car.

On some models a round **companion flange** is attached to the rear end of the transmission main shaft, which sticks out the back end of the transmission. On other models a splined **sleeve yoke** fits into the rear end of the transmission and meshes with splines on the rear end of the transmission main shaft.

If there's a problem with your manual transmission, specialized tools (hydraulic press, transmission jigs, special wrenches, etc.) are required to repair the inner workings, so it's really beyond our means.

When transmission problems develop, I suggest taking the truck to Toyota or a transmission shop for repair. The money you save by wrestling it out and in probably wouldn't be worth the effort involved. Buying a used transmission from a salvage yard and installing it yourself might save you enough money to make it worth your while. But, whether you have your transmission rebuilt or you buy a used one, be sure it comes with a written guarantee that covers the parts and the labor charges for removing and installing it again if it's defective.

Since the truck must be raised as high as possible, don't even think about removing and installing the transmission yourself unless you have a hydraulic floor jack, two good jackstands and a paved surface to work on. A lot of wiggling, prying, jostling and swearing goes on, and unless the truck is securely braced a bad accident could happen.

4WD TRANSFER CASE

On 4WD models a **transfer case** is attached to the right rear side of the transmission. The transfer case contains gears similar to those in the transmission. When the 4WD selector lever is in the 4WD position, the gears in the transfer case are linked to the gears in the transmission.

DRIVESHAFTS

A long hollow steel **driveshaft** (also called a *propeller shaft*) with **universal joints** (U-joints) on each end connects the rear end of the transmission to the **rear differential**.

There are two different types of rear driveshafts on Toyota trucks. All short bed models, and all 4WD models except '84-'86 long bed 4WD models, have a **one piece driveshaft** that connects the rear end of the transmission directly to the front end of the differential. All long bed 2WD models and '84-'86 long bed 4WD models have **two piece driveshafts**. On two piece driveshafts there are two separate driveshafts attached end to end between the transmission and differential. The rear driveshaft is understandably called the **rear driveshaft**, but the front driveshaft (for some reason) is called the **intermediate shaft**. The two shafts are supported where they connect by a **center support bearing** (center bearing, carrier bearing).

A **universal joint** (U-joint) on the end of each driveshaft provides flexibility that enables the driveshaft to turn while the differential moves up and down. The X-shaped U-joints are mounted between **end yokes** that are welded to the ends of the driveshaft and either a **sleeve yoke** or **flange yoke**.

'75-'78 long bed models and all 4WD models: The front end of the driveshaft is attached to a **companion flange** on the rear end of the transmission.

'75-'78 short bed models and all '79-'87 2WD models: A **sleeve yoke** on the front end of the driveshaft slips into the rear end of the transmission. An **oil seal** in the transmission prevents transmission oil from leaking out around the sleeve yoke.

4WD models: A short driveshaft, which I'll call the **4WD driveshaft**, connects the front of the transfer case to the front differential. The 4WD driveshaft has a **U-joint** and **flange yoke** on the front end and a **double Cardan joint** and **flange yoke** on the rear end. A double Cardan joint consists of two U-joints mounted in a steel case. Unfortunately when the double Cardan joint wears out you have to replace the whole driveshaft.

The U-joints and double Cardan joint provide flexibility in the driveshafts so they can move up and down while being turned by the engine. More about U-joints—how they work, how to check them and how to lubricate them—is in Chapter 5, Procedure 3, Step 9. Removing the driveshafts for U-joint replacement is easy. See Procedure 6.

REAR AXLES

Splined ends on the inboard end of the **rear axle shafts** mesh with splines in the **differential gear assembly**. The rear wheels attach to the outboard ends of the axles. How to remove and install the rear axles is covered in Procedures 4 and 5.

THE DIFFERENTIAL

The rear differential gear assembly (also called the differential carrier assembly or just the differential) is located midway between the rear wheels in the large differential housing (also called the pumpkin or third member).

In my humble opinion the differential assembly is one of the all-time niftiest mechanical inventions. Here's why. Power from the engine is delivered to the **drive pinion shaft** in the differential by the driveshaft. The differential divides the power equally for delivery to the two rear wheels on all models, and to the two front wheels on 4WD models when the 4WD is engaged. A **worm gear** on the end of the drive pinion shaft meshes with a large **ring gear** inside the differential. The ring gear in turn meshes with gears connected to the two axles, which run out to the left and right wheels. The differential's magic is in how it delegates the power to the two driving wheels.

As the truck goes around a corner, the outside wheel has to travel further than the inside wheel, right? If the axle was one piece with no differential, the inside wheel would drag slightly and wear out the tire very quickly. But the ring and pinion gears work in conjunction with small **spider gears** so the two drive wheels can rotate at different speeds while maintaining about equal driving power. Amazing, eh?

4WD Front differential: On 1979-85 4WD models, the front differential is essentially the same as the rear differential. In 1986, Toyota changed the front differential to a flexible axle setup that has two short axles sticking out the sides of the differential gear assembly. **Axle shafts** with **inboard joint tulips** (tulips) on the inboard ends and **Constant Velocity Joints** (CVJs) on the outboard end connect the differential to the front wheels. How to check and repair the front axle shafts is in Chapter 12.

As long as they are kept full of fresh gear oil, differentials are unlikely to ever cause problems. I have included a procedure for removing the differential gears, mainly so you can change to a limited slip differential, which will give your truck more traction than the original differential (Procedure 7). There's more about these traction improvers in Chapter 14.

The rear differential carrier assembly on all models and the front differential carrier assembly on '79-'85 4WD models can be removed easily for repair or replacement without removing the entire differential housing (Procedure 7). The front differential on '86-'87 4WD models is a much more difficult unit to deal with, so have the professionals repair or replace it for you.

PROCEDURE 1: CHECK AND ADJUST CLUTCH PEDAL

Condition: Routine maintenance; OR you were directed here by the clutch troubleshooting guide in Chapter 4.

Tools and Materials: Ruler or tape measure, 10mm and 14mm wrenches, pliers or Vise Grips, maybe a Friend.

Step 1. Check and Adjust Clutch "Free Play."

Set your ruler or tape measure perpendicular to the clutch pedal pad so you can measure how far the clutch pedal moves toward the floorboard before resistance is felt. Push lightly on the pedal with a fingertip until you feel a very slight increase in resistance. The pedal should move slightly but not more than ¼" before you feel resistance. The distance, called the **pushrod freeplay**, is necessary to be sure the clutch pushrod is not constantly in contact with the piston in the master cylinder. Look at the Pushrod Free Play Table to see if the adjustment is correct. If it isn't, loosen the locknut on the clutch pushrod with a wrench, then use pliers to screw the rod in or out until the pushrod free play is correct. Tighten the locknut.

Push further on the pedal until you just start to feel a significant increase in resistance. Eyeball your tape or ruler. This distance is the **pedal free play**. Look at the Pedal Freeplay Table to see if the adjustment is correct.

If the pedal moves more or less than the figures given in the foreplay. . .I mean, Free Play Table before resistance is felt, something is out of whack. 1975-78 models and 1979-80 4WD models should do Step 2 to check and adjust the clutch release fork. 1979-87 2WD models and 1981-87 4WD models should do Procedure 2 to bleed the clutch system.

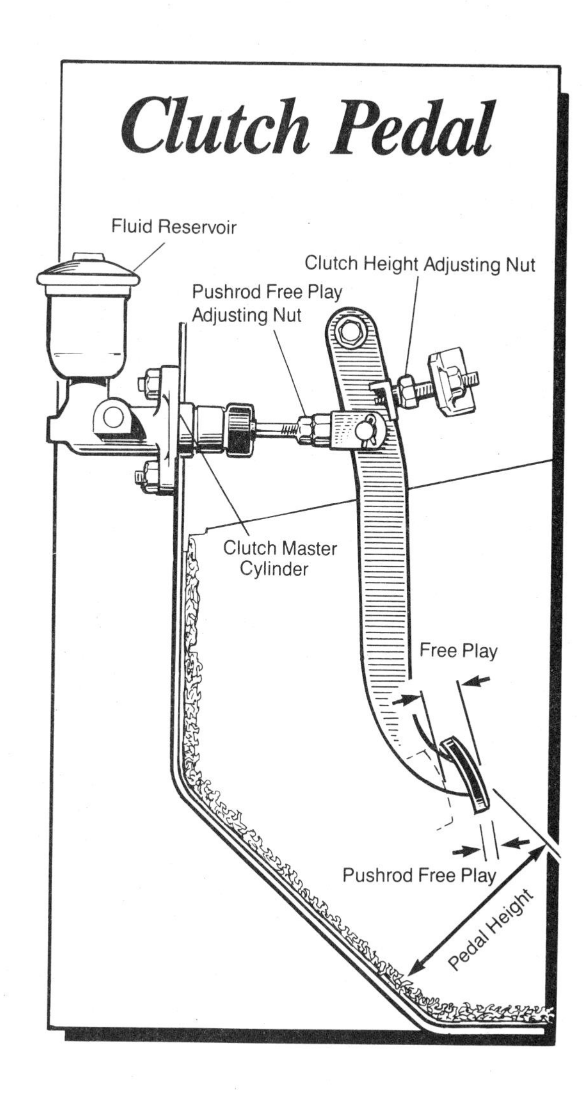

CLUTCH SPECIFICATIONS

Pushrod Free Play		
1975-78	.20"	5mm
1979-87	.04-.20"	1-5mm
Pedal Free Play		
1975-78	1-1.7"	25-45mm
1979-87 2WD	3/16-5/8"	5-15mm
1979-80 4WD	1-1-3/4"	25-45mm
1981-87 4WD	3/16-5/8"	5-15mm

Step 2. Check and Adjust Clutch Fork Free Play.

This step is only for '75-'78 2WD and '79-'80 4WD models.

If you're not sure where the clutch slave cylinder is located, have Friend press and release the clutch pedal while you crawl under the right side of the truck and watch for movement. You'll see a **pushrod** in the **slave cylinder** pushing on the **clutch release fork** on the side of the transmission bell housing. A **spring** with hooked ends is attached between

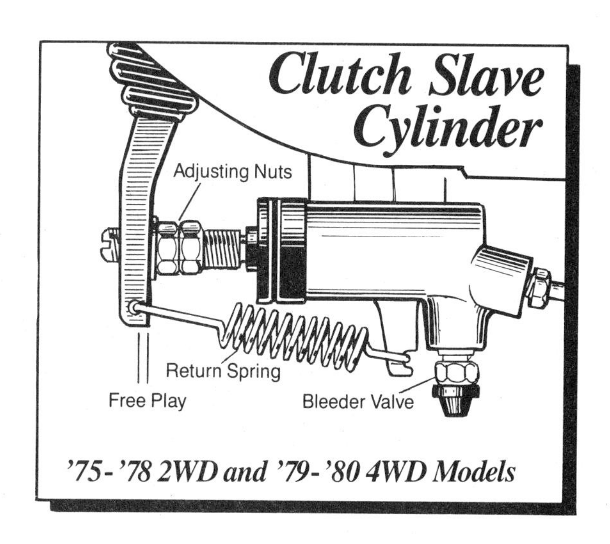

'75-'78 2WD and '79-'80 4WD Models

the fork and slave cylinder. Unhook one end of the spring, then measure the distance the clutch release fork can be pulled away from the end of the pushrod. The distance should be between 5/64" and 1/8". In other words, if there's a slight gap, no adjustment is necessary. Reconnect the spring and you're finished. If there is a large gap, or no gap at all, here's how to adjust the clutch release fork free play:

There are two nuts on the pushrod right next to the release fork. The nut farthest from the release fork is a locknut to hold the other nut and the pushrod in position. Loosen the locknut, then use a wrench to hold the other nut while you use a screwdriver in the end of the pushrod to screw it in or out of the nut until the adjustment is correct. Tighten the locknut against the other nut. Reconnect the spring between the fork and slave cylinder. If the spring is missing, replace it with a new one.

PROCEDURE 2: BLEED HYDRAULIC CLUTCH SYSTEM

Bleeding the clutch system is essentially the same as bleeding the brake system. To find out how to bleed a hydraulic system, please read through Chapter 7, Procedure 1, before bleeding the clutch system.

If you are here to change the clutch fluid, start with Step 2, then do Step 1.

Condition: There's little or no resistance on the clutch pedal; OR the clutch has to be pumped several times before you can shift gears; OR the clutch master or slave cylinder has been disconnected or removed; OR the clutch fluid in the clutch fluid reservoir disappeared.

Tools and Materials: 10mm box end wrench, glass jar, about 18 inches of 3/16in inside diameter clear plastic tubing, Friend.

Step 1. Bleed Clutch System.

Fill the clutch fluid reservoir with fresh DOT3 or 4 brake fluid.

Crawl under the right side of the truck and locate the clutch slave cylinder. It's bolted to the right side of the transmission bell housing, just to the rear of the starter. Find the bleeder valve on the slave cylinder and remove the rubber cap, if there is one. Fit a 10mm box end wrench onto the bleeder valve, then slip one end of your clear plastic tubing onto the valve nipple. Have Friend slowly pump the clutch pedal a few times, then hold the pedal to the floor. When Friend yells that the pedal is down, you open the bleeder valve at least a quarter of a turn. You'll see fluid and maybe bubbles rushing through the clear plastic tube. When fluid stops coming out of the slave cylinder, tighten the bleeder valve. Friend can let the pedal up now. Have Friend pump again and hold the pedal down while you open and close the bleeder valve. Repeat this until there are no bubbles in the clear plastic tubing, or until the fluid is clean and clear if you're replacing the fluid.

When the clutch has been bled, be sure the bleeder valve is tight and the rubber cap is installed, if you have one. Fill the clutch reservoir with fresh fluid to the MAX line or to the dotted line below the MAX line.

Step 2. Replace Hydraulic Clutch Fluid.

If you are here to change the fluid, use a baster or syringe to suck the old fluid out of the reservoir, then fill the reservoir with fresh brake fluid. Go through the bleeding steps described in Step 1 and keep bleeding until the fluid in the clear plastic tube is clean and fresh looking.

PROCEDURE 3: REMOVE, REBUILD, INSTALL CLUTCH MASTER CYLINDER AND/OR SLAVE CYLINDER

Condition: Clutch pedal offers little or no resistance and shifting gears is more difficult than forgetting Nixon's face; OR you have to pump the clutch pedal several times in order to shift gears; OR you've noticed brake fluid leaking out of the clutch master or slave cylinder; OR the slave cylinder is being removed for transmission removal.

Tools and Materials: 10mm flare nut wrench, 12mm socket, ratchet and extension, small screwdriver, medium screwdriver, pliers, flashlight or drop light, rags, brake grease or lithium soap base glycol grease, pint of DOT3 or 4 brake fluid, fine steel wool, rubbing or denatured alcohol, solvent, carburetor or brake cleaner, safety glasses, maybe master cylinder or slave cylinder rebuild kit or new master or slave cylinder.

Step 1. Remove Clutch Master Cylinder.

Peek up under the dash so you can see where the clutch pedal is connected to the pencil-size master cylinder pushrod. The U-shaped clevis on the rear end of the pushrod is attached to the clutch pedal with a clevis pin. Use pliers to remove the cotter pin or hairpin-type clip in the end of the clevis pin, then slide the clevis pin out of the clevis. Crawl out from under the dash and give your back a rest.

Working in the engine compartment, use a 10mm flare nut wrench to unscrew the union fitting that attaches the metal line to the clutch master cylinder. Use a 12mm socket, ratchet and ratchet extension to remove the two 12mm nuts that attach the master cylinder to the firewall. Gently pull the metal line away from the master cylinder just far enough so you can remove the cylinder.

Step 2. Remove Clutch Slave Cylinder.

Use a 10mm flare nut wrench to unscrew the nut that attaches the metal line to the slave cylinder. If there's a spring connecting the slave cylinder to the end of the clutch release fork, use pliers to unhook the spring.

Now remove the two 12mm bolts that attach the slave cylinder to the transmission bell housing. Pull the slave cylinder off the bell housing.

Step 3. Clean and Inspect Inside of Clutch Master or Slave Cylinder.

Before disassembling the master or slave cylinder, clean the outside with solvent, carburetor cleaner or brake cleaner.

Master cylinder: Use a socket and extension to remove the bolt in the bottom of the reservoir, then pull the reservoir off the master cylinder.

Pull the rubber boot off the rear end of the master cylinder, then insert a small screwdriver between the end of the cylinder and the snap ring that fits in a groove on the inside of the cylinder. Hold a finger over the end of the master cylinder while you pry the snap ring out of its groove. The finger will prevent the snap ring from flying off and smacking you in the face. Now you can remove the snap ring, the push rod and the large washer that's on the push rod.

Slave cylinder: Pull the rubber boot off the end of the cylinder. The push rod will come off with the boot.

EVERYONE: Tap the mounting ear of the cylinder on a block of wood to jar the piston out of the cylinder. If the piston refuses to come out, you'll have to take the cylinder to a service station and have them blow compressed air into the hole where the fluid line was connected to pop the piston out.

Once the piston is out, use fresh brake fluid and a rag to clean the inside of the cylinder. Look inside the cylinder for scratches or corroded areas. Very light scratches can probably be buffed out with steel wool, but deep scratches mean the cylinder should be replaced. If you see any dark spots or corroded areas, use a small screwdriver to probe the areas to see if they are small pits. If you find any pits the cylinder must be replaced. The pits, caused by water and crud in the fluid, are probably the reason you're messing with the cylinder.

If the cylinder looks OK, dip a piece of steel wool in alcohol and push it into the wheel cylinder. Stick a screwdriver into the center of the steel wool and twist it around and around so the steel wool tangles with the screwdriver—but don't let the blade touch the side of the cylinder. Put a good shine on the inside of the cylinder. Don't push the steel wool backward and forward—only 'round and 'round until the cylinder is nice and smooth.

When the cylinder is clean, inspect it for scratches and corrosion pits again. If the inside of the cylinder is nice and smooth, you can rebuild the cylinder. If there's any doubt, replace the cylinder.

Step 4. Rebuild Master or Slave Cylinder.

Look at the piston to see how the little lip on the rubber cups point toward one of the ends. Remember how they are pointed so you can install the new cups exactly the same way.

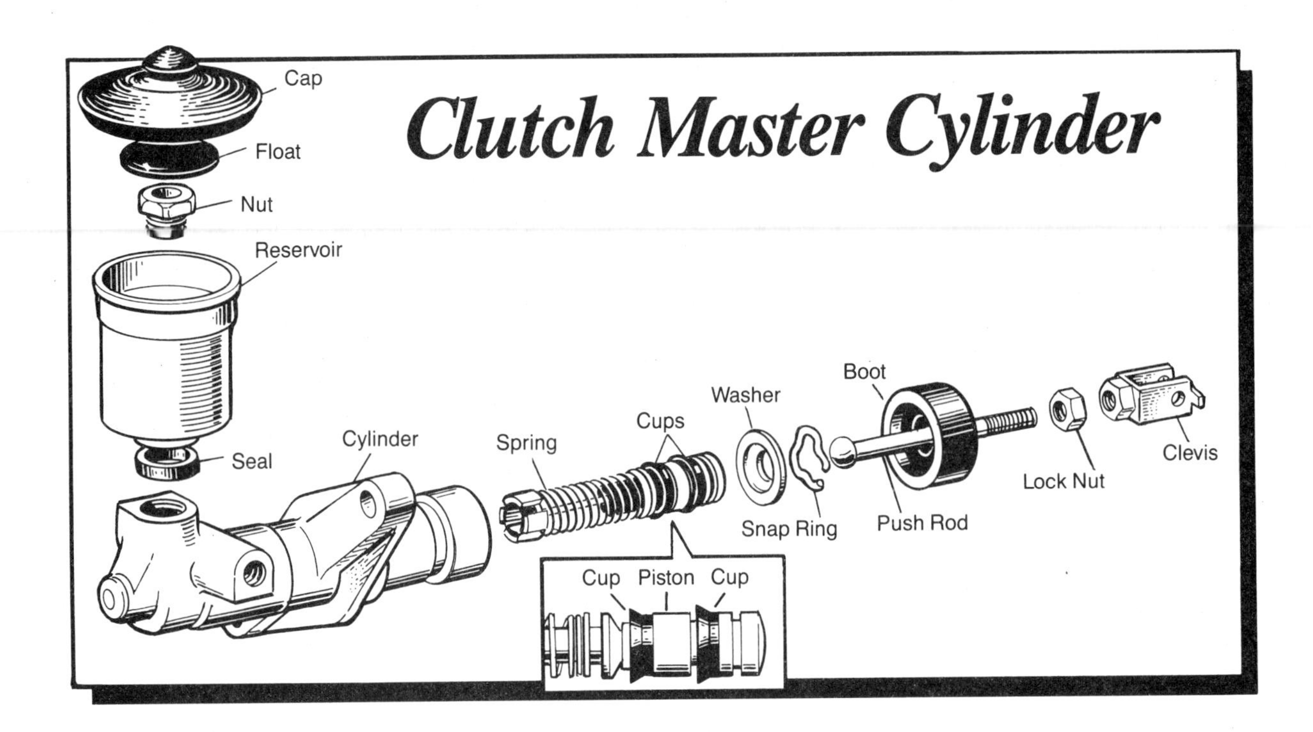

Remove the old, tired rubber cups from the end of the piston. If one of the cups is slightly larger than the other one, make a note which cup goes where so you can install the new cups in the proper place during reassembly. Pry them off with a small screwdriver, being careful to avoid scratching the piston. Clean the piston with the steel wool and alcohol. Dry the pistons thoroughly with a clean rag or paper towel, then blow into the cylinder to remove traces of the steel wool. Wipe out the cylinder with another clean rag or paper towel to remove any moisture that your hot little breath might have left in there.

Wash your hands thoroughly to remove any traces of grease. Break out your can of brake fluid and pour a little in a clean container. Dip a corner of a clean rag or your forefinger in the brake fluid and thoroughly swab out the inside of the cylinder.

Take the cylinder rebuild kit out of the box and put the two round rubber cups and the clean piston in the container with brake fluid. Don't soak the large end boot. After the parts have soaked for a few minutes, take them out of the brake fluid and lay them on a clean rag or paper towel.

Master cylinder: Slide one of the rubber cups onto the end of the piston so the lip points toward the spring. Wiggle the cup into the groove closest to the spring. Install the other cup the same way into the groove closest to the end of the piston. If your rebuild kit has a small packet of grease, coat the rubber cups, the area under the lips, the tiny groove near the end of the piston and the end where the push rod fits with the grease. If the packet didn't come with grease, use lithium soap base glycol grease or brake grease to lubricate the cups and piston. If you don't have any grease, just be sure the piston and cups are thoroughly covered with brake fluid.

Set the front end of the cylinder on a block of wood or table top and insert the end of the piston without rubber cups into the cylinder. When the cups reach the cylinder you'll have to wiggle the piston while pushing it into the cylinder. Hold the piston in the cylinder while you fit the push rod and large washer into the cylinder. Push down on the push rod while you fit one side of the snap ring into its groove. Use a screwdriver to pry the rest of the snap ring into the groove. Fit the rubber boot onto the end of the master cylinder. Now go to Step 5 to install the master cylinder.

Slave cylinder: Look closely at the two rubber cups. One is slightly smaller than the other. Carefully install the smaller cup onto the piston so the little lip faces toward the pushrod end. Now install the larger cup so the lip faces away from the pushrod end. Look at the illustration. If the rebuild kit has a little packet of grease, smear the grease all over the piston, under the lips of the cups, and in the end where the push rod fits. If the packet didn't come with grease, use lithium soap base glycol grease or brake grease to lubricate the cups and piston.

If you don't have any grease, just be sure the piston and cups are thoroughly covered with brake fluid.

If there was a small spring in your slave cylinder, fit the small end of the spring onto the small nub on the end of the piston.

Wiggle the piston into the cylinder. Fit the rubber boot onto the end of the cylinder. The push rod has a groove where the boot fits. Insert the longer end of the push rod into the boot so the boot fits into the groove on the push rod. Now go to Step 6 to install the slave cylinder.

Step 5. Install Clutch Master Cylinder.

Gently pull the metal line out of the way while you fit the master cylinder onto the two mounting studs on the firewall. Fit the line into the cylinder and screw the nut in several turns by hand. It helps to wiggle the cylinder a little while screwing the nut in. Be sure it's going in straight.

Install and tighten the two 12mm nuts that secure the cylinder to the firewall, then use the flare nut wrench to tighten the nut on the metal line.

Creep back under the dash and get ready to connect the clevis to the clutch pedal. Fit the U-shaped clevis onto the clutch pedal, align the holes, then slip the clevis pin through the holes. Install the hairpin clip or cotter pin into the end of the clevis pin. If you have a cotter pin, bend the ends around the pin. Be sure to bleed the clutch system (Procedure 2), then check the pushrod freeplay (Procedure 1).

Step 6. Install Clutch Slave Cylinder.

Hold the slave cylinder in its installed position while you carefully screw the nut on the metal line into the cylinder several turns with your fingers. When you are sure the nut has started straight, install and tighten the two slave cylinder mounting bolts. Use the flare nut wrench to tighten the fluid line nut. If your model had a spring between the cylinder and clutch release fork, use pliers to install the spring.

Be sure to bleed the clutch system (Procedure 2).

'75-'78 models and '79-'80 4WD models: Check and adjust the clutch fork free play (Procedure 1, Step 2).

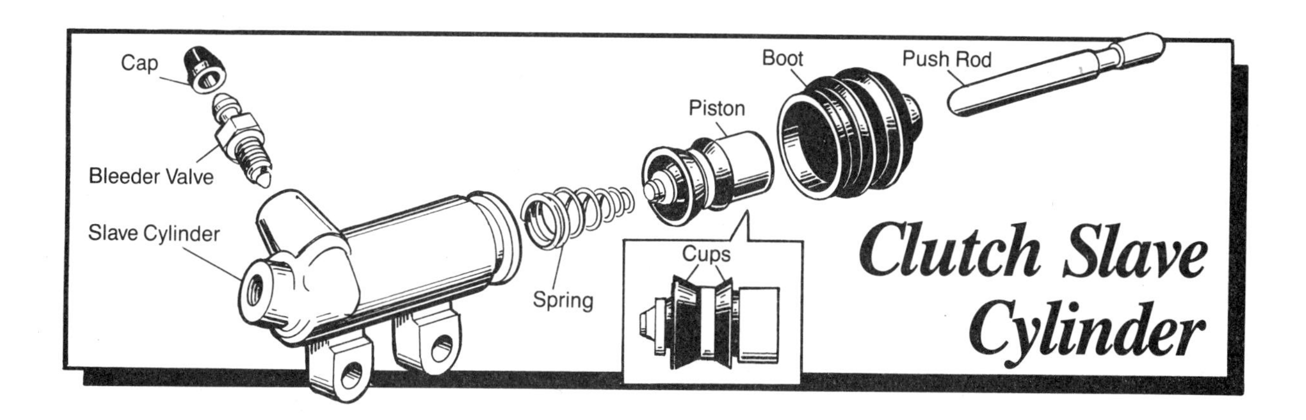

PROCEDURE 4: REMOVE AND INSTALL REAR AXLE, REAR AXLE BEARINGS AND REAR AXLE OIL SEALS (EXCEPT '86-'87 MODELS WITH DUAL REAR WHEELS)

Since several special tools are required to remove the rear axle hubs on 1986 and 1987 models with dual rear wheels, you'll have to take your "dualie" to the Toyota dealer or a garage that specializes in Toyotas and have them replace the rear axle bearings and oil seals. Removal and installation of the rear axles on these models is covered in Procedure 5.

Condition: Rear wheel bearing or oil seal is worn out; OR you're removing the differential gears; OR rear axle is broken.

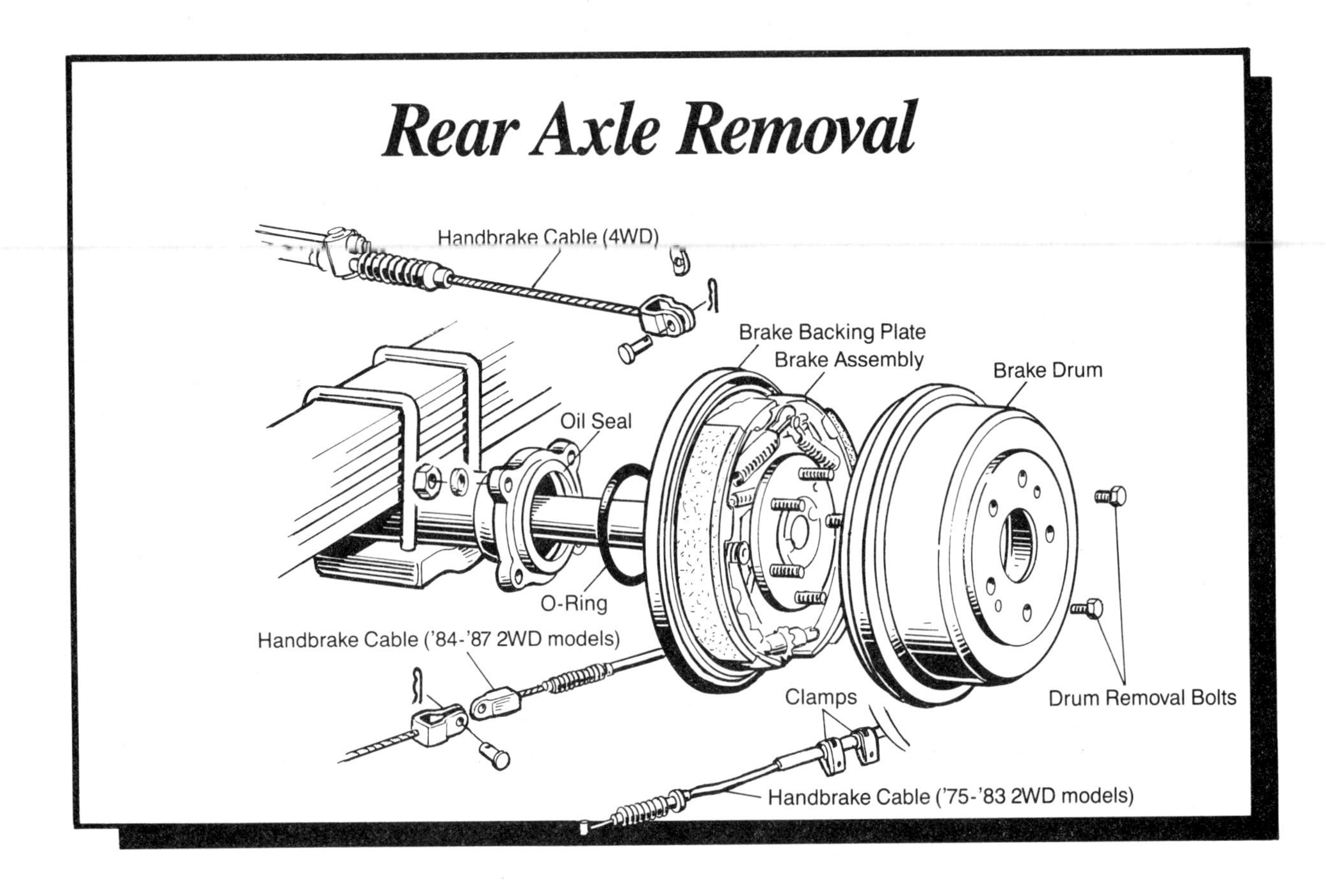

Tools and Materials: Jack, jackstands, medium phillips and regular screwdrivers, 12mm wrench, 14mm box end wrench, 24mm socket, ratchet, 10mm flare nut wrench, rags, brake bleeding tools listed in Chapter 7, Procedure 1, maybe some or all of the following: new wheel bearing, axle, oil seal, O-ring, marking pen, large screwdriver or seal puller, multi-purpose grease, gear oil.

Remark: If a rear wheel bearing or outer oil seal is worn out you can remove the axle, then take it to Toyota or a machine shop to have the old bearing pressed off and the new bearing pressed on.

Step 1. Drain Differential Oil.

See Chapter 5, Procedure 15, Step 6, to drain the differential oil. If you are only removing one axle, you can block the truck so the side you are working on is higher than the other and you won't have to drain the oil.

Step 2. Chock, Jack, Block and Remove Rear Wheel(s) and Brake Drum(s).

Loosen the rear lug nuts, then jack up the rear of the truck and put it on jackstands. Remove the rear wheels.

If there's a screw on the outboard side of the brake drum, remove it, then pull the drum off the axle. If the drum doesn't come off easily, see Chapter 7, Procedure 6, Step 2.

Step 3. Disconnect Parking Brake Cable.

4WD models: Locate the U-shaped clevis that connects the parking brake cable to the bell crank lever on the inboard side of the brake backing plate. Use pliers to remove the cotter pin that secures the clevis pin, then pull the pin out of the clevis. Tuck the handbrake cable out of the way.

2WD models: There are two ways to accomplish the divorce. . . I mean separation. You can either disconnect the rear end of the cable from the brake backing plate, which entails removing the brake shoes, or you can leave the cable attached to the backing plate and remove the entire cable from the truck.

I prefer removing the brake shoes (which prevents them from accidentally getting contaminated with oil), then disconnecting the cable from the brake backing plate so the long cable isn't following the axle around getting in the way. Also, there's less crawling around under the truck this way. The Toyota manuals recommend removing the cable from the truck. I've included instructions for doing it both ways.

Disconnect parking brake cable from brake backing plate: To see how to remove the rear brake shoes, see Chapter 7, Procedure 8, for '75-'78 models, '79-'85 4WD models and Cab and Chassis models, or Procedure 9 for '79-'87 2WD models (except C&C), and '86-'87 4WD models. Stash the shoes where they won't get oily or greasy.

2WD models: Once the shoes are off, locate the two bolts that attach the parking brake cable to the brake backing plate. Remove the bolts, then wiggle the cable out of the backing plate. Tuck it away from the end of the differential so it's out of the way.

Remove parking brake cable on 2WD models: Follow the stiff cable going forward out of the brake backing plate and remove the 12mm bolts and clamps that attach it to the frame. You'll come to a place where the cable is attached with a U-shaped spring clip. Use pliers to wiggle the spring clip off the cable. Now, to disconnect the front of the cable from the equalizer bar, pull the cable forward and the equalizer bar rearward so you can slide the cable up through the slot in the top part of the equalizer bar. See Chapter 7, Procedure 16, Step 3, if you need further instructions on removing the parking brake cable.

'84-'87 2WD models: Follow the stiff parking brake cable forward from where it attaches to the brake backing plate. You'll come to a U-shaped clevis. Use pliers to remove the cotter pin that secures the pin in the clevis, then pull the pin out.

Step 4. Disconnect Brake Line.

Use a 10mm flare nut wrench to disconnect the brake line from the wheel cylinder at the top of the brake backing plate. Unscrew the nut all the way but don't pull the brake line out of the wheel cylinder.

Step 5. Remove Backing Plate Nuts.

Use a 14mm box end wrench or socket and ratchet to remove the four nuts that attach the brake backing plate to the end of the differential housing.

Step 6. Remove Axle.

Pull the backing plate and axle out of the differential housing a few inches. You'll see the inner oil seal in the end of the differential housing. Now pull the axle out of the differential housing being very careful not to damage the inner oil seal, unless you're here to replace it anyway.

Remove the rubber O-ring that fits on the end of the differential housing.

If you are removing both axles, use an indelible pen or paint to mark them "left" and "right" so you won't get them confused during installation.

If you're here to replace the wheel bearing or one of the oil seals, see the next step.

If you are removing the axles so you can remove the differential gears, lay the axles and backing plates somewhere safe where they won't get stepped on. Be careful that no oil gets spilled on the brake shoes, if they are still on the backing plate.

Step 7. Replace Wheel Bearing, Inner and Outer Oil Seals.

If you are here to replace the wheel bearing and/or the outer oil seal, take the axle to the Toyota dealer or a machine shop and have them remove the snap ring, then press the backing plate off the axle and remove the old bearing and outer oil seal.

While the bearing and seal are removed, have the dealer or shop check the bearing case for wear or damage. If necessary, the bearing case can be replaced by screwing nuts on the four bolts until they are flush with the ends of the bolts, then tapping the bolts out of the backing plate. When installing a new bearing case, be sure to install the two longer bolts in the two upper bolt holes and the two shorter bolts in the bottom holes. The top surface of the bearing case is flat and the other three sides are slightly rounded.

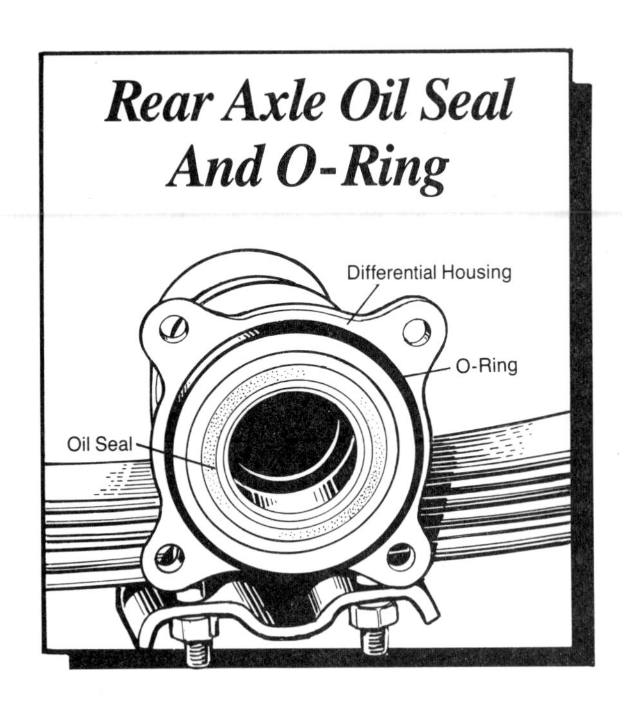

If the bearing case is OK, or once it has been replaced, have a new bearing and outer oil seal installed in the backing plate, then press the backing plate onto the axle.

If you are here to replace the inner seal, use a seal puller or large screwdriver to pry the seal out of the end of the differential housing. Use a clean rag to clean the surface where the seal fits, then push a new seal into the differential housing. The flat side of the seal goes toward the outside. Use the blunt end of a ratchet extension and a hammer to tap around the outer edge of the seal until it's fully seated. Once the seal is in, smear multi-purpose grease on the little rubber seal lips.

Step 8. Install Rear Axle.

Install a new O-ring around the inner oil seal case. Slide the axle into the differential housing, being very careful not to damage the inner oil seal or the oil deflector that's inside the differential housing. You'll have to rotate the end of the axle a little to get the splines to engage in the differential. Fit the brake line into the wheel cylinder as you wiggle the four bolts through the holes in the differential housing, then install and tighten the four nuts to 51 ft.lbs.

Tighten the brake line nut with your fingers until you're absolutely certain it's going in straight, then tighten the nut with the flare nut wrench.

'75-'83 2WD models: If you disconnected the parking brake cable from the brake backing plate, wiggle the cable end into position, then install and tighten the two mounting bolts.

EVERYONE: Install the brake shoes if you removed them (Chapter 7).

'84-'87 2WD and all 4WD models: Now reconnect the clevis to the bell crank (4WD) or parking brake cable (2WD). Use a new cotter pin and wrap the ends around the clevis pin.

'75-'83 2WD models: If you removed the parking brake cable, reattach it to the frame with the clamps and bolts, then fit the end of the cable into the equalizer bar.

EVERYONE: Install the brake drum and brake drum screw, if you have one. Install the wheel and snug the lug nuts with the lug wrench.

Bleed the brake system (Chapter 7, Procedure 1). This is critical, so don't forget it.

After the brakes have been bled, lower the truck off the jackstands and torque the lug nuts to 65-87 ft.lbs. Install the differential drain plug, then fill the differential with fresh gear oil if you drained it.

PROCEDURE 5: REMOVE AND INSTALL REAR AXLES AND REPLACE OUTER OIL SEAL ON 1986-87 TRUCKS WITH DUAL REAR WHEELS

Condition: You want or need to replace the differential carrier assembly, OR the outer oil seal is leaking.

Tools and Materials: Phase 1 tool kit, jack and jackstands, two 8x1.25mm bolts at least a couple of inches long, new axle gaskets, silicone gasket sealer, a new outer oil seal if yours is leaking.

Step 1. Remove Axle.

Set the parking brake, chock the front wheels, then jack up the rear of the truck and put it on jackstands. Remove the six nuts and washers around the outer edge of the axle. Install two 8x1.25 bolts into the threaded holes in the axle and tighten the bolts one full turn. Tap on the end of the axle with a hammer to free the little cone washers that are around the six mounting studs. Tighten the two bolts until you can pull the axle out of the hub. Support the weight of the axle as you pull it out so the oil seals aren't damaged. Remove the two bolts.

Step 2. Replace Outer Oil Seal.

The outer oil seal is just inside the hub opening. Use a small puller or large screwdriver to pry the old seal out of the hub, then use a clean rag to clean the oil seal mounting surface inside the hub. Fit the new seal into position with the flat side out and push it into the hub. Use the blunt end of a ratchet extension and hammer to evenly tap around the outer edge of the seal until it's fully seated in the hub.

Step 3. Install Axle.

Scrape all traces of the old gasket from the mating surfaces of the hub and axle. Smear a light coat of silicone sealer on the new gasket, then fit it onto the six studs on the hub.

Smear some multipurpose grease on the lips of the oil seal, then carefully insert the axle into the hub so it doesn't damage the oil seal. You'll have to turn the axle back and forth until the splines on the end engage with the splines in the differential. Wiggle the axle onto the mounting studs, then install the cone washers, lockwashers and nuts. Tighten the nuts to 25 ft.lbs.

Lower the truck off the jackstands.

PROCEDURE 6: CHECK U-JOINTS AND DRIVESHAFTS, REMOVE AND INSTALL DRIVESHAFTS

Read the rap at the beginning of this chapter to see which type driveshaft you have.

All models have a long, black **driveshaft tube** connecting the rear end of the transmission to the rear differential. Some long bed models have two driveshafts connected end to end, with a U-joint in the center. A carrier bearing (center bearing) supports the two shafts where they connect. A U-joint on the ends of each driveshaft allows it to rotate smoothly even though the transmission and differential aren't perfectly aligned.

Condition: Vibration that increases as the speed of the truck increases or loud clunks when taking off in FIRST or REVERSE, both indicating worn U-joints; OR the driveshaft tube is dented or bent; OR you're removing the transmission or rear differential (all models) or the front differential (4WD models).

Tools and Materials: To check the U-joints and driveshafts: flashlight or drop light, maybe jack and jackstands, chalk or marker. To remove and install the driveshafts: two 14mm wrenches, 4WD models need a 12mm socket and ratchet, rags, jack and jackstands. To remove the intermediate driveshaft on '75-'78 short bed models and '79-'87 2WD Long Bed models you'll need an oil drain pan.

Remarks: If the U-joints are worn out, remove the driveshaft and take it to the Toyota dealer or a machine shop to have new U-joints installed. If the driveshaft is bent, a machine shop can replace the tube for you, or you might find a good used driveshaft at a salvage yard. New ones are expensive.

Always mark the ends of the driveshaft and whatever it's bolted to so you can install it in the same position during reassembly.

Step 1. Chock, Jack and Block.

If your truck is 4WD, has a lift kit, or has even slightly oversize tires you probably won't need to put it on jackstands to remove the 4WD driveshaft. It all depends on the size of the spare tire around your waist. Be sure and chock the wheels and set the handbrake even if you don't jack it up. Put the gearshift lever in NEUTRAL.

OK, if there's a clearance problem between you and the bottom of the truck, set the handbrake, chock the wheels, then jack up the rear of the truck (if you're removing the rear driveshaft) or the front of the truck (if you're removing the 4WD driveshaft) and put it on jackstands. Put the transmission and transfer (4WD) gearshift levers in NEUTRAL. On 4WD models set the hubs to the unlocked position if you are removing the 4WD driveshaft.

Step 2. Check Driveshaft and U-joints.

Check U-joints: A U-joint consists of an X-shaped piece of steel called a **cross** that has four grease filled cups on the ends containing needle bearings. U-shaped pieces of steel called **yokes** are attached on opposite sides of the cross. The U-joint cups fit into holes in the ends of the yokes and are secured by C-shaped clips. As the needle bearings and bearing surfaces on the ends of the cross wear away, slack develops and the U-joint should be replaced with a new one. Fortunately, Toyota U-joints are very durable and rarely need to be replaced. If you find a worn U-joint, remove the driveshaft (Step 3) and take it to the Toyota dealer or a machine shop and have them install the new U-joint(s). U-joints should be checked regularly, and here's how you do it.

Hold the yoke on one side of the U-joint with one hand while twisting the yoke on the other side of the joint. Look for movement where the cross disappears into the cups in the yokes. If you see any movement, the U-joint is worn and should be replaced. If there's enough movement so you hear a click when twisting the yokes, install a new U-joint before driving the car! New U-joints are relatively inexpensive, but if one breaks while cruising down the road, the driveshaft will flail about under the car, damaging the yokes and other delicate things like brake lines. If the rear driveshaft U-joint breaks, the driveshaft might even fall off the truck, causing frantic havoc on a busy freeway.

Check the driveshaft tubes for dents. Even a slight dent can cause severe vibrations.

If you have a two-piece driveshaft, hold the rear shaft while you twist on the intermediate shaft. Look and feel for looseness between the two shafts. If you hear a click or feel looseness, the splines connecting the two shafts might be worn out. Also check the rubber mounting around the center bearing that supports the two shafts where they connect. It should hold the driveshafts firmly. If the rubber is torn, remove the driveshafts and have the Toyota dealer or a garage replace it for you.

OK, that concludes the tests. If you found anything amiss, see the following steps to correct the problem.

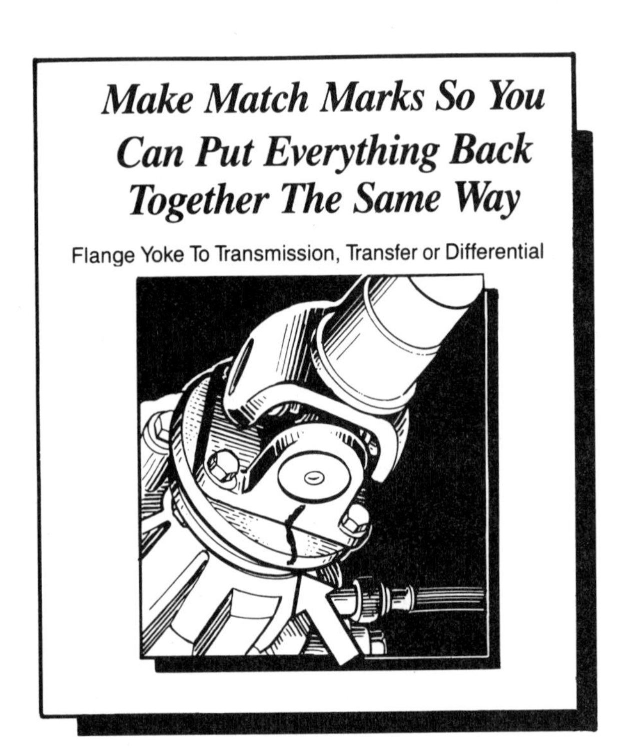

Make Match Marks So You Can Put Everything Back Together The Same Way

Flange Yoke To Transmission, Transfer or Differential

Step 3. Remove Rear and Intermediate Driveshafts.

'79-'87 2WD models: Place a catch pan below the rear end of the transmission because when the driveshaft is removed some oil might spill out.

EVERYONE: Crawl under the rear of the truck with two 14mm wrenches and chalk or a marker. The rear end of the driveshaft is bolted to a round companion flange on the differential. If you have a two-piece driveshaft, the front end of the rear shaft is attached to the rear of the intermediate shaft via a flange yoke.

To remove the rear driveshaft, locate four bolts and nuts that attach the flange yoke on the rear end of the shaft to the companion flange on the front end of the differential. Use your marker to make a line on the flange yoke and companion flange so you can bolt them back together in the same position.

Hold the bolt heads with a wrench while you remove the nuts. Rotate the flange so you can get to all four. If the transmission is in gear or you didn't jack up the rear of the truck, you won't be able to turn the driveshaft. Check the gearshift lever and/or jack up one of the rear wheels if you can't get to all four bolts and nuts. When the nuts are all removed, support the weight of the driveshaft while you remove the bolts. Then gently lower the rear end of the shaft. Don't pull the shaft toward the rear of the truck.

'79-'87 short bed 2WD models: Support the front end of the shaft and pull it straight out of the transmission. Lower it to the floor. Now you can drag it out from under the truck.

'75-'79 short bed models, '79-'83 and '87 4WD models: The front end of the driveshaft is attached to a companion flange on the transmission. It's almost exactly like the differential connection. Mark and then remove the front end of the driveshaft just as you did the rear end.

People with two-piece driveshafts: If you're removing the rear shaft of a two-piece driveshaft, mark the front flanges just as you marked the rear, then unbolt the rear shaft from the intermediate shaft and lower it to the floor.

Intermediate shaft: If you are removing the intermediate shaft, remove the two bolts that attach the center support bearing the frame. Lower the rear end of the shaft to the floor.

'79-'87 long bed 2WD models: The front end of the intermediate shaft is connected to the transmission with a sleeve yoke. Just support the weight of the front of the shaft and pull it straight out of the transmission. A little oil might leak out, so have a catch pan or pile of rags to catch it.

'75-'78 models and all 4WD models: If the front end of your intermediate shaft is attached to a flange on the transmission, mark the two flanges so you can install them in the same position, then remove the four bolts and nuts. Lower the shaft to the floor.

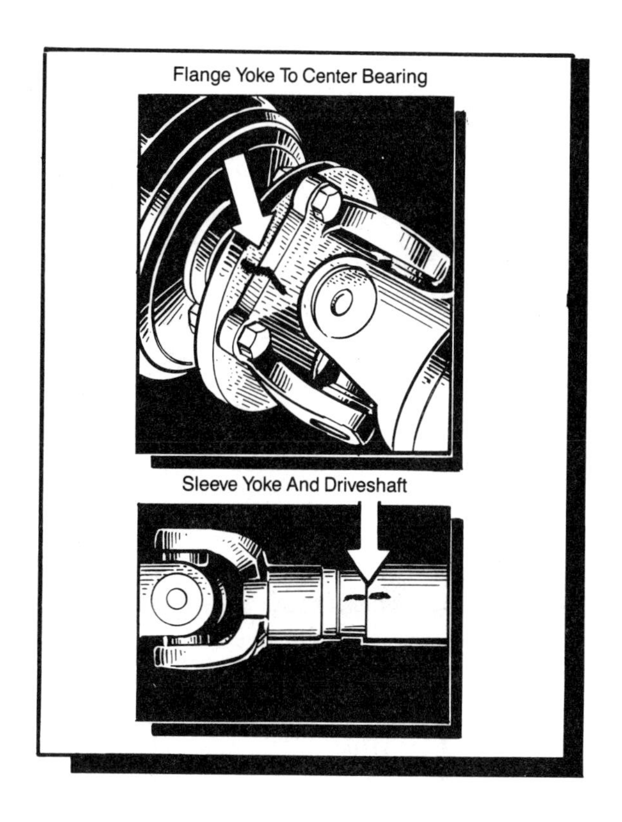

EVERYONE: If you removed the shaft for repair, haul it to Toyota or a machine shop and let them do the work. If you removed the shaft so you could remove the transmission, stand the shaft(s) upright in a corner or somewhere out of the way so they don't get stepped on.

Step 4. Install Rear and Intermediate Driveshafts.

Before installing the driveshafts, first clean the mating surfaces of the flange yokes, companion flanges, and/or the inside and outside of the sleeve yoke.

If the front of your one piece driveshaft or intermediate shaft has a sleeve yoke on the front end, align the splines in the sleeve yoke with the splines on the shaft in the transmission, then carefully slide the yoke straight into the transmission.

If the front end of your one-piece driveshaft or intermediate shaft has a flange yoke, align the marks you made on the flange yoke and transmission flange, then install and tighten the four bolts and nuts.

One piece driveshaft: Hold the rear end of the driveshaft up to the differential flange. Align the match marks you made on the flange yoke and companion flange, then reattach the rear end of the driveshaft to the

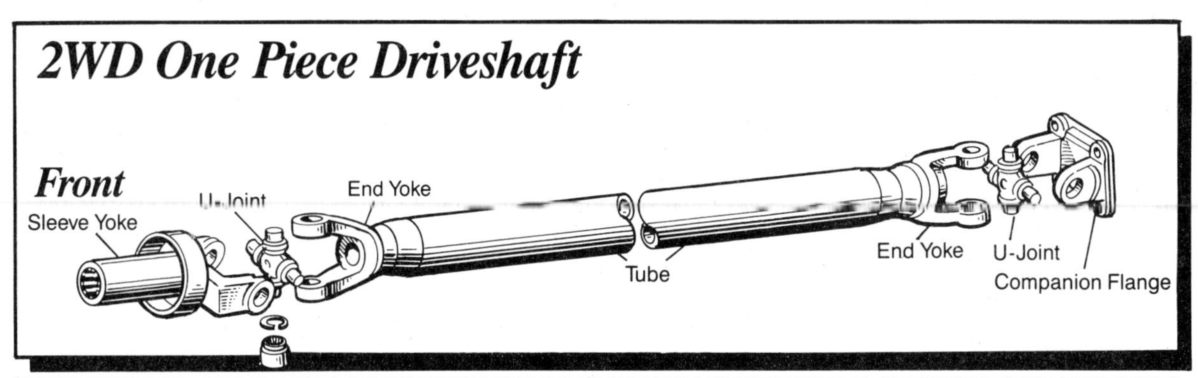

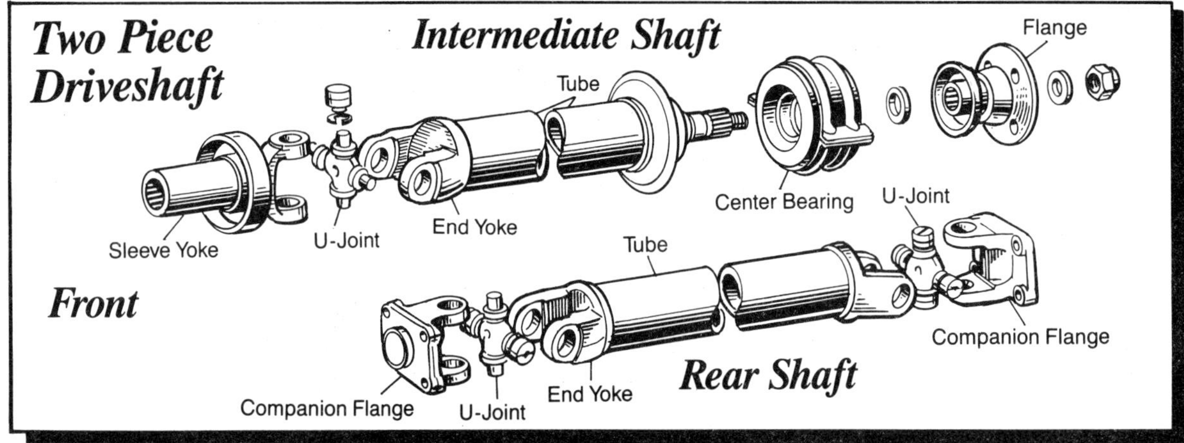

differential with the four bolts and nuts. Hold the bolt heads with one wrench while you tighten the nuts with the other wrench. That's all there is to it. Lower the truck to the ground.

Two piece driveshaft: Lift the rear end of the intermediate shaft up to the frame and hold it there while you install and tighten the two center support bearing bolts to 27 ft.lbs.

Next, align the match marks on the rear end of the intermediate shaft and front end of the rear shaft. Install and tighten the four nuts and bolts to 54 ft.lbs. If you don't have match marks because you replaced one of the driveshafts or the part that was marked, install the rear shaft so the grease zerks in the U-joints are pointed the same direction as the grease zerks in the front driveshaft. This way the zerks are all accessible without having to roll the truck forward or backward more than once.

Finally, lift up the rear end of the rear driveshaft and align the marks on the flange yoke and differential flange. Install and tighten the four bolts and nuts to 54 ft.lbs.

Step 5. Remove and Install 4WD Driveshaft.

Crawl under the right side of the truck with a piece of chalk, paint and small brush or indelible marking pen, 12mm socket and ratchet and two 14mm box end wrenches.

The double Cardan joint is protected by a shield. Remove the four 12mm bolts from the shield, then remove the bottom half of the shield. Make a mark on the flange yokes and flanges on both ends of the driveshaft. Use the two 14mm box end wrenches to remove the four bolts and nuts that attach the front end of the shaft to the differential. Gently lower the front end, then remove the four bolts that attach the double Cardan joint to the transfer case. Lower the 4WD driveshaft to the floor. Careful, it's heavier than it looks.

If you removed the driveshaft because the U-joint or double Cardan joint is worn out, take it to Toyota or a machine shop and see if they can save it. If the double Cardan joint is worn out, you'll probably have to replace the whole driveshaft. You can probably reuse the sleeve yoke and front U-joint if they are still in good condition.

To install the 4WD driveshaft, clean the mating surfaces of the flange yokes and flanges where they fit together. Hold the double Cardan end of the driveshaft in position so the match marks you made on the flanges are aligned. Install the bolts into the flanges, then install the nuts. Align the match marks for the front end of the shaft and front differential, then install the four bolts and nuts. Hold each bolt with one wrench while you tighten the nut with another wrench to 54 ft.lbs. on all models except turbos. Torque the nuts on turbo models to 61 ft.lbs. Lower the truck and you're finished.

PROCEDURE 7: REMOVE AND INSTALL REAR DIFFERENTIAL CARRIER ASSEMBLY (GEARS) ON ALL MODELS AND THE FRONT DIFFERENTIAL CARRIER ASSEMBLY ON '79-'85 4WD MODELS

Condition: Rear differential is howling like a wolf; OR gears inside the differential have broken; OR you want to change the differential gear ratio; OR you want to change to a limited slip type differential.

Tools and Materials: Jack, jackstands, drain pan, Phase 1 tool kit, new differential carrier gasket, silicone gasket sealer, rags, fine file, gear oil.

Step 1. Drain Differential Oil.
Chapter 5, Procedure 15, Step 6, tells you how.

Step 2. Chock, Jack, Block, Remove Rear Wheels.
Park on level ground and chock the front wheels. Loosen the rear lug nuts a little, then jack up the rear end of the truck and put it on jackstands. Remove the rear wheels, then release the parking brake.

Step 3. Remove Driveshaft.
Remove the driveshaft (Procedure 6, Step 3). If you have a two piece driveshaft, only remove the rear shaft.

Step 4. Remove Axles.
See Procedure 4, to remove the rear axles on all models except '86-'87 C&C models with dual rear wheels. Procedure 5 tells you how to remove the axles on '86-'87 C&C models with dual rear wheels.

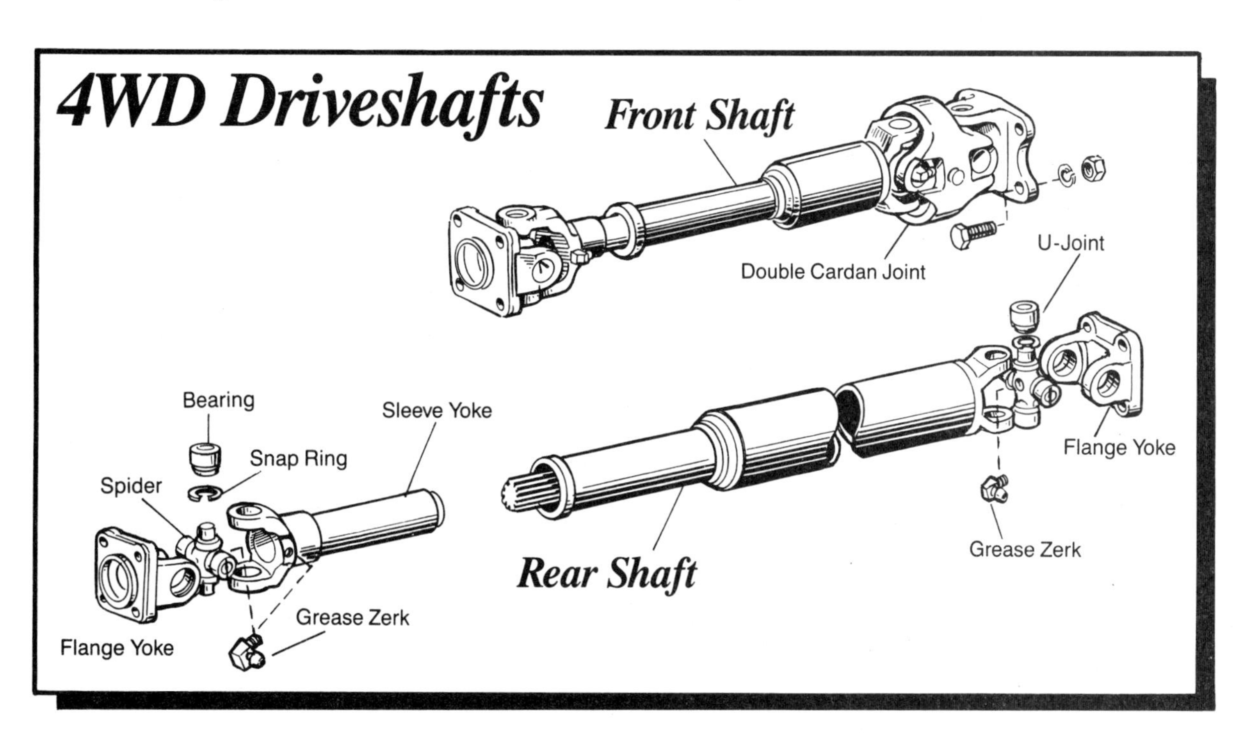

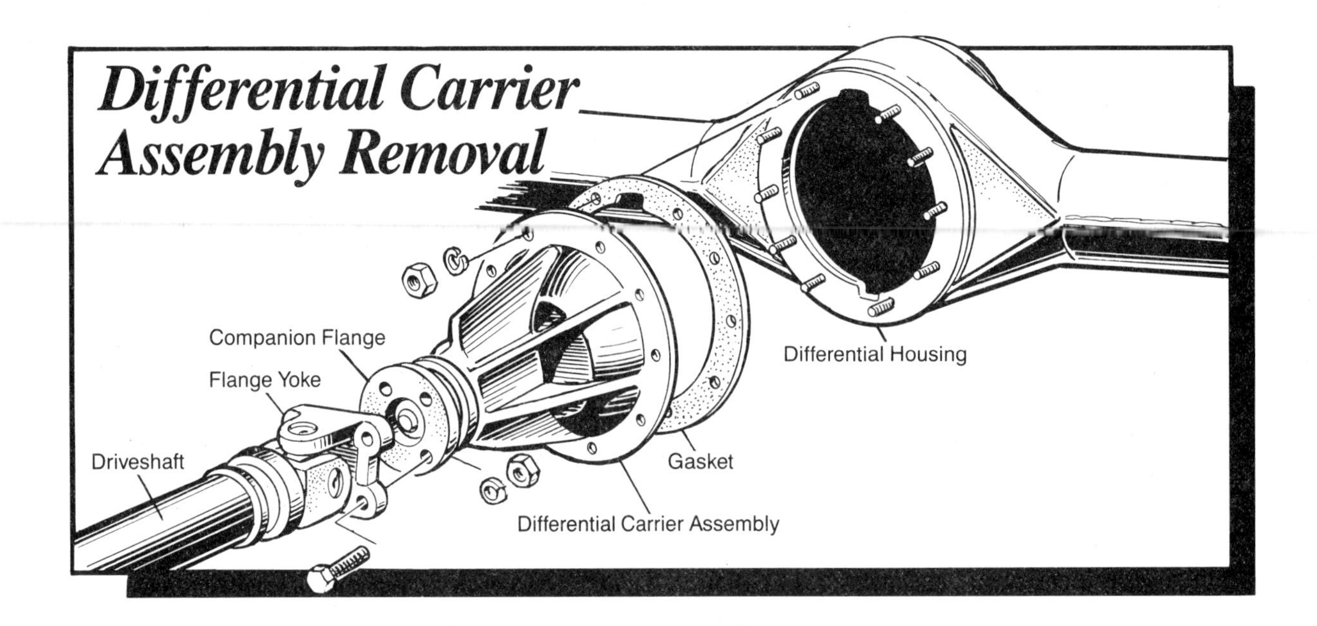

If you are removing the front differential carrier assembly on a '79-'85 4WD model, see Chapter 12, Procedure 11.

Step 5. Remove Differential Carrier Assembly.

Remove the ten or so nuts that attach the differential carrier assembly to the differential housing, then pull the differential carrier assembly out of the housing. Watch out, it's kind of heavy. If it's stuck, use a plastic or rubber mallet to tap on the sides until it pops free. Haul it away to be rebuilt or replaced.

Step 6. Install Differential Carrier Assembly.

First thoroughly clean the mating surfaces on the differential housing and the carrier assembly. Feel all the way around the surface for metal burrs, old gasket sealer, etc. If you find anything, gently smooth it off with a fine file. Use a clean rag to wipe out any crud that's in the bottom of the differential housing.

Coat both sides of a new differential carrier gasket with silicone gasket sealer, then fit the gasket onto the bolts on the differential housing.

Carefully fit the carrier assembly into the differential housing. Install the nuts and tighten them in a crisscross pattern. The proper torque is 18 ft.lbs. except for trucks with dual rear wheels (dualies). If your truck is a dualie, torque the nuts on the rear differential to 23 ft.lbs.

Install the axles: Chapter 12, Procedure 11, for '79-'85 4WD front differential. In this chapter, see Procedure 4 for trucks with single rear wheels, or Procedure 5 for '86-'87 C&C models with dual rear wheels.

Install the driveshaft (Procedure 6, Step 4 or 5).

Install the wheels and snug the lug nuts. Lower the truck to the ground and torque the lug nuts to 65-87 ft.lbs. Install the differential drain plug, then fill the differential with fresh gear oil (Chapter 5, Procedure 15, Step 6).

Bleed the brake system (Chapter 7, Procedure 1). Don't skip this or you won't have any brakes.

PROCEDURE 8: REMOVE AND INSTALL MANUAL TRANSMISSION, CLUTCH, THROWOUT BEARING, PILOT BEARING, REAR CRANKSHAFT SEAL (PHASE 2)

This is a Phase 2 procedure, so I'm assuming you are a somewhat experienced mechanic. Therefore the instructions are more abbreviated and there will be more things left to your ingenuity than with most procedures in this book.

Due to complexities beyond our control, this procedure does not cover removal and installation of automatic transmissions. Take it to the pros.

Please read the rap at the beginning of this chapter about clutches, transmissions and driveshafts.

Condition: Some or all of the clutch components are worn out; OR the rear crankshaft seal is leaking; OR the transmission isn't working properly.

Tools and Materials: Phase 1 tool kit, hydraulic floor jack, transmission jack, jackstands, exhaust pipe gasket for the manifold connection, clutch alignment tool, block of wood about ¾" thick and six inches long, tape, dust mask or respirator, transmission oil, solvent, rags, carb or brake cleaner, multi-purpose grease, silicone gasket sealer, maybe a file.

For safety and convenience, I urge you to borrow or rent a transmission jack before removing the transmission. Transmission jacks are much wider at the bottom so they are more stable and they often have a strap to tie around the transmission so it can't roll off the jack.

Remark: If the clutch has been slipping or chattering, for insurance it's a good idea to replace the clutch disc, pressure plate, pilot bearing, throwout bearing and rear crankshaft seal while the transmission is out so you won't have to remove it again for a long time (hopefully).

Step 1. Get Ready To Remove Transmission.

Disconnect the negative battery terminal (Chapter 8, Procedure 1, Step 3).

'75-'78 models: Drain about a gallon of antifreeze from the radiator, then disconnect the upper radiator hose from the radiator (Chapter 6, Procedure 2, Step 2).

Disconnect the accelerator torque rod that goes across the rear of the engine. Unhook it from the pivot mechanism that's bolted to the firewall (Chapter 9, Procedure 3, Step 2). This will prevent the rod from being bent by the EGR valve when the rear of the engine is lowered.

EVERYONE: Remove the upper mounting nut from the starter (Chapter 8, Procedure 10, Step 3).

Crawl into the cab and put the gearshift lever in NEUTRAL. If there is a plastic console around the gearshift lever, remove the phillips screws that attach it, then remove the console. Remove the carpet around the gearshift lever(s) if it's in the way. If the rubber gearshift boot is attached to the floorboard with a retainer, remove the screws, then the retainer. Pull the rubber gearshift lever boot up the shaft away from the floorboard. If there is another, smaller rubber boot at the base of the lever, pull it up the lever also.

Look down into the hole in the floorboard and you'll see either four bolts or a round, bulbous retainer around the base of the lever. If you have the four bolts, remove them, then pull the lever up and out of the transmission. If you have the round bulbous retainer, here's how to remove it: Press down on the retainer and turn it about 1/6 turn *counterclockwise*, then pull the gearshift lever up out of the transmission. If necessary, use a couple of screwdrivers to turn it.

4WD models: Pull the rubber boot(s) on the 4WD shift lever up away from the floor. Use needlenose pliers to remove the clip around the base of the lever, then lift the lever out of the transfer case. If you can't get the clip off, remove the four bolts around the base of the lever, then lift the lever off the transfer.

EVERYONE: Chock, Jack and Block the front end of the truck (Chapter 2, Procedure 1). Be sure the truck is resting solidly on good jackstands because there's a certain amount of wiggling, jiggling, pushing, pulling and swearing involved in removing and installing the transmission.

Drain the transmission oil on all models and the transfer case oil on 4WD models (Chapter 5, Procedure 15, Steps 4 and 5). If you are here only to replace the clutch, you don't have to drain the transmission or transfer case, but it's probably time to change the oil anyway and there's less chance of making a mess with an empty tranny.

If your driveshaft bolts to the rear end of the tranny, just remove the bolts, slide the shaft rearward far enough to separate it from the tranny, then tie the front end of the shaft to the exhaust pipe so it's out of the way. If your driveshaft slides into the rear of the tranny you'll have to remove the driveshaft from the truck (Procedure 6, Step 3).

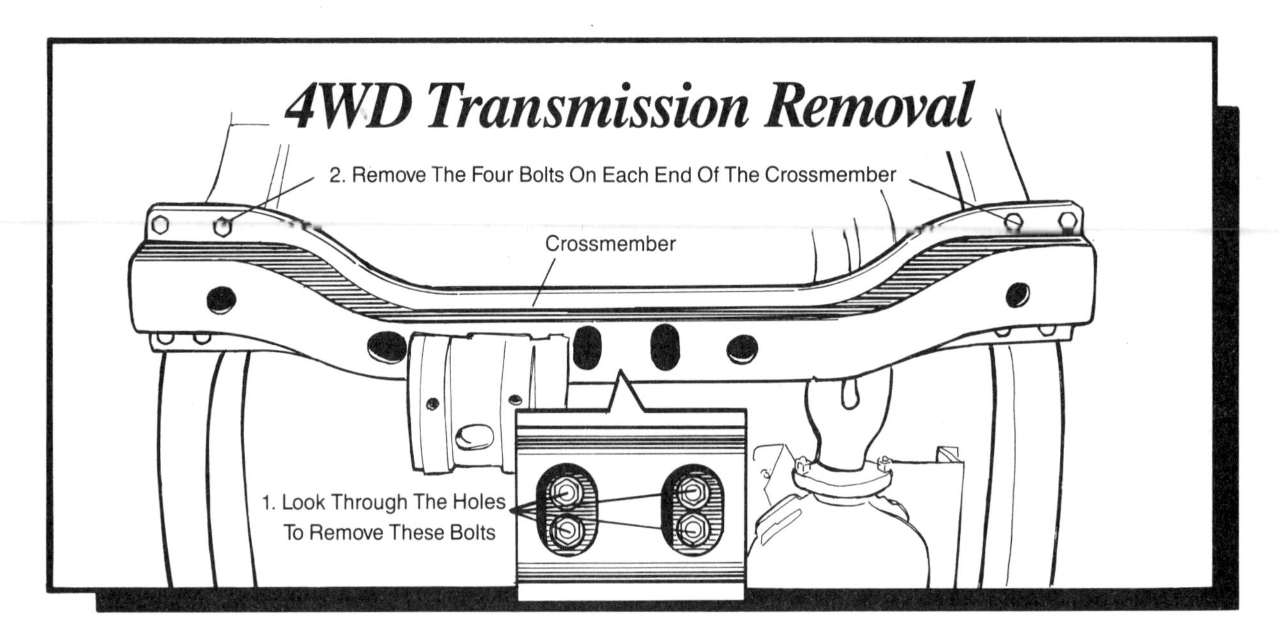

4WD models: Remove the 4WD driveshaft (Procedure 6, Step 5).

EVERYONE: The **speedometer cable** is that stiff pencil-size cable that's screwed into one side of the tranny. Use pliers to unscrew the knurled nut on the end *counterclockwise*, then pull the cable out of the tranny and tuck it somewhere out of the way.

The **back-up light switch** is screwed into one side of the tranny and has a plastic wire connector with wires sprouting from it. Disconnect the plastic connector and tuck it out of the way. On 4WD models there will also be a **4WD indicator switch** light to label, then unplug. Look for other electrical switches on the tranny. If you find any, label and then disconnect them.

Remove the bolts that attach the **clutch slave cylinder** to the right side of the bell housing (Procedure 3, Step 2). Don't disconnect the metal fluid line from the cylinder. On some models you'll need to disconnect the **spring** between the slave cylinder and **clutch release fork**. Remove the bolts that attach the **fluid line bracket** to the bell housing.

Now remove the lower mounting bolt for the starter. Lay the starter and slave cylinder beside the engine.

Remove the three nuts that attach the **exhaust pipe** to the **exhaust manifold**, then remove the bolt and **exhaust pipe clamp** (and heat shield on '75-'78 models) that attaches the exhaust pipe to the **exhaust pipe support bracket** (Chapter 10, Procedure 6, Step 2). Remove the bolts that attach the support bracket to the left side of the bell housing. Push the exhaust pipe toward the left side as far possible, then use rope or whatever to tie it there.

Tape a piece of wood about ¾" thick to the crossmember that's right below the engine on 2WD models or to the front differential on 4WD models. The block of wood will prevent the engine oil pan from being dented. On '75-'78 models the block keeps the rear of the engine from dropping so low that the EGR valve gets crushed against the firewall.

'75-'78 models and 4WD models: There are two holes in the bottom of the crossmember that supports the rear end of the transmission. Through the holes you'll see two or four bolts screwed vertically into the bottom of the rear transmission bracket. Remove the vertical bolts. Place the jack under the tranny and jack it up just enough so it isn't resting on the crossmember. Remove the bolts at each end of the crossmember and remove the crossmember. Lower the transmission so the engine rests on the piece of wood.

'79-'87 2WD models: A crossmember beneath the rear end of the tranny has a flat **horizontal bracket** bolted to the front side. Just above the horizontal bracket is the rear transmission mount. Remove the four vertical bolts that attach the rear transmission bracket to the horizontal bracket.

Use a jack to raise the transmission slightly, then remove the horizontal bolts that attach the horizontal bracket to the crossmember. Now remove the bolts that attach the rear transmission bracket to the rear end of the transmission. Remove the transmission bracket. Lower the transmission so the engine rests on the piece of wood.

EVERYONE: Now comes the fun part; remove all the bolts around the front edge of the transmission bell housing that attach the housing to the engine. You'll need a long extension and sockets to reach some of them. 14mm and 17mm swivel sockets make the job easier. The two lower bolts on each side attach the bell housing to steel stiffener plates.

Once the bolts are out, look for other things that might be attached to the transmission. If you find anything, label and then disconnect it.

OK, lets see if we can pluck the tranny out by its roots. Put the transmission jack (or hydraulic floor jack) under the center of the transmission and raise it until it supports the weight of the tranny. Don't raise it so high it's lifting the engine.

2WD Transmission Removal

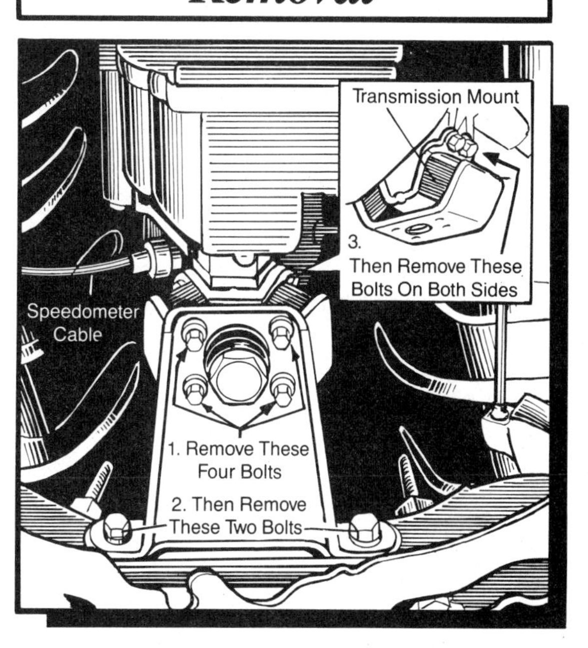

'75-'78 models and 4WD models: Pull the tranny toward the rear of the truck until the mainshaft sticking out the front clears the pressure plate. Hold the tranny so it can't roll off the jack while you lower it to the floor. Drag the tranny out from under the truck.

'79-'87 2WD models: Pull the tranny toward the rear of the truck until the mainshaft sticking out the front clears the pressure plate. The top of the tranny on some models must be rotated about 45 degrees to the right before you can pull it rearward. Once the mainshaft is clear of the pressure plate, lower the front of the transmission until you can push it forward far enough for the rear end to clear the crossmember. Drag the tranny out from under the truck.

EVERYONE: While the tranny is out it's a good idea to inspect the clutch parts. If you are here only to replace the transmission and aren't going to inspect the clutch parts, skip down to Step 11 to install the new or rebuilt tranny.

Step 2. Remove and Inspect Clutch Disc, Pressure Plate and Flywheel.

Wear a dust mask or respirator while dealing with the clutch.

If there's a possibility you are going to use the same pressure plate again, use a punch and hammer or indelible marker to mark the edge of the pressure plate and flywheel so you can install the pressure plate in the same position on the flywheel.

Loosen the six bolts around the edge of the pressure plate one turn at a time until the pressure plate is loose, then remove the bolts. Pull the pressure plate and clutch disc off the flywheel.

Feel for ridges and grooves on the friction surface of the flywheel and pressure plate where the clutch disc rubs. If you feel grooves or see dark, blotchy looking spots, the pressure plate should be replaced and the flywheel should be resurfaced to insure maximum disc life. Most garages automatically have the flywheel resurfaced to be sure it's OK. If the friction surface on the flywheel is smooth with no dark spots, you can install a new disc and pressure plate.

Now check the clutch disc. The rivets that attach the friction surface to the disc should be at least .012" below the friction surface. If the friction surface has worn down almost to the rivets, or there is oil or grease on the friction surface, the disc must be replaced. If the clutch was slipping or if there's any doubt about the condition of the pressure plate and disc, have the pros check it or go ahead and replace it. You don't want to remove the tranny again, do you?

Step 3. Check Pilot Bearing.

Look in the center of the flywheel for the small round pilot bearing. Press your finger against one edge of the inner steel ring and rotate the bearing *counterclockwise*. The bearing should turn smoothly with no resistance. If the bearing feels rough or has resistance to turning, replace it for sure (Step 7).

Step 4. Check Throwout Bearing (clutch release bearing).

Look at the transmission main shaft inside the transmission bell housing. The throwout bearing is mounted to the clutch release fork and can slide forward and backward on the main shaft.

Push against the front edge of the bearing while turning it in both directions. If you feel resistance or roughness in the bearing, replace it (Step 9).

Step 5. Summary.

If any of the clutch parts look at all questionable, or if the clutch parts have over 60,000 miles, it's a good idea to replace them while you're here.

Step 6. Remove Flywheel.

Use a large screwdriver to wedge between the teeth on the outer edge of the flywheel and the engine block to keep the flywheel from turning while you remove the six flywheel mounting bolts, then pull the flywheel off the engine. Watch out, it's heavy.

Once it's off, take it to a machine shop and have it resurfaced. This will smooth the wrinkles out so the new clutch disc will work better and last longer. The people at the machine shop will probably install a new pilot bearing for a couple of bucks and save you the hassle.

If you're here to replace the rear crank seal, see Step 8. If you are replacing the pilot bearing, go on to the next step.

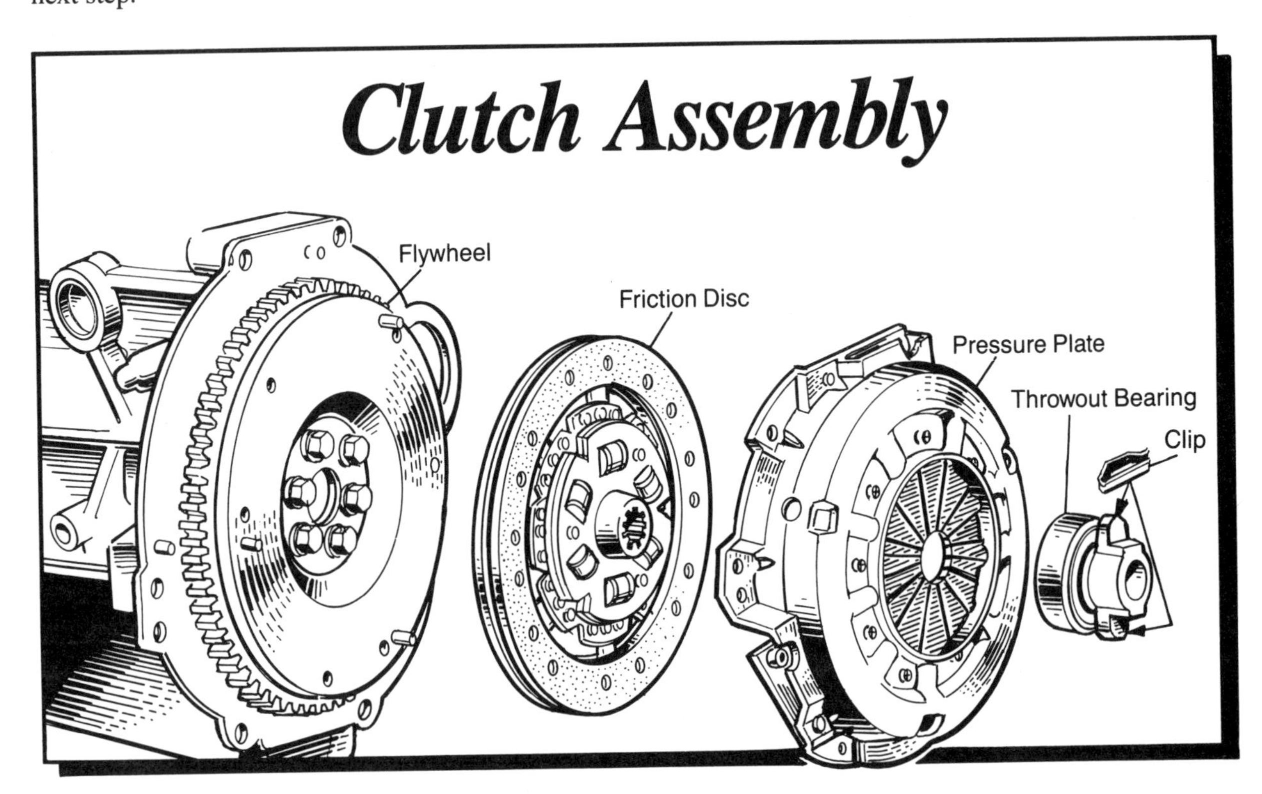

Step 7. Replace Pilot Bearing.

The pilot bearing is in the center of the flywheel. If the flywheel is still on the engine you'll have to borrow, buy or rent a bearing puller with very small jaws to remove the pilot bearing.

If the flywheel is off the engine, use a hammer and punch or a socket with a slightly smaller diameter than the bearing to tap the bearing out toward the clutch side of the flywheel.

Coat the outer edge of the new pilot bearing with oil. Then, from the clutch side of the flywheel, use a hammer to gently tap the new pilot bearing into the flywheel until it's flush with the flywheel. Only tap on the outer edge of the bearing and not in the center. Now lay the old bearing on the new bearing and use it to tap the new bearing into the flywheel until it stops. Tap the old bearing out of the flywheel if it's stuck. Once the new bearing is installed, check that it rotates smoothly.

Step 8. Replace Crankshaft Seal.

This step is for people with leaking rear crankshaft seals.

Once the flywheel has been removed, you'll see an aluminum seal retainer bolted to the rear of the engine, around the crankshaft. The seal is that rubber thing in the space between the crankshaft and seal retainer. To remove the old seal, use a knife to carefully cut part of the seal away where it contacts the crankshaft. Next, wrap tape around the end of a small screwdriver, about ¼" from the tip. Slide the tip of the screwdriver between the crank and seal and lever the seal out of the holder. Be careful that the screwdriver doesn't scratch the crankshaft.

Wrap a small rag or paper towel soaked with solvent, carb cleaner or brake cleaner around the end of a small screwdriver, then use it to clean the seal mounting surface in the seal retainer. Grab the new seal and smear some multipurpose grease on the little lips that contact the crankshaft. Don't get any of the grease on the seal surface that contacts the seal retainer. Grease would make it slippery and it might pop out of the holder.

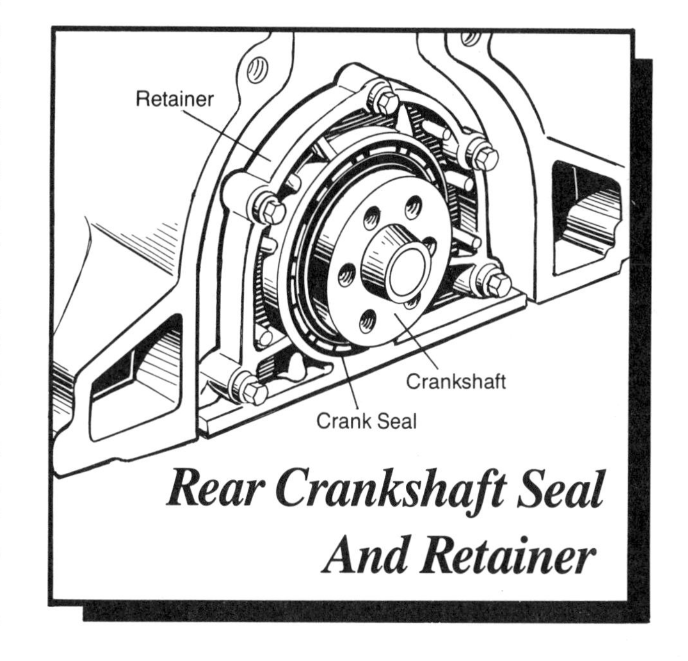

Rear Crankshaft Seal And Retainer

Clean your hands, then hold the seal up to the seal retainer with the flat side toward you, away from the engine. Use your thumbs and forefingers to push on the seal to get it started evenly into the holder. Push all around the edge of the seal until it's flush with the holder. You might need to use the end of a socket extension and hammer to tap around the outer edge of the seal to make it seat completely. If the seal gets bent, throw it away and get another one.

If you can't get the seal out or in, here's how to remove and install the seal retainer.

Use a socket and ratchet to remove the mounting bolts around the rear edge. You'll also need to remove two bolts that attach the oil pan to the bottom of the seal retainer. Gently pry the seal retainer off the engine, being careful not to tear the oil pan gasket. If the gasket tears, you'll need to remove the oil pan and replace the gasket (Chapter 13, Procedure 4). Once the oil seal retainer is off, lay it on two blocks of wood spread far enough apart that you can tap the old seal out through the flywheel side.

Use a rag and solvent, carb cleaner or brake cleaner to clean the seal surface in the retainer and the mating surfaces of the seal retainer and engine block. Scrape off any traces of the old gasket. Flip the holder over so the flywheel side is up, then lay the new seal on the hole. Use your fingers and thumbs to press the seal into the holder. If necessary, use something blunt like the end of a socket extension and hammer to tap the seal in as far as it will go. You can lay a clean block of wood on the seal, then hammer on the block to drive the seal in.

Smear a very thin coat of silicone gasket sealer on each side of a new oil seal retainer gasket and lay it on the seal retainer. Smear gasket sealer on the bottom of the retainer. Pack grease into the edge of the seal that contacts the crankshaft.

Wiggle the seal retainer and seal onto the crankshaft. Be sure the little lips on the seal don't get broken. Install and tighten the seal retainer bolts to 9 ft.lbs. (Don't forget the ones for the oil pan.) Careful! They are small bolts so don't overtighten them.

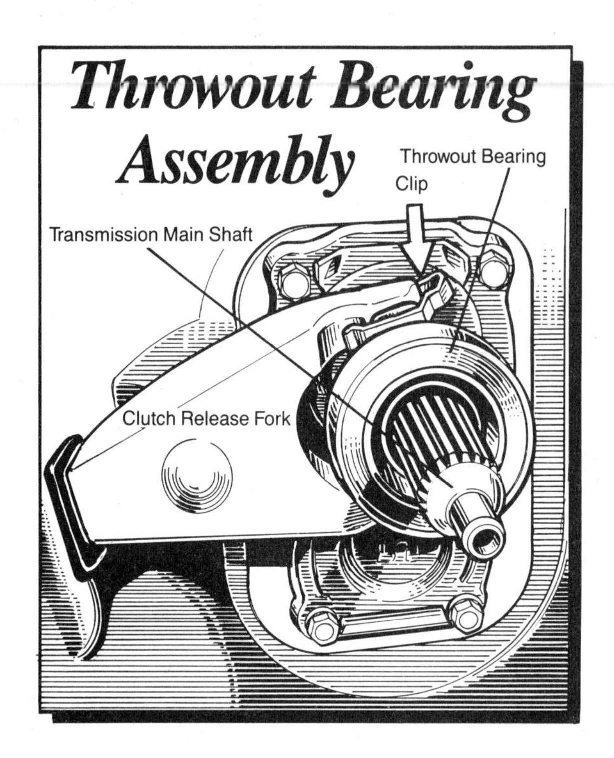

Step 9. Replace Throwout Bearing.

The throwout bearing is that round thing that fits around the splined shaft sticking out of the front end of the transmission. It's attached to the clutch release lever with two flat clips or wire clips.

To remove the throwout bearing, use a small screwdriver or needlenose pliers to remove the clips from the little ears on the sides of the throwout bearing holder. Note how they are attached so you can install them the same way. Slide the bearing and holder off the transmission shaft.

If you don't have a vise or two blocks of wood handy, take the throwout bearing and holder to the machine shop and have the old bearing removed and the new bearing pressed on.

If you have a vise or a couple of wood blocks, support the sides of the throwout bearing so the bearing holder is hanging down. Use a flat punch or screwdriver to tap the holder out of the inside of the bearing. It isn't real tight and usually taps out easily.

Check the old bearing to see which side was out, then use a punch or screwdriver and hammer to tap the new bearing onto the holder the same way. Only tap on the thick inner race of the bearing, not on the rounded part. Tap it on all the way.

Use a rag to clean the shaft on the transmission where the throwout bearing fits. Spread a very thin coat of grease on the shaft. Dab grease on the two dimples on the backside of the bearing holder, then slide the bearing holder onto the shaft so the bearing is toward the front. Hook the two small clips over the ears on the sides of the bearing holder so the holder is clipped to the clutch release fork. If you have the wire-type clip, be sure the end of the clip is securely fastened in the hole on the front of the bearing holder.

The throwout bearing must be able to move easily on the transmission shaft or it will wear out quickly. Here's how to check it.

Push rearward on the end of the clutch release level to force the bearing toward the front end of the shaft, then pull forward on the lever. The throwout bearing should slide smoothly on the shaft. If you feel resistance as the bearing slides back and forth on the shaft, remove the clips and slide the throwout bearing and its holder off the shaft. Check the inner surface of the holder where you tapped while removing the holder from the bearing. The tapping may have created burrs along the edge. If necessary, use a file to remove the burrs, then reinstall the bearing and holder.

Step 10. Install Flywheel, Clutch Disc and Pressure Plate.

Fit the flywheel onto the end of the crankshaft, then install the six bolts. Use your biggest screwdriver in the gear teeth to prevent the flywheel from turning while you torque the flywheel bolts to 68 ft.lbs. for '75-'78 models or 80 ft.lbs. for '79-'87 models.

Hold the clutch disc against the flywheel with the spring side and/or the longer part of the splined center part of the disc toward the rear of the truck. Align the marks you made on the pressure plate and flywheel (if you are using the old pressure plate), then install the six pressure plate bolts. Tighten the bolts just enough that you can move the clutch disc up and down with a screwdriver and it will stay where you put it.

In order to mate the transmission and engine, the splined hole in the clutch disc must be aligned almost perfectly with the pilot bearing in the flywheel. There are two ways to do it: You can borrow, buy or maybe rent a clutch alignment tool that you insert into the clutch disc and pilot bearing while tightening the pressure plate bolts. Or, you can very carefully eyeball the clutch disc and pilot bearing until they are aligned. Use the alignment tool if possible.

OK, align the clutch disc and pilot bearing, then evenly tighten the pressure plate bolts one turn at a time in a crisscross pattern to 14 ft.lbs.

Step 11. Install Transmission.

Drag the transmission under the truck and lift it onto the transmission jack.

'79-'87 2WD models: Raise the transmission until the rear end can slide over the crossmember. If you had to twist the top of the tranny about 45 degrees to the right to get it out, you'll need to twist it that way again before it will slide onto the crossmember. Use the jack to raise the front of the tranny and push it forward until the transmission main shaft is aligned with the hole in the pressure plate. Turn the tranny upright if you tilted it, and align it with the engine.

'75-'78 models and 4WD models: Jack the tranny up until it is aligned with the engine.

EVERYONE: Gently push forward on the tranny while guiding the transmission shaft into the pressure plate. Now comes the wiggling, jiggling and swearing. Wrestle the tranny around until it fits against the rear of the engine. Gently lift, lower and push the rear end of the tranny side to side until the transmission main shaft aligns with the pilot bearing. If necessary you can use a block of wood on the Toyota jack or hydraulic floor jack to raise the rear end of the engine. When everything is aligned, the tranny will pop right in. Remember, Perseverance Furthers! If after a lot of wiggling, jiggling and swearing the tranny still refuses to go in that final inch, the clutch disc probably isn't aligned correctly and the transmission shaft is hitting the pilot bearing. You'll have to pull the tranny back out and check the clutch disc alignment again.

When the bell housing is touching the engine all the way around, install the top two transmission mounting bolts and the one just below the starter and snug them down. Round up the bolts that screw into the stiffener plate brackets on the lower sides of the bell housing. Install and snug down those bolts. When all the bolts are snug, torque the transmission mounting bolts to 53 ft.lbs. and the stiffener bolts to 27 ft.lbs.

'79-'87 2WD models: Use the jack to raise the transmission high enough to fit the rear mounting bracket to the bottom rear of the transmission. Torque the four bolts to 19 ft.lbs. Install the bracket that bolts horizontally to the crossmember and torque the bolts to 32 ft.lbs. Lower the transmission and install the four bolts into the bottom of the bracket. Torque the bolts to 9 ft.lbs.

'75-'78 models and 4WD models: Raise the tranny high enough so you can install the crossmember below the rear end. Tighten the crossmember bolts to 70 ft.lbs. Lower the rear end of the transmission onto the crossmember and install the mounting bolts that attach the transmission to the crossmember. Tighten the bolts to 9 ft.lbs.

EVERYONE: Now you can remove the block of wood that's taped to the crossmember or front axle. Whew, the hard part is over, so take a break if you want and light 'em if ya got 'em.

Install a new exhaust pipe gasket onto the bottom of the manifold, then fit the exhaust pipe onto the three studs. Install the nuts and torque the nuts to 46 ft.lbs. Next, install the exhaust pipe bracket to the bell housing and torque the upper bolt to 27 ft.lbs. and the lower bolt to 51 ft.lbs. Install the exhaust pipe clamp and tighten the bolt.

Wiggle the starter into position, then install and tighten the lower mounting bolt. Fit the clutch slave cylinder onto the bell housing, then install and tighten the mounting bolts to 9 ft.lbs. Be sure the end of the push rod is in its place at the end of the clutch release fork. Install the spring clip that secures the clutch fluid line to the bracket. If your slave cylinder had a spring between the cylinder and the clutch release fork, use pliers to install it now.

Reconnect the speedometer cable and back up light switch to the transmission. On 4WD models you'll also need to reconnect the 4WD indicator light switch. Reconnect any other switches that you disconnected.

Install the driveshaft (Procedure 6, Step 4). If you have 4WD, also do Procedure 6, Step 5, to install the 4WD driveshaft.

Fill the transmission and transfer case (4WD) with fresh gear oil (Chapter 5, Procedure 15, Steps 4 and 5).

Lower the truck off the jack stands, then install the upper starter mounting bolt. Install the air cleaner if you removed it.

Smear some multipurpose grease on the bottom end of the transmission shifter lever, then fit the lever into the top of the tranny. If your setup has four bolts around the base of the lever, install and tighten the four bolts that attach the lever to the tranny. If your setup has the rounded retainer, align the slot in the retainer with the little tab, push the retainer down as far as possible, then turn it *clockwise* until it locks into place.

If your model has a plastic console around the gearshift lever, install it now.

4WD models: Insert the 4WD shift lever into the top of the transfer case. Then, depending on how you removed the lever, use needlenose pliers to install the retaining clip, or install the four bolts.

'75-'78 models: Connect the upper radiator hose to the radiator. Tighten the radiator drain valve, then fill the radiator with coolant (Chapter 6, Procedure 3, Step 3). Reconnect the accelerator torque rod to the pivot mechanism on the firewall. Be sure the linkage is locked into place.

EVERYONE: Reconnect the battery cable to the negative battery terminal.

Look around the truck for things that still need to be done. When you're satisfied everything's finished, go for a test drive. Check that the clutch engages properly and the gears shift smoothly.

Step 12. One More Thing.

Whew! Now do Chapter 5, Procedure 4, Step 20. You'll be glad you did.

CHAPTER 12
SUSPENSION, STEERING AND FRONT AXLES

You've probably followed a car on a rough road, or driven beside a car on a bumpy freeway, and noticed how the car's wheels were moving up and down, following the contour of the road, yet the body of the car (and the passengers) were traveling along relatively smoothly. The phenomenon you were witnessing was Suspension In Action! Without a suspension system, even small bumps would just about jar your teeth out and larger bumps would cause your truck to be frequently airborne, making it impossible to steer. A suspension system that's in good order makes your ride both comfortable and safe.

Steering is lumped in with suspension because they are interrelated; in fact, they share several parts in common. Together they affect how your truck deals with the road. The steering "geometry" is designed so your truck has a tendency to want to go straight ahead. Wear in the various steering parts, or parts that have been knocked out of adjustment or bent by off-roading or hitting curbs after late nights out on the town, change the geometry of the system. These changes are evident in many ways: the truck wanders mindlessly across the road, impulsively darts here and there, wears the tires in funny patterns or makes nerve-wracking noises on rough roads. These are the symptoms. Now you get to play Doctor with your truck to diagnose and cure its ills. Procedure 1 tells you how to check the various suspension and steering parts.

Before jumping into how Toyota suspension and steering work, let me first describe a few of the interrelated parts.

STEERING KNUCKLES

The heart of the front suspension and steering on your truck is a heavy chunk of metal called a **steering knuckle** (or just *knuckle*). There's a steering knuckle on each side of the truck, next to the brakes. On 4WD models, holes for the front **axle shaft** are machined into the sides of the knuckles. On 2WD models the **axle** is built right into the knuckle.

All of the front suspension and steering components, as well as the front axles, wheel bearings, brakes and wheels, are attached directly or indirectly to the two steering knuckles. Pretty important chunk of metal, eh?

2WD models and '86-'87 4WD models: The top and bottom of each knuckle are attached to **upper** and **lower suspension arms** with **ball joints**.

'79-'85 4WD models: The steering knuckles are mounted to the outboard ends of the front differential housing.

BALL JOINTS

A **ball joint** is not a round marijuana cigarette. Nor is it a house of ill repute. It's a vital part of your steering/suspension setup. It's made of two pieces: a round steel ball with an end that's threaded like a bolt (a stud), and a steel socket that surrounds the ball. The socket also has a threaded bolt or nut-like end or a mounting plate attached to it. When the "bolt" (stud) on the ball is attached to one part of the truck and the attaching part of the socket is secured to a different part of the truck, the two parts are securely connected yet free to pivot all around the radius of the ball. The flexibility offered by the ball joints allows the different parts of the suspension and steering to change relative positions even though they are securely attached to one another. It's exactly how your hip and shoulder joints work, except that the material is steel instead of bone.

On all 2WD and '86-'87 4WD models, ball joints are located at the top and bottom of each steering knuckle. They allow the wheels to move up and down and turn. I'll call this type the **steering ball joint** or just ball joint.

On all models a 90-degree ball joint is at the end of each tie rod, so I'll simply call this type of ball joint a **tie rod end**. (The tie rods will be described in detail along with other parts of the steering system in the Steering description ahead.)

As the metal parts of the ball joint gradually wear away, the balls become loose in the sockets, causing excessive play (movement) in the steering and/or suspension.

Properly maintained ball joints and tie rod ends are usually good for well over 100,000 miles and, in fact, generally outlive the truck. You should check them periodically, though, and Procedure 1 tells you how.

FRONT SUSPENSION

To give your suspension the flexibility to move up and down following the contour of the road, a spring of some sort must be used. Toyota trucks have used three different types of springs over the years: coil springs, leaf springs and torsion bars. Here's when and where they are used:

'75-'78 models: The front suspension system uses a strong heavy-duty **coil spring** mounted between the suspension arms, near each front wheel. When a wheel hits a bump, the lower suspension arm compresses the spring, allowing the wheel to travel over the bump without lifting the rest of the truck. It's pretty easy to remove the coil springs, but special tools and finesse are required to install them. So if you suspect a problem with the coil springs, have the Toyota dealer or a garage check and repair them for you.

'79-'85 4WD models: The outer ends of the front differential are attached to the center of strong steel **leaf springs**. The ends of the leaf springs are attached to the frame. When a front wheel encounters a bump, the leaf springs flex (bow) a little to absorb the jolt. As time goes by, the leaf springs might begin to sag and lose their ability to absorb bumps. How to replace the leaf springs is in Procedure 14. Spring modification kits are discussed in Chapter 14.

'79-'87 2WD and '86-'87 4WD models: The front suspension consists of two strong steel **torsion bars** mounted front-to-rear, one near each front wheel. The rear end of each torsion bar is bolted securely to the body and the front end is mounted to the upper or lower suspension arm. When a wheel hits a bump or hole, the suspension arm twists the torsion bar and the flexing of the bar absorbs the jolt.

Torsion bars very rarely, if ever, break or bend. If you suspect a problem with your torsion bars, have the Toyota dealer or a garage check and repair them.

REAR SUSPENSION

On all models, each end of the rear differential is attached to the center of slightly arched steel **leaf springs**. The ends of the leaf springs are attached to the frame of the truck. When a rear wheel hits a bump, the arched leaf springs flex a little to absorb the shock. The leaf springs can become weak with age and/or hauling too many heavy loads. How to replace the leaf springs is in Procedure 14. Spring modification kits are listed in Chapter 14.

SHOCK ABSORBERS

Double action (up and down) shock absorbers are mounted between the frame and each wheel. The **shock absorber** has a dual purpose—it helps the springs or torsion bars absorb the shock of irregularities in the road such as potholes, tree stumps, armadillos, etc., and also "dampens" the springs so the truck doesn't continue bouncing after hitting a bump.

The top of each shock absorber is bolted to a bracket on the frame. The bottom ends of the front shock absorbers are bolted to the lower suspension arm on models with **coil springs** or **torsion bars**, or to the **differential housing** on models with leaf springs. The bottom ends of the rear shock absorbers are mounted to brackets on the rear differential housing.

STEERING

Power steering is offered as an option on Toyota trucks. The hydraulic system that operates the power steering is very complex and should be serviced by the Toyota dealer or a garage, not mortals like you and me. Other than the hydraulics on the steering box, the system is similar to the regular steering system that I'm about to describe.

The **steering wheel** is attached to a long **steering shaft** that goes through the hollow **steering column** to an **intermediate shaft** in the engine compartment. The intermediate shaft connects the steering shaft to the **steering gearbox unit**. Inside the gearbox unit, a **worm gear** meshes with gear teeth on a strong heavy steel bar called a **sector shaft**. An adjusting bolt allows you to keep the worm gear and sector shaft gear meshed properly. Here's how the steering box is connected to the rest of the steering system:

2WD and '86-'87 4WD models: A short **pitman arm** connects the steering box to a long steering **relay rod**. A short **tie rod** with a ball joint on each end connects each end of the relay rod to a short knuckle arm on each steering knuckle. A movable **idler arm** mounted to the frame supports the tie rod and relay rod on the right side of the truck. When the steering wheel is turned, it moves the relay rod toward the right or left side of the truck. The relay rod moves the tie rods, which in turn pivot the steering knuckles on the ball joints.

'79-'85 4WD models: A short strong **drag link** connects the pitman arm on the steering box to the rear end of a knuckle arm bolted to the top of the left steering knuckle. A long tie rod with a ball joint on each end connects the front end of the knuckle arm to another knuckle arm on the right steering knuckle. When the steering wheel is turned, the drag link pushes or pulls on the left knuckle arm, which rotates the steering knuckle. The long tie rod connecting the two steering knuckles causes the two knuckles to rotate in the same direction.

ALIGNMENT

Your front wheels have three attitudes toward the road: **caster**, **camber** and **toe-in**. Although you can't adjust the three attitudes at home, I'll explain their functions anyway.

Caster works kind of like the front wheels on supermarket shopping carts (when they work as they should, which is seldom). The wheels roll behind and below a pivot shaft, which helps the wheel decide which way it is going. In other words it makes the wheel "center-seeking"; it follows the lead of the pivot shaft.

Camber is the angle the wheels have to the road off the vertical plane. As you face the front of the car, the bottoms of the tires are slightly closer together than the tops (or they should be if things are right).

The toe-in, just like a pigeon-toed kid, is set so the wheels will run straight on the highway. Friction of the tires on the road tends to force them into the wall-eyed (toed out) position, so you want them slightly toed-in to counter this force. If they're wall-eyed, you will have steering and handling problems—the car will want to wander.

On Toyotas the front toe-in is adjusted by changing the length of the tie rods. It's done with the truck standing still by screwing the tie rod ends further onto or off of the tie rods. Special expensive equipment is required to check the caster, camber and toe-in, so you have to take your truck to the Toyota dealer or an alignment shop to have it checked and adjusted.

There's actually a fourth attitude, which operates when you're turning a corner. It's called **steering axis inclination**. The steering knuckles are tilted so the tops of the housings are closer together than the bottoms when you look at them from the front end of the car, just the reverse of the wheel camber. This inclination is done for you by those clever Toyota engineers so that some semblance of proper wheel attitude is maintained when you zip around corners.

All this doesn't amount to diddly squat to you as long as it works OK, right? The attitudes are designed for proper road handling, safety, and minimal tire wear. They do fine until wear catches up with them, then comes the uneasy feeling that the truck is doing more steering than you are, or the tires start wearing in funny patterns. Make a maintenance habit of running through Procedure 1 every 12,000 miles to locate and eliminate looseness (play) in the suspension and steering systems. You should be able to feel the play in plenty of time to do something about it.

PROCEDURE 1: CHECK SUSPENSION AND STEERING

Condition: Regular 12,000 mile maintenance; OR your truck feels like a small boat on a stormy sea as you sail down the road; OR you hear clanks, clunks or bangs every time you hit a bump; OR the tires are wearing in funny patterns.

Tools and Materials: Tire gauge, hard level ground, flashlight, safety glasses, Friend. '84-'87 2WD and '86-'87 4WD models will also need a long bar (use the handle for the hydraulic jack if it's removable) and a short block of wood.

Step 1. Check Tire Pressure.

Check the tires and inflate them to the proper pressure. Chapter 5, Procedure 4, Step 15, tells you how. Read the rap on tires and tire pressure in Chapter 5 if you haven't already.

Step 2. Check Shock Absorbers.

Park the truck on hard level ground and get the wheels pointing straight ahead. Bounce each corner of the truck up and down a few times by pushing on the fender or end of the bumper. Pay particular attention to the first bounce. If the truck bounces easier on the first push, then becomes harder, or continues to be easy to bounce, the shocks have reached the end of the trail. Healthy shocks will resist your efforts equally on each push and the truck will not move up and down more than twice when you stop pushing and let go.

The rear shock absorbers are long metal tubes bolted between the truck's frame and a bracket on the rear differential housing. Be sure the truck is in gear and the handbrake is on, then slide under the rear. Look at the shocks where the smaller bottom part disappears into the larger top part. Any sign of wetness there means a seal inside the shock is broken allowing the shock oil to leak out. The shock is doomed and should be replaced.

Procedure 2 tells you how to do it.

To check the front shock absorber, kneel in front of one of the front tires and look under the fender. (On '75-'78 models you'll have to peek through the coil spring to see the shock absorber.) Like the rear shocks, if you see oily wetness on the smaller part of the shock, it means the fluid is leaking and the shock should be replaced (Procedure 3).

Step 3. Check Steering Damper ('80-'87 models).

A **steering damper**, which is a shock absorber mounted horizontally between the frame and steering system, helps absorb sudden sideways shocks to the front wheels and prevents steering wheel shimmy. If you lie down and look under the front of the truck, the steering damper will be right in front of you. One end of the damper is attached to the frame and the other end is attached to the relay rod on 2WD and '86-'87 4WD models, or to the tie rod on '79-'85 4WD models.

Grab the steering damper and shake it to check that the ends are securely attached. Tighten the bolts and/or nuts if they appear loose (Procedure 4, Step 2). If the steering wheel shimmies while driving, or there is oil or dampness near the center of the steering damper where the small part fits into the larger part, replace the steering damper (Procedure 4).

Step 4. Check for Clanks, Clunks and Bangs.

Clanks, clunks and bangs when you hit bumps mean something is loose. Tracking down some rattles would turn even Sherlock Holmes into a babbling idiot. Usually it's the exhaust system or something rolling around in the cab or bed, but let's check the suspension to be sure.

If the clanks and bangs are coming from the rear, put the truck in gear (or PARK), set the handbrake, chock the wheels, put on your safety glasses, and squeeze under the rear. Don't jack it up.

Grab the bottom end of a rear shock absorber just above the mounting bolt and shake it like you're strangling a cobra. Try to move the shock up and down and side to side. Next, grab the shock near the top and strangle that cobra again. Check both rear shocks. Look for looseness in the rubber grommets at the top and bottom of the shock. Check both sides and tighten the shock nuts or bolts if the grommets are loose (Procedure 2, Step 3). If any of the grommets are AWOL, cracked or can't be tightened, try to round up new or used ones and install them. If you can't find new grommets, the shock will have to be replaced (Procedure 2). While you're under the rear of the truck, bump the exhaust pipe around a little with your hand (use a rag if the pipe is hot) to see if it's loose and hitting something. Clunks or squeaks? Turn to Chapter 10 to correct exhaust system problems.

Check the mounting bolts that attach the leaf springs to the frame. If the springs appear to be loose, check the bolts and bushings for wear (Procedure 14).

If clanks and bangs are coming from the front of the truck, there's a slight possibility one of the front shocks isn't securely bolted to the suspension arm or the mounting bracket. Check them just as you checked the rear shocks (above) and tighten the bolts and nuts, or replace the grommets or shock absorber.

'79-'85 4WD models: A thumb-size **torque rod** with large bushings on each end connects the top left side of the front differential housing to the front of the frame. Grab the torque rod and shake it to see if the bushings are worn out. If you detect looseness in the ends of the torque rod, remove it and replace the bushings (Procedure 13).

Step 5. Vibrations or Shimmies.

Vibrations in the truck, or steering wheel shimmies (steering wheel moves rapidly side to side), that increase in intensity as the truck's speed increases can mean one of several things.

1. A tire is out of balance. A fairly small glob of mud/clay stuck to one of the wheels from off-roading can make a wheel alarmingly out of balance, so check the inside and outside of the wheels for crud. Wash them off if you find anything. If the truck still has bad vibrations, have the tires dynamically balanced by Toyota or an alignment shop.

2. The front wheel alignment (toe-in) is incorrect. Are the front tires wearing out faster on either the inside

or outside edge? If so, have the alignment checked by Toyota, an alignment shop or tire shop, not a department store garage.

3. Ball joints, wheel bearings or bushings in the front suspension are worn. We'll check all these in the next few steps.

4. The driveshaft might be bent, out of balance or have worn U-joints. See Chapter 11, Procedure 6, Step 2.

3. On '79-'85 4WD models the birfield joints in the front axles might be worn out. Procedure 10 tell you how to remove the axle and check the joint.

4. On '80-'87 models a loose steering damper could rattle and allow the steering wheel to shimmy (Procedure 4).

5. On '86-'87 4WD models a tulip joint or CVJ (constant velocity joint) on the front axles might be worn. You'll feel a solid vibration in the seat of your pants rather than steering wheel shimmy. Procedure 15 tells how to check tulips and CVJs.

Step 6. Check the Steering Wheel Free Play.

Be sure the front tires are pointed straight ahead for this test.

Open the driver's window and turn the steering wheel as you watch the left front wheel (the key has to be turned to the first click to release the steering lock). Move the steering wheel right and left a little. How much does the steering wheel move before the front tire starts to move? This slack in movement is called **steering play** and should be no more than 1-1/8" for 1975-78 models or 1-3/16" for 1979-87 models. Does the steering wheel move more than it should? Either the steering box needs to be adjusted or the ball joints (on models with ball joints) and/or tie rod ends are worn. Here's how to adjust the steering box on models without power steering.

Point the front wheels straight ahead. The idea is to reduce the free play so it's within the specifications without making the steering wheel feel rough when you turn it, so it might take a couple of tries for you to get the adjustment correct.

OK, locate a nut on top of the steering gearbox that has a slotted screw in the center. Hold a screwdriver in the slot to prevent the screw from turning while you loosen the lock nut *counterclockwise* about ½ turn. Turn the screw about ¼ turn *clockwise*, then hold the screw in that position while you tighten the lock nut. Check the steering wheel free play again. If the steering wheel becomes hard to turn or you feel a roughness while turning it, loosen the lock nut and turn the screw 1/8 turn *counterclockwise*, then tighten the lock nut. Try turning the steering wheel again. If it's still not right, keep adjusting. If there's still too much steering play after adjusting the steering box, check the steering linkage.

Step 7. Check Pitman Arm, Tie Rod Ends, Relay Rod and Idler Arm.

Pitman arm: Find the short shaft mounted to the bottom or side of the steering box. That's the pitman arm and it connects the steering box to the relay rod on 2WD and '86-'87 4WD models, or to the drag link on '79-'85 4WD models. To check the pitman arm, grab it and shake it hard while watching for movement at each end. If you notice looseness at the steering box end it means the bearings in the steering box are worn. Have the Toyota dealer or a garage replace the steering box. If there's looseness at the opposite end from the steering box, it means the ball joint on the relay rod on 2WD models or on the pitman arm itself on '86-'87 4WD models is worn out. Procedure 9, Step 1 tells you how to replace the relay rod and Procedure 9, Step 2, tells you how to replace the pitman arm. '79-'85 4WD models, be sure to check the drag link (below).

Tie rod ends: To check the tie rod ends for play, put on your safety glasses, grab a flashlight and slide under the front of the truck (be sure the wheels are chocked, the handbrake is on and the transmission is in FIRST or PARK). Just inside the front of each front tire is a tie rod end (it's inside the rear of the front tires on '75-'78 models). It connects the knuckle arm on the steering knuckle to the tie rod. Another tie rod end is on the other end of the tie rod. Remember, there is a short tie rod on each side of the truck on 2WD and '86-'87 4WD models. '79-'85 4WD models have one long tie rod that connects the two steering knuckles.

Grab a tie rod near the end and try to move it side to side while watching the rubber part of the tie rod end. Push up and pull down on the bottom of the tie rod end. If the rubber moves while you're pushing or pulling, it means the ball is loose in the socket.

Here's another way to check the tie rod ends: have Friend rock the steering wheel back and forth while you watch the tie rod ends. There should be NO movement in the rubber. You should be able to twist the tie rod end a little—that's normal.

Check all the tie rod ends the same way. Replace the tie rod end(s) if your test tells you any of the ball joints in the tie rod ends are loose (Procedure 8).

Relay rod: On 2WD and '86-'87 4WD models, check the joints on each end of the relay rod the same way you checked the tie rod ends. **2WD models:** If either of the relay rod ends is loose, replace the relay rod (Procedure 9, Step 1). **'86-'87 4WD models:** If the joint on the left end (driver's side) of the relay rod is loose, replace the pitman arm (Procedure 9, Step 2). If the joint on the right end (passenger's side) of the relay rod is loose, replace the idler arm (Procedure 9, Step 3).

Idler arm: On 2WD and '86-'87 4WD models, locate the idler arm attached to the right end (passenger's side) of the relay rod. Grab the arm and try to move it up and down. If you notice any looseness in the relay arm, remove it and have new bushings installed (Procedure 9, Step 3).

Drag link: On '79-'85 4WD models, find the long rod that connects the pitman arm on the steering box to the knuckle arm on top of the left steering knuckle. That's the drag link. Shake both ends of the drag link to check for looseness. Have Friend rock the steering wheel back and forth while you watch the ends. If the ends seem loose and sloppy, see Procedure 9, Step 4, to adjust or repair the drag link ends.

EVERYONE: If there's excessive play in the steering wheel but the pitman arm and tie rod ends (everyone), the relay rod and idler arm (2WD and '86-'87 4WD models), and the drag link ('79-'85 4WD models) all check out OK, be sure to do Steps 7 and 8 to check the ball joints, wheels, wheel bearings and steering knuckle bearings for looseness.

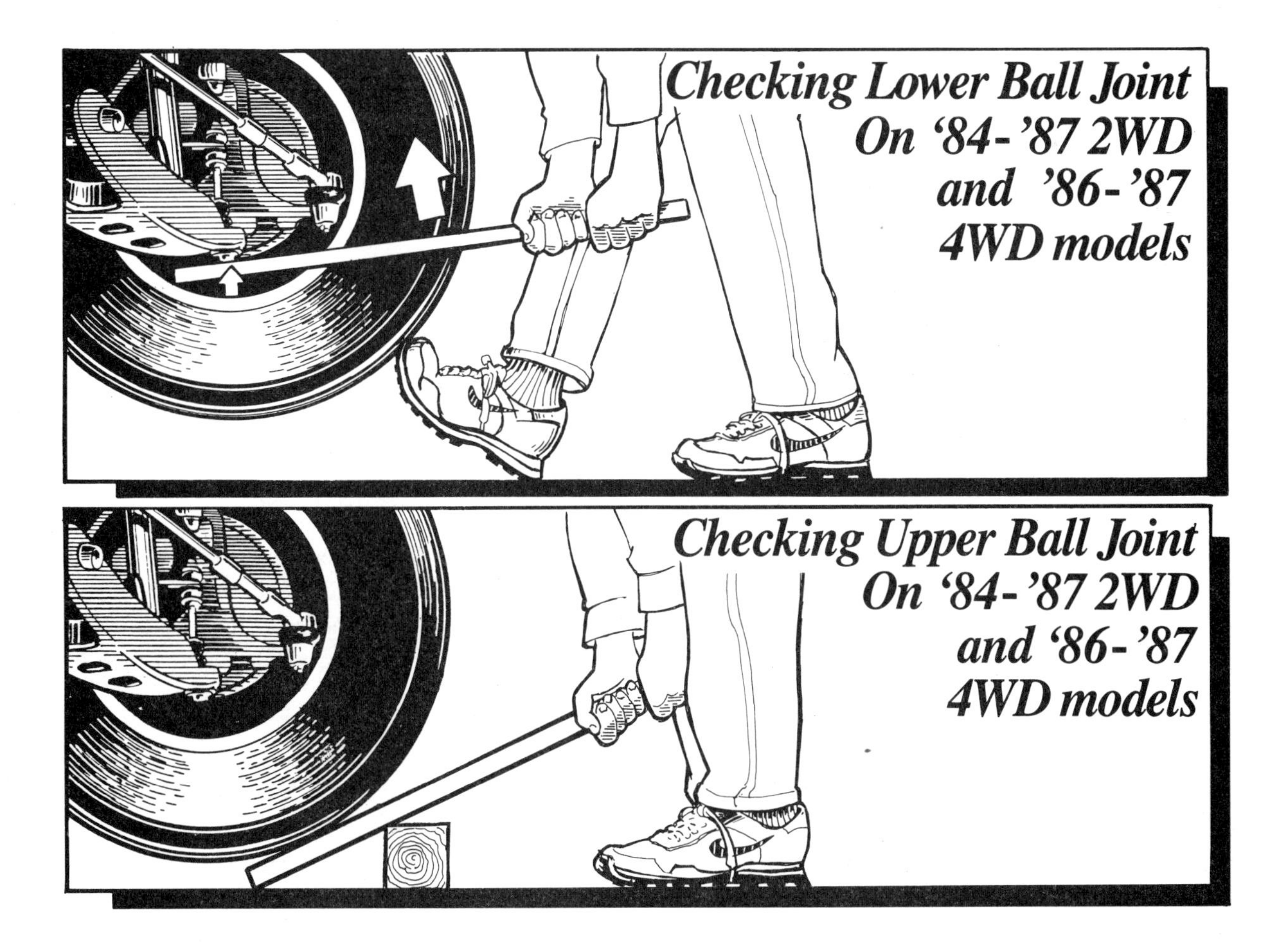

Step 8. Check the Steering Ball Joint.

If you have a '79-'85 4WD, you don't have steering ball joints, so skip to Step 8 to check the steering knuckle bearings.

Chock the rear wheels, set the handbrake, then jack up the front of the truck and put it on jackstands so the front wheels are about two inches off the ground (see Chapter 2, Procedure 1). The front wheels must be off the ground and pointed straight ahead for this test.

2WD and '86-'87 4WD models: The steering ball joints connect the top and bottom of the steering knuckle to the suspension arms. Here's how to test the ball joints for play.

'75-'83 2WD models: The truck is resting on jackstands with the front wheels off the ground, right? Put a hydraulic jack or the Toyota jack beneath the lower suspension arm on the side you're getting ready to check. Put a short block of wood on top of the jack, then gently raise the jack against the suspension arm until you see the truck start to lift off the jackstand. Lower the jack until the truck is barely resting on the jackstand again. Have Friend push on the brake pedal to eliminate any wheel bearing play.

Grab the bottom of one of the front tires, then try to push it up and down while feeling for any looseness. Now push and pull on the bottom of the tire. Feel any looseness? If the wheel feels solid, the ball joints are good. If you feel a little play when you try to move the tire, have Friend wiggle the tire the way you did while you watch the ball joints. If you see the rubber dust boots move more than .091" (in other words, a barely perceptible amount), the loose ball joint should be replaced (Procedure 11). Lower the jack that's under the suspension arm, then check the ball joints on the other side of the truck.

While the truck is blocked up, try wiggling the tire again without Friend's foot on the brake. Feel any looseness now? If so, see Step 8.

'84-'87 2WD and '86-'87 4WD models: To check the lower ball joint, put the end of a long bar against the inside of the front wheel, then raise the bar so it's against the bottom of the ball joint. Pull up on the bar while watching the ball joint for movement. If the ball joint moves more than .091" (a barely perceptible amount), replace it (Procedure 12).

To check the upper ball joint, place a short block of wood a couple of inches in front of one of the front tires. Stick your long bar beneath the front of the tire, then push down so the bar is resting on the block of wood. Pry up on the wheel while watching the upper ball joint for movement. Again, if the ball joint moves more than .091" (a barely perceptible amount), replace the ball joint. Check the ball joints on the other side of the truck the same way.

While the truck is jacked up, grab the bottom of each front tire and try to move it in and out, then up and down. If you can feel any looseness in the wheel, see Step 8.

EVERYONE: Check the rubber boots on all of the ball joints, tie rod ends, relay rod ends, pitman arm and idler arm. Replace them with new boots from Toyota if they are cracked, torn or missing. On some models the dust boot and ball joint are inseparable, so you'll have to replace the ball joint if the boot is torn.

Step 9. Check Wheels and Wheel Bearings, Steering Knuckle Bearings ('79-'85 4WD models).

The truck must be jacked up and resting on jackstands for this test (Chapter 2, Procedure 1).

Ask Friend to hold the steering wheel steady while you grasp one of the front wheels at the 9 and 3 o'clock positions. Rock the tire back and forth and feel for movement. Try the 12 and 6 o'clock positions. If the wheel bearing is loose, you'll feel movement in all directions and you've probably been hearing some low pitched growls and rumbling coming from the front of the truck as you drive. See Procedure 5 to check and adjust the wheel bearings.

2WD and '86-'87 4WD models: If there was movement in the wheel when you rocked it back and forth in Steps 6 and 7, but the ball joints checked out OK, the wheel is loose on the hub (check the lug nuts for tightness) or the wheel bearings are out of adjustment or shot. See Procedure 5.

'79-'85 4WD models: If you feel looseness while rocking the wheel at the 12 and 6 o'clock positions, have friend rock the wheel while you watch the top and bottom of the steering knuckle. If you see the steering knuckle moving while friend rocks the wheel, the bearings in the top and bottom of the steering knuckle are worn. See Procedure 11.

Step 10. Finishing Up.

Lower the truck if it's on jackstands. Now that you've diagnosed the suspension and steering, let's remedy any maladies that you observed.

PROCEDURE 2: REPLACE REAR SHOCKS

Condition: Rear shocks or shock bushings have expired.

Tools and Materials: Phase 1 tool kit, two new rear shock absorbers, penetrating oil.

Remarks: Always replace both rear shocks at the same time or the truck's handling characteristics will change frightfully.

If the rubber grommets are worn out but the shock seems good otherwise, try to buy new grommets or round up some used ones and install them.

Step 1. Locate Shock Mounting Bolts or Nuts.

At the top and bottom of each rear shock you'll see a castellated (castle) nut with a cotter pin locking it in place ('75-'78 models) or a bolt and washer ('79-'87 models).

Step 2. Release Upper Shock Mount.

Put wheel chocks in front of and behind the front wheels. Jack up the rear of the truck and put it safely on jackstands. 4WD models have a lot of clearance, so you probably don't need to jack and block them. Be sure the handbrake is set and transmission is in FIRST or REVERSE (manual) or PARK (automatic).

'75-'78 models: Use pliers to remove the cotter pins from the castellated nuts on each shock absorber.

EVERYONE: Squirt penetrating oil around the nuts or bolt heads. Use a socket and ratchet to unscrew the bolts or nuts *counterclockwise* a little at a time. They're usually pretty tight, so you might have to use a cheater bar (a two- to three-foot-long piece of pipe) on the ratchet handle for added leverage. Use a husky ½" drive socket and ratchet if you have them.

We want to avoid breaking anything, so if a bolt or nut seems to tighten while you're unscrewing it, douse everything with penetrating oil, then screw the bolt or nut back in a little. Douse everything with penetrating oil again and unscrew it a little. Repeat the in-and-out routine as many times as necessary. When the bolt or nut is off, wrestle the shock off its bracket.

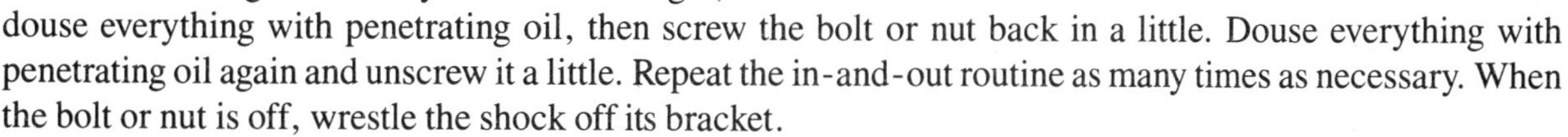

Remove the upper bolt or nut from the other shock absorber. Remove the lower bolts or nuts the same way.

Step 3. Install Shock Absorber.

Before installing a new shock, hold it upright the way it will be installed. Hold the bottom end and extend the top end as far as it will go, then push the top of the shock down until it hits bottom. Do this a few times to purge the air from the shock oil. (This isn't necessary if you're installing gas-filled shocks.) Compare the resistance in the new shocks to each other and to the resistance in the old shocks. If the new shocks aren't equally hard to pump or aren't significantly harder to pump than the old shocks, you either bought some cheap dime store shocks or the new shocks are defective. Return them and get some good ones. Don't laugh, two out of the last four "major brand" shocks I've tried to install were defective!

Clean the threads of the mounting bolts and nuts with a wire brush, then give them a light coat of oil.

Slide the bottom end of the shock onto the bracket. Get the bottom bolt or nut started, then install the top bolt or nut and get it started. Install the other shock the same way. When you're sure all the threads are straight, torque the bolts or nuts. Here's how tight to torque them:

MODEL	TORQUE
'75-'78	25-40 ft.lbs.
'79-'83 All	14-22 ft.lbs.
'84-'87 2WD	19 ft.lbs.
'84-'87 4WD	47 ft.lbs.

Lower the truck if it's on jackstands, then go for a ride. Quite a difference, eh?

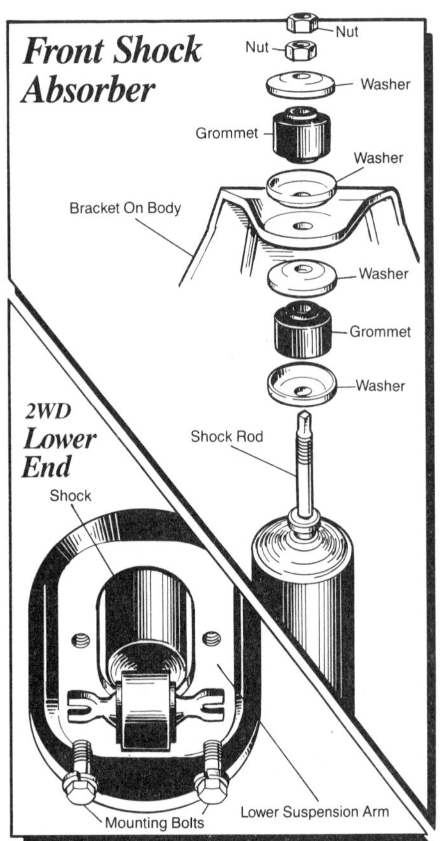

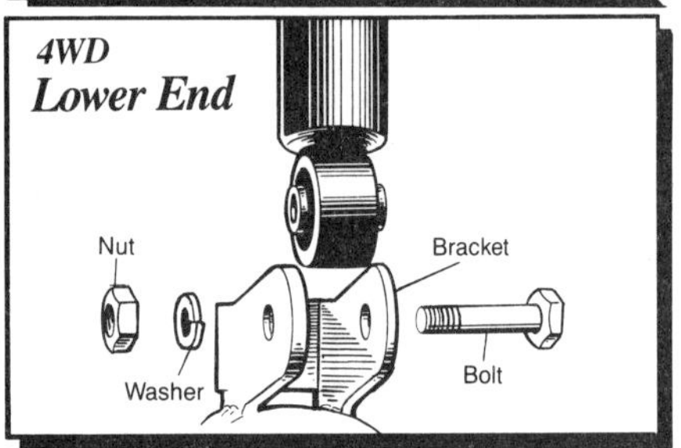

PROCEDURE 3: REPLACE FRONT SHOCKS

Condition: Front shocks are worn out; OR the shock must be removed to replace suspension parts.

Tools and Materials: Phase 1 tool kit, rags, maybe new shock absorbers.

Step 1. Chock, Jack and Block.

Loosen the front lug nuts a little, jack up the front of the truck and put it on jackstands (Chapter 2, Procedure 1). Remove the front wheels.

Step 2. Locate and Remove Upper Shock Mounting Nuts.

A threaded rod sticking out of the upper end of the shock absorber fits through a bracket on the frame. Looking into the wheel well, you might need to move a little rubber flap hanging down from the body to see the bracket and shock mounting nuts. Two nuts attach the threaded rod to the bracket. You'll see a series of washers and rubber grommets on either side of the mounting bracket. Make a note of the washer and rubber grommet arrangement above and below the mounting bracket. (Some models don't have a washer on top of the lower grommet.)

Note that there are two nuts on the threaded rod and the end of the rod is flattened on two sides. Squirt some penetrating oil on the nuts, then use a 14mm wrench to hold the bottom nut while you remove the top nut with another 14mm wrench or socket.

Hold the flattened part of the rod with a crescent wrench, Vise Grips or large pliers while you remove the bottom 14mm nut. Remove the large washer (note which side is top), then remove the rubber pad, then remove the second large washer. Next remove the mounting bolt(s) that attach the bottom end of the shock.

2WD models: The lower end of the shock is attached to the bottom of the lower suspension arm with two 12mm bolts. You have to look through a hole in the bottom of the suspension arm to see them. The bolts fit through slots on the ends of a bracket attached to the bottom of the shock absorber.

Use a socket and ratchet to remove the two bolts, then pull the shock down and out of the suspension arm.

4WD models: The lower end of the shock fits into a bracket on top of the differential housing ('79-'85 models) or the lower suspension arm ('86-'87 models) and is held in place with a bolt and nut. Squirt penetrating oil on the threaded end of the bolt and all around the nut. If the nut isn't welded to the bracket, hold the nut with a box end wrench while you use a socket and your longest ratchet to turn the bolt head *counterclockwise*. Use a ½" drive ratchet and socket, if you have them, because the nut is probably very tight. When the nut is off, tap the bolt out of the bracket and shock absorber. Be careful and don't damage the threads on the bolt. Wiggle the shock out of the bracket.

Step 3. Install Front Shock Absorber.

Clean the threads of the mounting bolts and nuts with a wire brush, then give them a light coat of oil. Before installing a new shock, hold it upright the way it will be installed. Hold the bottom end and extend

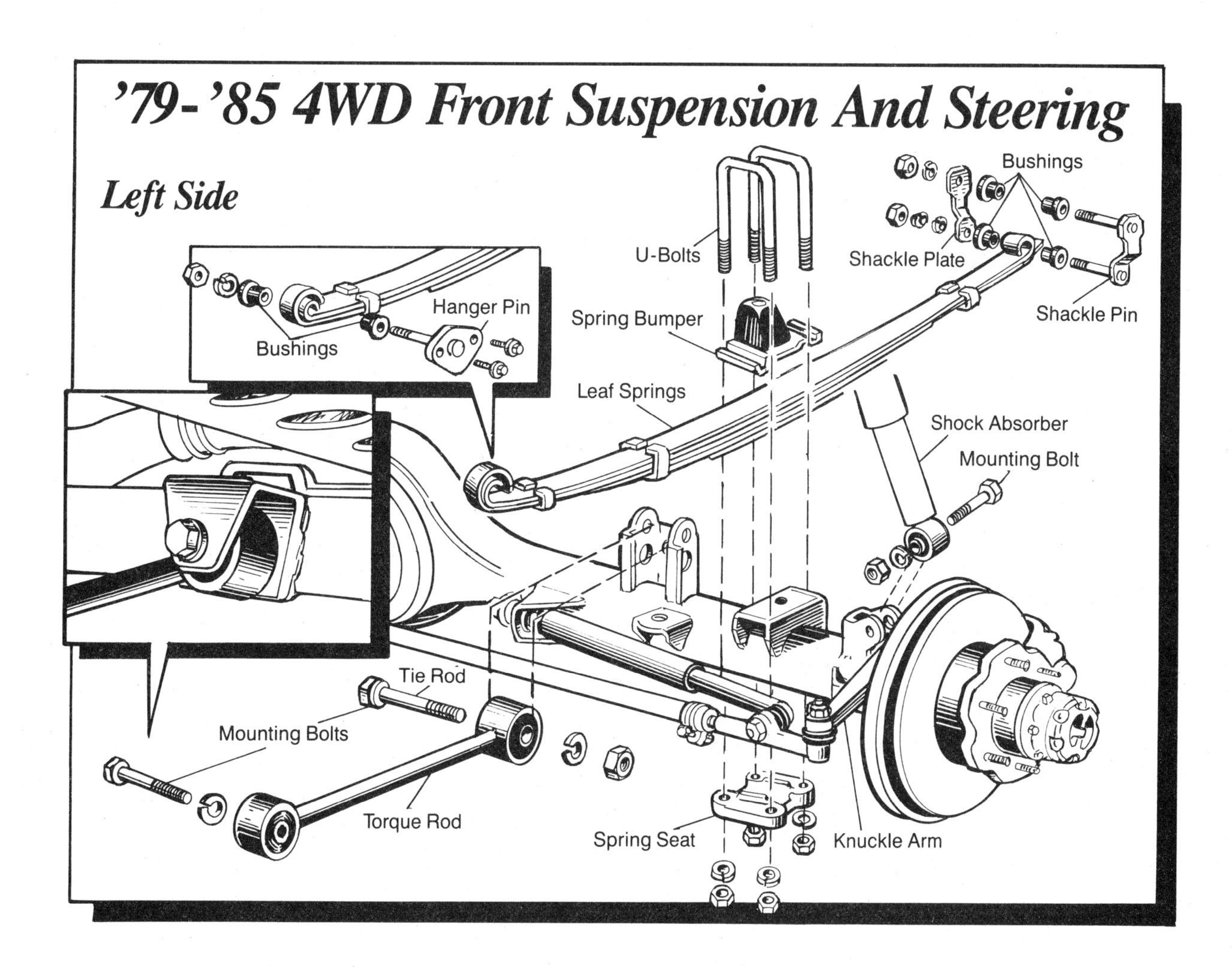

the top end as far as it will go, then push the top of the shock down until it hits bottom. Do this a few times to purge air from the shock oil. (This isn't necessary if you are installing gas-filled shocks.) Compare the resistance in the new shocks to each other and to the resistance of the old shocks. If the new shocks aren't equally hard to pump, or aren't significantly harder to pump than the old shocks, you either bought some cheap dime store shocks or the new shocks are defective. Return them and get some good ones.

OK, to install the front shocks, extend the shock as far as possible, then install a large washer, a rubber grommet and a second large washer (if your model has one) on the threaded rod. The concave side of the large washers face the rubber grommet. In other words, install the new ones just like the old ones were installed.

2WD models: Stick the shock into its hole in the lower suspension arm, then guide the threaded rod through the hole in the upper bracket.

4WD models: Guide the threaded rod on the top of the shock into its bracket on the frame and the bottom of the shock into its bracket on the suspension arm or differential housing.

EVERYONE: Install another large washer on the threaded rod, then another grommet, then another washer. The concave sides of the large washers face the grommet. Screw one of the mounting nuts onto the threaded rod to hold it in place while you install the mounting bolt in the bottom of the shock.

2WD models: Install the two bolts in the slots in the bottom shock bracket and screw them into the suspension arm. Tighten the bolts to 13 ft.lbs.

4WD models: Fit the shock mounting bolt through its hole in the shock and bracket and screw it into the nut (if yours is welded to the bracket) or install the lockwasher and nut. Tighten the bolt or nut to:

MODEL	TORQUE
'79-'83 models	26-39 ft.lbs.
'84-'85 models	70 ft.lbs.
'86-'87 models	101 ft.lbs.

EVERYONE: Torque the nut at the top of the shock to 18 ft.lbs., then install the locknut (top nut) and tighten it while holding the bottom nut with another wrench.

Now install the shock on the other side of the truck.

When both shocks are installed, put the front wheels on and snug the lug nuts with a wrench. Lower the truck, then torque the lug nuts to 65-87 ft.lbs. Now go for a nice smooth ride.

PROCEDURE 4: REMOVE AND INSTALL STEERING DAMPER ON 1980-87 MODELS

Condition: Steering damper is worn out; OR you are removing the relay rod (2WD models) or the tie rod (4WD models).

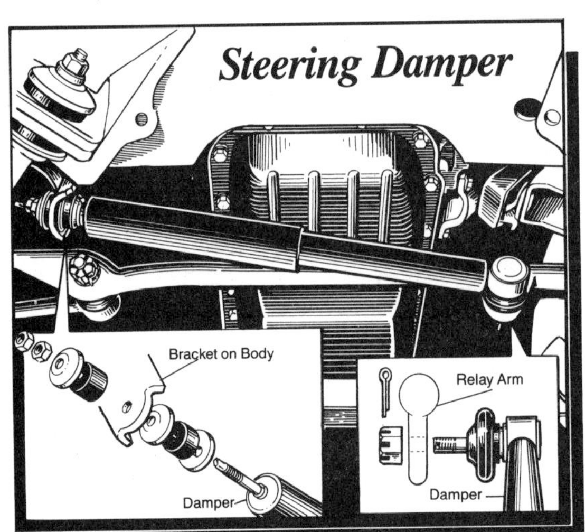

Tools and Materials: Two 12mm wrenches, tie rod puller or pickle fork, maybe a new steering damper, pliers or crescent wrench.

Step 1. Remove Steering Damper.

First, disconnect the steering damper from the relay rod or tie rod. Use pliers to remove the cotter pin from the castle nut, then remove the castle nut. Use a tie rod puller or pickle fork between the steering damper and rod to separate the steering damper from the rod. If you are planning to reuse the steering damper, be careful not to tear the rubber dust boot. Now remove the other end of the damper.

2WD and '80-'85 4WD models: Use a 12mm wrench to hold the nut closest to the bracket while you use another 12mm wrench to remove the nut on the end of the threaded rod. Use pliers or a crescent wrench to hold the end of the threaded rod while you remove the second nut. Remove the metal washer and rubber grommet. Now you can pull the steering damper out of the bracket.

'86-'87 4WD: Use a wrench to hold the bolt head while you remove the nut. Pull the end of the steering damper out of the bracket.

Step 2. Install Steering Damper.

Fit the ball joint-type end of the steering damper into its hole on the relay rod or tie rod and screw the castle nut on a few turns to hold it while you install the other end.

2WD and '80-'85 4WD models: Install a washer, then a rubber grommet, then another washer onto the end of the damper. The concave sides of the washers face the grommet. Next fit the end of the damper into the bracket. Install a grommet, then a washer with the concave side facing the grommet. Install one of the two mounting nuts (if your setup has two) onto the threaded rod and torque it to 9 ft.lbs. If you have two mounting nuts, use a wrench to hold the one that's already installed while you install and tighten the other nut.

'86-'87 4WD models: Fit the end of the damper into its bracket, then insert the mounting bolt. Install the nut and tighten it to 9 ft.lbs.

EVERYONE: Tighten the castle nut to 43 ft.lbs., then install a cotter pin through the nut. If necessary, tighten the nut a little more so the pin will fit. Wrap the ends of the cotter pin over the end of the castle nut.

PROCEDURE 5: REMOVE AND INSTALL FRONT AXLE HUB AND DISC

Condition: Brake disc is gouged or grooved and needs to be machined smooth (turned) or replaced; OR the wheel bearings need to be packed with fresh grease; OR the hub must be removed so you can remove the steering knuckle and/or ball joints.

Tools and Materials: Phase 1 tool set, can of high temperature wheel bearing grease, rags, paper towels, old newspapers, maybe new wheel bearings and grease seals, brake cleaner or alcohol.

'78-'83 2WD and all 4WD models: You will need a pint of brake fluid and the brake bleeding tools listed in Chapter 7, Procedure 1.

2WD models: You will need a 30mm (1-3/16") socket to remove and install the front axle nuts.

4WD models: You will need the tools listed in Procedure 6 to remove the 4WD hubs and a thin-walled 54mm (2-3/16") socket to remove the axle nuts. You might be able to rent a big socket—just so it has thin enough walls to fit inside the axle hub. The Toyota dealer sells the sockets (special tool number SST 09607-60020) for around $40, or you can order one from Northwest Off-Road Specialties, Inc. for about $15. (See Chapter 14 for Northwest Off-Road's catalog and address.) Models with manual locking hubs will need two new lockwashers for the axle nuts.

4WD models with automatic locking hubs: You will need a 5mm allen wrench and a strong T25 torx socket to remove the automatic locking hubs. A torx socket is a splined steel rod that fits into the splined end of a torx screw.

Remark: Once the truck is jacked up and the wheels are removed, it's a good idea to spread newspapers under the front axles to keep grease, oil and brake fluid off the floor and, even more importantly, to help keep dirt out of the bearings, hubs and brake parts that you remove.

Step 1. Chock, Jack and Block.

Chock the rear wheels, set the handbrake, loosen the front wheel lug nuts a little, then jack up the front of the truck and put it on jackstands. Remove the front wheels.

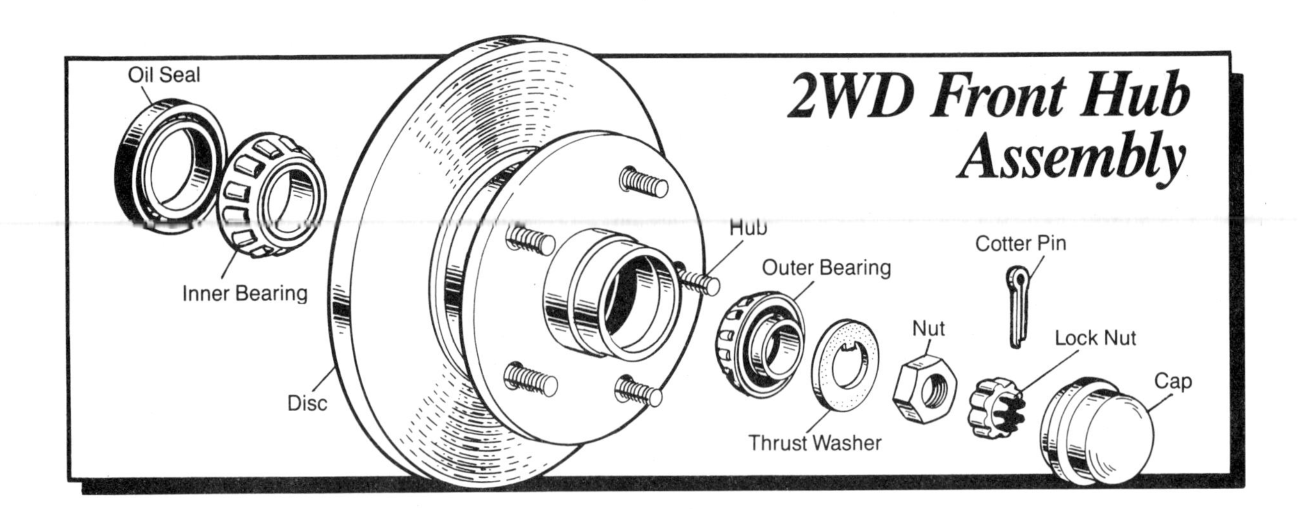

Step 2. Remove Calipers and Torque Plate.

See Chapter 7, Procedure 5, Steps 1-4 to remove the brake calipers. If yours are the kind that you can remove and hang by a string or wire, don't disconnect the brake line from the caliper. If yours are the kind that must be disconnected from the brake line to remove, plug the ends of the brake lines with the rubber bleeding valve caps to prevent the fluid from leaking out and to keep dirt from entering the line. Stash the calipers where they are safe from dirt and grease.

If your model has a torque plate wrapped over the disc, you'll have to use a ½" drive 17mm socket and ratchet to remove the two bolts that attach the torque plate to the steering knuckle. Pull the torque plate off the knuckle.

Step 3. Remove Axle Hub and Disc.

Mark the axle hubs "left" or "right" as you remove them. If you remove the wheel bearings from the hub, keep track of which hub they came from so you can install them in the same place during reassembly.

4WD models: See Procedure 6 to remove the 4WD hubs. When the hubs are off, come back here to remove the axle hub.

2WD models: Fit the tip of a medium size screwdriver into the gap between the axle hub and the little cap on the end of the axle. Use a hammer to gently tap on the screwdriver until the cap moves out a little. Do the same thing in several places around the edge of the cap until you can pull it off.

Use pliers to remove the cotter pin sticking through the axle nut ('75-'78 models) or through the funny-shaped **nut lock** ('79-'87 models). Remove the nut lock, if your model has one. Now use a 30mm socket or large pliers to remove the axle nut (*counterclockwise*). Leave the large flat washer on the axle.

To remove the hub, put your thumbs on the flat washer while you grab the hub with your fingers and pull it off the axle. Support the weight of the hub while you pull it straight out and off the axle. If you just drag the hub off the axle, the inner grease seal might get damaged. Once the hub is off the axle, pull the flat washer and outer bearing out of the outboard side of the hub and lay them on something clean, then cover them with a clean rag or paper towel.

'79-'87 4WD models with free wheeling hubs: Look at the large **lock nut** on the end of the axle. Find the place where a thin **lock washer** tab is bent over one of the flat sides of the lock nut. Use a screwdriver and hammer to tap the tab away from the lock nut, then use a 54mm socket to remove the nut. Pull the lock washer off the axle, then remove the **adjusting nut** that's left on the axle.

'79-'87 4WD models with automatic locking hubs: Use a 54mm socket to remove the large axle nut.

All 4WD models: Support the weight of the hub while you pull it straight out and off the axle. If you just drag the hub off the axle, the inner grease seal might get damaged.

EVERYONE: The wheel bearings are the round things in the center of the hub that the axle goes through. Look for white gooey-looking stuff that would indicate water has gotten inside the bearings. See any? If you do, the wheel bearings should be repacked and the grease seals replaced (Procedure 7). The grease seals are the round things in the inboard side of the hub, right next to the inner wheel bearings. If the grease seals are hard, cracked or torn they should be replaced (Procedure 7). Everything OK? Proceed . . .

If you are here to repack the bearings with fresh grease, see Procedure 7.

If you are here to remove the steering knuckle, set the hub aside and cover it with a clean rag or paper towel so dirt won't get in the bearings, then skip down to Procedure 10 for 2WD and '86-'87 4WD models or Procedure 11 for '79-'85 4WD models.

If you are removing the hub so you can replace the disc, see Step 4.

If you are removing the hubs so the discs can be turned, the grease seals and wheel bearings must be removed (Procedure 7, Step 2). Once the seals and bearings are out, haul the hubs to the Toyota dealer or a brake shop to have them turned.

The minimum legal (and safe) thickness for the disc is:

BRAKE TYPE	INCHES	MILLIMETERS
S-16	.453	11.5
FS17	.827	21
K-Type	.748	19
PD60	.945	24
'79-'85 S12+8	.453	11.5
'86-'87 S12+8	.748	19

Replace the disc (Step 4) if it's worn out. Thin discs can't dissipate the heat properly and thus warp easily.

Step 4. Replace Disc.

'81-'85 4WD models: The disc is attached to the hub with the lug studs and two bolts. To replace the disc you'll need to have the Toyota dealer, a garage or a machine shop press the lug studs out of the hub for you. Remove the two bolts that attach the disc to the hub, then remove the disc.

Fit a new disc onto the hub and install and tighten the two bolts to 34 ft.lbs. Have the lug bolts pressed back into the hub, then check the torque on the two bolts. That's all there is to it.

EVERYONE (except '81-'85 4WD models): The bolts between the lug studs attach the disc to the hub. Depending on the model, the bolt heads are either on the inboard or outboard side of the hub. Remove the five or six 14mm bolts that attach the disc to the hub. Remove the old disc, then fit a new disc onto the hub. Lightly

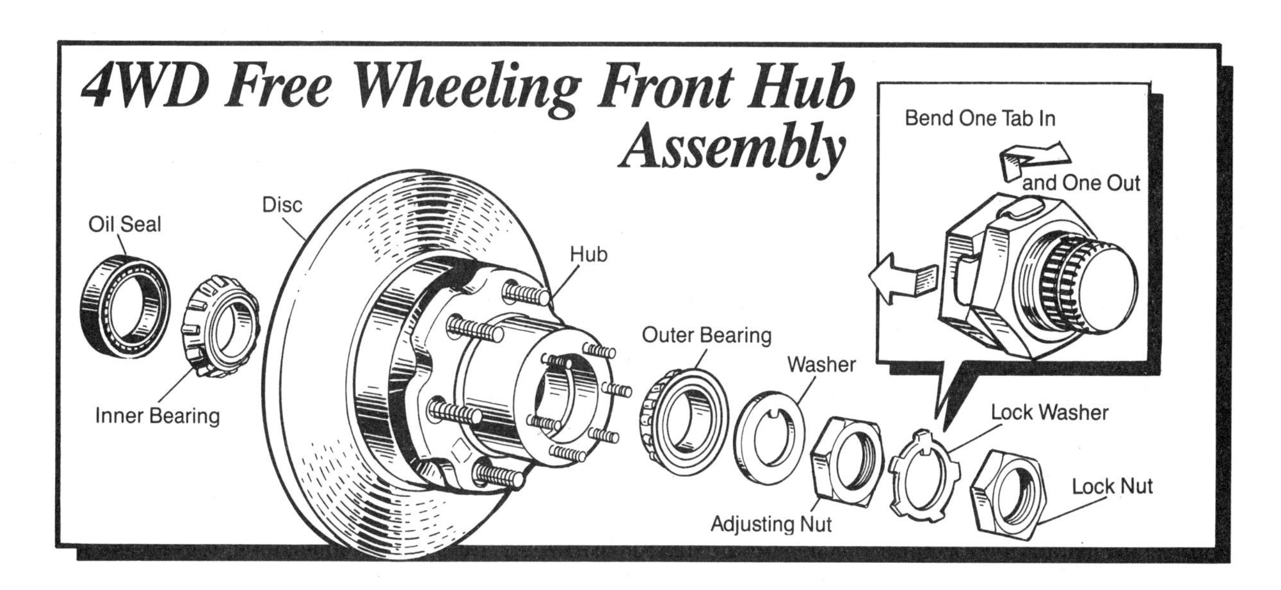

oil the bolt threads, then screw them in and torque them in a crisscross pattern to 12 ft.lbs., then around again to 22, and finally to the figure for your year and model listed in the table below.

MODEL	BRAKE TYPE	TORQUE
'75-'83	S16	29-39 ft.lbs.
'79-'84	K-Type	40-54 ft.lbs.
'79-'80 4WD	S-12+8	29-39 ft.lbs.
'84-'85 2WD	PD60 & FS17	47 ft.lbs.
'86-'87	All types	47 ft.lbs.

EVERYONE: It's a good idea to have the new discs turned (machined) before installing them. Even though the disc is made of heavy steel, mounting it to the hub often distorts it slightly, which could cause brake squeal.

When you are ready to install the axle hub, see Step 5. This would be a good time to repack the wheel bearings with fresh grease (Procedure 7). Come back here to install the hubs.

Step 5. Install Axle Hub.

Use brake cleaner or alcohol to clean the brake disc (even if it's new) and all of the caliper mounting hardware that your model has—things like the mounting bolts and torque plate. Lightly oil the threads on the mounting bolts, then wipe excess oil off with a clean rag. Clean your hands before installing the clean disc and hub.

2WD models: The bearings and grease seal have been installed, right? OK, put your thumbs on the flat washer and grab the hub with your fingers. Gently slide the hub onto the axle, being very careful that the axle doesn't damage the grease seal. Push the hub all the way on. Next, install the axle nut and torque it to 22 ft.lbs. Rotate the hub frontward and backwards a few times to seat the bearings, then loosen the axle nut until it can be turned by hand. Torque the nut to 22 ft.lbs. again and rotate it back and forth a few more times. Then loosen the nut again until you can turn it by hand.

OK, now for the final adjustment. Use one hand on the socket to tighten the axle nut as tight as you can. Don't use the ratchet. Rotate the hub to check that it turns smoothly with a slight resistance. If you have a spring scale for weighing fish, hook the scale onto one of the lug studs and see how much force is required to turn the hub. It should only take between 19.4 and 60 ounces of pull to make the hub turn. If the hub turns with excess resistance, loosen the axle adjusting nut slightly and try the hub again.

Grab the hub and try to move it in and out on the axle. There should be no looseness. If you feel a looseness when you push and pull on the hub, tighten the axle adjusting nut slightly.

When the hub turns smoothly and there's no looseness, fit the nut lock onto the axle nut on '79-'87 models. Then fit the cotter pin through the axle. If the notches in the axle nut ('75-'78 models) or nut lock ('79-'87 models) aren't aligned with the hole in the axle, turn the nut slightly so the hole and notches are aligned, then insert the cotter pin. Bend one of the cotter pin ends over the end of the axle nut to lock it in place.

Hold the round cap on the end of the hub while you tap it in with your hand. Finish installing it by tapping a screwdriver all around the raised ridge on the cap until it is fully seated against the hub.

No torque plates? You can go back to the brake chapter to install the calipers.

Models with FS17 and PD60-type brakes: Skip down to Step 6 to install the torque plates (caliper holders).

4WD models: Fit the axle hub on the spindle, then install the outer bearing. If you have free wheeling hubs, install the thrust washer and then the axle nut. If you have automatic locking hubs, you don't have a thrust washer so just install the axle nut.

Tighten the axle nut to 43 ft.lbs., then turn the hub forward and backward a few times to seat the bearings. Loosen the adjusting nut until you can turn it by hand.

'79-'83 4WD models: Tighten the nut again to 3 to 5 ft.lbs.

'84-'87 4WD models: Tighten the nut again to 18 ft.lbs.

All 4WD models: Check that the hub turns smoothly with a slight resistance. If you have a spring tension gauge or spring scale for weighing fish, hook one end of the scale on a lug stud and check that it takes 6.2 to 12.6 pounds of force to turn the hub. If it takes less than 6.2 pounds to turn it, tighten the adjusting nut slightly and check it again. If it takes more than 12.6 pounds of force, slightly loosen the nut and check it again.

When the hub turns smoothly with a slight resistance, try to move it in and out on the axle. If you feel any looseness, tighten the adjusting nut slightly. OK, the hub turns smoothly with no looseness, right?

Models with automatic locking hubs can go to Procedure 6, Step 6, to install the 4WD hubs now. Models with free wheeling hubs must do the next paragraph.

Models with free wheeling hubs: Install a new lock washer so the tab on the inner edge fits into the groove on the axle, then install the lock nut as tight as you can with your fingers. Use a screwdriver and hammer to bend one of the lock washer tabs inward over one of the flat sides of the adjusting nut. Torque the lock nut to 58-72 ft.lbs. ('79-'83 models) or to 33 ft.lbs. ('84-'87 models). Turn the hub again to check that it turns smoothly without excessive resistance.

Do Procedure 6, Step 4, to install the 4WD hubs, then go to Chapter 7, Procedure 5, Step 4A, to install the calipers.

Step 6. Install Torque Plate.

FS17 and PD60 brakes: Fit the torque plate over the disc so the two bolt holes are aligned with the bolt holes in the steering knuckle. Screw in the two 17mm mounting bolts, then torque them to 80 ft.lbs. See Chapter 7, Procedure 5, Step 4B, to install the calipers.

PROCEDURE 6: REMOVE AND INSTALL 4WD HUBS

First, I need to define some terms. The **axle hub** (also called the **wheel hub**) is the large steel hub on the front axle that contains the wheel bearings. The brake disc is bolted to the axle hub, and the tire and wheel are bolted to the **lug studs** mounted in the axle hub. On 4WD models a **4WD hub body** bolted to the outboard side of the axle hub contains a mechanism that locks the axle hub to the front axle when you want 4WD. A **hub cover** covers the outboard end of the 4WD hub body.

Free wheeling hubs or **automatic locking hubs** refer to the type of mechanism in the 4WD hub body that locks the axle hub to the axle. Free wheeling hubs have a control handle built into the hub cover that you must turn to the LOCK position to lock the axle hubs to the axle. Automatic locking hubs don't have control handles built into the ends of the hubs. They lock the axle hub to the axle automatically when you engage the 4WD. Be sure you are following the instructions that apply to the kind of hubs on your truck.

OK, here's how to remove, inspect and install the 4WD hubs.

Condition: Difficulty engaging or disengaging the free wheeling hubs; OR the automatic hubs aren't engaging or disengaging; OR you need to remove the 4WD hubs in order to remove the axle hubs.

Tools and Materials: 12mm socket and ratchet, four inches or longer extension for the ratchet, brass bar at least ½" diameter and six inches long, hammer, wheel bearing grease, new 4WD hub gasket and hub cover gasket, flat nosed external snap ring pliers, cleaning solvent, rags.

Free wheeling hubs also require a 10mm socket and a very small screwdriver.

Automatic locking hubs also require a 5mm allen wrench, a strong T25 torx socket and needlenose pliers.

Remark: It takes special tools to disassemble automatic locking hubs. If yours aren't working right, you can remove the old ones and install new ones (Steps 5-8), or remove them and take them to the Toyota dealer for repair.

When replacing free wheeling 4WD hubs, you can buy new ones from the Toyota dealer or replace them with Warn Hubs from a parts store for about half the cost. Warn makes an "economy" steel and plastic hub and a higher quality steel and brass hub. Go for the high quality ones if you can afford them.

Step 1. Chock, Jack and Block.

If you are removing the 4WD hubs so you can remove the axle hubs you'll need to chock the rear wheels, set the handbrake, loosen the lug nuts a little, jack up the front of the truck and put it on jackstands (Chapter 2, Procedure 1).

If you are here only to remove and install the 4WD hub bodies and don't need to remove the axle hubs (and discs), the 4WD hubs can be removed and installed with the wheels on the truck, so you won't need to jack up the front end and put it on jackstands.

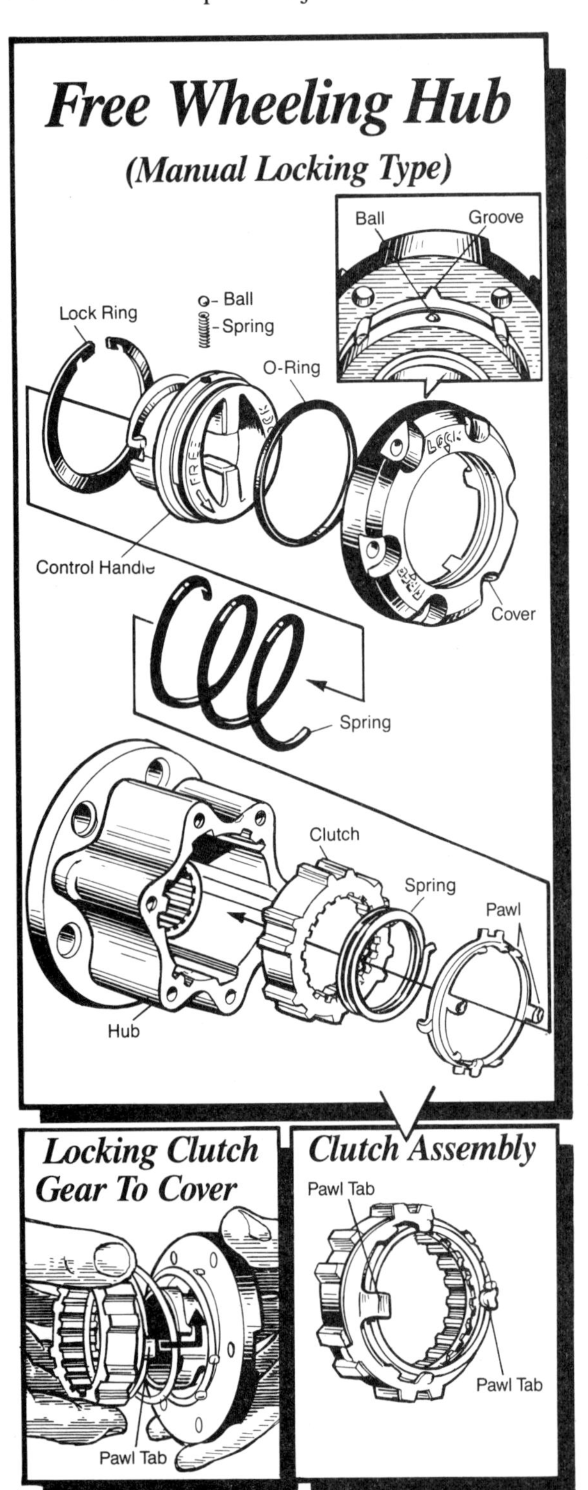

Step 2. Remove and Check Free Wheeling Hub Covers.

Set the control handle on the 4WD hubs to the FREE position, then use a 10mm socket and ratchet to remove the six bolts that attach the cover to the hub. Pull the cover and control handle off the hub.

Inspect hub cover and clutch assembly: The round gear-looking thing attached to the inboard side of the hub cover is the clutch assembly. To check it grab the hub cover and slowly turn the control handle to the LOCK position. The clutch assembly should move clockwise and jump away from the cover. Push the clutch assembly back against the cover and turn the control lever to the FREE position. The clutch should stay next to the hub cover. If the clutch doesn't move away from the cover or won't stay locked against it, either the large spring or the pawl that holds it is broken or worn out.

It there is water inside the hub, or the grease is a whitish color, either the hub cover gasket or a little rubber O-ring between the cover and control lever is leaking. You'll replace the gasket during reassembly, so here's how to replace the O-ring.

Hold the clutch cover in your left hand with the clutch gear facing you. Push in on the gear and turn it *clockwise*. If the gear stops turning, push it in again and keep turning it *clockwise*. The gear and spring will pop off the cover. Wipe the grease off the inside of the cover, then use a very small screwdriver to hook one of the notches in the flat snap ring on the inside of the cover. Push the notch toward the center and lift at the same time. The end of the spring will pop out of its groove. Wiggle the rest of the snap ring out of the groove. Now you can push the control handle out of the cover. Be careful not to loose the tiny ball and spring at the edge of the lever right next to arrow. Remove the ball and stash it somewhere safe. The spring will probably stay inside the handle.

Use the small screwdriver to remove the old O-ring that's in a groove around the edge of the handle. Install a new O-ring in the groove, then check that it isn't crooked or twisted. Smear a light coat of grease on the O-ring, then put a little dab in the hole where the tiny ball fits.

Hold the handle so the hole is at the top, then set the little ball into its hole. There are two grooves in the cover aligned with the FREE and LOCK positions. Fit the handle into the cover so the little ball goes into one of the grooves. Push the handle into the cover until the outer surface is even with the outside of the cover. Insert one end of the snap ring into the groove, then push the rest of the spring down until it's completely in the groove. See if the handle moves smoothly back and forth from the FREE to the LOCK position.

Set the handle to the FREE position, then fit the flatter end of the large spring onto the inside of the hub cover.

One side of the clutch gear has a spring wound inside, held in place by small metal tabs. The other side of the clutch gear is flat. Fit the side of the gear with the spring into the large spring on the cover so the metal tabs are aligned with the slots in the cover. Push the clutch toward the cover, making sure the tabs fit into the slots, then turn the gear *counterclockwise* to lock it into place. If the gear doesn't stay right next to the cover, push and turn it *counterclockwise* some more.

Step 3. Remove and Inspect Free Wheeling 4WD Hub Parts.

Locate the snap ring around the end of the axle. Use flat-nosed snap-ring pliers to spread the ends of the snap ring just enough to pull it off the axle.

Next use a 14mm socket and ratchet to remove the six nuts around the base of the 4WD hub. Use a brass bar and hammer to tap on the ends of the six studs to loosen the cone-shaped washers that are around each stud. Don't tap on the 4WD hub to remove it! Pull the cone washers off the studs, then pull the hub body off the axle hub. Remove the gasket that fits between the hub body and the axle hub.

Use solvent and clean rags to remove the grease from the hub. To check the 4WD hub parts, inspect the splines on the inside and the gear teeth on the outside of the inner hub. The teeth on the outside of the inner hub mesh with the teeth on the inside of the clutch to lock the hub to the axle when the hubs are in the LOCK position. If any of the splines or teeth are chipped or missing, the hub should be replaced.

Try to move the inner hub in and out toward the ends of the hub. If you feel more than a minute amount of play, the hub is worn. If the play is easily felt the hub should be replaced.

Now let's fit the cover onto the hub and install a couple of the mounting bolts finger-tight. Here's how to install the cover. Two of the grooves on the inside of the 4WD hub don't have a tooth in the center. They are "blank," so to speak. Look at the grooves on the edge of the clutch, nearest to the cover. You'll see that tabs for the pawl fit between two pairs of teeth. The teeth with the pawl tabs must go into the two "blank" grooves in the 4WD hub. If the cover is installed in any other position, it won't fit against the 4WD hub correctly.

OK, set the control handle to the FREE position and check that the clutch gear is right next to the cover. If it isn't, push in on the gear and turn it *clockwise*. Fit the cover on the hub and install a couple of the mounting bolts. The inner hub should turn freely inside the hub. Check it. Now set the control handle to LOCK and try to turn the inner hub. It should be locked to the hub. If it isn't, the clutch mechanism isn't working properly. Have the experts check it for you or replace the hub. Everything appears to be in good condition? Good.

Set the control handle to FREE, then remove the two mounting bolts and pull the cover off the hub. Smear multi-purpose grease all over the inner hub and clutch gear, and in the grooves inside the hub. Do Step 4 to install the hub.

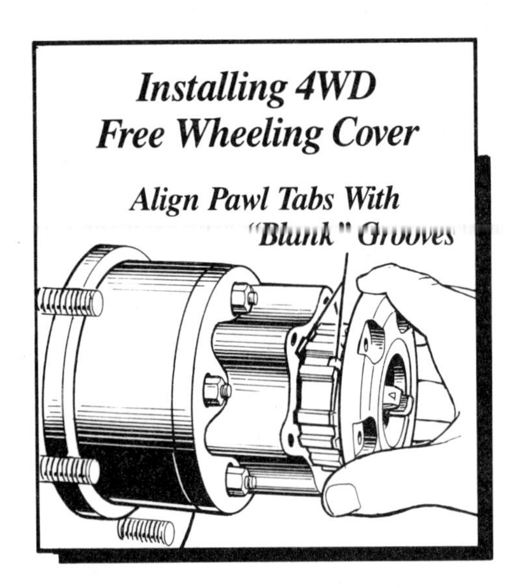

Installing 4WD Free Wheeling Cover

Step 4. Install Free Wheeling Hub.

Fit a new 4WD hub gasket onto the studs on the axle hub. Install the hub body onto the studs so the stubby knock pin sticking out of the axle hub between two of the studs fits into one of the small holes on the inboard side of the 4WD hub. Install the six cone washers and nuts, then tighten the nuts to 23 ft.lbs.

Screw an 8x1.25mm bolt into the hole in the end of the axle shaft. Grab the bolt head with pliers and pull the axle toward you while you use snap ring pliers to install the snap ring in its groove near the end of the axle. Be sure the snap ring is seated all the way around. Now remove the bolt.

Now set the control handle to the FREE position. Push the clutch toward the cover and turn it counterclockwise to lock it in position. Smear wheel bearing grease on the teeth and splines of the clutch assembly. Be sure the grease gets in all the grooves.

Notice that two of the grooves on the inside of the 4WD hub are missing a tooth in the center. They are "blank." On the grooves on the edge of the clutch nearest to the cover, you'll see that tabs for the pawl fit between two of the pairs of teeth. The pawl tabs must go into the two "blank" grooves in the 4WD hub or you won't be able to get the cover on completely. Got it? Good.

Hold a new hub cover gasket in position while you fit the hub cover onto the 4WD hub. Install and snug down the six 10mm bolts. Careful! They only get torqued to 7 ft.lbs.; don't overtighten them or the little bolts will break.

Now check that you can turn the control lever back and forth from FREE to LOCK.

Step 5. Remove Automatic Locking Hubs.

Use a 5mm allen wrench to remove the six screws in the hub cover.

If you need to remove the 4WD hub, remove the bolt that's screwed into the end of the axle. Next, remove the six 14mm nuts at the base. Use a brass bar and hammer to tap on the end of the studs until the cone washers are loose enough to remove. Pull the 4WD hub off the axle hub. Don't tap on the hub to remove it. Once the hub is off, the round part that's left on the axle hub is the brake assembly for the automatic locking hub.

If you are here only to check the automatic locking hubs, you don't need to remove the hub brake assembly. Skip down to Step 6 to check the little brake shoes.

If you are here to remove the axle hub, use needlenose pliers to gently squeeze the ends of the spring in the brake assembly. Don't squeeze any harder than necessary or the spring will be weakened. Turn the spring to a position so one of the torx screws is between the ends of the spring. Use the torx socket to remove the screw. Turn the spring and remove the other two torx screws the same way. Now you can pull the brake assembly off the axle hub. See Step 6 to check the thickness of the brake shoes.

Step 6. Check Brake Assembly for the Automatic Locking Hubs.

To check the brake assembly, gently squeeze the ends of the spring together and pull it slightly out of the drum. Don't pull the shoes all the way out. Now use a micrometer to measure the thickness of the brake shoes. No micrometer? You'll have to use a feeler gauge. The brake shoes must be at least .040" (1mm) thick. If the shoes are OK, use the needlenose pliers to squeeze the spring and push the shoes all the way back into the brake shoe. If the shoes have worn so they are thinner than .040", replace the brake assembly. See Step 7 to install the brake assembly.

Step 7. Install Brake Assembly for Automatic Locking Hubs.

To install the brake assembly, the axle hub adjusting nut must be positioned correctly. If you've turned the hub adjusting nut, the bearing preload must be adjusted (Procedure 5, Step 5) before installing the brake assembly. If the adjusting nut hasn't been moved, or you've already adjusted the preload, check that the adjusting nut is aligned exactly the same as one of the two illustrations.

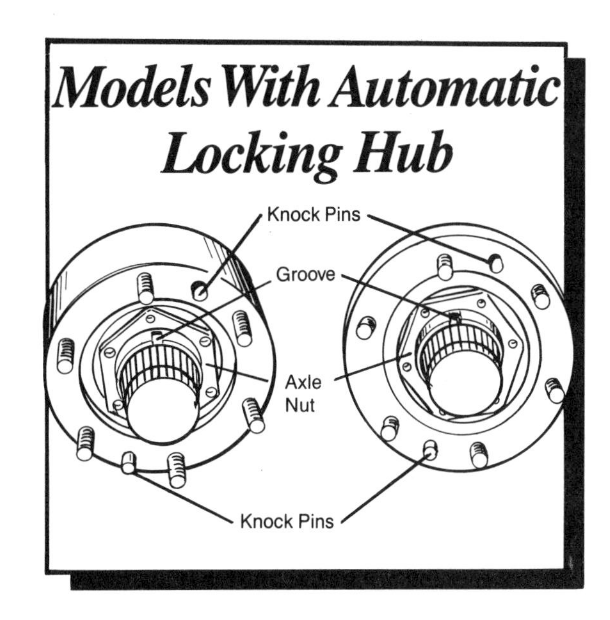

Grab the brake assembly and hold it so the small tab on the inner edge is at the top. Use the needlenose pliers to move the spring in the brake assembly so one of the holes in the brake assembly is aligned with one of the holes in the adjusting nut. Slide the brake assembly onto the axle so the tab fits into the groove on the axle. Push it all the way against the adjusting nut. Look through the holes in the brake assembly to see if they are aligned with the holes in the adjusting nut. If they aren't, remove the brake and turn the adjusting nut slightly, then install the brake assembly and check the holes again. When the holes are aligned, install one of the torx screws and tighten it to 61 inch pounds. If you don't have an inch pound torque wrench, torque it to 5 ft.lbs. Get it as close to the proper torque as possible. Now move the spring and install and torque the other two torx screws the same way. Install the screws so they are an equal distance apart. When the screws are torqued, check that the brake shoe is as far into the drum as possible. See Step 8 to install the 4WD hub.

Installing Automatic Locking Hub

Align The Inner Cam Protrusion With One Of The Knock Pin Holes

Inner Cam Protrusion
Knock Pin Hole
4WD Hub
Knock Pin Hole

Step 8. Install Automatic Locking Hub.

Look at the inboard side of the automatic locking hub. You'll see two smaller holes around the outer edge that don't go all the way through the hub. These are knock pin holes for the knock pins that are in the axle hub. Turn the inner hub so the small tab is aligned with one of the knock pin holes. Then move the larger tabs so they are equally spaced on each side of the smaller tab.

Use needlenose pliers to move the spring in the brake assembly to a position so the gap between the spring ends is aligned with the knock pin on the axle hub.

Fit the hub body onto the axle hub so the tab on the inner hub fits between the ends of the brake spring. The knock pin should fit into the knock pin hole. Check that the 4WD hub fits against the axle hub. If the 4WD hub and axle hub don't touch all the way around, remove the 4WD hub and check that everything is aligned correctly (as described above), then reinstall the hub. It might help to rotate the axle slightly so the axle splines are aligned with the splines in the hub.

When everything fits perfectly, install the six cone washers, lock washers and nuts. Torque the nuts in a criss-cross pattern to 23 ft.lbs.

Install the bolt and plate washer in the end of the axle. Torque the bolt to 13 ft.lbs. Finally, hold a new cover gasket in place while you install the cover and the six allen bolts. Torque the bolts to 7 ft.lbs.

Step 9. Finish the Job.

If you removed the wheels, install them and snug the lug nuts with a wrench. Lower the truck off the jackstands, then torque the lug nuts to 65-87 ft.lbs. If you disconnected any brake lines, be sure to bleed the brake system (Chapter 7, Procedure 1).

PROCEDURE 7: CLEAN, INSPECT, REPACK, INSTALL NEW FRONT WHEEL BEARINGS

Condition: Routine maintenance; OR a front wheel bearing has broken or worn out.

Tools and Materials: Phase 1 tool kit, safety glasses and dust mask, high temperature wheel bearing grease, several rags or paper towels, spray can of brake cleaner or solvent, stiff brush, wash pan, two new grease seals. 4WD models with free wheeling hubs will need two new lock plates for the axle nuts.

If you need to replace any of the wheel bearings, you'll need the following tools. To remove the outer races for the old bearings and install new outer races, you need a ½" to 1" diameter copper, brass or aluminum rod (called a "drift"), at least six inches long.

Remarks: Different brands of grease are likely to be incompatible. They cause each other to deteriorate or liquify, which reduces the lubricating effect. So, clean all the old grease out of the bearings and housings before packing them with new grease.

Keep track of where the wheel bearings were installed so you can put all the pieces back in the same places during reassembly.

Caution! While repacking or replacing the wheel bearings, don't get any grease on the brake pads. If you accidentally do, use brake cleaner to remove it or replace the pads with new ones.

Step 1. Chock, Jack, Block, and Remove Wheels and Calipers.

Flip to Chapter 7, Procedure 5, Steps 1-4, to get the truck on jackstands with the front wheels and brakes removed. If your calipers are the kind you can hang by a rope or wire, DON'T disconnect the brake lines. Please read the **Caution! Warning!** in the remarks at the start of Chapter 7.

2WD models: See Procedure 5, Steps 2 and 3, in this chapter to remove the front axle hubs. Once the hubs are off, come back here to replace the bearings.

4WD models: See Procedure 6 to remove the 4WD hubs, then see Procedure 5, Step 3 to remove the axle hubs. Once the hubs are off, come back here to repack or replace the bearings.

Step 2. Remove Wheel Bearings.

The axle hubs are off the truck, right? If not, you skipped Step 1.

Lay the hub on a clean cloth or newspaper with the lug studs pointing down. Lay a hammer handle or thin piece of wood across the disc. Use a screwdriver to pry the inner grease seal out of the inboard side of the hub. Just push the tip of the screwdriver under the rubber part of the seal, then push it down against the hammer handle or block of wood to pry the seal out. Do this in several places around the seal and it will pop out. Now you can remove the inner bearing. Remember to keep track of which side of the truck the bearings were on so you can put them back in the same place during assembly. If the inner wheel bearing is still in the hub, pull it out now and skip down to Step 3.

Sometimes the inner wheel bearing stays on the axle when the axle hub is removed. If your inner wheel bearing is still on the axle, use your two largest screwdrivers to gently pry the bearing off the axle. Gently, I said. Hook the ends of the screwdrivers behind the bearing cage on opposite sides, then lightly push the handles toward the truck. The screwdrivers will pivot on the dust cover and pry out on the bearing. You might need to twist the screwdrivers so the tips pry against the bearing cage. If the bearing still refuses to budge, you'll need to buy, rent or borrow a gear puller, or else put everything back together and take it to Toyota or a garage to have the bearings packed or replaced. It's cheaper to find a puller.

Replace the bearing with a new one if the puller bends the bearing cage (the thing that holds the rollers in) while removing the bearing.

Step 3. Clean and Inspect Wheel Bearings.

The bearing that fits into the axle hub from the inboard side is the inner bearing, and the one you install from the axle nut side of the hub is the outer bearing. The inner bearing is always larger than the outer one.

Each bearing has two races, an inner and an outer. The **outer bearing race** is pressed tightly into the hub and stays there until you knock it out with a drift (punch, dull chisel, copper, brass or aluminum rod). The **inner bearing race** is the part that fits between the axle and the rollers in the bearing cage. You can usually slide the inner race (and bearing) off the axle with your fingers or pry it off with screwdrivers.

Use a stiff parts cleaning brush or old toothbrush and solvent to clean the bearings until they shine. Grab your spray can of brake cleaner or carb cleaner and clean the places the brush can't reach.

Wipe the old grease out of the hub with rags or paper towels. Spray brake cleaner or solvent in the bearings to wash away all traces of the old grease. Dry the inside of the hub with clean rags or paper towels.

Check the outer bearing races (inside the axle hub), the inner races (the part that fits between the axle and the rollers), and the rollers in the bearings for cracks, chips and scratches. The races and rollers should be bright and shiny. A brown or blue color means the bearings have been overheated, probably due to lack of grease or dirty installation. Get a new bearing if any of the races or rollers are cracked, chipped, scratched or discolored, or if the rollers are too loose inside the cage. (If the rollers fall out of the cage, you need a new bearing for sure.) Step 5 tells you how to install new bearing races in the axle hub.

When you're through cleaning the bearings, throw the greasy rags in the trash outside. DON'T pile them in a corner of the garage, because greasy or oily rags have a weird ability to burst into flames!

Step 4. Pack Wheel Bearings with Grease.

Wheel bearings all nice and shiny? They must be completely dry of water, solvent, and brake or carb cleaner before packing. Whether original or new, the bearings have to get packed before they're installed.

Here comes the fun part. Put a glob of wheel bearing grease about the size of a golf ball in the palm of one hand. Press the larger side of the bearing into the glob of grease over and over until grease oozes through the rollers. The grease should come out around the smaller side of the bearing. The idea is to pack the grease into the spaces around all the bearings. Rotate the bearing a little and keep packing until grease is oozing out all the way around. Pack the other bearing(s) the same way. Lay the packed bearings on a clean paper towel or rag. Be sure to keep track of which hub they came out of. Don't you wish you could do this every day?

Clean all the old grease off the axle. The inside of the axle hub has been spotlessly cleaned, right?

Pack grease inside the hub until it's level with the edge of the wheel bearing races. If you accidentally get grease on the disc where the brake pads rub, clean it off with solvent or brake cleaner. If your truck is 2WD, pack grease in the round axle cap until it's about half full.

Now you can go to the assembly step to put the whole mess back together. Do Step 5 if you're installing new wheel bearings, or Step 6 if you're installing the old bearings. Clean your hands before fondling the other parts or the pages of this book. Thank you.

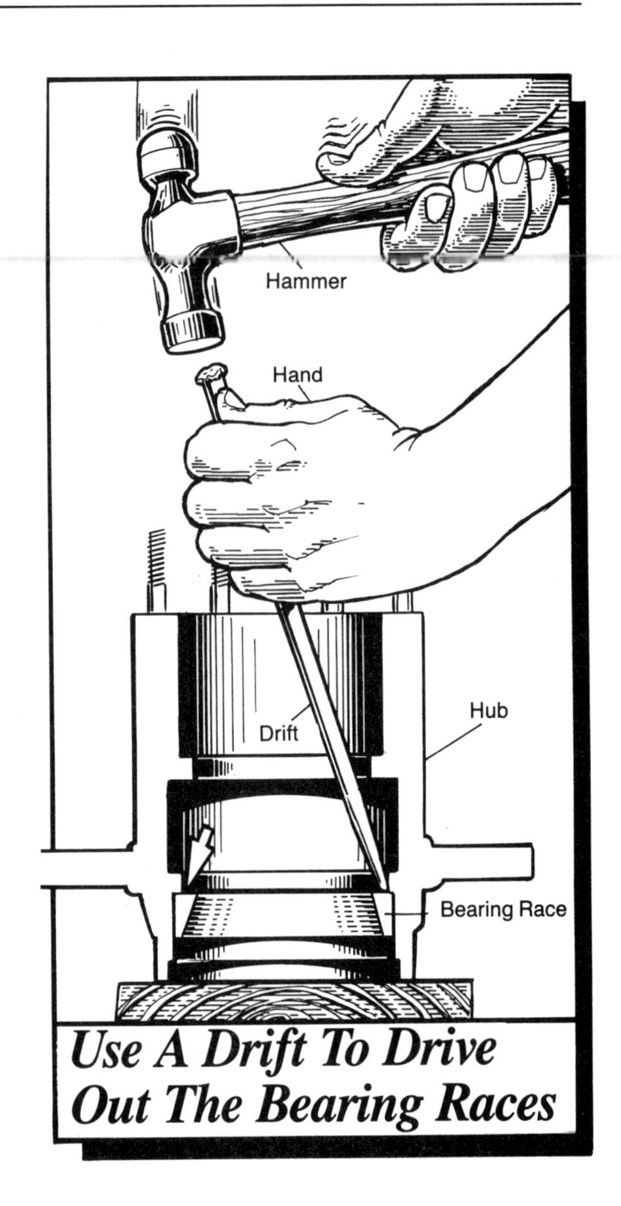

Use A Drift To Drive Out The Bearing Races

Step 5. Install New Wheel Bearings.

If you bought new bearings to install in the drums, you've made sure you bought the right ones, eh? You should have new bearings with exactly the same numbers stamped on them as the old bearings—or a darn good explanation from the parts man about why the numbers are different.

OK, to install new bearings, first you have to knock the old outer races out of the hub, then put new ones in. Yes, it's tempting to leave the old outer races in the hub and just slide in a new bearings, but don't. The life of the new bearings will be shortened drastically.

To remove the old outer races, put on your safety glasses, then stick a finger into the hub and locate the inner edge of the bearing race. It sticks up a little higher than the inside of the hub. Got it? Lay the hub so the lug studs are sticking up. Slide a couple of blocks of wood under the hub so there's room to remove the bearing race out the bottom of the hub. Don't block the bearing hole with the blocks.

Put a drift (preferably a copper, brass or aluminum rod) inside the drum and against the lip on the inner race. In a pinch a screwdriver, dull chisel or flat nosed punch will work. Tap all around the inside circumference of the race until it begins to move out of the hub. Keep tapping around the race until it falls out. Have a look at the illustration. Then turn the hub over and tap the other race out the same way.

Before installing the new bearing races, use brake cleaner or solvent to remove all traces of old grease from inside the hub. Lay the new outer race in its hole so the thicker, heavy side of the race goes in first. LIGHTLY tap all around the edge with a hammer until the race starts going into the hub. Remove the race if it gets crooked and start again. Once the edge of the race is flush with the hub, put the drift on the edge of the race and continue tapping all around the circumference until it's fully seated in the hub. Don't let the drift slip and scratch the bearing surface. The sound the hammer makes will change from a ding to a dong when the race hits bottom. Or is it a dong to a ding? Anyway, remove and install any other outer races the same way.

Now pack the new bearings with grease if you haven't already (Step 4).

Step 6. Put It All Back Together.

What an exhilarating experience packing wheel bearings is! I wish I could have been there to watch. Is the mess all cleaned up? Now let's put it all back together.

Slide the freshly packed inner (larger) wheel bearing into the inboard side of the hub. The smaller edge goes in first.

Before installing the new inner seal, be sure it looks just like the old one. Match 'em up. If it matches, press the new grease seal into the hub with your thumbs. The "open" side of the seal with a groove in it goes toward the inside of the hub and the smooth side with the "lips" faces away from the hub. Use a drift or ratchet extension and hammer to gently tap all the way around the outer edge of the seal to seat it completely. Put grease in the lips of the seal, then use a clean rag or paper towel to wipe away the excess grease around the seal with a clean rag.

Stand the hub on its edge and insert the outer (smaller) bearing in its hole. Keep greasy fingers away from the friction surface on the disc.

2WD models: Fit the large flat washer into the outer hole in the hub.

EVERYONE: Grab the hub so your fingers won't get pinched between the hub and dust plate. While holding the outer bearing in with your thumbs, line up the hole in the hub with the axle and slide the hub straight onto the axle. Wiggle it all the way on.

Now do Procedure 5, Step 5 to install and adjust the axle nuts. That procedure will also tell you when and how to put the other parts back together.

PROCEDURE 8: REMOVE AND INSTALL TIE RODS

First a bit of orientation (just in case you skipped the first part of this chapter).

2WD and '86-'87 4WD models: There is a short tie rod on each side of the truck. One end of each tie rod attaches via a ball joint (called a tie rod end) to the steering knuckle arm and the other end of the tie rod is attached to a long relay rod via another tie rod end.

'79-'85 4WD models: One long tie rod with a ball joint (called a tie rod end) on each end connects the two steering knuckle arms.

Condition: Tie rod end ball joints are worn out; OR you need to release the tie rod end for steering knuckle or steering ball joint removal.

Tools and Materials: Safety glasses, phase 1 tool kit, a new cotter pin for each tie rod end removed, regular and needlenose pliers, a tie rod puller or pickle fork. (You can probably rent a puller or pickle fork.)

If you need to disassemble any tie rods to replace the tie rods or tie rod ends, you'll need a tape measure and some chalk or paint.

Remark: If you plan to use the tie rod end again, I recommend using a tie rod puller rather than a pickle fork because pickle forks tend to tear up the rubber dust boots. If a dust boot gets torn during removal, replace it with a new one from the Toyota dealer.

If a tie rod end is removed from the tie rod for the installation of new parts or whatever, you'll need to have the front end alignment checked by the Toyota dealer or an alignment shop after it's all back together.

Step 1. Chock, Jack and Block.

Put chocks in front of and behind the rear wheels. Loosen the front wheel lug nuts a little, then jack up the truck and put it on jackstands. Remove the front wheels.

Step 2. Remove Tie Rod.

2WD models: Use chalk or paint to label the tie rods "left side" and "right side" if you are removing both. Also mark which end is inboard and which is outboard.

EVERYONE: Use chalk or paint to make a mark on each end of the tie rod(s) in line with the ball joint stud. You'll need to know which way the stud points if you are replacing any of the tie rod ends.

Use needlenose pliers to straighten the bent end of the cotter pin that goes through the tie rod end castle nut. Pull the cotter pin out, then use a 19mm wrench to unscrew the castle nut from the ball joint.

Use a tie rod puller or pickle fork to separate the tie rod end from the knuckle arm or relay rod. Pullers and pickle forks are less expensive than replacing a tie rod end that's damaged during removal. See Chapter 15 if you need instructions for using a puller. A pickle fork consists of a steel rod with two tapered forks on one end. The forks fit between the ball joint and whatever it's attached to. When you use a hammer to tap on the end, the tapered forks force the ball joint stud out of its hole. The hazard of using a pickle fork instead of a puller is that the rubber dust boot on the ball joint is more likely to be torn. If you tear a dust boot, replace it with a new one from the Toyota dealer.

If you can't get a puller or pickle fork, you can try using two hammers to break the ball joint free. Screw the castle nut back onto the ball joint stud until it's even with the end of the stud. Put on your safety glasses, then squirt some penetrating oil around the ball joint stud where it goes through the steering knuckle or relay rod. Wait a few minutes for the penetrating oil to seep in, then use the two hammers to simultaneously smack the sides of the knuckle arm or relay rod through which the ball joint fits. The ball joint stud should pop out. Be careful not to hit the side of the castle nut or any of the brake parts. I've never had much success with this method, but all the old mechanics swear by it. Maybe I have bad ball joint Karma.

If all else fails, or if you're getting a new tie rod end anyway, unscrew the castle nut, turn it over so the notched part is toward the tie rod end and screw it on until the nut is even with the end of the stud. Put a block of wood on the nut, then hit the block *squarely* with the hammer and the tie rod end hopefully will pop out. Remove the castle nut. If the stud turns with the nut, lightly tap the ball joint back up into its hole and hold it there while you unscrew the castle nut.

If you are removing the whole tie rod or the relay rod, remove the other end of the tie rod now.

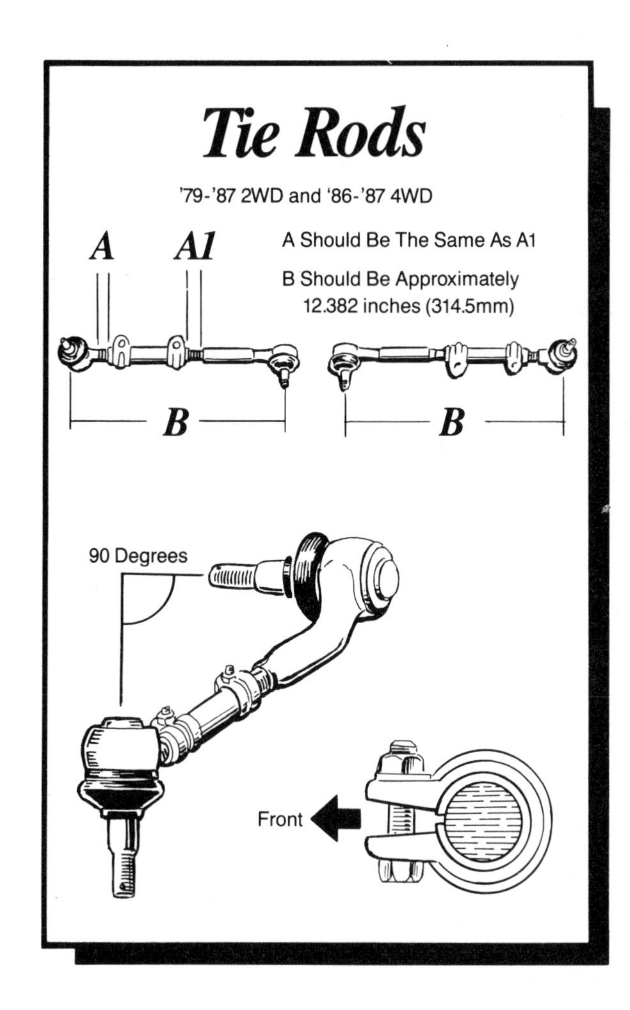

Step 3. Remove Tie Rod End from Tie Rod.

'75-'78 models: Measure the distance between the center of the tie rod ends. Write the measurement down somewhere because you'll need it during reassembly.

EVERYONE: Only remove one tie rod end at a time from the tie rod so you can use the opposite end for measurement. You'll see what I mean when it's time to install one of the tie rod ends.

Use a socket and ratchet to remove the bolt that secures a clamp near the end of the tie rod. Now you can unscrew the tie rod end from the tie rod. One of the tie rod ends will have left hand threads. This means you turn it *clockwise* the remove it and *counterclockwise* to install it.

Step 4. Install Tie Rod End on Tie Rod.

Screw the tie rod end into the tie rod until there are the same number of threads left outside the tie rod as there are on the opposite tie rod end. In other words, screw the tie rod end into the tie rod the same amount the other tie rod end is screwed in, or as near as possible. If I've totally confused you, look at the illustration. Distance A should equal distance A1.

If you are replacing both tie rod ends, replace the other end the same way.

Install the clamp bolts in the clamps and position them so the clamp ends are aligned with the slots in the tie rod. Don't tighten the clamp bolts yet. Now twist one of the tie rod ends ¼ turn so the ball joint studs are pointing in the same direction. Adjust the studs so they are sticking straight out of the ball joint, perpendicular to the tie rod. Use a tape measure to check the distance between the centers of the two studs. Here's how long the tie rods should be:

'75-'78 models: The tie rods should be as close as possible to their original lengths. You wrote the measurements down somewhere, right?

'79-'87 2WD models and '86-'87 4WD models: The distance should be about 12.4 inches (314mm).

'79-'85 4WD models: The distance should be approximately 47.25 inches (120cm)

EVERYONE: If the distance between the two studs isn't correct, hold the tie rod ends so they can't turn while you turn the tie rod. Turning it one way will shorten the distance between the ball joint studs and turning it the other way will lengthen the distance. When the distance is correct, twist the tie rod end that you twisted earlier back ¼ turn so the ball joint stud is aligned with the mark you made on the tie rod. The studs will now be 90 degrees to one another. Align the ends of the clamps with the slots in the tie rods. Now tighten the two clamp bolts to 19 ft.lbs. (2WD models and '86-'87 4WD models) or 27 ft.lbs. ('79-'85 4WD models).

Step 5. Attach Tie Rod End To Steering Knuckle Arm (and to the Relay Rod on 2WD and '86-'87 4WD Models).

Clean all traces of grease, oil and dirt from the tapered ball joint studs and their holes in the steering arm and relay rod, if you have a relay rod.

'75-'78 models: The tie rod ends fit into the bottoms of the knuckle arms and the front of the relay rod. The longer tie rod end goes on the knuckle arm and the shorter tie rod end attaches to the relay rod.

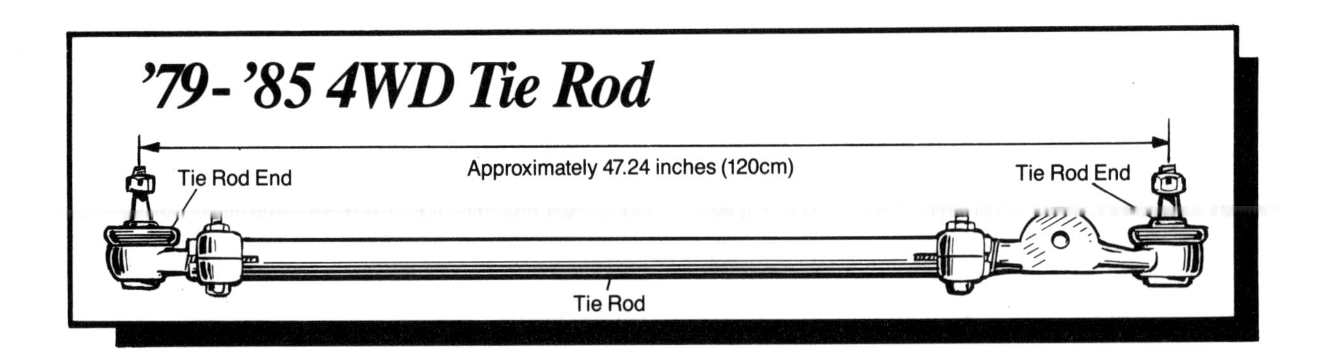

'79-'85 4WD models: Stick the tie rod end studs into the holes in the knuckle arms from the bottom. Screw the castle nuts on as far as you can with your fingers.

'79-'87 2WD models and '86-'87 4WD models: The shorter tie rod end fits into the top of the knuckle arm and the longer tie rod end fits into the rear of the relay rod. If your tie rod ends are the same length, install the tie rod the way it was originally. Install the castle nuts and tighten them with your fingers.

EVERYONE: Torque the castle nuts to 67 ft.lbs. If the stud turns with the nut, use a hammer to tap the tie rod end a little further into the knuckle arm or relay rod. Torque the nuts, then tighten it a bit further if necessary in order to slide a new cotter pin through the hole in the stud. When the cotter pin is in, wrap the ends around the castle nut.

Step 6. Finish Up.

Put the wheels on the truck, snug the lug nuts with your wrench, lower the car and torque the lug nuts to 65-87 ft.lbs. If you removed any tie rod ends from the tie rod(s) or replaced any tie rods, you'll need to have the wheel alignment checked by Toyota or an alignment shop.

PROCEDURE 9: REMOVE AND INSTALL RELAY ROD, PITMAN ARM, IDLER ARM AND DRAG LINK

'79-'85 4WD models don't have idler arms. Only '79-'85 4WD models have drag links.

Condition: Relay rod, pitman arm, idler arm or drag link is worn and loose, causing excessive play in the steering wheel, uneven tire wear or steering wheel shimmy.

Tools and Materials: To remove and install the pitman arm or idler arm you'll need: Phase 1 tool set, tie rod end puller or pickle fork, pitman arm puller, maybe new ball joints (if your pitman or idler arm has a worn out ball joint attached to it), maybe new bushings for the idler arm. You can probably rent a tie rod end puller or pickle fork and pitman arm puller. The pitman arm is attached to the steering box with a 36mm nut, so you'll probably need to rent a socket to remove and install it.

To remove and install the drag link you'll need pliers, a large screwdriver, maybe a crescent wrench or Vise Grips, molybdenum disulphide lithium base grease, maybe new rubber dust protector, ball stud seats and/or springs.

Step 1. Remove and Install Relay Rod (2WD and '86-'87 4WD models).

To remove the relay rod, separate the tie rod ends from the relay rod (Procedure 8, Steps 1-2), separate the relay rod from the pitman arm (Step 2 in this procedure), and separate the rod from the idler arm (Step 3 in this procedure). '80-'87 models will also need to separate the rod from the steering damper (Procedure 4, Step 1). Replace the relay rod if it's bent, or if the ball joints on the ends are loose (2WD models only).

To install the relay rod, connect the rod to the idler arm (Step 3 in this procedure), connect the rod to the pitman arm (Step 2 in this procedure), and connect the tie rod ends to the relay rod (Procedure 8, Step 5, in this chapter). '80-'87 models also must connect the steering damper to the relay rod (Procedure 4, Step 2, in this chapter).

Step 2. Remove and Install Pitman Arm.

To remove the pitman arm, remove the huge nut and lockwasher that attach it to the steering box. Use a pitman arm puller to separate the pitman arm from the steering gear box.

2WD and '86-'87 4WD models: Remove the cotter pin and castle nut that attach the end of the pitman arm to the relay rod. Use a tie rod puller or pickle fork to separate the pitman arm from the relay rod.

'79-'85 4WD models: See Step 4 to separate the pitman arm from the drag link.

EVERYONE: If your model has a worn out ball joint on the end of the pitman arm, you'll have to buy a new arm from the Toyota dealer.

To install the pitman arm, locate matchmarks on the pitman arm and steering box sector shaft. Fit the pitman arm onto the shaft so the marks are aligned, then install the lockwasher and nut. Torque the nut to 90 ft.lbs. (2WD models) or to 130 ft.lbs. (4WD models).

2WD and '86-'87 4WD models: Connect the other end of the pitman arm to the relay rod and torque the castle nut to 67 ft.lbs. If necessary, tighten it a little further to install the cotter pin through the castle nut. Bend the ends of the cotter pin over the end of the nut.

'79-'85 4WD models: Connect the other end of the pitman arm to the drag link (see Step 4).

Step 3. Remove and Install Idler Arm.

To remove the idler arm, use pliers to remove the cotter pin from the ball joint on the end of the arm. Use a socket and ratchet to remove the castle nut, then use a tie rod puller or pickle fork to separate the idler arm from the relay rod. Remove the two or three bolts and nuts that attach the idler arm bracket to the frame. Remove the idler arm.

If you removed the idler arm because the shaft is loose, take it to the Toyota dealer or a machine shop and have them install new bushings and seals.

To install the idler arm, attach it to the frame with the two or three bolts, nuts and lock washers. Torque the nuts or bolts to the following specifications:

MODEL	TORQUE
'75-'78 models	25-36 ft.lbs.
'79-'87 2WD models	48 ft.lbs.
'86-'87 4WD models	70 ft.lbs.

Now attach the end of the idler arm to the relay rod. Install the castle nut and tighten it to 65 ft.lbs. ('75-'78 models) or to 43 ft.lbs. ('79-'87 models). Tighten it a little further if necessary to install the cotter pin through the castle nut. Bend the ends of the cotter pin over the end of the castle nut.

Step 4. Adjust, Remove and Install Drag Link on '79-'85 4WD models.

The drag link connects the pitman arm on the steering box to the knuckle arm on the left steering knuckle. If the ends of the drag link appear to fit loosely, try removing the cotter pins from the ends, then use a large screwdriver to tighten the plug in the end of the drag link *clockwise* (as viewed from the end of the drag link). You might have to use a crescent wrench (if your screwdriver shaft is square) or Vise Grips on the screwdriver shaft to turn the plug. Tighten the plug as far as you can, then loosen it 1⅓ turns. Is the excess play gone now? If so, there's no need to remove the drag link. If the excess play is still there, or you need to remove the pitman arm, you'll need to remove the drag link. Here's how.

Use chalk or paint to mark the drag link so you'll know which end is front and which is rear. To remove the drag link, use pliers to remove the cotter pins from each end. Use a screwdriver to unscrew the plugs in the ends of the drag link, (*counterclockwise* as viewed from the end). You might have to use a crescent wrench or

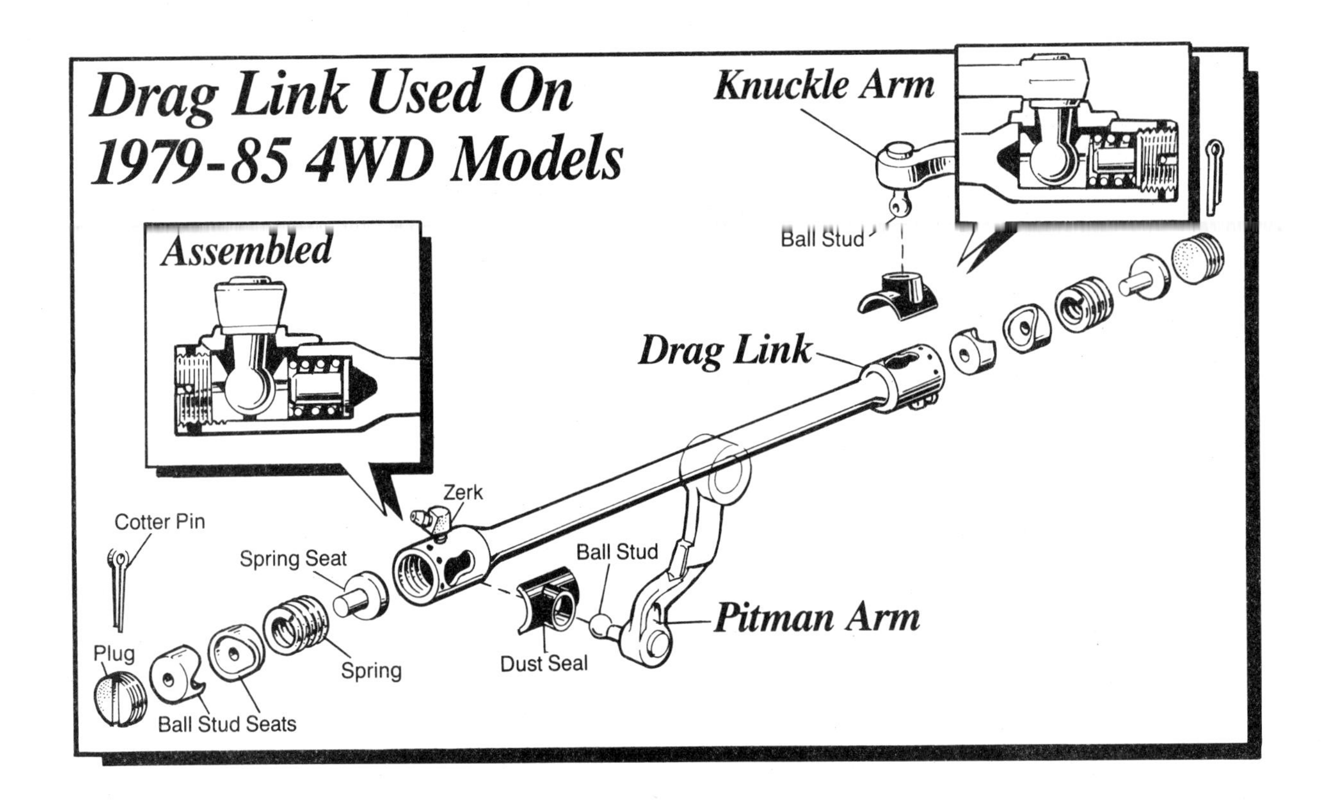

Vise Grips on the screwdriver shaft to turn the plug. Once the plugs are out, you can wiggle the drag link off the pitman arm and knuckle arm.

If the drag link was loose and causing excess play, either the ball stud seats or the ball studs are worn out. Remove the ball seats, spring and spring seat from each end of the drag link. Keep the parts separate and marked for which end they came out of. Use solvent and rags to clean all of the parts you removed. Check the parts for wear. If you're not sure what to look for, take them to the Toyota dealer or a garage for their opinion. While you're there, pick up replacement parts for whatever was worn out. Don't forget to get new rubber dust seals if yours are worn out or disfigured.

To put the drag link back together, install the parts for the pitman arm end first. Smear the ball stud on the pitman arm and the ball stud seats with molybdenum disulphide lithium base grease. Insert the spring seat, then the spring, then the ball stud seat into the drag link so the rounded part faces the slot in the drag link. Install the drag link with the dust seal onto the pitman arm. Then insert the other ball stud seat and plug. Tighten the plug as tight as you can, then loosen it 1⅓ turns. Install the cotter pin and bend the ends over the end of the drag link.

To install the knuckle arm end of the drag link, smear the ball stud and stud seats with molybdenum disulphide lithium base grease, then insert one of the ball stud seats into the drag link. Install the drag link with its dust seal onto the knuckle arm, then install the other ball stud seat, then the spring, then the spring seat, and finally the plug. Use a large screwdriver to tighten the plug as tight as you can, then loosen it 1⅓ turns. Install the cotter pin and bend the ends over the end of the drag link.

Use your grease gun to pump a few shots of grease into each end of the drag link. That's all there is to it.

PROCEDURE 10: REMOVE AND INSTALL STEERING KNUCKLE ON '79-'87 2WD AND '86-'87 4WD MODELS

Condition: Routine maintenance; OR you need to replace the bushings in the knuckle; OR you need to remove the steering knuckle in order to get to the ball joints.

Tools and Materials: Phase 1 tool kit, ball joint puller or pickle fork, new cotter pins for the dust cover mounting bolts, a can of molybdenum disulphide lithium base grease, maybe new wheel bearings, wheel bearing grease seals and/or ball joints, feeler gauges, snap ring pliers.

'79-'83 2WD and all 4WD models: You will also need a can of DOT3 or 4 brake fluid, a can or jar to catch brake fluid in, baggies and rubber bands and the brake bleeding tools listed in Chapter 7, Procedure 1.

2WD models: You'll need new cotter pins for the axle nuts.

'86-'87 4WD models: You will need an 8x1.25mm bolt, new dust cover oil seals, maybe new bushings and spacers for the knuckles, a spray can of carburetor cleaner (or other cleaner that contains toluene or trichloroethylene), and a tube of Three Bond 1324 or Loctite 271.

Step 1. Remove Front Wheels and Brakes.

Do Chapter 7, Procedure 5, Steps 1-4. I'll see you back here when the brakes are off.

Step 2. Remove Axle Hub.

See Procedure 5, Steps 2 and 3, in this chapter to remove the axle hub, then come back here.

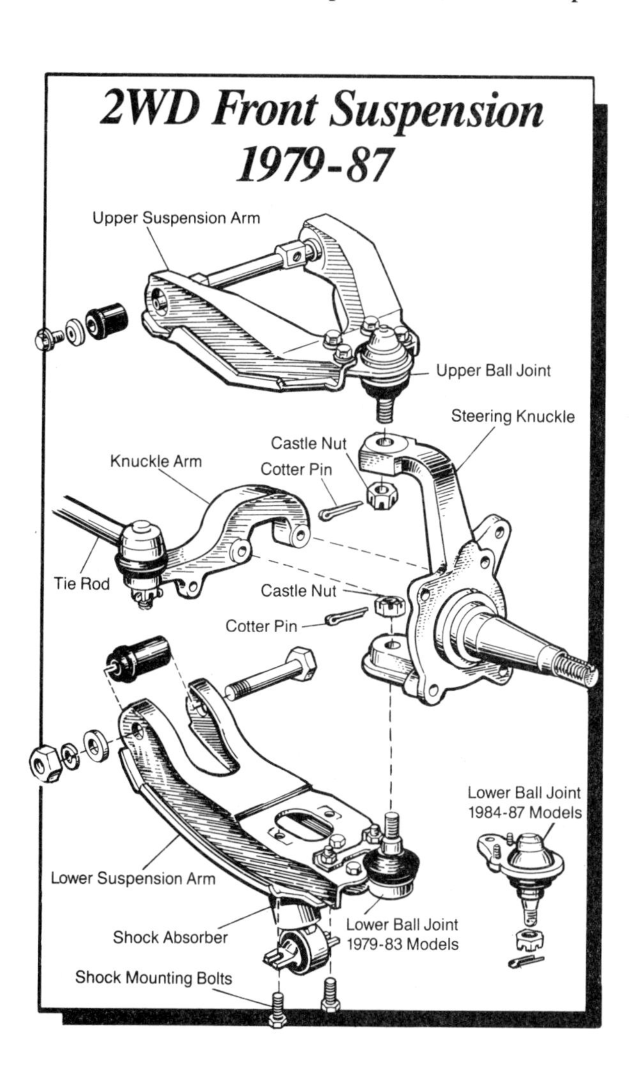

Step 3. Remove Brake Dust Cover.

2WD models: Locate the four 14mm nuts near the center of the dust cover. Use pliers to remove the cotter pins, then use a wrench to hold the bolt heads on the inboard side of the dust cover while you remove the nuts. Pull the cover off the knuckle.

The upper bolts also attached the brake line bracket to the steering knuckle and the lower two bolts attached the knuckle arm to the steering knuckle. Move the brake line bracket and brake line, and the knuckle arm, away from the knuckle so they are out of the way. You can skip down to Step 6 now.

4WD models: Seven or eight bolts near the center attach the dust cover. Use a socket and ratchet to remove the bolts, then remove the oil seal and dust cover.

Step 4. Remove Steering Knuckle Arm.

'86-'87 4WD models: Use a 19mm socket and your longest ratchet or breaker bar to remove the two bolts that attach the knuckle arm and brake line bracket to the steering knuckle. Wiggle the knuckle arm, tie rod and brake line bracket out of the way. Note that the two mounting bolts have a special coating. Be sure that these bolts attach the knuckle arm during reassembly.

Step 5. Check Thrust Clearance on '86-'87 4WD Models.

Install an 8x1.25mm bolt in the end of the axle. Use pliers to pull on the bolt head while you use feeler gauges to measure the clearance between the little spacer on the axle and the end of the steering knuckle. The clearance should be between .003" and .027" (.075-.690mm). If the gap is more than .039" (1.0mm), have the Toyota dealer replace the outside and inside bushings in the steering knuckle once it's off the truck. If the clearance is between .027" and .038", the bushings are marginal but might last a while longer.

Step 6. Separate Steering Knuckle from Ball Joints.

2WD models: Slide your floor jack or the Toyota jack under the outer end of the suspension arm. Raise the jack until you see the suspension arm move slightly upward. Don't jack it up any higher.

Use pliers to remove the cotter pins from the upper and lower ball joint castle nuts. Depending on the castle nut size, use a 19mm or 22mm socket and a ratchet to remove the castle nuts.

Use a ball joint puller or pickle fork to separate the lower ball joint from the steering knuckle. Then use the puller or pickle fork to separate the upper ball joint from the steering knuckle. Wiggle the steering knuckle off the truck.

If you're using a pickle fork, you will probably need to use your biggest hammer to beat on it. Unless you are replacing the ball joints, be careful not to tear the rubber dust boots.

'86-'87 4WD models: Disconnect the bottom end of the shock absorber from the lower suspension arm. Just remove the nut and bolt that attaches it to the bracket.

Look for a vertical bolt sticking up out of the lower suspension arm. The upper end of the bolt is attached to the end of the stabilizer bar, which curves around to the lower suspension arm on the opposite side. Remove the nut, bolt, retainers, grommets, and collar to disconnect the end of the stabilizer bar from the lower suspension arm.

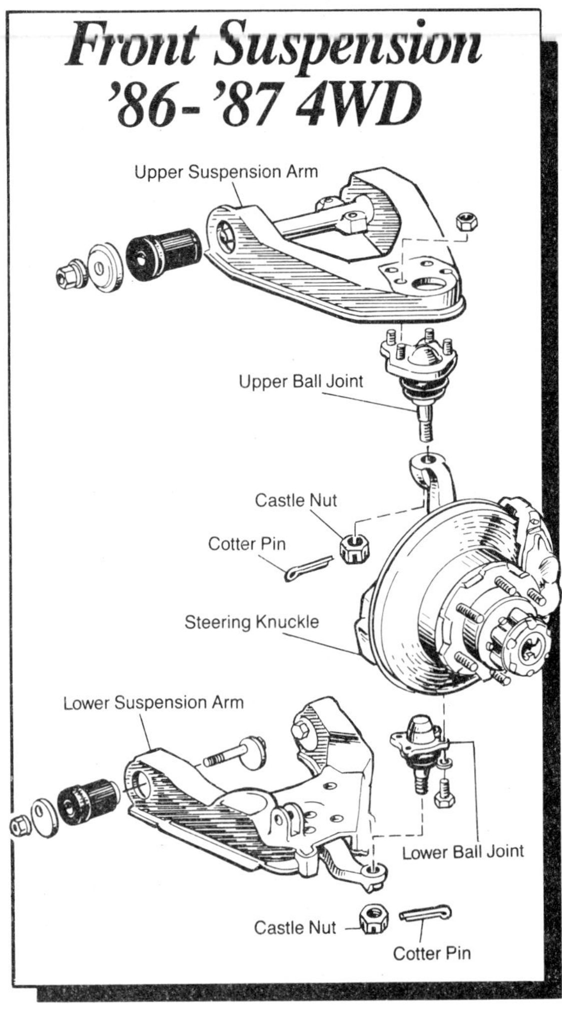

Front Suspension '86-'87 4WD

Use snap ring pliers to remove the snap ring from the end of the axle. Pull the little spacer off the axle.

Use pliers to remove the cotter pin from the upper ball joint, then use a socket and ratchet to remove the castle nut. Use a ball joint puller or pickle fork to separate the steering knuckle from the ball joint. If you are using a pickle fork, you'll probably need to use your biggest hammer to smack the pickle fork.

The lower ball joint is attached to the steering knuckle with four 14mm bolts. Use a socket and ratchet to remove the bolts.

Use your foot to push down on the lower suspension arm while you wiggle the steering knuckle off the ball joints. The steering knuckle is now liberated.

If you need to remove the front axle, see Chapter 11.

If the clearance between the steering knuckle and spacer was larger than it should be, take the knuckle to the Toyota dealer and have new bushings installed.

EVERYONE: If you are here to remove the ball joints, go to Procedure 12.

Step 7. Install Steering Knuckle and Dust Cover.

2WD models: Fit the upper end of the steering knuckle onto the upper ball joint. Install the castle nut and snug it down. We'll tighten it later.

Use the jack to support the lower suspension arm. Align the lower ball joint with its hole in the steering knuckle while you push down on the upper suspension arm and steering knuckle. Install the castle nut on the lower ball joint. (You might have to use the jack to raise the lower suspension arm a little.)

Torque the upper castle nut to 80 ft.lbs. and the lower castle nut to 105 ft.lbs. If necessary, tighten the nuts a little further so you can install a new cotter pin through the slots in the nut. Wrap the ends of the cotter pin over the ends of the ball joint studs.

Fit the dust cover onto the steering knuckle so the cut out part is toward the rear. Install the knuckle arm with two bolts and nuts but don't tighten them yet.

If the dust cover is secured with two bolts from the outboard side, install the bolts and torque them to 80 ft.lbs.

If the brake line bracket was attached with the two upper dust cover bolts, fit the bracket into place, then install the bolts and nuts. Torque the nuts to 80 ft.lbs., then tighten them a little further if necessary so you can install new cotter pins through the nuts. Bend the ends of the cotter pins around the nuts.

Tighten the lower nuts to 80 ft.lbs. If necessary, tighten the bolts a little further so you can install new cotter pins through the slots in the castle nut. Bend the ends of the cotter pins around the bolts.

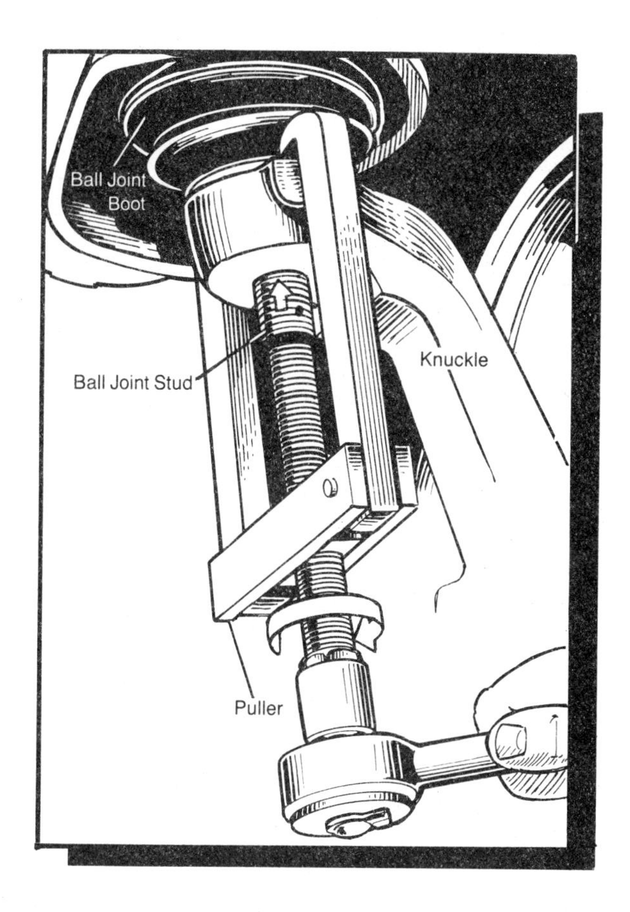

'86-'87 4WD models: Smear some molybdenum disulphide lithium base grease on the smooth part of the axle where it fits into the axle hub. Use your foot to push down on the lower suspension arm while you fit the knuckle onto the axle and the upper and lower ball joints.

Install and tighten the four 14mm bolts that attach the lower ball joint to the steering knuckle. Torque the bolts to 43 ft.lbs. Install the castle nut onto the upper ball joint stud. Torque the nut to 105 ft.lbs.

Install the spacer on the end of the axle, then install the 8x1.25mm bolt in the end of the axle. Use pliers on the bolt to pull the axle toward you while you use snap ring pliers to install the snap ring. Be sure the snap ring is seated in the groove all the way around.

If you replaced the bushings in the steering knuckle, recheck the clearance between the knuckle and spacer the same way you checked it during disassembly. The standard clearance should be between .003" (.075mm) and .027" (.690mm). If it isn't, replace the spacer. There are two spacer sizes available. One is .070" (1.80mm) and the other is .088" (2.25mm). Use the spacer that will bring the clearance into the standard range.

If necessary, use a jack to raise the stabilizer bar high enough to install the retainers, cushions and collar (see the illustration). Torque the nut to 19 ft.lbs.

Fit the bottom end of the shock absorber into its bracket, then install the mounting bolt and nut. Torque the nut to 101 ft.lbs.

Use a spray can of carburetor cleaner or some other cleaner that contains toluene or trichloroethylene to clean the knuckle arm mounting bolts. Coat the threads of the bolts with Three Bond 1324 or Loctite 271. Connect the knuckle arm and the brake line bracket to the steering knuckle, then torque the bolts to 120 ft.lbs. Install the dust cover with a new dust cover oil seal and torque the bolts to 13 ft.lbs.

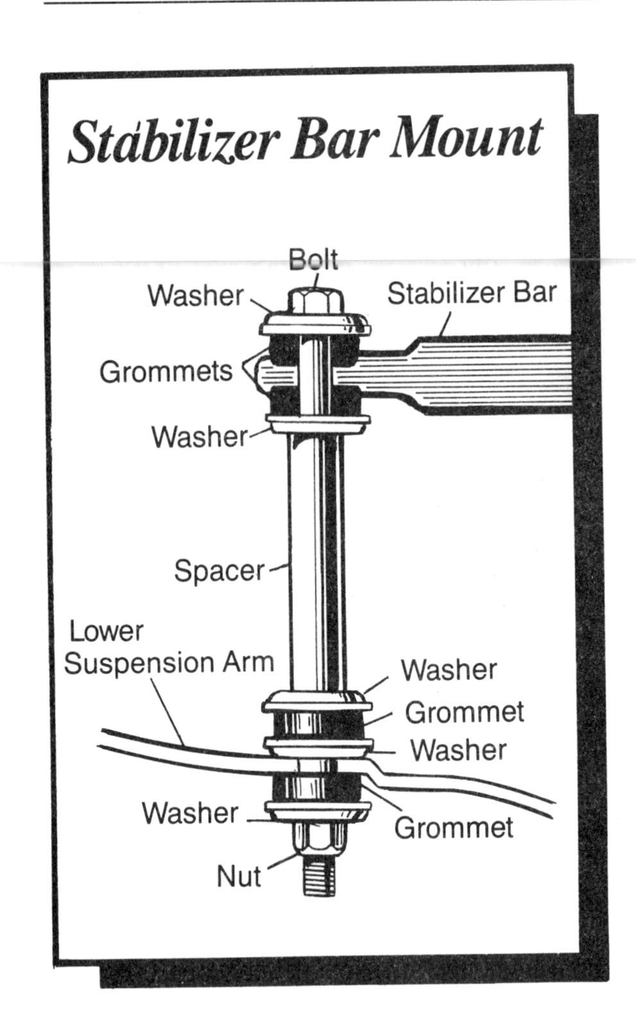

Step 8. Finish Up.

See Procedure 5, Step 5, to install the axle hubs, torque plates, brake calipers, pads, and finally the wheels. If you disconnected any brake lines, be sure to bleed the brake system after everything is all back together (Chapter 7, Procedure 1).

When you're finished, take the truck for a test drive. If you hear unusual noises on the side you've worked on, or the truck pulls to one side, something wasn't reassembled right. This is rare, but don't drive the truck until you've got it together correctly.

Have the front wheel toe-in checked by Toyota or an alignment shop.

PROCEDURE 11: REMOVE AND INSTALL STEERING KNUCKLE AND FRONT AXLE ON '79-'85 4WD

If you are here because the differential housing or a steering knuckle is broken and must be replaced, take the truck to the Toyota dealer for the repairs. Special tools and expertise are required to set the steering knuckle alignment and knuckle bearing preload after either of these parts is replaced.

You can repack or replace the bearings and/or the front axle, and replace the oil seal between the differential and steering knuckle.

Condition: Differential oil is leaking from one or both of the steering knuckles indicating the oil seal between the differential and steering knuckle is worn out; OR noise and/or vibration in the front end makes you suspect the birfield joint (constant velocity joint) in the front axle is worn or broken; OR excess steering wheel free play was traced to the steering knuckle arm.

Tools and Materials: Phase 1 tool set, tie rod end puller or pickle fork, brass bar (drift) at least ½" diameter and six inches long, new cotter pins for the tie rod ends, a can of molybdenum disulphide lithium base grease, dust cover gasket, knuckle spindle gasket, oil seal set, maybe new knuckle bearings, snap ring pliers, solvent, rags, baggies, marking pen.

You will also need a can of DOT3 or 4 brake fluid and the brake bleeding tools listed in Chapter 7, Procedure 1.

If you disassemble the birfield joint (constant velocity joint) on the front axle, you'll need two new snap rings for the axle shaft. If the joint is worn out, you'll need a new axle assembly.

If you need to replace the oil seal in the differential housing, you will need a slide hammer type seal puller with long thin jaws.

Remark: You can buy a front end rebuild gasket set from Toyota that contains most of the gaskets you'll need. If you buy the set, check that all the gaskets and seals are there before leaving.

New birfield joints from Toyota are very expensive. You might be able to buy rebuilt units through your local parts store.

Step 1. Remove Front Wheels and Brakes.
Do Chapter 7, Procedure 5, Steps 1-4A. I'll see you back here when the brakes are off.

Step 2. Remove Axle Hub.
See Procedure 6 to remove the 4WD hub, then do Procedure 5, Step 3, in this chapter to remove the axle hub.

Step 3. Remove Brake Dust Cover.
There are seven or eight bolts near the center of the dust cover. Use a socket and ratchet to remove the bolts. Pull the dust seal cover, dust seal and dust cover off the knuckle.

Step 4. Remove Axle Spindle and Axle Shaft.
Using a brass bar, tap against one of the flat sides of the spindle to move it back and forth to loosen it. The spindle will gradually come off the steering knuckle.

Use a clean rag to wipe the grease off the bushings in the spindle. Check the bushings for wear and damage. If something's amiss, take the spindles to the Toyota dealer or a machine shop and have new bushings installed.

Now that the spindle is off you'll be able to see a large lump (the **birfield joint**) on the axle. To remove the axle, turn it so one of the flat sides on the birfield joint is at the top, then pull the axle out of the steering knuckle.

Step 5 tells how to disassemble, clean, inspect and reassemble the birfield joint. If you don't need to take the joint apart, stash the axle where it won't trip someone or get stepped on, then skip down to Step 6.

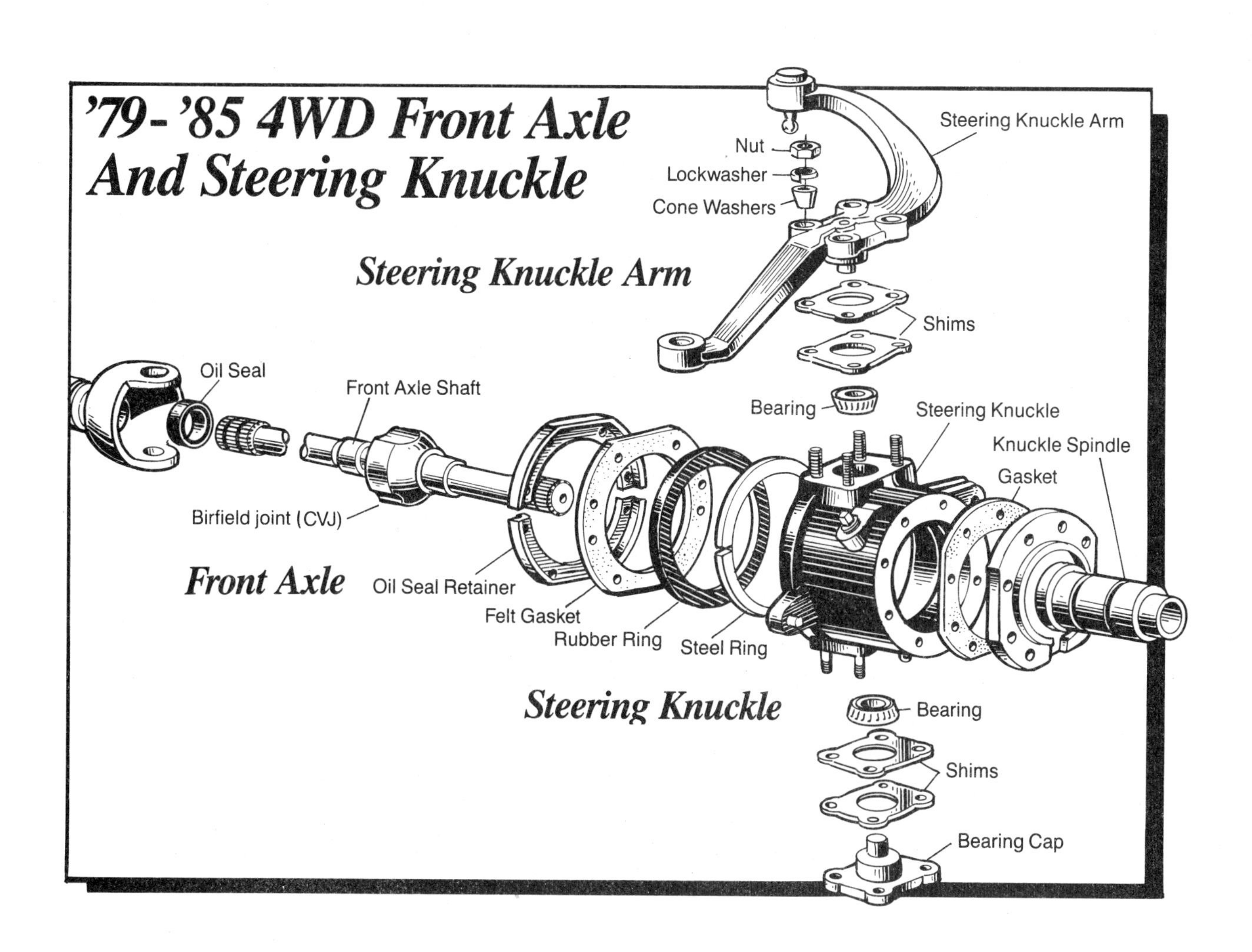

Step 5. Clean, Inspect, Reassemble Birfield Joints.

The birfield joint consists of an inner race that slips onto the splined end of the long inner shaft. An outer race is attached to the inboard end of the short outer shaft. Ball bearings fit between a cage and the inner race. The ball bearings allow the inner and outer shafts to change positions while still being solidly connected.

To disassemble the birfield joint, clamp the long inner shaft in a vise. Place the end of a brass drift against the inner race, then use a hammer on the drift to tap the race off the shaft. You'll probably have to beat on it pretty hard to get it off. Catch the outer shaft as it comes off the inner shaft.

Hold the outer race while you tilt one edge of the inner race and cage out of the outer cage. Remove the ball bearing that's exposed when you tilt the race and cage. Go around the inner race tilting it so you can remove the other ball bearings. When the balls are all removed, find two openings in the cage that are larger than the others. Fit two of the protrusions on the outer race into the two large openings, then turn the cage so it's perpendicular to the outer race. Pull the inner race and cage out of the outer race.

Fit two of the lumps on the inner race into the large openings and pull the inner race out of the cage.

Use solvent and rags to clean the ball bearings, cage and the inner and outer races. Inspect the parts for wear. Are the ball bearings bright and shiny? Are there grooves worn into the inner and outer races? Does it look like the ball bearings are wearing into the cage? Shiny places in the race and cage that have been "polished" by the balls are OK. If any abnormalities are found, replace the worn parts with new ones.

Before reassembling the birfield joint, coat the parts with molybdenum disulphide lithium base grease. Insert the inner race into the cage so the protruding end of the inner race is toward the wide side of the cage (see the illustrations). Fit the cage and inner race into the outer race by inserting two protrusions on the outer race into the two large openings in the cage. Rotate the cage and inner race so the wide side of the cage and the side of the inner race with protrusion is facing the outside of the outer race (see the illustration).

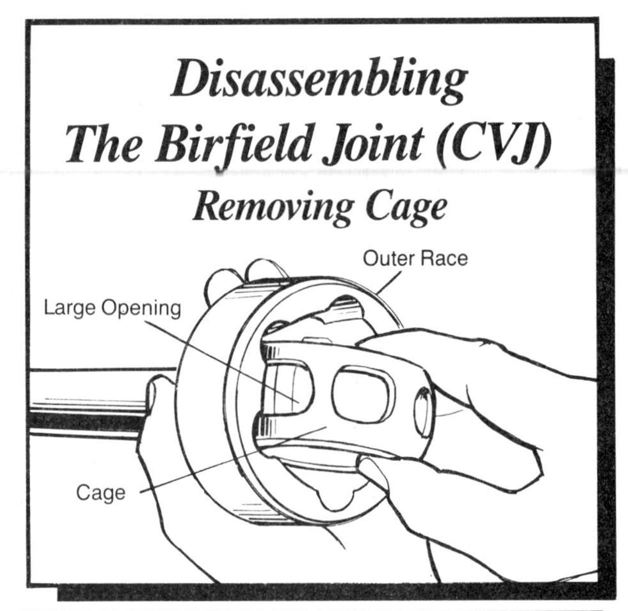

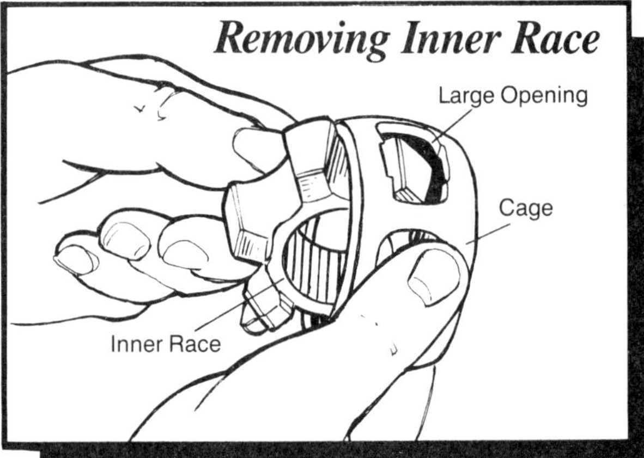

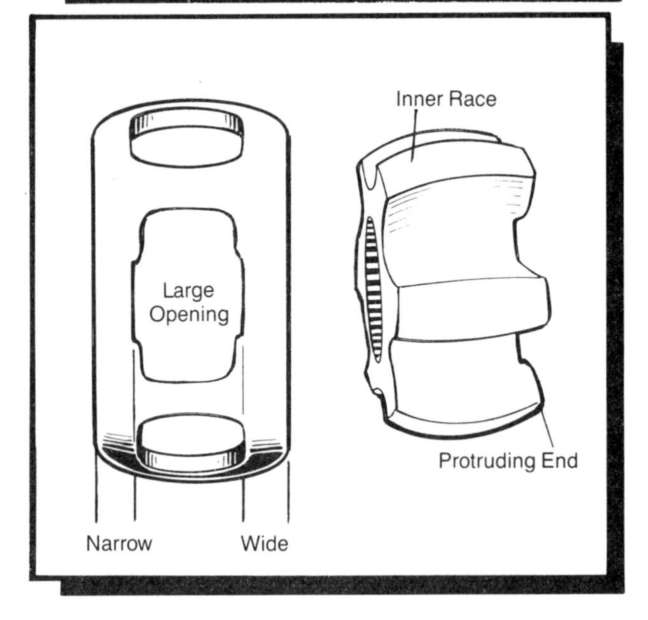

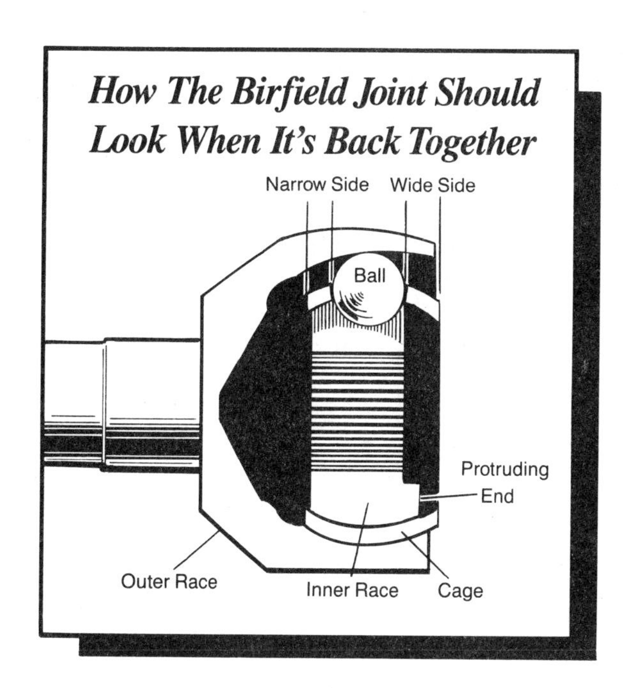

Use snap ring pliers to remove the old snap rings from the end of the long inner shaft. Fit new snap rings onto the end of the inner shaft where the old snap rings were. The smaller snap ring goes closest to the end of the axle. Clamp the short outer shaft vertically in a vise so the outer race is straight up. While you install the long inner shaft into the inner race of the outer shaft, use a very small screwdriver to compress the snap ring closest to the end of the shaft so it can slide through the inner race of the outer shaft. Once the shaft is installed the snap ring will expand and lock the two shafts together. Tug on the long inner shaft to be sure it can't be pulled out.

Step 6. Remove Steering Knuckle Arm.

Remove the cotter pin and castle nut from the tie rod end, then use a tie rod puller or pickle fork to separate the tie rod from the knuckle arm (Procedure 8, Step 2).

If you are working on the left side, disconnect the drag link from the knuckle arm (Procedure 9, Step 4).

Remove the four nuts and lock washers from the top of the knuckle arm.

Use a hammer to gently tap up on both ends of the knuckle arm. You want to lift the knuckle arm evenly, so don't hit it very hard. Remove the cone washers from the mounting studs, then lift the arm off the knuckle. The upper knuckle bearing is probably on the bottom of the knuckle.

There will be one or two shims between the arm and knuckle. Baggie the shims and mark them "left" or "right" side and "top" or "bottom" so you'll know exactly where they came from.

Step 7. Remove, Clean, Inspect Steering Knuckle.

Once the knuckle arm is off, remove the eight bolts around the inboard side of the knuckle that attach the oil seal retainer. Between the retainer and knuckle there is a felt gasket, then a rubber ring, then a metal ring. Pry off the upper and lower halves of the oil seal retainer, then pry the gaskets and metal ring away from the knuckle.

Push down on the steering knuckle and tilt the bottom end toward you. Pull the knuckle off the end of the differential housing.

Use rags or paper towels to scoop as much grease as possible from inside the knuckle, then use solvent and a parts cleaning brush to clean the outside of the knuckle and to remove all of the old grease from inside the knuckle. Dry the knuckle with a clean rag. Clean the knuckle arm and bearing with the solvent and brush, then dry them with a clean rag.

Use a rag or paper towels to clean the end of the differential housing, then inspect the bearing races in the holes at the top and bottom. If you can't clean the races so they shine, or if you notice any chips, cracks or dark areas on the races, the bearings should be replaced.

Inspect the bearing on the knuckle arm and the one in the bottom of the knuckle. If the rollers are chipped, scratched, dark colored or fit too loosely in the bearing cage, they should be replaced. Remove the bearing cap on the bottom of the knuckle, then see Procedure 7, Step 5, to replace the bearing races in the end of the differential housing. You remove and install them the same way you remove and install outer bearing races in the axle hubs.

Step 8. Remove and Install Oil Seal in Differential Housing.

If gear oil was leaking out of the steering knuckle, the little oil seal in the differential housing is broken or worn out. To replace it you'll need a slide hammer-type seal puller with long jaws.

Fit the seal puller into the seal, then expand the jaws so they are locked against the seal. Hammer the seal out of the housing.

Coat the rubber edges of the new seal with grease, then fit it into its hole in the housing. Use your brass drift or a long ratchet extension and hammer to tap all around the edge of the seal until it seats against the housing.

Step 9. Install Steering Knuckle.

Scoop up a glob of molybdenum disulphide lithium base grease, then use your fingers to pack it into the ends of the bearings until it squishes out the opposite ends. Smear the grease on the bearing races in the differential housing.

Clean your hands, then install the oil seal set onto the differential housing. First install the felt dust seal, then the rubber ring, then the steel ring. You'll have to fit one end of the steel ring over the end of the housing, then work around the ring pushing the rest of the ring on as you go.

Fit the steering knuckle onto the differential housing. You'll have to tilt and twist it to make fit over the end of the housing. Fit the shims onto the top of the knuckle, then hold the knuckle arm so the holes are aligned with the studs on the knuckle. Use a hammer to gently tap the knuckle arm down onto the knuckle. Be sure the arm is going on straight or the bearing could be damaged. Install the cone washers, lock washers and nuts onto the mounting studs. Tighten the nuts to 71 ft.lbs. Grab the knuckle arm and move the knuckle back and forth to check the bearings. It should take between 6.6 and 13.2 pounds of force to move the knuckle. If the knuckle is hard to turn, either the bearings are damaged or you forgot to install the shims. Correct the problem before going on with the assembly. Everything's OK? Continue.

Reconnect the tie rod to the knuckle arm (Procedure 8, Step 5). If you are working on the left side, reconnect the drag link to the knuckle arm (Procedure 9, Step 4).

Now install the two halves of the oil seal retainer onto the inboard side of the knuckle. Be sure the flat sides of the felt gasket are at the top and bottom, and the bolt holes are aligned with the holes in the knuckle. Install the eight bolts and snug them with a wrench.

Step 10. Install Axle and Spindle.

To install the axle, smear molybdenum disulphide lithium base grease all over the outside of the birfield joint, and inside the steering knuckle. Gently insert the longer end through the steering knuckle, being careful not to damage the oil seal in the differential housing. Turn the axle so one of the flat sides of the birfield joint is up, then push the axle all the way in. You might have to turn the axle back and forth a little to align the splines.

Pack molybdenum disulphide grease into the steering knuckle until it's about three-fourths full. Use a clean rag to wipe the mounting surfaces on the steering knuckle, spindle, brake dust cover and dust cover retainer.

Place a new spindle gasket in position on the knuckle, then fit the spindle onto the knuckle so the flat sides are at the sides and bottom. The round part goes at the top. Install the dust cover, a new dust cover gasket and finally the dust cover retainer. Install the spindle mounting bolts and torque them in a criss-cross pattern to 38 ft.lbs.

Step 11. Finish the Job.

Now see Procedure 5, Step 5, to install the axle hubs (this would be a good time to repack the bearings), brake calipers, pads, and finally the wheels. Be sure to bleed the brake system after everything is back together (Chapter 7, Procedure 1).

When you are finished, take the truck for a test drive. If you hear unusual noises on the side you've worked on, or the truck pulls to one side, something wasn't reassembled right. This is rare, but don't drive the truck until you've got it together correctly.

Have the front wheel toe-in checked by Toyota or an alignment shop.

PROCEDURE 12: REMOVE AND INSTALL STEERING BALL JOINTS ON 2WD AND '86-'87 4WD MODELS

This procedure is not for '79-'85 4WD models.

Condition: You detected looseness in one or more of the steering ball joints when checking the suspension or steering; OR you need to remove the steering knuckle.

Tools and Materials: Phase 1 tool kit, ball joint puller or pickle fork, 22mm socket, new cotter pins for the castle nuts, maybe new ball joints, baggies, rags, wire brush.

'75-'83 2WD models require a small block of wood (a short piece of 2x4 will do).

'75-'83 2WD and all 4WD models will need a pint of DOT3 or 4 brake fluid and the brake bleeding tools listed in Chapter 7, Procedure 1.

Remarks: Friction between the tapered ball joint stud and its hole in the suspension arm or the steering knuckle is what prevents the stud from turning while you tighten the castle nut—so clean all traces of grease and oil from the tapered surfaces of the stud and hole with a clean, dry rag before installing the ball joint. Once the ball joint stud is in its hole, give the opposite end of the ball joint a couple of light taps with a hammer to seat the stud. Install the castle nut and tighten it with a wrench. Tap on the ball joint some more if the stud turns.

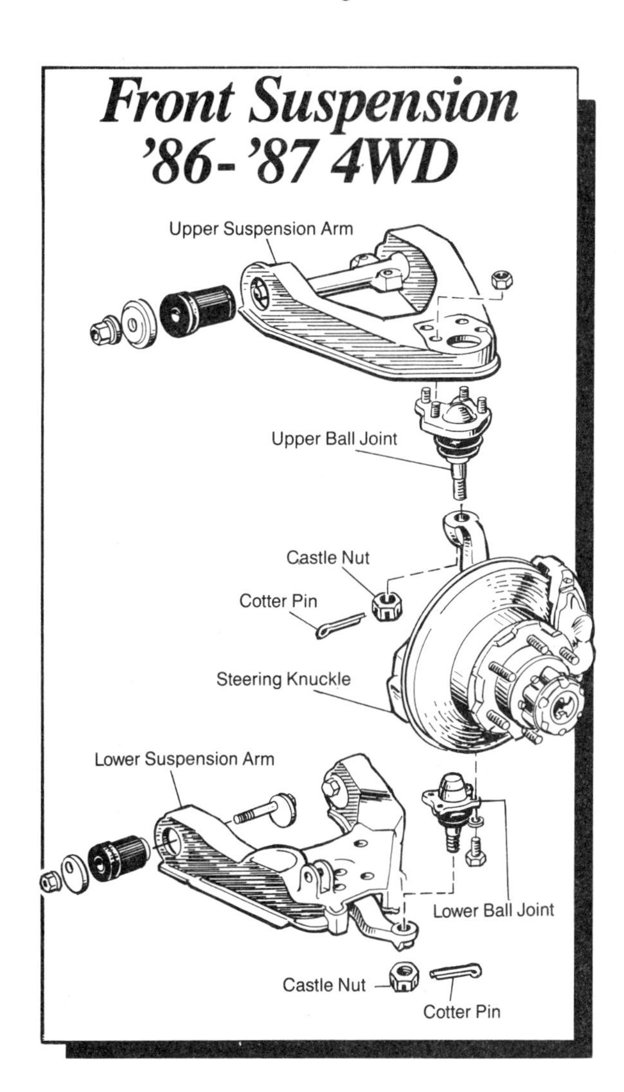

Step 1. Chock, Jack and Block.

Loosen the front lug nuts a little, then jack up the front of the truck and put it safely on jackstands. Remove the front wheels.

Step 2. Remove and Install Ball Joints on '75-'83 2WD models.

Remove lower ball joint: Place a small block of wood on your floor jack or Toyota jack and put it beneath one of the lower suspension arms. Raise the jack until you see the suspension arm move upward slightly. Don't raise it any higher.

Use pliers to remove the cotter pin from the castle nut on the lower ball joint, then use a socket and ratchet to remove the castle nut. Separate the ball joint from the lower suspension arm with a ball joint puller or pickle fork. If you are using a pickle fork, use your biggest hammer to beat on the end of the fork. Try to avoid tearing the rubber ball joint dust boot.

Locate the bolts and nuts that attach the ball joint to the end of the lower suspension arm. Hold the bolt heads with a wrench while you remove the nuts. Three of the bolts and nuts are 12mm and one bolt and nut is 14mm. Now wiggle the lower ball joint off. If necessary, raise the jack a little.

If you need to remove the upper ball joint, do it now while the lower ball joint is off. Here's how.

Remove upper ball joint: Locate the brake line junction just below the upper ball joint. A rubber hose connects to a metal line and the two are attached to a bracket with a spring clip. Hold the nut on the end of the rubber hose with a 17mm open end wrench while you use a 10mm flare nut wrench to unscrew the nut on the metal brake line. Don't bend the metal line. When the nut is loose, use pliers to wiggle the spring clip off the bracket. Put the brake bleeder cap or a plastic baggie on the end of the metal line to keep dirt out of the line. Put a plastic baggie over the end of the rubber brake hose to keep dirt out. Prop the rubber hose out of the way.

Use pliers to remove the cotter pin in the castle nut, then use a socket and ratchet to remove the castle nut.

Use a ball joint puller or pickle fork to separate the ball joint from the steering knuckle. Be careful not to damage the metal brake line. If you are using a pickle fork, you'll probably need to use your biggest hammer to beat on the end of it.

Hold the ball joint mounting bolt heads with a wrench while you use a socket and ratchet to remove the mounting nuts. Now you can pull the ball joint off the suspension arm.

Install upper ball joint: Clean the mud, dirt and old grease off the suspension arm, then fit the new ball joint onto the arm just like the old one was installed. Install the mounting bolts and nuts and torque them to 20 ft.lbs.

Wipe off any traces of grease from the ball joint stud and the hole in the steering knuckle where the stud fits. Fit the ball joint stud into the hole on the steering knuckle, then install and tighten the castle nut to 85 ft.lbs. If necessary, tighten it a little more so you can install a new cotter pin through the slots in the castle nut and the hole in the ball joint stud. Wrap the ends of the cotter pin over the end of the castle nut.

Remove the baggies from the brake hose and line. Fit the rubber hose through the bracket and screw the nut on the line into the hose with your fingers until you are sure the nut is going in straight. Wiggle the spring clip into the slot to secure the brake line. (You might have to tap it in with a hammer.) Now use the 10mm flare nut wrench to tighten the brake line nut. When everything is back together, be sure and bleed the brake system (Chapter 7, Procedure 1). Install the lower ball joint if you removed it.

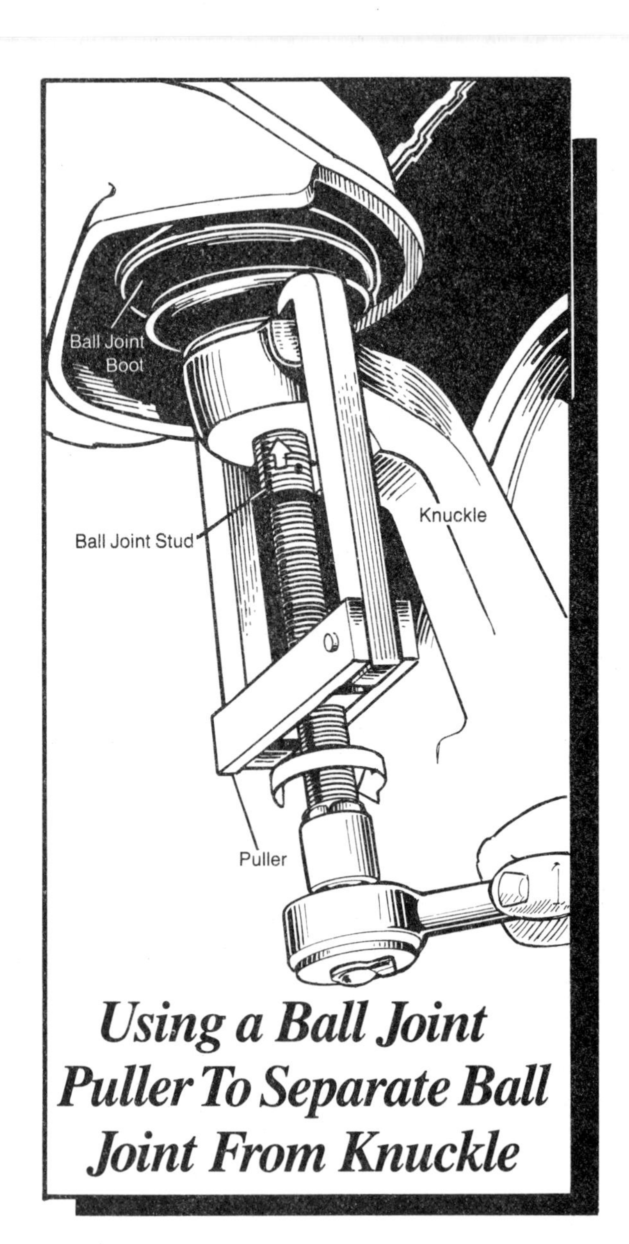

Using a Ball Joint Puller To Separate Ball Joint From Knuckle

Install lower ball joint: Fit the lower ball joint between the lower suspension arm and steering knuckle. Install and tighten the ball joint mounting nuts and bolts. Torque the 12mm bolts and nuts to 20 ft.lbs. and the 14mm bolt and nut to 32 ft.lbs.

Wipe any traces of grease from the ball joint stud and its hole in the steering knuckle. Fit the ball joint stud into its hole in the knuckle and install the castle nut. Tighten the castle nut to about 100 ft.lbs., then tighten it further until you can fit a new cotter pin through the slots in the nut and hole in the ball joint stud. Wrap the ends of the cotter pin around the castle nut.

EVERYONE: Install the wheel and snug the lug nuts, then lower the truck off the jackstands. Torque the lug nuts to 65-87 ft.lbs. If you disconnected any brake lines, be sure to bleed the brake system (Chapter 7, Procedure 1).

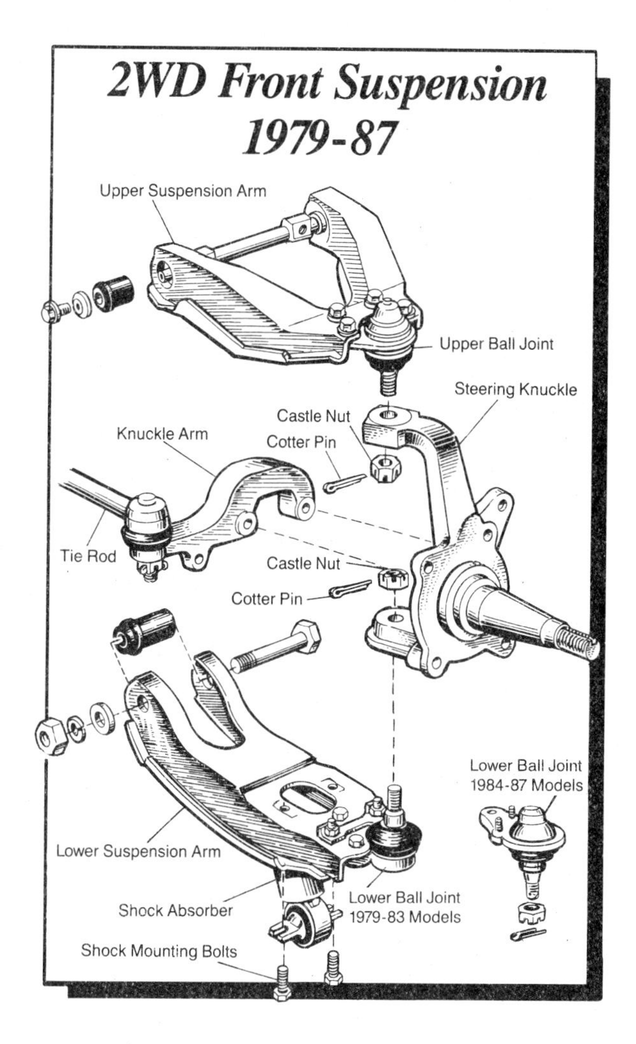

Step 3. Prepare to Remove Ball Joints on '84-'87 2WD models and '86-'87 4WD models.

To remove the ball joints you must first remove the following parts: 4WD Hubs (on 4WD models), brake calipers, wheel hubs, steering knuckles. Here's where to look for the instructions:

4WD models: See Procedure 6 in this chapter to remove the 4WD hubs.

EVERYONE: See Chapter 7, Procedure 5, Steps 1-4, to remove the brake calipers.

Once the calipers are off, see Procedure 5 in this chapter to remove the wheel hub and brake disc.

Once the wheel hub and brake disc are off, see Procedure 10 in this chapter to remove the steering knuckle.

Once the steering knuckle is off, see the next step to replace the ball joints.

Step 4. Remove Lower Ball Joints on '84-'87 2WD and '86-'87 4WD.

'84-'87 2WD models: Squirt some penetrating oil on the bolts and nuts that attach the ball joints to the suspension arms. Hold the bolt heads with a wrench while you use a socket and ratchet to remove the ball joint mounting nuts. If you are removing both ball joints, put the bolts for the upper and lower ball joints in separate baggies and label them upper or lower.

'86-'87 4WD models: Use pliers to remove the cotter pin from the lower ball joint castle nut, then use a socket and ratchet to remove the castle nut. Now use a ball joint puller or pickle fork to separate the ball joint from the lower suspension arm.

Step 5. Remove Upper Ball Joints on '84-'87 2WD and '86-'87 4WD Models.

Use a wrench to hold the bolt heads while you remove the nuts that attach the upper ball joint to the upper suspension arm.

Step 6. Install Upper and Lower Ball Joints on '84-'87 2WD and '86-'87 4WD models.

Use a wire brush and/or rag to clean the ball joint mounting surfaces on the suspension arms and steering knuckle.

Fit the upper ball joint into position on the suspension arm, then install the mounting bolts and torque them to 20 ft.lbs. ('84-'87 2WD models) or 25 ft.lbs. ('86-'87 4WD models).

'84-'87 2WD models: Fit the lower ball joint onto the suspension arm, then install and tighten the nuts to 51 ft.lbs.

'86-'87 4WD models: Fit the lower ball joint stud into its hole in the lower suspension arm. Install and torque the castle nut to 105 ft.lbs. If necessary, tighten it further so you can install a new cotter pin through the castle nut and ball joint stud. Bend the ends of the cotter pin over the end of the castle nut.

Step 7. Finish the Job on '84-'87 2WD and '86-'87 4WD models.

Once the ball joints are on, it's time to put all those other parts back on.

See Procedure 10 in this chapter to install the steering knuckle and dust cover.

See Procedure 5, Steps 5 and 6, in this chapter to install the wheel hub and torque plates (if your model has torque plates).

Now see Chapter 7, Procedure 5, Steps 4-6 to install the brake calipers.

4WD models: See Procedure 6, this chapter, to install the 4WD hubs.

EVERYONE: Finally, put the wheels on and snug the lug nuts. Lower the truck and torque the lug nuts to 65-87 ft.lbs. If you disconnected any brake lines, be sure to bleed the brake system (Chapter 7, Procedure 1).

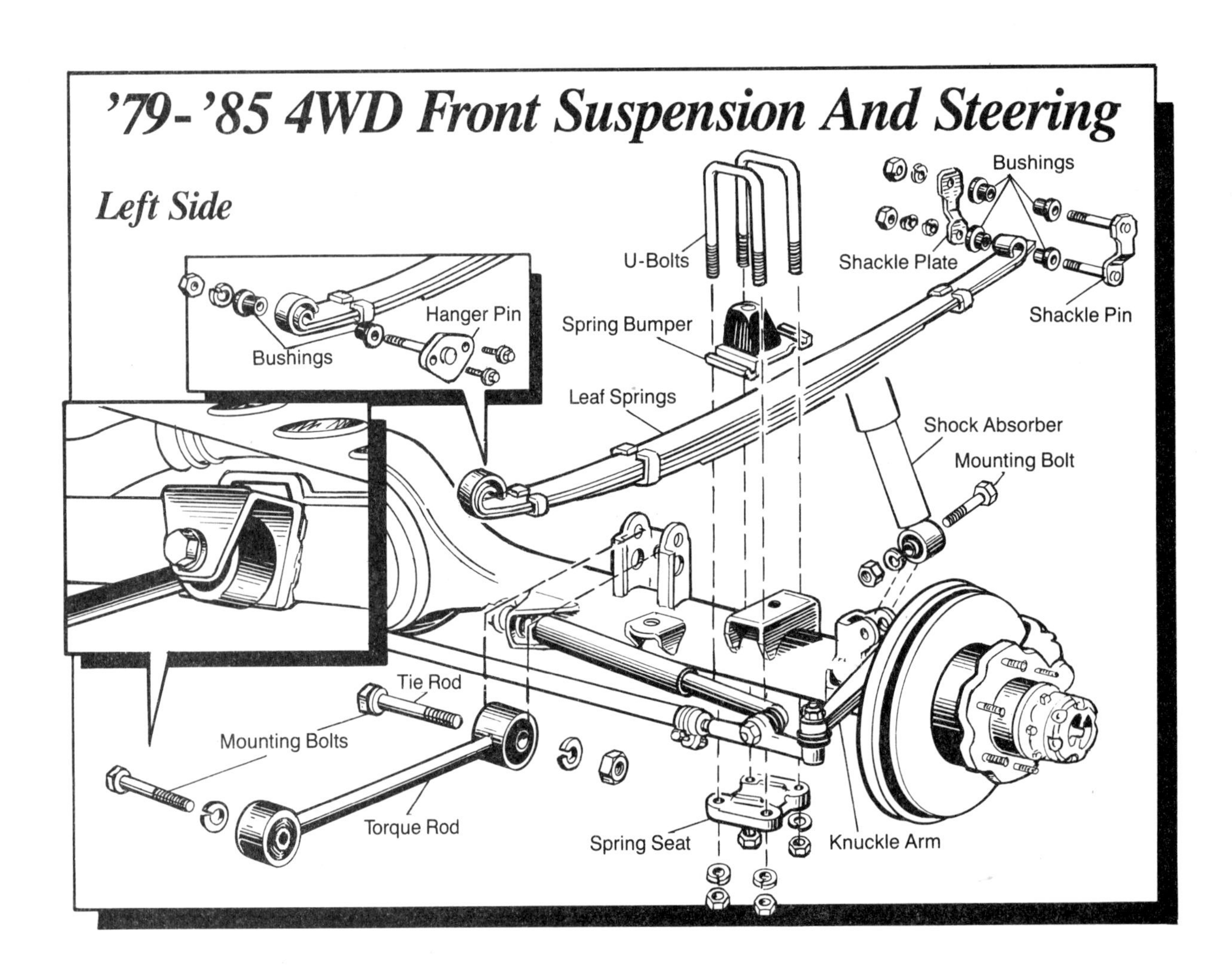

PROCEDURE 13: REMOVE AND INSTALL TORQUE ROD ON '79-'85 4WD MODELS

The torque rod is a short steel bar with bushings installed in each end. One end of the rod is attached to a bracket on the front differential housing, and the other end is attached to a bracket on the truck's frame. The torque rod stabilizes the front differential and prevents spring deformation (wrap up) under hard accelerations. If the bushings in the torque rod wear out, you'll hear a clunk when you accelerate or decelerate while in 4WD.

Condition: Bushings in the torque rod are worn out; OR you are removing the front differential housing.

Tools and Materials: Two 19mm wrenches or sockets and ratchet, maybe new torque rod or torque rod bushings.

Step 1. Remove and Install Torque Rod.

Use a 19mm wrench to hold the bolt head while you remove the nut on each end of the torque rod. Tap the bolts out of the bracket, then remove the torque rod.

Replace the torque rod if it's bent. The bolts should fit snugly in the bushings. If the bushings are worn, take the rod to the Toyota dealer or a machine shop to have the old bushings pressed out and new bushings pressed into the rod.

To install the torque rod, fit it into the brackets on the differential housing and frame. Install the bolts and nuts and tighten the nuts with your fingers. Now bounce the front of the truck up and down a few times to stabilize the bushings. Hold the bolt heads with a wrench while you torque the nuts to 87-122 ft.lbs.

PROCEDURE 14: REMOVE AND INSTALL LEAF SPRINGS (FRONT ON '79-'85 4WD MODELS, REAR ON ALL MODELS)

Condition: Springs are sagging or broken; OR the bushings in the springs or spring shackles are worn out; OR you are installing a lift kit.

Tools and Materials: Phase 1 tool kit, hydraulic jack, jackstands, maybe new springs, spring bushings or mounting bolts, chalk or paint. If you remove the springs on both sides of the truck at the same time you'll need two sets of jackstands.

Step 1. Chock, Jack and Block.

Park on level ground, set the handbrake, put the gearshift lever in FIRST or REVERSE (manual) or PARK (automatics).

If you are removing the rear leaf springs, put chocks in front of and behind the front tires. If you are replacing the front springs ('79-'85 4WD models), put chocks in front of and behind one of the rear tires.

Loosen the lug nuts a little, then use a hydraulic jack under the round part of the differential housing to raise the truck.

Front spring removal: Place jackstands under the frame just behind the rear end of the leaf springs. Lower the truck onto the jackstands, then remove the front wheels.

Rear spring removal: Place jackstands under the frame just in front of the front end of the leaf springs. Lower the truck onto the jackstands, then remove the rear wheels.

Step 2. Remove This and That.

Shock absorbers: Disconnect the bottom of the shock absorbers from the differential housing (Procedure 2, Step 2 for rear shocks, Procedure 3, Step 2 for front shocks).

If you are removing the rear leaf springs, skip down to Step 3.

Stabilizer bar: Locate the long U-shaped stabilizer bar attached to each side of the differential housing near the front. The thumb-size bar connects to a vertical bolt that's attached to brackets on the housing. Hold

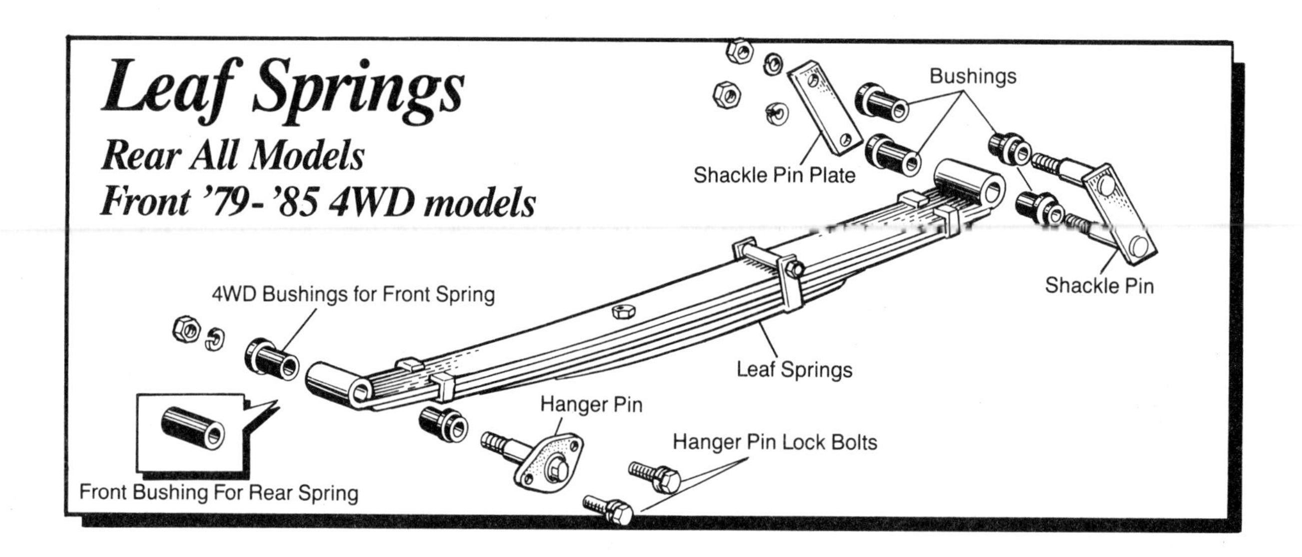

the bolt head with a wrench while you use a socket and ratchet to remove the nut. Once the nut is off, lift the bolt and push up on the stabilizer bar so you can screw the nut back onto the bolt above the bracket. This way you don't have to remove all those washers, grommets and spacers that are on the bolt. Disconnect both sides the same way.

Drag link: See Procedure 9 in this chapter to disconnect the drag link from the knuckle arm.

Brake line: Use a 10mm flare nut wrench to disconnect the brake tube from the brake hose near the top of the brake dust cover. Now use pliers to remove the spring clip so you can disconnect the hose from the dust cover. Remove the rubber dust cap from the brake bleeder valve and stick it on the end of the metal brake line so the brake fluid won't leak out. To keep dirt out of the rubber brake hoses, cover the ends with plastic baggies and secure them with rubber bands.

Step 3. Remove Leaf Spring.

Place the hydraulic jack under the differential housing on the side you are working on. Raise the jack until it barely touches the bottom of the differential housing.

Squirt penetrating oil on the threads of the U-bolts. Use a 19mm socket and ratchet to remove the nuts and washers on the bottoms of the U-bolts. Remove the U-bolts, spring seat and spring bumper (4WD models) from the leaf spring. As you remove them, use chalk or paint to mark them "left" and "right," "front" and "rear," so you can install everything in the same position during reassembly.

Slowly lower the jack until the leaf spring is barely clear of the differential housing. If you lower the jack too much, the spring will come crashing down when the mounting bolts are removed.

The hangar pin attaches the spring to the frame at the front, and the shackle pin (two bolts connected with a metal strap) attaches the spring to the frame at the rear.

Use a socket and ratchet to remove the nut from the inboard end of the hangar pin. Remove the nuts from the shackle pin bolts. If you have two bolts securing the hangar pin to the frame, remove the two bolts and pull the hangar pin out of the spring. The spring will drop down to the differential housing. Remove the lower bolt in the shackle pin. Now you can pull the spring out from under the truck.

Inspect the bushings in the frame and both ends of the leaf springs for wear and cracks. Check the leaf springs for broken leaves and weakness. Replace any bushings that are broken or worn. If you can't remove the bushings from the spring ends, have the Toyota dealer or machine shop press the old bushings out and new ones in.

If any leaves are broken you can have them replaced by the Toyota dealer or a garage, or you can buy a new set of springs. If you are faced with leaf spring repair or replacement, I suggest that you send for some of the catalogs listed in Chapter 14 to compare their prices to the Toyota dealers prices. You might be able to get new springs and shock absorbers for the price of springs from Toyota. If you're going to install a lift kit, now's the time to do it.

Step 4. Install Leaf Springs.

Fit bushings into the frame and into both ends of the springs, then wiggle the spring into position above the differential housing. Install the hangar pin and tighten the two bolts to 9 ft.lbs. (if your model has the two bolts). Install the nut on the hangar pin and tighten it with your fingers. Don't use a wrench yet. Install the shackle pins and shackle pin plate. Install and tighten the nuts with your fingers, not a wrench.

Raise the differential until it touches the bottom of the springs. Remember the marks you put on the U-bolts, spring seat and spring bumper (if your model has a spring bumper) during disassembly? Use the marks so you install the parts in their original positions. Set the spring bumper on the spring (if you have one). Fit the two U-bolts onto the differential housing. If you have a spring bumper, fit the U-bolts into the grooves on the bumper. Fit the spring seat onto the bottom of the U-bolts so the differential housing fits into the groove. Install the U-bolt mounting nuts and lock washers. Evenly tighten the U-bolt nuts in a criss-cross pattern to 90 ft.lbs. The length of exposed threads below each nut should be the same.

Step 5. Install This and That.

Shock absorber: See Procedure 2, Step 3, in this chapter to install the rear shock absorber or Procedure 3, Step 3, to install the front shock.

If you are replacing the rear springs you can skip to Step 6.

Drag link: See Procedure 9, Step 4, in this chapter to connect the drag link to the knuckle arm.

Stabilizer bar: If the grommets, washers and spacer came off the vertical bolt during disassembly, here's how it all goes back together. Remember that the concave side of the metal washers face the rubber grommets. Starting from the bolt head you should have a metal washer, a rubber grommet, then the end of the stabilizer bar, another grommet, then another washer. Next comes the long spacer, then a washer, a rubber grommet and another washer. This is where the bolt fits through the bracket on the differential housing. Below the bracket there's another grommet, a washer and the mounting nut. Hold the bolt head with a wrench while you torque the nut to 19 ft.lbs. Hold that nut with a wrench while you install and tighten the lock nut against it.

Brake line: Remove the plastic baggies and rubber cap from the brake line and hose. Fit the rubber hose into the brake line bracket, then screw the brake line nut into it. Screw the nut in with your fingers until you are sure the threads are straight. Use a 17mm open end wrench to hold the nut on the rubber hose while you use a 10mm flare nut to tighten the brake line nut. Get it good and snug but don't overtighten it. Pull the brake hose through the bracket while you fit the spring clip into its slots.

Stabilizer Bar Mount

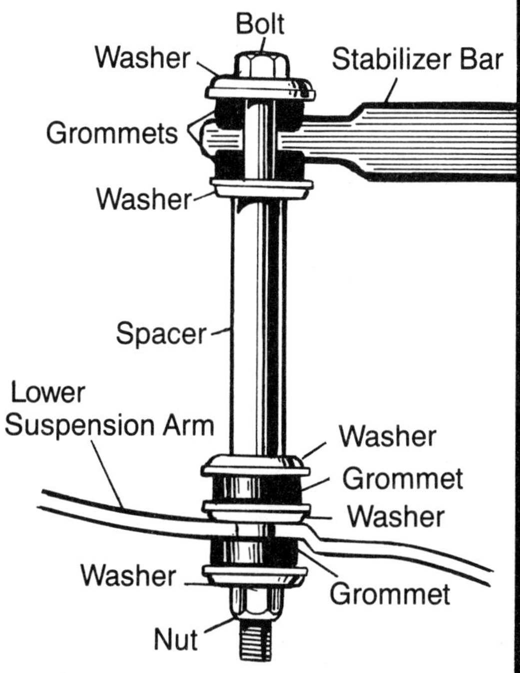

Step 6. Finish the Job.

Install the wheels and snug the lug nuts with a wrench. Raise the truck and remove the jack stands. Lower the truck and torque the lug nuts to 65-87 ft.lbs.

Bounce the end of the truck where you installed the spring up and down several times to stabilize the suspension. Crawl under the truck and torque the hanger pin nut and the shackle pin nuts to 67 ft.lbs.

If you disconnected any brake lines, be sure to bleed the brakes (Chapter 7, Procedure 1). Then go for a ride.

PROCEDURE 15: CHECK TULIP JOINTS AND CVJS

This procedure is only for 1986 and 1987 4WD models.

Condition: Routine maintenance; OR you feel a solid vibration that increases with speed; OR you hear a knocking sound when making sharp turns; OR you hear a clunk when you let the clutch pedal up.

Tools and Materials: Jack and jackstands, safety glasses, rags.

Remarks: Drive train vibrations caused by worn tulip joints, CVJs, U-joints, bent driveshafts or axleshafts are harsh, solid vibrations felt in the seat of your pants. The vibration intensity increases with car speed. (Vibrations caused by improper wheel balance or wheel alignment are softer and you feel them more on the steering wheel.) It's difficult to check the tulips and CVJs because they normally have a little looseness (play) in them. It's a good idea to check them while they're in good condition to get a feel for the proper amount of play. Then you'll be able to detect wear when it occurs. The CVJ and axleshaft are inseparable and must be replaced as a unit.

Step 1. Quick CVJ Check.

Find a large deserted parking lot where you can drive in circles. Turn the steering wheel either direction as far as it will go, then make a few slow circles while listening for clanks and clunks. Turn the steering wheel the other direction and try again. No sounds? The CVJs are probably good.

If you hear clunks while turning but the clunk goes away when the wheels are straightened out, or you're here from the 12,000 mile tune-up procedure, do Step 2.

Step 2. Check Tulips and CVJs.

Chock the rear wheels, set the handbrake, then jack up the front of the truck and put it on jackstands. Put the transmission in NEUTRAL.

To locate the inboard tulip joints and CVJs, crawl under the front of the car. Look at the inboard side of each front wheel for a black, wavy rubber boot. That's the **CVJ boot**. The large end of the CVJ boot is attached to the CVJ. The **axleshaft** is a steel rod a little larger than your thumb coming out of the inboard end of the CVJ boot. Further inboard the shaft disappears again into the rubber **inboard tulip joint boot**.

Check CVJs: Try to push and pull the axleshaft into and out of the CVJ while watching for play (movement) where the shaft disappears into the CVJ boot. You might be able to move the shaft in and out very slightly. Hold the front wheel while you twist the axleshaft as if you're screwing and unscrewing it. At most, the amount of play you can see and feel in the joint should be very slight.

Evaluation: If the axleshaft moves in and out more than 1/16", can be twisted more than a barely perceptible amount, and/or makes dry-sounding clunks when you move it, the joint is worn or needs to be cleaned and repacked with grease (Procedure 16). It's worthwhile to try cleaning and greasing the joint before replacing it because they're very expensive. If fresh grease doesn't quiet the joint, it should be replaced (Procedure 17).

Check tulip joints: Tulip joints are normally a little wobbly on the axleshaft. The only check you can do is the "twist test," like you did with the CVJs. Hold the round tulip with one hand while twisting the axleshaft with the other. If there's more than a slight movement and/or you hear a dry clunk or click when twisting the shaft, the tulip should be cleaned and greased (Procedure 16). If there's more than a slight amount of play between the axle and tulip joint, the joint should be replaced (Procedure 16).

Lower the truck when you're through checking, cleaning and greasing, or replacing the tulips and/or CVJs.

PROCEDURE 16: REMOVE AND INSTALL INBOARD TULIP JOINT AND BOOT

This procedure applies only to 1986-87 4WD models.

Replacing the inboard tulip joints and CVJs or their rubber boots is dirty and greasy, but not too difficult.

Condition: A tulip joint or CVJ is worn out; OR a tulip joint or CVJ boot is torn; OR the tulip joint is being removed so you can install a new CVJ boot or CVJ.

Tools and Materials: Safety glasses, Friend, maybe new tulip joint(s) or tulip joint boots and clamps, tulip joint grease (see Remarks), hammer, punch, external snap ring (circlip) pliers, two 17mm box end wrenches, 17mm socket and ratchet, very small screwdriver, medium screwdriver, pliers, flashlight or droplight, vinyl tape or silver duct tape, LOTS of rags and/or paper towels, jack and jackstands.

Remarks: The tulip joint must be removed from the axle to be cleaned and greased, or to replace the CVJ or either of the boots.

If you're replacing a boot, fresh grease should be supplied with the boot kit. If you can't get the Toyota grease, use molybdenum wheel bearing grease.

Clean the parts around the tulip joint and CVJ to prevent dirt from getting into the joint while repacking them and/or replacing the boots. Use your garden hose or cruise down to the carwash.

I've seen "split" boots advertised for other makes of cars that have CVJ and tulip-type joints. I'm sure they will be available for Toyotas soon, if not already. The split boots enable you to replace a boot without disconnecting the axle. You just cut the old boot off the joint, wrap the split boot around it, then glue the edges together. I've never used a split boot because I always clean and grease the joint when a boot breaks. However, split boots would probably be handy to have in the spare parts stash if you do a lot of off-roadin'. They should at least keep dirt out and possibly save the joint until you get back to civilization where you could install a regular type boot.

Caution: Wear safety glasses while working under the truck.

Step 1. Get Ready.

Chock the rear wheels and set the handbrake, then jack up the front of the truck and put it on jackstands.

Step 2. Separate Tulip Joint from Differential.

Put your safety glasses on and crawl under the side of the truck. You'll see that each tulip joint is bolted to the differential with six bolts and nuts. The hardest part of separating the joint from the differential is keeping the axle from turning while you loosen the nuts. There are two ways to accomplish the task: have Friend sit in the truck (it's solidly on jackstands, right?) and press on the brake pedal while you loosen the nuts. The other way is to fit a wrench on the bolt head, then prop the wrench against the frame while you use another wrench to loosen the nuts. You have to get the wrench in a certain position to do this. Use your longest 17mm wrench or ratchet handle to loosen the nuts because they are on tight. You'll have to rotate the axle to get

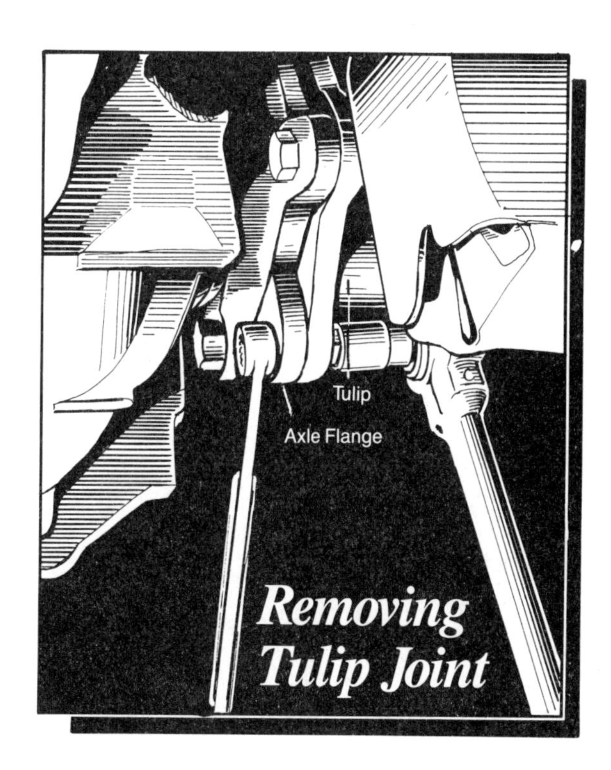

Removing Tulip Joint

to all six nuts. OK, remove the six nuts from the tulip joint.

Once the nuts are off, pry the tulip off the studs. It's a tight squeeze so you'll have to wiggle and twist the joint around until you find a position that allows it to be pulled down away from the differential.

If you're removing the complete front axle from the truck, do Procedure 17, Steps 3 and 4 to release the outer end of the axle from the hub. Procedure 17, Step 5 tells you how to remove the axle from the truck.

If you're here to replace the tulip or one of the axle boots, go on to the next step.

Removing Tulip Or CVJ Boot Clamp

Pry The Band Apart

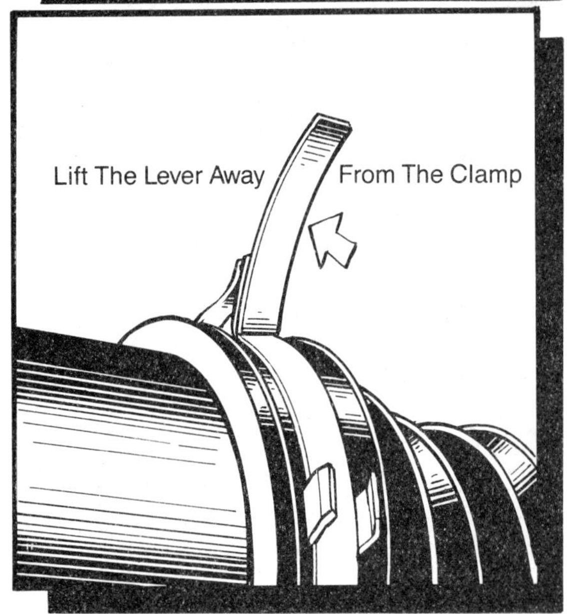

Step 3. Remove Tulip Joint and/or CVJ Boot Clamps.

Before removing the tulip joint you must mark the joint and axle so you can put them back together in exactly the same position. Here's how. Clean the axle and joint so you can use an indelible marking pen or paint to make a heavy line on the axle shaft and one on the outer part of the tulip.

The boot clamps have a split-band around the clamp that holds a thicker, lever-like part of the clamp. The clamps can be reused if they aren't bent or funky. If someone has replaced the boot before, they may have replaced the original type clamps with large hose clamps. If necessary, you can use hose clamps, nylon tie wraps or plastic zip ties in place of the boot clamps. If you use hose clamps, use the ones with the smallest clamp screw you can find.

To remove the boot clamps, find the small band that wraps around the clamp. There's a split in the center part of the band. Pry the band open with a small screwdriver or knife, then lift up on the lever that was held by the band. Lift the lever far enough to wiggle the clamp off the boot. Remove both clamps on the boot, then twist and slide the boot away from the tulip joint or CVJ.

Step 4. Remove Tulip Joint.

Now that the boot is out of the way, pull the tulip joint off the end of the axle. Now you can see the greasy innards. The thing on the end of the axle with three round knobs is called the tripod joint. Look at the inside of the tulip joint and you'll notice grooves for the tripod joint on the inside of the housing. Wipe some of the grease away from the end of the axle so you can see the snap ring that secures the tripod joint to the axle. Before removing the tripod joint, use your punch and hammer to make matchmarks on the end of the axle and on the round part of the tripod joint that surrounds the axle.

Hold a finger on the end of the axle while you

use external snap ring pliers to remove the circlip from the end of the axleshaft. Your finger will keep the circlip from flying off. When the circlip is off, use a hammer and brass or aluminum drift to tap the round part of the tripod joint off the axle. Tap a little in one spot, then rotate the axle so you can tap on the other two spaces between the knobs.

If you're replacing the tulip joint boot or CVJ boot, slide the tulip boot off the axle now. Otherwise, leave it on the axle.

Step 5. Clean, Inspect, Grease Tulip Joint.

Use rags or paper towels to wipe as much grease as possible from the tripod joint and from inside the tulip joint and boot. If needle bearings fall out of the tripod joint, or if the knobs are bluish-colored instead of clear and bright (you should be able to see your reflection in them), the tripod and tulip joints should be replaced with new ones. Feel the grooves inside the tulip where the tripod joint fits for worn or rough places. If you can feel a slight ridge where the tripod has worn into the tulip, replace the tulip and tripod. Everything look good?

If you have a tube of grease, press the nozzle end of the tube against the ends of the tripod joint where you can see the little needle bearings. Squeeze the tube so grease oozes out the other end of the bearing. Squeeze grease into each ball all the way around. Smear grease all over the outside of the tripod joint.

If the grease you're using isn't in a tube, put a golf ball size glob of the stuff in the palm of one hand. Mash the ends of the tripod balls down into the grease until it oozes out the other end. Smear grease all over the tripod joint. If you aren't replacing the CVJ boot, skip down to Step 7.

Tripod Joint Removal

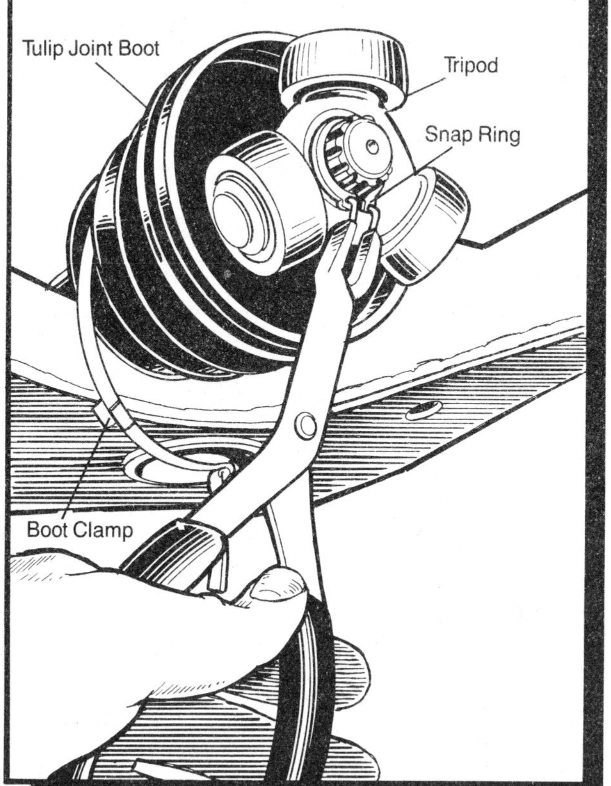

Step 6. Replace CVJ Boot.

If you are replacing the CVJ boot, remove the two clamps on the boot just like you did on the tulip boot. Use a rag to clean the axle, then slide the CVJ boot off the axle.

It's difficult to thoroughly pack the CVJ with fresh grease, so just pack as much as you can into the metal housing.

Step 7. Install CVJ and Tulip Joint Boots and Tulip Joint onto the Axle.

Put a very thin coat of grease in the grooves of the boots where the clamps fit. It makes the clamps easier to tighten. Now wrap a layer or two of silver duct tape or vinyl tape around and over the end of the axle so the boots won't be damaged during installation. Make sure the axle is clean so dirt won't get in the boots.

If you removed the CVJ boot, slide it onto the axle, then pack it with grease (Toyota says .43-.45 pounds).

Slide the boot onto the CVJ. Fit the large and small CVJ boot clamps into position on the boot but don't tighten them yet.

To install the tulip joint, slide a clamp for the small end of the tulip boot onto the axle (if you removed the old one), then slide the small end of the boot on (if you removed the boot). Remove the tape from the end of the axle.

Look at the tripod joint and axle for the punch marks you made. Find 'em? The other side of the tripod joint is beveled right next the splines. Align the match marks you made, then slide the tripod onto the axle. Check that the marks are aligned. If you forgot to mark the tripod joint, can't find the mark, or you're installing a new tripod, install the joint onto the axle with the beveled side toward the CVJ.

Use the brass or aluminum drift to gently tap the tripod onto the axle far enough to install the circlip. Only tap on the round part between the balls—not on the balls. Use snap ring pliers to install the circlip into the groove. To be sure the circlip is seated properly, tap a screwdriver against the clip all the way around.

Pack grease into the tulip joint (Toyota says .60-.62 pounds, but I don't know how you would weigh it). If you're installing a new boot, there are probably fresh grease and new clamps in the kit. Pack all the grease that came in the kit, or a baseball size blob of molybdenum wheel bearing grease, into the boot and spread it around.

Slide the small end of the boot into the groove on the axle. Wipe the grease off the outside of the tulip, then fit the big end of the boot over the edge of the tulip so the ridge inside the boot fits into the groove on the outside of the housing.

Step 8. Install Boot Clamps.

Fit the boot clamps into the grooves on the boot. It's best to tighten the large clamp first so the grease doesn't get out of the boot and dirt doesn't get in. Be sure the boot is properly seated in the groove on the tulip, CVJ or axle before you tighten the clamp. Here's how to tighten the clamps:

Press the lever down into the band and hold it there while you use a screwdriver to bend the sides of the band over the lever. Use pliers to squeeze the sides of the band together gently until the two sides touch. Give the band a tap or two with the hammer to be sure it's tight. Tighten the large clamps on the boot(s).

If you are using hose clamps, fit the clamp into the groove on the boot, then use a screwdriver to tighten the clamp. Be sure the clamp is in the groove all the way around. If the clamp is too wide to fit in the groove, it might slip off the boot—get a narrower clamp.

Wait until the tulip joint is attached to the differential before tightening the clamp on the small end of the boot. Now you can install the tulip on the differential.

Step 9. Attach Tulip Joint to Differential.

Wiggle the tulip onto the studs on the differential. Sounds easy, eh? Actually, you'll need to pry the tulip away from the studs as far as possible (which ain't that easy) in order to get it onto the studs. Keep trying—you'll get it. Install and tighten the nuts to 61 ft.lbs. Either have Friend push on the brake pedal or put a wrench on the bolt heads and prop it against the frame to keep the axle from turning while torquing the nuts.

Step 10. Finish Up.

Slide the smaller end of the tulip or CVJ boot into the groove on the axle, if it isn't there already. If the boot is distorted and part of it won't pop out, there's a vacuum inside that must be relieved. Slide a very small screwdriver under the edge of the small end of the boot, then lift the edge so air can enter the boot. Be careful not to tear the boot with the screwdriver. Pull out on the indentation in the boot if necessary.

When the boot is straight, be sure the ridge on the inside of the boot is in the groove on the axle. Slide the small clamp into its slot on the boot and tighten it the same way you tightened the large clamp (Step 8).

Use clean rags to wipe the grease off the tulip joint, boot and axle. Lower the truck, clean your tools, throw the greasy rags in the outside trash can, then clean your hands, and you're finished. Now that you've been through the ordeal once and know what you're doing, the next time you replace a boot, tulip or tripod joint, it will be a lot easier.

PROCEDURE 17: REPLACE CVJ AND FRONT AXLE SHAFT ON 1986-87 4WD MODELS

The CVJ and axle are inseparable, so unfortunately they must be installed as a complete unit.

Condition: CVJ is worn out; OR front axle is bent.

Tools and Materials: Same as Procedure 16 to remove the tulip and boots, plus those listed in Procedure 6, to remove the free wheeling or automatic locking hubs.

Step 1. Chock, Jack and Block.

Chock the rear wheels, set the handbrake, then slightly loosen the lug nuts on the side you're removing. Jack up the front of the truck and put it on jackstands. Gently push on the car to be sure it's securely on the jackstands.

Step 2. Separate Tulip Joint from Differential.

See Procedure 16, Step 2, in this chapter to separate the tulip joint from the differential.

Step 3. Remove Free Wheeling or Automatic Locking Hub.

See Procedure 6, to remove the free wheeling hub or automatic locking hub, whichever you have.

Step 4. Remove Snap Ring and Spacer.

Hold a finger over the outboard end of the axle while you use external snap ring pliers to remove the snap ring. Pull the spacer off the axle.

Step 5. Remove Front Axle.

Crawl under the truck and wiggle the axle out of the steering knuckle. If you removed the axle to get to the

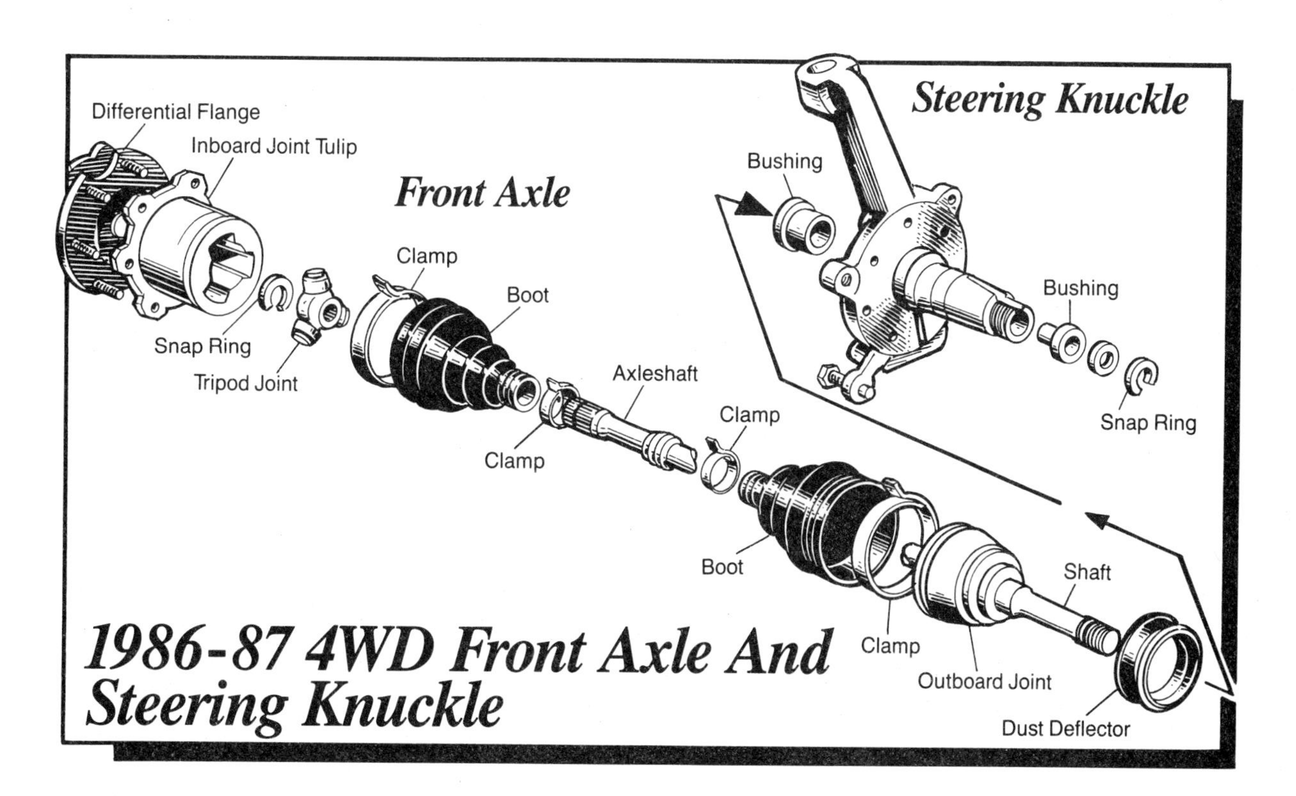

1986-87 4WD Front Axle And Steering Knuckle

steering knuckle, go back to the steering knuckle removal procedure. If you removed it because the CVJ was worn out, remove the tulip joint if it's still good (Procedure 16, Step 4), then install it on the new axle (Procedure 16, Step 7).

Step 6. Install Axle.

If you are installing a new axle, be sure it has a dust deflector on the outboard end of the CVJ. If the new axle doesn't have a deflector, use a screwdriver and hammer to remove the deflector from the old axle and install it on the new one. If the deflector is broken, bent or torn, replace it with a new one.

Smear some molybdenum disulphide lithium base grease on the outboard end of the axle (the part that goes into the steering knuckle), then slip that end of the axle through the hole in the steering knuckle. Wiggle it in as far as it will go. Be careful not to damage the boots. Fit the tulip joint onto the studs on the differential (Procedure 16, Step 9). Install the six nuts, but don't tighten them yet.

Now crawl out from under and install the spacer onto the outboard end of the axle. Use snap ring pliers to install the snap ring into its groove. Be sure the snap ring is seated all the way around the shaft.

Install the free wheeling or automatic locking hub, depending on your setup (Procedure 6, Step 4, for freewheeling hubs or Procedure 6, Step 7, for automatic locking hubs).

Crawl back under the truck and torque the six nuts on the tulip joint to 61 ft.lb. To keep the axle from turning, have Friend push on the brake pedal or use a wrench on the bolt heads to prop against the frame.

OK, things are looking a little more normal now. The only parts left to install are the wheels. Install the wheels and snug the lug nuts with a wrench. Lower the truck off the jackstands, then torque the lug nuts to 65-87 ft.lbs. You deserve a gold star (or a purple heart?) for your efforts!

CHAPTER 13
ENGINE REPAIR

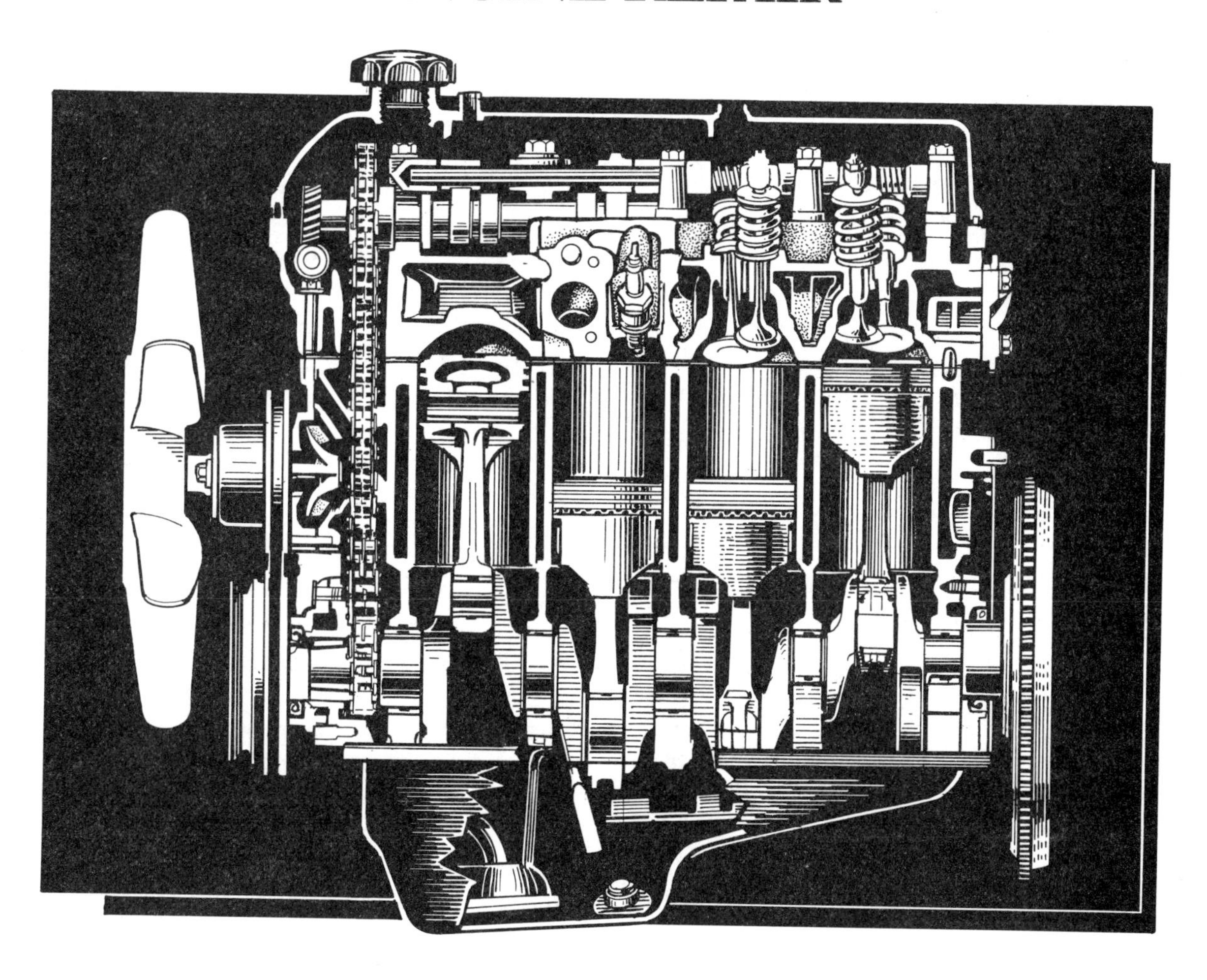

This chapter is about how to remove and install the distributor, front crankshaft seal, oil pump, oil pan and oil pick-up tube. If the rear crankshaft seal is leaking, see Chapter 11, Procedure 8.

After considerable deliberation and conversations with several Toyota mechanics and people who do their own car and truck repair, I decided not to include cylinder head or engine removal in this manual. Because there have been so many variations in the hoses, wires and components attached to the engines, it would almost require a separate book to be as specific as I would want to be about how to disconnect and reconnect everything. With proper maintenance, Toyota engines tend to last indefinitely, often outlasting the truck itself, so if the maintenance procedures in this book are performed regularly, it's unlikely that the engine will ever need to be removed.

If you determine that the cylinder head needs to be removed (because the head gasket is leaking, for a valve job, or to replace the piston rings or rod bearings) and you want to do the work yourself, I suggest that you buy the official Toyota Repair Manual for your model year. The manuals have lots of pictures and brief step-by-step descriptions that most people with a little mechanical experience should be able to follow. How and where to get the manuals is listed at the end of Chapter 3.

PROCEDURE 1: REMOVE AND INSTALL DISTRIBUTOR

The distributor sticks out of the front left side of the engine and has five high-tension electrical wires plugged into its cap.

Condition: Distributor bushings are worn out; OR mechanical advance mechanism isn't working; OR distributor plate is stuck; OR oil is leaking out around the base of the distributor.

Tools and Materials: 12mm and 19mm sockets, ratchet, long screwdriver, phillips screwdriver, small file or hammer and punch. If the spark plug wires aren't numbered you'll need masking tape and an indelible marker.

Step 1. Mark Distributor.

'79-'87 20R and 22R models: Use a phillips screwdriver to loosen the clamps that attach the large rubber hose to the end of the air cleaner snout. Remove the hose.

EVERYONE: Use your fingers or a long screwdriver to unclip or unscrew the clips or mounting screws for the distributor cap, then wiggle the distributor cap off. (See Chapter 5, Procedure 9, Step 2, for more detail.)

See Chapter 5, Procedure 5, Step 3, to set the engine to top dead center (TDC) firing position for cylinder #1. Be sure the rotor is pointing to the #1 spark plug terminal and the notch in the crank pulley is aligned with the 0 mark on the engine. On '75-'77 models the line on the engine should point to the right (passenger's side) notch on the crank pulley.

Use paint or a marker to make a line on the distributor or vacuum advance unit showing where the rotor points when the engine is set at TDC firing position for #1 cylinder.

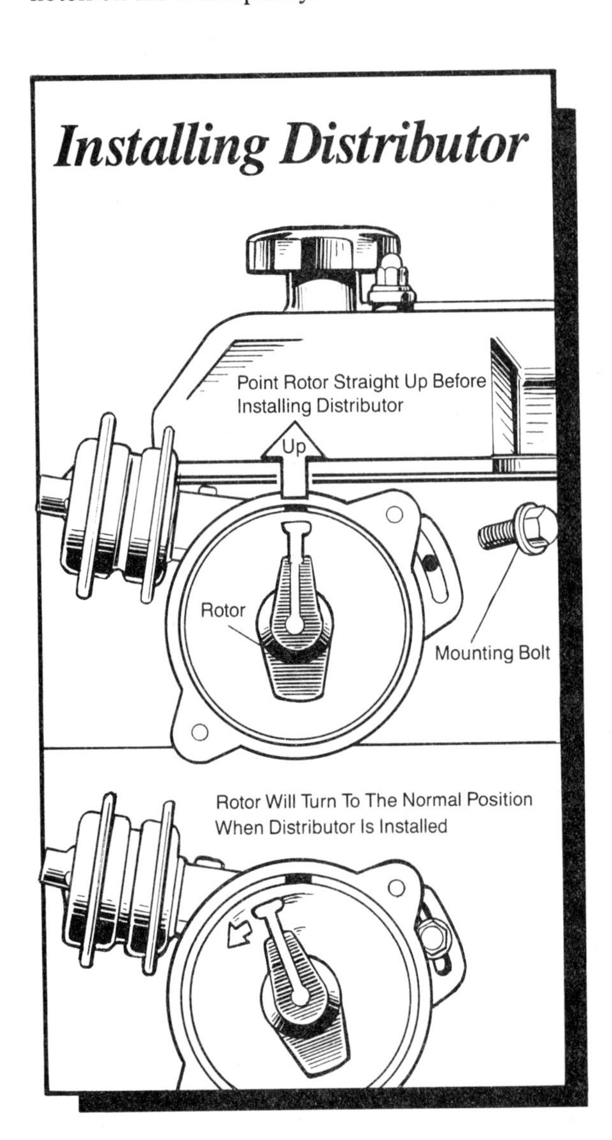

Step 2. Remove Distributor.

Follow the small wires from the distributor to a plastic connector. Pull the connector out of its clip, then separate the two halves of the connector. You'll probably have to lift on a tab while pulling the connector apart.

If you have a vacuum hose or two attached to a round vacuum advance mechanism on the front of the distributor, grab the distributor end of the hose(s) and twist it/them off the vacuum fitting(s). If there are two hoses, label and mark them "inner" and "outer" as you remove them.

'79-'87 models: Pull the engine oil dipstick out of its tube and wipe it off with a clean rag. Stash the dipstick somewhere safe, then cover the dipstick tube on the engine with the clean rag.

EVERYONE: Use a 12mm wrench or socket, ratchet and ratchet extension to remove the distributor mounting bolt. Don't move the distributor while removing the bolt. Once the bolt is out, use a hammer and punch or nail to make a small mark on the distributor housing right next to the hole for the mounting bolt. The mark will serve as a preliminary setting when the distributor is installed.

OK, now comes the big moment! Grab the distributor and wiggle it out of the cylinder head. Watch the rotor as you remove the distributor—it will rotate clockwise so it is pointing straight up.

If you removed the distributor because oil was leaking out around the base, replace the rubber O-ring on the shaft. Just wiggle the old one off, then coat the new O-ring with oil and slide it onto the housing until it fits neatly into its groove.

If the bushings in the distributor are worn out, the mechanical advance unit in the distributor wasn't working, or the distributor drive plate is stuck, haul the distributor to the Toyota dealer or auto electric shop for repair.

Step 3. Get Ready to Install the Distributor.

The engine must be set to Top Dead Center (TDC) firing position for cylinder #1. If you set the engine in that position before removing the distributor, and haven't turned the engine since, skip down to Step 4.

If you aren't sure that the engine is set right, remove the valve cover (Chapter 5, Procedure 8, Step 3). Use the 19mm socket on the crank pulley to rotate the engine *clockwise* (as viewed from the front) until the notch on the crank pulley is aligned with the 0 mark on the engine. On '75-'77 models, the line on the engine should be aligned with the right (passenger's side) notch on the pulley.

Grab the front two rocker arms on top of the engine and wiggle them up and down to see if they are slightly loose. If they are, the engine is at TDC firing position for cylinder #1. You can skip down to Step 4 to install the distributor.

If the rocker arms are tight, use the socket and ratchet to turn the crankshaft one complete turn *clockwise* (as viewed from the front). Align the notch and the 0 or line on the engine again. Then try the rocker arms. They should be slightly loose. Do Step 4 to install the distributor.

Step 4. Install Distributor.

Lightly oil the gear on the end of the distributor and the rubber O-ring. Install the rotor on the distributor shaft, making sure it is on correctly. (See Chapter 5, Procedure 9, Step 8, if you aren't sure.)

Fit the gear end of the distributor into the cylinder head a couple of inches. Turn the distributor so the slot for the mounting bolt is toward the rear and the mark you made is aligned with the bolt hole. Turn the rotor so it points straight up.

Next, wiggle the distributor into the cylinder head. The rotor will turn slightly counterclockwise as the distributor is installed. Check that your mark is aligned with the bolt hole. The rotor should be pointing to the line you made for the #1 spark plug wire. If it isn't, remove the distributor and try again.

When you are sure the distributor is installed correctly, install the mounting bolt so it's snug but don't tighten it yet.

Reconnect the distributor wiring connector halves making sure they lock together, then snap the connector into its clip. Insert the dipstick.

Check the points gap (Chapter 5, Procedure 11, Step 2) or the air gap (Chapter 5, Procedure 10, Step 2).

If your distributor has a plastic dust shield, remove the rotor and install the shield, then install the rotor again.

If you are using the old distributor cap, use a knife blade or small metal brush to clean the terminal posts on the inside. Check the cap for cracks and replace it if you find any.

If you are installing a new distributor cap, transfer the wires one at a time from the old cap to the new one. Be sure the wires end up in exactly the same positions on the new cap. See Chapter 5, Procedure 9, Step 9, if you need further instructions.

Fit the cap onto the distributor, then tighten the two mounting screws or fit the clips into place.

'79-'87 20R and 22R models: Install the rubber hose onto the air cleaner snout and whatever the front end was attached to. Tighten the phillips screws.

Fit the vacuum line(s) onto their fitting(s) on the vacuum advance unit on the distributor.

'75-'77 models: If you have a dwell meter, see Chapter 5, Procedure 11, Step 3, to check the points dwell.

EVERYONE: Now do Chapter 5, Procedure 12, to set the ignition timing. Once the timing is set, you're finished!

PROCEDURE 2: REMOVE AND INSTALL FRONT CRANKSHAFT OIL SEAL

The front crankshaft seal fits between the crankshaft pulley and the oil pump housing. Rubber "lips" around the inner edge of the seal press against the pulley shaft to prevent engine oil from leaking out. Eventually the lips wear out and the seal must be replaced. Amazingly, the rubber can wear a groove into the steel pulley! If the groove gets too deep, the pulley must be replaced.

Condition: Oil is leaking out around the crankshaft pulley.

Tools and Materials: 10mm, 12mm, 14mm and 19mm sockets and ratchet, ¾" drive ratchet or breaker bar to remove the pulley bolt, 3" to 6" ratchet extension, medium screwdriver, new front crankshaft seal, multi-purpose grease, probably a cheater bar (a piece of pipe to fit over the ratchet or breaker bar handle to give you more leverage). Maybe new drive belts.

Step 1. Get Ready.

Chock the rear wheels, set the handbrake, then jack up the front of the truck and put it on jackstands (Chapter 2, Procedure 1).

4WD models: There is probably enough clearance under the front of the truck that you won't need to put it on jackstands. Just be sure the rear wheels are chocked and the handbrake is on.

EVERYONE: Remove the skid plate and/or splash pan that covers the bottom front of the engine compartment. They are held on by 12mm bolts.

Step 2. Remove Crankshaft Pulley Bolt.

This is the most difficult part of the job. If you can't get the pulley nut off, you'll have to take the truck to the Toyota dealer or a garage and have them loosen it for you.

Here's the method I've devised for locking the engine while I remove the crank bolt. Stick a 3/8" drive ratchet extension at least three inches long through the front of one of the slots in the crank pulley. Now fit the 19mm socket and ratchet or breaker bar onto the crankshaft pulley bolt head and turn it *counterclockwise* (as viewed from the front of the truck). The extension will hit one of the oil pump mounting bolts and lock the pulley. Put the cheater bar on the ratchet or breaker bar and loosen the bolt. If you can't get it loose, you'll have to take the truck to the pros.

Step 3. Remove Fan, Drive Belts and Crankshaft Pulley.

See Chapter 6, Procedure 4, Step 2, to remove the fan. When the fan is off, see Chapter 8, Procedure 3 to remove all of the drive belts. Inspect the belts while they are off and replace them if you find cracks, frayed edges or oil spots. It's a good idea to replace the belts if they are more than three years old. (Better to do it now than at the side of the road.)

Once the belts are removed, pull the crank pulley off the crank. If it's stuck, put a large screwdriver behind the pulley on each side and lever it off the crank.

Step 4. Remove and Install Front Crankshaft Oil Seal.

Stick the tip of a medium size screwdriver under the inner edge of the oil seal, then push the handle toward the rear of the truck to lever it out. If necessary, put a hammer handle under the screwdriver blade for added leverage.

Use a clean rag to clean the oil seal mounting surface inside the front of the oil pump housing. Also clean the crank pulley and inspect the surface where the seal rubs. There is probably a small groove worn into the pulley by the oil seal. If the groove is deeper than a barely noticeable scratch, the pulley should be replaced. If you aren't sure whether the groove is too deep or not, get a second opinion from the pros.

Smear some multipurpose grease into the little rubber lips around the inner surface of the new oil seal. Fit the seal onto the front of the engine so the smooth side is toward the front. Press it in as far as you can push it

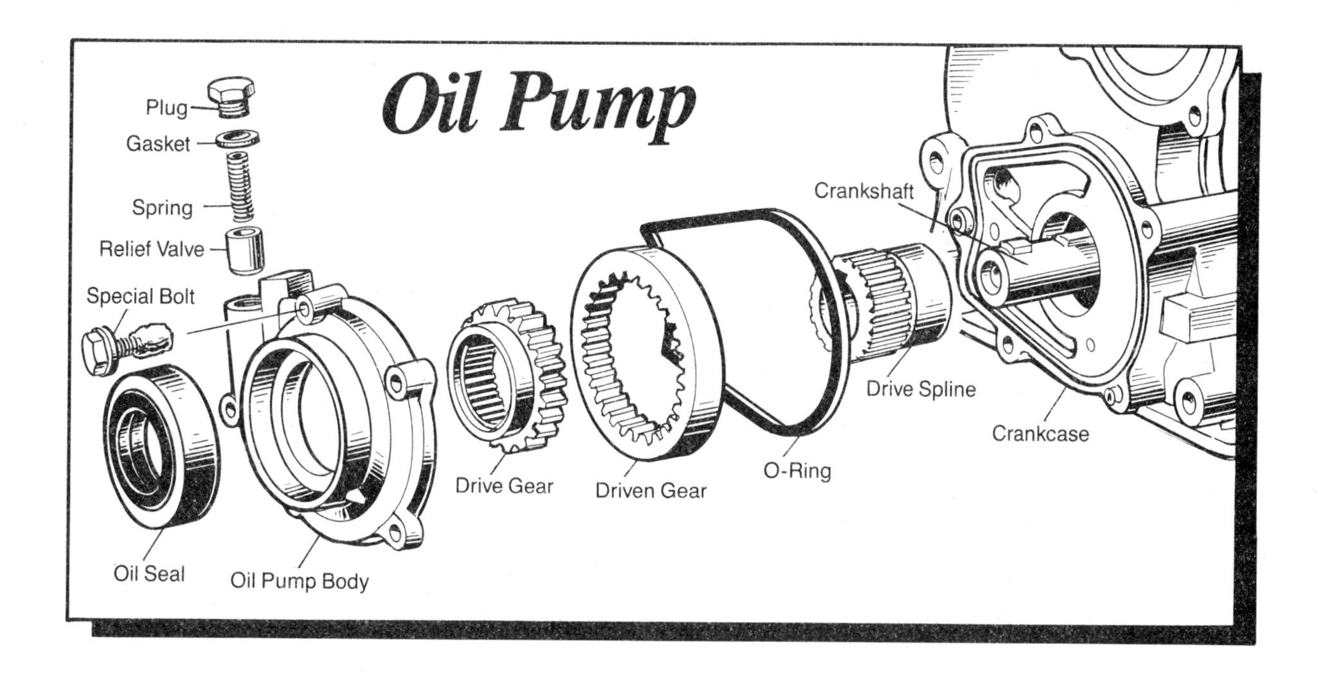

with your fingers. Be sure it's going in evenly all the way around. Tap all around the edge of the seal with a hammer until it's flush with the front of the timing chain cover. Be careful not to bash the end of the crankshaft or the radiator with the hammer.

Step 5. Install Crankshaft Pulley.

Align the groove in the pulley with the woodruff key in the crankshaft, then fit the crank pulley onto the crankshaft. Install the mounting bolt. Use the ratchet extension through a slot in the pulley to lock it the way you did when removing the pulley bolt. Torque the pulley bolt to 116 ft.lbs. Don't forget to remove the ratchet extension!

Step 6. Do This and That.

Install and adjust the drive belts (Chapter 8, Procedure 3). If you install new belts, be sure and check them after the engine has run for five to ten minutes.

Install the fan and tighten the four 10mm nuts (Chapter 6, Procedure 4, Step 4).

Install the splash pan and/or skid plate, then lower the truck off the jackstands, if you raised it.

PROCEDURE 3: REMOVE, INSPECT AND INSTALL OIL PUMP

The timing chain cover is that large chunk of aluminum on the front of the engine. The water pump is bolted to the upper part of the cover and the oil pump is bolted to the lower part. The crankshaft pulley mounts on the end of the crankshaft that passes through the oil pump.

Condition: Oil pump is leaking; OR oil pressure light flickers; OR oil pressure gauge indicates lower than normal oil pressure.

Tools and Materials: 10mm, 12mm, 14mm, 19mm and 22mm sockets, ¾" drive ratchet or breaker bar, 3" to 6" ratchet extension, screwdriver, probably a cheater bar (a piece of pipe to fit over the ratchet or breaker bar handle to give you more leverage), new front crankshaft seal, multi-purpose grease, new oil pump O-ring, Three Bond 1324 sealer (Toyota Part No. 08833-00070) or Loctite 242 or 271 (get it in a parts store), maybe new oil pump and/or drive belts, solvent, parts cleaning brush, rags, safety glasses.

To check the oil pump you'll need a set of feeler gauges and a straightedge ruler.

Step 1. Get Ready.

Do Procedure 2, Steps 1 to 3, to remove the fan, drive belts and crankshaft pulley. When all that stuff is off, come back here and we'll remove the oil pump. Don't forget to wear your safety goggles.

Step 2. Remove Oil Pump.

Use a 22mm socket to loosen the bolt on the top right side of the oil pump. The **relief valve** and **spring** are lurking below the bolt.

Remove the five 12mm bolts that attach the oil pump to the timing chain cover. As you remove the bolts, lay them in order so you'll know which bolt goes where when you put the oil pump back on.

When the oil pump is removed, about a cup of oil will drain out, so place a catch pan or pile of rags beneath the oil pump to catch the oil.

Feel along the bottom edge of the oil pump for a little lip that hangs down slightly farther than the front of the engine. Place the tip of a screwdriver against the rear of the lip and give it a couple of taps with a hammer. The oil pump should move away from the engine slightly. Try to wiggle the pump off with your hands. If it's stuck, use the screwdriver to carefully pry the pump off the engine without scratching the mating surfaces. Don't let the oil drip in your face!

Once the pump is off, pull the **drive spline** off the crankshaft.

Step 3. Inspect Oil Pump.

Wiggle the smaller **drive gear** out of the pump housing, then remove the larger **driven gear**. Use a clean rag or paper towel to wipe them clean. Inspect the teeth on both gears for cracks, chips or more wear along one side of the teeth than on the other. Replace the oil pump if you find any of these abnormalities.

Insert the tip of a screwdriver below the outer edge of the oil seal and pry it out of the pump body.

If the outside of the pump body is covered with crud and filth, use solvent and a stiff brush to clean it. Pour fresh solvent over it to flush away any remaining dirt.

Remove the oil pressure relief valve bolt, washer, spring and relief valve. Use a rag to clean the relief valve, then inspect it for scratches. If you find any, replace it with a new one.

Inspect the pump body for cracks. Look for scratches on the smooth inner surface where the outside of the driven gear rubs and on the sides of the crescent shaped chunk of aluminum. Replace the pump if there are more than the slightest signs of scratches.

Check the teeth on the drive spline for wear. Replace it if grooves have worn into the teeth.

Fit the drive and driven gears into the pump. Whip out your feeler gauges and measure the clearance between the pump body and the outside of the driven gear. There are four places where the pump body is slightly grooved, so don't check in those places. The maximum clearance allowable between the body and driven gear is .008" (0.2mm).

Now check the gap between the teeth of the drive gear and driven gear and the crescent-shaped thing. The maximum clearance is .012" (0.3mm).

Lay a straight edge across the gears and measure the gap between the two. The maximum clearance is .006" (0.15mm) between the gears and the straight edge.

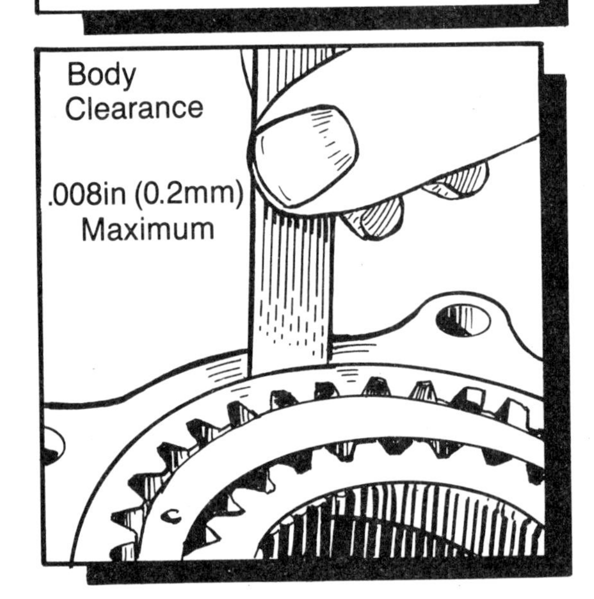

Replace the oil pump if any of your measurements were larger than the maximum figure.

If the rubber O-ring is still in its groove in the timing chain cover, pull it out. Use a clean rag to wipe off the front of the timing chain cover, then check the cover for cracks. In the unlikely event that you should find something amiss, drag the truck to the Toyota dealer or a garage and have the cover replaced. They will have to remove the cylinder head and oil pan to replace it.

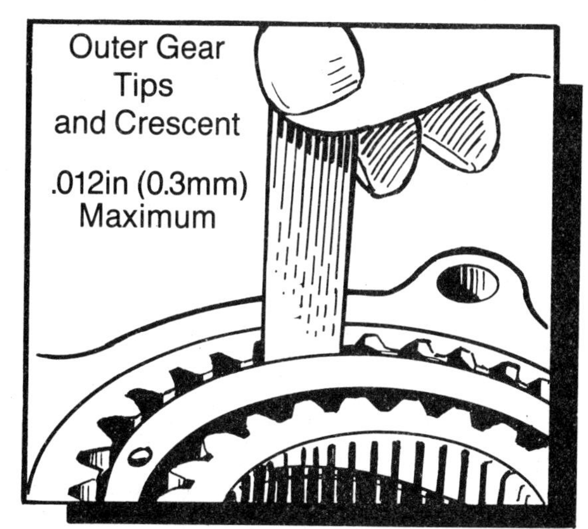

Step 4. Install Oil Pump.

Be sure all the parts for the oil pump and the timing chain cover are spotlessly clean. Douse all the parts with fresh solvent to be sure, then dry everything with clean lint-free rags. Use a wire brush to clean the threads on the mounting bolts. Spread a light coat of antiseize compound on the threads of the two long bolts and the two bottom bolts. Don't put any oil on the short top bolt.

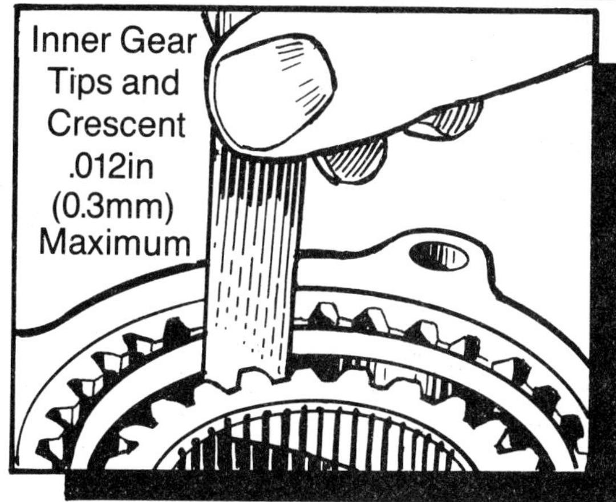

Remove the drive and driven gears from the pump body. Lay the pump body on a clean surface with the front side facing up. Fit the new crankshaft oil seal into its hole so the smooth side is up. Press the seal in with your fingers until it's flush with the pump body. If necessary, lay a clean flat board across the seal, then tap on the board with a hammer. Pack multipurpose grease into the groove between the two rubber lips on the inner surface of the seal where it rubs against the crank pulley.

Coat the relief valve with fresh oil. Install the relief valve, then the spring into the pump body. Fit the washer onto the bolt, then install the bolt and snug it down. You'll have to tighten it after the pump is installed.

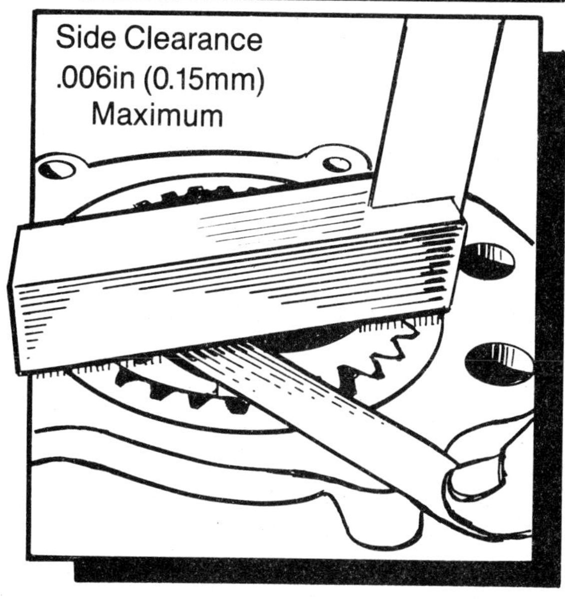

Coat the drive and driven gears, and the inner surface of the pump body, with fresh oil. Fit the driven gear into the housing and spin it around to be sure it turns smoothly. Now fit the drive gear into the body so the little lip is toward the front of the pump. The two gears should be flush with the inner surface of the pump body. Turn the drive gear to be sure everything is sliding smoothly.

Spread some fresh oil on the drive spline teeth, then fit it onto the crankshaft so the splined end is toward the front. You'll have to align the groove with the woodruff keys on the crank. Slide it all the way on.

Put a light coat of oil or grease on the new O-ring to hold it in place while you install the pump.

Fit the O-ring into its groove on the timing chain cover, making sure it is in the groove all the way around.

Hold the oil pump so the timing marks are at the top and slip the pump onto the timing chain cover. Two of the holes fit onto little collars sticking out of the timing chain cover. Gently wiggle the oil pump until it fits against the cover.

Squirt some Three Bond 1324 (Toyota Part No. 08833-00070) or Loctite 271 or 242 on the threads of the short top bolt. Install the bolt and tighten it with your fingers. Next install the two long bolts on the upper right and left sides and snug them with your fingers. Finally, install the two bottom bolts. Use your torque wrench to tighten the top bolt to 18 ft.lbs., the two long bolts to 14 ft.lbs, and the two bottom bolts to 9 ft.lbs. Tighten the 22mm bolt that covers the oil pressure relief valve on the top right side of the oil pump.

Step 5. Do This and That.

Do Procedure 2, Step 5. Install and adjust the drive belts (Chapter 8, Procedure 3), then install the fan and tighten the four 10mm nuts (Chapter 6, Procedure 5).

Start the engine and watch the oil pressure light or gauge. It will take a few seconds for the oil pump to fill and start pumping, so don't panic. Once you're sure you have oil pressure, check the bottom of the pump for leaks. There might be a few drops of oil from the assembly lubrication. Wipe the oil off and watch for more. If the pump stays dry, install the splash pan and/or the skid plate.

If the pump keeps leaking, the O-ring must have fallen out of its groove. You'll have to remove the pump and install another new O-ring.

If the oil pressure light doesn't go out or the gauge doesn't show pressure within 30 seconds, turn the engine off. Try it again after a couple of minutes. If there's still no oil pressure, you must have forgotten to install one of the gears. Remove the pump and check it.

If you installed new drive belts, be sure to check the tension after the engine has run for five to ten minutes. Adjust them again if they have loosened.

PROCEDURE 4: REMOVE AND INSTALL OIL PAN

The oil pan is that black, bulbous thing covering the bottom of the engine crankcase. It's attached with a plethora of bolts and a couple of nuts.

Condition: Oil pan is leaking; OR you need to clean the oil pick-up screen.

Tools and Materials: The tools and materials listed in Chapter 5, Procedure 3, for changing the engine oil. You will also need 12mm and 14mm wrenches and sockets, ratchet, ratchet extension, a thick strong putty knife, several single edge razor blades, solvent, hammer, safety glasses.

If you remove the oil pick-up tube, you will need a new oil pick-up tube gasket.

'84-'87 models: You will also need a hydraulic floor jack, a short block of wood and a tube of gasket sealer from the Toyota dealer (Part No. 08826-00080).

Remark: You'll be working under the truck, so don't forget to wear your safety glasses.

Step 1. Get Ready.

Chock the rear wheels, set the handbrake, put the gearshift lever in FIRST (manual) or PARK (automatic). Drain the engine oil into a catch pan (see Chapter 5, Procedure 3).

2WD models: Jack up the front of the truck and put it on jackstands (Chapter 2, Procedure 1).

4WD models: There is probably enough room under the truck so that you won't need to jack it up and put it on stands. If you decide to jack it up, see Chapter 2, Procedure 1.

EVERYONE: Remove the splash pan and/or skid plate from beneath the engine, if you have them. They are attached with 12mm bolts.

Step 2. Remove Idler Arm and Crossmember on '79-'83 2WD Models.

See Chapter 12, Procedure 9, Step 3, to remove the two or three bolts and nuts that attach the idler arm to the frame. You won't need to disconnect the arm from the relay rod, just from the frame. Pull the steering linkage down and forward as far as possible so you'll have room to remove the oil pan.

Remove the four bolts and nuts that attach the crossmember that runs side to side beneath the oil pan. It connects the two lower suspension arms. Remove the crossmember.

Step 3. Remove Engine Mount Bolts and Raise Engine on '84-'87 models.

On each side of the engine, toward the front, there are rubber and steel motor mounts. From underneath the truck, locate two 14mm bolts on the slanted part of each mount and remove the bolts.

Place a block of wood on a hydraulic jack, and jack up the front end of the transmission until the engine has risen about one inch.

Step 4. Remove Oil Pan.

Remove all of the bolts and nuts from around the edge of the oil pan. Use a hammer to tap a strong thick putty knife between the oil pan and engine crankcase, then gently pry on the oil pan with the putty knife. You'll probably need to do this in several places around the oil pan, especially at the corners. Don't pry so hard with the putty knife that the oil pan gets bent out of shape—it will never seal right if it's bent. Just keep tapping it in and pry a little, then move to a different spot and do it again. Eventually you'll be able to pry the pan off the engine.

Step 5. Clean and Inspect the Oil Pan.

Use a knife or single edge razor blades to scrape the old gasket off the oil pan and the mounting surface on the engine. Be sure all traces of the old gasket are removed. Next, use solvent and a stiff parts cleaning brush to clean the oil pan. Clean the mounting surface on the engine with a rag.

Inspect the mounting surfaces on the pan and engine for cracks, metal burrs or deep scratches. Use a flat file to smooth off any abnormalities.

If the oil pan is cracked or severely dented, replace it. You can probably find a good used one at a junk yard.

Step 6. Remove, Inspect and Install Oil Pick-up Tube.

The oil pick-up tube is bolted to the bottom of the engine. A round oil strainer is attached to the end of the tube.

To remove the pick-up tube, locate the mounting bolts that attach the end of the tube and the oil strainer supports to the crankcase. Remove the bolts, then gently pull the tube and strainer off the engine. Use solvent and a brush to remove all traces of crud from the tube and strainer. Pour fresh solvent through the tube and strainer to flush out any residue. Use a knife or razor blade to remove all traces of the old gasket from the engine and the end of the tube. Clean the mounting surface on the engine with a clean rag.

To install the oil pick-up tube and strainer, fit a new gasket on the end of the tube and install the bolts to hold it in place. Screw the two bolts into the engine, then install the bolt(s) that attach the strainer bracket. Tighten the bolts to 9 ft.lbs.

Step 7. Install Oil Pan.

'75-'84 models: Look on the bottom of the crankcase where the timing chain cover attaches to the front and where the rear crankshaft oil seal retainer attaches to the rear. You need to spread gasket sealer on the new oil pan gasket where it fits against these joints. To be sure where the sealer goes, hold the gasket up to the crankcase so it matches the contour of the crankcase.

Lay the new oil pan gasket on the clean oil pan so the shape of the gasket matches the oil pan and all the bolt holes are aligned. Spread gasket sealer on the corners where the gasket will fit against the timing chain cover and oil seal holder joints. Hold the gasket in place with your fingers while you fit the oil pan onto the crankcase.

Install the bolts and nuts and tighten them to 9 ft.lbs. If you don't have a torque wrench, put your hand on the head of the ratchet and snug the bolts down. Don't overtighten them or the gasket will break.

'85-'87 models: Use the gasket sealer you got from the Toyota dealer on the oil pan and engine crankcase. Once you've put the sealer on the crankcase and oil pan, you must install the pan within five minutes or you'll have to remove the sealer completely and start all over.

Install the nozzle on the tube of gasket sealer, then cut the end off so the opening is approximately ¼" (5mm). Put a bead of the gasket sealer along the bottom of the joints between the crankcase and the timing chain cover on the front of the engine, and between the crankcase and oil seal retainer on the rear. See the illustration to see where to put a bead of gasket sealer on the oil pan.

Fit the oil pan onto the crankcase and install the mounting bolts and nuts. Torque them to 9 ft.lbs. No torque wrench? Put your hand on the head of the ratchet and snug them down. If you overtighten the bolts the gasket might break, so be gentle.

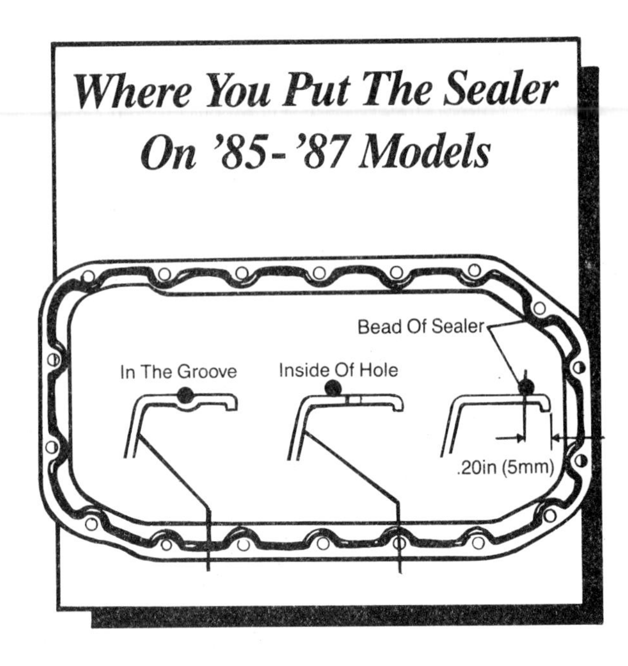

Step 8. Finish the Job.

'79-'83 2WD models: Fit the crossmember into place, then install and tighten the four mounting bolts.

Fit the idler arm onto the frame and install the mounting bolts. Tighten the bolts to 26-36 ft.lbs. on '75-'78 models or 37-41 ft.lbs. on '79-'83 models.

'84-'87 models: Lower the jack until the slanted parts of the motor mounts barely touch. Install and tighten the four mounting bolts. Get them tight. Then lower the jack completely.

EVERYONE: Install the splash pan and/or the skid plate with the 12mm bolts.

Be sure the oil drain plug is installed and tightened, then see Chapter 5, Procedure 3, to replace the oil filter and refill the crankcase with fresh engine oil.

Lower the truck if you put it on jackstands. Start the engine and check for leaks around the oil pan. If it's leaking, snug down the oil pan mounting bolts a little more. Check it once a week for about a month to be sure no leaks have developed. That's all folks.

CHAPTER 14
MODIFYING YOUR TOYOTA

If you want to make your truck look more "bitchin" or be a "rad" performer, you're in the right place. This is the chapter where you can spend all that money you've been saving by doing your own maintenance and repairs. Hopefully you'll even make your truck safer in the process.

Thanks to the ever increasing popularity of Toyota trucks, there are almost unlimited sources of modification products available for your Toy. Your truck is like a blank canvas to an artist or an instrument to a musician: it's just waiting to be used to create an original work of art. About the only limitation is the size of your pocketbook.

Determining how you want your truck to look and perform, and then organizing the modifications into a logical step-by-step order, will make the most efficient use of your time and money. Set weekly, monthly or yearly goals and pigeon-hole the money for buying the parts. It's easier to save a little at a time rather than having to cough up a big wad all at once.

Toyota trucks are balanced when they come from the factory—"balanced" in the sense that the suspension is designed to handle the power produced by the engine. If you increase engine performance too much without also the beefing up the suspension, the delicate balance is destroyed. The added power will get you in off-road places that the factory suspension wasn't designed to handle, and premature failure will result (usually at the worst possible time). Added power will also propel you around corners faster than the factory suspension was designed to handle, and you'll end up like an upside-down turtle in the ditch.

What I'm getting at is that for safety, the suspension should be beefed up before, or at the same time as, you increase the horsepower of the engine.

I've broken this chapter into three parts. First I'll go through some of the most popular appearance modifications and tell you what's involved in making the changes yourself, and where to turn for help if you get stuck.

The second part deals with suspension, and the third part of the chapter covers engine modifications that can change your Toyota into a slightly hopped-up street racer, a gorilla off-roader, or a fire-breathing full-on racer. In all three sections I start with the cheapest, easiest and/or most important changes you can do. Then I gradually go deeper and deeper into the more expensive, more difficult, and more exotic modifications. Most of the products listed in this chapter are "bolt-on" items that can be installed with the hand tools listed in Chapter 3. I'll warn you of items that require special tools or abilities

At the end of the chapter I've included a list of companies who specialize in selling appearance and performance goodies for Toyota trucks, and a few magazines that have good technical articles about the latest equipment items available and how to install some of them.

PLEASE NOTE!

In this chapter I'm only informing you of the products available for modifying your truck to fit your individual taste and needs. I cannot guarantee or be responsible for how your truck will perform, possible damage to the truck, or personal injury resulting from the installation of these products. In some states it is illegal to make engine modifications that affect the emission control devices, so check the laws in your state before making any engine changes.

If you want to make a "monster" truck out of your Toyota, you're in the wrong place. Granted, it's fun to watch monsters like Big Foot crush cars on TV, but those trucks have very specific limitations and aren't suited to do anything but crush cars. I'll leave those modifications to people who can afford to sink megabucks into a truck that can only go a few yards at very slow speeds.

Also, this chapter will not help you make a "low rider." If you lower a car or truck with independent front suspension, which most Toyota trucks have, it will upset the delicate geometry and cause steering and tire wear problems. Thanks.

PART 1: APPEARANCE MODIFICATIONS

PAINT STRIPES

Probably the quickest, cheapest and easiest way to change your truck's appearance is by adding fancy "paint" stripes. These stripes are actually heavy duty tape usually made by the 3M company. A strong adhesive substance on the back of the tape holds it securely to the body. You can purchase the stripes at auto parts stores, the Toyota dealer (or most other new car dealers), or through some of the magazines and catalogs listed at the end of the chapter. I've also seen attractive tape stripes from boat companies used effectively on cars and trucks.

The trick to installing the stripes is getting them on exactly where you want them. Take your time when laying out the design and make small pencil marks where the stripes should end up. Once the protective sheet of paper is removed and the stripe is on, it's very difficult to move.

Removing paint stripes is a tedious job due to the strength of the glue. A low power hair dryer or commercial paint and varnish removal heat gun helps soften the sticky stuff so it comes off a little easier. Be careful not to overheat the paint or it will blister. Residual glue can be removed with denatured alcohol.

BUMPERS

Bumpers come in a variety of sizes and shapes that can dramatically change the appearance of your truck. There are black or chrome traditional style bumpers, and the newer tube-type bumpers with one, two or three 2" or 3" diameter tubes stacked one on top of the other. Some front bumpers have built in brush guards of various sizes to protect the grille and headlights when you wander off the road. And some even have built-in winches to save you when you wander too far off the road. Front bumpers with brush guards usually have places to mount driving lights.

Most rear bumpers have built-in trailer hitches. If the body and/or suspension has been raised by using a lift kit, a "drop hitch" must be installed on the bumper to lower the trailer hitch to normal trailer towing height.

When buying bumpers, find out what gauge steel was used in construction. I suggest using .109" thick material as a minimum. .124" is even better.

Installing bumpers is very straightforward and only involves unbolting the old bumper (if there is one), then bolting the new one in place. If you plan to tow heavy trailers, I suggest having heavy duty mounting brackets for the bumper installed to prevent side to side movement. Any good welding shop can make the braces.

ROLL BARS

Besides changing the appearance of your truck, roll bars might just save your life! A nice combination. Like tubular bumpers, heavy duty roll bars are usually made of 2" or 3 inch diameter black or chrome tubes welded together. Also, like bumpers, roll bars are made out of tubes of different thickness. Minimum thickness of the bars should be .109".

In the catalogs, roll bars are described as single, double, triple, etc. which indicate how many tubes are in the vertical part and how many are in the diagonal support. For instance, a triple double means there are three vertical tubes and two diagonal braces. Most roll bars have built in brackets or holes for mounting high intensity driving or off-road lights.

A recent variation on the roll bar includes brackets for attaching two long diagonal braces between the top of the roll bar and the rear of the truck bed. A bracket provided on the diagonal bars allows mounting a spare tire or two in the bed so it's handier. There are also bed-mounted spare tire holders that aren't attached to the roll bar. If you install oversize tires, the spare might not fit under the bed, so it must be mounted in the bed. Removing the spare from under the truck also slightly increases the rear ground clearance. Instructions for installing the roll bars are usually included in the kit.

AUXILIARY DRIVING AND OFF-ROAD LIGHTS

Auxiliary lights make night driving much safer. Especially driving off-road or in Mexico.

Driving lights and off-road lights come in an assortment of sizes, shapes, and power. The lenses are normally white, with yellow fog lenses optional. Lights are rated in watts; normal sealed beam headlights are about 60-65 watts on high beam and 55 watts on low beam. Halogen headlights are about 65 watts high beam and 35-55 watts on low beam. Auxiliary driving lights are around 100 watts, which makes them illegal for highway use in some states. Off-road lights start at about 130 watts and go all the way to 210 watts! Needless to say, off-road lights should not be used when driving on the highway.

If you want to install several auxiliary lights across the top of the truck without drilling any holes, light bars that attach to the rain gutters are the answer.

Putting high wattage driving or off-road lights on your truck can overburden the electrical system if they aren't installed properly. Heavy gauge wire, fuses and in some cases electrical relays are necessary to prevent frying things. I recommend getting a wiring kit that includes all the hardware for adding the lights. Installation instructions will probably come with the kit.

CAMPER SHELLS

There are basically two kinds of camper shells available: molded fiberglass or aluminum siding over a wood frame. Each has advantages and disadvantages. The fiberglass shells are very durable and seem to last forever, but they usually are not insulated, so they're colder. Water tends to condense on the inner surface, making things a bit damp and musty. The aluminum campers are usually insulated, keeping you warmer and cozier, but they don't seem to survive the stresses of being bounced and twisted around in the back of the truck as well as the fiberglass type.

SUNROOFS

Sunroofs are nice, fairly inexpensive, and an easy way to make the cab of the truck seem larger and less claustrophobic. Installation should be done by professionals because even a small goof could mean a wet and miserable cab every time it rains or snows.

TIRES AND WHEELS

The kind of tires and wheels you get for your truck should be determined by the kind of driving you want to do, not by how good they look on the truck. No matter what those flashy white letters say, they won't do a thing for performance.

All tires are something of a compromise because none of them work "the best" in all situations. Steel radials provide excellent traction and cornering on hard surface roads, but just don't have the "bite" needed when the surface is soft. Combination tires are middle-of-the-road, so to speak, and give acceptable performance on hard surfaces, as well as added traction when you leave the pavement. Genuine off-road tires for soft surfaces have large, aggressive treads with widely spaced tread lugs so they can get a good bite on whatever is available. On the highway, however, the off-road tires are noisy, rough riding, and wear out quickly. Fortunately, there is a wide variety of all three types available.

Once you decide which type of tire you want, you need to determine what size you need. Unless you're making a low-rider, you'll probably want to install taller and wider tires and wheels than the originals. How big a tire will fit on your Toy? There are two factors to consider: clearance between the tires and wheels, and the body, brakes and suspension parts of the truck; and the effect the larger tires will have on the overall gear ratio of the truck.

Clearance: Where there's a will there's a way to make almost any tire size fit your Toyota—by trimming the fenders, lifting the body and/or suspension, or a combination of all three. But keep in mind, lifting the body and/or suspension too much makes the truck unsafe.

Gear ratio: The larger the tire, the lower the engine rpm will be at any given speed, and thus the less power you'll have with the standard gear ratios. Since engines are most efficient when operating at approximately 60 to 80 percent of their peak horsepower, oversize tires can lower the rpm range so much that the engine is actually lugging instead of cruising along in its optimum range. You can increase the tire size somewhat without sacrificing too much power or efficiency, but beyond a certain point you have to change the gear ratio in the differential(s) to keep your truck healthy and efficient.

If you're considering changing to much larger tires than the originals, I suggest you send for the Dick Cepek Catalog listed at the end of this chapter. It has charts and formulas for determining wheel clearance and gear ratios for the different size tires for your Toyota.

Here's what all those mysterious letters and numbers on tire sidewalls mean.

Tires used to say 2 ply, 4 ply, etc. on the side which told you how many plies (layers) of material were built into the carcass of the tire. Tires are now rated by "load range." Here's what the different load ranges mean: A=2 ply, B=4 ply, C=6 ply, D=8 ply, E=10 ply and F=12 ply. The higher the load range, the stronger the tire. Also, the higher the load range the stiffer the tire, so heavy duty tires make for a rougher ride.

The government has developed a Tire Grading System (TGS) which is put on the sticker on new tires to help compare the countless brands and types of tires. Here's how to use the TGS.

Treadwear: This number gives you an idea of how much mileage to expect from a tire. The numbers are given in tens from 40 to 230. Unfortunately the numbers don't relate to how many thousands of miles the tire will last; they are relative numbers and mean that a tire graded 150 should give you 50 percent more mileage than one graded 100, and so on. The actual mileage you get will depend on how you drive and where you live.

Traction: Traction, graded A, B or C, indicates the tire's ability to stop on wet surfaces. Tires graded A will stop on a wet road in the shortest distance. Tires rated C have poor traction, not the kind you want.

Temperature Resistance: This is also graded A, B or C. Tires rated A run cooler than those rated B or C and therefore are less likely to blow out or have tread separation if driven over long distances at highway speeds.

Here are some more clues so you'll know what the letters and numbers on tires mean: A tire with 195/70SR-15, for example, is 195mm at its widest part (the cross section, not necessarily the tread width). The 70 is the tires "aspect ratio," which means the tire's height is 70 percent of the width (thus it's a 70 series tire). The S means the tire is able to sustain a given high speed. No letter before the R is lowest, S is higher, H is higher still, and V is highest. The R stands for radial. And finally, the 15 stands for the diameter of the wheel in inches. Whew. So the tire size is designated by a combination of inches, millimeters, percentage and some arbitrary letters. No wonder buying tires is a chore.

If you change to taller or wider tires, you'll probably want to change wheels. And there are hundreds of different styles to choose from. Three things must be considered when buying wheels: whether they are compatible with tubeless tires, the wheel width, and the amount of offset (if any).

Compatibility: Any wheels will work if you plan to use tubes and tube-type tires. If you plan to use tubeless tires, be sure the wheels are made for tubeless tires.

Width: Generally speaking, the wheel width should be approximately two inches narrower than the cross-section of the tire. Be sure and ask the dealer if the tires and wheels you select are compatible.

Offset: Wheel offset refers to the relationship of the wheel center to the wheel rim. Negative offset means the rim of the wheel is moved inward, making the car's track narrower. Positive offset means the rim is further outward, giving the car a wider track, which will make the truck corner better. Wheels with too much negative offset will probably rub on the brake calipers an '/or tie rod ends. Too much positive offset can cause the tires to rub on the fenders and create greater strain on the wheel bearings and hubs.

STEREO SYSTEMS

Although a good stereo system doesn't change the way your truck looks or performs, it can make driving a lot more fun. It can also represent a significant investment of your hard-earned cash.

Besides the physical size of the stereo and your bank account, the combinations of radios, tape decks, CD players, amplifiers, equalizer/boosters, speakers, etc., are almost endless. When buying a stereo system, the confusing part is rationally comparing the features on comparably priced models. You need some cold hard facts and specifications that you can mull over while sitting by the fireplace instead of in a crowded showroom with several radios blasting and a hungry salesman breathing down your neck. Unfortunately, the choice is often made under these adverse conditions.

Recently I've found a better way to shop for stereos. I highly recommend sending for the Crutchfield catalog listed at the end of the chapter. The catalog could qualify as a textbook about selecting and installing stereo systems because it explains what the different components do, which components will fit into your truck without cutting any sheet metal, which ones require modification, which antenna to use, and most importantly, what all those technical specifications mean. For example, which is best, a higher or lower number for the FM sensitivity rating of a radio? Answer: A lower number means the radio is more sensitive! And at some time or other we've all wanted to know what "Wow and Flutter" really means. Crutchfield even has a toll free telephone hot line so you can call for help or advice.

I recommend getting the catalog and doing your homework about the specifications for the large number of brands and models they sell. You'll be able to narrow down the products that fit your needs and budget to a few makes and models. Then, if possible, go to your local stereo dealer to listen to those components and to compare the dealer's prices to those in the catalog. Go for the best deal.

PART 2: SUSPENSION

SHOCK ABSORBERS

The quickest, easiest, and usually the cheapest suspension improvement is the installation of a good set of shock absorbers. The most popular kind these days are the nitrogen gas-filled shocks that are guaranteed to last forever. They are a great improvement over the original Toyota shocks.

If you get serious about off-roading (or just want your truck to look like you're serious), you can install adapters so two or three shocks can be bolted to each wheel. Some shocks even have competition yellow or glow-in-the-dark boots to make sure everyone will notice them.

STEERING DAMPERS

A heavy duty or double steering dampers should be installed to help keep oversized tires from wandering and reduce steering wheel shimmy. It's a simple job to replace the original damper on '80-'87 models (Chapter 12, Procedure 4). To install a steering damper on '75-'79 models, you'll have to get one with brackets for attaching it to the frame and the relay rod on 2WD models, or to the frame and tie rod on 4WD models.

STABILIZER BARS

Heavy duty front and rear stabilizer (anti-sway) bars will improve cornering, giving less body roll and better tire adhesion. They also add stability when driving in crosswinds with a tall camper mounted in the bed.

The size of the bars must be coordinated, "balanced," between the front and rear, so don't install a heavy duty bar on the rear without first installing a larger bar than the original one on the front. You can order stabilizer bars and other suspension parts through the Addco catalog listed at the end of the chapter.

SPRINGS

Toyota ½ ton trucks are designed to carry about 1,100 pounds without straining the suspension system. If your truck is used mainly as a beast of burden to haul heavy loads, overload springs can be added to the rear leaf springs to increase the hauling capacity.

Stiffer arched springs can be installed on the rear of all Toyota trucks and on the front on '79-'83 4WD models. Heavy duty torsion bars can be installed on '79-'87 2WD and '84-'87 4WD models. The arched springs and/or heavy duty torsion bars will result in about a one- to two-inch lift and increase the axle travel so the wheels stay on the ground more while blasting over rough terrain.

LIFT KITS

I don't recommend installing lift kits that raise the truck body or suspension more than four inches from the original height. Larger tires and a four-inch suspension lift give Toyota trucks a significant increase in ground clearance without making them too top heavy and dangerous. Chapter 12, Procedure 14, tells you how to remove and install leaf springs. Check the laws for your state to see how much you can legally lift your truck.

TRACTION BARS

If you hop up the engine and/or install oversize tires, it's a good idea to install traction bars on the rear springs to prevent the rear differential from rolling up the springs under heavy power.

BRAKES

If you increase your truck's ability to GO, you should also consider improving its ability to WHOA. Semi-metallic brake pads and shoes that don't fade under hard use are offered in some of the catalogs listed at the end of the chapter.

LIMITED SLIP DIFFERENTIALS

The traction of your truck on soft or slippery terrain can be significantly increased by installing a limited slip (posi-traction) unit in the differential(s). These units direct more power to both rear tires, rather than only to whichever tire turns the easiest as the original differential does. Some of the limited slip differentials are available in different ratios to compensate for the the installation of larger tires. Also available are Detroit Locker differentials that offer 100 percent traction to both rear wheels, regardless of how slippery the road surface might be.

PART 3: ENGINE MODIFICATIONS

Adding a few mild performance parts like a Weber carburetor, a more efficient exhaust system and, on '75-'77 models, an electronic breakerless ignition system, will increase the performance (and maybe even the gas mileage) without necessitating suspension modification. However, if you go beyond these simple modifications, beef up the suspension first, as described in Part 2.

Before modifying any engine, do a compression check to be sure it's sound.

WEBER CARBS

I've installed Weber carbs on several cars and invariably been thrilled with the noticeable increase in power, smoother operation throughout the rpm range, and generally a slight improvement in gas mileage (when I drive normally). Weber is the official carburetor of the Toyota Off-Road Racing Team, which has done very well the past several years.

If you live anywhere but California, you can legally install any Weber on your Toy. If you live in California, you'll have to get a "Street Lethal" setup that incorporates all of the original factory emission control devices into a model 033B Weber carb.

Like your original Toyota carb, the 033B Weber is a two barrel "progressive" carb. Progressive means one barrel supplies the fuel air mixture to the engine until the gas pedal is about ⅔ of the way to the floor. Pushing your foot down into the final ⅓ opens the second barrel for added punch.

Original Toyota carbs are rated at 190 cfm (cubic feet per minute) on 20R engines and 326 cfm on 22R engines. Weber carbs with 32mm primary and 36mm secondary barrels (32/36 mm) are rated at 325 cfm. Obviously the 20R engine will benefit greatly with a 32/36mm Weber; it will seem like a much larger engine. 22R engines will respond much smoother and quicker because the secondary barrel is opened mechanically rather than by a vacuum diaphram, but you'll only notice a slight improvement in power.

The internal circuits of each barrel of a Weber act like two carbs in one: a low speed (idle) circuit feeds the engine the proper mixture up to approximately 2500 rpm, and a high speed (main) circuit takes care of the engine's needs in the higher rpm range. Both circuits are tuneable by changing the jets. The Weber kits are pre-jetted for stock engines. If you make other modifications to the engine like free flow exhaust system, high lift cam, high compression pistons, etc., you you'll need to change the jets in the Weber so it compliments the other modifications.

To get a dramatic power increase in a 22R engine you'll need to use one of the other carbs listed later, or a 38DGAS (38mm) or 40DFAV (40mm) Weber. These models are rated at around 400 cfm and both barrels open simultaneously rather than progressively. Now we're gettin' serious!

There are two ways to install a Weber on your Toy. You can get an inexpensive adapter that allows you to bolt the carb to the original intake manifold, or you can install an Offenhouser dual port intake manifold. Some of the Toyota performance experts swear there's a significant performance improvement in using the Offenhouser manifold, while other experts are a bit skeptical, saying the adapter works just as well. I suggest trying the adapter first (it's pretty cheap), then if you still want more, try changing manifolds.

OTHER CARBURETORS

The carburetors listed in this section are for the very serious racer or off-roader. Other modifications such as exhaust headers and high performance camshafts must also be installed to take advantage of these carbs.

Weber makes DCOE series 40mm and 45mm high performance side draft carburetors that you install in pairs, giving you a total of 160mm or 180mm carburetor barrels. You must change the intake manifold to install these carbs.

Mikuni carbs are also high quality, high performance carbs that will make your Toy leap tall rocks in a single bound. Mikunis are side draft carbs that require a special manifold.

There's also an American style Holley 4 barrel carb and Offenhouser manifold available for Toyota trucks.

EXHAUST SYSTEM

After adding a larger carb (or carbs) to get more fuel and air into the cylinders, a larger free-flow exhaust system should be installed to carry away the increased volume of burned gases. Otherwise "back pressure" of the exhaust gas can rob the engine of 15-20 percent of its horsepower.

High performance exhaust manifolds, called headers, are designed so the pulses of exhaust gases from each cylinder helps pull the exhaust gases from each of the other cylinders.

The diameter of the header pipes can affect the performance of the engine at different rpm levels. 1-3/8" tubing for the header pipes and a 2" or 2½" exhaust system seems to provide the most power in the lower and middle rpm range—where most people need it.

Free flow mufflers also help reduce exhaust restriction. The most common type recommended by the pros is called a "turbo" design muffler. Interestingly, the turbo muffler is so named because its use first became popular on turbocharged Chevy Corvairs made in the '60s.

CAMSHAFTS

The lobes on the camshaft open the intake and exhaust valves to allow the air and fuel mixture to enter the cylinders and the exhaust gases to exit. The lobes can be modified to allow the valves to open earlier and farther than the original Toyota camshaft, and close them later.

Mild-performance camshafts can increase the power throughout the rpm range. High performance camshafts are designed to increase the power for certain rpm ranges: low range for increased torque for off-road use, high range for high speed competition. Heavier valve springs should be installed if a modified camshaft is installed.

FOR THE TRULY SERIOUS

The following products are for the all-out, go-for-broke road racer or off-roader.

Turbochargers and Superchargers: In engine dynomometer tests the installation of a supercharger on a stock '81 22R engine raised the horsepower (at the rear wheels) from 58 hp up to 128 hp. WOW! Over twice the horsepower! Torque at the rear wheels also increased from 111 ft.lbs. to 228 ft.lbs. The installation looks like a pretty straightforward bolt-on operation. Now for the bad news: the conversion is quite expensive.

Installing a turbocharger will also increase the horsepower significantly, but not as much as the supercharger. A turbo conversion kit costs roughly half of what the supercharger costs.

V-6 and V-8 Conversions: Kits are available for installing a 231 cubic inch Buick V-6 or a 350 cubic inch Chevy V-8 engine in your Toyota truck. Since Toyota introduced its own V-6 in 1988, the V-6 kits will probably go the way of the Edsel. Chevy V-8s are good strong engines and I like them a lot, but if you really want a truck with a V-8, why not just buy a Chevy (or Ford) to start with?

CATALOGS

Listed below are a few catalogs that either cater specifically to Toyota trucks or contain valuable information that is applicable to Toyota trucks. There are lots more available; all you have to do is send for them. If you know of other companies that provide good service and products for Toyota trucks, have them send me a catalog at John Muir Publications, P.O. Box 613, Santa Fe, New Mexico 87504. If possible I'll include them in the next edition of this manual. Thanks.

NORTHWEST OFF-ROAD SPECIALTIES, INC., 1999 Iowa Street, Bellingham, Washington 98226.

These nice folks deal exclusively in Toyota 4WD truck appearance and performance products. They not only sell products, they develop and manufacture some of them, then go off-roadin' to see if they can withstand the abuse 4WD trucks are subjected to. Call (206) 676-1200 for a catalog.

DOWNEY OFF ROAD MANUFACTURING, 10001 South Pioneer Boulevard, Santa Fe Springs, CA 90670.

Downey supplies appearance and modification parts for 2WD and 4WD pickups, Toyota Tercel SR5 and the famous Toyota Landcruiser.

Downey designs and manufactures most of the products they sell, then tests them in major off-road races. They are closely associated with the Toyota factory off-road racing team. To get their catalog, call (213) 949-9494. The catalog costs $3.00, but if you tell them you found out about them in this book they will probably let you have the catalog for FREE.

DICK CEPEK TIRES, 17000 Kingsview Ave., Carson, CA 90746.

In addition to having excellent articles and charts about how to select tires and wheels, the catalog tells you how to figure out your differential gear ratio so you'll know how large of tires you can install without sacrificing power and economy, or what differential gear ratio you should install to handle the tires you want to install.

The catalog has all kinds of off-road camping and emergency supplies, handbooks about off-road driving, maps, winches, suspension kits (springs and shock absorbers), roll bars, bumpers, auxiliary lights, and lots of army surplus-type gear. I love this catalog. (Where else can you order a genuine 49er gold mining pan made of plastic?) The catalog costs $2.00, but it's well worth it. Send your two bucks to the address listed above, or call (213) 217-1213 and charge it to your credit card.

ADDCO INDUSTRIES, INC., Watertower Road, Lake Park, Florida 33403.

ADDCO designs and manufactures high performance suspension parts like stabilizer (anti-sway) bars and shock absorbers. An excellent little pamphlet called *HANDLING: What It Is—and How to Get It* comes with the catalog. Call (305) 844-2531.

CRUTCHFIELD, 1 Crutchfield Park, Charlottesville, Virginia 22906.

This is the catalog mentioned in the Stereo section. It really will help sort out the advantages and disadvantages of the various components available these days. Also available but not listed in the catalog (as of the printing of this book), are wiring harness kits for installation of power amplifiers and speakers in '82-'87 Toyota pickups.

To order the free catalog, call (800) 336-5566.

MAGAZINES

There are several monthly magazines available for pickup owners. These magazines often feature excellent articles on what's available for Toyota pickups and articles on how to install various accessories. Unfortunately, the magazine publishers don't keep an index of past articles, so the information is only available for the month of publication, then it's gone.

You can either subscribe to the magazines or browse through them at the local supermarket or bookstore and only buy issues that have articles applicable to Toyota trucks. Here are some of the magazines I check out when doing my grocery shopping:

FOUR WHEELER, Four Wheeler Publications.

4 WHEEL & OFF-ROAD, Peterson Publications.

4WD ACTION, McMullen Publishing.

TRUCKIN', McMullen Publishing.

CHAPTER 15
MECHANIC'S TIPS, SECRETS, ODDS 'N ENDS

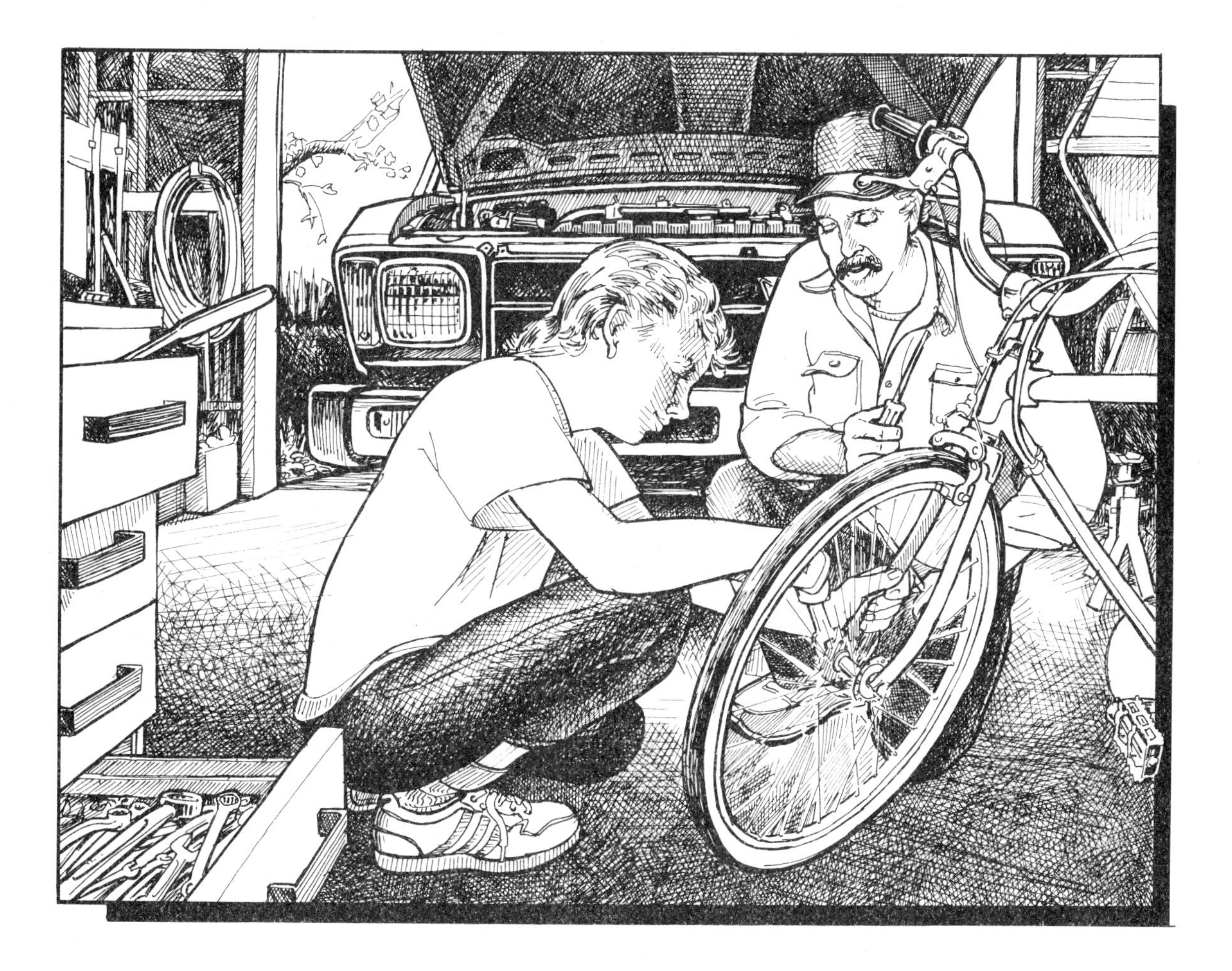

This chapter is a grab bag of know-how to help get you past unexpected and unwelcome circumstances like broken bolts, stripped threads, having to use a brake drum or gear puller, etc. The *conditions* under which you need the procedure are stated in the procedure's name and, since they're all short, the *tools and materials* required for the procedures will be found within the procedure or steps. Don't forget your goggles when dealing with stuck or stubborn bolts, wheel puller, etc., where you'll be using a hammer or hacksaw.

PROCEDURE 1: HOW TO CURE HICCUPS

Pour a glass of fresh water and put a drinking straw in it. (There's probably a leftover straw from the local fast food cesspool in the glove box, under the seats, etc.) Set the glass on a table, stick a finger firmly into each ear, then drink the water through the straw. Like magic, the hiccups are gone. I've never seen this method fail! What other automotive repair manual gives you practical, down-to-earth information like this?

PROCEDURE 2: HOW TO USE A VOLT/OHM METER (VOM)

Small Volt/Ohm meters are readily available, and relatively inexpensive, at your local electronics store. (Is there a town in the world that doesn't have a dear old Radio Shack?) You don't need a big fancy one to check out your truck. Just be sure it will measure at least 15 volts DC and has an OHM scale.

Condition: You need to check the voltage of the battery; OR you're checking the charging system; OR you're checking for juice at the fuse box or one of the electrical components; OR you're checking a fuse or wire to see if juice can go from one end to the other (continuity check).

Tools and Materials: A Volt/Ohm meter (also called a VOM).

Remark: The VOM you have may use slightly different names or symbols for the various scales, but they all measure the same electrical phenomena: AC and/or DC *volts*, and resistance in *ohms*.

A good VOM will test a number of things, but I'm going to limit the explanation to things that are applicable to your truck: *DC Volts*, *Continuity* and *Resistance*.

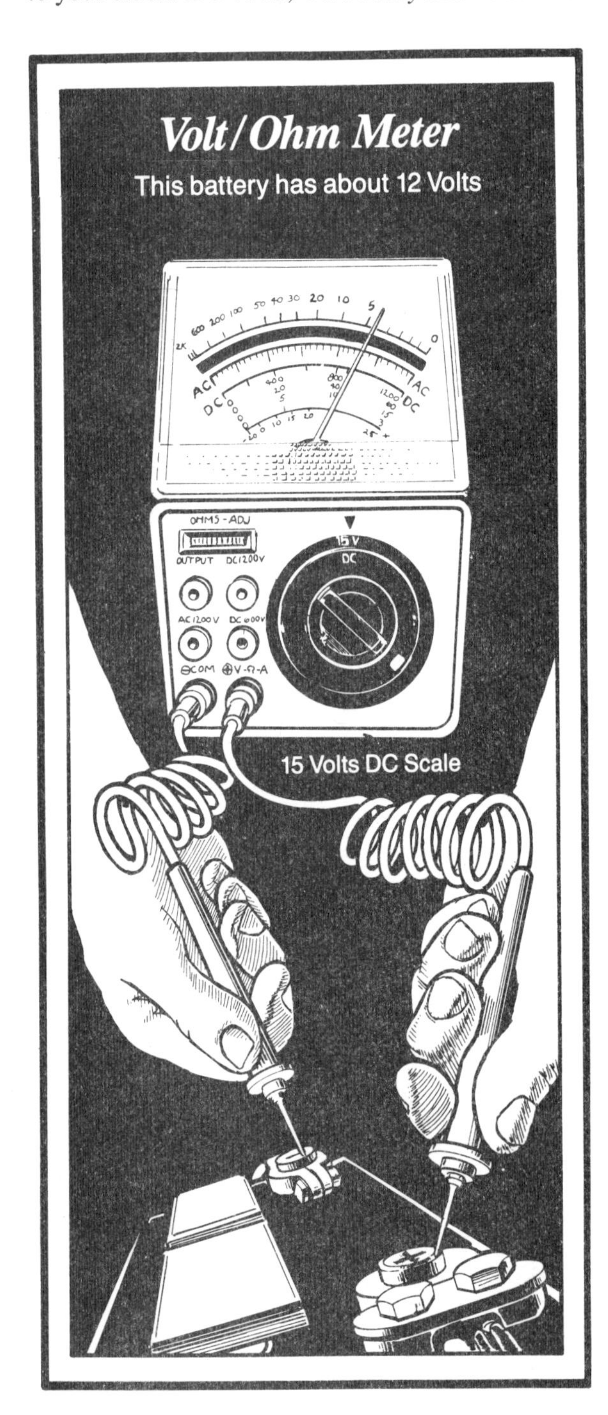

Caution: The VOM is a very sensitive instrument, and you should just touch the probes lightly to whatever you're testing so you can quickly see if you have the dial set at the wrong scale (the needle will jump all the way across). Setting the VOM to the wrong scale can burn it out. Never test for continuity or resistance on anything that's plugged into a battery or wall outlet. If you're testing voltage and have the VOM set to DC volts, and the needle takes a dive to below zero, you have the *wrong polarity* so switch the probes around—that is, put one where the other was. Don't try to check the voltage of the large spark plug or coil wires with a VOM: you might fry the meter.

Step 1. Set Up Volt/Ohm Meter.

Most Volt/Ohm meters require one or two small flashlight batteries. Be sure yours has good batteries before using it to do tests on your truck.

Untangle the two VOM wires. You'll notice that the plastic insulator on one end of each wire is longer than the one on the other end. The longer insulator end is called a **probe** and the shorter insulator end is called a **jack**. Plug the jack for the red wire into the positive (+) **VΩA hole** on the meter. Now plug the jack for the black wire into the negative (-) **COM hole** on the meter.

Step 2. How to Measure Voltage.

Set up your VOM according to Step 1, Since your truck has a 12-volt DC electrical system, set the selector knob on the VOM to the next higher DC volt setting above 12 volts (probably 15 volts DC; your VOM might say DC V, Volts DC, etc.). To find the proper scale on the meter for your setting, look at the column of numbers under the DC on the meter. Find the number that corresponds to your selector knob setting (probably 15). The numbers across the scale on the same row as that number are the ones you use to read the voltage of the component being checked. Look at the illustration of my VOM (if you don't have one handy) so you'll know what I'm talking about. In the illustration the selector knob is set at 15 DC V (volts) and the needle is showing 12 volts (two lines to the right of the 10).

To check the voltage in the battery, touch the *black* probe to the *negative* (-) battery terminal and the *red* probe to the *positive* (+) battery terminal. If the battery has any juice in it, the needle on the meter will move to the right telling you how many volts the battery is putting out. If it's less than 12 volts, the battery needs a charge. Doing this test with the engine running should give you a higher reading, like about 13.5 to 14.5 volts, if the alternator and voltage regulator are working properly.

Step 3. Checking for Juice in a Wire.

To see if there's juice in any wire on your truck (except spark plug and coil wires), turn the ignition switch and the switch for the component being tested ON. Touch the red probe to the metal on the end of the wire and the black probe to bare metal on the car body or engine. The VOM will show how many volts are present in the wire. No volts? Either the wire or component isn't getting any juice or is shorted out, or there may be a loose connection.

Step 4. How to Check for Continuity.

Caution: This is not a test to see if the battery or a component is getting juice. Turn the switch to whatever you're testing OFF or disconnect the negative (-) battery cable clamp to be sure it's not getting juice. Use this test to see if electricity is *capable* of flowing through a wire, fuse, ground connection, etc.

Set up your VOM as described in Step 1. Turn the selector knob to the RX10, RX100, or RX1K position in the OHMS section. To adjust the VOM, touch the metal ends of the two probes together. The needle should swing toward the zero (0) on the right side of the OHMS scale on the meter. If the needle doesn't point to the 0, turn the *Ohms Adjust knob* until the needle points to the 0.

Now you can test wires, fuses, paper clips, your body, etc., to see if electricity can flow from one probe, through whatever you're testing, to the other probe. To check continuity in a fuse, you must remove it from its receptacle. Touch a probe to each end of the fuse. If the needle swings to zero, the fuse is OK; if it stays at *infinity* (∞), the fuse is blown. Use the VOM in the same way to test for continuity through any wire or component, touching the probes to the opposite ends of the electrical connector (juice path) you want to test.

Let's play with the VOM for a while. With the selector knob set at the RX1K position, touch the two probes together. The needle goes to 0 so there's no resistance to the flow of electricity and you have continuity. Check a paper clip, belt buckle, or anything metal that isn't connected to a source of electricity. If the needle goes to the 0 on the OHMS scale, you have continuity. If the needle doesn't move, there is no continuity or you're testing something that's non-conductive (incapable of carrying electricity). If the needle moves part way toward the 0 and stops, electricity is capable of flowing through the object, but there's a resistance to the flow (see Step 5).

Step 5. Test for Resistance.

Some wires and electrical gizmos on your truck are designed to have a certain amount of resistance to the flow of electricity. For instance, the coil and spark plug wires on most trucks have a built in resistance factor to help eliminate electrical static on the radio. The wires work fine as long as the resistance is within a prescribed range, but when the resistance becomes greater than it's supposed to be, the current flowing through the wires to the coil or spark plug(s) will be insufficient to "fire" the plug efficiently.

If you're handy with a VOM and have the Toyota workshop manual for your model, you can check the resistance of almost every wire and electrical component on the truck, then compare your meter readings to the specifications in the manual. Space doesn't allow me to include all the specifications for all the years and models. Here's how you use a VOM to check wires for resistance.

Set up the VOM as described in Step 1. Set the selector knob at RX1K. The R stands for resistance (to the flow of electricity), the X means times (as in multiplication), and the 1K stands for 1000. Touch the probes to the palm of your hand about one inch apart. Don't worry, you won't get zapped. If you have a sweaty palm, the needle will move just a little. A dry palm probably won't move the needle. Lift off the probes, lick your palm and try again. The needle will probably move to about 200 on the OHMs scale. Multiply 200 times 1000 (1K) and you get 200,000 ohms resistance in one inch of wet palm skin. If the probes are clean and you haven't used them on a battery, touch the probes to your tongue and see what the resistance is. There's probably less resistance on your tongue than your sweaty palm because more moisture is present (water is a good conductor).

PROCEDURE 3: HOW TO USE A TORQUE WRENCH

Torque is measured in foot pounds (ft.lbs.), inch pounds (in.lbs), or meter kilograms (Mkg). I assume you have a ft.lbs. torque wrench. Inch pounds can be converted to ft.lbs. by dividing by 12. The U.S. ft.lb. represents the number of pounds applied to the end of a wrench one foot long, (more technically, the leverage one foot away from the center of the nut or bolt you are turning).

Torque wrenches come in three basic types: one slips or clicks when the preset torque is reached, another has a dial you read as you turn, and the third (cheapest and most common) type has a skinny rod coming up from the head of the wrench with a point on the end that points to numbers (the torque you've reached) on a calibrated arc scale on the handle. Here's how to use all these kinds of torque wrenches:

First, be sure the bolt and/or nut threads are clean and lightly oiled. Find the correct torque value; these are given right in the procedure you're dealing with. Attach the correct socket, then hold the torque wrench and socket firmly on the nut or bolt with one hand on the head (socket end) of the wrench. Stay clear of the pointer rod if your wrench has one. Get yourself in position where you can see the reading clearly on the arc scale or dial. Pull on the handle of the torque wrench with a steady, slow pull until the pointer or dial needle points to the correct number, or until you hear a click (depending on type). Don't add extra torque "just to be sure." Trust your torque wrench! If you're doing a set of bolts or nuts (such as the lug nuts, nuts on the head or clutch housing bolts), first run all the bolts in the series up to about half the final torque, then up to ¾ of the final torque, then up to the final torque all around. Go around again to be sure none were missed.

PROCEDURE 4: STARTING A NUT

Here are a few tricks to getting a nut started on a bolt or stud, especially if you can't see the place where you are working and have to feel. Use your index finger to hold the nut on the end of the stud and twist the nut around with your thumb and second finger. Twist it *counterclockwise* a little until you feel the threads slip into place, then *clockwise* to screw it on.

If the threads are so bunged up on a stud that the nut won't start, tap it a little with a small hammer as you turn it with a box end wrench until it's down one thread; then it should go on with the wrench.

If the space around a nut is too confining to let you turn the nut with your fingers, hold the nut onto the end of the stud with your forefinger and turn it on with the point of a screwdriver. Use a wrench to tighten it.

If the bolt you are putting a nut on tends to turn, you can often wedge the bolt with a small screwdriver or knife blade to hold it still while you start the nut.

PROCEDURE 5: TIGHTENING THINGS HELD ON BY MORE THAN ONE BOLT OR NUT

Anywhere a part is held on with more than one bolt or nut, never tighten first one nut or bolt all the way, then the next one. Always tighten them gradually in sequence: first tighten one a little, then the one opposite the first one a little, then one next to the first one a little, and so on until they are all fairly tight. This puts equal stress on the part or parts. Do the final tightening the same way until they are all tightened or torqued. This will save you broken assemblies and distorted plates, such as the cylinder heads and clutch pressure plate.

PROCEDURE 6: TOUGH OR BROKEN NUTS, SCREWS AND BOLTS

First, be absolutely certain you are turning the nut, bolt or screw the right direction to remove it. Bolts and screws turn *counterclockwise* as viewed from the head. Nuts turn *counterclockwise* as viewed from the threaded end of the bolt, stud or screw.

Step 1. Dealing with Tight Nuts.

If you have a nut that refuses to budge, sprinkle it repeatedly with penetrating oil ("holy water") and let it soak for a few minutes. WD-40 isn't technically penetrating oil, but it's often thin enough to do the job. Marvel Mystery Oil and Liquid Wrench also work well, but my favorite is Sili-Kroil.

If possible, use a six-point box end wrench or six-point socket to get a better grip on the nut and to avoid rounding off its corners. (Open-end wrenches and 12-point sockets are more likely to slip, damaging the nut.) Find a cheater bar (a piece of pipe large enough to slide over the wrench) and slip it onto the wrench handle for added leverage. Pull *counterclockwise* on the end of the cheater bar.

Caution: Cheater bars and the wrench handles they hold tend to slip; make sure the socket or wrench is securely on the nut or bolt head, and the cheater pipe is well over the shaft of the wrench handle.

If the points on a nut or bolt head get rounded off, try Vise Grip or Channel Lock pliers first (see Chapter 3: *Tools*). If they don't work, take the next smaller size socket out of the box, file down the sides of the nut a little and jam the socket down on the nut with a hammer. Sprinkle a little more holy water while mumbling whatever incantations one mumbles while sprinkling holy water, then put the ratchet on the socket and turn the nut off.

When all else fails, use a hacksaw or chisel to cut off one side of the nut. Make the cut parallel to the stud, then use the Vise Grips to unscrew what's left of the nut.

Step 2. Dealing with Stubborn Bolts and Screws.

Repeatedly sprinkle the bolt or screw with penetrating oil and let it soak. Give the head of the bolt or screw a few solid whacks straight on the head with a hammer. The straighter the blows, the more effective they will be. If you can't get to a screw with the hammer, fit the screwdriver blade into the slot, then rap on the other end of the screwdriver. You hope the hammering will jar the threads loose so the bolt or screw can be removed. If a tight bolt still won't move, use a cheater bar on the wrench as described in Step 1.

If the corners of a bolt get rounded off so the wrench slips, try using Vise Grips or Channel Lock pliers. If that fails, file down the sides of bolt head, then jam the next smaller socket on with a hammer and try the ratchet again. (You may have to use the hammer and a screwdriver or chisel to get the bolt out of the socket once you've unscrewed it.)

If the slot in a screwhead gets widened and tapered so the screwdriver slips out easily when you try to turn it, try straightening the sides of the slot with a hacksaw or small file, then use a larger screwdriver. If you can grab the screwhead with Vise Grips, clamp them on, then use the Vise Grips and screwdriver together to turn the screw.

When the slots on phillips head screws disappear, use a hacksaw to cut a slot in the head, then use a regular screwdriver. If you can grab the head with Vise Grips, clamp them on and use the Vise Grips and screwdriver together. Another technique is to clamp the Vise Grips onto the shaft of the screwdriver as a turning handle. This allows you to use maximum force to hold the screwdriver in the slots. Remember, *counterclockwise* to unscrew it.

Step 3. Broken Bolts or Screws.

If a bolt or screwhead breaks off and there's still a stub of it left sticking out, soak it with penetrating oil, then smack the stub squarely on the head with a hammer a few times. Use Vise Grips or Channel Locks to grab the stub and turn it out. If you have access to a propane torch and the stub is in a place where there's absolutely no danger of starting a fire, heat up the area around the stub (not the stub itself), then try removing it with Vise Grips or Channel Locks.

If the bolt or screw is broken off flush with whatever it's screwed into, you'll need to round up an electric drill, drill bits, center punch, and a gizmo called an "easy out" of the right size for your broken bolt or screw. Your friendly parts store counterperson should be able to tell you which size to use. Tap the center punch exactly in the center of the broken part, then drill a small hole straight through the center of the bolt. If you drill a crooked hole, the easy out probably won't work and you also run the risk of damaging the hole threads. Have Friend help you align the drill bit so it's straight while you drill the hole.

Next, drill the hole to the proper size for the easy out. The proper drill bit size should be stamped on the side of the easy out, or ask the partsperson what size to use. Use the hammer to tap the easy out into the hole, then use a crescent wrench to gently unscrew the broken bolt. Be very careful not to break the easy out. You'd be in real trouble then, because easy outs are made of super-hard material and can't be drilled out. If you're not up for all this, take the car or the part with the broken bolt to a garage or machine shop and have them remove the broken bolt or screw.

PROCEDURE 7: DEALING WITH BROKEN OR STRIPPED STUDS

A stud is a headless bolt with threads on both ends—what a way to go through life! Studs you might have to deal with are on the cylinder head where the intake and exhaust manifolds attach. If the nut is rusted to the stud so the stud comes out when you unscrew the nut, buy and install a new stud and nut. Put *Loctite* (a compound you find at the parts store) on the threads before screwing it in so it won't come out the next time.

Step 1. Removing and Installing Studs.

Studs are removed and installed using two nuts locked together on the exposed stud threads, or by *very careful* use of Vise Grips or pliers on the non-threaded (middle) portion of the stud.

To use the two-nut method, screw two nuts onto the stud far enough so the end of the stud sticks through the outside nut. Lock the nuts by tightening them toward each other with two wrenches. Remove the stud by turning the inside nut *counterclockwise* with your wrench. Install the stud by turning the outside nut *clockwise*.

If you're removing a stud with stripped threads, just grab it with Vise Grips or Channel Locks and unscrew it. You'll be putting in a new stud anyway.

When using Vise Grips or pliers to install good or new studs, be careful not to damage the threads on either end. Grab it only at the unthreaded place in the middle. Be sure the threads you're screwing the stud into are clean and in good condition. Grab the stud as close to the center as possible and don't squeeze any tighter than necessary.

Step 2. Removing Broken Studs.

Follow the instructions in Procedure 6, Step 3, for removing broken bolts and screws.

Step 3. Other Troubles with Studs.

When you're tightening a nut on a stud and the nut keeps turning without tightening, you have a stripped nut, a stripped stud or a stud that's pulling out. First remove the nut from the stud, either pulling or prying it off as you turn it, then examine both the nut and the stud for stripping—flat and mashed places on the threads. Perhaps the stud is unhurt and all you need is a new nut. If the stud is stripped, you have to remove the stud and replace it with a new one from the Toyota dealer (Step 1).

If the stud itself pulls out as you tighten the nut, the threads that hold the stud are usually stripped. You'll need to have the Toyota dealer, a garage, or a machine shop drill and tap (thread) the hole for a larger stud. Better yet, have them install a *Helicoil* into the stripped hole so you can use the original stud. I prefer Helicoils because they're made of tough steel and are less likely to strip out again later.

PROCEDURE 8: MECHANICS' QUICK DWELL TEST

For those of you with breaker-type distributors, this is a quick way to set the points dwell without having to put everything back together and start the engine between checks.

You'll need a Friend for this one. Hook up the *dwell gauge*, then pull the *coil wire* out of the center of the distributor cap and ground it with your jumper wire (clip the other end to a piece of bare metal on the car). Remove the distributor cap and rotor, then slightly loosen the *points holding screws*. Insert the tip of a medium screwdriver between the *nipples* and *slot*.

Be sure the transmission is in NEUTRAL or PARK and the handbrake is ON, then have Friend crank the engine. Adjust the point gap with the screwdriver while watching the dwell meter. When the dwell is correct for your car's specifications, tell Friend to stop cranking the engine. Tighten the points holding screws, then have Friend crank the engine again and check the dwell reading again. When the dwell is right on, have Friend turn the ignition OFF. Install the rotor and distributor cap. Unclip the jumper wire and plug the coil wire back into the distributor cap. Disconnect the dwell gauge and you're finished.

PROCEDURE 9: HOW TO USE A PULLER (WHEEL, GEAR, DRUM, ETC.)

A puller is a device that grabs onto something and pulls it off or out. There are several types of pullers and many "special application" pullers. They usually have a large bolt in the middle that does the pulling and various types of arms and legs that grab onto what they were built to pull.

A **drum puller** is one built to pull brake drums or discs; they usually have a round *plate* or three *arms* that attach to three lug studs with lug nuts. A "tower" that holds the large bolt through its center is positioned against the end of the axle. Turning the bolt with a wrench forces the arms to pull the drum off the axle.

A word of caution about wheel and drum pullers. When you tighten the center bolt on the puller and the drum or disc doesn't seem to budge, there is a lot of pent-up energy in the puller. The puller could conceivably come flying off. So be sure to wear safety glasses and stand to one side while tightening the large bolt.

A **gear** or **bearing puller** has two or three arms with hooks (jaws) on the ends. The hooks hook over the back of the gear or bearing so when the large screw is turned, the gear or bearing is pulled off the shaft it's mounted on. The same rules apply as for the wheel and drum pullers.

You might need a three arm (jaw) puller to remove stubborn brake drums or brake discs, and a two arm (jaw) puller to remove the tie rod ends and ball joints. You can usually find a variety of pullers at your local equipment rental place; if you take one home and find you can't make it fit, take it back. These people are usually understanding and will often help you with further advice on selecting and using pullers. Just ask.

PROCEDURE 10: HOW TO SPLICE ELECTRICAL WIRE AND REPLACE WIRE CONNECTORS

Step 1. Simple Splice.

If you're making a wire longer by adding a piece of wire to it, be sure the wire you're adding is the same gauge as, or thicker than, the wire you're adding it to. If it's a narrower gauge, it may overheat at that point.

Strip about ½" of plastic insulation away from the end of each wire. Use a *wire stripping tool* if you have one. If not, a knife or, in an emergency, your teeth will do. Make *certain* all the juice is off to any wire still attached to the car, and be extra careful not to nick or cut the wire still inside. Twist the bare wire strands on the exposed ends a couple of times so they're wrapped up tight with no loose strands sticking out. Arrange the two wires so they form an X and touch at the points where the insulation ends and the bare wire begins. Hold that point tight with a thumb and forefinger while you twist the two wires together into a spiral shape. Fold the spiral onto the insulation of one of the wires, then give the wires a little tug to test the strength of the splice. Wrap *insulating tape* (electrician's black tape) around one of the wires, starting about an inch back from the bare wires. Keep wrapping the tape round and round toward the bare wires until they're covered, then continue wrapping the tape about an inch past the splice. If the tape doesn't seem to stick too well, cut another piece that's a little longer and spiral wrap again going the opposite direction.

Step 2. Install Wire Connector.

Wire connectors are available individually or in plastic packets at your local auto supply store. If one comes detached from its wire, it's easy to put on a new one. If you're splicing two wires together and have a new insulated in-line wire connector handy, or you're replacing a connector on the end of a wire, first strip the insulation from the end(s) of the wire(s) as described in Step 1. Stick the twisted bare wire into the wire hole end of the connector, then squeeze that end of the connector with wire stripping pliers or regular pliers. Squeeze the end of the connector as tight as you can. If you're splicing two wires together, install the other wire in the other end of the connector, the same as you did with the first, and squeeze with the pliers. Test with a slight tug to make sure the wires are securely attached.

PROCEDURE 11: REPLACE SPEEDOMETER CABLE

To get to the speedometer cable, you must first remove the instrument panel in the dashboard. See Chapter 8, Procedure 4, Step 8, to remove the panel. Gently pull the panel toward you until you can reach behind and disconnect the speedometer cable. It's directly behind the speedometer gauge. Find a little tab on the end of the cable and press on the tab while you pull the cable out of the gauge. (Careful of all those wires under there!)

Inside this cable is a smaller wire cable with a square end. Gently twirl the square end of the cable with your fingers. If it twists slightly and then stops, the cable is probably good and it's the speedometer that isn't working. Have Toyota or a garage fix or replace it for you. If the cable twists freely with your fingers, give it a little tug to see if it pulls out of the housing. If the inner cable comes completely out, the cable is broken and needs to be replaced. Here's how.

Follow the speedometer cable through the firewall into the engine compartment. The other end of the cable attaches to one side of the *transmission*, with a plastic or metal ring that you unscrew with your fingers. Unscrew the ring, using pliers if necessary, then release any plastic clips that secure the cable to the truck body or engine parts. Pull the old cable through the firewall into the engine compartment.

Push the speedometer end of the new cable through the hole from the engine side. Thread the cable through the wires and stuff so you can attach it easily to the rear of the speedometer. Insert the end of the cable into the speedometer, then wiggle the plastic end on until it locks into place. Fit the rubber grommet around the cable so water and air can't come in through the hole in the firewall. Attach the other end of the cable to the transmission; turn the ring down snugly with your fingers. Reattach the cable to the body and/or engine with the plastic clips. Drive the car and see if the speedometer works now. It should.

PROCEDURE 12: REMOVE AND INSTALL INSIDE DOOR PANELS (TO GET AT LOCKS, LATCH MECHANISMS, WINDOW CRANKS, ETC.)

Inside your doors are the works for the window crank, lock, door handle mechanisms and maybe a radio speaker. The door panel is made of fiberboard covered with vinyl and/or fabric, and is held on with clips and the door hardware (handles, armrest). It's easy to remove the door panel so that you can get at what's inside. Replacing the window crank or the inside door handle is easy, but replacing the window operating mechanism or the outside door handle is rather complicated and should be done by the professionals.

Use Step 1 alone if you need to replace a broken window crank. Step 2 tells you how to remove and install the armrests. Step 3 tells you how to remove and install the panel to get to the inside door handle or install a speaker.

Step 1. Remove and Install Window Crank.

The window crank is attached to the window operating mechanism inside the door with a U-shaped clip. Roll the window all the way up and notice that the crank points up at about a 45 degree angle. When you put the crank back on, install it in the same position.

You'll need a rag or towel to reach between the window crank and the plastic trim ring to remove the clip. Here's how. Turn the crank so the handle part is pointing straight down. Push the plastic trim ring away from the bottom of the crank while you insert the edge of a rag between the two. Grab the rag on both sides a few inches away from the crank and pull up on the rag. Slide the rag back and forth across the bottom of the crank while pulling up on the rag. The U-shaped clip will wiggle up and out of the crank. Sometimes it flies out, so be ready to catch it. Once the clip is off, the window crank will slide right off. You can remove the trim ring now.

To install the window crank, fit the plastic trim ring into its hole in the door panel. The clip usually gets stretched a little during removal, so squeeze the clip and bend it so the sides are almost touching. Now fit the clip into the slots on the sides of the window crank so the open end of the clip is toward the handle. Fit the crank onto the shaft, then wiggle the crank while you push it toward the door. When the clip snaps into its groove on the shaft, the crank is installed. If the crank comes off easily, bend the clip so the sides are closer together before installing it on the crank, then push the crank onto the shaft again.

Step 2. Remove and Install Armrests.

The armrest is held on by two or more phillips screws. On some models you may have to pry off a little rubber or plastic plug with a regular screwdriver to get at the screw heads. The screws go up through the armrest at a slight angle. Unscrew the screws and the armrest should come right off.

To install the armrest, hold it in position while you install the two screws. It's a little tricky to get the screws started, but perseverance will further.

Step 3. Remove and Install the Door Panel.

Before removing the door panel you must first remove the window crank (Step 1), the armrest (Step 2) and the plastic trim around the door handle. Here's how to remove the door handle trim: Pull the door handle toward the inside as far as possible while you remove the phillips screw located in the center of the plastic trim. Remove the screw and wiggle the trim over the handle.

The panel is attached to the door with little clips around the edges. To remove it, put tape on the end of a screwdriver so it won't scratch the paint, then slide the screwdriver between the panel and the door. Twist the screwdriver side to side. One of the clips should pop out of its hole in the door. Slip your fingers behind the panel and pull toward you while you get the screwdriver as close as possible to the next clip. Pop that clip with the screwdriver. Now go around the bottom and sides of the panel, placing your fingers or the screwdriver as close as possible to the clips to avoid breaking the panel. The top of the panel either is secured with clips like the sides and bottom, or it hooks over the top edge of the door. If you have them, remove the clips along the top edge. When all the clips have been released, gently lift the panel away from the door. On some models you'll have to lift up slightly on the trim along the top of the panel, then use the screwdriver to unhook the top edge. If you've removed the panel to install speakers, install them now. Be sure the speakers won't get crunched when you roll the windows down.

To remove the inside door handle, remove the bolts at the front and rear of the handle. Pull the handle away from the door and disconnect the long thin rod. To install the handle, connect the rod to the inside then fit the handle on the door. Install and tighten the two mounting bolts.

To install the door panel, fit it into position over the window operating shaft and inside door handle. If yours is the type that hooks over the top edge of the door, be sure the panel is securely hooked all along the top edge. Align the clips with the holes in the door, then push them in one at a time. Tap around the outer edge of the panel with your fist to seat them fully. Install the armrest, window crank and door handle trim, and you're finished.

PROCEDURE 13: SOME TIPS FROM POOR RICHARD'S RABBIT BOOK

Remark: The following jewels of wisdom were stolen from Richard Sealey's masterpiece, *How To Keep Your Volkswagen Rabbit Alive*. Although they were written for Rabbits, they are equally applicable to Toyotas.

Need a Drop of Oil?

Should you be out in the proverbial boonies and stuck for a spot of oil, remove the dipstick and use the oil adhering to the tip. Clever, huh?

The world record for transferring a pint of oil from the engine to a container using the "one-drop-at-a-time" method is 4 hours, 26 minutes, 12 seconds. (Richard Sealey holds the record.)

Drive Belt Broken?

If one of the drive belts ('"fan belts") on the front of the engine breaks and you don't have a spare, you can substitute the leg of a nylon stocking or pair of tights for a belt. That is, if you're wearing nylon stockings or tights (or have a stray pair floating around in the back seat). Remove the tights and cut one of the legs off close to the crotch. Pull the liberated leg into a long, thin "belt" and slip it around the pulleys just as you would a real drive belt. Tie a square knot to attach the ends of the stocking leg. Snug it down as tight as possible. Cut off any excess nylon. Should work fine till you get to civilization.

Buy a new belt at the next parts store you pass. If you don't have a nylon stocking, woven nylon string such as used with camping gear will sometimes work, if you can tie it tight enough. A friend carries a stocking or leg from a panty hose in his on-board emergency tool kit. He's too cheap to carry a spare drive belt, and says he likes to help damsels in distress. The nylon stocking emergency drive belt fits any car.

Gas Tank Leak?

During one of my travels, I bounced off a sand dune into a pile of rocks, which put four tiny holes into the Rabbit's gas tank. Since welding equipment is hard to find in the middle of the Mojave, I whipped out a bar of Dial and had at the tank. If this disaster should happen to you, rub bar soap into the offending split or pin-hole. Of course, if you've trashed out your gas tank on a rock and there's a huge gash in it, this method won't work. However, it works beautifully for small holes. Continue rubbing the soap into the holes until the gas no longer flows. Repair the gas tank as soon as you have tools. The temporary repair on the Rabbit has lasted three years. You might say it's part of a continuing experiment.

Shelter

Let me dispel one myth. It isn't a good idea to keep a car in a heated garage. It's lovely to have heat when working on a car, but storing a car in one is not so good. If the car underbody is coated with salt from winter roads, the warmth of the surrounding atmosphere will accelerate the rusting process. Rinse off salt and dirt from beneath the car before putting it into any garage, warm or freezing. (You'd think that after 100 years, and the scheming of thousands of engineers, they'd have come up with truly rust-proof production cars. Even fiberglass Corvettes can develop frame rot.)

If you know of other time-saving and/or labor-saving tips, please let me know. ASA NISI MASA!

A

B

C

N

O

P

R

S

W

Z

Other Books from John Muir Publications

Travel Books by Rick Steves

Asia Through the Back Door, 4th ed., 400 pp. $16.95
Europe 101: History, Art, and Culture for the Traveler, 4th ed., 372 pp. $15.95
Mona Winks: Self-Guided Tours of Europe's Top Museums, 2nd ed., 160 pp. $10.95
Rick Steves' Best of the Baltics and Russia, 1995 ed. 144 pp. $9.95
Rick Steves' Best of Europe, 1995 ed., 544 pp. $16.95
Rick Steves' Best of France, Belgium, and the Netherlands, 1995 ed., 240 pp. $12.95
Rick Steves' Best of Germany, Austria, and Switzerland, 1995 ed., 240 pp. $12.95
Rick Steves' Best of Great Britain, 1995 ed., 192 pp. $11.95
Rick Steves' Best of Italy, 1995 ed., 208 pp. $11.95
Rick Steves' Best of Scandinavia, 1995 ed., 192 pp. $11.95
Rick Steves' Best of Spain and Portugal, 1995 ed., 192 pp. $11.95
Rick Steves' Europe Through the Back Door, 13th ed., 480 pp. $17.95
Rick Steves' French Phrase Book, 2nd ed., 112 pp. $4.95
Rick Steves' German Phrase Book, 2nd ed., 112 pp. $4.95
Rick Steves' Italian Phrase Book, 2nd ed., 112 pp. $4.95
Rick Steves' Spanish and Portuguese Phrase Book, 2nd ed., 288 pp. $5.95
Rick Steves' French/German/Italian Phrase Book, 288 pp. $6.95

A Natural Destination Series

Belize: A Natural Destination, 2nd ed., 304 pp. $16.95
Costa Rica: A Natural Destination, 3rd ed., 400 pp. $17.95
Guatemala: A Natural Destination, 336 pp. $16.95

Undiscovered Islands Series

Undiscovered Islands of the Caribbean, 3rd ed., 264 pp. $14.95
Undiscovered Islands of the Mediterranean, 2nd ed., 256 pp. $13.95
Undiscovered Islands of the U.S. and Canadian West Coast, 288 pp. $12.95

For Birding Enthusiasts

The Birder's Guide to Bed and Breakfasts: U.S. and Canada, 288 pp. $15.95
The Visitor's Guide to the Birds of the Central National Parks: U.S. and Canada, 400 pp. $15.95
The Visitor's Guide to the Birds of the Eastern National Parks: U.S. and Canada, 400 pp. $15.95
The Visitor's Guide to the Birds of the Rocky Mountain National Parks: U.S. and Canada, 432 pp. $15.95

Unique Travel Series

Each is 112 pages and $10.95 paperback.
Unique Arizona
Unique California
Unique Colorado
Unique Florida
Unique New England
Unique New Mexico
Unique Texas
Unique Washington

2 to 22 Days Itinerary Planners

2 to 22 Days in the American Southwest, 1995 ed., 192 pp. $11.95
2 to 22 Days in Asia, 192 pp. $10.95
2 to 22 Days in Australia, 192 pp. $10.95
2 to 22 Days in California, 1995 ed., 192 pp. $11.95
2 to 22 Days in Eastern Canada, 1995 ed., 240 pp $12.95
2 to 22 Days in Florida, 1995 ed., 192 pp. $11.95
2 to 22 Days Around the Great Lakes, 1995 ed., 192 pp. $11.95
2 to 22 Days in Hawaii, 1995 ed., 192 pp. $11.95
2 to 22 Days in New England, 1995 ed., 192 pp. $11.95
2 to 22 Days in New Zealand, 192 pp. $10.95
2 to 22 Days in the Pacific Northwest, 1995 ed., 192 pp. $11.95
2 to 22 Days in the Rockies, 1995 ed., 192 pp. $11.95
2 to 22 Days in Texas, 1995 ed., 192 pp. $11.95
2 to 22 Days in Thailand, 192 pp. $10.95
22 Days Around the World, 264 pp. $13.95

Other Terrific Travel Titles

The 100 Best Small Art Towns in America, 224 pp. $12.95
Elderhostels: The Students' Choice, 2nd ed., 304 pp. $15.95
Environmental Vacations: Volunteer Projects to Save the Planet, 2nd ed., 248 pp. $16.95
A Foreign Visitor's Guide to America, 224 pp. $12.95
Great Cities of Eastern Europe, 256 pp. $16.95
Indian America: A Traveler's Companion, 3rd ed., 432 pp. $18.95
Interior Furnishings Southwest, 256 pp. $19.95
Opera! The Guide to Western Europe's Great Houses, 296 pp. $18.95
Paintbrushes and Pistols: How the Taos Artists Sold the West, 288 pp. $17.95
The People's Guide to Mexico, 10th ed., 608 pp. $19.95
Ranch Vacations: The Complete Guide to Guest and Resort, Fly-Fishing, and Cross-Country Skiing Ranches, 3rd ed., 512 pp. $19.95
The Shopper's Guide to Art and Crafts in the Hawaiian Islands, 272 pp. $13.95
The Shopper's Guide to Mexico, 224 pp. $9.95
Understanding Europeans, 272 pp. $14.95
A Viewer's Guide to Art: A Glossary of Gods, People, and Creatures, 144 pp. $10.95
Watch It Made in the U.S.A.: A Visitor's Guide to the Companies that Make Your Favorite Products, 272 pp. $16.95

Parenting Titles

Being a Father: Family, Work, and Self, 176 pp. $12.95
Preconception: A Woman's Guide to Preparing for Pregnancy and Parenthood, 232 pp. $14.95
Schooling at Home: Parents, Kids, and Learning, 264 pp., $14.95
Teens: A Fresh Look, 240 pp. $14.95

Automotive Titles

The Greaseless Guide to Car Care Confidence, 224 pp. $14.95
How to Keep Your Datsun/Nissan Alive, 544 pp. $21.95
How to Keep Your Subaru Alive, 480 pp. $21.95
How to Keep Your Toyota Pickup Alive, 392 pp. $21.95
How to Keep Your VW Alive, 25th Anniversary ed., 464 pp. spiral bound $25

TITLES FOR YOUNG READERS AGES 8 AND UP

American Origins Series

Each is 48 pages and $12.95 hardcover.
Tracing Our English Roots
Tracing Our French Roots (available 7/95)
Tracing Our German Roots
Tracing Our Irish Roots
Tracing Our Italian Roots
Tracing Our Japanese Roots
Tracing Our Jewish Roots
Tracing Our Polish Roots

Bizarre & Beautiful Series

Each is 48 pages and $14.95 hardcover, $9.95 paperback.
Bizarre & Beautiful Ears
Bizarre & Beautiful Eyes
Bizarre & Beautiful Feelers
Bizarre & Beautiful Noses
Bizarre & Beautiful Tongues

Environmental Titles

Habitats: Where the Wild Things Live, 48 pp. $9.95
The Indian Way: Learning to Communicate with Mother Earth, 114 pp. $9.95
Rads, Ergs, and Cheeseburgers: The Kids' Guide to Energy and the Environment, 108 pp. $12.95
The Kids' Environment Book: What's Awry and Why, 192 pp. $13.95

Extremely Weird Series

Each is 48 pages and $9.95 paperback, $14.95 hardcover.
Extremely Weird Bats
Extremely Weird Birds
Extremely Weird Endangered Species
Extremely Weird Fishes
Extremely Weird Frogs
Extremely Weird Insects
Extremely Weird Mammals
Extremely Weird Micro Monsters
Extremely Weird Primates
Extremely Weird Reptiles
Extremely Weird Sea Creatures
Extremely Weird Snakes
Extremely Weird Spiders

Kidding Around Travel Series

All are 64 pages and $9.95 paperback, except for *Kidding Around Spain* and *Kidding Around the National Parks of the Southwest*, which are 108 pages and $12.95 paperback.
Kidding Around Atlanta
Kidding Around Boston, 2nd ed.
Kidding Around Chicago, 2nd ed.
Kidding Around the Hawaiian Islands
Kidding Around London
Kidding Around Los Angeles
Kidding Around the National Parks of the Southwest
Kidding Around New York City, 2nd ed.
Kidding Around Paris
Kidding Around Philadelphia
Kidding Around San Diego
Kidding Around San Francisco
Kidding Around Santa Fe
Kidding Around Seattle
Kidding Around Spain
Kidding Around Washington, D.C.

Kids Explore Series

Written by kids for kids, all are $9.95 paperback.
Kids Explore America's African American Heritage, 128 pp.
Kids Explore the Gifts of Children with Special Needs, 128 pp.
Kids Explore America's Hispanic Heritage, 112 pp.
Kids Explore America's Japanese American Heritage, 144 pp.

Masters of Motion Series

Each is 48 pages and $9.95 paperback.
How to Drive an Indy Race Car
How to Fly a 747
How to Fly the Space Shuttle

Rainbow Warrior Artists Series

Each is 48 pages and $14.95 hardcover. ($9.95 paperback editions available 4/95.)
Native Artists of Africa
Native Artists of Europe
Native Artists of North America

Rough and Ready Series

Each is 48 pages and $12.95 hardcover. ($9.95 paperback editions available 4/95.)
Rough and Ready Cowboys
Rough and Ready Homesteaders
Rough and Ready Loggers
Rough and Ready Outlaws and Lawmen
Rough and Ready Prospectors
Rough and Ready Railroaders

X-ray Vision Series

Each is 48 pages and $9.95 paperback.
Looking Inside the Brain
Looking Inside Cartoon Animation
Looking Inside Caves and Caverns
Looking Inside Sports Aerodynamics
Looking Inside Sunken Treasures
Looking Inside Telescopes and the Night Sky

Ordering Information

Please check your local bookstore for our books, or call **1-800-888-7504** to order direct. All orders are shipped via UPS; see chart below to calculate your shipping charge for U.S. destinations. **No post office boxes please; we must have a street address to ensure delivery.** If the book you request is not available, we will hold your check until we can ship it. Foreign orders will be shipped surface rate unless otherwise requested; please enclose $3 for the first item and $1 for each additional item.

For U.S. Orders Totaling	Add
Up to $15.00	$4.25
$15.01 to $45.00	$5.25
$45.01 to $75.00	$6.25
$75.01 or more	$7.25

Methods of Payment

Check, money order, American Express, MasterCard, or Visa. We cannot be responsible for cash sent through the mail. For credit card orders, include your card number, expiration date, and your signature, or call **1-800-888-7504**. American Express card orders can only be shipped to billing address of cardholder. Sorry, no C.O.D.'s. Residents of sunny New Mexico, add 6.25% tax to total.

Address all orders and inquiries to:
John Muir Publications
P.O. Box 613
Santa Fe, NM 87504
(505) 982-4078
(800) 888-7504